Beirut ★

L E B A N O N

Damascus ★

★ Tyre

S Y R I A

GOLAN
HEIGHTS

Haifa ●

Lake
Tiberias

Nazareth ●

I S R A E L

Nablus ●

WEST
BANK

Jordan R.

Tel Aviv ●

★ Amman

Jerusalem ★

Gaza ●

Hebron ●

Dead
Sea

GAZA
STRIP

Rafah ● Beersheba ●

J O R D A N

Eilat ●
Taba ● ● Aqaba

S A U D I

A R A B I A

Gulf of Aqaba

0   50   100   150   200   250 km

0   50   100   150 miles

Chazaud

Sharm el Sheik ●

Red Sea

THE IRON WALL

The
IRON WALL

Israel and the Arab World

AVI SHLAIM

W · W · NORTON & COMPANY
New York   London

Photo Credits: National Photo Collection, Government Press Office, Jerusalem: 1, 2, 4, 5, 6, 7, 8, 9, 10, 12, 13, 17, 18, 19, 20, 24, 25, 26, 28, 29, 30, 31, 33, 34, 35, 36. AP/Wide World Photos: 14, 16. Corbis/AFP: 37. Corbis/Bettmann: 3, 11, 15, 21, 22. Corbis/David Rubinger: 23. Corbis/Reuters: 27, 32.

For information about permission to reproduce selections from this book, write to Permissions, W. W. Norton & Company, Inc., 500 Fifth Avenue, New York, NY 10110

The text and display of this book are composed in Galliard
Composition and manufacturing by the Haddon Craftsmen, Inc.
Book design and cartography by Jacques Chazaud

Library of Congress Cataloging-in-Publication Data

Shlaim, Avi.
The iron wall : Israel and the Arab world / Avi Shlaim.
p. cm.
Includes bibliographical references and index.
ISBN 0-393-04816-0
1. Arab-Israeli conflict. 2. Israel-Foreign policy. I. Title.
DS119.7.S4762 1999
956.04—dc21   99-23121
CIP

W. W. Norton & Company, Inc., 500 Fifth Avenue, New York, N.Y. 10110
www.wwnorton.com

W. W. Norton & Company Ltd., 10 Coptic Street, London WC1A 1PU

1 2 3 4 5 6 7 8 9 0

To the memory of my father
Joseph Shlaim, 1900–1971

CONTENTS

Illustrations follow page 264

LIST OF MAPS

PREFACE

The establishment of the State of Israel, on 14 May 1948, was one of the most momentous events in the history of the twentieth century. This book is a study of the first fifty years of Israeli foreign policy, with a particular focus on Israel's relations with the Arab world. A great deal has been written on the subject, much of it from a pro-Israeli perspective. Israel has been considerably more successful than its Arab opponents in putting across its rendition of events. But the Israeli version, like any nationalist history, is one-sided and self-serving. "A nation," said the French philosopher Ernest Renan, "is a group of people united by a mistaken view about the past and a hatred of their neighbors." The Israelis are no exception.

For many years the standard Zionist account of the causes, character, and course of the Arab-Israeli conflict remained largely unchallenged outside the Arab world. The fortieth anniversary of the establishment of the State of Israel, however, was accompanied by the publication of four books by Israeli historians who challenged the traditional historiography of the birth of the State of Israel and the first Arab-Israeli war. The four books are Simha Flapan's *The Birth of Israel: Myths and Realities*, Benny Morris's *The Birth of the Palestinian Refugee Problem, 1947–1949*, Ilan Pappé's *Britain and the Arab-Israeli Conflict, 1948–51*, and my own *Collusion across the Jordan: King Abdullah, the Zionist Movement, and the Partition of Palestine*. Collectively the authors came to be called the Israeli revisionist, or new, historians.

Revisionist historiography has focused on the events surrounding the birth of Israel and the 1948 Arab-Israeli war. My aim in the present book is to offer a revisionist interpretation of Israel's policy toward the Arab world during the fifty years following the achievement of statehood. I should state at the outset that this is not a comprehensive history of the Arab-Israeli conflict but a study of Israel's policy toward the Arab world. Consequently, the emphasis throughout is on Israel—on Israeli perceptions, Israeli attitudes, Israeli thinking, and Israeli behavior in the conflict. The structure of the book is chronological, but I have tried to provide a critical analysis of Israeli foreign policy and not simply a chronology of events. Like the British historian E. H. Carr, I believe that the main task of the historian is not to record but to evaluate.

Carr also described the writing of history as a perpetual dialogue between the historian and his sources. A word about the sources used in the writing of this book might therefore be of some interest. The secondary literature on this subject is vast, and all the books and articles that I cite in the footnotes are also listed in the bibliography. But wherever possible I have preferred to rely on primary sources, whether in English, French, Hebrew, or Arabic. Since the subject matter of the book is foreign policy, the most relevant category of primary source material consists of official government documents. The student of foreign relations is well served both by the Israel State Archives in Jerusalem and by the excellent series it publishes under the title *Documents on the Foreign Policy of Israel*. Israel adopted the British thirty-year rule for the review and declassification of foreign policy documents. Arab governments only open their records for research, if they open them at all, in a haphazard and arbitrary manner. It is very much to Israel's credit that it allows researchers access to its internal documents and thereby makes possible critical studies such as the present one.

The real problem for me has not been the imbalance between the documents available from the Israeli side and those from the Arab side but rather the fact that, under the thirty-year rule, I was able to consult Israeli documents only up to the mid-1960s. I had to choose between covering the early period in depth and attempting a more comprehensive treatment of half a century of Israeli foreign policy despite the relative dearth of official documents on the more recent period. I chose the latter course. It is for others to judge whether the attempt to provide an overview has been successful.

In writing this book I have made extensive use of interviews with policymakers and participants in the events described here: officials, parliamentarians, ministers, soldiers, and one king. Again, I am only too well aware of the problems and pitfalls associated with oral history, such as faulty memory, self-serving accounts, distortions, and deliberate falsifications. Nevertheless, I am a great believer in oral history not as a substitute for written sources but as a complement to them. Most of the interviews were held in 1981–82 when I spent a year in Israel gathering material for a book on politics and the management of national security in the first twenty-five years of statehood. I ended up writing *Collusion across the Jordan,* which focused on Israeli-Jordanian relations during the three decades that culminated in King Abdullah's murder in 1951. So I was left with a treasure trove of interview material, which I put to use for the first time in the present volume.

The individuals I interviewed, Israelis as well as others, are listed in the bibliography. I am grateful to all of them for sparing the time to see me and for answering my questions. But I consider myself particularly fortunate to have had a two-hour interview with the late King Hussein bin Talal of Jordan in December 1996. The interview dealt with King Hussein's relations with Israel from 1953 to 1996. It was the first time that the king spoke on the record about his meetings with Israeli leaders prior to the conclusion of the Israeli-Jordan peace treaty in October 1994.

At various stages in the long journey that ended with the publication of this book, I received support from institutions and individuals that it is my pleasure to acknowledge. My greatest debt is to the British Academy for awarding me a two-year research readership in 1995–97 and for giving me a research grant. The readership freed me from my teaching and administrative duties at the University of Oxford, while the grant enabled me to travel, to visit archives, and to employ research assistants. Without the generous support of the British Academy this book could not have been written.

I am also grateful to my colleagues in the International Relations Department at Oxford for making it possible for me to take extended leave and to Dr. Erica Benner for taking over my teaching.

The part of the research that I enjoyed most was the time I spent in distant, dusty archives. But some of the work had to be delegated, and I am grateful for all the help I received from three very dedicated research assistants. Leanna Feldman gathered material in the Ben-Gurion Archive in Sede-Boker, Ariela Abramovici in the Israel State Archives in Jerusalem, and Dr. Michael Thornhill in the Public Record Office in Kew. In addition to working in the PRO, and in various Oxford libraries, Michael Thornhill rendered invaluable assistance as an adviser, administrator, accountant, editor, and proofreader.

A large number of Israeli friends have helped me in various ways, but three deserve a special mention. Dr. Zaki Shalom, of the Ben-Gurion Research Center, shared with me his knowledge and his extensive private collection of materials on Israeli foreign and defense policy. Dr. Moshe Shemesh, of the same center, educated me on Arab strategies toward Israel and spent many evenings, when he was supposed to be on vacation with his family in Oxford, poring over Arabic documents with me. Dr. Mordechai Bar-On, a former soldier and a scholar, has been a never-ending source of information, ideas, and arguments.

A number of friends and former students read the first draft of this book and gave me the benefit of their opinion. Sudhir Hazareesingh and Ngaire Woods read the early chapters and made constructive comments. Karma Nabulsi and Raad Alkadiri read the entire manuscript with great care and made extremely helpful suggestions for improving it. I am very much in their debt.

Elizabeth Anderson typed successive drafts of what must have looked like an interminable manuscript with exemplary patience, skill, and good cheer. Marga Lyall compiled the bibliography. Otto Sonntag copyedited the typescript intelligently, imaginatively, and with meticulous attention to detail.

My thanks go to the staff at W. W. Norton: to Donald Lamm for his wise editorial direction, to Drake McFeely for his unfailingly good advice and support, and to Sarah Stewart for being so helpful in so many different ways.

Finally I wish to thank my wife, Gwyn Daniel, for continuing to be interested in my work after twenty-five years of marriage, for many stimulating conversations, incisive criticism, perceptive comments, and encouragement throughout many seasons.

All the above institutions and individuals deserve a share of the credit for this book, if any credit is due. For the shortcomings that remain, I alone am responsible.

Avi Shlaim
May 1999
Oxford

CHRONOLOGY

29 Nov. 1947	UN resolution for the partition of Palestine.
14 May 1948	Proclamation of the State of Israel.
15 May 1948– 7 Jan. 1949	First Arab-Israeli War.
Feb.–July 1949	Arab-Israeli armistice agreements signed.
April–June 1949	First round of Lausanne talks under the auspices of the Palestine Conciliation Commission.
11 May 1949	Israel admitted to UN membership.
9 Dec. 1949	General Assembly votes for internationalization of Jerusalem.
13 Dec. 1949	Knesset decides to hold its sessions in Jerusalem.
4 April 1950	Jordan annexes West Bank, including East Jerusalem.
25 May 1950	Britain, France, and U.S. issue Tripartite Declaration on regulating the supply of arms to the Middle East.

12 Feb. 1951	Israel begins Huleh drainage work in DMZ with Syria.
4 April 1951	Syria attacks Israeli patrol in al-Hamma.
2–6 May 1951	Israeli-Syrian clashes in Tal al-Mutilla.
23 July 1952	Free Officers' revolution in Egypt.
18 Aug. 1952	Ben-Gurion welcomes Egyptian revolution in the Knesset.
9 Oct. 1952– 27 May 1953	Syrian-Israeli talks on the division of the DMZs.
2 Sept. 1953	Israel starts work on Jordan River project. Syria complains to Security Council.
1 Oct. 1953	President Eisenhower appoints Eric Johnston to mediate in water dispute.
15 Oct. 1953	The Qibya raid.
7 Dec. 1953	Moshe Sharett succeeds David Ben-Gurion as prime minister.
17 April 1954	Colonel Nasser becomes prime minister of Egypt.
July 1954	The Lavon affair, or "the mishap"—activation of Jewish sabotage ring in Egypt.
28 Sept. 1954	Egypt seizes Israeli ship *Bat Galim* at Port Said.
19 Oct. 1954	Britain signs Suez base evacuation agreement with Egypt.
21 Feb. 1955	Ben-Gurion returns to government as minister of defense.
24 Feb. 1955	Iraq and Turkey sign the Baghdad Pact.
28 Feb. 1955	IDF raid on Gaza.
5 April 1955	Britain joins the Baghdad Pact.
9 Aug. 1955	Elmore Jackson embarks on his mission of conciliation.

27 Sept. 1955	Nasser announces the Czech arms deal.
20 Oct. 1955	Egypt and Syria sign mutual defense treaty.
2 Nov. 1955	Ben-Gurion again becomes prime minister.
11 Dec. 1955	Operation Kinneret.
Dec. 1955–March 1956	The Anderson mission.
6 April 1956	UN secretary-general begins shuttle to reestablish the Israeli-Egyptian armistice.
13 June 1956	British complete evacuation of their forces from Suez.
18 June 1956	Sharett resigns as foreign minister.
24–26 June 1956	The Vermars conference.
26 July 1956	Egypt nationalizes the Suez Canal Company.
30 Sept.–1 Oct. 1956	The St.-Germain conference.
22 Oct. 1956	Defense pact signed by Egypt, Syria, and Jordan.
22–24 Oct. 1956	The conference of Sèvres.
29 Oct.–7 Nov. 1956	The Suez War.
5 Nov. 1956	USSR threatens use of force, including rockets, if Britain, France, and Israel do not halt attack on Egypt.
5 Jan. 1957	Anti-Communist Eisenhower Doctrine proclaimed.
10 March 1957	IDF withdraws to armistice line with Egypt.
1 Feb. 1958	Syria and Egypt merge to form the United Arab Republic (UAR).
14 July 1958	Revolution in Iraq.
15 July 1958	American deployment to Lebanon; British deployment to Jordan.

28 Sept. 1961	Syrian coup leads to dissolution of UAR.
8 March 1963	Ba'thist coup in Syria.
16 June 1963	Ben-Gurion resigns and Levi Eshkol succeeds.
13–17 Jan. 1964	First Arab summit meeting in Cairo decides on Jordan River diversion.
29 May 1964	Creation of the Palestine Liberation Organization (PLO).
5–11 Sept. 1964	Second Arab summit, Alexandria.
23 Feb. 1966	Left-wing coup in Syria followed by increased PLO activity against Israel.
9 Nov. 1966	Syria and Egypt sign mutual defense treaty.
13 Nov. 1966	Israeli raid on West Bank village of Samu.
7 April 1967	Israeli aircraft shoot down seven Syrian MiGs.
15 May 1967	Nasser deploys troops in Sinai.
19 May 1967	Nasser requests withdrawal of UN Emergency Force from Sinai.
22 May 1967	Nasser closes the Straits of Tiran to Israeli shipping.
26 May 1967	Abba Eban meets President Johnson after talks with de Gaulle and Wilson.
30 May 1967	Egypt and Jordan sign mutual defense pact in Cairo.
1 June 1967	Government of national unity formed in Jerusalem.
5–10 June 1967	The Six-Day War.
27 June 1967	Israel annexes East Jerusalem.
26 July 1967	Allon Plan presented to cabinet.

28 Aug.–2 Sept. 1967	Arab League summit at Khartoum.
22 Nov. 1967	UN Security Council passes Resolution 242.
26 Feb. 1969	Levi Eshkol dies and is succeeded by Golda Meir.
March 1969– Aug. 1970	The Israeli-Egyptian War of Attrition.
9 Dec. 1969	The Rogers plan is announced.
22 Dec. 1969	Israel rejects the Rogers plan.
19 June 1970	The second Rogers initiative.
7 Aug. 1970	Israeli-Egyptian cease-fire under the Rogers initiative.
Sept. 1970	"Black September": Jordan crushes Palestinian fedayeen.
28 Sept. 1970	President Nasser dies and Sadat succeeds.
4 Feb. 1971	Sadat presents proposal for an interim settlement.
8 Feb. 1971	Jarring's questionnaire to Israel and Egypt.
4 Oct. 1971	The third Rogers plan.
15 March 1972	King Hussein unveils federal plan for a United Arab Kingdom.
22–26 May 1972	Nixon-Brezhnev summit meeting in Moscow.
18 July 1972	Sadat expels Soviet military advisers from Egypt.
6–26 Oct. 1973	The Yom Kippur War.
22 Oct. 1973	UN Security Council Resolution 338 calls for direct negotiations.
21 Dec. 1973	The Geneva peace conference.

18 Jan. 1974	The Israeli-Egyptian disengagement agreement is signed.
10 April 1974	Golda Meir resigns and is succeeded by Yitzhak Rabin.
31 May 1974	The Israeli-Syrian disengagement agreement is signed.
26–29 Oct. 1974	Arab League summit at Rabat recognizes PLO as "the sole legitimate representative of the Palestinian people."
13 April 1975	The outbreak of the Lebanese civil war.
1 Sept. 1975	Israeli-Egyptian interim agreement, Sinai II.
1 June 1976	Syrian military intervention in Lebanon.
4 July 1976	IDF frees Israeli passengers hijacked to Entebbe.
17 May 1977	Rise to power in Israel of right-wing Likud party.
1 Oct. 1977	Joint statement by the U.S. and USSR for reconvening the Geneva peace conference.
19–21 Nov. 1977	Sadat's visit to Jerusalem.
2–5 Dec. 1977	Arab front of steadfastness and opposition meets in Tripoli.
14 Dec. 1977	Cairo conference opens.
16 Dec. 1977	Begin unveils Palestinian autonomy plan in Washington.
25–26 Dec. 1977	Begin-Sadat summit at Ismailia.
11 Jan. 1978	Israel-Egyptian military committee convenes in Cairo.
14 March 1978	IDF launches Operation Litani in southern Lebanon.

19 March 1978	UN Resolution 425 calls for Israeli withdrawal from Lebanon.
13 June 1978	IDF withdraws from Lebanon after UNIFIL deployed.
18–19 July 1978	Leeds Castle conference in UK.
5–17 Sept. 1978	The Camp David conference.
17 Sept. 1978	Israel and Egypt sign the Camp David Accords.
12 Oct. 1978	Blair House conference opens in Washington.
2–5 Nov. 1978	Arab League summit in Baghdad denounces the Camp David Accords.
1 Feb. 1979	The Islamic revolution in Iran.
26 March 1979	Israel-Egypt peace treaty is signed at the White House.
21 Oct. 1979	Moshe Dayan resigns as foreign minister over conduct of Palestinian autonomy negotiations.
5 May 1980	Ezer Weizman resigns as defense minister.
17 Sept. 1980	Outbreak of war between Iraq and Iran.
4 June 1981	Begin and Sadat meet in Sharm el-Sheikh.
7 June 1981	Israeli bombs the Iraqi nuclear reactor near Baghdad.
30 June 1981	The Likud is reelected.
6 Oct. 1981	President Sadat is assassinated and Mubarak succeeds.
30 Nov. 1981	U.S. and Israel sign memorandum of understanding on strategic cooperation.
14 Dec. 1981	Israeli annexation of the Golan Heights.
18 Dec. 1981	U.S. suspends the agreement on strategic cooperation with Israel.

26 April 1982	Israeli withdrawal from Sinai completed.
3 June 1982	Attempted assassination of the Israeli ambassador in London.
6 June 1982	Israeli invasion of Lebanon.
13 June 1982	IDF begins siege of West Beirut.
21 Aug. 1982	PLO fighters are evacuated from Beirut.
1 Sept. 1982	President Reagan announces a new peace plan for the Middle East.
14 Sept. 1982	President Bashir Gemayel is assassinated.
16 Sept. 1982	The massacre of Sabra and Shatila.
17 May 1983	Israel and Lebanon sign agreement.
28 Aug. 1983	Menachem Begin resigns and Yitzhak Shamir succeeds.
5 March 1984	Israeli-Lebanese agreement abrogated by President Amin Gemayel.
14 Sept. 1984	National unity government under Shimon Peres takes office.
10 June 1985	Israel withdraws from Lebanon, but forms "security zone" in the south.
11–12 Sept. 1985	Peres-Mubarak summit conference in Cairo.
1 Oct. 1985	Israel bombs PLO headquarters in Tunis.
9 Dec. 1985	Start in Geneva of international arbitration on Taba.
15 April 1986	American air attack on Libya.
20 Oct. 1986	The rotation agreement is implemented: Shamir replaces Peres as prime minister.
25–27 Feb. 1987	Second Peres-Mubarak summit conference in Cairo.

11 April 1987	The Peres-Hussein London Agreement.
9 Dec. 1987	Outbreak of the *intifada*.
4 March 1988	George Shultz launches his peace initiative.
18 July 1988	End of Iran-Iraq war.
31 July 1988	King Hussein announces Jordan's disengagement from the West Bank.
1 Nov. 1988	Likud wins elections.
15 Nov. 1988	Palestine National Council in Algiers conditionally accepts UN Resolutions 181, 242, and 338.
14 Dec. 1988	Arafat accepts U.S. terms for talks with the PLO.
10 Oct. 1989	James Baker presents his five-point plan.
12 Oct. 1989	Ta'if accord to end the Lebanese civil war.
15 March 1990	Labor quits national unity government.
20 June 1990	U.S. suspends dialogue with the PLO.
2 Aug. 1990	Iraq invades Kuwait.
16 Jan.–28 Feb. 1991	The Gulf War.
March 1991	President Bush announces major new Middle Eastern peace initiative.
30–31 Oct. 1991	Middle Eastern peace conference convenes in Madrid.
10 Dec. 1991	Bilateral Arab-Israeli peace talks begin in Washington.
25 Dec. 1991	Dissolution of the USSR.
23 June 1992	Labor defeats Likud in Israeli elections.
16 Dec. 1992	Israeli deportation of 416 Hamas activists.
19 Jan. 1993	Knesset repeals ban on contacts with the PLO.

25 July 1993	Israel launches Operation Accountability in southern Lebanon.
10 Sept. 1993	Israel and PLO exchange letters formally recognizing each other.
13 Sept. 1993	Israel-PLO Declaration of Principles on Palestinian self-government is signed in the White House.
25 Feb. 1994	Massacre of Palestinians at Tomb of the Patriarchs in Hebron.
4 May 1994	Israel and PLO reach agreement in Cairo on the application of the Declaration of Principles.
25 July 1994	Washington Declaration ends state of war between Israel and Jordan.
26 Oct. 1994	Israel and Jordan sign a peace treaty.
23 Dec. 1994	Israeli and Syrian chiefs of staff hold talks in Washington.
2 Feb. 1995	First summit between leaders of Egypt, Jordan, PLO, and Israel.
28 Sept. 1995	Israeli-Palestinian Interim Agreement on the West Bank and the Gaza Strip (Oslo II) is signed.
4 Nov. 1995	Rabin is assassinated and Peres succeeds.
27 Dec. 1995	Israeli-Syrian talks at Wye Plantation near Washington.
5 Jan. 1996	Hamas master bomb maker Yahya Ayyash ("the engineer") is assassinated by Israel.
21 Jan. 1996	First Palestinian elections.
25 Feb. 1996	A Hamas suicide bomber blows up a bus in Jerusalem.
2–4 March 1996	Four Hamas suicide bombs kill 59 Israelis.

13 March 1996	Antiterrorist summit of 27 states is held in Sharm el-Sheikh.
11 April 1996	Israel launches Operation Grapes of Wrath in southern Lebanon.
24 April 1996	The Palestinian National Council amends the Palestinian National Charter.
29 May 1996	Binyamin Netanyahu defeats Peres in Israeli elections.
25 Sept. 1996	Clashes following opening of tunnel in the Old City of Jerusalem.
13 Nov. 1996	Third Middle East Economic Conference opens in Cairo.
15 Jan. 1997	The Hebron Protocol is signed.
18 March 1997	Construction begins of Jewish housing at Har Homa in East Jerusalem.
14 May 1998	Israel celebrates its 50th anniversary.
23 Oct. 1998	Netanyahu and Arafat sign the Wye River Memorandum.
14 Dec. 1998	The Palestinian National Council lays to rest the goal of destroying Israel.
20 Dec. 1998	Israel's government suspends the implementation of the Wye River Memorandum.
22 Dec. 1998	The Knesset decides to hold new elections.
17 May 1999	Ehud Barak defeats Netanyahu in Israeli elections.

THE IRON WALL

PROLOGUE

The Zionist Foundations

IN 1907 YITZHAK EPSTEIN, a Russian-born teacher who had settled in Palestine, published an article entitled "A Hidden Question" in the Hebrew periodical *Ha-Shiloah*. Its subject was the attitude of the Jews toward the Arabs of Palestine. "Among the grave questions raised by the concept of our people's renaissance on its own soil," wrote Epstein, "there is one that is more weighty than all the others put together. This is the question of our relations with the Arabs." This question, he added, "has not been forgotten, but rather has remained completely hidden from the Zionists, and in its true form has found almost no mention in the literature of our movement."[1] Epstein's anxiety was brushed aside by the majority of his Zionist contemporaries. But the hidden question came back to haunt the Zionist movement and the State of Israel throughout the first fifty years of its existence.

ZIONISM AND THE ARAB QUESTION

The Zionist movement, which emerged in Europe in the last two decades of the nineteenth century, aimed at the national revival of the Jewish people in its ancestral home after nearly two thousand years of exile. The term "Zionism" was coined in 1885 by the Viennese Jewish writer Nathan Birnbaum, Zion being one of the biblical names for Jerusalem. Zionism was in essence an answer to the Jewish problem that derived from two basic facts: the Jews were dispersed in various countries around the world, and in each country they constituted a minority. The Zionist solution was to end this anomalous existence and dependence on others, to return to Zion, and to attain majority status there and, ultimately, political independence and statehood.

Ever since the destruction of the First Temple in 586 B.C. and the exile to Babylon, the Jews yearned to return to Zion. This yearning was reflected in Jewish prayers, and it manifested itself in a number of messianic movements. Modern Zionism, by contrast, was a secular movement, with a political orientation toward Palestine. Modern Zionism was a phenomenon of the late nineteenth-century Europe. It had its roots in the failure of Jewish efforts to become assimilated in Western society, in the intensification of antisemitism in Europe, and in the parallel and not unrelated upsurge of nationalism. If nationalism posed a problem to the Jews by identifying them as an alien and unwanted minority, it also suggested a solution: self-determination for the Jews in a state of their own in which they would constitute a majority. Zionism, however, embodied the urge to create not merely a new Jewish state in Palestine but also a new society, based on the universal values of freedom, democracy, and social justice.

The father of political Zionism and the visionary of the Jewish state was Theodor Herzl (1860–1904), a Hungarian-born Jew who worked as a journalist and a playwright in Vienna, the capital of the Austro-Hungarian Empire. Herzl was an assimilated Jew with no particular interest in Judaism or Jewish affairs. It was the virulent antisemitism surrounding the Dreyfus Affair in the early 1890s, which he covered as the Paris correspondent of a Vienna daily newspaper, that aroused his interest in the Jewish problem. He concluded that assimilation and emancipation could not work, because the Jews were a nation. Their problem was not economic or social or religious but national. It followed rationally from these premises that the only solution was for the Jews to leave the diaspora and acquire a territory over which they would exercise sovereignty and establish a state of their own.

This was the solution advocated by Herzl in the famous little book he published in 1896, *Der Judenstaat,* or *The Jewish State.*[2] The Jews, he insisted, were not merely a religious group but a true nation waiting to be born. The book provided a detailed blueprint for a Jewish state but left open the question whether the site for the proposed state should be Palestine, on account of its historic associations, or some vacant land in Argentina. The publication of *The Jewish State* is commonly taken to mark the beginning of the history of the Zionist movement. It firmly identified the author's name with political Zionism, with the view that the Jewish question was a political question with international ramifications and that it therefore needed to be attacked in the forum of international politics. This was in contrast to the practical Zionism of Hovevi Zion, the Lovers of Zion, who had started in 1881 in a number of Russian cities, against the background of persecution and pogroms, to promote immigration and settlement activities in Palestine. The publication of *The Jewish State* also catapulted Herzl into a position of leadership in Jewish affairs, a position he retained until his death in 1904.

In line with his explicit political orientation, Herzl convened the First Zionist Congress, in 1897 in Basel, Switzerland. The congress was initially scheduled to take place in Munich because it had kosher restaurants. But the leaders of the Munich Jewish community declined to act as hosts, arguing that there was no Jewish question and that the holding of a congress would only supply ammunition to the antisemites. The Basel Program stated, "The aim of Zionism is to create for the Jewish people a home in Palestine secured by public law." By adopting this program the congress endorsed Herzl's political conception of Zionism. The Basel Program deliberately spoke of a home rather than a state for the Jewish people, but from the Basel Congress onward the clear and consistent aim of the Zionist movement was to create a state for the Jewish people in Palestine. To his diary Herzl confided, "At Basel I founded the Jewish State. If I said this out loud today, I would be answered by universal laughter. Perhaps in five years, and certainly in fifty, everyone will know it."[3]

The publication of *The Jewish State* evoked various reactions in the Jewish community, some strongly favorable, some hostile, and some skeptical. After the Basel Congress the rabbis of Vienna decided to explore Herzl's ideas and sent two representatives to Palestine. This fact-finding mission resulted in a cable from Palestine in which the two rabbis wrote, "The bride is beautiful, but she is married to another man."

This cable encapsulated the problem with which the Zionist movement had to grapple from the beginning: an Arab population already lived on the land on which the Jews had set their heart.[4] The received view is that the Zionist movement, with the exception of a few marginal groups, tended to ignore the Arabs who lived in Palestine and constituted what came to be called the Arab question. Some critics add that it was this ignorance of the Arab population by the Zionists that prevented the possibility of an understanding between the two national movements that were to claim Palestine as their homeland. It is true that the majority of the early Zionists exhibited surprisingly little curiosity about the land of their devotions. It is also true that the principal concern of these Zionists was not the reality in Palestine but the Jewish problem and the Jewish association with the country. It is not true, however, to say that the Zionists were unaware of the existence of an Arab population in Palestine or of the possibility that this population would be antagonistic to the Zionist enterprise. Although vaguely aware of the problem, they underestimated its seriousness and hoped that a solution would emerge in due course.

Herzl himself exemplified the Zionist tendency to indulge in wishful thinking. He was certainly aware that Palestine was already populated with a substantial number of Arabs, although he was not particularly well informed about the social and economic conditions of the country. He viewed the natives as primitive and backward, and his attitude toward them was rather patronizing. He thought that as individuals they should enjoy full civil rights in a Jewish state but he did not consider them a society with collective political rights over the land in which they formed the overwhelming majority. Like many other early Zionists, Herzl hoped that economic benefits would reconcile the Arab population to the Zionist enterprise in Palestine. As the bearers of all the benefits of Western civilization, the Jews, he thought, might be welcomed by the residents of the backward East. This optimistic forecast of Arab-Jewish relations in Palestine found its clearest expression in a novel published by Herzl in 1902 under the title *Altneuland (Old-Newland)*. Rashid Bey, a spokesman for the native population, describes Jewish settlement as an unqualified blessing: "The Jews have made us prosperous, why should we be angry with them? They live with us as brothers, why should we not love them?"[5] This picture, however, was nothing but a pipe dream, a utopian fantasy. Its author completely overlooked the possibility that an Arab national movement would grow in Palestine in response to the Zionist drive to transform the country into a Jewish national home with a Jewish majority.

In defense of Herzl it should be pointed out that at the end of the nineteenth century Palestine was a province of the Ottoman Empire, and an Arab national movement was only beginning to develop there. Still, his preference for playing the game of high politics was unmistakable. His most persistent efforts were directed

at persuading the Ottoman sultan to grant a charter for Jewish settlement and a Jewish homeland in Palestine. But he also approached many other world leaders and influential magnates for
help in promoting his pet project. Among those who granted him
an audience were the pope, the king of Italy, the German kaiser,
and Joseph Chamberlain, the British colonial secretary. In each
case Herzl presented his project in a manner best calculated to appeal to the listener: to the sultan he promised Jewish capital, to the
kaiser he intimated that the Jewish territory would be an outpost
of Berlin, to Chamberlain he held out the prospect that the Jewish
territory would become a colony of the British Empire. Whatever
the arguments used, Herzl's basic aim remained unchanged: obtaining the support of the great powers for turning Palestine into
a political center for the Jewish people.

In its formative phase, under the direction of Herzl, the Zionist
movement thus displayed two features that were to be of fundamental and enduring importance in its subsequent history: the
nonrecognition of a Palestinian national entity, and the quest for
an alliance with a great power external to the Middle East.
Bypassing the Palestinians was the trend in Zionist policy from
the First Zionist Congress onward. The unstated assumption of
Herzl and his successors was that the Zionist movement would
achieve its goal not through an understanding with the local
Palestinians but through an alliance with the dominant great
power of the day. The weakness of the Yishuv, the pre-
Independence Jewish community in Palestine, and the growing
hostility of the Palestinians combined to make the reliance on a
great power a central element in Zionist strategy. The dominant
great power in the Middle East changed several times in the course
of the twentieth century; first it was the Ottoman Empire, after
World War I it was Great Britain, and after World War II it was the
United States. But the Zionist fixation on enlisting the support of
the great powers in the struggle for statehood and in the consolidation of statehood remained constant.

CHAIM WEIZMANN
AND THE BRITISH CONNECTION

The chief architect of the alliance between the Zionist movement
and Great Britain was Chaim Weizmann (1874–1952). The charter that Herzl had unsuccessfully sought from the Ottoman Turks

was secured by Weizmann from the British in 1917 in the form of the Balfour Declaration. Weizmann forged the alliance with Britain and made it the cornerstone of Zionist policy in the course of a long and distinguished career that spanned the first half of the twentieth century.

Born in Russia, Weizmann went to university in Berlin and Geneva and was active in the Zionist movement from its inception, attending some of the early congresses. In 1904 he moved to London and took up a faculty post in chemistry in the University of Manchester, but in the middle of World War I he transferred to London to direct a special laboratory the British government had created to improve the production of artillery shells. In London he promoted the Zionist cause by making contacts and converts in the highest political circles. His remarkable skills in diplomacy and persuasion swiftly carried him to the top. In 1920 he was elected president of the World Zionist Organization, and he was to retain this office, with an interruption from 1931 to 1935, until 1946. When the State of Israel was created, he served as its first president until his death in 1952.

One of Weizmann's early contributions was to resolve the ongoing dispute between the political Zionists and the practical Zionists. The political Zionists, following in Herzl's footsteps, gave priority to diplomatic activity to secure international support for a Jewish homeland in Palestine. The practical Zionists, on the other hand, stressed the organization of Jewish immigration to Palestine, land acquisition, settlement, and the building of a Jewish economy there. The debate was not just about means but about the true meaning of Zionism. At the Eighth Zionist Congress, in 1907, Weizmann presented a new term, "synthetic Zionism," and argued that the two approaches supplemented each other, representing, in effect, two sides of the same coin. The policy implication of the new term, that the two approaches should be practiced simultaneously, seemed to satisfy both factions.

Most of Weizmann's own efforts were directed at enlisting the British government's support for the Zionist project in Palestine. He had no direct knowledge of the Arab problem and no distinctive policy of his own for dealing with it. In general it seemed to him that the Arabs of Palestine were not a separate political community with national aspirations of its own but a tiny fraction of the large Arab nation, and he also expected that economic self-interest would temper their opposition to Zionism. About the moral superiority of the Jewish claim over the Arab claim to a homeland in Palestine, he never entertained any doubt.

To a very great extent Weizmann's attitude toward the Palestine Arabs was shaped by his broader strategy of gaining British support for Zionism. The deeper and more complex his negotiations with the British government became in the course of World War I, the less attention he paid to the local difficulty with the Palestine Arabs. To elicit British support for what he ambiguously termed a Jewish commonwealth in Palestine, he minimized the danger of organized Arab resistance. In making his case, however, he appealed not only to the British imperial interest in having a friendly nation in a region of great strategic importance but also to British idealism. His efforts were crowned with success when, on 2 November 1917, Foreign Secretary Arthur J. Balfour wrote to Lord Rothschild a letter that said,

> His Majesty's Government view with favour the establishment in Palestine of a national home for the Jewish people, and will use their best endeavours to facilitate the achievement of this object, it being clearly understood that nothing shall be done which may prejudice the civil and religious rights of existing non-Jewish communities in Palestine, or the rights and political status enjoyed by the Jews in any other country.

The Balfour Declaration, as this letter came to be known, represented a major triumph for Zionist diplomacy. At the time of its issue, the Jewish population of Palestine numbered some 56,000 as against an Arab population of 600,000, or less than 10 percent. Considering that the Arabs constituted over 90 percent of the population, the promise not to prejudice their civil and religious rights had a distinctly hollow ring about it, since it totally ignored their political rights. Britain's public promise to the Jews could not be reconciled either with its earlier promise to Hussein the sharif of Mecca to support the establishment of an independent Arab kingdom after the war in return for an Arab revolt against the Ottoman Empire or with the secret Sykes-Picot agreement of 1916 to divide the Middle East into British and French spheres of influence in the event of an Allied victory. These irreconcilable wartime promises returned to haunt Britain on the morrow of the Allied victory. As far as Weizmann was concerned, however, the Balfour Declaration, despite all its ambiguities and limitations, handed the Jews a golden key to unlock the doors of Palestine and to make themselves the masters of the country.

In the aftermath of the war, Weizmann's attitude toward the Palestine Arabs continued to be governed by the need to retain

British backing for the fledgling Jewish national home. Having sponsored a Pan-Arab movement under the leadership of the sharif of Mecca during the war, Britain had no sympathy with the idea that the Arabs of Palestine formed a distinct political entity. Its policy was to make the Hashemite princes, the sons of the sharif of Mecca, rulers of semi-independent Arab states. Prince Faisal, commander of the Arab revolt against the Turks, became the king of Syria, but after the French ejected him from their sphere of influence, the British procured for him the Iraqi throne. Abdullah, his elder brother, was appointed ruler of the emirate of Transjordan, created by Britain in 1921. Iraq and Transjordan thus became the two main pillars of Britain's empire in the Middle East in the aftermath of World War I (see map 1).

It took Weizmann no time at all to orient himself on the new map of the Middle East. Taking his cue from the British, he disregarded the claims of the Palestine Arabs and strove to reach agreement with the Hashemite rulers of the neighboring Arab countries. This was the basis of the agreement he signed with Faisal on 3 January 1919. It endorsed the Balfour Declaration and envisaged "the most cordial goodwill and understanding" between Arabs and Jews in realizing their national aspirations in their respective territories in Palestine. The agreement had a very short life, however, because it ran counter to public opinion in the Arab world. Whether or not Faisal had the authority to sign an agreement affecting the Palestine Arabs in the first place, he was forced by his own nationalist followers to declare that the separation of Palestine from Syria was not acceptable and that Zionist aspirations for a state clashed with Arab ideas. In Arab eyes the main result of the Weizmann-Faisal intermezzo was to identify Zionism as the ally of British imperialism in the Middle East and as an obstacle in their own struggle for self-determination.

In the period 1918–20 the Zionists put forward their own maximalist interpretation of the Balfour Declaration. They wanted international recognition of the Jewish claim to Palestine, and they wanted the Jewish national home to stretch across both banks of the river Jordan. When Weizmann was asked at the Paris peace conference what was meant by a Jewish national home, he famously replied, "To make Palestine as Jewish as England is English." He was careful, however, not to speak openly in terms of a state, so as not to give substance to the charge that the Jewish minority planned to make itself master over the Arab majority. Although a Jewish state with a Jewish majority was his ultimate and unchanging aim, he believed in working toward this goal in a gradual, evolutionary, and nonprovocative fashion.

Weizmann's policy toward the Palestine Arabs is usually described as moderate, but it was moderate in style much more than in substance. Although patient and prudent and willing to listen to the Arabs, he was uncompromising in his defense of Jewish interests in Palestine. He was prepared to accept the Arabs as partners in running Palestine through an elected council based on parity between the two communities, but he did not accept them as equal partners in negotiations on the future of the country. According to him, these negotiations had to be conducted exclusively between Britain and the Jews.

Small wonder that Jewish-Arab relations deteriorated seriously after the Balfour Declaration was issued. Weizmann's assumption

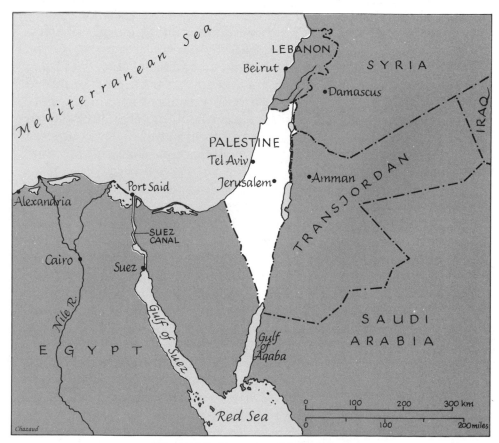

The Middle East after World War I

that the Palestine Arabs would remain politically passive and that the Arab-Jewish conflict would find its resolution on the social and economic plane turned out to be mistaken. A Palestinian national movement emerged in the interwar period, partly in response to the Zionist challenge. Under the leadership of Hajj Amin al-Husseini, the grand mufti of Jerusalem, the Palestinian national movement became not only active but aggressive in its opposition to Zionism. The mufti systematically rejected all the compromise proposals put forward by the British, instigated riots and disturbances against the Jews, and led a full-scale revolt in 1936–39 against the British authorities and their Jewish protégés.

Weizmann turned out to be equally mistaken in his assumption of the essential identity between British and Jewish interests in Palestine. Mounting Arab resistance, with occasional outbursts of violence, forced Britain to reassess its own wartime commitments to Zionism. The result was a gradual retreat from the promise embodied in the Balfour Declaration and a more evenhanded policy toward the two warring communities in Palestine. Winston Churchill's white paper of 1922 limited British support for the Jewish national home in three significant ways: it laid down for the first time economic criteria for Jewish immigration, it proposed elected institutions based on proportional representation instead of parity, and it excluded Transjordan from the area available for Jewish settlement. This adverse shift in British policy continued throughout the interwar period, reaching its climax in the white paper of 1939.

Weizmann's disappointment with the British was as bitter as that of any other Zionist leader. His response, however, was characteristically prudent and pragmatic. Having staked everything on the British connection, he recognized that there was now no alternative to continuing reliance on the mandatory power if the national home was to survive. This is why he opposed a showdown with Britain: there was simply no way the Zionists could impose on Britain their own interpretation of what the Balfour Declaration entailed. His advice was to continue to build the Jewish national home step by step, immigrant by immigrant, settlement by settlement.

This advice did not command unanimous assent in the Zionist camp. In the early 1920s, against the background of growing Arab militancy and British moves to appease the Arabs, voices were raised in favor of revising the official policy of the Zionist movement. The most powerful voice was that of Ze'ev (Vladimir) Jabotinsky.

ZE'EV JABOTINSKY
AND REVISIONIST ZIONISM

Ze'ev Jabotinsky (1880–1940) was an ardent Jewish nationalist, the founder of Revisionist Zionism, and the spiritual father of the Israeli right. Born in Odessa to a liberal Russian Jewish family, he worked as a journalist in Rome and Vienna and at an early age began to devote his outstanding skills as a writer, orator, and polemicist to the Zionist cause. During the First World War he persuaded the British to form Jewish volunteer units within the British army and himself served as an officer in the Zion Mule Corps in Egypt.

In 1921 Jabotinsky was elected to the Zionist Executive. From the very start he was at odds with Chaim Weizmann, whose principal sparring partner he remained for the rest of his life. In 1923 he resigned from the Zionist Executive, charging that its policies, especially its acceptance of the 1922 white paper, would result in the loss of Palestine. At successive Zionist congresses Jabotinsky established himself as one of the great orators of his day and as the chief spokesman for the opposition. He formed a new party, the World Union of Zionist Revisionists in 1925, and the youth movement Betar. After a decade in opposition to the official leadership of Zionism, he and his group seceded from the movement altogether and established the New Zionist Organization, which elected him as its president. Jabotinsky strongly opposed the partition of Palestine. Growing militancy led him to take over the leadership of the dissident military organization, the Irgun. He died in America in 1940 on a mission to organize Jewish participation in the Allied war effort. Jabotinsky was an exceptionally talented and versatile man, an original thinker and ideologue, and a powerful political leader. His followers worshiped him, while his enemies detested him with equal passion.

Although the Revisionist movement was dominated to a large extent by Jabotinsky and his ideas, it was not a one-man show. It gained significant grassroots support in the 1920s, during a period of crisis in the history of Zionism. The Balfour Declaration had inspired great hopes that Zionism would be speedily fulfilled with the help of Great Britain, but Britain's postwar policy produced a mood of disappointment and disillusion in the Yishuv. Jabotinsky tapped into this mood to build his movement and to articulate the ideology of Revisionist Zionism.

One of the paradoxes of this phase in Zionist history is that there was no fundamental difference between Jabotinsky and Weizmann regarding the role of Great Britain. Both men, in different ways, were disciples of Theodor Herzl in that they both assumed that the support and protection of a great power were absolutely indispensable in the struggle for statehood. Jabotinsky's strong pro-Western orientation stemmed from his distinctive worldview. He rejected the romantic view of the East and believed in the cultural superiority of Western civilization. "We Jews have nothing in common with what is denoted 'the East' and we thank God for that," he declared. The East, in his view, represented psychological passivity, social and cultural stagnation, and political despotism. Although the Jews originated in the East, they belonged to the West culturally, morally, and spiritually. Zionism was conceived by Jabotinsky not as the return of the Jews to their spiritual homeland but as an offshoot or implant of Western civilization in the East. This worldview translated into a geostrategic conception in which Zionism was to be permanently allied with European colonialism against all the Arabs in the eastern Mediterranean.

The root cause of Jabotinsky's dispute with the official Zionist leadership was his conception of the Jewish state. He laid down two principles that formed the core of the Revisionist Zionist ideology and its political program. The first was the territorial integrity of Eretz Israel, the Land of Israel, over both banks of the river Jordan within the original borders of the Palestine mandate. The second was the immediate declaration of the Jewish right to political sovereignty over the whole of this area.

This maximalist definition of the aims of Zionism once again raised a question: Did the Arabs of Palestine constitute a distinct national entity and, if so, what should be the Zionist attitude toward them and what should be their status within the projected Jewish state? Jabotinsky's answer is contained in two highly important articles he published in 1923 under the heading "The Iron Wall." They gave the essence of Revisionist theory on the Arab question and provided its fighting slogan. The first article is entitled "On the Iron War (We and the Arabs)." It begins on a personal note in which Jabotinsky engagingly described his emotional attitude to the Arabs as one of "polite indifference." But he went on to reject, as totally unacceptable, any thought of removing the Arabs from Palestine. The real question, he said, switching to a philosophical mode, was whether one could always achieve peaceful aims by peaceful means. The answer to this question, he insisted, depended without a doubt on the attitude of the Arabs toward Zionism, not on Zionism's attitude toward them.

Jabotinsky's analysis of the Arabs' attitude led him to state categorically, "A voluntary agreement between us and the Arabs of Palestine is inconceivable now or in the foreseeable future." As most moderate Zionists had already found out, there was not the slightest chance of gaining the agreement of the Palestine Arabs to turn Palestine into a country with a Jewish majority. This was because they regarded their country as their national homeland and wanted to remain its sole owners. Jabotinsky turned sharply against those Zionists who portrayed the Palestine Arabs either as fools who could be easily deceived by a watered-down version of Zionist objectives or as a tribe of mercenaries ready to give up their right to a country in exchange for economic advantage: "Every indigenous people," he wrote, "will resist alien settlers as long as they see any hope of ridding themselves of the danger of foreign settlement. This is how the Arabs will behave and go on behaving so long as they possess a gleam of hope that they can prevent 'Palestine' from becoming the Land of Israel."

Having explained the logic of Palestinian hostility to Zionism, Jabotinsky turned to the policy implications. One option, he noted, was to offer the non-Palestinian Arabs money or a political alliance in return for their agreement to Jewish control of Palestine. This option was rejected for two reasons. First, it would do nothing to modify the implacable hostility of the Palestinian Arabs to Jewish colonization. Second, to pledge Jewish money and political support to the Arabs of the Middle East would be to betray the European colonial powers, especially Britain, and this would be a suicidal act. Jabotinsky therefore concluded,

> We cannot promise any reward either to the Arabs of Palestine or to the Arabs outside Palestine. A voluntary agreement is unattainable. And so those who regard an accord with the Arabs as an indispensable condition of Zionism must admit to themselves today that this condition cannot be attained and hence that we must give up Zionism. We must either suspend our settlement efforts or continue them without paying attention to the mood of the natives. Settlement can thus develop under the protection of a force that is not dependent on the local population, behind an iron wall which they will be powerless to break down.

This, in a nutshell, was Jabotinsky's policy regarding the Arab question: to erect an iron wall of Jewish military force. On the need for an iron wall, he claimed, there was agreement among all Zionists. The only slight difference was that "the militarists" wanted an iron wall constructed with Jewish bayonets, whereas "the vegetarians" wanted it built with British bayonets. But they all wanted an iron wall. Constant repetition of Zionist willingness to negotiate with the Arabs was not only hypocritical but harmful, and Jabotinsky regarded it as his sacred duty to expose this hypocrisy.

Toward the end of the article Jabotinsky went to some length to dispel any impression his analysis might have given that he despaired of the prospect of reaching an agreement with the Arabs of Palestine:

> I do not mean to assert that no agreement whatever is possible with the Arabs of the Land of Israel. But a voluntary agreement is just not possible. As long as the Arabs preserve a gleam of hope that they will succeed in getting rid of us, nothing in the world can cause them to relinquish this hope, precisely because they are not a rabble but a living people. And a living people will be ready to yield on such fateful issues only when they have given up all hope of getting rid of the alien settlers. Only then will extremist groups with their slogans "No, never" lose their influence, and only then will their influence be transferred to more moderate groups. And only then will the moderates offer suggestions for compromise. Then only will they begin bargaining with us on practical matters, such as guarantees against pushing them out, and equality of civil and national rights.

The article concluded with a profession of faith that peaceful coexistence between Arabs and Jews in Palestine would be possible, but only as a result of the construction of an impregnable wall:

> It is my hope and belief that we will then offer them guarantees that will satisfy them and that both peoples will live in peace as good neighbors. But the sole way to such an agreement is through the iron wall, that is to say, the establishment in Palestine of a force that will in no way be influenced by Arab pressure. In other words, the only way to achieve a settlement in the future is total avoidance of all attempts to arrive at a settlement in the present.[6]

Moderate Zionists criticized the article, especially on the grounds that it was written from an immoral standpoint. Jabotinsky therefore wrote a second article, entitled "The Morality of the Iron Wall," in which he turned the tables on his critics. From the point of view of morality, he held, there were two possibilities: either Zionism was a positive phenomenon, or it was negative. This question required an answer before one became a Zionist. And all of them had indeed concluded that Zionism was a positive force, a moral movement with justice on its side. Now, "if the cause is just, justice must triumph, without regard to the assent or dissent of anyone else."

A frequent argument against Zionism was that it violated the democratic right of the Arab majority to national self-determination in Palestine. Jabotinsky responded that the Jews had a moral right to return to Palestine and that the enlightened world had acknowledged this right. He then turned to the argument that the method of the iron wall was immoral because it tried to settle Jews in Palestine without the consent of its inhabitants. He pointed out that since no native population anywhere in the world would willingly accept an alien majority, the logical conclusion would be to renounce altogether the idea of a Jewish national home. Even to dream of a national home would then become immoral. The article concluded with an assertion of the morality of the iron wall: "A sacred truth, whose realization requires the use of force, does not cease thereby to be a sacred truth. This is the basis of our stand toward Arab resistance; and we shall talk of a settlement only when they are ready to discuss it."[7]

Although "On the Iron Wall" became the bible of Revisionist Zionism, its real message was often misunderstood, not least by Jabotinsky's own followers. For him the iron wall was not an end in itself but a means to the end of breaking Arab resistance to the onward march of Zionism. Once Arab resistance had been broken, a process of change would occur inside the Palestinian national movement, with the moderates coming to the fore. Then and only then would it be time to start serious negotiations. In these negotiations the Jewish side should offer the Palestinians civil and national rights. Jabotinsky did not spell out in this article what precisely he meant by "national rights," but other pronouncements suggest that what he had in mind was political autonomy for the Palestinians within a Jewish state. What does emerge from the article is that he recognized that the Palestine Arabs formed a distinct national entity and that he accordingly considered them entitled to some national rights, albeit limited ones, and not merely to individual rights.

In the realm of ideas Jabotinsky was important as the founder of Revisionist Zionism. In the realm of politics his impact was much greater than is commonly realized. For it was not only Revisionist Zionists who were influenced by his ideas but the Zionist movement as a whole. "On the Iron Wall," in the words of one perceptive observer, should be treated as "a forceful, honest effort to grapple with the most serious problem facing the Zionist movement and as a formal articulation of what did become, in fact, the dominant rationale for Zionist and Israeli policies and attitudes toward the Arabs of Palestine from the 1920s to the late 1980s."[8]

The Zionist movement was not a monolithic political movement but a collection of rival political parties, the largest being the Labor Party, which was inspired by Marxist ideas and socialist ideals. One fundamental difference between Labor Zionism and Revisionist Zionism related to the use of force. Labor Zionists were reluctant to admit that military force would be necessary if the Zionist movement was to achieve its objectives. Jabotinsky faced up to this fact fairly and squarely. He went further in suggesting a reversal of the Zionist order of priorities. Labor Zionists wanted to proceed toward statehood by immigration and settlement and accorded a lower priority to the building up of a military capability. Jabotinsky never wavered in his conviction that Jewish military power was the key factor in the struggle for a state. It was the Labor Zionists who gradually came around to his point of view without openly admitting it. So in the final analysis the gap was not all that great: Labor leaders, too, came to rely increasingly on the strategy of the iron wall.

David Ben-Gurion
and the Triumph of Pragmatism

Labor Zionism's shift toward the premises and strategy of the iron wall is best illustrated by the career of David Ben-Gurion (1886–1973), the builder of Yishuv's military power and the founder of the State of Israel. Born as David Green in Plonsk, Poland, he developed at an early age a passionate commitment to socialism and Zionism and in 1906 left for Palestine to work as a farmhand. He was initially active in the socialist Zionist Po'ale

Zion party, which joined with other groups to form Ahduth Ha'avodah in 1919 and merged with Hapoel Hatza'ir in 1930 to form Mapai, the Israeli Labor Party. He quickly rose to positions of political prominence in the trade union movement, the Labor Party, and the Zionist movement. From 1921 to 1935 he served as the secretary-general of the Histadrut, the General Federation of Labor in Palestine. In 1935 he was elected chairman of the Jewish Agency Executive and held this post until the State of Israel was born in 1948. From 1948 until his retirement in 1963, except for one short interval, he served as Israel's prime minister and minister of defense

Throughout his long political career Ben-Gurion was involved deeply and continually in the Arab question. He often spoke out on the subject and published countless articles and books. Sifting through this material, however, is a largely futile exercise because a wide gulf separated his public utterances on the Arab question from his private convictions and because he was, above all, a pragmatic politician. Ben-Gurion's public pronouncements in the 1920s and early 1930s tended to conform to the labor movement's official position, which held that the Arabs of Palestine did not constitute a separate national entity but were part of the Arab nation and that, moreover, there was no inherent conflict between the interests of the Arabs of Palestine and the interests of the Zionists. Zionism's only conflict, so the socialist argument ran, was a class conflict with the Arab landowners and effendis, and this conflict would be resolved when the Arab peasants realized that their true interests coincided with those of the Jewish working class.

Privately Ben-Gurion did not share this class analysis or its optimistic forecast. What distinguished his approach to the Arab problem was unflinching realism. Already as an agricultural laborer he recognized the problem's acuteness. His fears and anxieties deepened when he realized that Arab opposition was grounded in principle and that it amounted to an utter rejection of the entire Zionist enterprise. Thus, at a very early stage in his career, Ben-Gurion came to the conclusion that the conflict between Zionism and the Arabs was inescapable and that it presented a formidable challenge.

Ben-Gurion's appreciation of the strength of Arab opposition led him to seek the support of an external power in order to compensate for the weakness of the Zionist movement. His orientation on a great power was practical rather than ideological. In the course of his career he advocated an Ottoman, a British, and an American orientation. Changes in orientation were dictated by the rise and fall in the influence of these great powers. When Britain supplanted the Ottoman Empire as the dominant power in Palestine, he followed Chaim Weizmann in advocating an alliance with Britain. Indeed, for Ben-Gurion an alliance with Britain was an indispensable condition for the success of Zionism. He regarded cooperation with Britain as more important than cooperation with the Arabs. Many of the proposals he made to the Arabs were made not out of real conviction but in order to please the British. The British wanted a Jewish-Arab understanding, so Ben-Gurion wanted to be seen to be working toward this end even when his proposals had no chance of being accepted by the Arabs. An anti-imperialist alliance with the Arabs was completely out of the question as far as he was concerned, although socialist ideology pointed in that direction.

The Arab Revolt, which broke out in April 1936, marked a turning point in the evolution of Ben-Gurion's attitude toward the Arab problem. For the first time he acknowledged openly the national character of the Arab opposition to Zionism. There is a great conflict, he told the Jewish Agency Executive on 19 May 1936. "We and they want the same thing: We both want Palestine. And that is the fundamental conflict."[9] Because ideologically less hidebound than his colleagues, he was willing to admit that in political terms they were the aggressors while the Arabs were defending themselves. But recognizing the deep-rooted character of the Arab Revolt did not incline him toward negotiation and compromise. On the contrary, it made him conclude that only war, not diplomacy, would resolve the conflict.

Ben-Gurion was committed to the full realization of Zionism regardless of the scale and depth of Arab opposition. In a letter to the Jewish Agency Executive of 9 June 1936, he insisted that peace with the Arabs was only a means to an end: "It is not in order to establish peace in the country that we need an agreement. Peace is indeed a vital matter for us. It is impossible to build a country in a permanent state of war, but peace for us is a means. The end is the complete and full realization of Zionism. Only for that do we need an agreement." Ben-Gurion maintained that an agreement with the Arabs regarding the final objective of Zionism was conceivable, but only in the long term: "A comprehensive agreement is undoubtedly out of the question now. For only after total despair on the part of the Arabs, despair that will come not only from the failure of the disturbances and the attempt at rebellion, but also as a consequence of our growth in the country, may the Arabs possibly acquiesce in a Jewish Eretz Israel."[10]

The similarity between Ben-Gurion's conclusion and that of Ze'ev Jabotinsky in the article "On the Iron Wall" thirteen years earlier is very striking. Both men regarded the Arabs of Palestine as a national movement that by its very nature was bound to resist the encroachment of Zionism on its land. Both realized that these Arabs would not willingly make way for a Jewish state and that diplomacy was therefore incapable of resolving the conflict. Both believed that the Arabs would continue to fight for as long as they retained any hope of preventing the Jewish takeover of their country. And both concluded that only insuperable Jewish military strength would eventually make the Arabs despair of the struggle and come to terms with a Jewish state in Palestine. Ben-Gurion did not use the terminology of the iron wall, but his analysis and conclusions were virtually identical to Jabotinsky's.

The British government responded to the outbreak of the Arab Revolt in Palestine by appointing a royal commission, with Lord Peel as chairman, to investigate the causes of the disturbances and to recommend a solution. The commission concluded that Jewish nationalism was as intense and self-centered as Arab nationalism, that the gulf between them was widening, and that the only solution was to partition the country into two separate states. In its final report of July 1937, the commission proposed a very small Jewish state of some 5,000 square kilometers, a large Arab state, and an enclave from Jerusalem to Jaffa under a permanent British mandate (see map 2).

For Ben-Gurion the Peel partition plan marked the beginning of the end of the British mandate in Palestine and the birth of a Jewish state as a realistic political program. The Zionist movement was divided in its response to the partition plan, not least because of the small size of the Jewish state and doubts regarding its viability. But at the Twentieth Zionist Congress, which met in Zurich in August 1937, a decision was reached to accept the plan as a basis for negotiations with the British government. This decision clearly implied that from then on the creation of an independent Jewish state would take precedence over a Jewish-Arab agreement. It was thus in line with the guiding principle that Ben-Gurion had laid down the preceding year—namely, that while they were continuing to strive for an agreement with the Arabs, the realization of Zionism must not be made dependent on it.

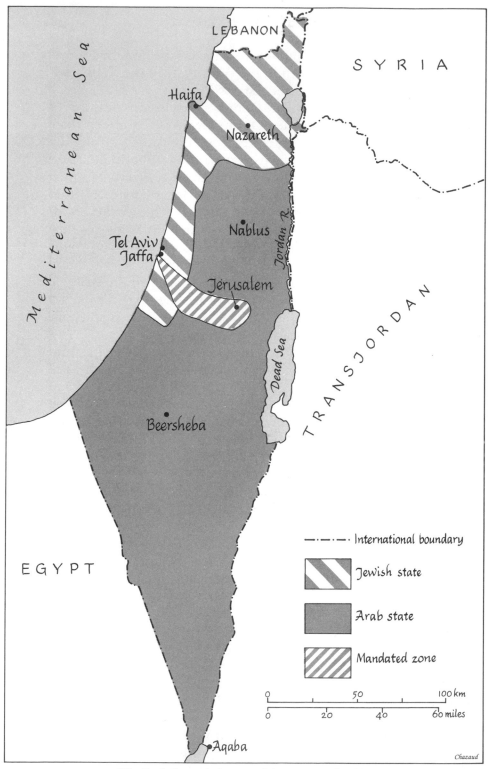

The Peel Commission partition proposal, 1937

The leaders of the pro-partition camp were Chaim Weizmann, David Ben-Gurion, and Moshe Shertok, the head of the Political Department of the Jewish Agency, who was to change his name to Sharett and become the first foreign minister of the State of Israel. Their main argument in favor of partition was that establishing an independent Jewish state even in a small part of Palestine was a more promising avenue for the realization of Zionism than any of the alternatives. Weizmann held that the Jews would be fools not accept the Peel plan even if the Jewish state was the size of a table-cloth. But whereas Weizmann accepted partition as part of a con-tinuing pro-British orientation, Ben-Gurion lost faith in Britain and valued the Peel plan for the opportunity it offered to build up the independent power of the Jewish community in Palestine.

Although Ben-Gurion accepted partition, he did not view the borders of the Peel commission plan as permanent. He saw no contradiction between accepting a Jewish state in part of Palestine and hoping to expand the borders of this state to the whole Land of Israel. The difference between him and the Revisionists was not that he was a territorial minimalist while they were territorial max-imalists but rather that he pursued a gradualist strategy while they adhered to an all-or-nothing approach.

The nature and extent of Ben-Gurion's territorial expansionism were revealed with startling frankness in a letter he sent to his son Amos from London on 5 October 1937. There Ben-Gurion pro-fessed himself to be an enthusiastic advocate of a Jewish state, even if it involved the partitioning of Palestine, because he worked on the assumption that this state would be not the end but only the beginning. A state would enable the Jews to have unlimited im-migration, to build a Jewish economy, and to organize a first-class army. "I am certain," he wrote, "we will be able to settle in all the other parts of the country, whether through agreement and mu-tual understanding with our Arab neighbours or in another way." Both his mind and his heart told Ben-Gurion, "Erect a Jewish State at once, even if it is not in the whole land. The rest will come in the course of time. It must come."[11]

The majority of Zionists followed Ben-Gurion in opting for partition and a Jewish state. At the Twentieth Zionist Congress, in Zurich, the arguments for and against partition were examined exhaustively. It was the first major public debate on partition and also the most serious and searching one in the history of Zionism. With so much at stake, both camps presented their case with great passion and conviction. The naysayers advanced three main arguments: the Promised Land of the forefathers and the Bible must not be compromised; the Yishuv was not yet ready to stand on its own feet; and Britain must be held firmly to its commitments under the Balfour Declaration and the mandate. Two hundred and ninety-nine delegates voted in favor of Ben-Gurion's proposal, 160 voted against, and 6 abstained. The debate thus ended with a strategic decision to support partition and the creation of a Jewish state in part of Palestine. At the end of the congress, Ben-Gurion presented himself for reelection as chairman of the Jewish Agency Executive for the specific purpose of working toward the establishment of a Jewish state. He was to devote the next ten years of his life to a single-minded pursuit of this goal.

THE STRUGGLE FOR STATEHOOD

The struggle for statehood was accompanied by many disagreements, but these were more about tactics than about the long-term goal. Ben-Gurion's own commitment to statehood did not waver in the face of Arab opposition or British prevarications. Having taken the initiative in proposing partition in 1937, the British government began to retreat from partition with the approach of World War II. The support of the Arab states and the Muslim world generally was much more crucial for Britain in the conflict with the Axis powers than the support of the Jews. A white paper of 17 May 1939 abruptly reversed British support for Zionism and for a Jewish state. It condemned the Jews to a status of permanent minority in a future independent Palestinian state. So the Zionist movement was driven to develop its own military power, through the paramilitary organization called the Haganah (which in Hebrew means defense), in order to combat Arab resistance. Having subscribed to a defensive ethos that had served it so well on the public relations front, it adopted a policy based on force in order to counter the use and the threat of force by its Arab opponents. The offensive ethos that had always been embedded in the defensive ethos had in any case become more prominent following the outbreak of the Arab Revolt.

At the same time the Yishuv mounted its own active resistance to the policy of the white paper that restricted Jewish land purchase and Jewish immigration to Palestine. The outbreak of World War II in September 1939 placed the Yishuv in an acute dilemma:

it was behind Britain in the struggle against Nazi Germany but at loggerheads with Britain in the struggle for Palestine. A way out of the dilemma was found, however, succinctly summed up in Ben-Gurion's slogan: "We will fight with the British against Hitler as if there were no white paper; we will fight the white paper as if there were no war."

During the war Ben-Gurion became ever more assertive about the Jewish right to political sovereignty, while denying this right to the Arab majority in Palestine. His solution to the Yishuv's demographic problem involved the migration to Palestine of two to three million Jews immediately following the end of the war. The Arab problem, he claimed, paled in significance compared with the Jewish problem because the Arabs had vast spaces outside Palestine, whereas for the Jews, who were being persecuted in Europe, Palestine constituted the only possible haven. He thus came to treat the Arab problem as merely one of status for the Arab minority within a state with a large Jewish majority.

The new concept of a Jewish state over the whole of Palestine found expression in the so-called Biltmore Program. At an extraordinary meeting of the American Zionists, attended by both Weizmann and Ben-Gurion, in the Biltmore Hotel in New York in May 1942, a resolution was adopted urging "that Palestine be constituted as a Jewish Commonwealth integrated in the structure of the new democratic world" after World War II. With this resolution the Zionist movement for the first time openly staked a claim to the whole of mandatory Palestine. The goal of a Jewish-Arab agreement was not abandoned, but it was now clearly expected to follow rather than to precede the establishment of a Jewish state or commonwealth.

The Biltmore Program was adopted before the full scale and the horror of the Nazi campaign for the extermination of European Jewry became known. Zionist leaders assumed that at the end of the war there would be millions of Jewish refugees in Europe whose plight would strengthen the case for a large Jewish state in Palestine. None of them foresaw the Holocaust, the most calamitous event in the annals of Jewish history, in which six million Jews would perish. In the end, however, the tragedy of European Jewry became a source of strength for Zionism. The moral case for a home for the Jewish people in Palestine was widely accepted from the beginning; after the Holocaust it became unassailable. The poet Robert Frost defined a home as the place where, if you have to go there, they have to let you in. Few people disputed the right of the Jews to a home after the trauma to which they had been subjected in Central Europe.

A much tougher kind of Zionism was forged in the course of World War II, and the commitment to Jewish statehood became deeper and more desperate in the shadow of the Holocaust. On the one hand, the Holocaust confirmed the conviction of the Zionists that they had justice on their side in the struggle for Palestine; on the other, it converted international public opinion to the idea of an independent Jewish state.

Ben-Gurion embodied the "fighting Zionism" that rose out of the ashes of World War II, and he wrested the leadership from the hands of Weizmann, who still adhered to "diplomatic Zionism" and to the alliance with Britain. Against Weizmann's advice the Zionist conference of August 1945 decided on a policy of active opposition to British rule, and in October an armed uprising was launched. The Haganah was instructed to cooperate with the dissident groups spawned by the Revisionist movement. The main group was the National Military Organization (the Irgun), which began to direct its operations against the British administration in Palestine after the publication of the white paper in 1939. Later that year, when the Irgun called off its campaign against the British, a split took place. The more militant wing, led by Avraham Stern, seceded from the Irgun to form Lohamei Herut Yisrael (Fighters for the Freedom of Israel), better known as Lehi, after its Hebrew acronym, or the Stern Gang. The Stern Gang was so hostile to the British that it sought contact with the Axis powers in order to drive the British out of Palestine. Although its members never exceeded three hundred, the Stern Gang was a considerable thorn in the flesh of the British. Between November 1945 and July 1946, the three underground organizations joined arms in what became known as "the movement of the Hebrew revolt."

A massive British military crackdown forced the Zionist leaders to call off the Hebrew revolt, and they instead tried to drive a wedge between Britain and the United States on the diplomatic front. Britain sought American support for its plan for self-governing Jewish and Arab cantons, a plan categorically rejected by the Zionists. To get America on their side, members of the Jewish Agency Executive decided in August 1946 to agree to consider the establishment of a Jewish state on an adequate part of Palestine. This decision signified the abandonment of the Biltmore Program and a return to the principle of partition. The decision was viewed not as a concession to the Arabs but as a means of gaining American support for the idea of a Jewish state. In February 1947 the British government, unable to come up with a solution on which both sides could agree, referred the Palestine problem to the United Nations.

On 29 November 1947 the General Assembly of the United Nations passed its historic Resolution 181 in favor of the partition of Palestine. In a rare instance of agreement during the Cold War, the United States and the Soviet Union voted for the resolution while Britain abstained. The resolution laid down a timetable for the establishment of a Jewish state and an Arab state linked by economic union, and an international regime for Jerusalem. Exceptionally long and winding borders separated the Jewish state from the Arab one, with vulnerable crossing points to link its isolated areas in the eastern Galilee, the coastal plain, and the Negev. The borders of these two oddly shaped states, resembling two fighting serpents, were a strategic nightmare (see map 3). No less anomalous and scarcely more viable was the demographic structure of the proposed Jewish state, consisting as it did of roughly 500,000 Jews and 400,000 Arabs.

Despite all its limitations and anomalies, the UN resolution represented a major triumph for Zionist diplomacy. While falling far short of the full-blown Zionist aspiration for a state comprising the whole of Palestine and Jerusalem, it provided an invaluable charter of international legitimacy for the creation of an independent Jewish state. News of the UN vote was greeted by Jews everywhere with jubilation and rejoicing. But the followers of Ze'ev Jabotinsky in the Irgun and the Stern Gang did not join in the general celebrations. A day after the UN vote, Menachem Begin, the commander of Irgun, proclaimed the credo of the underground fighters: "The partition of Palestine is illegal. It will never be recognized. . . . Jerusalem was and will for ever be our capital. Eretz Israel will be restored to the people of Israel. All of it. And for ever."[12]

The Jewish Agency officially accepted the UN partition plan, but most of its leaders did so with a heavy heart. They did not like the idea of an independent Palestinian state, they were disappointed with the exclusion of Jerusalem, and they had grave doubts about the viability of the Jewish state within the UN borders. Nevertheless, the UN resolution represented a tremendous gain of international support for the establishment of a Jewish state—hence their decision to go along with it.

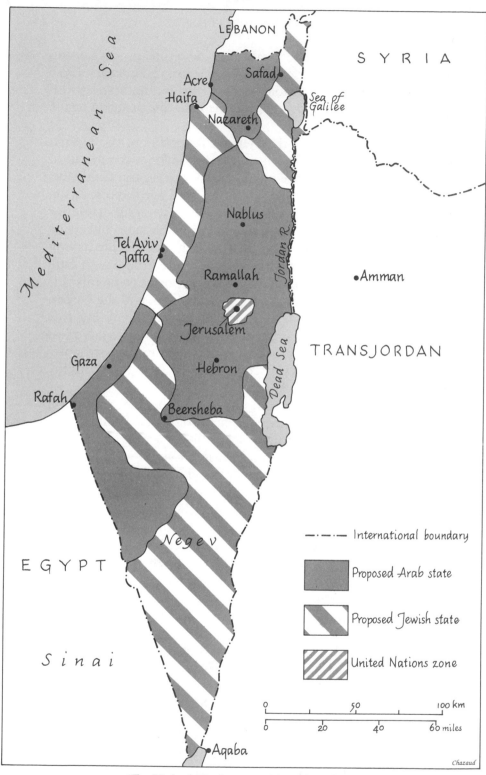

The United Nations partition plan, 1947

The Palestine Arabs, who unlike the Jews had done very little to prepare themselves for statehood, rejected the UN partition plan out of hand. The Arab Higher Committee, which represented them, denounced the plan as "absurd, impracticable, and unjust." The Arab states, loosely organized since 1945 in the Arab League, also claimed that the UN plan was illegal and threatened to resist its implementation by force. On 1 December the Arab Higher Committee proclaimed a three-day strike, which was accompanied by violent attacks on Jewish civilians. The UN vote in favor of partition thus provided not just international legitimacy for creating Jewish and Arab states but, unintentionally, the signal for a savage war between the two communities in Palestine.

1

The Emergence
of Israel

1947–1949

THE STATE OF ISRAEL was born in the midst of a war with the
Arabs of Palestine and the neighboring Arab states. This war,
which Israelis call the War of Independence and Arabs call *al-
Nakba,* or the disaster, had two phases. The first phase lasted from
29 November 1947, when the UN passed the partition resolution,
until 14 May 1948, when the State of Israel was proclaimed. The
second phase lasted from 15 May 1948 until the termination of
hostilities on 7 January 1949. The first and unofficial phase of the
war, between the Jewish and Arab communities in Palestine, ended
in triumph for the Jews and tragedy for the Palestinians. The second and official phase, involving the regular armies of the neighboring Arab states, also ended in a Jewish victory and a
comprehensive Arab defeat.

THE UNOFFICIAL WAR

The key figure on the Israeli side throughout the first Arab-Israeli
war was David Ben-Gurion. As the strongman of the Yishuv, Ben-
Gurion relentlessly concentrated power in his own hands. In 1946
he assumed the defense portfolio in the Jewish Agency Executive
and immediately started preparing the Yishuv for a military confrontation with the Arabs, which in his view was inescapable. He
accepted the UN partition plan, but he did not accept as final the

borders it laid down for the Jewish state. Although he valued international support, especially that of the United States and the Soviet Union, for the idea of a Jewish state, he did not expect statehood to be delivered on a silver platter. Realizing that ultimately the Jews would have to fight for their state, he wanted a clear-cut Jewish military victory. That is why he assumed personal responsibility for directing the military struggle and left it to Moshe Sharett to conduct, in New York, the diplomatic campaign for a Jewish state. Ben-Gurion also enjoyed the strong support of Golda Meir (formerly Meyerson) during the struggle for independence. Born in Russia in 1898 and educated in Milwaukee as a teacher, Mrs. Meir in 1921 emigrated to Palestine, where she rose through the ranks of the trade unions to a prominent position in the Labor Party. In 1946, when Moshe Sharett was arrested by the British, Mrs. Meir became acting head of the Political Department of the Jewish Agency. In 1947–48 she assumed responsibility for fund-raising in the United States, freeing Ben-Gurion to concentrate on the military side of the struggle.

Acceptance of the UN plan implied acceptance of a Palestinian state, but in practice the Zionist leaders preferred to seek an understanding with one of the rulers of the neighboring Arab states. They had their greatest success with their neighbor to the east, with King Abdullah of Transjordan. Did they have any diplomatic alternative? Did they have a Palestinian option in 1947–49? The answer to this question must be no, because under the leadership of Hajj Amin al-Husseini the Palestinian national movement remained as uncompromising in its opposition to Zionism in the late 1940s as it had been over the preceding quarter of a century.

The Zionists were looking for an Arab leader who would accept the principle of partition, agree to a Jewish state, and be willing to coexist peacefully with such a state after its establishment. In 1947 there was only one Arab leader who fit the bill—King Abdullah. Friendly relations had existed between Abdullah and the Zionists ever since the establishment of the emirate of Transjordan in 1921. Abdullah made a realistic appraisal of the balance of power between the Zionist movement and the Arab national movement. He may not have fully understood the ideology that propelled the Jews to strive so relentlessly for an independent state in Palestine, but he knew a going concern when he saw one. Abdullah and the Zionists saw in each other a means to an end. For Abdullah the Zionists represented a potential source of support for realizing his dream of Greater Syria. For the

Zionists, Abdullah offered a means of breaking the chain of Arab hostility that surrounded them on all sides. Abdullah and the Zionists spoke the same language, the language of realism, but from different scripts. Hashemite-Zionist friendship was underpinned by having a common protector in Britain and a common enemy in Hajj Amin al-Husseini. To both sides Palestinian nationalism posed a threat, and they therefore had a common interest in repressing it. As the British mandate over Palestine was approaching its inglorious end, the two sides made an effort to coordinate their strategies.

On 17 November 1947, twelve days before the UN met to decide the fate of Palestine, Golda Meir, representing the Jewish Agency in Sharett's absence, secretly met with King Abdullah in Naharayim, on the river Jordan, and reached a broad understanding with him. Abdullah began by outlining his plan to preempt the mufti, to capture the Arab part of Palestine, and to attach it to his kingdom, and he asked about the Jewish response to this plan. Mrs. Meir replied that the Jews would view such an attempt in a favourable light, especially if Abdullah did not interfere with the establishment of a Jewish state, avoided a military confrontation, and appeared to go along with the United Nations. She did not promise Abdullah any active Jewish support in his bid to annex the Arab part of Palestine adjacent to his kingdom. Rather, the understanding was that he would take it himself, the Jews would set up their own state, and, after the dust had settled, the two parties would make peace. This meeting did not commit either side formally to a particular course of action, certainly not in advance of the UN decision. But it did result in a meeting of minds and laid the foundations for a partition of Palestine along lines radically different from the ones eventually envisaged by the United Nations.[1]

The situation in Palestine rapidly deteriorated following the UN vote on 29 November in favor of partition. Arab guerrilla attacks began to be launched against Jewish targets. Ben-Gurion was convinced that these attacks were merely a prelude to a full-scale military confrontation with the regular armies of the neighboring Arab states. On 1 and 2 January 1948, he met with his senior civilian and military advisers, and these meetings helped shape Jewish strategy in the evolving conflict. The Arab experts of the Jewish Agency downplayed the military danger posed by the local Arabs and called for political flexibility in dealing with them. The commanders of the Haganah, on the other hand, advocated hard-hitting military reprisals. Ben-Gurion himself shared the latters' opinion that their best bet under the circumstances was not to contain and localize the trouble but to escalate the military conflict. Consequently, the Haganah embarked on a policy of "aggressive defense" accompanied by economic subversion and psychological warfare.[2]

Plan D, prepared by the Haganah chiefs in early March, was a major landmark in the development of this offensive strategy. During the preceding month the Palestinian irregulars, under the inspired leadership of Abdel Qader al-Husseini, cut the main road between Tel Aviv and Jerusalem and started to gain the upper hand in the fighting with the Haganah. After suffering several defeats at the hands of Palestinian irregulars, the Haganah chiefs decided to seize the initiative and go on the offensive. The aim of Plan D was to secure all the areas allocated to the Jewish state under the UN partition resolution as well as Jewish settlements outside these areas and corridors leading to them, so as to provide a solid and continuous basis for Jewish sovereignty. The novelty and audacity of the plan lay in the orders to capture Arab villages and cities, something the Haganah had never attempted before. Although the wording of Plan D was vague, its objective was to clear the interior of the country of hostile and potentially hostile Arab elements, and in this sense it provided a warrant for expelling civilians. By implementing Plan D in April and May, the Haganah thus directly and decisively contributed to the birth of the Palestinian refugee problem.

Palestinian society disintegrated under the impact of the Jewish military offensive that got under way in April, and the exodus of the Palestinians was set in motion. There were many reasons for the Palestinian exodus, including the early departure of the Palestinian leaders when the going got tough, but the most important reason was Jewish military pressure. Plan D was not a political blueprint for the expulsion of Palestine's Arabs: it was a military plan with military and territorial objectives. However, by ordering the capture of Arab cities and the destruction of villages, it both permitted and justified the forcible expulsion of Arab civilians.[3] By the end of 1948 the number of Palestinian refugees had swollen to around 700,000. But the first and largest wave of refugees occurred before the official outbreak of hostilities on 15 May. The bulk of the refugees ended up on the West Bank, in the Gaza Strip, and in neighboring Arab countries, especially Transjordan, Syria, and Lebanon.

The collapse of Palestinian resistance prompted the Arab League to commit the regular armies of the member states to the struggle against partition, thus reversing an earlier decision merely to finance and arm the local Arabs.[4] On the Jewish side the turn of the tide reinforced the conviction that military force offered the only solution to the Arab problem. An American proposal in the first week of May for an unconditional cease-fire and the extension of the mandate by ten days to give time for on-the-spot negotiations in Palestine was turned down by the Jewish Agency. A British proposal for a truce in Jerusalem was similarly frustrated by persistent evasiveness on the part of the Jewish Agency.

The diplomatic efforts of the Jewish Agency were directed not at a truce with the Palestinians but at dissuading King Abdullah from joining in the Arab League plan for invading Palestine upon expiration of the British mandate. On 11 May, Golda Meir, disguised as an Arab woman, made the dangerous journey to Amman in a last-ditch effort to salvage the agreement she had reached with the king at their meeting six months earlier. The king received his nocturnal visitor cordially, but he looked depressed, troubled, and under a great deal of pressure. His suggestion that Palestine remain undivided, with autonomy under his crown for the areas in which the Jews predominated, was rejected by Mrs. Meir out of hand. She suggested that instead of Abdullah's new offer they should adhere to their original plan for the partition of Palestine. Abdullah did not deny that they had an agreement, but he explained that the situation had changed and that he was now unable to stand against the current for military intervention in Palestine. Mrs. Meir warned the king that the Jews had dramatically increased their military strength in recent months and that, while willing to respect the UN borders in the event of peaceful partition, they would fight everywhere and with all their force in the event of war. The king urged her to think again about his offer and to contact him anytime before May 15. Her parting words were that his offer was totally unacceptable and that if he reneged on their agreement and chose war, they would meet again after the war.[5]

On 12 May the Provisional State Council was called upon to decide finally whether to accept the American proposal for an armistice and postpone the declaration of independence or to carry out the original plan of proclaiming the establishment of a Jewish state upon expiration of the British mandate. It was to this meeting that Golda Meir reported on the failure of her mission to

Amman. Moshe Sharett communicated the advice he received in Washington from Secretary of State George Marshall to postpone the declaration of independence and avoid a military showdown with the Arabs. The military chiefs presented a rather pessimistic appraisal of the military situation and warned that the chances of victory and defeat were equally balanced. This estimate that the Yishuv had only a fifty-fifty chance of survival was based on the assumption that it would have to withstand a concerted attack by all the Arab armies, including Transjordan's Arab Legion.[6]

Despite the risks, Ben-Gurion threw all his weight behind an immediate proclamation of independence, so as not to miss the historic opportunity. The proposal to reject a truce and proclaim independence was supported by six members of the Provisional State Council and opposed by four. It was also decided, following Ben-Gurion's strongly expressed preference, not to indicate the borders of the new state in the declaration of independence, in order to leave open the possibility of expansion beyond the UN borders. The name of the new state was to be Israel.

At four o'clock in the afternoon on 14 May 1948, in front of a large crowd of notables in the museum of Tel Aviv, David Ben-Gurion read out the Declaration of Independence and proclaimed the establishment of the Jewish state in Palestine to be called Medinat Israel—the State of Israel. The Declaration of Independence pledged that the State of Israel would be based on the principles of liberty, justice, and peace as conceived by the Prophets of Israel; would uphold the full social and political equality of all its citizens, without distinction of religion, race, or sex; and would loyally uphold the principles of the UN Charter. It specifically promised equal rights to the Arab inhabitants of the State of Israel and extended the hand of peace to all the neighboring Arab states.

A picture of Theodor Herzl hanging at the center of the main hall appeared to gaze down on the group of leaders who had come together to fulfill the vision of the Jewish state that he had articulated fifty years earlier at the First Zionist Congress, in Basel. From the beginning Herzl envisaged the need to enlist the support of a great power, and this vision too was translated into reality. The United States was the first country to recognize the State of Israel, with President Harry Truman acting against the advice of the State Department. The Soviet Union followed suit. Israel was thus born with two godfathers, the two superpowers of the postwar era, which were beginning to supplant the European powers in the

Middle East. Yet Israel faced an immediate threat from its angry Arab neighbors. "Its fate," wrote Ben-Gurion laconically in his diary, "is in the hands of the defense forces."[7]

THE WAR OF INDEPENDENCE

On 15 May the regular armies of Egypt, Transjordan, Syria, Lebanon, and Iraq invaded Palestine, reinforcing the Palestinian irregular forces and the Arab Liberation Army, which was sponsored by the Arab League. Israel was thus born in the midst of war. The first aim of its foreign policy was survival. The Haganah was renamed the Israel Defense Force (IDF), and the Irgun and the Stern Gang were later disbanded and merged with the IDF.

Israel's War of Independence was long, bitter, and very costly in human lives. It claimed the lives of 6,000 soldiers and civilians, or 1 percent of the entire Jewish population of around 650,000. The war consisted of three rounds of fighting punctuated by two UN-decreed truces. The first round lasted from 15 May until 11 June, the second from 9 to 18 July, and the third from 15 October until 7 January 1949.

The conventional Zionist version portrays the 1948 war as a simple, bipolar no-holds-barred struggle between a monolithic Arab adversary and a tiny Israel. According to this version, seven Arab armies invaded Palestine upon expiration of the British mandate with a single aim in mind: to strangle the Jewish state as soon as it came into the world. The subsequent struggle was an unequal one between a Jewish David and an Arab Goliath. The infant Jewish state fought a desperate, heroic, and ultimately successful battle for survival against overwhelming odds. During the war hundreds of thousands of Palestinians fled to the neighboring Arab states, mainly in response to orders from their leaders and in the expectation of a triumphal return. After the war, the story continues, Israel's leaders sought peace with all their heart and all their might, but there was no one to talk with on the other side. Arab intransigence was alone responsible for the political deadlock that persisted for three decades after the guns fell silent.

This popular-heroic-moralistic version of the 1948 war has been used extensively in Israeli propaganda and is still taught in Israeli schools. It is a prime example of the use of a nationalist version of history in the process of nation building. In a very real sense history is the propaganda of the victors, and the history of the 1948 war is no exception.

To say this is not to suggest that the conventional Zionist version of the first Arab-Israeli war is based on myth rather than on reality. On the contrary, this version is largely based on historical facts, but it is a selective and subjective interpretation of these facts. It is precisely because this version corresponds so closely to the personal experience and perceptions of the Israelis who lived through the 1948 war that it has proved so resistant to revision and change.

Following the release of the official documents, however, this version was subjected to critical scrutiny.[8] The two main claims about the official phase of the 1948 war concern the Arab-Israeli military balance and Arab war aims.

As far as the military balance is concerned, it was always assumed that the Arabs enjoyed overwhelming numerical superiority. The war was persistently portrayed as a struggle of the few against the many. The desperate plight and the heroism of the Jewish fighters are not in question. Nor is the fact that they had inferior military hardware at their disposal, at least until the first truce, when illicit arms supplies from Czechoslovakia decisively tipped the scales in their favor. But in mid-May 1948 the total number of Arab troops, both regular and irregular, operating in the Palestine theater was under 25,000, whereas the IDF fielded over 35,000 troops. By mid-July the IDF mobilized 65,000 men under arms, and by December its numbers had reached a peak of 96,441. The Arab states also reinforced their armies, but they could not match this rate of increase. Thus, at each stage of the war, the IDF significantly outnumbered all the Arab forces arrayed against it, and by the final stage of the war its superiority ratio was nearly two to one. The final outcome of the war was therefore not a miracle but a reflection of the underlying Arab-Israeli military balance. In this war, as in most wars, the stronger side ultimately prevailed.[9]

As far as Arab war aims are concerned, the older generation of Israeli historians have maintained that all the forces sent to Palestine were united in their determination to destroy the newborn Jewish state and to cast the Jews into the sea. In this they simply expressed the prevalent perception on the Jewish side at the time. Now, it is true that the military experts of the Arab League had worked out a unified plan for the invasion, but King Abdullah, who was given nominal command over all the Arab forces in Palestine, wrecked this plan by making last-minute changes. His objective in sending his army into Palestine was not to prevent the establishment of a Jewish state but to make himself the master of the Arab part of Palestine. There was no love lost between Abdullah and the other Arab rulers, who resented his expansionist ambitions and suspected him of being in cahoots with the enemy. Each of the other Arab states was also moved by dynastic or national interests, which were hidden behind the fig leaf of securing Palestine for the Palestinians. The inability of the Arabs to coordinate their diplomatic and military plans was in no small measure responsible for the disaster that overwhelmed them.[10] Israel's leaders knew of these divisions and exploited them to the full following the official outbreak of hostilities, just as they had exploited them previously.[11]

If one focuses on the military operations in 1948, as countless historians have done, one sees the familiar picture of Israel pitted against the entire Arab world. But if one probes the politics of the war, a more complicated lineup emerges. In the case of Ben-Gurion it is essential to understand his political objectives because these were usually at variance with his declared objectives. Indeed, it was his political objectives that largely determined Israel's military conduct during the war and its borders at the end of the war.

Ben-Gurion had a grand strategy, which he presented to the general staff on 24 May, ten days after the Declaration of Independence, and which stressed a number of key points. First, he had a clear order of priorities: Jerusalem, Galilee in the north, and the Negev in the south. Second, he preferred an offensive to a defensive strategy. Third, his method for dealing with the hostile Arab coalition, and one that became a central tenet in Israel's security doctrine, was to pick off the Arabs one by one: to attack on one front at a time while holding on in the other fronts. Fourth, he wanted to force a showdown with Jordan's Arab Legion, in the belief that if the mighty legion could be defeated, all the other Arab armies would rapidly collapse.[12]

At this early stage in the war there was a deep difference between Ben-Gurion and his generals. He regarded the Arab Legion as the number one enemy, whereas they saw the Egyptian army as the primary threat. He wanted to concentrate the bulk of Israel's forces in and around Jerusalem, whereas they wanted to give priority to the southern front. Clearly, Ben-Gurion did not consider himself to be bound by the earlier agreement with Abdullah once Abdullah himself had retreated from it. The earlier agreement had in any case not covered Jerusalem, which under the UN plan was supposed to become a separate body, or *corpus separatum,* under an international regime. The battle for Jerusalem was initiated by

an Israeli offensive a few days before the end of the British man-
date, and it was in response to this offensive that, on 17 May, King
Abdullah ordered the Arab Legion to move to the defense of the
Old City.[13]

Once the Israeli offensive had been halted, the focal point of
the battle moved to Latrun, a hill spur with fortifications that
dominated the main route from Tel Aviv to Jerusalem. The UN
partition plan allocated Latrun to the Arab state, but the strategic
importance of Latrun was such that Ben-Gurion was determined
to capture it. Against the advice of his generals, he ordered three
frontal attacks on Latrun, all of which were beaten off by the Arab
Legion before the UN truce ended the first round of fighting.

To the embattled Israelis the truce was, in the words of General
Moshe Carmel, like "dew from heaven." They used it to recruit
more soldiers, retrain, reorganize, and rearm. Count Folke
Bernadotte, the UN mediator, presented proposals for a settlement on 27 June, but they were rejected by both sides. On 17
September, a day after Bernadotte submitted his second report to
the UN, he was assassinated in Jerusalem by members of the ultranationalist Stern Gang, who regarded the Swedish nobleman as
an agent of the British government. The triumvirate that ordered
the assassination of the UN mediator included Yitzhak Shamir,
the future prime minister of Israel. Stern Gang and Irgun units
continued to pursue independent policies in Jerusalem, over which
Jewish sovereignty had not been proclaimed. They rejected the
truce and planned to fight on in order to establish "Free Judea"
outside the State of Israel. The assassination of Bernadotte forced
the government to crack down on the dissident organizations and
to merge them with the IDF. Bernadotte's assassins were never
brought to justice.

When Egypt violated the truce on 8 July, the IDF was ready to
launch its counteroffensive. The main target of the counteroffensive was the Arab Legion. Operation Danny aimed to eliminate the
Lydda-Ramle wedge, which threatened the road to Jerusalem, and
to widen the corridor to Jerusalem by capturing Latrun and
Ramallah. All these places had been assigned by the UN to the
Arab state and fell within the perimeter held by the Arab Legion.
Lydda and Ramle, which had been left virtually undefended, were
captured by the IDF on 12 July and their inhabitants forced to
flee. In Latrun, Ramallah, and the Old City of Jerusalem, the Arab
Legion successfully defended its positions. Very significantly, however, it made no attempt to capture any territory assigned to the

Jewish state. All the other Arab armies lost ground to Israel. Israel improved its position immeasurably as a result of the ten days' fighting: it seized the initiative and retained it until the end of the war.

In the second half of the war, the special relationship between Israel and Jordan slowly began to reassert itself. In the summer of 1948 their armies came to blows, but even at the height of the war the two countries remained, in Uri Bar-Joseph's apt phrase, "the best of enemies."[14] Throughout the war King Abdullah continued to pursue limited objectives and made no attempt to encroach on Jewish state territory. Ben-Gurion, for his part, showed no similar restraint and, in the first two rounds of fighting at least, acted according to the old adage *"à la guerre comme à la guerre."* During the long second truce, however, he had time to reflect on the advantages of adhering to the original agreement to divide western Palestine between Israel and Transjordan, an agreement that Abdullah showed every sign of wanting to restore.

On 26 September, Ben-Gurion proposed to the cabinet a major military offensive to capture large chunks of the West Bank. By this time the IDF had the military capability to capture the entire West Bank, all it needed was the order to move. In the cabinet six ministers voted for the proposal and six voted against, and the plan was consequently shelved. Ben-Gurion described this decision as a cause for "mourning for generations to come." But he must have had second thoughts about the wisdom of his own proposal, because he did not bring it up again. Those who knew him suggested several reasons for his decision not to press for the capture of the West Bank or a large part of it. First and foremost, he feared British military intervention under the terms of the Anglo-Jordanian defense treaty. Second, he estimated that the inhabitants of the West Bank would not run away, and he was reluctant to include a larger number of Arabs than was strictly necessary within the borders of the Jewish state. Third, he knew that the capture of a large part of the West Bank would irreversibly destroy the special relationship with King Abdullah. Whatever his motives, Ben-Gurion bore the ultimate responsibility for the political decision to leave the bulk of the West Bank in the hands of King Abdullah.[15]

After the plan for a military offensive on the eastern front was abandoned, Ben-Gurion showed growing interest in the idea of an offensive against the Egyptian army, which still occupied much of the Negev. Precisely at that time Israel received a peace feeler from the Egyptian royal court, which was anxious to extricate itself from the Palestine imbroglio. Kamal Riad, an emissary for King Farouk, met in Paris with Elias Sasson, head of the Middle East department at the Israeli Foreign Ministry, a native Arabic speaker and a leading moderate. Riad suggested Egypt's de facto recognition of Israel in return for agreement to Egypt's annexation of a large strip of territory in the Negev.[16] Moshe Sharett wanted to explore this peace feeler, but Ben-Gurion bluntly brushed it aside. The cabinet was divided between those ministers who had an orientation toward peace with Egypt and those, like Ben-Gurion, who inclined toward peace with Transjordan. On 6 October, Ben-Gurion presented to the cabinet his proposal for renewing the war against Egypt, without even mentioning the Egyptian peace feeler. Instead, he stated that relations between Transjordan and Egypt were so strained that the Arab Legion was unlikely to intervene if Israel renewed the fighting against Egypt. On 15 October, Israel broke the cease-fire and launched an attack on the Egyptian forces in the south. By the time of the cease-fire on 7 January 1949, the entire Negev was in Israeli hands. Throughout the war between Israel and Egypt, the Arab Legion remained neutral. Israel and Transjordan certainly emerged from the war as the best of enemies.

The special relationship between Israel and King Abdullah was thus a major factor in determining the course and outcome of the first Arab-Israeli war. This factor is largely ignored in Zionist historiography, because it does not sit easily with the heroic version of the war in which little Israel stands alone against the entire Arab world. Abdullah's meetings with Golda Meir were common knowledge in Israel long before the release of the official documents. The usual argument against Abdullah is that when the moment of truth came, he went back on their agreement and joined in the all-out Arab effort to destroy the newly born Jewish state. A closer analysis of the 1948 war, however, reveals that Abdullah remained remarkably loyal to his original understanding with Golda Meir. Moreover, the special relationship with Abdullah was exploited by Israel shrewdly and skillfully in breaking the chain of hostile Arab states, in deepening the divisions in the Arab coalition, and in playing its members off against one another. Had this special relationship not existed, Israel would have been unlikely to achieve such a comprehensive and decisive victory in the first Arab-Israeli war.

Israel emerged from the war economically exhausted but with superior organization and morale, a tremendous sense of achievement, and a confident outlook on the future that formed a solid foundation for the development of parliamentary democracy. The first general election for the 120-member Knesset, or parliament, was held on 25 January 1949. A system of proportional representation was adopted, which encouraged the proliferation of small parties and resulted in coalition governments because no party ever achieved an absolute majority. Mapai won some 36 percent of the votes, the left-wing Mapam 15 percent, the United Religious Party 12 percent, the right-wing Herut Party 11.5 percent, the General Zionists 5 percent, the Progressive Party 4 percent, the Communists 3.5 percent, and the Sepharadim 3.5 percent, the rest of the votes being divided among a number of smaller parties. Following the elections, David Ben-Gurion formed a coalition government consisting of Mapai, the Religious, the Progressive, and the Sephardi parties. The three senior posts remained unchanged, with Ben-Gurion as prime minister and defense minister, Moshe Sharett as foreign minister, and Eliezer Kaplan as finance minister. Mapai thus retained a virtual monopoly in the defense and foreign affairs sphere, and it succeeded in excluding the extreme left and the extreme right from power.

As the moderate American Zionist leader Nahum Goldmann noted in his autobiography, the military victory of 1948 had a marked psychological effect on Israel:

> It seemed to show the advantages of direct action over negotiation and diplomacy. . . . The victory offered such a glorious contrast to the centuries of persecution and humiliation, of adaptation and compromise, that it seemed to indicate the only direction that could possibly be taken from then on. To brook nothing, tolerate no attack, cut through Gordian knots, and shape history by creating facts seemed so simple, so compelling, so satisfying that it became Israel's policy in its conflict with the Arab world.[17]

Nowhere was the psychological effect of victory more pronounced than in the case of David Ben-Gurion. Ben-Gurion had always tended to think about the Arab-Israeli conflict in terms of the underlying military balance of power. In 1948 it was only natural that he should concentrate on the military struggle. But toward the end of 1948 successive IDF victories called for some forward political planning. Sharett instructed the Middle East department in the Foreign Ministry to explore various plans for a Palestinian government. Ben-Gurion, on the other hand, actively discouraged political planning of any kind while pressing Israel's military advantage. As a result, Israel's Arabists felt increasingly marginalized and frustrated. This is evident from a letter sent on 2 November 1948 by Yaacov Shimoni, the deputy head of the Foreign Ministry's Middle East department, to his boss, Elias Sasson, who was in Paris at the time conducting a dialogue with various Arab and Palestinian officials. Shimoni complained that Ben-Gurion "seeks to solve most of the problems by military means, in such a way that no political negotiations and no political action would be of any value."[18]

With a victorious army behind him, Ben-Gurion ignored not only the advice of the political experts but also the calls of the UN for a cease-fire. At the end of December he launched a second offensive in the south, Operation Horev, with the aim of throwing the Egyptian army back across the international border. The IDF penetrated into Sinai and reached the outskirts of El-Arish, but heavy American pressure compelled it to retreat and to leave the Gaza Strip in Egyptian hands. Both sides accepted the Security Council's call for a cease-fire on 7 January 1949 and agreed to begin armistice negotiations.

ARMISTICE AGREEMENTS

Armistice negotiations between Israel and the neighboring Arab states got under way with the help of Dr. Ralph Bunche on the island of Rhodes on 13 January 1949. The UN had appointed Bunche acting mediator to Palestine after the assassination of Count Bernadotte. To this difficult task the black American official brought all the outstanding diplomatic skills that were soon to be recognized by the award of the Nobel Peace Prize. Israel negotiated bilaterally with each of the neighboring Arab states, beginning with Egypt, and concluded a separate armistice agreement with each of them. The roll call was impressive: the agreement between Israel and Egypt was signed on February 24; that between Israel and Lebanon, on March 23; that between Israel and Jordan, on April 3; and that between Israel and Syria, on July 20. Each set of negotiations had a distinctive character, conditioned by military and political circumstances peculiar to that front. What all the negotiations had in common was that they were conducted under the auspices of the UN.[19]

The negotiations between Israel and Egypt started on 13 January and lasted six weeks. The advantage Israel enjoyed by virtue of its victory in the war and military control over most of the Negev was offset to some extent by the force of UN resolutions that worked in Egypt's favor. On some of the issues on the agenda, the Israeli delegation was internally divided: the military representatives led by General Yigael Yadin felt that the government's position was too accommodating, whereas the diplomats led by Dr. Walter Eytan, the director general of the Foreign Ministry, warned that the government's line was not flexible enough.

On February 24 the armistice agreement formally terminating the state of belligerency between Israel and Egypt was signed. Both sides had to move a long way from their opening position to make this agreement possible. Israel had to agree to an Egyptian military presence in the Gaza Strip and to the demilitarization of El-Auja. But the agreement secured Israel's control over the Negev, strengthened its international position, helped establish its credentials for UN membership, and paved the way to similar agreements with the other Arab states.

Negotiations between Israel and Lebanon began on 1 March and lasted three weeks. In private talks the Lebanese had told the Israelis that they could not be the first Arab state to negotiate directly with Israel but that they expected to be the second one. They also said that they were not really Arabs and that they had been dragged into the Palestine adventure against their will. When the official talks began, the IDF occupied a narrow strip of Lebanese territory containing fourteen villages. Israel was willing to withdraw to the international border but only on the condition that the Syrian army similarly withdraw from a patch of territory it still occupied on the east bank of the Sea of Galilee. In the end the attempt at linkage between the Lebanese and Syrian fronts was abandoned. Ben-Gurion thought that it was in principle undesirable to link one Arab country with another and that Israel's interest would be better served by dealing with each Arab country on a strictly bilateral basis. He also felt that an armistice agreement with Lebanon would improve Israel's international standing and place it in a stronger position to negotiate with Jordan.

The armistice negotiations between Israel and Jordan differed from the preceding negotiations with Egypt and Lebanon and the negotiations with Syria that were to follow. The negotiations were affected by the unique features of the Jordanian front, by Iraqi control over part of the front, and by the special political relationship between King Abdullah and the Jewish state. Having gained military control over the West Bank, Abdullah set in motion a process of creeping annexation that culminated in the Act of Union in April 1950. Arab disapproval of his policy of annexing the West Bank made Abdullah all the more dependent on the goodwill of Israel. Indeed, he counted on Israel to help him mobilize international support, and especially American support, for incorporating the remains of Arab Palestine into his kingdom. This was the background to the renewal of direct contact between the two sides in the autumn of 1948.

Jerusalem, the most explosive flashpoint along the entire eastern front, provided the starting point for talks between the two sides. Ben-Gurion was ready to offer a real cease-fire in Jerusalem in order to draw Abdullah into comprehensive peace negotiations. In November 1948 direct contact was established between the two local commanders in Jerusalem, Lieutenant Colonel Moshe Dayan and Lieutenant Colonel Abdullah al-Tall. These contacts led to the signing of a "sincere and absolute cease-fire" in Jerusalem on 30 November. On Ben-Gurion's part this step represented the quiet abandonment of the goal of bringing the whole of Jerusalem under Israeli sovereignty in favor of the much more modest goal of partitioning Jerusalem between Israel and Jordan. Such a partitioning seemed the most realistic strategy at the time for warding off persistent pressure from the great powers and the UN for the internationalization of the city.

On the subject of the West Bank, opinion was divided. Elias Sasson thought that Israel should support Abdullah's plan to annex it. The military experts considered the cease-fire line on the West Bank untenable and feared that by negotiating with Abdullah Israel would forfeit its military option. Although reluctant to give open support to Abdullah's annexation of the West Bank, Ben-Gurion also wanted to end the war and he told the cabinet on 19 December, "The only solution perhaps is Abdullah." Members of the left-wing Mapam party objected to annexation and still supported the establishment of an independent Palestinian state. The cabinet decided to open armistice negotiations with Jordan, but without any advance commitment to support the king's annexationist plans and without abandoning the possibility of a military operation.[20]

When direct talks between the two sides began on 26 December, the Arab Legion was also in control of parts of the southern Negev. In the course of the talks, it became clear that

Abdullah would not willingly withdraw from these positions. The Israeli leaders therefore planned a military operation to push the Arab Legion back to its side of the international border. They hoped to carry out this operation after the signing of the armistice agreement with Egypt and before the commencement of armistice negotiations with Jordan. Having had the benefit of Jordanian neutrality during the war with Egypt, the Israeli leadership counted on Egyptian neutrality during the planned offensive against Jordan. But the attempt to delay the start of the negotiations with Jordan did not succeed.

Official armistice negotiations under the chairmanship of Dr. Bunche opened on 4 March 1949 and lasted a month. Abdullah wanted to conduct the real armistice negotiations with Israel's representatives privately and secretly in his winter palace at Shuneh. He therefore sent relatively junior army officers to the talks at Rhodes, which thus were little more than a puppet show. Only a day after the opening of the show, Israel launched Operation Uvda (Fait Accompli) to extend its control of the southern Negev down to Eilat. Operation Uvda plunged the armistice negotiations into deep crisis, but the facts it created could not be reversed.

Another crisis occurred toward the middle of March when Jordan and Iraq agreed that the Arab Legion would take over the positions held by the Iraqi army in the northern sector of the West Bank. Israel seized the opportunity to bring heavy pressure on Abdullah to yield a sizable strip of territory in the Wadi Ara area. It was made clear to Abdullah that Israel was prepared to resort to military force if its demands were not accepted, and once again he caved in.

The Israeli-Jordanian general armistice agreement, accompanied by maps, was signed in Rhodes on 3 April 1949. The border in the south corresponded to the international border; that on the Iraqi front reflected Abdullah's concessions; and that in Jerusalem was based on the "sincere and absolute cease-fire" of 30 November. Article 8 empowered a special committee, composed of representatives of the parties, to deal with all the outstanding problems, such as the movement of traffic on vital roads and access to the holy places in the Old City of Jerusalem.

The armistice agreement with Jordan represented a major victory for Israeli diplomacy. "Coercive diplomacy" might be a more appropriate term, since the negotiations were accompanied by the threat, and actual use, of military force. This combination of diplomacy and force secured for Israel significant territorial and strategic gains in the Negev and in the Wadi Ara area. To avert a military clash, Abdullah had to retreat. Yet, at the same time, by signing the armistice agreement, Israel implicitly recognized his rule over a large portion of the territory that the UN had allocated to the Palestinian state. The agreement was signed in the name of the Hashemite Kingdom of Jordan, the first time that this name was used officially. Palestine and Transjordan gave way to Israel and the Hashemite Kingdom of Jordan, and the official nomenclature reflected the new reality. Arab Palestine, or what remained of it, was officially designated as West Jordan, or more colloquially as the West Bank, while former Transjordan was known from then on as East Jordan, or the East Bank. In a very real sense, therefore, the signing ceremony at Rhodes represented the official demise of Arab Palestine. On both sides the general expectation was that the armistice agreement would soon be followed by an overall peace settlement.

After Jordan came Syria's turn to negotiate an armistice with Israel. Of all the Arab countries, Syria proved the toughest nut to crack. The negotiations were the most protracted, lasting from 5 April to 20 July. In the course of the fighting, Syrian forces had established a number of bridgeheads on Israeli territory, north and south of the Sea of Galilee, and all the IDF attempts to push them back across the international border ended in failure. Israel was thus in a weak military position at the start of the talks, but its international position was bolstered by the three armistice agreements it had already concluded under the auspices of the UN and by its admission to UN membership in May.

Syria was in a strong military position but internally unstable. On 30 March, less than a week before the start of the armistice talks, Colonel Husni Zaim, the chief of staff, overthrew the regime in a bloodless coup. This coup set the pattern for military intervention in Arab politics and for the overthrow of the old order that was held responsible for the loss of Palestine. Although Zaim had promised his co-conspirators a fight to the finish against Zionism, once he captured power he made a determined effort to come to terms with Israel. He openly declared his ambition to be the first Arab leader to conclude a peace agreement with Israel and offered repeatedly to meet with Ben-Gurion to work together toward this end.[21]

The first phase of the armistice negotiations ended in deadlock because the opening positions of Israel and Syria were wide apart and neither side was prepared to budge. Israel insisted on unconditional Syrian withdrawal to the international border, whereas Syria insisted that the existing cease-fire line should become the new border. To break the deadlock, Zaim came up with a proposal of startling audacity. He wanted to skip altogether the armistice talks and proceed directly to the conclusion of a peace treaty, with an exchange of ambassadors, open borders, and normal economic relations. As an additional incentive, Zaim offered, in the context of an overall settlement, to settle 300,000 Palestinian refugees, nearly half the total number, in northern Syria. Syria at that time had about 100,000 refugees, so the offer entailed the permanent resettlement in Syria of an additional 200,000 refugees who had ended up in other Arab states. In return he asked for a modification of the international border to give Syria half the Sea of Galilee. Zaim also offered to meet Ben-Gurion face-to-face in order to break the logjam in the lower-level talks.[22]

Ben-Gurion rejected Zaim's overture out of hand. He instructed the Israeli representatives to tell the Syrians bluntly that first they had to sign an armistice agreement on the basis of the old international border, and only then would Israel be prepared to discuss peace and cooperation.[23] He also kept under active review military plans for ejecting the Syrian forces from their positions on the Israeli side of the international border.[24] As no progress was achieved, the armistice negotiations were suspended on 17 May.

Zaim's next move was to communicate to Israel through a UN channel a secret offer that included the following elements: a cease-fire based on the existing military lines, a peace settlement within three months based on the old international border, and the settlement of 300,000 Palestinian refugees in Syria. The demand for redrawing the international border had evidently been dropped. Moshe Sharett, who reported this development to the cabinet on 24 May, attached the greatest importance to Zaim's offer, particularly to the idea of settling 300,000 refugees, and he pressed for a high-level meeting with Zaim. Ben-Gurion, on the other hand, suspected that this might be a diplomatic trap and persisted in his refusal to meet with Zaim. Ben-Gurion read to the cabinet his reply to Bunche, who had urged him to grant Zaim's request for a meeting. It stated that Ben-Gurion was prepared to meet with Colonel Zaim to promote peace between their two countries but that he saw no point in such a meeting until the Syrian representatives to the armistice talks had declared unequivocally their readiness to withdraw to the prewar lines.[25]

Bunche then seized the initiative with a compromise proposal that satisfied both sides. His proposal was to demilitarize the area between the international border and the cease-fire lines following the withdrawal of the Syrian forces from their forward positions. This proposal compensated Syria for staging a complete withdrawal while freeing Israel of the presence of Syrian troops on its territory. Bunche's compromise formula was both complicated and ambiguous on many important issues, such as the status of the demilitarized zones. It was to be the source of endless disputes and clashes in the coming years. But it enabled Israel and Syria finally to sign an armistice agreement on 20 July. Three weeks later Husni Zaim was overthrown in a bloody military coup.

With the conclusion of the agreement between Israel and Syria on 20 July, the Rhodes armistice negotiations were completed. The first Arab-Israeli war was officially over. In the course of the war, Israel had expanded its territory from the 55 percent of mandatory Palestine allocated to it by the United Nations to 79 percent. Israel also succeeded in expelling all the Arab forces from Palestine with the exception of the Arab Legion, which remained in control of the West Bank. This sealed the fate of the UN plan for an independent Palestinian state. The Palestinians were left out in the cold. The name Palestine was erased from the map (see map 4). Interestingly, the postwar settlement was based on the same principle that King Abdullah and Golda Meir had agreed to in November 1947: the partition of Palestine at the expense of the Palestinians. It was a striking example of the unsentimental *realpolitik* approach that had dictated Israel's conduct throughout the first Arab-Israeli war.

THE ELUSIVE PEACE

The armistice agreements were intended to serve as steps on the road to peace. An identical preamble to all four agreements stated that their purpose was "to facilitate the transition from the present truce to a permanent peace in Palestine." Yet not in a single case did the armistice agreement turn out to be the precursor to a formal peace settlement. Why was there no political settlement between Israel and its neighbors after the guns fell silent? Why did peace prove to be so elusive? This is one of the most contentious issues in the debate about 1948.

The traditional Zionist answer to this question can be summed up in two words: Arab intransigence. According to this version,

Israel following the armistice agreements, 1949

Israel's leaders strove indefatigably for a peaceful settlement of the conflict after the terrible ordeal of 1948, but all their efforts foundered on the rocks of Arab intransigence. Israel's leaders were desperate to achieve peace, but there was no one to talk to on the other side. An impenetrable wall of Arab hostility presented them with a situation of *ein breira,* of having no choices whatsoever with respect to the pursuit of peace.

Revisionist Israeli historians, on the other hand, believe that postwar Israel was more intransigent than the Arab states and that it therefore bears a larger share of the responsibility for the political deadlock that followed the formal ending of hostilities. At the core of the revisionist version of events is the notion of *yesh breira,* of there having been real political choices to be made by Israel with respect to future relations with the Arabs. The real question facing Israel at that critical point in its history was not whether peace with its Arab neighbors was possible but at what price.

Evidence for the revisionist interpretation comes mainly from official Israeli sources. The files of the Israeli Foreign Ministry, for example, burst at the seams with evidence of Arab peace feelers and Arab readiness to negotiate with Israel from September 1948 on. The two key issues in dispute were refugees and borders. Each of the neighboring Arab states was prepared to negotiate directly with Israel and to bargain about borders.

On the other central issue, that of Palestinian refugees, individual Arab states had less freedom of action. Here there was a clear and consistent Pan-Arab position, binding on all the members of the Arab League. The position was that Israel alone had created the refugee problem and that it must not be allowed to evade its responsibility for solving this problem. The solution had to be along the lines of UN resolutions that gave the refugees themselves the choice between returning to their homes and receiving compensation for their property from Israel. The collective position permitted individual Arab states to cooperate with the United Nations Relief and Works Agency (UNRWA) for Palestine and the Near East, but only on condition that this cooperation did not compromise the basic rights of the refugees.

Israel's position on the Palestinian refugee problem was diametrically opposed to that of the Arab League. Israel claimed that the Arabs had created the problem by starting the war and that Israel itself was not responsible in any way. It therefore did not accept the UN resolutions that gave the refugees the right of return or, alternatively, the right to compensation. Israel was prepared to cooperate with international agencies in searching for a solution to the refugee problem but only on condition that the bulk of the refugees were resettled outside its own borders.[26] In the propaganda war accompanying the conflict, Israeli spokesmen repeatedly charged that the Arab governments were interested not in solving the refugee problem but only in making political capital out of it. There was some truth in this charge: having lost the war, Arab governments used whatever weapons they could find to continue the struggle against Israel, and the refugee problem was a particularly effective weapon for putting Israel on the defensive in the court of international public opinion. On the other hand, the collective position of the Arab League was based not on political expediency but on principle.[27] Each Arab government had it own policy toward the refugees living on its territory. The Jordanian government had a policy of rehabilitating the Palestinian refugees, giving them Jordanian citizenship, and integrating them into the life of the nation. The Egyptian government, by contrast, did very little for the 200,000–300,000 refugees who lived in the Gaza Strip, and refused to give them Egyptian citizenship. But no Arab government felt at liberty to proceed to a separate peace with Israel in total disregard for the rights of the Palestinian refugees.

If the Pan-Arab position on the refugee problem was one constraint on any separate peace deal with Israel, Arab public opinion was another. It is important to distinguish in this connection between the Arab publics and the Arab rulers. Hatred and hostility at the popular level toward the Jewish state intensified beyond measure in the aftermath of the loss of Palestine and the experience of military defeat. Arab rulers, on the other hand, displayed remarkable pragmatism in the wake of the same events. Indeed, after the sobering experience of military defeat at the hands of the infant Jewish state, they were prepared to recognize Israel, to negotiate directly with it, and even to make peace with it. Each of these rulers had his territorial price for making peace with Israel, but none of them refused to talk.

On the Israeli side, military power expanded the margins for political choice. Here the dominant figure was the prime minister, by virtue both of his position and of his personality. In peace, as in war, Ben-Gurion kept policy-making firmly in his own hands. He did not encourage debate in Mapai or in the government of the various political options available to Israel at the end of the War of Independence. Nor did he want to air in public the pros and cons of the rival orientations on Egypt, on the Palestinians, and on

Jordan. And to a very large extent he succeeded in maintaining a monopoly over the making of high policy in the sphere of defense and foreign affairs. It was he who mostly determined Israel's grand strategy and national priorities at the end of the war. While the institutional trappings of prime ministerial power helped Ben-Gurion maintain tight control over policy-making toward the Arabs, even more important was the fact that he was articulating a policy with which most of the Israeli elite, and especially the army, were in agreement.

Peace with the Arabs was certainly something Ben-Gurion desired, but it was not his main priority at this particular time. His top priorities were the building of the state, large-scale immigration, economic development, and the consolidation of Israel's newly won independence. He thought that the armistice agreements met Israel's essential needs for external recognition, security, and stability. He knew that for formal peace agreements Israel would have to pay by yielding territory to its neighbors and by agreeing to the return of a substantial number of Palestinian refugees, and he did not consider this as a price worth paying. Whether Ben-Gurion made the right choice is a matter of opinion. That he had a choice is undeniable.

Thus an important factor in the failure to proceed from armistice agreements to contractual peace agreements was Ben-Gurion's inflexibility. And the major reason for this inflexibility was his belief that time was on Israel's side. On 29 May 1949 he expounded this view to the cabinet. He prefaced his remarks by pointing out that the failure to attain formal peace with the Arabs should not be seen as a great disaster. On all of the great questions, time worked to Israel's advantage: borders, refugees, and Jerusalem. In the first place, with the passage of time the world would get used to Israel's existing borders and forget about the UN borders and the UN idea of an independent Palestinian state. Similarly, in respect to the Palestinian refugees, Israel's position continued to improve despite moral pressure from the UN to allow them to return. The same was true of Jerusalem. People were getting used to the existing situation and beginning to see the absurdity of the idea of suddenly establishing an international regime over the city.

Then came double-talk: "It is true that these things should not prevent us from accelerating the peace, because the issue of peace between us and the Arabs is important, and it is worth paying a considerable price for it. But when the matter is dragged

out—it brings us benefits, as the mufti helped us in the past."
Only in the case of Egypt, continued Ben-Gurion, were really serious efforts for peace called for. The reasons given were that no
objective conflict of interests existed between the two countries; a
large desert separated them; and "Egypt is the only state among
the Arab countries that constitutes a real state and is forging a
people inside it. It is a big state. If we could arrive at the conclusion of peace with it—it would be a tremendous conquest for us."
It was highly revealing that even when talking about the attainment of peace, Ben-Gurion inadvertently used the military terminology of conquest. In any case, his conclusion was clear enough:
"But in general we need not regret too much that the Arabs refuse
to make peace with us."[28]

Moshe Sharett was more seriously committed to the pursuit of
peace because he felt that in the long run Israel could not live in
splendid isolation, nor could it afford to forgo the manifold economic benefits that only peace could bring. Ben-Gurion agreed
with Abba Eban, who doubled as ambassador to the United States
and to the UN, that the armistice agreements were perfectly adequate, that by seeming in a hurry to get peace Israel would only
encourage the Arabs to expect concessions on borders and
refugees, and that it would therefore be better to wait a few years,
because there would always be opportunities to talk to Arab leaders.[29] In an interview with Kenneth Bilby, the correspondent of the
New York Herald Tribune, Ben-Gurion succinctly summarized his
contradictory position: "I am prepared to get up in the middle of
the night in order to sign a peace agreement—but I am not in a
hurry and I can wait ten years. We are under no pressure whatsoever."[30]

Ben-Gurion's response to Arab peace feelers has to be seen in
the light of this conviction that Israel's bargaining position could
only improve with the passage of time. That is why he rejected
King Farouk's peace feeler in late September 1948 and Husni
Zaim's peace overture in the spring of 1949. Zaim was desperate
for a direct high-level dialogue, but there was no one to talk to on
the other side. Ben-Gurion turned down all his invitations to par-
ley, and eventually time ran out for him. There is, of course, no
way of knowing what might have happened had Zaim managed to
prolong his hold on power. But during his brief tenure he gave
Israel every opportunity to bury the hatchet and lay the foundations for peaceful coexistence. If his overtures were spurned, if his
constructive proposals were not put to the test, and if an oppor-

tunity for a breakthrough had been missed, the responsibility must be attributed not to Zaim but to Israel. And the responsibility can be traced directly to that whole school of thought, of which Ben-Gurion was the most powerful proponent, which maintained that time was on Israel's side and that Israel could manage perfectly well without peace with the Arab states and without a solution to the Palestinian refugee problem.

2

Consolidation

1949–1953

IN THE PERIOD 1947–49 the Zionist movement had been the main agent working to transform the status quo in the Middle East. In 1949, having achieved independence, the State of Israel became a status quo power. It accepted the postwar status quo and worked to preserve it in the face of Arab attempts to change it. The two main aspects of this status quo were demographic and territorial. Within the territory of the State of Israel at the end of the War of Independence, there were 716,000 Jews and 92,000 Arabs, 700,000 of the country's Arab inhabitants having ended up as refugees in the neighboring Arab countries in the course of the war. Israel's commitment to the new demographic status quo took the form of firm opposition to the return of the refugees.

THE STATUS QUO

The postwar territorial status quo was established by the armistice agreements that Israel signed with Egypt, Lebanon, Jordan, and Syria in the first half of 1949. All but one of these agreements attracted broad popular and parliamentary support. The exception was the agreement with Jordan. In the Knesset debate on 4 April, the government came under heavy fire from both right and left over this agreement. Two motions of no confidence in the government were put on the agenda, one by Herut and one by

Mapam. The critics charged that the armistice agreement was tantamount to recognizing the incorporation of the West Bank and the Old City of Jerusalem into Abdullah's kingdom. The right-wing Herut party, formed after the dissolution of the Irgun by Menachem Begin and other disciples of Ze'ev Jabotinsky, adhered to the Revisionist Zionist ideology that claimed that the Jewish people had a historic right to the whole Land of Israel. Begin moved his first motion of no confidence on the grounds that the government of Israel abandoned to the Hashemite Kingdom of Transjordan a huge portion of the western part of the motherland.[1]

David Ben-Gurion had a very low opinion of Menachem Begin and the other advocates of historic borders and the whole Land of Israel, referring to them disparagingly as verbal maximalists.[2] In the Knesset, Ben-Gurion told Begin that it was preferable to have a democratic Jewish state without the whole of the Land of Israel than to have the whole land without a Jewish state. A Jewish state, he argued, was not possible over the whole Land of Israel if that state was also to be democratic, because the number of Arabs there exceeded the number of Jews. The choice was between a democratic state of Israel in part of the land and a Jewish state over the whole land and the expulsion of its Arab inhabitants.[3]

Ben-Gurion's left-wing opponents, Mapam and the Communists, charged him with opening Israel up to Anglo-American influence by allowing King Abdullah to take over the West Bank. Tawfiq Toubi, an Arab member of the Israeli Communist Party, described the armistice agreement as the cornerstone of the policy pursued by Ben-Gurion's government throughout the War of Independence, the policy of active resistance to the establishment of an independent Palestinian state. Mapam's motion rejected the agreement on the grounds that it recognized King Abdullah's annexation of the parts of the Land of Israel and the expansion of Anglo-American imperialism into these parts.[4] Mapam halfheartedly advocated the capture of the West Bank and the creation there of an independent Palestinian state under the leadership of "progressive elements" that would make peace with Israel. It even suggested mobilizing Palestinian fighters and supporting them in their struggle to establish their own state.

This suggestion led Ben-Gurion to observe that it was not Israel's responsibility to create a state for the Arabs of Palestine. "We are not contractors for the construction of an independent

Palestinian state," he said sarcastically. "We believe this is a matter for the Arabs themselves."[5] Ever the realist, Ben-Gurion had reduced his thinking to one simple rule in his diary entry for 18 January 1949: "Peace is vital—but not at any price. Peace with the existing, not the imaginary, Arabs. No war for an Arab state. No war to place a particular Arab group in power. If such a war is needed, let it be a war between Arabs and Arabs and not with us."[6]

In the final stages of the War of Independence, Yigal Allon, the commander of the southern front, had pressed on Ben-Gurion various plans for the conquest of the West Bank, but Ben-Gurion rejected all of them. He knew that the West Bank contained a substantial number of refugees in addition to its own inhabitants, and he feared the consequences of a takeover. In the circumstances of 1949, with the overriding imperative of absorbing immigrants on a large scale, he regarded the armistice agreements as a very promising beginning to the quest for security and international recognition. Fully prepared to make peace on the basis of the new territorial status quo, he was hopeful that the armistice agreements would pave the way to peace.[7] Initially at least, Ben-Gurion accepted the armistice agreements in their entirety. He was a purist in this respect. He saw the agreements as marking a definite end of the war, and he expected them to be honored to the letter by both sides.

Nor was there any serious difference of opinion between the Foreign Ministry and the defense establishment regarding the new territorial status quo. Some members of the latter felt that Israel had not exploited its military advantage to the full and that, in Yigal Allon's phrase, "Israel had won the war but lost the peace."[8] But this was a minority view. The predominant view of the Israeli establishment—the cabinet, the Foreign Ministry, and the Defense Ministry—was that Israel needed more people, not more land. As for the armistice agreements, the consensus was that they represented a very positive step toward peace and that peace was indeed just around the corner.[9]

It soon became clear, however, that Israel and the Arabs interpreted the armistice agreements very differently. Israel maintained that the agreements gave Israel three indisputable rights. The first right was to an absolute cease-fire, which would be binding not only on regular armies but also on irregular forces and civilians. The second was to have the cease-fire lines treated as international borders for all intents and purposes, pending the conclusion of final peace agreements. This meant full sovereignty over Israeli territory, the only limitation being on the introduction of armed forces into the demilitarized zones. The third right was to settle Jews on all the land within its domain and to develop the economy without taking into account the rights of the previous owners who had become refugees.

The Arabs, on the other hand, claimed three rights under the armistice agreements. First, they held that the agreements did not terminate the state of war with Israel and that they were therefore not precluded by international law from denying Israel freedom of navigation, imposing an economic boycott on it, and waging a propaganda campaign against it. Second, they insisted that the armistice lines were only cease-fire lines and not international borders and that Israel was therefore subject to restrictions on its rights to develop the demilitarized zones and to exploit their water resources. Third, they argued that the armistice agreements did not cancel the rights of the displaced Palestinians to return to their lands and that Israel's use of that land was therefore not legitimate. Moreover, they claimed, the Palestinians were entitled to struggle against the occupation of their land, and the Arab states were under no obligation to curb this struggle.[10]

The task of reconciling these two radically different interpretations and of converting the armistice agreements into peace treaties was entrusted by the United Nations to the Palestine Conciliation Commission (PCC). The PCC invited Israel and its neighbors to a conference at Lausanne, which lasted with breaks from April until September 1949. The Israelis were reluctant participants, for they saw the conference from the start as a sterile diplomatic move and did not pin any hopes on it.[11] As far as procedure was concerned, Israel preferred direct bilateral negotiations with each of the Arab parties to the dispute, whereas the PCC could offer only indirect negotiations between Israel and the Arab delegations as a whole. As for the substance, it was predictable that Israel would come under pressure to make concessions for the sake of peace when its fundamental position was to preserve the demographic and territorial status quo. The Israelis therefore approached the Lausanne conference in a cautious and defensive mood; they spent all their time fending off pressures from the PCC and the U.S. government, and they breathed a collective sigh of relief when the conference ended inconclusively. The entire conference, in the words of one member of the Israeli delegation, was "an exercise in futility."[12]

The Arab governments also approached the Lausanne conference in an uncompromising mood. They had succeeded, to some
extent, in closing ranks in the face of the common foe and the bitter consequences of defeat; they coordinated their policies; and
they presented a united front in their dealings with the PCC.
Having rejected the UN partition resolution of 29 November
1947, they now wanted to put the clock back and to use it as the
basis for a settlement with Israel. The postwar status quo was totally unacceptable to them as a basis for a settlement. Their position was in fact considerably more extreme than it appeared to be
at the time. Determined by the Arab League, it was binding, at
least in theory, on all the member states. An internal report of the
secretary-general of the Arab League reveals that the official position was that the territory of the Jewish state should be as defined
in the UN partition resolution, but with two provisos. First, some
parts of this Jewish state should be severed to make room for the
refugees who did not exercise their right to return to their original homes. Second, if Israel chose to keep some of the territories
it captured in the war, it had to compensate the Arabs by turning
over to them other parts that had been allocated to the Jewish state
by the UN.[13] In short, the Arab League, in the aftermath of a war
its members had lost, proposed to allow Israel even less territory
than the UN cartographers had done in 1947.

At the Lausanne conference the two main bones of contention
were refugees and territory. Israel's position on the former was
clear and emphatic: the Arab states were responsible for the
refugee problem, so responsibility for solving it rested with them.
Israel was willing to make a modest financial contribution toward
the resolution of this problem but only as part of an overall settlement of the conflict and only if the refugees were to be resettled
in Arab countries. On the second issue Israel's position was that
the permanent borders between itself and its neighbors should be
based on the cease-fire lines, with only minor adjustments.[14]

The Arab representatives refused to negotiate with Israel directly and insisted on dealing with the PCC as a single, unified delegation. They wanted to place the refugee problem at the top of
the agenda, arguing that Israel was alone responsible for the
Palestinian exodus. They also demanded that all the refugees be
given a choice between returning to their homes and receiving
compensation. Israel's suggestion that permanent borders be based
on the cease-fire lines was rejected out of hand, and each Arab delegation demanded far-reaching changes in its country's border
with Israel.

Secret meetings were initiated by Israeli officials with individual members of the Arab delegations, but they failed to produce any progress and only brought recriminations from the PCC. The PCC accused the Israeli officials of going behind its back; the Israelis replied that it was the commission's own procedures that forced them to seek direct contact with their Arab counterparts. Elias Sasson reported to his superiors on the seriousness of the situation and urged them to adopt a different approach. Israel, he argued, could not expect the Arab states to meet all its demands in full if Israel itself was not prepared to move some way toward meeting theirs.

At first Moshe Sharett rejected Sasson's advice, but unrelenting American pressure induced him to propose to the cabinet the issuing of a declaration stating Israel's willingness to take back 100,000 refugees. This number included around 30,000 refugees who had already been permitted to return to rejoin their families. Yet Ben-Gurion opposed this proposal on the grounds that it would not satisfy either the Americans or the Arabs and would be harmful to Israel's security. The cabinet eventually authorized Sharett to try out a watered-down version of his proposal on the Americans. The Americans welcomed the idea but expressed disappointment at the small number of refugees Israel was prepared to take back. The Arabs considered the offer to accept 100,000 refugees wholly inadequate, and the official talks at Lausanne once again reached a dead end.

The failure of the Lausanne conference came as no surprise to Israel. It only served to reinforce the conviction that direct bilateral talks held out more promise of progress than mediation by third parties. At Lausanne, Israel succeeded in defending the status quo but failed to make any progress toward an accommodation with its neighbors. In the second half of 1949 Ben-Gurion's tough line continued to prevail. This line held that Israel could not afford to make concessions for the sake of peace, let alone concessions that might harm its security, and that for the time being the armistice agreements provided a satisfactory substitute for peace.

One vital issue on which the PCC had failed to make Israel budge was the status of Jerusalem. Jerusalem was of tremendous importance to the Jewish people because of its biblical, religious, and spiritual associations. It was also at the heart of the Jewish state's aspiration to be "a light unto the nations." But Israel's diplomatic posture in regard to Jerusalem was singularly uncomfortable. By accepting the UN partition resolution, the Jewish Agency had accepted the provision for placing Jerusalem under an international regime. Nevertheless, the newborn Jewish state desperately wanted Jerusalem to be its capital. At the end of 1948 Jerusalem was effectively partitioned along the cease-fire line between Israel and Jordan. Toward the end of 1949 the threat of internationalization loomed ever more ominously on the horizon. Two unholy alliances were engaged in the political battle for the Holy City. Israel and Jordan were allies in the fight to keep their respective parts of the Holy City in their own hands. Against them emerged an alliance of three blocs of countries that favored internationalization: nearly all the Muslim states, the Vatican and the Catholic states, and the Soviet Union and its satellites.

While Israel's diplomats were conducting a vigorous campaign against internationalization, the cabinet waged a vigorous internal debate. The prime minister wanted to declare Jerusalem as the capital of Israel and to move as many government offices as possible there; the foreign minister urged caution. On 5 December 1949 the prime minister read a statement in the Knesset designed to make it absolutely clear that Israel would never accept foreign rule over Jerusalem. He agreed to UN supervision of the holy places but added, "At the same time, we see it as our duty to declare that Jewish Jerusalem is an organic and inseparable part of the State of Israel—as it is an inseparable part from Israel's history, Israel's faith and the soul of our people. Jerusalem is the heart of hearts of the State of Israel." The statement, however, failed to deter the supporters of internationalization. On 9 December the UN General Assembly adopted by a large majority a resolution that called for treating Jerusalem as a separate entity and placing it under UN rule.

The UN decision rekindled the debate inside the Israeli cabinet. The prime minister reacted with Churchillian defiance, in deeds as well as words. He proposed a vehement denunciation of the UN resolution as well as immediate practical measures to establish facts on the ground and to assert Israel's sovereignty. Sharett, from New York, agreed to the practical measures but opposed the declaration of war against the UN. After a stormy debate the cabinet approved the text of the declaration submitted by the prime minister with only minor amendments. At a meeting of Mapai members of the Knesset, there was again a large majority in favor of the prime minister's proposal. Accordingly, on 13 December, from the podium of the Knesset, Ben-Gurion announced the decision to move the Knesset and the government offices from Tel Aviv to Jerusalem. No time was wasted between the announcement of this decision and its implementation.

Sharett reacted to his triple defeat—in the UN, in the cabinet, and in the party—by tendering his resignation as foreign minister in a cable from New York. Ben-Gurion, however, refused to accept it and Sharett stayed at his post. Sharett's dramatic step was intended to signal his displeasure at the government's moves and its disregard for his authority. It was also meant to warn his colleagues that ill-thought-out declarations could harm Israel's prestige and international standing. Sharett's own view was that the UN resolution was impracticable and bound to fall by the wayside and that it was therefore unwise and unnecessary for Israel to embark on a collision course with the world organization. Ben-Gurion rejected these arguments. He took a much more serious view of the UN resolution and thought that Israel's response should be immediate and emphatic. The supreme goal in his eyes was to secure Jerusalem as Israel's capital, and for this he was prepared to risk a clash with the UN.

It was not apparent at the time even to Ben-Gurion's close party colleagues that his assertive public posture concealed deep inner doubts and anxieties. To his diary he confided that the decision over Jerusalem was one of the most difficult and fateful decisions he had ever been called upon to make, for it involved not just defiance of the UN but a confrontation with the Muslim, Catholic, and Soviet worlds. It was a campaign in which Israel, for the first time in its short history, was pitted against the entire world. If the world had its way, reasoned Ben-Gurion, 100,000 Jews would have been placed outside the boundaries of the State of Israel. Moreover, the loss of Jerusalem would only be a beginning. It would be followed by international pressure to take back the refugees and to place other religious places under international supervision; the end result would be loss of independence and anarchy. Jerusalem was thus the all-important test case. If Israel defeated the UN resolution, the question of borders would be solved and the pressure to repatriate the refugees would cease: "Our success in Jerusalem solves all the international problems around the State of Israel."[15]

Subsequent events were to show that Ben-Gurion greatly inflated the dangers inherent in the UN resolution. Equally unfounded were his hopes that success in Jerusalem would solve all of Israel's international problems. Israel won this particular battle, but the war over Jerusalem was to continue for decades. So did the pressures on Israel to cede territory and to take back the refugees. Sharett's assessment of the challenge was much more balanced and realistic. The unresolved disagreement on this issue was to cast a long shadow on the relationship between the two men.

PEACE TALKS WITH JORDAN

The Cold War led to growing great-power involvement and rivalry in the Middle East. This in turn complicated the search for a settlement between Israel and the Arabs. During the Lausanne conference, for example, Israel was subjected to strong pressure by the American members of the PCC to make concessions to the Arabs. Although the PCC was not disbanded, Lausanne signaled the UN's failure to bring about a comprehensive settlement of the Arab-Israeli dispute. Peace talks continued after Lausanne, but they were for the most part secret talks between Israel and individual Arab states.

Of the various bilateral talks, those with Jordan were the most protracted and promising.[16] Secret meetings between Israel and Jordanian delegates at Lausanne paved the way to direct negotiations that began in November 1949 and continued intermittently until King Abdullah's death in July 1951. Most of the meetings took place in the king's winter palace at Shuneh, near the Allenby Bridge. The main Jordanian participant in the talks, apart from the king, was Samir Rifai, who was minister of the royal court and later prime minister. Israel's principal representatives in the talks were Reuven Shiloah and Elias Sasson of the Foreign Ministry. Some of the talks were also attended by Walter Eytan, the director general of the Foreign Ministry, Yigael Yadin, the chief of staff, and Major General Moshe Dayan. When Elias Sasson became minister in Turkey, his son, Moshe Sasson, took his place in order to provide an element of personal continuity in the relations with King Abdullah.[17] Sir Alec Kirkbride, the British minister in Amman, gave the following gloss on these high-level talks:

> The visitor [Reuven Shiloah] used to travel down from Jerusalem in a car sent by the King, dine at the royal table with the Prime Minister and then retire with the latter to an antechamber for discussions which seemed to be interminable. King Abdullah used to stay up for as long as he could keep his eyes open in the hope that some positive result might emerge. The exchange usually terminated at about three o'clock in the morning after which Shiloah went back across the lines. I marvelled at the amount of time the two participants managed to take up with their discussions.[18]

The first phase of the talks got under way in November 1949, the aim being an overall peace settlement. On the Israeli side it was hoped that peace with Jordan would be valuable in itself but also open the road to peace with Egypt and Lebanon. However, the government's latitude for making concessions was restricted by various domestic considerations. Mapam and the Communists objected to negotiations with Jordan because they regarded Abdullah as a British puppet, while Herut was militantly opposed to recognizing his sovereignty over the West Bank because it claimed this area as part of the Land of Israel. Ben-Gurion appears to have shared both the left's suspicion of Abdullah and his British masters and the right's unease about giving up Israel's claim to the whole of mandatory Palestine. But as a pragmatic politician he realized that no peace would be possible without some Israeli concessions, and he was ready for border changes based on the exchange of territory.[19]

In the talks Rifai stressed that the king needed a peace he could defend in front of the Arab world, and he demanded first of all the southern Negev and, very much as a second best, a land corridor from Jordan to the Mediterranean coast under full Jordanian sovereignty. A major breakthrough was achieved on 13 December when Israel eventually offered the king access to the sea. At this meeting a paper entitled "The Principles of a Territorial Settlement" was drafted. Its principles included the partition of Jerusalem, transfer of the west bank of the Dead Sea to Israeli sovereignty, border modifications in the Latrun area, and, most important, a land corridor from Hebron to Gaza under Jordanian sovereignty. The offer of a corridor, however, was subject to three conditions: Israel would enjoy free crossing at a number of points, Jordan would maintain no army and erect no military installations in the corridor, and the Anglo-Jordanian treaty would not apply to the corridor.

Only a week after this dramatic breakthrough, the talks ran into a major crisis. The main sticking point was the width of the corridor: the Jordanians demanded a few kilometers, whereas the Israelis conceded no more than fifty to a hundred meters. Another problem was that Israel offered only three kilometers of seafront in an area covered with sand dunes and unsuitable for a port. Ben-Gurion instructed the Foreign Ministry to inform Abdullah in writing that his conception of a corridor was utterly unacceptable and that if he wanted to continue the talks he would have to come forward with a new proposal. Samir Rifai interpreted this move as an indefinite postponement of the negotiations. Throughout the talks Rifai was much more inflexible and demanding than his master.

The second phase of the talks began in mid-January 1950 as a result of a royal initiative. Having failed to achieve an overall settlement, the negotiators lowered their sights to an agreement over Jerusalem. Israel was represented by Shiloah and Dayan. The Israelis said at the outset that their fundamental aim was still an overall peace and that this aim dictated their approach to the Jerusalem problem. Here too, however, an impasse was reached because the Jordanians demanded the restoration of the Arab quarters in the New City and offered only limited concessions in return. A third phase in the talks began in the middle of February and reached a climax with the initialing of a nonaggression pact on 24 February.

The idea of a five-year nonaggression pact was put forward by King Abdullah himself at a meeting at Shuneh on 17 February in a dramatic personal intervention to save the talks from shipwreck. Since Rifai was evasive, the king dictated his proposal to Shiloah. Its main elements were the conclusion of a nonaggression pact between Israel and Jordan for five years, based on the existing borders as demarcated in the armistice agreements; guarantees to the UN that Israel and Jordan would respect the right of worship of all religions in the holy places in Jerusalem; special compensation to the inhabitants of Jerusalem for their property; negotiations to renew the commercial relations between the two countries and a free zone for Jordan at the port of Haifa; permission to all property owners to return to Israel or send a lawyer to dispose of their property; and the appointment of mixed committees to work out the details of a final settlement.

The Israeli government accepted the king's proposal as a basis for negotiations, and the next meeting at Shuneh was held on 24 February. The Jordanian government was represented by Fawzi al-Mulki, the minister of defense, in addition to the king and Rifai. The king asked Shiloah to read out his proposal for Mulki's benefit so that they could discuss it and make his personal text more precise. After the revision had been completed, two clean copies of the agreement were produced, whereupon the king turned to Rifai and Mulki first and Shiloah and Dayan next and told them to initial both copies, adding with a smile, "You will sign and I will serve as a witness." It was agreed that to the next meeting the two delegations would bring draft agreements based on this directive, with a view to producing a unified text. The king showed much joy and hailed the agreement as a turning point in the negotiations, as indeed it was.

But it was a turning point in the history of Israeli-Jordanian relations at which history failed to turn. Four days later there was another meeting to go over the two draft agreements. The Israelis had produced a long and legalistic text, but at least it addressed all the points in the king's proposal. The Jordanian text, on the other hand, substituted "modification of the armistice" for "nonaggression pact" and omitted any mention of "freedom of commerce and trade." The Israelis made it clear that they had no intention of signing a second edition of the armistice agreement, and despite the king's best endeavors the meeting ended without any agreement being reached.

At the next meeting on 7 March, it was evident that the king had not been able to overcome his government's opposition to a separate agreement with Israel. Jordan was being subjected to a hostile propaganda campaign and faced expulsion from the Arab League for its dealings with Israel. The king was prepared to disregard this pressure, but his government was not. At the meeting the king explained that Jordan had been forced to slow down the pace but that this slowing down meant the suspension rather than the rupture of the talks. The Israelis experienced disappointment verging on despair—so much attempted and so little achieved. Yet they did not blame the king for the failure of their joint efforts. Sharett in particular saw Abdullah as representing the trend toward reconciliation with Israel, against the dominant trend in the Arab world in favor of nonrecognition of the reality of Israel, and he gave him full credit for showing the courage of his convictions.

While the talks were suspended, the situation along Israel's long and unnatural border with Jordan steadily deteriorated, culminating in an armed clash between the IDF and the Arab Legion at the end of the year. In the absence of the restraining discipline of peace talks, the IDF adopted a very aggressive policy for dealing with incursions into Israeli territory that were carried out mainly by Palestinian refugees for economic reasons. Thus diplomatic deadlock led to military escalation, which in turn encouraged hopes of territorial expansion, at least in some quarters.

A conference of Israel's ambassadors in July 1950 provided the setting for one of the earliest confrontations between the proponents of peace based on the status quo and the proponents of territorial expansion. Moshe Sharett dwelled in his address on the need for peace and normal relations with the country's neighbors. He stressed that peace with Jordan was important not just as an end in itself but, given Jordan's reasonable position on the refugee question, a precedent for a peace settlement that did not involve the return of the refugees. Major General Dayan, who followed the foreign minister, questioned the value of formal peace agreements with the Arab countries. Only Jordan had a concrete interest in peace, he pointed out, because it stood to receive compensation. The other Arab states were not compelled by any practical reasons to make peace with Israel; on the contrary, their prestige would be harmed by making peace. From Israel's point of view, claimed Dayan, it was more important to penetrate the region economically, to become part of the Middle Eastern economy, than to achieve formal peace. Dayan went on to suggest that instead of negotiating a formal peace treaty with Jordan and paying the price for it, Israel should capture all the territory up to the Jordan River. The suggestion was made obliquely rather than directly, but it met with a firm rebuttal from the foreign minister. "The State of Israel," said Sharett, "will not get embroiled in military adverturism by deliberately taking the initiative to capture territories and expand. Israel would not do that, both because we cannot afford to be accused by the world of aggression and because we cannot, for security and social reasons, absorb into our midst a substantial Arab population . . . We cannot sacrifice Jewish fighters, nor can we harm others in an arbitrary fashion merely in order to satisfy the appetite for expansion."[20]

In April 1950 Jordan formally annexed the West Bank, and in December Abdullah suggested the resumption of negotiations with Israel. These talks were conducted by Shiloah and Rifai, who had become prime minister in the meantime. The aim of the talks was full implementation of the armistice agreement, especially Article 8, which gave Israel the right of access to the humanitarian institutions, like the university and the hospital, on Mount Scopus, and to the Wailing Wall, in the Old City of Jerusalem. There was a territorial dispute over Naharayim in the north and Wadi Arava in the south, and the king promised to implement Article 8 as a first step to peace if these disputes could be settled to Jordan's satisfaction. By this time, however, Ben-Gurion had come to question not just the feasibility but even the desirability of a political settlement with Jordan. To Shiloah, who came to consult him before a meeting with Abdullah on 13 February 1951, Ben-Gurion gave no fewer than seven reasons for his doubts. First,

Jordan was not a natural or stable political entity but a regime based on one man who could die any minute and who was entirely dependent on Britain. Second, a political settlement with Jordan was liable to get in the way of a settlement with Egypt. Third, an accord with Abdullah without peace with Egypt could not lift the siege that Israel faced on the continents of Asia, Africa, and Europe. Fourth, such an accord would reinforce Britain's hold in the surrounding area. The fifth reason was presented in the form of a question: "Do we have an interest in committing ourselves to such ridiculous borders?" Sixth, an accord with Egypt would settle Israel's relations with the entire Arab and Islamic world and yield important economic links. Finally, Egypt was a natural and stable country, which had no real conflict with Israel.[21] The clear implication was that preference should be given to Egypt over Jordan in the search for peace.

Ben-Gurion's lack of commitment to a political settlement with Jordan was a major factor in the failure of the talks. The talks continued literally until Abdullah's dying day, but ground was lost rather than gained. An exchange of official notes between Shiloah and Rifai in April 1951 failed to solve any of the outstanding problems and created new ones in connection with Mount Scopus. In May relations between the two countries reached an impasse at the official level. Contact was maintained, but there was no meeting of minds and no real negotiations took place. The king had been doing all the running for some time, but even his intervention and attempt to mediate between Shiloah and Rifai did not save the talks. Although the king's determination to move forward to a settlement with Israel never faltered, he was increasingly isolated and powerless in the quest for peace. His offer to go to Jerusalem and meet the Israeli prime minister in person provoked a stony silence. Ben-Gurion, for his part, showed no imagination and no vision in his approach to Jordan. All he would agree to was minor border changes based on reciprocity, while what the king needed was a generous deal that would vindicate his stand in favor of Arab acceptance of Israel. The quest for an overall settlement was thus doomed essentially because Israel was too strong and inflexible while Abdullah was too weak and isolated.

It was a sad story with a tragic ending. On Friday, 20 July 1951, King Abdullah was murdered by a Muslim fanatic outside the al-Aksa Mosque in the Old City of Jerusalem. With the king's death the era of personal diplomacy in Jordanian-Israeli relations came to an end. On hearing the news, Ben-Gurion's first thought was to seize the opportunity to rectify the mistakes of 1948 by changing the border with Jordan. He asked his military advisers to prepare a contingency plan for the capture of the West Bank. Not content with this plan, Ben-Gurion considered an approach to Britain to permit Israel to capture the whole of the Sinai peninsula in order to turn the Suez Canal into an international waterway. The expulsion of the Egyptians from Sinai could make way for British bases there. The more Ben-Gurion thought about the idea of capturing Sinai with the help of the British, the more he liked it, especially since the Sinai peninsula, unlike the West Bank, was not densely populated with Arabs.[22] In the end he had to abandon the idea of joint Anglo-Israeli action against Egypt until five years later, and the capture of both Sinai and the West Bank was left to Ben-Gurion's successors sixteen years later.

Abdullah's assassination thus caused something of a change in Ben-Gurion's thinking. Until 1951 he had accepted the territorial status quo and done nothing to disturb it. Once Abdullah was removed, his own commitment to the status quo began to waver and he indulged in dreams of territorial expansion. The murder also made him more pessimistic about the prospects of peace with the rest of the Arab world. He concluded that peace with the Arabs could not be attained by negotiation; instead, they would have to be deterred, coerced, and intimidated.

King Abdullah's murder was a critical episode in the history of Israeli-Arab relations. Ben-Gurion summed up its impact during talks on Arab policy held over a year later: "We did have one man who we knew wanted peace with Israel. We tried to negotiate with him, but the British interfered, and then a bullet came and put an end to the business. With the removal of the Abdullah factor, the whole matter was finished."[23]

CONFLICT WITH SYRIA

If King Abdullah was the most moderate Arab ruler in relation to Israel, the Syrians were Israel's most intransigent and implacable enemies. At least that was the popular perception in Israel. It is usually forgotten that Israel enjoyed a year and a half of peaceful relations with Syria after the conclusion of the armistice agreement in July 1949 and that the first military clash, in the spring of 1951, was a Syrian response to an Israeli attempt to change the status quo in the border area. Nor is it widely known that in the early

1950s serious, if ultimately unsuccessful, negotiations took place between Israel and Syria in an attempt to resolve peacefully the differences between them.[24]

The Israeli-Syrian armistice line was conducive to conflict because it crossed the sources of the Jordan River that were vital to Israel, because of the intricate topography of the border area, and, above all, because it contained three demilitarized zones (DMZs) whose status had not been clearly defined in the armistice agreement (see map 5). The root cause of the dispute between Israel and Syria and of their armed clashes was the question of sovereignty in the DMZs. Syria maintained that these zones must remain under UN supervision until the conclusion of a peace agreement. Israel, on the other hand, insisted that they lay within its sovereign territory and that it was only precluded from introducing arms into them. The armistice agreement itself merely called for the resumption of normal civilian life in these zones, pending the conclusion of a final peace settlement. It said nothing about Israeli sovereignty over them. The UN men were therefore broadly in agreement with the Syrians and in disagreement with the Israelis about the legal status of the DMZs.

There were only a handful of Jewish settlements in the DMZs and a substantial population of Syrian farmers, and Israel feared that Syria would manipulate this population to extend its influence. Israel therefore embarked on an energetic and ruthless policy of creating facts on the ground in the DMZs immediately after the signature of the armistice agreement. The two principal architects of this policy were Moshe Dayan, who served as the IDF staff officer for armistice affairs in 1949–50, and Yosef Tekoah, the director of armistice affairs at the Foreign Ministry and another leading hawk. Tekoah had studied international law at Harvard and could always be relied on to produce legal arguments to justify even the most outrageous Israeli actions. He adopted the uncompromising approach of the defense establishment, which was much more concerned with extending Israel's control over land and water resources than with its image abroad. The IDF men regarded him as one of them, as a military man in civilian clothes. Indeed, he was their Trojan horse inside the predominantly Anglo-Saxon diplomatic fraternity. In his view the basic function of Israeli diplomacy was to serve the country's security needs.

In Tekoah, Ben-Gurion found a man after his own heart. Ben-Gurion saw full control over the DMZs as a vital Israeli security need. He therefore wanted to squeeze the Syrians out of the

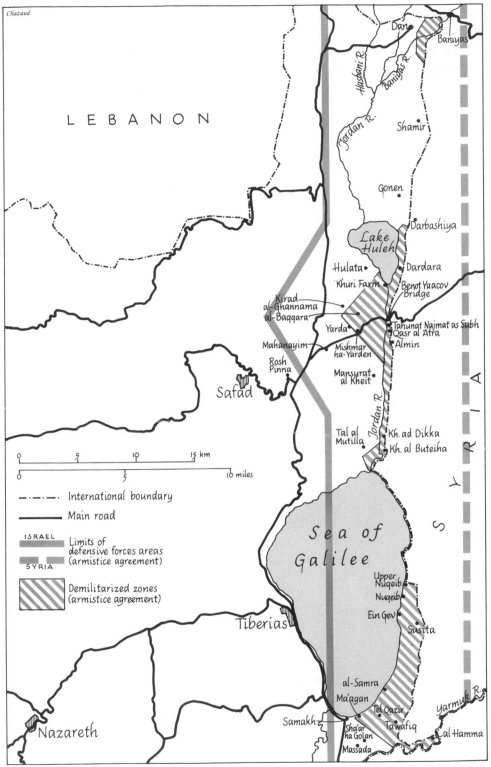

Israel-Syria armistice lines

DMZs even if this was not in line with the spirit or the letter of the armistice agreement. Here his policy was not to preserve the territorial status quo but to change it.[25] This policy had three principal aims: to establish physical control over the disputed territories, to contain Syrian influence, and to do away with UN supervision. To achieve the first aim, Israel purchased land from the Syrian villagers, developed Jewish settlements, established new agricultural settlements, built fortifications around them, and introduced soldiers disguised as civilians or policemen. To achieve the second aim, Israel seized an opportunity in March 1951 to move forcibly several hundred Bedouins who refused to accept Israeli identity cards from the central DMZ to Arab villages in northern Israel. In pursuit of the third aim, Israel refused to recognize the jurisdiction of the UN over civilian activities and even placed roadblocks to stop the UN men from entering the DMZs. Both Syria and the UN observers felt deceived and were disturbed by the direction of Israeli policy.

In early 1951 Israel embarked on a major development project: the draining of Lake Huleh, designed to reclaim 15,000 acres for cultivation. Although the lake itself was just outside the DMZ, the first stage of this project involved work on Arab-owned land in the central DMZ. As long as the work was carried out on Jewish-owned land, even inside the DMZ, Syria raised no objections. But when the tractors reached the land of the Arab villages, Syria complained to the Syrian-Israeli Mixed Armistice Commission (MAC). Major General William Riley, chairman of the MAC, rejected the Syrian claim that the project would give Israel a military advantage, but he also ordered work to be suspended until a mutual agreement was reached on compensation for the Arab landowners. Israel interpreted this ruling rather selectively and embarked on a policy of brinkmanship that led to a rift with the UN and to a violent incident with the Syrians. A meeting between the deputy chiefs of staff of Syria and Israel on 26 March failed to resolve the dispute and even raised the level of tension.

On 30 March, at a meeting chaired by the prime minister from which the foreign minister was absent because of illness, it was decided to continue the drainage work, to refrain from military action but return fire, and to take a series of practical steps to assert Israeli sovereignty in the central DMZ. One of these steps was the forcible evacuation of the eight hundred inhabitants of two Arab villages from the DMZ. The UN men condemned this action. Informal talks followed and some progress was achieved. A meeting of the MAC was arranged for 4 April. On that very day, however, a high-level decision was taken by the IDF to send a patrol of soldiers dressed up as policemen to al-Hamma at the farthest end of the southern DMZ. The patrol was intended to show the flag in an area that was under complete Syrian domination. The Syrian army responded violently, by shooting and killing seven members of the patrol and hampering the evacuation of the rest.

The sending of the patrol to al-Hamma was severely attacked by members of the Knesset Committee for Defense and Foreign Affairs and senior officials in the Foreign Ministry. IDF leaders were criticized for failing to consult the political experts and for not taking into account the political consequences of military decisions. Sharett considered the sending of the patrol "a very rash and ill-considered action" and accused those responsible of an astonishing lack of sensitivity and of knowingly sending men to their death. He also suggested closer coordination on a day-to-day basis between the IDF and the Foreign Ministry in the management of armistice affairs.[26]

The cabinet met on 5 April and, in the absence of the foreign minister, accepted the prime minister's recommendations to destroy three Arab villages inside the DMZ, bomb from the air the Syrian post and police station in al-Hamma, boycott the MAC, and lodge a complaint with the UN Security Council on the murder of the seven "policemen." This response to an incident Israel had provoked was amazingly aggressive. It was the first time that the Israeli Air Force (IAF) had gone into action since the conclusion of the armistice agreements. These actions were intended to clear Arab civilians from the border area, to signal Israel's determination not to accept any restrictions on the sovereignty it claimed in the DMZs, and to deter the Syrians from resorting to military force again.

The Syrians, however, were not deterred. In early May, Syrian forces crossed the central DMZ and occupied Tal al-Mutilla, a strategic hill north of the Sea of Galilee, one mile west of the armistice line. The IDF succeeded in recapturing this hill in a poorly executed operation that cost the lives of forty soldiers and damaged the morale of the army. Israel complained to the UN, but on 18 May the Security Council condemned Israel for its attack on al-Hamma, ordered it to bring back the Arab inhabitants it had expelled from the DMZ, and made resumption of the drainage work conditional on the agreement of the chairman of the MAC. The negotiations with General Riley were protracted and acrimonious, causing delays and changes in the project, which was considered to be of great importance to Israel's economic development. The whole experience convinced Ben-Gurion that relations with Syria were a zero-sum game and that Israel should act unilaterally to complete the Huleh drainage project. When the project was completed, and after much bloodshed and damage to Israel's international standing, the experts concluded that it was not just unnecessary but actually damaging to Israel's agriculture and ecology.

The military confrontation between Israel and Syria ended in May, but without resolving the key issue of sovereignty over the DMZs. A month later the Syrians suggested to the MAC's Israeli delegate high-level political talks on the division of the DMZs. The Israeli delegate rejected the idea on the grounds that Syria had no right to interfere in the affairs of the DMZs but was later persuaded to convey the offer to his government. Sharett looked favorably upon this offer, but Shiloah deemed it full of dangers and the army men warned that agreement to negotiate with the Syrians on the DMZs would in itself constitute recognition of certain Syrian rights in these areas. In their view the Syrian offer was motivated solely by the desire for territorial gains rather than by the desire for a comprehensive review of the relations between the two countries. Israel agreed to talks but on the condition that they not be confined to the border question. The agenda proposed by Israel, including economic relations and a peace treaty, was not acceptable to the Syrians, and consequently the meeting did not take place.

Syria's attitude toward Israel changed when Adib Shishakli, the deputy chief of staff, seized power in November 1951. Shishakli, who was strongly pro-American, wanted an accommodation with Israel to enable him to concentrate on internal reform and reconstruction. As a first step he sought to consolidate Syria's de facto control of parts of the DMZs with a formal agreement to be negotiated within the MAC. After protracted negotiations about the agenda and the level of the talks, a meeting was held, on 9 October 1952, in Hotel Shulamit in Rosh Pina, north of the Sea of Galilee. The Israeli delegation was headed by General Dayan, who had been appointed head of Northern Command in June, while the Syrian delegation was headed by Lieutenant Colonel Rassan Jadid. UN observers attended the meeting at Syria's insistence, but after a formal session they retired and left the two delegations to carry on direct talks. The Syrians proposed a division of the DMZs between the two sides along a line that would lie on the east side of the lakes and the Jordan River. Israel's delegation did not rule out such a division but insisted that an agreement could only be part of a general peace settlement or a nonaggression pact or at least that it be described as a step away from the armistice agreement in the direction of peace. The Syrians preferred to talk in terms of amending the existing armistice agreement by mutual consent. The meeting ended without any decision but with an understanding that the talks would continue.

On reading the reports of the meeting, Sharett felt that the Israeli position was unreasonable. Any disinterested person who read these reports, he minuted, would conclude that while the Syrians showed goodwill and tried to resolve the disagreements between the two sides on important matters, the Israelis dwelled on formal questions and legal issues. It was true that the Syrians stood to gain more. Nevertheless, as far as method was concerned, the Syrians strove to solve the problem in a simple and practical manner, whereas the Israelis complicated the matter with legal niceties that verged on sophistry.[27]

Ben-Gurion disagreed with Sharett on a number of counts. First, he pointed out that the Syrians demanded territories and water rights to which they were not entitled. Although these territories were demilitarized, they were part of the Land of Israel, and they were under de facto Israeli control. Second, the question was not whether to negotiate on the DMZs or within what framework but what the Syrians were offering in return for the territories they were demanding for themselves. Third, he agreed entirely that they should not insist upon a nonaggression pact, because that was already included in the armistice agreement. On the other hand, he did not agree that the liquidation of the territorial dispute with Syria would be an important achievement, because any dispute could easily be resolved if one side accepted the demands of the other. In conclusion, Ben-Gurion noted that Israel should not enter into any official negotiations on the liquidation of the DMZs as long as Syria did not offer compensation for Israel's concessions. Above all, Israel must not give up its exclusive right to the Jordan River and the Sea of Galilee without an appropriate Syrian return, which in his view it was unrealistic to expect.[28]

It was decided to continue the talks with the Syrians but to prepare Israel's position more carefully and to consult with water experts. It was agreed to accept the Syrian position that the talks be conducted within the framework of the armistice agreement. And it was also agreed in principle to give up small areas if Israel's vital interests, from the strategic and settlement points of view, could be preserved. Nine meetings took place between 15 January and 27 May 1953, under UN auspices and with American encouragement, in an effort to reach an agreement on the division of the DMZs between the two countries. The meetings alternated between the Syrian customhouse near the Benot Yaacov Bridge and Rosh Pina. In addition to the formal talks in the presence of the UN observers, there were numerous informal conversations. No agreed record of the discussions was kept, but the Israeli delegates compiled a full report on each meeting for their superiors.

At the eighth meeting, on 13 April, the Syrian delegates seemed very anxious to move forward and offered Israel around 70 percent of the DMZs. Significant results were achieved and a number of suggestions and summaries put in writing, but they required decisions by the two governments. The Israeli cabinet convened on 26 April to consider the latest Syrian suggestions for the division of the DMZs. Simha Blass, head of Israel's Water Planning Authority, was invited to this meeting. Dayan showed Blass the Syrian suggestions on a map. Blass told Dayan that although most of the lands that Israel was expected to relinquish were not suitable for cultivation, the map did not suit Israel's irrigation and water development plans. If the international boundary in the Banias area was moved, he explained, Israel's control over this water source would be affected. Dayan, who had previously accepted the map, now deferred to Blass's superior knowledge in water questions. Ben-Gurion asked Blass to see him before the cabinet meeting. Blass gave his reasons for objecting to the map, again focusing on the water rather than the land issue. Ben-Gurion responded by saying that these considerations were important but that peace was even more important. He added that since Israel was in conflict with all the Arab states, it was important that at least one Arab state signed some kind of an agreement with Israel.

Blass outlined his objections for the third time in front of the full cabinet. Ben-Gurion then presented at some length his own views on the matter. To Blass the other ministers seemed like polite and frightened children in a kindergarten. Anyone who wanted to say anything raised his hand hesitantly since the authority of the prime minister was so overpowering. On this occasion he spoke in favor of the proposal despite its limitations. He also stressed the importance of developing the northern region for the future of Israel and the need for quiet and avoidance of conflicts over the next ten years. The cabinet decided to continue the negotiations with the Syrians but to take into account the points and reservations made by Blass.[29]

Although phrased in a positive manner, this decision appears to have killed the negotiations. It involved changes to the preliminary accord and new conditions that made it difficult to go forward. At the last two meetings, on 4 and 27 May, Israel presented its new conditions. These were rejected by Syria, and the negotiations ended without agreement.

The failure of these high-level talks calls for an explanation. Superficially, it may appear that opposition from the Israeli military sealed the fate of the Syrian proposals, but this was not the case. The military was quite willing to surrender small peripheral areas over which it had no effective control for the sake of establishing full mastery of the bulk of the areas on the western side of the international border. Some senior officials in the Foreign Ministry were worried that the giving up of land would set an unfortunate precedent for future peace negotiations. But Sharett's approach was thoroughly pragmatic. He thought that if limited territorial concessions were indispensable for the settlement of a major source of friction, the price was worth paying. Ben-Gurion too did not rule out territorial concessions in principle but only insisted on reciprocity. The obstacle on the road to agreement was not land but water rights. That a set of proposals that had the support of the political and military elite was emasculated because it did not satisfy the requirements of a water expert seems surprising. It suggests lack of leadership and lack of statesmanship on Ben-Gurion's part when it came to the crunch. In the final analysis, it was Israel's insistence on exclusive and unfettered rights over the lakes and the Jordan River that seems to have upset the applecart. An opportunity for an agreement with a major adversary existed and was allowed to slip away. Yet the fact that the negotiations came so close to success is in itself significant because it shows that, contrary to popular Israeli perceptions, Syria was capable of behaving in a practical, pragmatic, and constructive fashion. There was definitely someone to talk to on the other side.

THE EGYPTIAN REVOLUTION

After the assassination of King Abdullah in July 1951, Israel shifted the focus of its peace efforts from Jordan to Egypt. It had always been a basic assumption of Israeli foreign policy that Egypt was the key to an accommodation with the Arab world. Egypt's history, size, national cohesion, and leadership position all combined to make it the preferred peace partner as far as Israel was concerned. Direct talks between Israeli and Egyptian representatives had been held at Rhodes, at Lausanne, and elsewhere. These talks suggested that Egypt would consider a nonaggression pact with Israel only in return for substantial territorial concessions in the Negev and the return of the Palestinian refugees. No serious politician in Israel was prepared to pay this price. Like Jordan, Egypt was ruled by a monarch, but whereas King Abdullah was moderate and pragmatic in his approach to Israel, King Farouk persisted in his hostility. It was he who had decided to commit the Egyptian army to the battle against Israel in May 1948 and who continued to resist reconciliation with Israel after the war except on his own terms.

The revolution of the Free Officers that toppled the monarchy in a bloodless coup on 23 July 1952 therefore kindled hopes that a new chapter was about to begin in Israeli-Egyptian relations. Farouk's overthrow, Sharett wrote "removes at least one obstacle to peace, which is wounded amour propre of a headstrong monarch."[30] One of the many complaints of the Free Officers was that the monarchy had pushed the Egyptian army into the Palestine imbroglio for dynastic reasons and without adequate preparations and supplies. The Free Officers declared their intention to turn their backs on Pan-Arab adventures and on the confrontation with Israel and to concentrate on domestic reform. They retained Ali Maher, a conservative royalist, as their civilian prime minister, and they acted to reduce border friction with Israel. Moreover, in ideological terms the new regime had much more in common with the socialist government in Israel than the old regime did. Ben-Gurion and his colleagues saw General Muhammad Naguib and his fellow officers not as potential collaborators but as true Egyptian nationalists who were likely to conclude that the conflict with Israel was not in their country's best interests. This analysis led them to pin all their hopes for peace on the new regime.[31]

On 18 August, in a speech in the Knesset, Ben-Gurion congratulated the Free Officers on their revolution and expressed his hope of a new beginning in Egyptian-Israeli relations. "There are no grounds," he said, "for any quarrel between Egypt and Israel. A vast expanse of desert stretches between the two countries and leaves no room for border disputes. There has never been, nor is there now, any reason for political, economic, or territorial conflict between the two neighbours. . . . The State of Israel wishes to see a free, independent, and progressive Egypt."

This public overture was soon followed up with a private message to the Revolutionary Command Council (RCC), which was headed by General Naguib. On 22 August, Shmuel Divon, the first secretary at the Israeli embassy in Paris, went to the residence of Ali Shawqi, the chargé d'affaires at the Egyptian embassy, and conveyed to him a proposal from the Israeli government. The proposal was to hold a secret meeting to discuss peace between the two countries or, if the Egyptian government preferred, preliminary parleys to explore the possibility of a peace settlement.[32] No direct response to this proposal was received from the RCC, but several messages of goodwill were conveyed by Egyptian diplomats and third parties. During the UN General Assembly session, Egyptian representatives stepped up their verbal attacks on Israel. These conflicting messages aroused Israeli suspicions that Naguib was playing a double game: that he was projecting an image of moderation that would enable Egypt to obtain arms and economic aid without taking any concrete steps toward a settlement with Israel.

Suspicion mingled with disappointment with the new regime. Many of the senior officials who gathered for a political consultation in the prime minister's office on 1 October bemoaned the lack of progress in the relations with Egypt and put forward various ideas for sustaining Israel's flagging peace offensive. Ben-Gurion, in his summing up, injected a note of skepticism. Israel's talk about peace was not a trick, he said,

> But at the same time we have to remember that there are limits to our desire for peace with the Arabs. This is one of our vital interests, but it is not the first and all-determining interest. First and foremost, we have to see to Israel's needs, whether or not this brings improvement in our relations with the Arabs. The second factor in our existence is American Jewry and its relationship with us (and the state of America since these Jews live in it). The third thing—peace with the Arabs. This is the order of priorities.[33]

Although peace with the Arabs was only the third priority, contacts with Egyptian diplomats continued. In late October, Shmuel Divon made contact with Abdel Rahman Sadeq, who had been sent by the RCC as press attaché to its Paris embassy. Sadeq cautioned that these meetings did not constitute official contact between the two countries, but he also revealed that he had been charged with sending reports directly to the RCC. Israel thus acquired an important channel for transmitting messages and suggestions to the Free Officers.[34] The Free Officers were unable to agree on a response to the bold Israeli peace overture, but they also wanted these contacts to continue. Consequently, the Paris channel remained open for well over two years.

Extremely interesting messages were exchanged through this channel in the first half of 1953. Within the RCC one of the principal supporters of continuing the contacts and moving toward an understanding with Israel was Colonel Gamal Abdel Nasser, who had served as a major in the Palestine war and had contacts with Israeli officers when his brigade was under siege in the Faluja pocket. Nasser was now the officer who monitored the contacts with the Israelis. It was to him personally that Sadeq reported and from him that he received his instructions.[35] At the end of January, Sadeq informed Divon that Nasser had instructed him to conduct the talks in the name of the RCC but to say that for the moment Egypt could not depart from the general Pan-Arab position on the Palestine question. In the meantime, Sadeq requested Israel's support in obtaining for Egypt economic aid from America, together with moral support for Egypt's demand for the withdrawal of British forces from the Suez Canal Zone. It was further emphasized that Nasser wanted this contact to be kept strictly secret and warned that otherwise it might have to be discontinued.[36]

After consulting the prime minister and the foreign minister, Reuven Shiloah instructed Divon to give the following reply. First, Israel welcomed the establishment of contact and empowered Divon to conduct it. Second, Israel regretted Egypt's unwillingness to depart from the hostile attitude of the Arab states. Third, Israel hoped for a fundamental transformation in the relations between the two countries but thought that at the very least Egypt should observe the armistice agreement and Security Council resolutions on freedom of navigation through the Suez Canal and the Gulf of Aqaba. Fourth, Israel was ready to assist Egypt in the economic sphere by placing an order for the purchase of five million dollars worth of cotton and other products if Egypt lifted the restrictions on the passage of Israeli oil tankers through the Suez Canal and the Gulf of Aqaba. Fifth, Israel sympathized with Egypt's wish to see the evacuation of the British forces and was willing to support Egypt in this matter if Egypt first improved

Egyptian-Israeli relations. Finally, Israel repeated its suggestion of a secret high-level meeting to remove the barriers to better relations between the two countries.[37]

On 13 May, Sadeq met Divon in the Hotel Reynolds in Paris, showed him a copy of a letter typed on official RCC stationery, addressed to Sadeq and signed by Nasser as Naguib's deputy. The letter explained that public opinion in Egypt and the Arab world made it prudent for the RCC to build its policy toward Israel gradually and that avoidance of aggressive statements against Israel was the first step in this direction. Nasser promised again that the RCC did not harbor any belligerent intentions, and he was glad that Israel accepted his word on the basis of mutual trust. He urged Israel to use its influence in America in support of Egypt's demand for the withdrawal of British forces and said that this would make it easier for the RCC to reach a final settlement with Israel. The RCC was grateful for the offer to buy Egyptian cotton but felt that this was premature. Finally, to demonstrate goodwill, the RCC proposed to examine the passage of Israeli ships and had already begun to ease restrictions.[38]

Nasser's message could be seen as highly significant because it marked the first time that the RCC apprised the government of Israel of its desire to take a series of steps to improve relations between the two countries and to pave the way to a final settlement. But this was not how Ben-Gurion saw it. In a terse letter to Sharett, he said that the Egyptian position could be summed up as follows: "We the Egyptians will continue our attacks on Israel together with all the Arab peoples, and Israel has to prove its goodwill toward us by buying cotton and mobilizing its influence in the United States for the benefit of Egypt." Ben-Gurion instructed Sharett to make two points clear to the other side: "(1) We would be prepared to mobilize our political influence on behalf of the Egyptian demands in the Suez matter, but only if we receive explicit commitments of free passages through Suez and to Eilat for Israeli ships and ships going to Israel. (2) As long as peace between us and Egypt is not secured—we would oppose the giving of arms to Egypt."[39]

Sharett's reply to Nasser was not as blunt as Ben-Gurion would have wished, but it conceded very little. Sharett and his advisers believed that Egypt's difficult circumstances should be exploited to find out once and for all whether Egypt was heading for a settlement. The purpose of Sharett's message was to make it unmistakably clear that Israel was not prepared to tolerate a prolonged game of empty promises and that Egypt would be judged not by its words but by its deeds. The practical test for Egypt was the granting of free passage through the Suez Canal and progress in other spheres toward a settlement. But a prior test of Egypt's intentions was agreement to a secret meeting at a higher level than the current one.[40]

No reply to Sharett's letter was received, but Divon later heard from his Egyptian contacts that the RCC decided not to ask for Israel's help in securing American economic aid, because it did not want to incur an obligation. Divon learned from Sadeq in October that Nasser was extremely concerned about secrecy and that he knew that the Israelis had told the Americans about their contacts with him. Nasser ruled out a high-level meeting with Israel until the Suez dispute had been resolved. Until then he hoped that the relations between Israel and Egypt would be characterized by mutual understanding. On the Israeli side, however, the suspicion persisted that the RCC had no intention of entering into serious peace negotiations.[41] By the end of the year, the high hopes that had been pinned on the Egyptian resolution had largely faded away.

INFILTRATION AND RETALIATION

Lack of progress in the secret talks between Israel and its neighbors was accompanied by a deteriorating situation on Israel's borders. Israel's defense planners made an important distinction between the problem of "basic security" and that of "day-to-day security." The former referred to a second round, to a full-scale attack by the regular armies of the Arab states that might imperil Israel's existence. The latter referred to provocations, hostile acts along the borders, and minor incursions into Israeli territory by civilians and irregular forces.[42] Following the conclusion of the armistice agreements in the summer of 1949, the IDF was reorganized into a small standing army with large reserves that could be mobilized at very short notice. This was the planners' solution to the threat to the country's basic security. Much more immediate, however, was the threat to its day-to-day security. This threat manifested itself mainly in the infiltration of Arab civilians across the armistice lines.

Infiltration was a direct consequence of the displacement and dispossession of around 700,000 Palestinians in the course of the 1948 war, and the motives behind it were largely social and eco-

nomic rather than political or military. Many of the infiltrators
were Palestinian refugees whose reasons for crossing the borders
included looking for relatives, returning to their homes, recovering material possessions, tending their fields, harvesting, and, occasionally, exacting revenge. Some of the infiltrators were thieves
and smugglers; some were involved in the hashish convoys; others
were nomadic Bedouins, more accustomed to grazing rights than
to international borders. There were acts of terror and politically
motivated raids, such as those organized by the ex-mufti Hajj
Amin al-Husseini and financed by Saudi Arabia, but they did not
amount to very much. According to the best available estimate,
during the 1949–56 period as a whole, 90 percent or more of all
infiltrations were motivated by social and economic concerns.[43]

As the years went by, a certain overlap developed between economic infiltration and political infiltration geared to killing and
injuring Israelis and spreading terror. The "free fire" policy
adopted by the Israeli army, border guard, and police in dealing
with suspects—a policy of shooting first and asking questions
later—contributed to this overlap. Faced with trigger-happy soldiers, infiltrators started coming in organized bands and responding in kind. Altogether between 2,700 and 5,000 infiltrators were
killed in the period 1949–56, the great majority of them unarmed.[44]

To point to the spontaneous character of much of the infiltration is not to deny that it posed a very serious problem for Israel
in general and for the border settlements in particular. Many of the
farmers in the border areas were recent immigrants from Arab
countries—Oriental Jews, as they were sometimes called—who
were undergoing a painful process of adjustment to their new environment. Infiltration across the border, which was usually carried
out at night, undermined their morale, placed their lives at risk, exacted a heavy economic toll, and raised the possibility of mass desertion. There was also the danger that the displaced persons
would try to reestablish themselves in their former homes and villages inside Israel. Infiltration, in short, posed a danger not only
to the country's day-to-day security but also to its territorial integrity.

To cope with this threat, Israel established new settlements
along the borders, razed abandoned Arab villages, and gave Arab
homes in towns like Jaffa and Haifa to new immigrants from
Central Europe, many of whom were Holocaust survivors. Israeli
units began patrolling the borders, laying ambushes, placing land

mines, and setting booby traps. A "free fire" policy toward infiltrators was adopted. Periodic search operations were also mounted in Arab villages inside Israel to weed out infiltrators. From time to time the soldiers who carried out these operations committed atrocities, among them gang rape, murder, and, on one occasion, the dumping of 120 suspected infiltrators in the Arava desert without water. The atrocities were committed not in the heat of battle but for the most part against innocent civilians, including women and children. Coping with the problems of day-to-day security thus had a brutalizing effect on the IDF. Soldiers in an army that still prided itself on the precept of "the purity of arms" showed growing disregard for human lives and carried out some barbaric acts that can only be described as war crimes.

In addition to operating within its own territory to check infiltration, Israel resorted to a policy of military retaliation against the countries from whose territory the infiltrators crossed the border, mainly Jordan and Egypt. These forays across the armistice lines were carried out by IDF units against Arab villages suspected of helping infiltrators. In effect they were a form of collective punishment against whole villages. The first full-scale attacks by the IDF were directed against the Jordanian villages of Falama and Sharafat in February 1951.

The raid against Falama was a resounding military failure. It was carried out by an IDF infantry battalion of 120 soldiers. On arrival at Falama the battalion encountered a dozen men from the Jordanian National Guard, who opened fire. The battalion beat a fast retreat. Its failure was symptomatic of the general decline in the IDF's combat ability after the end of the 1948 war. After Falama a series of retaliatory raids were carried out by the IDF across the border with Jordan and in the Gaza Strip. Conducted at night, all of these raids were aimed at civilian targets. And nearly all of them failed to accomplish their mission. Even when they were a success from the operational point of view, their impact was very limited and the underlying problem persisted. It was a difficult period for the IDF. Its morale, vigilance, and performance were all at a low ebb.

While failing to achieve its objectives, the policy of military retaliation greatly inflamed Arab hatred of Israel and met with mounting criticism from the international community. The Western powers regarded the policy as destabilizing and disruptive to their plans for the defense of the Middle East against the Soviet Union, so they put strong pressure on Israel to desist. Israel acted on the precept that the best form of defense is attack. It placed all the blame for the tension and violence along the borders at the doorstep of the Arab governments. The official line was that Palestinian infiltration into Israel was aided and abetted by the Arab governments following the defeat of their regular armies on the battlefield; that it was a form of undeclared guerrilla warfare designed to weaken and destroy the infant Jewish state; that Israel was thus the innocent victim of Arab provocation and aggression; and that its military reprisals were a legitimate form of self-defense.

The Israeli portrayal of the attitude of the Arab governments was grossly inaccurate and unfair. There is strong evidence from Arab, British, American, UN, and even Israeli sources to suggest that for the first six years after the war, the Arab governments were opposed to infiltration and tried to curb it. Each Arab government dealt with this problem in its own way, with varying degrees of success. The Lebanese authorities transferred many of the Palestinian refugees northward, to camps in Beirut, Tyre, and Sidon, and effectively sealed the border with Israel. The Syrian authorities also exercised strict control over their border with Israel, and infiltration was rare. The Egyptian authorities kept a quarter of a million Palestinian refugees incarcerated in a tiny strip of territory in Gaza, but they pursued a consistent policy of curbing infiltration until 1955.

Jordan had the longest and most winding border with Israel, with the largest number of civilians on both sides. Some Jordanian villages were divided down the middle by the armistice line; usually their houses were on the Jordanian side of the line and their lands on the Israeli side. The upshot was border crossings on a massive scale, constant tension and turmoil, frequent Israeli military reprisals, countless Jordanian proposals to improve security in the border areas, and a singular failure to stem the tide of infiltration.

The murder of King Abdullah in July 1951 was followed by a period of political uncertainty in the Hashemite Kingdom of Jordan, but his son Talal and his grandson Hussein, who ascended the throne in May 1953, continued the long-standing Hashemite tradition of favoring peaceful coexistence with their Jewish neighbors. Hussein became king at the age of eighteen. At that time, by his own admission, he did not know much about the thinking of the Israeli leadership, but he was very puzzled by the violence of Israel's response to minor incursions over the armistice line. These responses, he recalled four decades later, "were extremely severe, extremely devastating, with attacks on villages, on police posts, and on people along the long cease-fire line, and obviously I was not very happy with that, and it caused us a great deal of difficulty in terms of the internal scene in Jordan." His puzzlement was all the greater given that the Jordanian authorities had been doing everything that they could "to prevent infiltration and to prevent access to Israel."[45]

A key figure alongside successive monarchs in Jordan was John Bagot Glubb, better known as Glubb Pasha, the British officer who commanded the Arab Legion. In that capacity Glubb did his best to halt infiltration into Israel and to prevent border incidents. In February 1952 Jordan signed a local commanders' agreement with Israel to prevent infiltration, and this agreement facilitated coexistence for the rest of the year. Glubb's constant refrain to anyone who would listen was that the Arab Legion was doing its level best to maintain a peaceful border with Israel. This refrain was also repeated in his many writings.[46]

Israel's response was that the Jordanian authorities were aiding and abetting border violations and that they alone must be held responsible for the progressive breakdown of the armistice regime. These charges were contradicted by the evidence available to the Israelis at the time. The evidence consisted not simply of declarations by Glubb but of the constructive and cooperative attitude displayed by all the Jordanian representatives within the Jordanian-Israeli Mixed Armistice Commission in dealing with the problems that kept cropping up. In general the Jordanians preferred to decentralize the system and let local commanders and police officers handle minor incidents on the spot, but the Israelis wanted all incidents to be dealt with by the central MAC machinery in Jerusalem. And Glubb had the impression that the Israeli speakers at meetings of the MAC were really addressing the people of Israel, the United Nations, or the American public rather than attempting to settle problems in a practical way.[47]

Secret Jordanian military documents captured by the Israeli army during the June 1967 war prove conclusively that Glubb's version of Jordanian policy is correct and that the Israeli version is utterly false. These documents reveal strenuous efforts on the part of the Jordanian civilian and military authorities in general and on the part of Glubb in particular to keep civilians from crossing the line. On 27 February 1952, for example, the minister of defense wrote to the prime minister to demand drastic steps to prevent infiltration, such as the imposition of severe punishment by the courts on those who were caught. Two reasons were given for this proposal: first, the property confiscated by the Jews was always worth more than that stolen by the infiltrators from the Jewish area, and, second, it would help limit acts of revenge by the Jewish forces on Arab lands.[48]

On 2 July 1952 Glubb attended a meeting with district commanders and concentrated his remarks on the important problem of infiltration. He estimated that if they adopted strict measures they should be able to keep 85 percent of the incidents from taking place. To this end he urged the district commanders to make greater efforts, show more vigilance, and monitor more closely the behavior of the police chiefs in their district.[49] The reasons given by Glubb for this policy are very similar to those given by the minister of defense. First and foremost, curbing infiltration was considered necessary for Jordan's sake, not for Israel's sake. Second, the Jews gained much more from confiscation in the Arab areas than the infiltrators gained from stealing from the Jewish area. Third, there was real fear that revenge would be exacted by Jewish units inside Jordan. Most striking is the high priority given to the border problem at the highest levels of the Jordanian government and armed forces.

Despite these strenuous efforts, tension along the border increased in the course of 1953. In January, Israel abrogated the Local Commanders Agreement and followed this up with two reprisal attacks inside Jordan. Even when these attacks were not successful from the military point of view, they caused loss of life and material damage to the Arab villages. The debate surrounding the policy of military retaliation intensified in 1953. At issue was the utility of this policy and the relative merits of alternative courses of action. Spokesmen for the defense establishment maintained that, under the existing circumstances, strikes against Arab villages were the most effective means of protecting Israel's day-to-day security. There was a general consensus that the Jordanian government must be held responsible for all armistice violations, despite the knowledge that some of the violations were caused by the dire conditions of the refugees who lived near the border. Reprisals were intended to compel the Jordanian government to act decisively and to put pressure on the villages to deny access to infiltrators. Additional reasons for the reprisals included the desire to forge the IDF into a fighting army again after the spell it spent in the doldrums and the desire to bolster the confidence of the border settlements.[50]

Domestic political considerations also played a part in the decisions to resort to military force in countering the challenge of infiltration. Opposition parties, especially Herut on the right and Mapam on the left, were critical of the government for its failure to provide effective protection to Israel's citizens. Mapai, the ruling party, was therefore more inclined to resort to demonstrative actions in order to avoid sliding down in the popularity stakes. Mapai was also influenced by public opinion in the country at large to respond more forcefully to Arab provocations. The political climate in the early 1950s was thus generally conducive to the use of force in dealing with the Arabs. Ben-Gurion personified this militant national mood, and within the government and the party he was the undisputed leader of the activist school. He wanted the IDF to strike hard at civilians across the border in order to demonstrate that no attack on Israeli citizens would go unpunished. His instinct was to let the military have its head and to sidestep the slow-moving machinery of the United Nations. In Hebrew the UN is called *Oom,* and Ben-Gurion showed his disregard for it by calling it *Oom-shmoom.*

The moderate school in opposition to Ben-Gurion was headed by Sharett. Military retaliation was the central issue in the debate between the activists and the moderates. The activists believed that the Arabs were interested in Israel's destruction, that they understood only the language of force, that Israel could not rely on the UN for her security, and that, in order to survive, the State of Israel had repeatedly to demonstrate its military power. In short, they believed in the policy of the iron wall. The moderates did not object to military retaliation in principle, but they wanted to use it in a more selective and controlled way and only after careful consideration of the likely political consequences. They were more sensitive to Arab feelings and to world opinion; they wanted to create a climate that would favor the possibilities of peaceful coexistence in the Middle East; they feared that frequent and excessive use of force would further inflame Arab hatred of Israel and set back the prospects of reconciliation. Abba Eban, who had to defend the official line at the UN, warned the government that the clashes and the tensions along the borders contradicted Israel's fundamental interest, which was the preservation of the territorial status quo established by the armistice agreements. Walter Eytan felt that the policy of reprisals completely failed to solve Israel's day-to-day security problems and advocated replacing it with defensive measures. He also disputed the IDF argument that the Arabs understood only the language of force.[51]

After every major incident of murder or sabotage, military retaliation was discussed by the cabinet. Usually, the prime minister and the foreign minister would find themselves on opposite sides of the argument. On a number of occasions Ben-Gurion proposed to the cabinet the launching of large-scale reprisals, and on one he put forward a plan for capturing villages across the border and keeping them until the Jordanians promised that the acts of murder would not be repeated. In support of his proposal Ben-Gurion pointed to the panic prevailing in the border settlements and the low morale of the army, and he stated that in vital security matters even friendly great powers should not be allowed to influence Israel's decisions. The cabinet was evenly divided between activists and moderates, so its decisions were commonly carried by a very narrow majority and some rested on an uneasy compromise between the two approaches.[52]

In the summer of 1953 Ben-Gurion, now sixty-eight and utterly exhausted, considered retiring from politics, at least for a year or two. In July he took three months' leave from the government to examine in depth the country's security situation and the state of affairs in the IDF. Moshe Sharett became acting prime minister, and Pinhas Lavon, a minister without portfolio, took over as acting minister of defense. When his leave was up, Ben-Gurion announced his decision to retire from his post for a couple of years and live in Sede-Boker, an isolated kibbutz in the southern Negev that was not affiliated with any political party.

Sharett had the thankless task of holding the party, the government, and the country together in the period preceding Ben-Gurion's formal resignation on 2 November 1953. The manner of Ben-Gurion's departure weakened the government and the authority of his successor. One of Sharett's first tasks as temporary prime minister was to deal with the crisis caused by Israel's project for the diversion of water from the Jordan River in the north to the parched lands of the Negev in the south. Two problems beset this project. First, the Jordan River was an international waterway, and all the riparian states enjoyed rights over it under international law. Second, as with the Huleh drainage project, some of the work was carried out in the demilitarized zone, south of the Benot Yaacov Bridge.

The driving force behind the diversion project was Moshe Dayan. Dayan knew that Israel had no legal right to divert the waters of the Jordan River and that if the matter was referred to the UN, the ruling would go against Israel. He therefore decided to create facts on the ground that the UN would be powerless to reverse. In July, before Ben-Gurion went on leave, the cabinet decided to divert the Upper Jordan and transport that water to the Negev. The execution of the cabinet decision, however, bore all the hallmarks of the Dayan technique. Bulldozers suddenly appeared and started digging up a canal in the DMZ in which to transport the water to the Negev. The cabinet had not determined the precise location of the diversion, and one water expert, Aharon Viner, proposed a suitable spot outside the DMZ. Dayan rejected his advice. Basing himself instead on the advice of the activist Simha Blass, Dayan chose to make the diversion not on Israeli territory but at a particular point inside the DMZ, fifty-four meters above sea level. Even had the diversion been made in the DMZ, the canal could have been dug outside the DMZ first and the connection to the river made later. But Dayan had a political aim in pursuing this engineering project. His broader purpose was to squeeze the Syrians out and establish complete Israeli control over the DMZ and the water sources in the north of the country.

Sharett decided to put the facts before Ben-Gurion. He went to a meeting with him, accompanied by Gideon Rafael. Dayan, supported by Yosef Tekoah, also went along to present his preferred plan. Sharett argued that the manner in which the project was being carried out was unwise, illegal, and provocative. Just as Ben-Gurion seemed on the point of conceding the force of these arguments, Tekoah interjected to say that the UN had no legal basis to intervene in this matter. Ben-Gurion turned to Sharett and said, "Your legal expert thinks that this has nothing to do with the UN." Influenced by Tekoah, Ben-Gurion ruled that the work should proceed and that the UN should be ignored. Sharett left the meeting in a very bitter mood and on the way back to the Foreign Ministry even talked about resigning. He knew that a clash with the UN was inevitable and that he would have to extricate Israel from the imbroglio.[53]

Syria complained to the Mixed Armistice Commission, and on 23 September Major General Vagn Bennike, chief of staff of the UN Truce Supervision Organization and chairman of the Israel-Syria MAC, addressed a letter to the government of Israel requesting the suspension of the work in the DMZ until an agreement between the parties concerned could be reached.

Israel's representative on the MAC insisted that the work was confined to Jewish-owned land in the DMZ, but when Sharett visited the area, he discovered that he too had been misled and that Arab-owned land was affected. Strong pressure was brought to bear on Israel by the United States to suspend work. When Israel refused, Secretary of State John Foster Dulles publicly announced the suspension of a grant-in-aid that Israel had requested. The Eisenhower administration had its own plan for the division of the water of the Jordan River between the riparian states, a plan inspired by the Tennessee Valley Authority. It also decided to send Eric Johnston, chairman of the Advisory Board for International Development, to try and mediate between the countries of the region and to reach agreement on water quotas.

Several proposals were made by Sharett to suspend the work temporarily in order to remove American and international pressure on Israel, but they could gain no majority backing in the cabinet. Abba Eban was critical of the government line on the grounds that it soured relations with the Eisenhower administration. It would have been better, in his view, to accept Bennike's request for a temporary suspension. Ben-Gurion rejected the criticism and set out his reasons in a long and revealing letter to Eban. He said he understood and shared Eban's concern about public opinion in the United States and the UN, but he went on to draw a distinction between secondary matters and matters of life and death. The waters of the Jordan River belonged to the second category, and they consequently had to stand firm in the face of external pressure. The letter also expressed attitudes that were common inside the Israeli defense establishment at the time: mistrust of the UN, suspicion of even friendly states and allies, willingness to stand alone, and use of past suffering as justification of present policies.[54]

On 25 October the cabinet, at Sharett's suggestion, decided to suspend the work to divert the water of the Jordan River while the matter was under consideration in the UN Security Council. Three days later Dulles announced the release of the $26 million grant-in-aid to Israel. The crisis with the United States was over, but the Security Council continued to debate this matter until 22 January 1954, when the Soviet Union vetoed a proposal of the Western powers. Work in the DMZ was not resumed, and a very different plan had to be worked out to carry water from the north of Israel to the south.

While Israel was in the dock at the Security Council in New York, the policy of reprisals took a nasty turn with an IDF attack on the Jordanian village of Qibya on the night of 14–15 October 1953. The order to attack was given by the acting defense minister, Pinhas Lavon, following the murder of an Israeli mother and her two children by infiltrators who had crossed the armistice line near Qibya. Lavon did not consult the cabinet and only casually informed Sharett of the order. At the meeting of the MAC on 15 October, the Jordanian representative denounced the murder, promised full cooperation in tracking down the perpetrators, and conveyed Glubb's request to Israel to refrain from retaliation. On hearing this report, Sharett telephoned Lavon and asked him to call off the attack. Lavon replied that he would consult Ben-Gurion. Lavon later claimed that he did indeed consult Ben-Gurion, who agreed with him—and that this meant it was two against one. Ben-Gurion himself later stated that he was on leave at the time and was not consulted but that had he been consulted he would have supported retaliation.

Lavon's order was executed by Unit 101, a small commando unit created in August to carry out special tasks. Unit 101 was commanded by an aggressive and ambitious young major named Ariel ("Arik") Sharon. Sharon's order was to penetrate Qibya, blow up houses, and inflict heavy casualties on its inhabitants. His success in carrying out this order surpassed all expectations. The full and macabre story of what had happened at Qibya was revealed only during the morning after the attack. The village had been reduced to a pile of rubble: forty-five houses had been blown up, and sixty-nine civilians, two-thirds of them women and children, had been killed. Sharon and his men claimed that they believed that all the inhabitants had run away and that they had no idea that anyone was hiding inside the houses.[55] The UN observer who inspected the scene reached a different conclusion: "One story was repeated time after time: the bullet splintered door, the body sprawled across the threshold, indicating that the inhabitants had been forced by heavy fire to stay inside until their homes were blown up over them."[56]

The Qibya massacre unleashed against Israel a storm of international protest of unprecedented severity in the country's short history. The cabinet convened on 18 October under the chairmanship of Ben-Gurion, who had just completed his three months' leave. Sharett, horrified by the scale and brutality of the action, proposed an official statement expressing regret over the action and its consequences. Ben-Gurion was against admitting that the IDF carried out the action and proposed issuing a statement to say that it was the irate Israeli villagers whose patience had been exhausted by the endless murders who took the law into their own hands. The majority of the ministers supported Ben-Gurion, and it was decided that he should draft the statement. In a radio broadcast the following day, Ben-Gurion gave the official version. He denied any IDF involvement, placed responsibility for the action on the villagers who had been provoked beyond endurance, and expressed the government's regret that innocent people had been killed.[57] This was not Ben-Gurion's first lie for what he saw as the good of his country, nor was it to be the last, but it was one of the most blatant.

The official version was not believed, and it did nothing to reduce the damage to Israel's image. On 24 November the Security Council passed a resolution condemning Israel for the Qibya operation and calling on it to refrain from such operations in future. Perhaps the most searing criticism came from the pen of Abba Eban after he had deployed his best rhetorical skills in defense of his country at the UN. In a letter to Sharett on 26 November, Eban wrote, "Sending regular armed forces across an international border, without the intention of triggering a full-scale war, is a step that distinguishes Israel from all other countries. No other state acts in this way. It was this, rather than the heavy casualties, that shocked the world."[58]

The principal perpetrators of the attack on Qibya, however, remained unrepentant. Lavon told the cabinet that he gave the order on the basis of a cabinet decision in June that empowered him to order reprisals. He also claimed that this reprisal was necessary in order to prevent the murder of more Israelis in the future. Ariel Sharon was well pleased with his handiwork. He thought the operation did a power of good to IDF morale. He also claimed that Ben-Gurion congratulated him on this operation. According to Sharon, the outgoing prime minister said to him, "It doesn't make any real difference . . . what will be said about Kibbiya [sic] around the world. The important thing is how it will be looked at here in this region. This is going to give us the possibility of living here."[59]

Sharon received his orders from Moshe Dayan, the main architect of the policy of reprisals and at this time chief of the operations branch of the General Staff. Dayan was flown to New York to advise Eban during the UN debate. He was accompanied by Gideon Rafael, whom Sharett had recently appointed counselor in charge of Middle Eastern and UN affairs. At the first meeting with the Israeli mission to the UN, Dayan analyzed the background of the operation. Continued terrorist raids, he said, made the escalation of Israeli counteraction unavoidable, and he predicted that the cycle of violence would eventually spark a full-scale war. He argued

that the terrorist incursions were sponsored by the Arab governments as an intermittent stage and not as a substitute for total war.
The perspective so bluntly depicted by Dayan only added to the
doubts and anxieties felt by the diplomats about the policy of
reprisals.[60]

Dayan's claim that the terrorists who provoked the reprisal
were sponsored and guided by the Arab Legion was blatantly self-
serving. It was also untrue. When Aryeh Eilan, an official in the
Foreign Ministry, asked Yehoshafat Harkabi, the deputy director of
military intelligence, for some clear documentary proof of the Arab
Legion's complicity, Harkabi answered that "no proof could be
given because no proof existed." Harkabi added that "having personally made a detailed study of the whole phenomenon of infiltration, he had arrived at the conclusion that Jordanians and
especially the Legion were doing their best to prevent infiltration,
which was a natural, decentralized and sporadic movement." To
this clear-cut message Eilan reacted by insisting that, whatever the
truth of the matter, since Israel's leaders had repeatedly gone on
record asserting Jordan's official complicity, Israeli spokesmen
must continue to support them: "If Jordanian complicity is a lie,
we have to keep on lying. If there are no proofs, we have to fabri-
cate them."[61] Dishonesty at the top evidently bred dishonesty and
mendacity at the lower levels of the government.

Qibya was the forerunner of many future disputes and disagreements on the policy of military reprisals, but the furor surrounding it did not affect Ben-Gurion's plan to retire. A special
meeting of the cabinet was held on 19 October to hear his defense
review. He submitted a detailed three-year plan with eighteen specific proposals for strengthening the IDF and enhancing the country's basic security. The plan was based on the assumption, which
he deemed incontestable, that the Arab states were preparing for
war with Israel. He estimated that the Arabs would be ready for a
second round in 1956, from the point of view of equipment, training, and unity of command.[62]

Moshe Sharett was impressed with Ben-Gurion's lecture,
which lasted two and a half hours. It was more profound than any
previous lecture he had heard him give on security matters, and it
was buttressed with precise facts and figures about the growing
strength of the Arab states. But as he listened to this survey, Sharett
reflected that a way had to be found for forestalling this danger by
nonmilitary means: "activating solutions to the refugee problem
by a bold and concrete offer on our part to pay compensation;

restoring good relations with the great powers; ceaseless struggle for an understanding with Egypt. Each of these courses of action is liable to take us into a vicious circle, and yet we are not exempt from struggling and trying."[63] It was a striking juxtaposition of the profoundly dissimilar philosophies of the outgoing and the incoming prime ministers. It was also a preview of the political program that Sharett planned to introduce after replacing Ben-Gurion at the helm.

On 7 December Ben-Gurion relinquished all his ministerial duties. Before proceeding to his desert retreat in Sede-Boker, though, he made a number of important appointments. He confirmed the forty-nine-year-old Pinhas Lavon in the post of minister of defense, promoted the twenty-nine-year-old Shimon Peres from deputy to director general of the Ministry of Defense, and, as his last official duty, appointed the thirty-seven-year-old Moshe Dayan IDF chief of staff. The three men had one thing in common: they were all ardent supporters of an activist defense policy. The outgoing prime minister counted on this trio to continue the tough defense policy he had established and to counter the conciliatory line of the man his party had chosen to succeed him, against his advice.

3

Attempts at Accommodation

1953–1955

THE THREE YEARS preceding the Suez War of October 1956 were an important and formative period in the evolution of Israel's policy toward the Arab world. Israel's leaders were deeply divided among themselves on the nature of the threat facing them and on the best way of safeguarding the country's security. There was no uniform perception of the character and magnitude of the Arab threat and no consensus on how it should be countered. Rather, Israel's behavior in the conflict was the product of an internal struggle between two schools of thought: one hawkish, the other dovish; one activist, the other moderate; one favoring retaliation, the other negotiation. These two schools were epitomized by David Ben-Gurion and Moshe Sharett, who alternated as prime minister during this eventful and critical period.

PERSONALITIES AND POLICIES

In Israel, Sharett is generally regarded as a weak, hesitant, and ineffectual politician, subservient to Ben-Gurion and totally overshadowed by him. Only a handful of Israelis would subscribe to the view that will be advanced here—namely, that Sharett was an independent and original thinker on the basic questions of Israeli security and, more important, that he represented a serious alternative to the dominant school of thought led by Ben-Gurion and inspired by him even during his temporary retirement to Sede-Boker, which lasted just over a year. The general tendency is to belittle Sharett and to use his name as a byword for appeasement and pusillanimity.

About the difference in personality and character between Ben-Gurion and Sharett there can be no doubt. In temperament and style they were as unlike as any two men could be. Sharett himself admitted, "There has been a temperamental incompatibility throughout. I am quiet, reserved, careful; Ben-Gurion is impulsive, impetuous, and acts on intuition. My capital C is Caution, Ben-Gurion's is Courage."[1] The incompatibility was between the decisive man of action and the master of quiet persuasion, between the authoritative leader who brooked no opposition and the open-minded intellectual who examined a problem from every conceivable angle and took considerable trouble to understand the other person's point of view.

Despite their temperamental incompatibility, Ben-Gurion and Sharett worked effectively in double harness for two decades and may even be said to have complemented each other. It was only from 1953 on, under the impact of the worsening security situation, that their policy differences moved into sharper focus while their personal relations grew more tense and troubled, ending in tragic rupture in 1956.[2]

At the heart of their policy differences lay dissimilar images of the Arabs. Ben-Gurion had surprisingly little knowledge of Arab culture and Arab history and no empathy whatever for the Arabs. Arabic was not among the half dozen languages he spoke. His experience of direct contact with ordinary Arabs was limited and did not inspire any trust in them or liking for them. His basic image of the Arabs was that of a primitive, fierce, and fanatical enemy that understood only the language of force. In his monumentally prolix speeches he repeatedly stressed the alienation and the gulf between "us" and "them." "We live in the twentieth century, they—in the fifteenth," he said in one speech. He took pride in the fact that "we created a proper society . . . amid the world of the Middle Ages."[3] Ben-Gurion could not conceive of a multi-ethnic society, embracing Jews and Arabs. He often compared Israel to a boat and the Arabs to a cruel sea and ruled out the possibility of harmony between them. His aim was to make the boat so robust that no storm or turbulence in the sea could capsize it.[4]

Sharett, by contrast, spent some of his childhood in an Arab village, spoke Arabic fluently, and was well versed in Arab history, culture, and politics. He had Arab friends and kept in touch with them. Persuaded that the Arabs could be trusted, he had the capacity to win their trust in political as well as in social relations. He viewed the Arabs as a people and not just as an enemy—a "proud and sensitive" people, as he once put it.[5] His image of the Arabs was more flexible than that of Ben-Gurion, and he was much more sensitive to the effect Israeli behavior had on Arab feelings. At a meeting of Mapai's Political Committee, Sharett came out against the view that the Arabs were primitive and wild and that their hatred of Israel was so deeply ingrained that it could hardly be made worse by specific Israeli actions. The Arabs, he said, have "extremely subtle understanding and delicate senses." It was true, he conceded, that "there is a wall between us and them and there is a tragic development in that this wall is getting taller. But, nevertheless, if this wall can be prevented from getting taller, it is a sacred duty to do so, if at all possible."[6]

On the broad terms of a settlement with the Arabs, there was no real difference between Sharett and Ben-Gurion. Both men believed that a settlement should be based on the status quo. Like Ben-Gurion, Sharett was unwilling to take back the bulk of the Palestinian refugees or to relinquish large tracts of territory, if that was the price demanded from Israel in exchange for a peace settlement with the Arabs. Unlike Ben-Gurion, he attached considerable value to patient and imaginative diplomacy, to conciliatory language, and to gestures of goodwill in an effort to whittle down Arab hostility. He did not wish to add any secondary causes to the basic cause of the conflict between the Arabs and Israel. If Arab hostility could not be eradicated, it was all the more necessary to try to moderate it and to keep open every possible line of communication and dialogue.

Another important component in the political outlook of Ben-Gurion and Sharett was their attitude to the "external factor." A cardinal tenet in Ben-Gurion's political creed was self-reliance. He had a tremendous faith in the capacity of the Jewish people to shape its own destiny in the Middle East by direct action and through the creation of facts. The corollary of self-reliance was disdain for the "external factor" in the creation and survival of the Jewish state. "We must wean ourselves," he wrote in 1954 in an article on the UN, "from the preposterous and totally unfounded and baseless illusion that there is outside the State of Israel a force and will in the world that would protect the life of our citizens. Our own capacity for self-defense is our only security."[7] Nothing else, however, expresses so pithily Ben-Gurion's indifference to the UN and international public opinion than his often quoted saying "Our future does not depend on what the Gentiles say but on what the Jews do."[8]

In sharp contrast to Ben-Gurion, Sharett was highly sensitive not only to what the Gentiles said but even more to what they did. He acknowledged that the UN had played an indispensable part in the creation of the State of Israel, and he was in favor of allowing it to play a larger and more effective role in the regulation of the Arab-Israeli conflict. He believed that international public opinion had a bearing on Israel's security and was, therefore, a factor worth taking into account. Above all, he was eager to enlist the sympathy and support of the Western powers in Israel's quest for security and peace. To this end he deemed it necessary to abide by the prevailing norms of international behavior and to refrain from actions that would fuel Arab hatred.

From 1953 on, the internal debate in Israel between the activists and nonactivists focused increasingly on the question of reprisals. Ben-Gurion and his followers advocated a policy of severe and prompt military retaliation in response to incursions across Israel's borders. Sharett was not opposed to retaliation in principle. His concern related chiefly to the negative long-term consequences that reprisals were liable to have on Israel's relations with the Arabs and on its international standing. While viewing them as unavoidable as a weapon of last resort in some situations, Sharett feared that reprisals would degenerate into an unthinking military routine. He insisted that the resort to force must be preceded by careful consideration of the questions of scale and timing within the framework of Israel's overall foreign policy aims in order to minimize its negative consequences for Israel's regional and international interests.

The appointment of Pinhas Lavon as defense minister was tantamount to planting a time bomb under Sharett's premiership. Sharett strongly opposed the appointment and yielded only because he would have had to relinquish the foreign affairs portfolio had he taken over the defense portfolio himself. The new defense minister was, in the words of Golda Meir, the minister of labor in the Sharett cabinet, "one of the most capable if least stable members of Mapai, a handsome, complicated intellectual who had always been a great 'dove' but who turned into the most ferocious sort of 'hawk' as soon as he began to concern himself with military matters." Golda Meir and many of her Mapai colleagues thought him extremely unsuitable for this sensitive ministry, because he had neither the experience nor the necessary judgment. They tried to point this out to Ben-Gurion, but he would not change his mind.[9]

The personal transformation that accompanied Lavon's move into the Defense Ministry astounded all those who knew him. The extreme moderation that had for many years marked Lavon as the antithesis to Ben-Gurion's hard-line stance was quickly replaced by equally extreme hawkishness. The socialist thinker turned into an apostle of *realpolitik;* the preacher of fraternity among nations gave way to an Arab-scorning nationalist. Lavon's unstable character, his desire to outshine Sharett, and his fear of being found lacking in courage in comparison with the army officers all contributed to his swift adaptation to the activist climate of his new post.

Lavon regarded the status quo as unsatisfactory and implied that it could be changed to Israel's advantage only by resort to military force. Israel, he argued, was at a unique disadvantage because it faced hostile neighbors on all sides and because its geopolitical situation was so vulnerable. Peace was not a practical possibility, since the Arabs had no interest in peace and Israel could not offer them anything concrete in return for peace. Moreover, thanks to the Cold War and their oil, the bargaining power of the Arabs was going up while that of Israel was going down. The Western powers were courting the Arabs rather than Israel. If Israel sought a final settlement of the conflict under these conditions, it was bound to be at Israel's expense. Running after a settlement could only produce a bad one. Lavon's conclusion was that Israel should be prepared to live for some time in a state of neither peace nor war. This would not enable it to achieve its national objectives but would at least leave the option of achieving them at a later date. In the meantime, Israel should pursue a threefold policy: prevent and delay a political settlement of the Arab-Israel dispute; stand firm on all Israeli rights and refuse to make any concessions; and respond with force to every act of force.[10]

What Lavon did not spell out publicly was that by national objectives he meant extending Israel's borders at the expense of its neighbors or that these objectives could be achieved, according to his own analysis, only by the use of military force. In other words, the opportunity he was waiting for was the opportunity to go to war, in order to rectify Israel's vulnerable geopolitical situation. He came close to admitting this at a meeting of Mapai's Central Committee in April 1954. If one looked at a war with the Arabs only from the military point of view, he told his colleagues in confidence, there was no time like the present: "Today would be better for us than tomorrow, and tomorrow would be better than the day after tomorrow, because tomorrow and the day after tomorrow our military position would be much graver than today. I cannot say: I do not want war. I say: I want it, and I wish there was a situation in which there were no Englishmen and no Americans, and there were only us and the Arabs, and we could do that."[11]

If the appointment of Lavon was one time bomb under Sharett's premiership, the appointment of Moshe Dayan as IDF chief of staff was another. Dayan belonged to a new generation of tough home-grown military commanders. Born in Degania, near the Sea of Galilee, in 1915, he joined the Haganah in his teens. In 1941 he lost his left eye in an Allied operation against the forces of Vichy France in Lebanon. During the 1948 war his battalion captured Ramle and Lydda, and he later became the governor of Jerusalem. The black patch over his left eye was his most distinctive trademark. Although a highly intelligent man and a very capable officer, he was also independent-minded and insubordinate by nature and, as such, could not be counted upon to respect the supremacy of civilian authority. Whereas the first three IDF chiefs of staff had all been politically independent, Dayan was an active member of Mapai, with a reputation for deviousness and political intrigue. Sharett opposed Dayan's appointment. He thought that Dayan acted as a soldier only in times of war but in peacetime was a political man and that his appointment would mean the politicization of the General Staff. There was also considerable opposition to Dayan's appointment from Mapai's partners in the government, but, as usual, Ben-Gurion had his way.[12] Dayan showed complete personal loyalty to Ben-Gurion, his mentor, patron, and father figure. After Ben-Gurion's retirement, Dayan and Shimon Peres, the director general of the Ministry of Defense, used to visit the old chief regularly in Sede-Boker to report on current affairs and get his advice. Neither of them displayed any such loyalty toward their official political chief.

Dayan was both an expansionist and an activist. He held the view that Israel's borders had to be expanded so as to rectify the omissions of the 1948 war. In particular he felt that the border with Jordan, which he himself had helped negotiate, was impossible to live with and had to be replaced by a natural border running along the Jordan River. He was an activist in the sense that for him the solution to Israel's security problems lay in direct military action to enhance the deterrent power of the IDF and to compel the Arab governments to curb infiltration from their territory into Israel. The premise behind this policy was that the only effective antidote to force is force—and not reliance on the goodwill of Arab neighbors or on the protection of external powers and international agencies.

Dayan's ideas on the paramount role of force in regulating relations between Israel and the Arabs were intimately connected to his conception of the nature of the conflict. He perceived the Arab-Israeli conflict as a struggle for survival between two communities whose interests were irreconcilable. Israel simply had no way of overcoming Arab opposition to its presence in the region. The conflict was consequently not susceptible to peaceful resolution. All Israel could realistically aspire to was to force the Arabs to desist from hostile acts despite their unalterably hostile attitude. Israel's only hope of survival lay in vigilance, strength, and determination. This conclusion was a recurrent theme in Dayan's public utterances. It was explicitly and eloquently stated in his oration at the funeral of Ro'i Rotberg, a young farmer from Kibbutz Nahal-Oz who was murdered by Arab marauders in April 1956:

Yesterday morning Ro'i was killed. The quiet of spring morning blinded him, and he did not see the murderers lying in wait for him along the furrow. Let us not today fling accusations at the murderers. What cause have we to complain about their fierce hatred for us? For eight years now, they sit in their refugee camps in Gaza, and before their eyes we turn into our homestead the land and villages in which they and their forefathers have lived.

We should demand his blood not from the Arabs of Gaza but from ourselves. . . . Let us make our reckoning today. We are a generation of settlers, and without the steel helmet and the gun barrel, we shall not be able to plant a tree or build a house. . . . Let us not be afraid to see the hatred that accompanies and consumes the lives of hundreds of thousands of Arabs who sit all around us and await the moment when their hand will be able to reach our blood. Let us not avert our gaze, for it will weaken our hand. This is the fate of our generation. The only choice we have is to be prepared and armed, strong, and resolute, or else our sword will slip from our hand and the thread of our lives will be severed.[13]

Dayan was clearly not insensitive to Arab feelings. He recognized the injustice that his country had inflicted on hundreds of thousands of Arabs. But his very empathy bred deep pessimism concerning the possibility of an accommodation with them. It was not self-righteousness but the conviction that Israel's survival was at stake that led him to reject any magnanimity. Dayan's was the philosophy of a man who was born in war, who lived all his life in war, and for whom war had always been the focus of his thought. His funeral oration epitomized the stark philosophy of the "Arab fighter," that is, the equivalent of what Americans used to call the Indian fighter, a type common in the second generation of settlers in a country where newcomers are forced to fight the native population.[14] His instinctive feeling that Israel was doomed to live in continual warfare and the grim outlook that followed from it made him the symbol of a whole generation of Israeli activists or "Arab fighters."

Dayan was closely associated with the policy of reprisals from the beginning. A man with strong and assertive character, he had few inhibitions and no moral qualms about the use of military force even against civilians. As early as June 1950 he defended at a meeting of the Mapai Secretariat and members of Knesset the policy of collective punishment against Arab villages suspected of harboring infiltrators and saboteurs. Harassing the village, including women, children, and elderly people, he said, "is the only method that proved itself *effective,* not justified or moral, but effective, when Arabs lay mines on our side."[15]

Dayan's appointment as chief of staff was a milestone in the development of Israel's military doctrine, the core of which was the policy of reprisals. Until his appointment reprisals were carried out in the context of day-to-day security. Their objective was to reduce infiltration. After his appointment they were carried out in the context of basic security. Their objective was to enhance the deterrent power of the IDF, to demonstrate Israel's military superiority to the Arab governments, and to dampen any hope on their part of destroying Israel. In other words, the objective of reprisals changed from helping keep a quiet border to enhancing Israel's basic security against the threat of attack by the regular armies of the Arab states.

The clearest manifestation of this change in military doctrine was the switch from a "countervalue" to a "counterforce" strategy. A countervalue strategy is directed against civilians; a counterforce strategy, against military targets. In this respect the massacre at

Qibya marked the turning point. Until then the reprisals were directed against Arab civilians and Arab villages. Thereafter civilians were no longer deliberately targeted. This counterforce strategy, quite apart from its incidental humanity in sparing innocent civilians, had the merit of being a more effective instrument for promoting basic security.

The most detailed and authoritative exposition of the rationale behind the revised policy of reprisals was given by Moshe Dayan himself in a talk to army officers in August 1955. The interplay between day-to-day security and basic security was his central theme. Victories and reverses in the minor battles along and across the border were, he stated, of great importance not only because of their direct effect on day-to-day security but also because of their influence on the Arabs' estimate of Israel's strength, and on Israel's faith in its own strength. The duty of the IDF was to ensure a peaceful life, and satisfactory conditions for work and production, in the border settlements and inside the country. This meant establishing rules of what was permissible and what was forbidden in the relations between Israel and its Arab neighbors.

> We could not guard every water pipeline from being blown up and every tree from being uprooted. We could not prevent every murder of a worker in an orchard or a family in their beds. But it was in our power to set a high price on our blood, a price too high for the Arab community, the Arab army, or the Arab governments to think it worth paying. . . . It was in our power to cause the Arab governments to renounce "the policy of strength" toward Israel by turning it into a demonstration of weakness.[16]

These were the premises that guided Dayan's conduct during his four years as chief of staff. Like Ze'ev Jabotinsky, Dayan wanted to build an iron wall of Jewish military strength. Like Jabotinsky, he wanted to use this wall to demonstrate to the Arabs their military inferiority. And like Jabotinsky, he hoped that the iron wall would eventually extinguish the hope in Arab minds of ever prevailing in the struggle against the Jewish community.

Dayan's talk also shows how close he was to Ben-Gurion in his outlook on the Arab-Israeli conflict in general and on the utility of military force as an instrument of national policy in particular. This is hardly surprising, since both men were proponents of the philosophy of the iron wall. Both believed that the Arabs posed a continuing threat to Israel's basic security, both implicitly accepted the notion that the end justified the means, and both regarded military force as the only effective means of ensuring Israel's survival.

The real incompatibility was between Dayan's aggressive and ruthless brand of military activism and the moderate line favored by Sharett. In an exceptionally perceptive talk given to a group of Mapai members at a closed meeting in October 1957, more than a year after he had left the government, Sharett presented the whole debate between the proponents and the critics of reprisals in the context of two conflicting Israeli schools of thought on the question of how to conduct relations with the Arabs. With characteristic fairness and objectivity, he presented the thinking of what might be termed the school of retaliation as well as his own criticisms of it. Against this he juxtaposed the school of negotiation, which he himself supported. Sharett did not underestimate the complexity of Israel's situation, nor did he pretend that there were any simple solutions. Nevertheless, he rejected the pessimistic premises of the first school because they completely ignored the impact of Israel's own behavior on the Arabs. He contested the conclusion that it was Israel's destiny to live in a beleaguered fortress defending itself and deterring its enemies by exclusive reliance on the sword. But neither did he believe that there was a shortcut to the solution of the Arab-Israeli problem.[17] What he did do during his premiership was grope for an alternative foreign policy that did not take Israel's position as a beleaguered fortress as its starting point but sought to whittle down the barriers separating Israel from its regional environment.

THE ACTIVIST CHALLENGE TO SHARETT

Sharett's first year as prime minister was difficult for Israel both on the political front and on the day-to-day security front. In the course of 1954 Israeli-American relations deteriorated as a result of the U.S. decision to supply arms to the Arab states and base its military plans for the defense of the Middle East increasingly on Iraq and Egypt. Israel as a consequence felt marginalized. Britain's agreement to withdraw its forces from the Suez Canal Zone also caused concern in Israel. Along Israel's borders the situation deteriorated, with more incidents of infiltration, theft, murder, and sabotage, which the UN Truce Supervisory Organization (UNTSO) was unable to prevent. These developments combined to make Israelis feel isolated and ignored, and this intensified the conflict between the two approaches. Sharett became active on the American diplomatic scene in an effort to stop military aid to the Arabs and to procure arms and a security guarantee for Israel. For Lavon, on the other hand, the solution lay in military activity to deter the Arabs.[18]

What made things worse was Lavon's refusal to accept Sharett's authority in defense matters. He treated Sharett as no more than foreign minister and tried to limit his intervention in what he considered his own departmental concerns. Lavon did not report to Sharett regularly on the IDF operations along the borders, and the reports that he did make were often partial and misleading.[19] Lavon also kept the cabinet in the dark on important aspects of defense policy and made no effort to gain the confidence and support of his colleagues. Toward the middle of 1954 Sharett began to convene a committee of five senior ministers from Mapai to discuss defense and foreign affairs. The main task of this committee, usually referred to as "the Committee of Five," was to adjudicate in disputes over defense policy. The committee members were Sharett, Lavon, Golda Meir, the minister of labor, Levi Eshkol, the minister of finance, and Zalman Aran, minister without portfolio. The existence of this committee was kept secret. Sharett's motive in convening it was to use senior party colleagues to try to restrain and control Lavon and avert an open clash with him in the cabinet. He also feared that a showdown with Lavon would split the party and create the conditions for Ben-Gurion's return.

On 31 January 1954, at Lavon's suggestion, an informal meeting took place in the prime minister's home with the Mapai ministers and the new chief of staff. According to Sharett's diary,

> Moshe Dayan unfolded one plan after another for "direct action." The first—what should be done to force open the blockade of the Gulf of Eilat. A ship flying the Israeli flag should be sent, and if the Egyptians bomb it, we should bomb the Egyptian base from the air, or conquer Ras al-Naqb, or open our way south of the Gaza Strip to the coast. There was a general uproar. I asked Moshe, "Do you realize that this would mean war with Egypt?" He said, "Of course."

All those present rejected this plan, and Lavon hastened to retreat. Dayan's second proposal was for military action against the Syrians to establish Israel's exclusive right to fish in the Sea of Galilee.

The third proposal was to cross the border into Syria and capture positions there in the event of an Iraqi incursion into Syria. Sharett made it absolutely clear that no action must be taken before a political decision was reached. But he was extremely worried by the line of thinking of the new chief of staff.[20]

When General Naguib, the figurehead of the Egyptian revolution, was challenged by Nasser and Adib Shishakli was overthrown by a military coup in Syria at the end of February 1954, Ben-Gurion was invited to a meeting with Sharett, Lavon, and Dayan for consultation on how Israel might react. The meeting took place in the library of Ben-Gurion's home in Tel Aviv. The library was cold, and the conversation did not warm Sharett's heart. Lavon proposed a military thrust in the south to detach the Gaza Strip from Egypt and an invasion of the demilitarized zone in the north, along the border between Israel and Syria. Ben-Gurion came out against any provocation of Egypt but favored sending the army into the demilitarized zone on the pretext that the anarchy in Syria forced Israel to protect its settlements. Sharett announced that he was firmly opposed to both plans because they were certain to unite the Western powers and the Security Council against Israel and were also likely to end in a humiliating withdrawal. Lavon looked depressed. He understood this to be the end of the matter.

Ben-Gurion seized the opportunity to float a pet scheme of his for dismantling Lebanon and helping create a Christian-Maronite state that would be allied to Israel. This scheme was part of a broader conception that called for Israeli cooperation with other minorities to counter Muslim predominance in the Middle East. Ben-Gurion said that the moment was right to encourage the Maronites to proclaim their own Christian state. Sharett pointed out that the Maronite community was internally divided and that the partisans of Christian separatism were weak and on the defensive. A Christian Lebanon would mean giving up Tyre, Tripoli, and the Bekaa Valley. Not only would this destroy the economic raison d'être of the state, but there was no political force capable of reducing Lebanon to its pre–World War I territorial dimensions. Ben-Gurion reacted to these arguments by accusing Sharett of excessive timidity. In his view it was worth spending a million dollars on such a project because it would bring about a decisive change in the Middle East; a new era would begin. Sharett was exhausted by the argument with Ben-Gurion, which he likened to struggling with a whirlwind.[21]

Sharett had resisted Lavon's proposal for the occupation of

the DMZ by insisting on his formal responsibility to bring the matter before the cabinet. At its meeting the following day, the cabinet roundly defeated Lavon's proposal. Lavon claimed that a great opportunity to strengthen Israel had been missed. Sharett retorted that the plan would have backfired and that an unnecessary entanglement had been avoided.[22] In the space of two days, Sharett had checked three plans for intervention. In the face of combined pressure from Ben-Gurion, Lavon, and Dayan, he stood his ground and mobilized the cabinet as a counterweight to the policies urged by the interventionists. The debate highlighted the tension between the tendency to take risky military initiatives and to subvert Arab regimes and the tendency to refrain from military adventures and to avoid intervention in the internal affairs of the neighboring Arab states.[23]

Ben-Gurion continued to attack the Sharett line, as did Lavon and Dayan. Sharett was constantly under pressure to authorize reprisals in order to avoid being discredited inside Mapai, in the Knesset, in the press, and in the country at large. Reports reached Sharett that the army leaders were growing restive and more militant and that they were heading for war. They were nervous in view of Western arms supplies to the Arabs, and their instinct was to force a showdown before the Arabs became too strong.[24] For Lavon, too, war was the hidden agenda. He did not openly advocate war, but his thinking pointed in that direction. One argument was that from the purely military perspective it was better to have war sooner rather than later. Another argument was that Israel should not refrain from taking any military action out of fear that it might lead to war. Sharett exposed the danger inherent in these arguments at a meeting of Mapai's Political Committee on 12 May. First, he pointed out that it was not enough to say that they wanted peace; the government, and especially the IDF, had to behave accordingly. Second, there was a danger of sliding into war even without wanting or planning it. Third, there was a profound difference between a war forced on Israel, as in 1948, and a war initiated by Israel—between a war of no choice and a war of choice. Fourth, even assuming a military victory in a war that Israel initiated, its demographic consequences might make it a Pyrrhic victory. Even if Israel captured the rest of Palestine up to the Jordan River, a mass exodus of Palestinians was unlikely to happen again. For his part, Sharett preferred the present border, with all its problems, to the annexation of the West Bank, with its million inhabitants.[25]

The scope for large-scale reprisals against Jordan was reduced both because of Sharett's restraining influence and because the Arab Legion stationed four battalions along the border to prevent incidents. Israeli army leaders, however, were not content to sit still. They developed a more covert and devious strategy for terrorizing the Jordanians. They sent into the West Bank small patrols that intercepted enemy units and carried out acts of murder and sabotage. To evade responsibility, the IDF spokesman would concoct a false version of the sequence of events, usually claiming that the provocation occurred inside Israel's territory or that an Israeli patrol crossed the border in hot pursuit of terrorists. Dayan admitted to Jon Kimche, a friendly British journalist, who relayed the words to Sharett, that "UN reports are often more accurate than ours."[26]

Lavon colluded with the IDF chiefs in concealing this covert strategy from Sharett and in feeding him false reports when incidents came to light, but Lavon himself was not informed about all the activities of the army, which was nominally under his ministerial control. Sharett demanded from Lavon a swift and accurate report on all IDF operations and on every incident, but all he got were promises that Lavon evidently had no intention of keeping. Indeed, by the beginning of July, Lavon boasted in front of the General Staff that no fewer than forty small military operations had been initiated since he had become minister of defense a year earlier. This meant on the average more than three operations a month. Lavon also boasted about the variety of the operations: "acts of robbery, laying mines, destroying houses, firing on vehicles, etc. . . . During these years more was done in the military sphere than in all the years of the struggle."[27]

An independent investigation carried out by Sharett revealed that despite his activism Lavon was in fact unable to exercise effective control over the army and that he lacked the courage to admit this to anyone. Sharett therefore summoned Dayan and ordered him "to put an end, once and for all, to this unruly behavior of crossing the border every Monday and Thursday, without any consideration of the malignant consequences."[28] Such orders rolled off like water off a duck's back. Sharett, on the other hand, was beginning to show the effects of his ceaseless struggle with his own defense establishment. In one of his nightmares he dreamed that he and his wife, Zipora, were sentenced to death by firing squad on a charge of betraying the state.[29]

On the international front Sharett fared rather better than on the home front. To resolve the water dispute between Israel and the Arab states, America launched an imaginative plan patterned after the Tennessee Valley Authority. A presidential representative, Eric Johnston, was sent to the area to persuade the parties to collaborate on this project, for which the United States was prepared to make funding available. The project was to develop hydroelectric facilities and an advanced irrigation network for the benefit of all the states and, in addition, to create fertile land capable of supporting up to 900,000 Palestinian refugees on the West Bank of the Jordan. It was hoped that Arab-Israeli collaboration on water would become the cornerstone of a broader settlement.

Eric Johnston and his team visited Israel in October 1953 and returned for a major round of talks in June 1954. The attitude of the defense establishment was typically negative and suspicious: it was believed that Johnston's purpose was to look for incriminating evidence against Israel and to curtail its rights. Sharett's attitude was characteristically flexible and constructive. He mastered the water brief as only he knew how to, and he conducted the negotiations himself. The only agreement that was reached concerned the allocation of water to Israel and its neighbors. Initially, Johnston had proposed 32 percent to Israel, 64 percent to Jordan, and a small quota to Syria. The final allocation was 45 percent to Israel and 55 percent to the Arabs. Lavon and the IDF opposed this agreement, but the majority of the cabinet supported the prime minister.

To Mapai's Political Committee, Sharett explained the thinking behind his approach. This thinking took into account Israel's water, security, economic development, and political interests. In general, Israel's relations with its neighbors were deteriorating, and here was one area where it was possible to move forward. For his part, he would have preferred direct cooperation with the Arabs, but that was not being offered. The only choice was between moving towards cooperation with them with American help and not moving forward at all. He chose the former for a number of reasons. First, Johnston's water allocation matched Israel's own original expectations. Second, given Israel's limited resources, this agreement gave Israel ample scope to work on its water development plans over the next ten to fifteen years. Third, it opened up the possibility of further American economic aid. Fourth, this was the beginning of coordination between Israel and the Arabs on a common project.[30]

Indeed, the Johnston plan for the allocation of water quotas was a unique example of agreement between Israel and its neighbors. The agreement was achieved not in direct negotiations but through a mediator. The subject matter of the agreement was contentious, but a compromise was reached. The Arab leaders refused to sign the agreement because, as a matter of principle, they were opposed to formal recognition of Israel. But both Jordan and Israel informed the Americans that they would treat the agreement as if it had been signed. And over the next decade both parties behaved in accordance with the provisions of the Johnston plan. Sharett's flexible approach had been vindicated.[31]

While Sharett was working with the help of America to promote practical cooperation with the Arabs, the army leaders continued to pursue aggressive policies that knowingly increased the risks of a slide toward war. Even Ben-Gurion apparently felt that his protégé was going too far. When Dayan told him on 8 June that he wanted a policy more activist than that of the government, he interrupted him and asked, "What is activism? What do you want, war?" Dayan described his approach as follows:

> I am against a war initiated by our side, but I am also against making concessions in any sphere, and if the Arabs, as a result, want war—I do not object. Their threat must not constitute a constraint on our actions. Such is the case with the diversion of the waters of the Jordan River. We must carry out the diversion. And if the Syrians open fire and try to prevent our work by force—we shall respond to them with force. The same goes for free passage through the straits of Eilat. We must use the straits. If the Egyptians resist with force—we should not recoil from war. The conception today in the government led by Moshe Sharett is to ask, "Are we in favor of war?" And when the answer is negative, the conclusion is that Israel must give way on anything whose realization is liable, because of Arab opposition, to lead to war.[32]

The policy differences between Dayan and Sharett were exacerbated by power struggles, personal antipathies, and disputes over jurisdiction within the defense establishment. This murky labyrinth of rivalries, intrigues, and mutual mistrust among the leading players constituted the domestic backdrop to "the mishap."

THE MISHAP

The external setting for the mishap was the agreement initialed by Britain and Egypt in July 1954 to withdraw the British forces from the Suez Canal Zone. Under the terms of the 1936 treaty, Britain maintained bases along the Suez Canal, and its agreement to evacuate these bases, following protracted and acrimonious negotiations, was a major triumph for the Free Officers in their struggle for independence. In Israel the reaction to the agreement was rather mixed. The military planners looked upon it as an unmitigated disaster. They believed that it would remove the barrier between Egypt and Israel, that it would be followed by Western military assistance to Egypt, that it would strengthen Egypt's military potential, and that it would seriously tilt the military balance in Egypt's favor. They were therefore convinced that the British withdrawal must be prevented by diplomatic or other means.

The Israeli Foreign Ministry's experts on Arab affairs believed that once Nasser achieved his central goal of freeing his country from the presence of foreign troops, he would adopt an "Egypt first" policy and become more amenable to a settlement with Israel. An Israeli attempt to foil the agreement was bound to fail and likely to backfire. The problem, as one of these experts noted in his memoirs, was that it had become the practice of Israel's policymakers to find ways of accommodating the views of the military. The more strongly the military pushed its position and plan of action, the more the compromise tilted in its direction. Implementation, moreover, was not well coordinated between the different branches of the government: "We were trying to ride two horses simultaneously, one named contact, and the other contest—we fell between the two."[33]

While the diplomats were conveying messages, Israeli military intelligence, headed at that time by Colonel Binyamin Gibli, struck a sudden and totally unprovoked blow against Egypt. A Jewish espionage ring, organized and directed by military intelligence, carried out a series of acts of sabotage inside Egypt in July 1954. These acts were intended to derail or postpone Anglo-Egyptian agreement.[34] On 2 July incendiary devices were placed in mailboxes in Alexandria, causing very little damage. The same tactic was used against American libraries and information offices in Cairo and Alexandria on 14 July, again with little effect. On 23 July, the anniversary of the start of the Free Officers' revolution, members of the ring set out to detonate their bombs in a number of cinemas showing British and American films and in a post office. One of these primitive devices started emitting smoke prematurely from the pocket of a member of the ring as he was about to enter the cinema. He was caught red-handed, and his capture led to the rounding up of the other members of the ring. They were all put on trial; in the end two members of the ring were executed, one committed suicide in prison, and the others were sentenced to long terms of imprisonment.

The political thinking that motivated this amateurish and incompetently executed operation was staggeringly crude. The purpose of the scheme was to fake anti-British and anti-American incidents, so making it plain to the West that the Nasser regime could not be trusted to protect Western personnel and property in Egypt. Britain, it was thought, would thereupon reconsider its decision to withdraw its forces from Suez, and its continuing presence would prevent Egyptian military adventures in the Middle East. The other aim was to put an end to the rapprochement between Egypt and the American government, which was working toward a regional military alliance centering on Baghdad and Cairo and linked to the West—a project considered prejudicial to Israel's security.

The bitter controversy over the question of who gave the order for this disastrous operation developed into a confrontation between the army officers and their political master. Dayan himself was in the United States when the order was given, and he had all along opposed the activation of the spy ring. Colonel Gibli claimed that Lavon gave him the order to activate this ring at a meeting in Lavon's house on 16 July. Lavon's wild activism and the excessive interest he had evinced in his ministry's sabotage files lent credence to this claim. But the operation had been set in motion two weeks before this meeting, and evidence that came to light subsequently revealed that Gibli resorted to forging documents and procuring false testimonies in order to clear himself and pin responsibility on Lavon. Lavon emphatically denied having given the order to activate the ring and claimed that far from being an indictment of him personally, the whole murky affair was the work of army officers who plotted to discredit him and undermine his position.

Lavon's own activism showed no sign of abating. During a cabinet discussion of the Anglo-Egyptian agreement, he "went crazy," suggesting that the armistice agreement with Egypt be renounced and that Israel capture the Gaza Strip.[35] Moreover, the officers in military intelligence showed no remorse for their botched operation in Egypt. They put forward proposals for action with the deliberate aim of provoking a war with Egypt.[36]

In September the IDF reluctantly went along with a Foreign Ministry plan to challenge the Egyptian closure of the Suez Canal to Israeli shipping by sending the *Bat Galim,* a small vessel of a few hundred tons, through the canal to Haifa under the Israeli flag. From the start it was expected that the vessel would be seized and that Egypt could then be put in the international dock. Since the blockade was a violation of the 1951 Security Council resolution, it was thought that the permanent members would have no option but to oblige Egypt to give way, thus opening the canal to Israeli shipping. On 28 September the *Bat Galim* was stopped at the southern entrance to the canal and its crew imprisoned. The Western powers, who were trying to get Egypt to join a defense pact at the time, did not appreciate the Israeli démarche. Nor were they prepared to imperil their improving relations with Egypt in a fruitless attempt to force Egypt to back down. Consequently, the Israeli move was a fiasco. All it did was demonstrate to the Egyptians that for the time being the blockade could be continued with impunity.[37]

Following the failure to break the Egyptian maritime blockade, Dayan began to bombard Sharett with proposals for pure military action, untainted by diplomacy, against Egypt and Jordan. The situation along the border with the Gaza Strip was getting out of hand, and Dayan wanted Sharett to recognize that the policy of restraint and the appeals to the UN observers and to the United States had not worked and to authorize military action. He added that "retail" military actions would not do; only a blow on a massive scale would galvanize the Egyptian authorities to take prompt and energetic measures to check the rising tide of violence. More specifically, he proposed a raid at night into Gaza City to blow up a major government building, the police headquarters, or the waterworks. Sharett, intent on presenting Israel as a peace-loving nation and on dissuading the Western powers from supplying arms to Egypt, rejected the proposal, because it was likely to prove to the world that Israel was bent on aggression and conquest.[38]

Dayan's next proposal was for a military reprisal against Jordan. On 27 September a flock of 480 sheep ended up on the Jordanian side of the demarcation line. The sheep were a specially selected superior flock, the pride of Kibbutz Ein Hashofet. The Israeli version of the story was that three thugs from a neighboring Arab village seized the flock in broad daylight and herded it across the demarcation line. According to the Jordanian version, the flock had simply strayed across the demarcation line toward greener pastures, probably when their shepherd closed his eyes for a minute or two, as shepherds were wont to do.

A UN observer to whom this story was reported immediately set to work on the case. Dayan, however, informed Sharett that failure to retaliate would be tantamount to abandoning the border area to acts of sabotage, murder, and robbery. He outlined to Sharett very precise plans for military action. Sharett said he understood the seriousness of the matter but wanted to give the UN men a chance to recover the sheep before he decided on the resort to force. While they were talking, Mrs. Dayan called to say that the flock had been returned. Both men breathed a sigh of relief; in the case of Sharett it was probably deeper and more genuine. But the next day he was informed that the message contained a small error—the word "not" had been omitted; the correct message was that the flock had not been returned. Later that day the IDF's chief of operations presented to Sharett a plan of action that conjured up the prospect of a bloody clash with the Arab Legion. Pinhas Lavon cut short his vacation to put all his weight behind this plan and the earlier plan for an attack on Gaza.[39]

On a Sunday afternoon, six days after the sheep had strayed, Lieutenant General E. L. M. Burns, the Canadian head of UNTSO, received an urgent summons to see the Israeli prime minister about the Ein Hashofet sheep. Sharett opened by observing that it might seem strange that a prime minister should call a senior UN official to confer on such a trivial matter, but a question of principle was involved. There were some people of great influence who held that Israel should always retaliate by force against acts of Arab violence or breaches of the armistice. He himself, and a majority in his government, believed in following the procedures laid down in the armistice agreement. This was the only time that Sharett spoke to Burns about the two trends in Israel's defense and foreign policy. However, many others who shared his view, mainly Foreign Ministry officials, propounded the same thesis. The implication was that Burns should support the party of negotiation in winning diplomatic success so that it might be able to hold its own against the party of retaliation.

After much running to and fro by Burns and his men, and after the customary wrangling between the delegates of the two sides, the flock was handed back twelve days after it had crossed the armistice line:

> There was more haggling of course: thirty-nine inferior Jordanian sheep were included in the 462 produced. Also, the Israelis claimed, fifty-five of their prize sheep were still

missing, including a particularly fine and valuable ram. The stragglers, or most of them, were turned over later. Last of all came the prize ram. The Israelis complained that he seemed to be very tired.[40]

The UN men were well pleased with the outcome of what they called Operation Bo-Peep, and so was Sharett. Although "only" 90 percent of the herd was recovered, this was achieved without a single shot being fired and without a single drop of blood being spilled. If the impatient army men had had their way, the matter could have ended in a political disaster for Israel. Meanwhile, the Gaza front remained quiet, despite Dayan's predictions about the dire consequences of military inaction.[41]

Instead, it was on the Syrian front that trouble next occurred. On 8 December a party of five Israeli soldiers was captured several kilometers inside Syria's territory. Under interrogation they told their captors that their mission had been to pick up a device for tapping a telephone line that had been installed by the IDF some time before. Following the capture of the group, Lavon ordered the Israeli Air Force to force a civilian Syrian airliner to land in Israel with the intention of using its passengers and crew as hostages pending the release of the Israeli soldiers. The story subsequently issued by the IDF spokesman, stating that the airliner had violated Israel's airspace and endangered its security, was pure fabrication. An international uproar ensued over this unprecedented act of air piracy by a government, and the plane, with its crew and passengers, had to be released forty-eight hours later. Sharett could no longer contain his anger. In a letter to Lavon he accused the heads of the army of stupidity and shortsightedness and ordered the minister to make it clear to all concerned that the government would not tolerate such manifestations of "independent policy" on the part of the security forces.[42]

Sharett went on to complain about the disinformation spread by army sources and the incitement of journalists to criticize the government. The chairman of the MAC ordered the Syrians to release the five Israeli soldiers, and Sharett looked forward to another "victory of political effort over the line of military thuggery."[43] Matters were made worse when Uri Ilan, one of the Israeli soldiers, the son of a prominent woman and former member of the Knesset, committed suicide in prison. There was an uproar in the Israeli press against the barbarity of the Syrians, kidnapping and torture being alleged. News of the suicide stirred considerable commotion in army circles, and criticism of the government reached a new pitch. In the Knesset a motion of no confidence in the government was introduced by Herut, and in the ensuing debate Chaim Landau led the attack by accusing the government of defeatism, cowardice, appeasement, and the like.

Sharett responded on 17 January 1955 with a forthright speech. He revealed the truth about the mission of the five soldiers by reading with emphasis the report of the MAC, which contradicted the IDF story that the soldiers had been kidnapped. He also presented the true facts about the forcing down of the Syrian airliner and thereby disposed of more lies spread by the army. He warned that by hitting others Israel ran the risk of being hit itself. He concluded with an indirect attack on Lavon by saying that Israel had to choose between being "a state of law and a state of piracy." Lavon retorted, in a subsequent debate in the Knesset, that the State of Israel was "a state of law and self-defense."

On 18 January 1955 two Israeli tractor drivers were murdered by Jordanian infiltrators in Ajour, an abandoned Arab village. The news hit Sharett like a bolt from the blue, and he immediately realized that retribution would be demanded and that this time he must grant it. "In recent months," he wrote in his diary, "I stopped and checked a great deal, I prevented several explosive acts and caused the public to become tense. I must not strain its patience beyond endurance. An outlet must be provided, otherwise there will be an outburst of fury, with many of my friends joining in." Two of his friends, Zalman Aran and Golda Meir, went to see him that evening; before Aran could finish a sentence, Sharett interrupted him to say that he had already authorized retaliation. Aran apologetically explained their intervention with reference to the wave of indignation that was sweeping through the country: the Cairo trial, *Bat Galim*, the Damascus prisoners, Uri Ilan's suicide, and now the double murder. Sharett said he knew all this but stated,

> Go and explain to every man in the street that the Cairo trial is of our making, and *Bat Galim* is one battle in a campaign, and the prisoners in Syria failed in an operation that we initiated, and that if Arabs had failed in our territory, we would have killed them on the spot without any argument, as we did with the legionnaires who innocently strayed into our strip of land near Mevo'ot Betar, and every one of them has a mother who mourns her son even if she is not a member of parliament like Piga Ilanit—go and explain all that. It is clear

that the Ajour murder was the last straw and the anger must
be assuaged. Only this is the logic, none other. I do not believe that, from the security point of view, retaliation will make
the slightest difference. On the contrary, I fear that it will
serve as the opening link in a new chain of bloodshed in the
border area.

Sharett's outburst was highly revealing of the latent function that
assaults on the enemy played in satisfying domestic public opinion.
It also highlighted the continuing gulf between the defense establishment's faith in the deterrent effect of these assaults and
Sharett's skepticism. In his view, raids across the border were a
double-edged sword. If he sometimes authorized raids, as in this
case, it was usually for domestic political reasons. He was not oblivious to the risks involved in slackening the reins: "The building I
have been constructing tenaciously for some months and all the
brakes I installed and the fences I erected—all this is liable to be
wiped out at one stroke, but I feel that I have no alternative, come
what may."[44]

To Sharett's great relief, something happened to make it unnecessary to go ahead with the plan to retaliate. On 23 January, in
the middle of a cabinet meeting, a message arrived to say that the
Jordanians had informed the MAC that they had captured some of
the murderers, all of whom had lived in the village of Ajour and
lost their homes in the 1948 war. After the cabinet meeting,
Sharett convened the Committee of Five and suggested calling off
the plan to launch a raid into Jordan that night. While Levi Eshkol
supported him, Lavon argued that this would not be well received
in the army. Golda Meir saw a purpose in reprisals if the culprits
could not be tracked down, but she was against killing innocent
people when the culprits had been found. Aran said nothing, and
Sharett concluded that the operation would be called off. The
army, meanwhile, had hoped that Sharett would not find out
about the arrest in time to stop the planned reprisal. "Curious
people," he observed in his diary, "who have become accustomed
to think that one cannot sustain the morale of the army without
giving it the freedom to shed blood from time to time."[45]

THE DIALOGUE WITH NASSER

The mishap of July 1954 had evidently not cooled the defense establishment's ardor for military activism. Strict military censorship

ensured that the botched operation could only be referred to vaguely as "the mishap." It would have been wise for Sharett to use the debacle to clean up Israel's military stables, but he lost this opportunity through dithering and procrastination. The Committee of Five was of no help to him in dealing with this difficult matter. On 26 October 1954, after the perpetrators of the Jewish ring were put on trial in Cairo, the committee met and decided to launch a campaign to discredit the Egyptian authorities and to make the release of the defendants Israel's top priority. Sharett played his part in the campaign. On 13 December, the day after the trial opened in Cairo, he made a statement in the Knesset in which he accused the Egyptian authorities of a plot, and of a show trial against a group of Jews whom he portrayed as the victims of false accusations. Yet the real victims of false accusations were not the Egyptian Jews but the Egyptian authorities.

Behind the scenes Sharett resumed the dialogue with Nasser. The Divon-Sadeq back channel was hardly used in the course of 1954, because of Egypt's preoccupation with negotiating Britain's withdrawal from the Suez Canal Zone. The terrorist attacks of July 1954 flatly contradicted all the earlier assurances of Israel's desire to see Egypt free and independent. These attacks seemed to confirm the worst Egyptian stereotypes about Jewish duplicity and double-dealing and the worst fears of devilish plots being hatched by Israel to undermine their national unity and independence.[46] Not knowing the intricate internal background to these attacks, the Egyptians could be forgiven for treating them as the manifestation of official government policy.

Nasser himself thought well of Sharett. He spoke of him as an honest and moderate man to one British diplomat.[47] Nasser's attitude toward Israel to date had been pragmatic and practical rather than ideological. He was restrained in public, and in private conversations with non-Arabs he seemed to accept the notion that one day there might be peace with Israel. But this did not mean that he was prepared to promote peace with Israel. The position of the Free Officers was still far too weak for him to contemplate taking any initiative in an area so sensitive and so open to criticism as Israel.[48] But his representatives cooperated with Israel through the MAC with the aim of reducing the tensions along the border, and he kept the Divon-Sadeq channel open even after the Israeli-sponsored undercover unit had planted bombs in Cairo and Alexandria.

Abdel Rahman Sadeq, who was as well placed as anyone to assess Nasser's attitude toward Israel in the early 1950s, described him as a very reasonable and open-minded man, but one who could get quite angry when he felt he was being deceived. Nasser was very angry when the plot to discredit the Free Officers' regime was uncovered, but he was prepared to believe that in this instance the Israeli secret service acted without Sharett's knowledge. He was even prepared to believe that the plot was intended by some hard-liners in the secret service to sabotage Sharett's efforts at a peaceful dialogue with the Revolutionary Command Council.[49]

In any case, when Sharett took the initiative to renew the dialogue, Nasser raised no objections. This time Sharett had a specific and urgent aim in mind: to save the lives of the members of the spy ring who were on trial before a military tribunal in Cairo. The prosecution was demanding the death sentence on the grounds that the defendants worked for an enemy country. Sharett knew that a death sentence would have a disastrous effect at home because the Israeli public had been led to believe that the defendants were innocent. He therefore used several channels to convey his earnest request to Nasser to use his influence to ensure that the death sentence was not passed. Divon and Sadeq resumed their meetings in Paris, while Maurice Orbach, a British Labour Party member of Parliament, was asked to go to Cairo to plead for the lives of the defendants.

These talks, which lasted from October 1954 until January 1955, were not confined to the *Bat Galim* and the Cairo trial but were extended to cover broader aspects of Israeli-Egyptian relations, such as the blockade of Israeli shipping in the Suez Canal and the Gulf of Aqaba, the situation along the borders, restraints on propaganda, solutions to the Palestinian refugee problem, and avenues for economic cooperation.[50] Through their representatives in Paris, Sharett and Nasser also exchanged unsigned private messages on plain paper. On 21 December, for instance, Sharett expressed his admiration for the idealism and tenacity shown by Nasser in the struggle to liberate his country from foreign domination; he suggested that Nasser might lift the maritime blockade as a first step toward the improvement of relations between their two countries; and he fervently hoped that no death sentence would be passed on the defendants in the Cairo trial.[51] Nasser replied ten days later,

> I have received your letter of 21.12.54. I have instructed my special emissary to transmit a verbal answer to the questions

you mentioned in your letter. I am very glad that you realize the efforts spent from our side to bring our relations to a peaceful solution. I hope that they will be met by similar efforts from your side, thus permitting us to achieve the results we are seeking for the benefit of both countries.[52]

A more detailed reply to the various Israeli suggestions and requests was given by Nasser to Maurice Orbach. Nasser listened attentively as Orbach presented a long brief prepared for him by Gideon Rafael of the Israeli Foreign Ministry. After discussing the matter with his colleagues, Nasser gave the following replies. First, he asked Orbach to convey his thanks and admiration to Mr. Sharett. Second, he stressed that the defendants at the Cairo trial were mercenaries of a foreign intelligence service, but he also promised to use his influence to secure sentences that were not inflammatory. Third, he indicated that the *Bat Galim* would be released but not allowed to pass through the Suez Canal. Fourth, he said that non-Israeli ships would be allowed to carry all cargoes, except war materials and oil, to Israel through the Suez Canal and the Gulf of Aqaba. Fifth, he said that hostile propaganda and political warfare would cease if Israel did the same. Sixth, he promised that every effort would be made to prevent border incidents if Israel did the same. Finally, he agreed to high-level talks, preferably in Paris, but on the condition that strict secrecy be observed.[53]

Nasser's agreement to high-level talks was most encouraging. Sharett chose Yigael Yadin, the former chief of staff who was studying in London, to represent Israel in the talks. With the help of Gideon Rafael, he also prepared for the talks some positive proposals, which included land passage through the Negev between Egypt and Jordan and the payment of compensation to help with the resettlement of the Palestinian refugees in the Gaza Strip.[54] The services of the American Central Intelligence Agency (CIA) were being offered to ensure the secrecy of the talks. But on December 22 the Israeli agent, Max Bennet, committed suicide in his Cairo cell, and on 27 January 1955 the military tribunal found eight of the remaining twelve defendants guilty and sentenced two of them to death. The Israelis were stunned by the news. Sharett canceled the high-level meeting, saying, "We will not negotiate in the shadow of the gallows."[55]

In his memoirs Gideon Rafael accused Nasser of duplicity and deception. He opined that the reply to Sharett was "typical of Nasser's delaying tactics which he perfected over the years into an art. . . . He would adjust the presentation of his views to the sensitivities of the ear of his interlocutor. Where necessary he would stress his willingness . . . to establish peaceful relations with Israel, but would avoid any act of commitment. Pretexts of inappropriate timing and expectations of unilateral gestures were the mainstays of his elusiveness."[56] None of these claims is supported by the documentary record. Indeed, they represent the opposite of the truth as it emerges from the documents. Nasser made no pretexts and did not ask Israel for any unilateral gestures. His reaction to the deeds perpetrated by Israel's military intelligence was almost unreasonably reasonable. He also showed himself to be a man of his word. He promised to release the *Bat Galim,* and he did. He promised to curb hostile propaganda and political warfare, and he did. Israel, meanwhile, did the opposite. Nasser promised to make efforts to prevent border incidents, and the records of Egyptian military intelligence show that he did. On the Cairo trial he said many things, but he never promised that there would be no death sentence. The official line was that the government could not intervene in the trial. Once the military tribunal passed a death sentence, Nasser could not easily commute it. A short time before, members of the Muslim Brotherhood had been convicted of similar terrorist acts and had been executed. As Nasser explained to numerous intermediaries sent by Israel to plead for clemency, it would have been politically disastrous for him to be seen to be more lenient toward Jewish than toward Muslim terrorists.

Perhaps the clearest indications of Nasser's sincere commitment to improving relations with Israel was his agreement to high-level talks. For Nasser this was a high-risk venture, yet it was not he but Sharett who called it off. Nasser informed the Israelis through the CIA that he did not regard the death sentences as a reason not to go ahead with the high-level meeting. He also wanted the Israelis to understand that, with all the goodwill in the world, under the circumstances he was unable to act differently. The Americans praised Sharett for the constructive agenda he had proposed, and they pressed him to go forward. Sharett's reply was negative. He said that Nasser was either two-faced or unable to keep his word, and either way he was not a serious partner for negotiations.[57]

This little-known episode in Israeli-Egyptian relations once again calls into question the official version that says that Israel always strove for direct contact and always met with Arab refusal. There is, of course, no way of telling what might have happened had the planned meeting taken place. Could it have led to a higher-level meeting with Nasser himself? Could it have prevented the subsequent escalation of the conflict? Could it have produced at least some of the ingredients for a breakthrough in the relations between Israel and the most influential of her Arab opponents? There are no answers to these questions. History does not disclose its alternatives. All one can say is that Nasser offered Israel a chance to talk and that this offer was spurned. One can add that Sharett's wavering played a part in missing this opportunity. Sharett did not rise to the occasion, displaying delaying tactics and timidity when boldness was called for. In the words of one of his own officials, Sharett failed to seize the bull by the horns when the bull offered his horns.[58]

At home Sharett continued to grapple with the consequences of the Cairo calamity. On 2 January 1955, after endless agonizing, he appointed a committee to investigate the facts behind the affair. The committee consisted of Yitzhak Olshan, a high-court judge, and Yaacov Dori, a former chief of staff. It received the forged evidence and false testimonies incriminating Lavon, although this did not become known until five years later. Dayan and Peres supported Gibli's versions and gave the committee evidence that ranged freely and critically over Lavon's deficiencies as minister of defense. Dayan confirmed that Lavon systematically deceived Sharett, but he was also commendably candid about his own role:

> I did not conceal my passive partnership in the deceiving of Sharett by Lavon. I explained that I knew that from time to time Lavon deceives Sharett (by not taking him into a matter), but if Lavon took this upon himself, I don't have to interfere. Moreover, I completely disagree with Sharett's political conception and see in his failure to authorize operations from time to time damage to the interests of the state; and I have no reason to help him in that beyond the call of duty.[59]

In the end Olshan and Dori were unable to reach a clear verdict. In their report they stated that they could not be sure beyond a reasonable doubt that Gibli did not receive the order to activate the undercover unit, but at the same time they were not certain that Lavon actually did give the orders attributed to him. Sharett had no doubt that even if Lavon had not given Gibli the specific order that led to the Cairo calamity, he bore the political and moral responsibility because "he constantly preached acts of madness and taught the army leaders the diabolic lesson of how to set the Middle East on fire, how to cause friction, cause bloody confrontations, sabotage targets and property of the great powers, and perform acts of despair and suicide." At the same time, Sharett was shocked by the general picture that emerged from the enquiry. "I would never have imagined," he confided to his diary, "that we could reach such a horrible state of poisoned relations, the unleashing of the basest instincts of hate and revenge and mutual deceit at the top of our most glorious ministry. I wander around like a sleepwalker, horror-stricken and lost, completely helpless. . . . What shall I do, what shall I do?"[60]

Lavon spared Sharett the need to decide, by submitting his resignation on 2 February. Ben-Gurion then came under heavy pressure from his party colleagues to replace Lavon and clear up the mess he left behind him. On 21 February, Ben-Gurion reemerged from Sede-Boker to assume the defense portfolio in the government, which continued to be headed by Sharett. To Walter Eytan and Gideon Rafael, his trusted aides at the Foreign Ministry, Sharett explained that this was the only way out of the crisis and then added calmly, "You understand, my friends, that this is the end of my political career." They tried in vain to talk him out of his somber mood. But events proved that his insight was greater than theirs.[61] In November of that year Sharett would hand the premiership back to Ben-Gurion. In June of the following year he would resign his post as foreign minister, and that would, in fact, be the end of his political career.

THE GAZA RAID

It has been suggested that on his return to the government Ben-Gurion intended to restore the balance between the school of negotiation and the school of retaliation, which had crystallized and collided with such disastrous consequences in the course of 1954.[62] But it would appear that he returned from his brief sojourn in Sede-Boker in a truculent and uncompromising mood, determined to restore the primacy of defense over foreign policy considerations in Israel's relations with the Arabs. He had reached the conclusion that Nasser was an implacable and dangerous enemy. He was accordingly determined to get tough with him and was impatient from the start with Sharett's policy of appeasement.[63] To Ze'ev Sharef, the cabinet secretary, Ben-Gurion said about Sharett,

"He is raising a generation of cowards. I will not let him. . . . I will not let him. This will be a fighting generation."[64]

From the beginning Ben-Gurion acted as if he were the prime minister. When Sharett visited him in Sede-Boker, he proposed the following formula: "Although defense takes precedence over everything else, constant efforts must be made to obtain peace." This meant that retaliation would be permitted even if it damaged the prospects of peace. He went on to suggest renewing the "coalition" between himself and Sharett, by which he understood a combination of their two separate lines. He even saw fit to underline in writing that he intended to pursue an independent defense policy. He was prepared to consult: "But consultation with the foreign minister is one thing, and persistent interference by the foreign minister and his officials in defense matters is another. To this I will not agree."[65] He accepted the collective responsibility of the cabinet and the supreme authority of the prime minister, but this did not mean that he accepted the approach of the prime minister in matters over which they were divided. He agreed only to a coalition with the foreign minister. The letter ended with a warning that if the foreign minister and his officials interfered in defense matters and the prime minister supported this interference, another defense minister would have to be appointed.

On 28 February, only a week after Ben-Gurion's return, he inaugurated his tough new defense policy with a devastating raid on Gaza, code-named Operation Black Arrow. During the night two IDF paratroop companies led by Ariel Sharon attacked and destroyed the Egyptian army headquarters on the outskirts of Gaza City, killing thirty-seven Egyptian soldiers and wounding thirty-one at the cost to themselves of eight killed and nine wounded. The ferocity of the attack, the material damage it caused, and, above all, the heavy casualties made this the most serious clash between Israel and Egypt since the signing of the armistice agreement in 1949.

Why did the Israelis strike this devastating blow? The four preceding months were a period of comparative tranquillity along the border. Two incidents involving infiltrators who penetrated deep into Israeli territory, stole documents, and killed a cyclist constituted the immediate occasion for the raid. After the second incident, the new minister of defense and the chief of staff went to see the prime minister. They said that there was no doubt that the infiltrators had been sent by Egyptian military intelligence, and they proposed an attack on an army base near Gaza. Dayan estimated that there would be about ten enemy casualties, and Ben-Gurion promised to tighten the reins in order to avoid excessive bloodshed. Sharett agreed. His reasons for approving the plan had to do exclusively with domestic politics. He felt that the public would not understand a failure to respond to the recent provocations, especially in the aftermath of the executions in Cairo. In fact, he regretted that Ben-Gurion would get the credit for a reprisal that he would have approved anyway.[66]

Ben-Gurion himself appears to have had much wider aims. In the first place, he probably wanted to dramatize his return to power and demonstrate that once again there was decisive leadership at the top. Second, he probably felt more strongly than Sharett that a vigorous settling of accounts with the Egyptians was necessary to assuage public indignation at home. Third, and most important, Ben-Gurion had come to the conclusion that Egypt's ascendancy within the Arab world under Nasser's dynamic leadership represented a serious threat to Israeli security, and he probably hoped to cut Nasser down to size by exposing the military impotence of his regime. Finally, the action formed part of Ben-Gurion's general strategy of inducing the Arabs to accept Israel's terms for peaceful coexistence by demonstrating that unless they did so, they would have to pay a painful price.

Sharett was stunned and utterly mortified when he heard the report about Operation Black Arrow. He realized instantly that the high number of casualties meant a change not just in the scope but in the very nature of the operation. He knew that Israel would be roundly condemned by the international community for its belligerence, and he dreaded the consequences for Egyptian-Israeli relations. Another cause for irritation was an IDF communiqué inspired by Ben-Gurion, which claimed that the clash occurred after an IDF patrol had been attacked by an Egyptian force inside Israeli territory. While Sharett had no evidence that he had been deliberately deceived about the likely level of casualties, he reproached Ben-Gurion for putting out a version of events that was patently untrue and that nobody was going to believe.

A postmortem at a cabinet meeting revealed very different reactions on the part of Ben-Gurion and Sharett not only to the Gaza operation but to the whole question of reprisals. Ben-Gurion emphasized the importance of displaying Israel's military superiority over the strongest Arab country, as well as the positive value of the Gaza operation in bolstering the confidence of the Israeli public and the army. The negative political effect he dismissed as being of no decisive weight since, regardless of how exemplary Israel's conduct might be, the Western powers would always side with the Arabs on account of their vast superiority in territory, population, and oil. Sharett assumed full responsibility for the raid, although the number of Egyptian soldiers killed was four times greater than what he had been led to expect. He did not deny the raid's positive impact at home, but he expected it to have an adverse effect on the secret talks with Egypt, which had shown some signs of progress recently, and on Israel's efforts to obtain arms and a security guarantee from the United States.[67]

For Israeli-Egyptian relations the Gaza raid had far-reaching consequences. In the words of Kennett Love, the American journalist who was close to Nasser,

> The Gaza Raid started a chain of reactions between Gamal Abdel Nasser of Egypt and David Ben-Gurion of Israel—raids, counter-raids, an arms race and new alignments with the Great Powers—which developed a drift toward war that neither human will nor political ingenuity was able to deflect. The raid transformed a stable level of minor incidents between the two countries into a dialogue of mounting fear and violence in which the distinction between measures of defense and acts of aggression faded and became invisible to the world at large.[68]

Nasser himself repeatedly described the Gaza raid as a turning point. He claimed that it destroyed his faith in the possibility of a peaceful resolution of the conflict with Israel, exposed the weakness of his army, and forced a change in national priorities from social and economic development to defense, a change that culminated in an arms deal with Czechoslovakia in September of that year. The raid demonstrated the military impotence of Nasser's regime just at the time when he needed to demonstrate its strength in order to ward off the threat to his leadership posed by the emergent Baghdad Pact, whose cornerstone had been laid with the signature of the Turkish-Iraqi treaty on 24 February. A few days earlier Nasser had proclaimed his resolute resistance to the Western-inspired Baghdad Pact. Now he accused Israel, which was excluded from and felt threatened by this regional defense scheme, of having acted as a tool of Western imperialism.[69]

Moreover, the repercussions of the raid were not confined to Nasser's internal position and international relations. Crowded in the Gaza Strip were around 300,000 Palestinian refugees from the 1948 war who for years had been demanding the right to be armed and organized into an army in preparation for recovery of their homeland. The Israeli attack sparked mass demonstrations and riots throughout the strip that raged on for three days. The indignant refugees stormed UN and Egyptian government buildings, smashed windows, burned vehicles, trampled on the Egyptian flag, and beat up Egyptian soldiers. "Arms" was the universal cry, "give us arms and we shall defend ourselves."[70] These demonstrations and mob violence called into question the ability of Nasser's regime to maintain its rule over this strife-ridden and volatile area. A military regime cannot suffer military humiliation without risk to its position at home. Nasser was stung, and his attention was thereafter fixed on Israel. From this point on, the Egyptian authorities, instead of curbing and repressing militancy in the Gaza Strip and infiltration into Israel, began to devise ways in which the refugees' demands to be armed could be channeled into forms of hostile action against Israel that would fall short of full-scale war.[71]

Sharett gave credence to Nasser's version of the impact of the Gaza raid.[72] He was one of a tiny handful of Israelis in official positions who did. The general view was that the Gaza raid was the pretext rather than the cause of Nasser's turn to the Soviet bloc for arms.

One of the casualties of the Gaza raid was Sharett's secret dialogue with Nasser. This dialogue was severely strained by "the mishap," but it was not irretrievably lost. The Gaza raid, on the other hand, dealt it a fatal blow. There are two pieces of evidence for this. Colonel Salah Gohar, the Egyptian representative to the MAC, which held an emergency meeting after the Gaza raid, told Yosef Tekoah in an informal conversation that Nasser had said to him in confidence that he was in personal contact with Israel's prime minister and that things had been going well, with a good prospect of a follow-up, but then came the attack on Gaza—and now "it's off."[73] The other piece of evidence is the closure of the Divon-Sadeq channel in the immediate aftermath of the Gaza raid in what was a very abrupt reversal of Nasser's position. Abdel Rahman Sadeq's code name was Albert. He and Divon had arranged a follow-up meeting in Paris in March. This meeting was canceled by Sadeq after the Gaza raid in a cable that simply said, "No. Albert."[74] And that was the end of the dialogue between Israel's moderate prime minister and Egypt's hitherto moderate president.

It is odd that Ben-Gurion did not even mention the Gaza raid in his memoirs and voluminous writings on this period. In his diary he wrote after hearing a report on the operation from Ariel Sharon, "In my opinion it was the summit of human heroism."[75] It may have been at the same time the summit of political folly, for Ben-Gurion's coercive strategy backfired disastrously. It only served to inflame Egyptian hostility, stiffen Egyptian defiance, and initiate a bloody cycle of violence and counterviolence that culminated in the Suez War.

Ben-Gurion and his defenders maintain that the Gaza raid was not the cause, but merely the excuse, for Nasser's switch from moderation to confrontation. They see post-Gaza developments as stemming not from the attack but from the inherently aggressive tendencies of Nasser's undemocratic regime.[76] There is no evidence to substantiate this contention and a great deal of evidence to refute it. The clearest manifestation of Nasser's switch to confrontation was the unleashing of guerrilla warfare in the form of fedayeen attacks on Israel. "Fedayeen" is the Arabic term for self-sacrificers. In August 1955 the fedayeen made their appearance on the Israeli scene. During the next fourteen months fedayeen units, recruited from among the Palestinian refugees in Gaza and trained for sabotage by Egyptian officers, carried out a series of attacks inside Israel. They laid road mines, ambushed vehicles, sabotaged installations, committed acts of murder, and struck terror into the heart of the civilian population. The fedayeen raids were only one reason prompting Israel to launch the Sinai Campaign, but they were an important one since no other method proved effective. They thus constitute a significant strand in the tangled history of this period.

That the Egyptian government began to organize the fedayeen units in the spring of 1955 is not in dispute. General Dayan construed this decision as a continuation of the previous Egyptian policy of heartily approving infiltration into Israel.[77] Nasser's version was that the formation of the fedayeen represented a reversal of his previous policy of restraint and that it was the raid on Gaza that brought about this reversal.[78] In other words, his claim is that in unleashing the fedayeen Egypt was not acting but reacting to Israeli aggression and that it was therefore Israel, not Egypt, that bore the responsibility for the subsequent escalation.

Records of Egyptian and Jordanian military intelligence captured by the Israeli army in the course of the 1956 and 1967 wars conclusively disprove Dayan's version and substantiate Nasser's version. These records show that until the Gaza raid, the Egyptian military authorities had a consistent and firm policy of curbing infiltration by Palestinians from the Gaza Strip into Israel and that it was only following the raid that a new policy was put in place, that of organizing the fedayeen units and turning them into an official instrument of warfare against Israel.

The Jordanian documents tell a similar story. From them we learn that it was only in June 1955 that Egyptian military intelligence began to sponsor infiltration into Israel from Jordanian territory. Here, however, there was no change in the official attitude toward infiltration. On the contrary, when the Jordanian authorities learned of the Egyptian attempt, they adopted even tougher and more comprehensive measures to counter it. These measures caused friction and tension between Jordan and Egypt.[79]

THE COALITION

The coalition that produced the Gaza raid also made it impossible to pursue a coherent or consistent policy in its aftermath. A spate of incidents and bloody clashes along the border with Gaza, which Sharett viewed as the inevitable consequence of the Israeli attack, was taken by Ben-Gurion as a sign of growing Egyptian bellicosity, which, if allowed to go unchallenged, would endanger Israel's basic security.

The most serious incident occurred on 25 March. A group of Egyptians reached Patish, a settlement of immigrants from Iran in the Negev, and attacked with automatic fire and hand grenades a house in which a wedding was taking place, wounding twenty and killing a young woman. Ben-Gurion summoned Dayan and told him that they should expel the Egyptians from the Gaza Strip, capture it, and keep it under Israeli rule. This suggestion surprised Dayan. In the past Ben-Gurion had consistently opposed the capture of Gaza because it contained 300,000 bitter and hostile refugees that the State of Israel could do without. This time, Ben-Gurion explained, their duty to protect the settlers, boost their confidence, and enable them to put down roots outweighed all other considerations. For Dayan military considerations were still all important, and on these grounds he opposed the idea.[80]

Notwithstanding these objections, Ben-Gurion submitted to the cabinet a far-reaching proposal, to which was attached a detailed operational plan, for the capture of the Gaza Strip and the expulsion of the Egyptians from the area. Ben-Gurion's case for his plan frightened Sharett in its narrowness and shortsightedness, for it presented the capture of Gaza as the final objective without delving into all the likely consequences and ramifications. In his summing-up before the cabinet, at the end of a heated debate on the proposal, Sharett stated his general preference for accepting Israel's existing borders, reducing the tension with neighbors, strengthening relations with the Western powers, and cultivating international sympathy. He conceded that urgent defense considerations could sometimes necessitate actions that would increase tensions between Israel and the Arab world and damage Israel's relations with the Western powers, but such actions, he thought, should be kept to a minimum rather than piled on top of one another. Within this general framework, he opposed Ben-Gurion's proposal as bound to make Israel seem the aggressor and liable to provoke war with Egypt and possibly bring British intervention under the Tripartite Declaration in support of Egypt. In addition, Sharett claimed that capturing the Gaza Strip would not solve any security problem, because even if half of the refugees living there fled or were made to flee to the Hebron Hills, their hatred for Israel would only be inflamed, breeding worse and more frequent acts of vengeance and despair.[81] The cabinet defeated the proposal by a vote of nine to four, but it did not escape Sharett's notice that the majority of their Mapai colleagues supported Ben-Gurion against him and that this would be the balance of forces within the party in the event of its being asked to make a fundamental choice between war and peace by giving or withholding consent for the capture of the Gaza Strip.[82]

Three days after the cabinet's final rejection of the Gaza plan, another murder prompted Ben-Gurion to submit a new dramatic proposal, this time for the abrogation of the armistice agreement with Egypt. He did not ask the cabinet to assume responsibility for canceling the armistice agreement but rather to announce that since Egypt destroyed it in practice by ignoring, inter alia, the Security Council's decision concerning freedom of shipping through international waterways, the cabinet did not regard the agreement as binding on Israel. Lest this be taken as a ploy for renewing his earlier proposal, he stressed that he was now proposing not a military step but a political one. The armistice, he claimed, had become a farce and a travesty to which Israel should not be a party. If Egypt wanted to conduct peace negotiations with Israel, it would be welcome; if not, Israel's hands must be free.

Sharett's impression was that Ben-Gurion was seeking relief in a bold and explosive move not preceded by cold analysis and calculation. He therefore launched an all-out war on Ben-Gurion's proposal. He even managed to surprise himself by the extreme lengths to which he could go in his moderation. In the first place, Sharett pointed to the difficulty of proving that the denial of maritime rights constituted a violation of the armistice agreement and to the additional difficulty of explaining why, if it was indeed a violation, Israel had waited four years before issuing the proposed declaration. Outsiders would see it as a pretext by Israel for freeing itself from the restrictions imposed by the armistice in order to embark on a campaign of territorial conquests. It would therefore call forth a chorus of international condemnation. Why should Israel take upon itself the responsibility for abrogating the armistice agreement? he asked. If, as Ben-Gurion claimed, the purpose behind it was to strike a demonstrative political posture and not to clear the way for military operation, it entailed only damage without any countervailing gains. The armistice agreement, argued Sharett, conferred international legitimacy on Israel's border; if Israel itself denounced it, Egypt might invade one of the border areas in the Negev, forcing Israel to fight and rely on the outcome of a new war. A clear decision had to be made regarding Israel's basic objective—either to consolidate the status quo or to seek a new resolution by an appeal to arms.

The cabinet's vote produced a draw: six ministers, all Mapai members, voted for renunciation of the armistice agreement, six ministers voted against, and the rest abstained. Ben-Gurion's proposal was not adopted, but neither was it decisively defeated. For Sharett the vote signaled a serious personal warning. He was saved from having to resign by the skin of his teeth, while the government he headed had come ominously close to inflicting a calamity on the country.[83]

Relations between Ben-Gurion and Sharett became progressively more strained, tense, and envenomed, causing the latter endless frustration and mental anguish. There were recurrent clashes over the respective jurisdictions of the Foreign Ministry and the defense establishment in the conduct of armistice affairs, over the role of the United Nations in these affairs, over relations with the Western powers, and, above all, over the question of reprisals. Ben-Gurion, who had come back from Sede-Boker to reassert a tough defense policy, found himself swimming against a current of moderation in the cabinet. His formal subordination to Sharett, which in no way reflected the true power relations between them, was an additional source of friction and complication. The approach of the general election, and the high probability that he would be asked to form the next government, moved Ben-Gurion to inform Sharett, bluntly in a private letter, of his decision to speak up from time to time in order to acquaint the nation with the principles of his foreign policy.

On the need for an American guarantee of Israel's security, there was no real difference between the two leaders. Discussions between the two countries began in August 1954 against the background of the Anglo-Egyptian agreement on Suez and the American decision to supply arms to Iraq. All that was envisaged at that stage was an American declaration or an exchange of letters between America and Israel. But after Iraq and Turkey took the first step toward the Baghdad Pact in February 1955, John Foster Dulles, the secretary of state, offered Israel a mutual defense pact, provided it undertook not to expand its borders by force and to refrain from military retaliation against its neighbors. Ben-Gurion and Sharett appeared willing to accept the first condition, but not the second. A mutual defense pact with a superpower was attractive as a way of ending Israel's international isolation, guaranteeing its territorial integrity and long-term security, and inducing the Arabs to settle peacefully their dispute with Israel. At his very first meeting with Edward Lawson, the new American ambassador, Ben-Gurion told him that the three things dearest to his heart were the security of Israel, peace in the Middle East, and friendship between Israel and America. It was in America's power, he added, to realize all three things in one move: by concluding a mutual defense pact with Israel.[84]

Most of the participants at a conference of ambassadors held in May 1955, including the prime minister and the defense minister, regarded a defense pact with America as a highly desirable goal in which considerable efforts should be invested. But it was recognized that America would stipulate conditions and that these might turn out to be unacceptable.[85] In the event, the conditions did prove unacceptable, and after the Czech arms deal was announced, Israeli diplomats shifted the emphasis in their discussion with the Americans from a defense pact to the supply of arms. One man, the IDF chief of staff, opposed the idea of a defense pact with America from beginning to end. He saw no need for an American guarantee of Israel's security and strongly opposed America's conditions that Israel forswear territorial expansion and military retaliation. In an informal talk with the ambassadors to Washington, London, and Paris, Dayan described military retaliation as "a life drug." First, it obliged the Arab governments to take drastic measures to protect their borders. Second, and this was the essence, it enabled the Israeli government to maintain a high degree of tension in the country and in the army. Gideon Rafael, also present at the meeting with Dayan, remarked to Sharett, "This is how fascism began in Italy and Germany!"[86]

Dayan was at least consistent in his creed of self-reliance and in his rejection of an external guarantee, which is more than can be said for Ben-Gurion. The latter was very interested in a pact with the United States but rather reluctant to pay the price for it. Forswearing reprisals was completely out of the question for him, while on some occasions he appeared to share Dayan's urge for territorial expansion. One such occasion was a meeting of senior officials convened by Ben-Gurion on 16 May. There he seized the possibility of an Iraqi invasion into Syria to revive his pet scheme for Israeli intervention in Lebanon with the aim of annexing the south and turning the rest of the country into a Maronite state.

Sharett pooh-poohed the idea. He thought that Ben-Gurion was hopelessly out of date in viewing Lebanon as a province of the Ottoman Empire in which the decisive majority of the population consisted of Christian-Maronites. He recalled an earlier debate with him on the subject in which he had tried to explain that the Maronites were internally divided, that they had no daring leaders, and that as allies they would turn out to be broken reeds. But Ben-Gurion was itching to intervene. He noted that there were also Druze in Lebanon, but he failed to explain why they should want to help the Maronites turn Lebanon into a Christian state.

As to the means by which the internal change in Lebanon could be brought about, it was Dayan who had a specific and characteristically cynical proposal to put forward:

All that is required is to find an officer, even a captain would do, to win his heart or buy him with money to get him to agree to declare himself the savior of the Maronite population. Then the Israeli army will enter Lebanon, occupy the necessary territory, and create a Christian regime that will ally itself with Israel. The territory from the Litani southward will be totally annexed to Israel, and everything will fall into place.

The only difference between Dayan and Ben-Gurion was that the former wanted to act immediately, whereas the latter was prepared to wait for the pretext of an Iraqi invasion of Syria. Sharett saw no point in embarking on a detailed discussion of Ben-Gurion's "fantastic and adventuristic plan," which was "surprising in its crudeness and divorce from reality," in front of his officers. He merely remarked that the suggestion meant not the strengthening of an independent Lebanon but a war between Israel and Syria and that it should be treated as such.

Having nipped the plan in the bud, Sharett reflected on the shocking lack of seriousness displayed by the military toward the neighboring countries in general and Lebanon's complex internal makeup in particular. "I saw clearly," he wrote in his diary, "how those who saved the state so heroically and courageously in the War of Independence would be capable of bringing a catastrophe upon it if they are given the chance in normal times."[87]

No less shocking was the double standard evinced by Ben-Gurion in the debate on Lebanon. The same man who was so touchy about Israel's independence and territorial integrity, and so quick to react to the slightest manifestation of foreign interference in its affairs, also showed complete disregard for the rights of other sovereign states. His plan for dismembering Lebanon was particularly reprehensible because it was not prompted by any provocation on Lebanon's part. The usual argument about responding to force with force could not be invoked in this context, for the simple reason that Lebanon scrupulously abided by all the provisions of the armistice agreement it had concluded with Israel in March 1949.

Dayan did not easily let go of the plan for intervention in Lebanon, for he combined stubbornness with ignorance in roughly equal portions. He persisted in pushing the plan to hire a Lebanese officer who would serve as a puppet in inviting the Israeli army to liberate Lebanon from its Muslim oppressors. To deflect Dayan from embarking on this "crazy adventure," Sharett charged the recently established interdepartmental committee on Lebanon with research tasks and the establishment of contact with the more independent-minded groups of Maronites who might be encouraged to lean on Israel.[88]

Whereas Lebanon did not pose any threat to Israel's day-to-day or its basic security, Egypt did. The problem of day-to-day security grew progressively more acute in the aftermath of the Gaza raid. But in the course of 1955 Ben-Gurion became convinced that Nasser posed a threat to Israel's security not merely on a day-to-day basis but also on the most fundamental level. He came to believe that Nasser was hell-bent on the destruction of Israel and that this danger had to be met head-on. Nasser was perceived by Ben-Gurion as a latter-day Saladin, as a military leader capable of uniting the Arab world and leading it into battle against its enemies. The specter of a united Arab world haunted Ben-Gurion, who also saw Nasser as the equivalent of the modern Turkish leader Mustafa Kemal Atatürk, a man capable of moving his people from backwardness to a position of towering strength that would endanger Israel's future. Like Anthony Eden, Ben-Gurion developed a personal obsession with Nasser and concluded that his removal was a matter of vital national interest.

The explosion of a mine near the border with Egypt in which four Israeli officers were injured in mid-May prompted Ben-Gurion to propose to the Committee of Five a military reprisal. Sharett let Golda Meir and Levi Eshkol speak first. Both of them thought that inaction was out of the question, because the settlers and the public expected the government to do something following the Egyptian provocation. Domestic political considerations were uppermost in the minds of all those present. Although no one said so, Sharett sensed that they all thought that inaction would deal Mapai a serious blow in the forthcoming elections, because thousands of voters would turn to the activist parties, Herut and Ahdut Ha'avodah. Ahdut Ha'avodah had split off from Mapam in 1954 over foreign policy differences. Mapam retained its socialist and pro-Soviet orientation. Ahdut Ha'avodah, though also a workers' party, was much more nationalistic. Yitzhak Tabenkin, its spiritual leader, upheld the ideology of Greater Israel, while Yigal Allon, one of its most prominent political leaders, was an advocate of an activist defense policy and an outspoken critic of Mapai. Sharett would have resisted this electoral consideration, but he stood alone. He said he was opposed to the proposal but would bow to the will of the majority. He hoped that one of his colleagues would point out the unfairness involved in expecting the prime minister to bear the responsibility for an action he opposed, but no one did.

In the course of the discussion, Ben-Gurion delivered a diatribe on Nasser's crimes as if he were addressing a public meeting rather than sitting in a room with a handful of senior colleagues. Nasser must be taught a lesson, he thundered, either "to carry out his duties or be toppled. It is definitely possible to topple him, and it is even a *mitzvah* [a sacred obligation] to do so. Who is he anyway, this Nasser-Shmasser?"[89]

Astonishingly, the decision to retaliate was taken not in the cabinet but in a party forum in which party political considerations were paramount. Sharett spent a sleepless night and contemplated resigning for the third time in a month. His position as prime minister was becoming untenable because of a Mapai decision to make the Committee of Five the final arbiter in matters of military reprisals. Now, whereas Sharett had a majority within the government for his moderate line, Ben-Gurion had a majority for his activist line within the Committee of Five. Sharett knew that he could not resort indefinitely to the support of his coalition partners while he remained in a minority inside his own party.

Nevertheless, he was so convinced that the decision to retaliate was unsound that he reopened the question with the other members of the Committee of Five the next day. One additional argument for restraint arrived in the morning, with an American offer to help Israel build a nuclear reactor. Sharett attached great importance to this offer because of its potential contribution both to nuclear research and to closer political relations with America, and he feared that it might be withdrawn if Israel persisted in acting aggressively. All his efforts to persuade his colleagues to change their mind, however, were to no avail. At the end of a hectic day, there was still a majority of four against one in favor of military action. Consequently, on the night of 19 May, an Israeli force attacked an Egyptian army post near the place of the mine incident, blew it up, and returned to base without inflicting or suffering any casualties. Although Sharett believed that the General Staff would see the raid as a victory over him, he was nevertheless greatly relieved that no blood had been shed.[90]

THE TRIALS AND TRIBULATIONS
OF A MODERATE

The results of the general election held on 20 July disappointed the leaders of the ruling party. Mapai lost 5 out of its 45 seats in the 120-member Knesset. Mapai's main and moderate coalition partner, the General Zionists, went down from 20 to 13 seats. The moderate socialist party Mapam, after losing its activist wing, won only 9 seats. The activist parties, on the other hand, did rather well. Ahdut Ha'avodah won 10 seats in what was its first electoral campaign. Herut increased its representation from 8 to 15 seats, making it the second-largest party after Mapai. Foreign policy was not the main issue in these elections, but Sharett's moderate line was widely thought to have contributed to the party's poor performance at the polls.

On the morrow of the elections there was a move in Mapai to replace Sharett with Ben-Gurion as party leader and prime minister. Ben-Gurion's condition for taking over was a change in policy. He convened his senior colleagues and proposed to say to them, "I will not participate in a government that goes against my views in defense policy, and if such a government is formed—I shall fight it."[91] At the meeting he outlined the main principles of his defense policy: strict observance of the armistice agreements, the search for peace with the neighboring Arab states, and no territorial expansion, because what Israel needed was more Jews, not more land. But if the other side violated the armistice agreements by force, Israel would respond with force. And if the other side disrupted shipping to and from Eilat by force, Israel would also resort to force.[92] Sharett said that in view of his well-known differences with Ben-Gurion over defense, his personal preference was not to be a member of the next government. He did not rule out serving under Ben-Gurion but also made it clear that he could not implement a foreign policy with which he profoundly disagreed. So the first order of business, he suggested, was to debate the basic issues in a wider party forum in order to formulate a clear position on policy.[93]

Sharett did not feel that he had failed as prime minister and therefore had to make way for a better man. Indeed, he was seething with resentment at being elbowed aside by his power-hungry colleague.[94] Foreign policy was the agenda of Mapai's Central Committee meeting on 8 August. At the meeting Ben-Gurion proceeded to launch a frontal attack on those people, meaning Sharett, whose sole concern was with "what the Gentiles will say." The Foreign Ministry's attempt to arrogate the authority to determine defense policy, he warned, spelled disaster for Israel's security. The Foreign Ministry, he insisted, should serve the Ministry of Defense and not the other way around. The latter's role was to make defense policy and the former's role was to explain this policy to the world.[95]

Sharett remained as the nominal head of the government until Ben-Gurion finally succeeded in assembling a new coalition in November 1955, but during this long period his position was rendered intolerable by the intensifying conflict with the militant defense minister. A major crisis erupted toward the end of August when Sharett revoked the grudging permission he had granted earlier for a small-scale IDF operation to blow up bridges along the Gaza–Rafah road.

The reason for revoking the order was an appeal for restraint from Elmore Jackson, a prominent American Quaker who had been asked by the Egyptians to undertake a secret mission aimed at promoting a political settlement or at least some acceptable modus vivendi between Egypt and Israel. Nasser told Jackson, at their meeting in Cairo on 26 August, that he had developed great confidence in Sharett and that there had been informal talks in Paris but that the vicious attack on Gaza, following Ben-Gurion's return to the cabinet as defense minister, led him to break off the informal talks. With the escalation of violence on the Israeli side, he had no choice but to respond. Now he did not know whether he had confidence in either Sharett or Ben-Gurion, but he was prepared to continue the discussion. At his meeting with Sharett and Ben-Gurion on 29 August, Jackson was told that there had been an increase of fedayeen attacks in Israel from the Gaza Strip and that in response an Israeli attack on Khan Yunis had been ordered. Jackson offered his assessment that the basic negotiation was still alive but that it might not be if the projected attack occurred. He had the impression that Sharett agreed with him, but Ben-Gurion was noncommittal.[96] Sharett revoked the order for the attack on Khan Yunis in order to give the indirect discussions with Nasser a chance.

Dayan recalled the units that had already crossed the border and then proceeded to Jerusalem to submit his resignation to the defense minister. In his letter Dayan observed that the gulf between the defense policy recently laid down by the cabinet and the policy he considered necessary made it impossible for him to continue to discharge his responsibility as chief of staff. Finding himself in complete sympathy with Dayan, Ben-Gurion convened a meeting of Mapai's ministers in the government. There he presented Dayan's letter of resignation and called for the adoption of a clear line—either the Sharett line or the Ben-Gurion line—because alternating between the two caused nothing but harm. Ben-Gurion expressed regret that he had suggested the Gaza raid, because it went against the prevailing political line. If the majority preferred Sharett's line, concluded Ben-Gurion, then that line should be adopted and adhered to. Having had his say, Ben-

Gurion walked out of the room and, as a sign of protest, stayed away from his office in the Defense Ministry for twenty-four hours. Sharett caved in. That very afternoon he convened a cabinet meeting, which, on his recommendation, approved Dayan's plan for an assault on the police station of Khan Yunis, at the southern end of the Gaza Strip. Dayan and Ben-Gurion returned to their posts, and the first large-scale operation since the Gaza raid was launched, claiming the lives of thirty-seven Egyptians and wounding forty-five others.[97]

Sharett was worn out by the constant struggle to restrain Ben-Gurion and his officers. Every incident along the border was followed by a proposal for military retaliation, and every time he mustered a cabinet majority to defeat the proposal, the activists stepped up their campaign to discredit him. It was not only proposals for retaliation that he had to contend with but also indirect and direct calls for a war against Egypt. Ben-Gurion's proposed solution to the border incidents was to summon General Burns, the head of UNTSO, and to warn him that either the Egyptians put an end to the murders or Israel would capture the Gaza Strip, expel the Egyptian forces, and guard the border by itself. Sharett retorted that this step involved a high risk of war and should therefore not be taken unless Israel was prepared for war and certainly not without an explicit decision by the cabinet.[98]

It thus came as a great shock to Sharett when some of the leading Foreign Ministry moderates who were close to him joined the activists in calling for a preventive war against Egypt. "Preventive war" was a misnomer, for there was no evidence that Egypt planned to attack Israel, yet the advocates of war always called it that. These advocates also assumed that a military defeat would bring about the downfall of the military regime headed by Nasser. In view of Nasser's popularity at home, this was an unsound assumption, but one shared by some of the anti-Nasser circles in the American government. On 12 October, Sharett received a long and grave telegram from Abba Eban. It reported that Eban, Reuven Shiloah, the counselor at the embassy, Katriel Salmon, the military attaché, and Gideon Rafael had reached the conclusion that Israel could not count on receiving arms or a security guarantee from the United States to balance the Soviet arms that Egypt was about to receive. Their advice, therefore, was that Israel should prepare for the possibility of initiating a preventive war in order to break the backbone of the Egyptian army before it became stronger and thus to defeat Nasser and his gang. In his diary

Sharett recorded his melancholy thoughts on reading the telegram: "What is our vision on this earth—war to the end of all generations and life by the sword?"[99]

Rafael later explained that Soviet penetration of the Middle East and the supply of Soviet arms to Egypt led him and his colleagues to conclude that Israel should develop a military option only as one way of dealing with the new situation. But Sharett was very angry with them.[100] He knew that planning for the possibility of a preventive war, even as just one of the options, could generate the momentum for going to war. For his part, Sharett resolved to do all he could to prevent the drift toward war and to preserve the peace that he deemed vital to Israel's future. He noted the similarity between a preventive war by Israel against Egypt and one by the United States against the Soviet Union and the inconsistency of those who were utterly opposed to the latter but willing to risk the former.[101] Isser Harel, the head of Mossad, Israel's foreign intelligence service, added his powerful voice to the ones calling for a preventive war. He handed Sharett a long and thorough memorandum on the subject of preventive war which he recommended unreservedly. The memorandum failed to shake Sharett's resolve to resist war, but it added to his mental anguish.[102]

Reassurance came from an unexpected quarter. On Saturday, 22 October, Sharett went to visit Ben-Gurion and found him ill in bed but mentally alert and vigorous. Ben-Gurion told him that he was opposed to "an initiated war." He had read Eban's cable, Harel's memorandum, and a memorandum by Yehoshafat Harkabi, the director of military intelligence, and he did not agree with their conclusions. This statement dramatically changed Sharett's mood and released him from the nightmare of the preceding few days. Less reassuring were the proposals that Ben-Gurion planned to put to the new government that was in the process of being formed: to retaliate forcefully against every Egyptian violation of the armistice agreement, to respond by sending the IDF into the demilitarized zone in El-Auja and keeping it there, and to capture part of the northern DMZ with Syria if the Syrians did not behave themselves. Sharett left without finding out whether Ben-Gurion intended merely to react to provocations or to provoke a war. In other words, he was not sure whether in saying he was opposed to "an initiated war" Ben-Gurion meant that he was against the initiative or against war as such.[103]

The next day Sharett set off on a trip to meet the French prime minister, Edgar Faure, in Paris, and the American, British, and

Soviet foreign ministers in Geneva. His purpose was to put pressure on the Western powers either to prevent the arming of Egypt or to restore the military balance by supplying arms to Israel. Save for the promise that he obtained from Faure for the supply of jet fighters and about which he was enjoined to remain silent, he returned empty-handed and deeply disillusioned.[104] His unsuccessful and highly publicized mission only served to underscore Israel's international isolation in the face of the rising tide of Egyptian military strength.

What Sharett did not know was that on the day of his departure for Paris, Ben-Gurion had another visitor. The visitor was Moshe Dayan, who had been recalled from his vacation in France to an urgent consultation with the sick, but mentally sharp, minister of defense. Dayan also visited Ben-Gurion at his sickbed in the President Hotel in Jerusalem. In his *Diary of the Sinai Campaign* Dayan revealed, "At the end of the talk, he, as Minister of Defence, instructed me, among other things, to be prepared to capture the Straits of Tiran—Sharm e-Sheikh, Ras Natsrani and the islands of Tiran and Sanapir—in order to ensure freedom of shipping through the Gulf of Akaba and the Red Sea."[105]

Although Dayan and Ben-Gurion met alone and no minutes of the meeting were taken, we know from the diary of the office of the chief of staff the nature of the other things Dayan alluded to in his book. Ben-Gurion outlined to Dayan the main elements of the defense policy of the new government and asked for his comments. In the ensuing discussion the new defense policy received its first formulation. Dayan conveyed the conclusions to his deputy and to the director of military intelligence on the same day. Three days later Dayan convened a special meeting of the General Staff to give basic guidelines for the IDF's work in the coming months. Dayan's lecture faithfully reflected the understanding he had reached with the minister of defense and prime minister in waiting:

> a) The basic solution to Israel's worsening security problem is the overthrow of Nasser's regime in Egypt. Various means can alleviate the situation temporarily or postpone the decision, but no solution, barring the absolute removal of Nasser from power, will remove the root cause of the danger threatening Israel.
>
> b) In order to topple Nasser's regime, it is necessary to arrive at a decisive confrontation with the Egyptians at the ear-

liest possible date, before the absorption of the Soviet arms in Egypt makes the operation too difficult or even impossible.

c) Supreme efforts must be made to acquire more arms and ammunition until the date of the clash, but one thing must not be made dependent on the other.

d) Despite the above, this conception fundamentally rejects the idea of a preventive war. A preventive war means an aggressive war initiated by Israel directly. . . . Israel cannot afford to stand against the entire world and be denounced as the aggressor. . . .

e) . . . Israel does not need to resort to provocation . . . Egypt itself supplies the provocations continually. Israel can make do with the method of detonation—that is to say, to stand on its rights stubbornly and uncompromisingly and to react sharply to every Egyptian aggression. Such a policy will in the end bring about an explosion.[106]

War was evidently too serious a business to be left to the elected politicians. Dayan's guidelines to the General Staff embodied a new defense policy that had not been vouchsafed to the prime minister. They also supplied the answer to the question that troubled Sharett. With complete clarity, they indicated that when Ben-Gurion said that he was opposed to "an initiated war," he meant that he wanted war but that he did not want Israel to initiate it directly. On 2 November, Sharett stepped down to make way for Ben-Gurion. His premiership was over, and so was the policy of accommodation with the Arab world that he had pursued in the face of such overwhelming opposition from his own defense establishment.

4

The Road to Suez

1955–1957

L IKE ALL PREVIOUS governments, that formed after the July
1955 elections was a coalition of disparate elements dominated by Mapai, but the task of forming it was more difficult than
usual. Not until 2 November was David Ben-Gurion able to present to the Knesset a coalition government embracing the
Progressives and the religious bloc on the right, and Mapam and
Ahdut Ha'avodah on the left. The absence of the General Zionists
and the presence of Mapam and the Ahdut Ha'avodah did not
make a perceptible difference in the government's foreign policy.
Major decisions continued, in practice, to be taken by the leaders
of Mapai and sometimes by Ben-Gurion alone.

MOSHE DAYAN WANTS WAR

Ben-Gurion resumed his old practice of combining the premiership with the defense portfolio. Moshe Sharett, with considerable
misgivings, agreed to serve as foreign minister. Moshe Dayan
gained greatly in influence as a result of the personnel changes at
the top. Although in theory he was supposed to implement the
policy determined by the government, in practice he played a large
and steadily expanding role in the making of national security policy. All three men were highly intelligent and dedicated and had
the best interests of their country at heart. All of them also recog-

nized that their country's basic security was affected by the Czech arms deal with Egypt. But they held very different views about the appropriate policy for preserving that security. Dayan wanted a preventive war against Egypt, Sharett was firmly opposed to war, and Ben-Gurion was undecided. It was to take a year almost to the day to resolve this question, and the Suez War was the answer.

Dayan's basic assumption was that a second round was inevitable and that Israel should therefore prepare for war and not for peace. His main concern was to ensure that the timing and conditions of the next war were convenient for Israel. Following the Czech arms deal this became a pressing concern. Dayan estimated that the Egyptian army would be in a position to fight a war in the summer or autumn of 1956. His aim was to force a showdown before the military balance shifted in Egypt's favor. He did not advocate launching a preemptive strike, because this would have cast Israel in the role of aggressor. Rather, his strategy was to use military reprisals on a massive scale in order to provoke Egypt to go to war before the country was ready. The aim of these reprisals was not to force the Egyptians to keep the border quiet but, on the contrary, to create the conditions for an early war. In order to prepare the IDF for full-scale war, Dayan considered it essential to keep it constantly engaged in military operations in peacetime. It was no coincidence that he referred to these operations not as reprisals or retaliations but as peacetime military operations. In short, Dayan wanted war, he wanted it soon, and he used reprisals both to goad the Egyptians into war and to prepare his army for that war.[1]

In contrast, Sharett's basic premise was that war with Egypt was not inevitable and that everything should be done to prevent it. Realizing the great potential for escalation inherent in the Arab-Israeli conflict, Sharett urged caution and restraint. He feared that provocative or careless behavior might lead to a major explosion. Although aware that the dangers confronting Israel were serious, he did not think that Israel's very survival was on the line. His policy aimed at containing the conflict and at minimizing the risks of escalation. Like Dayan, Sharett understood very well that the policy of reprisals carried a high risk of escalation. The difference was that Dayan needed escalation to bring about war, whereas Sharett sought to avoid escalation in order to prevent war.[2]

Another major difference between Sharett and Dayan concerned the acquisition of arms. Both men were of course strongly committed to arms procurements for the IDF, but they went about it in very different ways. Sharett believed that the best chance of persuading the Western powers to supply arms to Israel lay in abiding by the rules of international law, cooperating with the UN observers, and behaving like a reasonable and responsible member of the international community. Dayan believed that if Israel behaved itself it would definitely not get arms, whereas if it misbehaved it might be given some arms as an incentive to behave better. He thought that Israel had a nuisance value, and he wanted to capitalize on this in order to induce the Western powers to give Israel arms in the hope that it would stay out of mischief. In other words, he considered military activism a factor more likely to help than to hinder the quest for arms.[3]

These initial differences over arms acquisition gradually developed into two rival foreign policy orientations. Although Sharett achieved the first breakthrough in France, he pinned his highest hopes on America. His foreign policy had an American orientation in that he sought political support, a security guarantee, and arms. Arms acquisiton was thus linked to a broader diplomatic strategy of working closely with America in the Middle East to promote common objectives, notably stability and peace. Shimon Peres, the director general of the Ministry of Defense, doubted all along that America would supply arms to Israel and worked assiduously to cultivate the French connection. In doing so, he went not through the normal diplomatic channels but directly to the French defense establishment. Dayan was quick to join Peres both in resorting to unorthodox methods and eventually in advocating a French orientation. At the beginning the question of orientation did not seem relevant to Israel's security needs. All of Israel's leaders agreed on the need to strengthen Israel's military capability, and they were willing to take arms from anywhere they could get them. Later it emerged that the source did make a considerable difference: France offered arms in the hope of inducing Israel to go to war against Egypt, whereas America allowed its allies to supply arms to Israel on condition that Israel did not go to war.

Unlike his protégé Dayan and his rival Sharett, Ben-Gurion did not have a clear or consistent line on the interrelated questions of preventive war, reprisals, arms acquisition, and foreign policy orientation. At the meeting on 23 October, Ben-Gurion had given Dayan the go-ahead for a policy designed to bring about a full-scale confrontation with Egypt and the overthrow of Nasser's regime. But it would take him the best part of a year to overcome his doubts and hesitations and to pursue his confrontational approach to Egypt to its logical conclusion.

The policy of confrontation with Egypt was announced by Ben-Gurion on 2 November 1955, when presenting his government to the Knesset. He began with the habitual expression of willingness to meet with any Arab leader to discuss a settlement, but he ended with a stern warning that the one-way war being waged against Israel by Egypt could not remain one-way for very long: "If our rights are assailed by acts of violence on land or sea, we shall reserve freedom of action to defend those rights in the most effective manner. We seek peace—but not suicide." To drive the message home, a large IDF brigade was dispatched that night to destroy Egyptian positions in al-Sabha, near the El-Auja demilitarized zone—a mission accomplished after the killing of fifty Egyptian soldiers and the capture of fifty others.

The assault on al-Sabha was the largest military operation carried out by the IDF since the end of the 1948 war. It was planned by Dayan as part of his overall strategy of prodding Nasser to go to war. On the night of the attack, as the last of the Egyptian positions were being captured, Dayan asked Ben-Gurion for permission to order his forces to stay in the captured positions, most of which were on Egyptian territory outside the DMZ, until the afternoon of the following day. His assumption was that keeping Israeli forces on Egyptian territory would provoke Nasser into ordering a counterattack. Ben-Gurion, however, rejected the idea, and the Israeli forces returned home, leaving behind a row of smoldering ruins.[4] About Dayan's personal loyalty to Ben-Gurion, there can be no doubt. Uzi Narkis, who was assistant to the chief of operations at the time, recalls standing with Dayan on top of Jebel Sabha when the battle was over, just before dawn. Narkis knew that Dayan was hoping for an Egyptian counterattack, so he suggested that they keep their forces there rather than return to base, that they "roll on" the battle. Dayan replied, "Ben-Gurion did not give me permission to do this, and I wouldn't do anything against his will."[5]

The supply of arms by the Soviet bloc to Egypt was followed by a diplomatic setback in the form of renewed Anglo-American pressure to promote a settlement of the Arab-Israeli dispute. Anglo-American suggestions for a settlement were outlined in Project Alpha in February 1955. The main elements of Alpha were as follows: linking Egypt to Jordan by ceding to them two triangles in the Negev without cutting Israel's link to Eilat; ceding to

Jordan certain problematic territories; dividing the DMZs between Israel and its neighbors; repatriation of a limited number of Palestinian refugees and compensation of the rest; an agreement on the distribution of the Jordan waters; termination of the Arab economic boycott; and Western guarantees for the new frontiers.[6] Project Alpha formed the background to a speech made by the British prime minister, Sir Anthony Eden, in April and a speech made by the U.S. secretary of state, John Foster Dulles, on 26 August. Israel categorically rejected the Anglo-American proposals.

Finally, in a speech in the Guildhall on 11 November, in more forthright language than that used by Dulles, Eden called for a compromise between the boundaries of the 1947 UN resolution and the 1949 armistice lines. He made it clear that London and Washington favored Israeli concessions in the Negev to enable Egypt and Jordan to establish a "land bridge" to each other without passing through non-Arab territory. For Israel this meant the loss of exclusive control over the Negev. In the Knesset, on 15 November, Ben-Gurion firmly rejected Eden's offer to mediate on this basis: "His proposal to truncate the territory of Israel for the benefit of its neighbors," he said, "has no legal, moral, or logical basis, and cannot be considered."

The Guildhall speech turned Israeli disillusion with Britain into hostility. Until the speech the dominant emotion was that Britain was misguided. After the speech Britain was seen as deliberately antagonistic. It was widely suspected that Britain's denial of arms was designed to make it impossible for Israel to refuse territorial concessions. Many Israelis, among them Ben-Gurion, believed that the British wanted the Negev transferred in whole or in part to Jordan for their own military purposes. And this suspicion heightened the defiant fervor with which Israeli leaders announced in and out of season that under no circumstances would Israel yield an inch of its territory.[7]

While the politicians and the diplomats were resisting Western pressures for territorial concessions, Dayan was thinking about territorial expansion. Dayan kept bombarding Ben-Gurion with proposals for direct military action. On 10 November, the day after the Guildhall speech, Dayan sent Ben-Gurion a memorandum calling for "an early confrontation with the Egyptian regime, which is striving for a war to destroy Israel, in order to bring about a change of the regime or a change in its policy." Among Dayan's specific recommendations were sharp reprisal actions against Egyptian or

Egyptian-directed acts of hostility, the immediate capture of the Gaza Strip, and preparations for the capture of Sharm el-Sheikh to break the blockade of the Gulf of Aqaba.

Dayan followed up this memorandum with a talk with Ben-Gurion three days later, urging military action as soon as possible. Ben-Gurion had already shown interest in action to break the blockade of Eilat and described it as "the great test." So at the talk Dayan presented Operation Omer, a plan to capture the Straits of Tiran.[8] The plan was to send a ship to the straits and, when the Egyptians opened fire, to send a mechanized forced down the eastern shore of the Sinai peninsula to capture the straits and to keep them. The plan also involved the use of naval and air power and paratroops. A special task force assembled under the command of Colonel Chaim Bar-Lev was expected to complete its preparations by the end of December. The planners knew that the operation could trigger a general war with Egypt, so the IDF had to be prepared for that eventuality.[9]

Perhaps because of the risk of war, and the risk of British intervention against Israel, Ben-Gurion showed none of his earlier enthusiasm for capturing the Straits of Tiran. He told Dayan that Operation Omer had to be postponed until the end of January because there was a prospect of obtaining arms from the United States. Dayan replied that he would rather fight immediately without American weapons than later with American weapons. He left with the distinct impression that Ben-Gurion had not yet settled on a definite policy, but that he tended to favor a political rather than a military solution.[10]

At length Ben-Gurion submitted the plan for capturing the Straits of Tiran to the cabinet, but despite his explanations the cabinet decided that the moment was not propitious. It added, however, that Israel should act "in the place and at the time that it deems appropriate." This decision was transmitted to Dayan, who responded with a letter to Ben-Gurion on 5 December urging the capture of the Straits of Tiran within one month. Dayan realized that postponing Operation Omer indefinitely was tantamount to its cancellation. It also amounted to a decision in principle against preventive war. Ben-Gurion's personal position was rather ambiguous. He had submitted the plan to the cabinet but did not put all his weight behind it. Nor did he fight back when a majority of the ministers, including the moderates in his own party, voted against it. It apparently suited him to look like an activist but to act like a moderate. The real activists felt that their best chance for war had been missed.[11]

OPERATION KINNERET

The year ended with a super-activist episode that was highly controversial at the time and for which no satisfactory explanation has ever been given—Operation Kinneret. On the night of 11 December a paratroop brigade under the command of Lieutenant Colonel Ariel Sharon raided the Syrian gun positions on the northeastern shore of Lake Kinneret, better known outside Israel as Lake Tiberias, or the Sea of Galilee. This was the IDF's fiercest and most brilliantly executed operation since the 1948 war. The paratroop brigade killed fifty Syrians and took thirty prisoners at the cost of six dead and ten wounded to itself. In the course of the battle all the Syrian positions were reduced to rubble.

Operation Kinneret was an unprovoked act of aggression by Israel. The three-pronged attack by land and sea was the product of prolonged planning and training. There was evidence to indicate that the raid was rehearsed and timed to perfection prior to execution. The backdrop to the raid was Syrian interference with Israeli fishing on the northeastern shore of the Sea of Galilee. The Syrians, however, fired not on the Israeli fishing vessels but merely on the patrol boats, and only when they came within 250 meters of the shore. Moreover, Operation Kinneret was not preceded by any unusual incidents. The Israelis were waiting for the slightest pretext to launch their carefully planned assault; when the Syrians proved uncooperative, the Israelis provoked the incident. On 10 December a police vessel was sent close to the shore, specifically in order to draw Syrian fire. A Syrian soldier fired a few shots that scraped some paint off the bottom of the patrol boat. No one was killed or wounded. This was the pretext for the IDF operation. Most observers agreed that the punishment was out of all proportion to the provocation. This judgment needs to be qualified in one respect: there was no Syrian provocation.[12]

The decision to authorize Operation Olive Leaves, the official name of the operation, had been made by Ben-Gurion alone. He had not consulted or informed the cabinet. Nor had he consulted anyone in the Foreign Ministry. Sharett was on a mission to the United States in a desperate bid to secure arms, and Ben-Gurion became acting foreign minister in addition to his other posts. On 27 November, Sharett had called Ben-Gurion to caution him that any reprisals could damage the negotiations, which had gotten off to a good start.[13] A definite American answer was promised by 12

December, and Ben-Gurion called Sharett and asked him to stay in Washington until he received the State Department's answer. Yet the day before the American answer was due, Ben-Gurion authorized the assault on the Syrian positions. Sharett made a bitter comment on the decision-making process: "Ben-Gurion the defense minister consulted with Ben-Gurion the foreign minister and received the green light from Ben-Gurion the prime minister."[14]

News of Operation Kinneret hit the Israeli public like a bolt from the blue. The ministers who read about it in the press were dumbfounded. Activists and moderates alike were critical of the scope and timing of the operation and of the prime minister's failure to consult them. They wanted to know why he had departed from the policy line that the cabinet had laid down, and they demanded that in future all military operations be submitted for approval. One minister charged that the IDF was pursuing an independent policy and trying to impose its policy on the government. Others speculated that the IDF had exceeded the orders it had been given by expanding the scope of the operation.

Ben-Gurion defended the IDF against these charges. But he himself was somewhat surprised by the results. When Dayan and Sharon reported to him, he seemed far from pleased and complained that the operation had been "too successful."[15] Ben-Gurion was largely to blame because he had not defined precisely the scope and purpose of the raid. It has been suggested that Ben-Gurion gave Dayan the order to do battle with the Syrians as a consolation prize for the postponement of Operation Omer. There is no evidence for this. According to Ariel Sharon, "Dayan's concept of this raid had gone well beyond the scale that Ben-Gurion had outlined to him."[16] Dayan had his own motives for ordering such a massive raid. In the first place, the Syrian army had never been defeated by the IDF, and by inflicting a crushing military defeat on it he wanted to break its image and its self-confidence. In addition, he wanted to put to the test the mutual defense pact that Syria and Egypt had concluded in October. If Nasser failed to rise to the challenge, the hollowness of his pledge would be exposed before the entire Arab world; if he did rise to it, this local incident might develop into a general confrontation with Egypt.[17]

Ben-Gurion must have known when he authorized the raid what the American reaction would be. This was presumably his reason for not consulting anyone in the Foreign Ministry or the cabinet. By authorizing the raid, he sabotaged not only Sharett's efforts to obtain American arms for Israel but also the orientation on America and the entire political strategy that went along with it. Uzi Narkis thought that this was Ben-Gurion's intention:

> I maintain that there was coordinated action here on the part of Ben-Gurion and Dayan to hurt Sharett. The scope of the operation was widened in order to deliver a body blow to Sharett. Between Dayan and Sharett there were no relations to speak of. Dayan was contemptuous of Sharett. Between the minister of defense and the chief of staff there was apparently a pact to cause Sharett to fail and to remove him from power. This was the first shot in the campaign against Sharett.[18]

A popular witticism in IDF circles at the time was that the biggest explosion of the Tiberias attack was that which went off under Moshe Sharett. Sharett himself was incandescent with rage when he heard the news. "My world became black, the matter of arms was murdered," he wrote in his diary.[19] In a cable of protest to Ben-Gurion, he did not pull his punches. He concluded the cable by questioning whether there was one government in Israel, whether it had one policy, and whether its policy was to sabotage its own efforts and foil its own objectives.[20] To Abba Eban, Sharett expressed his suspicion that Ben-Gurion had sanctioned the Kinneret raid in order to deny him a personal victory in the quest for arms. In his autobiography Eban gives the following account of the crisis:

> My own feeling is that whatever remnants existed of Sharett's ability to work with Ben Gurion went up in flames in Galilee that night. I, too, found it impossible to understand how Ben Gurion could reconcile two such lines of action. On the one hand he had asked Sharett to make a big effort to secure a breakthrough on our arms request. On the other hand, he had authorized a military operation of such strong repercussion as to make an affirmative answer inconceivable. I thought that an error of judgment had been made. I said so frankly in a long letter to Ben Gurion in January 1956 after we had gone through the routine of discussion and condemnation in the Security Council. I got an immediate reply through his secretary saying: "I fully understand your concerns about the Kinneret operation. I must confess that I, too, began to have my doubts about the wisdom of it. But when I read the full text of your brilliant defense of our action in the Security

Council, all my doubts were set at rest. You have convinced
me that we were right, after all."

I regarded this somewhat mischievous reply as being as
close to repentance as I was likely to secure from Ben Gurion.
My discussion with Jerusalem was not a defense of diplomacy
against military needs. There was a clash between two military
needs—the need for retaliation and the long-term need for
defensive arms. It seemed to me that the short-term objective
had triumphed unduly over our long-term aims.[21]

Sharett himself was still fuming with anger on his return home,
after his mission had been aborted. To Colonel Nehemia Argov,
Ben-Gurion's military secretary, who greeted him at the airport,
Sharett blurted, "You stabbed me in the back!"[22] To Mapai's senior leadership Sharett described the Kinneret raid as "a dastardly
act."[23] Sharett reported on his mission to Washington to Mapai's
Political Committee on 27 December. He was well aware that
Dayan was leading a campaign against the American option and for
launching a war against Egypt. It was also reported to Sharett that
at a meeting of the General Staff the chief of staff said that the present government would not declare war but that the army could
nevertheless bring about war through border clashes.[24] So in his
speech Sharett forcefully stated the case against going to war:

> I am against preventive war because it can turn into general
> war, to a ring of fire all around us, rather than be restricted to
> war with Egypt. I am against preventive war because that
> which did not occur in the War of Independence may occur,
> namely, intervention by a foreign power against us. . . . I am
> against preventive war because it means measures by the UN
> against us. I am against preventive war because it means injury
> and damage at home, the destruction of settlements, and the
> spilling of much blood.[25]

Sharett then turned to the ruinous effect of the Kinneret raid.
"Satan himself could not have chosen a worse timing," he ex-
claimed, his voice high-pitched in anger. Ben-Gurion was sitting at
the side of the room, having declined the chairman's invitation to
sit at the head of the table. According to Gideon Rafael, who was
sitting next to him, when he heard the word Satan, "he jerked as
if he had been hit by a bullet, then leaned back without uttering a
sound. I could physically feel how the word had hurt him. The audience gasped, as if witnessing a tightrope walker losing his bal-

ance. . . . [T]he brittle Ben Gurion-Sharett relationship had reached breaking-point."[26]

The damage to Israel's international standing was serious. Some observers even questioned the sanity of the Israeli policy-makers. The glaring disproportion between the scale of the Kinneret operation and its alleged cause put Israel in a worse light than usual. In the Security Council debate on this incident, Israel was more isolated than it had been in any previous debate. The eleven members of the Security Council outdid one another in denouncing Israel and in expressing their appreciation of Syria's moderation and restraint. On 19 January 1956 the Security Council passed a resolution that strongly condemned the latest incident, recalled earlier Israeli violations of the armistice agreements, called on Israel to respect these agreements, and threatened sanctions in the event of further violations.[27]

The costliest consequence of the Kinneret raid, however, was the American refusal to supply arms to Israel. Ben-Gurion argued that Dulles would not have given arms to Israel even if the raid had not taken place. Sharett and Eban thought that this was a silly argument because even if Dulles had already made up his mind, it was a gross mistake for Israel to hand him the perfect excuse for saying no. Ben-Gurion thought that Dulles was simply stringing Israel along over both the security guarantee and arms. By resorting to military action, Ben-Gurion signaled that if its interests were ignored, Israel would accept no restraint and behave as it pleased. Sharett and Eban wanted to wait a few days for the promised reply from Dulles without giving him an easy way out. They felt that Ben-Gurion's impulsiveness ruined their patient and painstaking diplomatic groundwork. Some of the other activists were much more extreme in their disregard for diplomacy. Moshe Dayan and Yosef Tekoah in particular were contemptuous of Eban and his diplomatic efforts. The Kinneret raid thus illustrated once again the rift between the defense establishment and the Foreign Ministry.[28]

The release of the official American papers for this period vindicated Sharett and Eban and conclusively disproved the claims of Ben-Gurion, Dayan, and the other defenders of the attack. On the eve of the attack, Dulles had decided to sell arms to Israel. He distinguished between defensive arms and offensive arms, such as tanks and planes, and proposed to deliver the former immediately and the latter at various stages in the following year. For the time being, he thought, the Tripartite Declaration of 1950 would give

Israel reasonable assurance against being attacked.[29] On 13 December, however, Eban was informed that a decision on Israel's request for arms had been postponed. The main reason given for the delay was the recent incident on the border with Syria.[30]

The official documents also reveal that Dulles was not as hostile to Israel as most Israelis thought and that he most certainly did not want to see it destroyed. His view was that efforts to match Israel's military power to that of all its Arab enemies would not guarantee its security. Only peace with the Arabs would enable Israel to survive in the long run. To attain peace, he held, Israel should be prepared to make territorial concessions and to take back 100,000 Palestinian refugees. Nor was Dulles as inflexible on the arms question as the Israelis made him out to be. He did think that Israel was entitled to receive Western arms of the same quality, if not in the same quantity, as Egypt was promised by the Soviet Union. But he was anxious to avoid polarization in the Middle East. He did not want the United States to become Israel's sole supplier of offensive arms or to abandon the Arab world to the Soviet Union. His solution to this problem was to encourage France and Canada to sell arms, especially fighter planes, to Israel. The Kinneret raid occurred just as Western policy on arms supplies was beginning to change in Israel's favor. It killed the prospect of direct U.S. military assistance to Israel.

On the question of war with Egypt, the majority in the cabinet also sided with Sharett. Ben-Gurion took it upon himself in mid-December not only to explain but to defend the government's position at a meeting of the General Staff. In his opening remarks he recognized the logic behind the contention that Egypt was getting stronger all the time and that unless they acted swiftly, they might miss the chance to deal Egypt a crushing blow. But he went on to elaborate on why the entire cabinet, himself included, opposed preventive war. The reasons encompassed the material damage and destruction inherent in war; the fear of British intervention on the side of Israel's enemies; and the danger that the perception of Israel as a threat to international peace would lead both East and West to deny arms and leave Israel weak and isolated in subsequent rounds of fighting with the Arabs. For all these reasons, concluded Ben-Gurion, the cabinet was right in opposing the initiation of war by Israel.[31]

As 1955 turned into 1956, the idea of a preventive war was no longer a serious topic of conversation in government circles. The debate had not been about "war or peace," because peace was not seen as an option at that time. The debate was between those who wanted to initiate war and those who wanted to exhaust every diplomatic avenue in order to restore the military balance of power between Israel and Egypt. Having embarked in late October on a strategy of actively bringing about a war with Egypt, Ben-Gurion began to have second thoughts toward the end of the year. About Nasser's intentions he had no second thoughts. Asked for his assessment of the security situation in mid-January 1956, he replied that he had no doubt whatever that Nasser was going to destroy the State of Israel the moment he felt that he had the power.[32] It was his awareness of the risks involved in unilateral Israeli action that led Ben-Gurion, at least for the time being, to abandon the policy of initiating war.

The Kinneret raid, which was intended to weaken Sharett, paradoxically increased his influence in the government, at least temporarily. Sharett thought that the IDF should be true to its name and serve only genuine defense purposes. He understood the importance of military power and spared no effort to acquire additional arms for the IDF, but he wanted this military power to be used for deterrence, not for attack.[33] The strength of Sharett's arguments became more widely appreciated in the cabinet in the aftermath of the Kinneret raid, for on 16 January Sharett wrote to Dulles to renew Israel's request for arms: "Arms of the same quality as Egypt is now getting is our only anchor of safety—the only effective deterrent to Egyptian aggression." This request was accompanied by an official undertaking: "I am authorized by my Government to state that, if given adequate arms, they will be used only for defensive purposes and that the avoidance of war and of any further deterioration in the stability of the area will be a primary consideration in our policy and action."[34] This was almost the exact opposite of the policy advocated by Moshe Dayan. The government was not threatening to cause trouble if denied weapons but to act responsibly if granted weapons.

THE ANDERSON MISSION

President Dwight Eisenhower launched a major personal initiative to explore the possibility of an understanding between Ben-Gurion and Nasser. He sent to the area Robert Anderson, a personal friend and a former deputy secretary of defense. The mission, code-named Operation Gamma, was prepared in November 1955 with the aim of negotiating a settlement and, if possible, arranging a direct meeting of the two leaders. Between December 1955 and March 1956, Anderson conducted three rounds of talks, shuttling between Cairo and Jerusalem via Athens and Washington in the utmost secrecy.[35]

In Israel, Operation Gamma was taken very seriously because of presidential involvement and the stature of the emissary, but its chances of success were not rated highly. Nasser's main concern seemed to be with ensuring that news of the mission did not leak out. He shared the secret with only two of his colleagues; they met with Anderson at night in a private flat and turned up at their offices the next morning to give the impression that nothing unusual was happening. But while Ben-Gurion and Nasser doubted that agreement was possible, each had his own agenda. Both needed American goodwill: Ben-Gurion in order to obtain arms, Nasser in order to obtain financial aid for the construction of the Aswan High Dam. Moreover, even if the talks failed, both had an interest in placing the onus for failure on the other side.

The substantive positions of the two sides in the talks did not present any surprises. Nasser demanded a substantial part of the Negev to allow for territorial contiguity between Egypt and Jordan. He also wanted Israel to give the Palestinian refugees a free choice between repatriation and resettlement with compensation. Ben-Gurion and Sharett were prepared to discuss minor territorial adjustments and a contribution to the settlement of the refugee problem, but only within the framework of direct peace negotiations.

Ben-Gurion attached the greatest importance to a face-to-face meeting with Nasser. He repeated the traditional Israeli claim that Arab refusal to recognize Israel's right to exist was the main stumbling block on the road to a settlement. Twelve years after the event Ben-Gurion took the unusual step of publishing the protocols of his talks with Robert Anderson. In these protocols Anderson is not described by name but only as "the emissary." Ben-Gurion published them first in a newspaper and then in a booklet under the title *Negotiations with Nasser*. His motive in publishing them was no doubt to show that he tried his best and that Nasser alone was responsible for the failure of the talks. But what emerges clearly from the protocols is Ben-Gurion's old tactic of projecting an image of reasonableness and placing the onus for the deadlock on the shoulders of his Arab opponents. This was the tactic that had served him so well in relation to the grand mufti, Hajj Amin al-Husseini, and other Arab leaders in the pre-Independence period. He tried it again with Nasser by relentlessly insisting on a one-to-one meeting as the only real test of the latter's intentions. No mediator, however noble and well intentioned, he said, could be a substitute for direct contact between the principal protagonists. If only he and Nasser could meet face-to-face, Ben-Gurion told Anderson, peace might be reached in two or three days. This seemed a reasonable proposition, but, as Ben-Gurion knew full well, there was not the remotest chance that Nasser would agree to it, because of the strong Arab taboo against recognizing Israel or talking to the enemy. One is forced to conclude that Ben-Gurion was simply trying to score points off his opponent.

Anderson tried his best to persuade Nasser to grant Ben-Gurion's wish for a high-level meeting, but Nasser rejected the idea. He said that the Egyptian people, the Egyptian army, and the Arab nation would not allow such a meeting. Nasser made two additional points. First, Israel was not just an Egyptian problem but an all-Arab problem, and Egypt had to keep in step with the other Arab states. Second, as far as Egypt was concerned, the only basis for a settlement with Israel was the UN partition resolution of 1947. This was, of course, a complete nonstarter for Israel.

Anderson recognized that there was no way of bridging the gap between the two sides and that his mission had failed. In his summing up of the mission, Anderson reported that Nasser mentioned four times the murder of King Abdullah. He was willing to talk to the United States, which could talk to Israel, but he could not take the risk of bringing an Israeli to Egypt. Eisenhower blamed both sides for the failure. Nasser was "a complete stumbling block," while the Israelis were "completely adamant in their attitude of making no concessions whatsoever in order to obtain peace."

Ben-Gurion regarded the Anderson mission as doomed to failure from the start.[36] He was convinced that Nasser was heading for war with Israel, and he desperately wanted American arms to balance the arms Egypt was getting from the Soviet Union. Even before Anderson arrived in Israel, Ben-Gurion sent Isser Harel, the head of the Mossad, on a secret mission to Washington, to talk to Allen Dulles, the director of the CIA and brother of John Foster Dulles. Harel's message was that the supply of arms to Israel would prevent war, whereas the denial of arms would force it to go to war. Harel also revealed that after hearing about the Czech arms deal he advised Ben-Gurion to take military action in order to defeat the Egyptian army and bring about Nasser's downfall. Ben-Gurion's rejection of this advice was presented by Harel as evidence of his reasonableness and moderation.[37]

While the Anderson mission was in progress, Ben-Gurion showed little interest in American mediation and kept pressing for arms. On 14 February he wrote to President Eisenhower, depicting Nasser as a threat to Western interests in the Middle East as well as to Israel's security, and protesting the denial of arms to Israel. At his last meeting with Anderson, on 9 March, Ben-Gurion sounded a note of alarm. To bring about peace was impossible, he said, but there was a way to prevent war. The only way to do so was to let Israel have defensive arms. If Israel got a negative reply to its request, "then we have only one task: to look to our security." Behind these words lurked the threat to resort to war if America persisted in refusing to supply arms.

Anderson's mission overlapped with the mission of Dag Hammarskjöld, the UN secretary-general, to the region. But whereas Anderson's aim was to promote a peace settlement between Israel and Egypt, Hammarskjöld had the much more limited aim of securing a cease-fire; and whereas Anderson's mission was secret, Hammarskjöld's was public. Hammarskjöld made three trips to the Middle East in 1956, in January, April, and July, meeting both Ben-Gurion and Nasser on each of these trips. His aim was to defuse the tension along the Israeli-Egyptian border and in particular to find a solution to the problem of the DMZ that straddled the border in El-Auja. Both sides had introduced troops and built fortifications in the DMZ in violation of the armistice agreement. From late October 1955 on, Israeli spokesmen took to calling this area Nitzana and to treat it as if it were part of Israel rather than a DMZ under the control of the UN. On 3 November, Hammarskjöld had submitted a three-point plan for resolving the dispute. Both parties accepted the plan, but the Israelis insisted that the Egyptians leave first whereas the Egyptians insisted that the Israelis get out first, and so the stalemate continued.

The negotiations with Hammarskjöld were accompanied by an internal debate in Israel. This was an important link in the long chain of disagreements between Ben-Gurion and Sharett over the armistice regime and relations with the UN. Ben-Gurion took personal charge of the negotiations and relied heavily on military advice, especially from Moshe Dayan. The specific question under consideration was whether to extend the Israeli presence in the

DMZ or to work with the UN secretary-general for a peaceful so-lution. Dayan and Yosef Tekoah pressed for turning the El-Auja DMZ into a part of Israel, just as they had done in the case of the DMZ along the Syrian border. Theirs was a policy of defying the UN and provoking the Egyptians for the sake of imposing unilat-eral Israeli control. Ben-Gurion was less extreme, but he was un-willing to withdraw from El-Auja both because of the question of sovereignty and because of its strategic importance, especially in time of war. Sharett, on the other hand, advocated strict obser-vance of the armistice agreement. He was opposed to the policy of constantly picking quarrels with Egypt since it also involved Israel in a confrontation with the UN. He accepted the status quo in the DMZ and thought that there was some scope for dialogue and compromise without sacrificing Israel's vital interests. His aim in the short term was to lower the tensions and create the conditions for a gradual improvement in Israeli-Egyptian relations.[38]

Dayan did not like the compromise with the UN and pressed for extending Israel's control over the DMZ through the intro-duction of additional soldiers masquerading as farmers. Ben-Gurion was persuaded to ask the cabinet to authorize the construction of two new "civilian" settlements in the DMZ. Fearing that this would exacerbate the dispute with Hammarskjöld over the implementation of his three-point plan, Sharett urged Ben-Gurion to hold fire until they could evaluate the entire situa-tion. Ben-Gurion forced the issue at a cabinet meeting on 18 March. He found himself once again in a minority, and his scheme was defeated.[39]

In early April incidents multiplied, and a substantial buildup of forces on either side of the border added to the general nervous-ness. The Security Council decided on 4 April to ask the secretary-general to investigate, on the spot, this rapidly deteriorating situation, and Hammarskjöld left at once for the Middle East. On the eve of his arrival, however, the IDF launched a heavy bom-bardment of Gaza City, ostensibly in reply to Egyptian shelling of a frontier settlement. Sixty Egyptian civilians were killed and over a hundred wounded. This in turn provoked a wave of fedayeen at-tacks from the Gaza Strip, causing numerous casualties and much damage well inside Israel.[40] Hammarskjöld found both Nasser and Ben-Gurion in an angry and truculent mood. Nasser had decided to retaliate in kind with the only effective weapon at his disposal, the sending of fedayeen inside Israel to kill civilians. He felt that Ben-Gurion would not be responsive to any other type of persuasion. He was adopting Ben-Gurion's own policy of "an eye for an eye."[41] Ben-Gurion thought that Hammarskjöld was biased in favor of Egypt, and the talks between them were acrimonious and unproductive. In the report on his mission to the Security Council on 9 May, Hammarskjöld was openly critical of Israel for violating the armistice agreements. Sharett was reduced to watching from the sidelines the steady deterioration in the relations between Israel and the world organization.

SHARETT'S FALL

Moshe Sharett was a balanced man in unbalanced times, a man of peace in an era of violence, a negotiator on behalf of a society that spurned negotiations, a man of compromise in a political culture that equated compromise with cowardice. His temperamental incompatibility with Ben-Gurion had been apparent for some time. But their recurrent clashes over policy had deeper roots in their outlooks on Israel's place in the world. Ben-Gurion was a great believer in the Jewish revolution. His principal tenet was self-reliance. He strongly believed that the revived Jewish nation in its historic homeland could make its own laws and be guided by its own, unique code of morality. Sharett put the emphasis on Jewish normality rather than on Jewish uniqueness. His principal tenet was international cooperation and the peaceful settlement of disputes. He strongly believed that international law and the prevailing norms of international behavior were binding on Israel, and it was his ambition to turn Israel into a respectable and responsible member of international society.

The tension between the leader of the moderate school and the leader of the activist school was fueled in the spring of 1956 by the conflict over the French connection. In essence, the alliance between Israel and France that developed during this period was one between the defense ministries of the two countries, bypassing both foreign ministries. As the head of the Foreign Ministry and the leading advocate of the Anglo-Saxon orientation, Sharett fought a losing battle against the chief proponents of the French orientation: Shimon Peres and Moshe Dayan. Since the alliance with France was predicated upon Israel's willingness to go to war against Egypt, the debate over orientation merged with that other great debate on the question of preventive war. Ben-Gurion was a slow convert to the French orientation, but once his mind was made up, he acted with characteristic speed and decisiveness in transferring complete control over the acquisition of arms from the Foreign Ministry to the Defense Ministry and in authorizing Dayan, on June 10, to go ahead with secret negotiations with France on far-reaching cooperation, including joint war operations against Egypt.[42]

The frontal clash between the policy of working for war against Egypt in collusion with France and working to preserve the peace in cooperation with the United States forced Ben-Gurion either to resign himself as head of the government or bring about the resignation of the foreign minister. By threatening the former, he exacted the latter and in mid-June 1956 Sharett tendered his resignation. Sharett's only demand was that a debate be held in a responsible party forum on the contending approaches that necessitated personnel changes, but Ben-Gurion kept such a debate from taking place by again threatening to resign. Consequently, the policy differences underlying Sharett's departure were never aired in a party forum. Nor were they aired in the cabinet. There Sharett frequently challenged specific proposals put forward by Ben-Gurion, but never the fundamentals of his Arab policy, in front of coalition partners.[43] In the Knesset, Ben-Gurion only hinted at the discord over policy by stating that the deterioration in the country's security persuaded him that the national interest now required close coordination between the Foreign Ministry and the Ministry of Defense, as well as new leadership in the former.[44]

The real reason behind Sharett's ouster was that he advocated an alternative to Ben-Gurion's militant policy in the conflict with the Arabs. In the cabinet, as we have seen, a majority of the ministers frequently rallied behind Sharett on crucial issues. During the six months when Ben-Gurion served as defense minister in the cabinet headed by Sharett, he suffered two major defeats: one on the proposal to capture the Gaza Strip and the other on his proposal for the renunciation of the armistice agreement. After Ben-Gurion replaced Sharett as prime minister, he suffered two more defeats at the instigation of his foreign minister: first the rejection of Operation Omer for the capture of the Straits of Tiran, then the rejection of the proposal to build new settlements in the El-Auja DMZ. All these decisions served to deflect Ben-Gurion from the militant course he was intent on pursuing, but he regarded it as utterly intolerable that measures supported by the majority of their party colleagues in the government were vetoed by a "Sharettist" majority consisting largely of non-Mapai ministers.[45]

Ben-Gurion was moving toward the conclusion that war with

Egypt was inevitable, and he knew that Sharett would oppose launching a preemptive strike. He also knew that Sharett would be capable of mobilizing a majority in the cabinet to veto a proposal to go to war. The decision to go to war had not yet crystallized in Ben-Gurion's mind, but he wanted to leave himself the option of imposing his will on the cabinet at a later date and was sufficiently ruthless to pay with someone else's career for this option.

By removing Sharett, Ben-Gurion purged a rival center of power and a focal point for opposition to his own policy within the party and the cabinet. In Golda Meir, who succeeded Sharett, he found a foreign minister after his own heart, for she accepted unquestioningly the supreme authority of the prime minister and his conception of the role of the foreign minister as essentially a spokesperson for the defense establishment. Her ignorance of international affairs was one of her main qualifications for the post, as Ben-Gurion was later to reveal, for it enabled his go-ahead lieutenants to bypass the Foreign Ministry and resort to unorthodox methods and unconventional channels in their quest for French arms.[46] Above all, Golda Meir accepted the need for preventive war, whereas Sharett's record strongly suggested that he would act as a brake on the drive to war. Sharett's departure was thus doubly significant: it marked the final collapse of the moderate school of thought on Israel's relations with the Arabs and the final triumph of the Ben-Gurionism, and it cleared the most serious internal stumbling block along the path that led Israel within a few months to a full-scale war with Egypt.

THE FRENCH CONNECTION

The war against Egypt was intimately connected with the French orientation in Israel's foreign policy. Ben-Gurion had temporarily dropped the idea of a preventive war against Egypt in the early months of 1956. America's final rejection of Israel's request for arms in April was a turning point for him. From that point on, he looked to France to satisfy Israel's needs for modern arms. Ben-Gurion did not choose France as an arms supplier and as an ally in preference to America. Only after the hope of receiving American arms had evaporated did he turn to France. The emergence of a French orientation in Israel's foreign policy was thus not a matter of deliberate choice but the result of the failure of the American orientation.[47] The idea of preventive war reemerged in the context of the ever closer relations with France.

Shimon Peres, the director general of the Ministry of Defense, was the principal architect of the French connection, or the bridge across the Mediterranean, as it was sometimes called. Peres was not an ideologue but a technocrat and an arch-pragmatist. He was not interested in foreign policy orientations but in obtaining arms for Israel. Practical considerations alone guided his actions. He asked himself how to break the ban on the supply of arms to Israel, and he came to the conclusion that France offered the best chance.[48]

The relationship between Israel and France began with the supply of arms, developed into political and military cooperation, and reached its climax in the joint war against Egypt. In the arms supply relationship, the first significant turn occurred in October 1955 when Prime Minister Edgar Faure promised Sharett two dozen Ouragan fighter planes, several transport planes, several scores of medium field artillery pieces, and a quantity of light arms. In early February 1956 a socialist government was formed in France by Guy Mollet in coalition with the radicals, whose representative, Maurice Bourgès-Maunoury, became minister of defense. Around that time Egypt stepped up its support for the Algerian rebels who were fighting through the Front de Liberation Nationale (FLN) for independence from France.

Having a common enemy in Egypt brought the two countries closer together. The French military had three priorities: Algeria, Algeria, and Algeria. Israel not only passed on what intelligence it had on Egyptian support for the Algerian rebels but also exaggerated the extent of this support. The French assumed that if only Nasser could be knocked out of the game, the Algerian rebellion would collapse. There was no solid basis for this assumption, but the Israelis nevertheless encouraged it. And as the Algerian rebellion gathered momentum, the French government became less inhibited about supplying arms to Israel even though this involved a contravention of the Tripartite Declaration of May 1950, of which France had been a signatory alongside Britain and the United States.

At first Christian Pineau, the socialist foreign minister, wanted to continue the old policy of dangling a carrot in front of Nasser in order to wean him away from the Algerian rebels. But the policy of the stick, advocated by Mollet and Bourgès-Maunoury, gained the upper hand in the spring. The stick was Israel, and the policy was to use Israel's power to threaten Nasser and pin him down in the Middle East. The long-term aim was to weaken Nasser, and to weaken the Pan-Arab movement, of which he had become the leader, in order to improve the chances of suppressing the Algerian rebellion.[49]

Over the summer close relations were developed between the French and Israeli defense establishments at different levels. The principals on the French side were Bourgès-Maunoury, Louis Mangin, his personal assistant, and Abel Thomas, the director general of the Defense Ministry. The principals on the Israeli side were Peres, Dayan, Major General Yehoshafat Harkabi, the director of military intelligence, and Yosef Nachmias, the Defense Ministry's representative in Paris. Personal relations between the officials of the two sides were friendly and good-humored. The diplomats of the two countries were the butt of many jokes. Peres was told by his opposite number to keep away from the Foreign Ministry officials because they did not make foreign policy but a policy that is foreign. The French generals did not spare Dayan their badinage about the eye he had lost in the service of the British against the Vichy regime in Syria during World War II. Dayan was clever, cynical, and devious, and all these qualities served him well in the task of excluding the Foreign Ministry officials, in cutting corners, and in overcoming political and legal restraints on the transfer of arms. "I don't care about prestige," he used to say, "particularly other people's prestige." Precisely because he was cynical, Dayan realized that French arms supplies to Israel were motivated not by altruism or socialist solidarity but by self-interest. "France will give us arms," he told Ben-Gurion, "only if we give it serious help in the Algerian matter. Serious help means killing Egyptians, nothing less."[50]

A formal, but secret, conference of the senior military echelons of the two sides was held toward the end of June in a château in Vermars, south of Paris. The Israeli delegation included Peres, Dayan, Harkabi, and Nachmias. In a carefully prepared introduction, Dayan spoke about the danger Nasser posed to the entire Middle East and North Africa. Nasser's goal, he said, was to eliminate all European influence from the region and to turn Egypt into a forward base for Soviet power. Israel had no general quarrel with the Arab world. Its quarrel was with Nasser, and its main aim was the overthrow of Nasser. Preventing the establishment of a Soviet base was an international as well as an Israeli interest. Israel was prepared for joint action with France against Nasser in the military and political spheres. The Arab empire that Nasser dreamed of could not rise without his subduing Israel first. As long as Israel existed, he could not realize his ambition. Every victory against Israel, however small, enabled Nasser to step up his activity on other fronts. Hence the importance of Israel remaining strong. For Israel the two critical needs were tanks and aircraft. Dayan indicated that he was convinced that in the end Nasser would attack Israel. He wanted to know whether the French were prepared to cooperate with the Israelis, directly or indirectly, with the aim of bringing down Nasser and strengthening Israel against an Egyptian attack.

The French replied that they accepted Dayan's analysis and his proposals, with one reservation—overthrowing Nasser was a political matter, and they had no authority to commit their government to this course of action. Joint action to foil Nasser's initiatives was as far as they could go. This was good enough for Dayan. The main thing, he said, was to prove to Nasser and his successors that the policy of destroying Western influence in the Middle East and the pro-Soviet tendency did not pay. An agreement was reached on intelligence cooperation and on joint operations such as blowing up the transmitters of Saut al-Arab, which disseminated Egyptian propaganda throughout the Arab world, and striking at the FLN bases in Libya. In return Israel was promised 72 Mystère planes, 200 AMX tanks, and large quantities of ammunition and spare parts. The bill came to more than $100 million, a vast sum in those days.[51]

When Ben-Gurion heard the list of French demands, he looked worried. He thought that the deal involved Israel's risking its very existence while France risked, at most, its position in North Africa. He asked for twenty-four hours to consult with Golda Meir and Levi Eshkol. The next day, 27 June, Ben-Gurion said to Dayan, "This is a slightly dangerous adventure but, what can we do, our entire existence is like that!" Ben-Gurion was opposed to hitting targets that would force Nasser to retaliate but otherwise gave his blessing to the deal. The cabinet was not informed.

The Vermars conference was a watershed. It provided an effective solution to the problem that had troubled Israel's defense planners since the Czech arms deal: the shift in the military balance in Egypt's favor. Israel's military superiority over Egypt was now guaranteed by the French. There was no longer any need for Israel to launch a preemptive strike. Egypt did not pose any serious threat. As far as Israel was concerned, that could have been the end of the matter.

The idea of a coordinated military offensive against Egypt emerged only after Nasser's nationalization of the Suez Canal

Company on 26 July, the fourth anniversary of the Free Officers' revolution. Nasser made his dramatic announcement following the abrupt cancellation of the American offer of funding to build the Aswan High Dam. Nasser's blow was aimed at the Western powers, not at Israel. Britain and France were most directly affected because they were the principal shareholders in the Suez Canal Company. America and Britain urged Israel to keep out of this dispute. Britain in particular was anxious to keep its dispute with Nasser from getting mixed up with the Arab-Israeli dispute. Any appearance of standing shoulder to shoulder with Israel over Suez would have been the kiss of death for Britain's position in the Middle East. Britain and France began to discuss joint military action to capture the canal, but the British insisted that Israel not be involved or even informed of this plan.[52] The Eden government persisted in its unfriendly attitude toward Israel. It rejected a French suggestion that it supply arms to Israel, on the grounds that this would unite the Arab states behind Nasser. It even saw fit to ask the Israeli government to refrain from any action against Egypt that might embarrass Britain.[53]

Although the nationalization of the Suez Canal Company did not directly concern Israel, Ben-Gurion's first thought on hearing the news was that it might provide an opportunity to bring about the fall of Nasser. He put out feelers to the CIA about joint action to topple Nasser but received a noncommittal reply. On 29 July, Dayan proposed to Ben-Gurion three possible lines of action to exploit the new situation: the capture of the entire Sinai peninsula right up to the Suez Canal, the capture of the Straits of Tiran, and the capture of the Gaza Strip. Ben-Gurion turned down these ideas on the grounds that the West would not support them, out of fear of the Soviet Union.[54] In his diary he wrote gloomily on the same day, "The Western powers are furious . . . but I am afraid that they will not do anything. France will not dare to act alone; Eden is not a man of action; Washington will avoid any reaction."[55]

Ben-Gurion was wrong about the French. Although the nationalization of the Suez Canal Company was completely legal, and although compensation was offered to the shareholders, the French were determined to hit back. If the French military suffered from an Algeria syndrome, the French politicians suffered from a Munich syndrome. Munich was the symbol of the appeasement of Hitler in the interwar period. Many of the leading ministers in Guy Mollet's government and their senior aides had been active in the resistance to Nazi Germany during World War

II. They regarded Nasser as a "Hitler on the Nile" and resolved that this time there would be no appeasement.

The day after the canal was nationalized, Bourgès-Maunoury asked Peres for an urgent meeting in his office. Peres took Yosef Nachmias along with him and was surprised to find the minister flanked by several generals poring over maps. "How long," asked the minister, "would it take the IDF to fight its way across the Sinai and reach the Canal?" Peres estimated that they could do it in two weeks. The minister followed with another question: "Would Israel be prepared to take part in a tripartite military operation, in which Israel's specific role would be to cross the Sinai?" Peres replied that he assumed that under certain circumstances they would be so prepared. The minister then briefed his visitor on the plans of Operation Musketeer, a joint Anglo-French scheme to land troops in the canal and reassert their rights by force. As they left, Nachmias said to Peres that he deserved to be hanged for speaking on a matter of such gravity without prior authorization. Peres replied that he would rather risk his neck than risk missing such a unique opportunity.[56]

On 18 September, Peres flew to Paris to expedite the purchase of arms. He also hoped for a frank talk with the French leaders about a common policy in the Middle East. In Paris, Bourgès-Maunoury reported to Peres that the British were very indecisive, that the plan for a joint operation with them might have to be abandoned, and that he was looking for other partners in the war against Nasser. He added that there were three different timescales: the French advocated immediate military action against Egypt, the British wanted to allow two more months for diplomatic action, and the Americans wanted a much longer period to undermine Nasser's regime without the use of military force. He assumed that Israel's timescale was closer to Britain's than to France's.

Peres replied that the partnership would be more important for Israel than the timing, and he suggested the establishment of personal contact at the level of ministers. Bourgès-Maunoury gave Peres a handwritten letter for Ben-Gurion with congratulations on his seventieth birthday. The letter included some carefully phrased sentences about the common danger from Egypt and his hope for active partnership for the good of both of their countries. Ben-Gurion wrote to thank Bourgès-Maunoury for his congratulations and added, "As for the three timescales, the one closest to our heart is in fact the French one." The significance of this last phrase can hardly be exaggerated, for it amounted to a positive preliminary response to the French soundings about a military partnership against Egypt.[57]

The birthday greetings from the French minister of defense went some way toward dispelling Ben-Gurion's fears of Western appeasement of Nasser. American efforts to find a peaceful solution to the Suez Canal Company dispute had greatly added to these fears. On 10 August, Ben-Gurion had written in his diary that Nasser was likely to emerge victorious from the dispute because the British did not seem ready to act against him, and without force he would not give up: "The growth in Nasser's prestige is bound to make him want to destroy Israel, not by a direct attack but first by a 'peace offensive' and an attempt to reduce our territory, especially in the Negev, and when we refuse—he will attack us."[58] Given this background, military action against Nasser seemed increasingly urgent.

At the end of September the French government decided to invite Israeli representatives to Paris to discuss joint military action against Egypt. The British were said to have approved the French plan to involve Israel on condition that the Israelis did not attack Jordan. In his diary Ben-Gurion described the French proposal as "possibly fateful," and he also reported it to the cabinet. In the cabinet discussion several fears were expressed: that Russia would send volunteers to help Egypt, that Britain would betray Israel, and that all the Arab states would join in the war. Ben-Gurion vigorously countered the arguments of the waverers. He was determined to prevent a "Sharettist" majority from forming again after Sharett had gone. He badly wanted an alliance with the Western powers, and he made it clear to the ministers that it was out of the question to let the chance slip by. The ministers accepted his recommendations and agreed to send a high-level delegation to France. Dayan remarked to Peres, "We are reaching the end of the beginning."[59]

A secret two-day conference opened on 30 September at St.-Germain. The conference raised French-Israeli contacts from the level of officials to the level of ministers. The Israeli delegation was headed by Foreign Minister Golda Meir and included Moshe Carmel, the transport minister, who represented Ahdut Ha'avodah in the cabinet, Peres, Dayan, and Dayan's chief of bureau, Lieutenant Colonel Mordechai Bar-On. The delegation's brief was to explore the possibilities of a partnership with France against Egypt. It was not authorized to make any definite political commitments. The French were also noncommittal, with Christian Pineau showing more reserve than Bourgès-Maunoury. Pineau seemed interested not in a joint action with Israel but in an Israeli attack that would provide the pretext for an Anglo-French operation against Egypt. Nevertheless, the talks ended with agreement on two points: further French military help to Israel, and the maintenance of consultations between the two sides.[60]

The plan for military action against Egypt created a vicious circle. Ben-Gurion was not prepared to act against Egypt without French participation. France was not prepared to act against Egypt without British participation. Britain was committed to joint military action with France but insisted on excluding Israel. In mid-July various attempts were made to break out of this vicious circle, with the French doing most of the running.

THE WAR PLOT AGAINST EGYPT

The French were the matchmakers in forging the secret pact to attack Egypt, and they displayed more energy, ingenuity, and guile in bringing the two parties together than the average matchmaker. On 13 October a Soviet veto put an end to the plan to impose on Egypt a Suez Canal users' association. The next day two Frenchmen paid a secret visit to the British prime minister at Chequers, his country residence, to propose a way out of the impasse. The two visitors were Albert Gazier, the acting foreign minister, and Maurice Challe, an air force general and the deputy chief of staff of the French armed forces. At this meeting the French general presented a plan of action that quickly became known as the Challe scenario. The plan was that Israel would attack Egypt in the area of the Suez Canal, and this would provide Britain and France with the pretext to intervene, ostensibly in order to separate the combatants and safeguard the canal.

Sir Anthony Eden liked the idea. According to Sir Anthony Nutting, the minister of state for foreign affairs, who was present at the meeting, "he could scarcely contain his glee."[61] For Eden this was the turning point. Until then he had been thrashing around. Selwyn Lloyd, the foreign secretary, was at the UN in New York, working out a peaceful solution of the dispute with Mahmoud Fawzi, his Egyptian opposite number. Eden did not like the idea of a diplomatic solution, but no alternative policy was available. Now there was an alternative, and Eden instantly switched from the diplomatic to the military path. He called Lloyd in New York and ordered him to drop everything and return home immediately.[62]

On 16 October, as soon as Lloyd arrived in London, Eden briefed him on the Chequers meeting and took him to a follow-up meeting in Paris. At the Palais Matignon, the official residence of the French prime minister, they met Guy Mollet and Christian Pineau and agreed to proceed along the lines of the Challe scenario, with Israel providing the pretext for allied intervention. The Frenchmen obtained a commitment from Eden, which he later confirmed in writing, that in the event hostilities developed between Egypt and Israel, Her Majesty's government would not come to the assistance of Egypt. The French immediately passed on this commitment to the Israelis to encourage them to play their part in the Challe scenario.[63] One obstacle on the road to the collusion had been cleared.

Ben-Gurion was greatly excited by the prospect of a military partnership with the Western powers against Egypt but extremely suspicious of the British in general and of Sir Anthony Eden in particular. Although he knew that the plan originated with General Challe, he repeatedly referred to is as "the British plan." He strongly resented the suggestion that Israel play the aggressor while Britain and France posed as the peacemakers. Israel, he repeated on a number of occasions, would not allow itself to be treated like a concubine. What he deeply longed for was a partnership between equals and an explicit coordination of military plans, preferably after a face-to-face meeting with Eden. When news of the Anglo-French summit meeting reached him, he wrote to Yosef Nachmias, "In connection with the arrival of the British representatives in Paris, you should contact the French immediately and ask them whether the meeting can be made tripartite. The Israeli representatives are ready to come immediately, in the utmost secrecy. Their rank will equal the ranks of the British and French representatives."[64]

The French understood that only a face-to-face meeting might allay Ben-Gurion's suspicions. Guy Mollet therefore invited Ben-Gurion to Paris and added that, if the need arose, a member of the British government would also be invited. Ben-Gurion replied that the "British" proposal was out of the question, but he was still willing to go if his visit would serve a useful purpose. He was haunted by the suspicions that Perfidious Albion would leave Israel in the lurch or even turn against it. Eden's letter specifically mentioned that different considerations would apply to Jordan in the event of hostilities, because Britain had a firm treaty with Jordan.[65] In his diary Ben-Gurion wrote, "It seems to me that the British plot is to embroil us with Nasser, and in the meantime bring about the conquest of Jordan by Iraq."[66] A secret source, known only to him and Peres, fed these suspicions that Britain was plotting against Israel and that it might even take military action against Israel under the terms of the Anglo-Jordanian Treaty.[67]

Dayan played a decisive part in persuading Ben-Gurion to go to the meeting in Paris. He pointed out that Britain and France did not need any help from Israel in order to defeat Egypt and that the only thing Israel could supply was a pretext for their intervention. This alone gave Israel a ticket of admission into the Suez campaign club. But even after he got on the plane sent for him by the French, Ben-Gurion remained very skeptical about the possibility of an understanding with the British. During the flight Ben-Gurion read books by Jewish historians that claimed, on the basis of evidence from the Byzantine geographer Procopius, that in ancient times a Jewish kingdom existed on the islands of Tiran and Sanafir, at the mouth of the Gulf of Aqaba. The Hebrew name of Tiran in those days was Yotvata. It did not take Ben-Gurion long to conclude, on the basis of this flimsy evidence, that Israel had a historic right to the Straits of Tiran, though as a reader of Greek he regretted not having Procopius in the original. The books were a gift from Moshe Dayan.[68]

The Israeli delegation to the secret talks included Ben-Gurion's military secretary, his doctor, Yosef Nachmias, Shimon Peres, Moshe Dayan, and Mordechai Bar-On. Bar-On, who had a degree in history, served as the secretary of the Israeli delegation and took copious notes throughout the conference. Several participants in the talks wrote about it subsequently, and Ben-Gurion recorded a great deal in his diary.[69] Bar-On, however, is the principal, most prolific, and most reliable chronicler of the conference.[70] The conference thus hatched not just the most famous but also the best-documented war plot in modern history.

The conference was held in a private villa in Sèvres, on the outskirts of Paris, and lasted from 22 to 24 October. At the ministerial level France was represented by Guy Mollet, Christian Pineau, and Maurice Bourgès-Maunoury; Britain, by Selwyn Lloyd. The first session started before the arrival of Lloyd, to enable the leaders of France and Israel to get to know each other and to have a preliminary discussion. Ben-Gurion opened the discussion by listing military, political, and moral considerations against "the British plan." His main objection was that Israel would be branded as the aggressor, while Britain and France would pose as peacemakers, but he was also exceedingly apprehensive about exposing Israeli cities to attack by the Egyptian air force. Instead, he presented a comprehensive plan, which he himself called "fantastic," for the reorganization of the Middle East. Jordan, he observed, was not viable as an independent state and should therefore be divided. Iraq would get the East Bank in return for a promise to settle the Palestinian refugees there and to make peace with Israel, while the West Bank would be attached to Israel as a semi-autonomous region. Lebanon suffered from having a large Muslim population, which was concentrated in the south. The problem could be solved by Israel's expansion up to the Litani River, thereby helping turn Lebanon into a Christian state. The Suez Canal area should be given international status, while the Straits of Tiran in the Gulf of Aqaba should come under Israeli control to ensure freedom of navigation. A prior condition for realizing this plan was the elimination of Nasser and his replacement with a pro-Western leader who would also be prepared to make peace with Israel.

Ben-Gurion argued that this plan would serve the interests of all the Western powers as well as those of Israel by destroying Nasser and the movement of Arab nationalism that he had unleashed. The Suez Canal would become an international waterway. Britain would restore its hegemony in Iraq and Jordan and secure its access to the oil of the Middle East. France would consolidate its influence in the Middle East through Lebanon and Israel, while its problems in Algeria would come to an end with the fall of Nasser. Even America might be persuaded to support the plan, for it would promote stable, pro-Western regimes and help check Soviet advances in the Middle East. Before rushing into a military campaign against Egypt, Ben-Gurion urged that they take time to consider the political possibilities. His plan might appear fantastic at first sight, he remarked, but it was not beyond the realm of possibility given time, British support, and good faith.

The French leaders listened patiently to Ben-Gurion's presentation but showed no disposition to be diverted from the immediate task of launching a military campaign against Egypt with British involvement. They assured Ben-Gurion that his plan was not fantastic but added that they had a unique opportunity to strike at their common enemy and that any delay might be fatal.

They also considered that while Eden himself was determined to fight, he faced growing opposition in the country and the cabinet, with Selwyn Lloyd showing a preference for a diplomatic solution. Lloyd was a reluctant conspirator. He did not like the idea of collusion with the Israelis and went to the meeting only because Eden had more or less ordered him to. His whole demeanor expressed distaste for the meeting, the company, and the agenda. He also found Ben-Gurion to be in a rather aggressive mood, indicating or implying that the Israelis had no reason to believe anything a British minister might say.

Whereas the purpose of the meeting was to discuss military action, Lloyd began by saying that, on the basis of his recent discussions with the Egyptian foreign minister, Mahmoud Fawzi, he estimated that a diplomatic solution to the dispute over the canal could be reached within a week. On the possibility of tripartite military action, Lloyd explained that his government could not go beyond the statement that Eden had made in the Palais Matignon on 16 October and subsequently confirmed in writing. In practical terms this meant that Israel would have to initiate a full-scale war and remain alone in the war for about seventy-two hours, while Britain issued an ultimatum to Israel that implied that Israel was the aggressor. It was, of course, precisely the role of the aggressor that Ben-Gurion did not want to play. The only encouraging element in what Lloyd had to say was the admission that his government wanted to destroy Nasser's regime. The one important drawback of a compromise with Egypt, he remarked, was that Nasser would remain in power. Lloyd defined the aim of any allied military operations as "the conquest of the Canal Zone and the destruction of Nasser."

When they got down to brass tacks, Ben-Gurion demanded an agreement between Britain, France, and Israel that all three should attack Egypt. He also wanted an undertaking that the Royal Air Force would eliminate the Egyptian air force before Israeli ground troops moved forward, because otherwise Israeli cities like Tel Aviv could be wiped out. Lloyd understood Ben-Gurion's anxiety but declined to cooperate directly with Israel. Throughout the meeting he tried to make it clear that an Israeli-French-British agreement to attack Egypt was impossible. All he agreed to was the French proposal that if Israel attacked Egypt, Britain and France would intervene to protect the canal. Since Ben-Gurion categorically rejected this proposal, the discussion reached a dead end.

At this critical juncture Dayan intervened to save the conference. Almost a year to the day had elapsed since Ben-Gurion had given him the order to provoke a war with Egypt. He was raring to go, with or without allies. Unlike Ben-Gurion, he discounted the danger of Israeli cities being bombed by the Egyptian air force. Having the whiff of battle in his nostrils, he was not about to go back quietly to his stable. The proposal he put forward was characteristically cunning. It envisaged an IDF paratroop drop in the Mitla Pass, thirty miles from the Suez Canal; an Anglo-French ultimatum to Egypt to evacuate its forces from the Canal Zone; and aerial bombardment of Egypt's airfields following the expected rejection of the ultimatum. The plan met both the British need for "a real act of war" to justify their intervention and Ben-Gurion's need for an escape route in the event that allied intervention failed to materialize. Lloyd had already given it as his private opinion that the gap between the Israeli attack and allied intervention could be reduced from seventy-two to thirty-six hours. The French now offered to station in Israel two squadrons of Mystère fighter-bombers and have two of their ships put into Israeli ports to protect Israeli's skies and coast in the first two days of fighting.

On the morning of 24 October, the third and last day of the conference, Ben-Gurion finally made up his mind to commit the IDF to the battle. In his diary he summarized the main considerations that led to this fateful decision. He thought that the operation had to be undertaken if Israel's skies could be effectively defended in the day or two that would elapse until the French and the British started bombing Egypt's airfields. The aim of destroying Nasser had pervaded the entire conference and was uppermost in Ben-Gurion's mind. "This is a unique opportunity," he wrote, "that two not so small powers will try to topple Nasser, and we shall not stand alone against him while he becomes stronger and conquers all the Arab countries . . . and *maybe* the whole situation in the Middle East will change according to my plan."[71]

When the negotiations and consultations were more or less completed, Ben-Gurion took the initiative in suggesting that a protocol be drawn up to summarize the decisions that had been reached and that this document be signed by the three parties and be binding on them.[72] The fact that the idea for drawing up a formal document came from Ben-Gurion is worth underlining because it is glossed over in the firsthand Israeli accounts of the meeting, presumably with the intention of minimizing his part in the collusion. A complete draft was prepared by a group of Israeli and French officials and presented to Patrick Dean, the deputy undersecretary at the Foreign Office, and Donald Logan, Selwyn Lloyd's private secretary, who came to represent Britain without their political master on the last day of the conference. Dean and Logan were surprised to see the draft because there had been no earlier mention of committing anything to paper. But Logan told Dean that it was an accurate record of what had been agreed, and both of them thought that it might be useful to have a record since otherwise misunderstandings could develop over what was a rather elaborate scenario.[73]

While the drafting was in progress, two other private conversations took place elsewhere in the villa. Ben-Gurion had a conversation with his French opposite number at which no one else was present. In his diary Ben-Gurion recorded the next day, "I told him about the discovery of oil in southern and western Sinai, and that it would be good to tear this peninsula from Egypt because it did not belong to her; rather it was the English who stole it from the Turks when they believed that Egypt was in their pocket. I suggested laying down a pipeline from Sinai to Haifa to refine the oil, and Mollet showed interest in this suggestion."[74] In the absence of any other record of this conversation, one is left with the impression that the Israeli prime minister was being his usual expansionist self, while his French counterpart was the polite host to the very end.

An even more intriguing conversation took place at the end of this one. It concerned French assistance to Israel in developing nuclear technology. Details of this second conversation emerged only in 1995 when Shimon Peres published his memoirs. The relevant passage reads as follows:

> Before the final signing, I asked Ben-Gurion for a brief adjournment, during which I met Mollet and Bourges-Maunoury alone. It was here that I finalized with these two leaders an agreement for the building of a nuclear reactor at Dimona, in southern Israel . . . and the supply of natural uranium to fuel it. I put forward a series of detailed proposals and, after discussion, they accepted them.[75]

The development of nuclear power was a subject dear to Ben-Gurion's heart. He saw in it a technological challenge that would help transform Israel into an advanced industrial state. The negotiations with the French were about a small nuclear reactor for civilian purposes. Nothing was said at this stage about possible military applications of this technology. But that was Ben-Gurion's ultimate aim: to produce nuclear weapons. He believed that nuclear weapons would strengthen Israel immeasurably, secure its survival, and eliminate any danger of another Holocaust.

Shimon Peres was the moving force behind the Israeli attempt to get French help in building a nuclear reactor. Pineau opposed this request, Bourgès-Maunoury strongly supported it, and Mollet was undecided. On 21 September, a month before the Sèvres meeting, Peres reached an agreement with the French on the supply of a small nuclear reactor. He used the occasion of Sèvres to try to commit France at the political level. The broaching of the nuclear issue by Peres at Sèvres could thus not have come as a complete surprise. A year later, in September 1957, when Bourgès-Maunoury was prime minister, France delivered to Israel a nuclear reactor with twice the capacity previously promised.[76]

Israel did not join in the Franco-British war plot in order to get a French nuclear reactor. The sensitive question of nuclear power was raised only toward the end of the conference and after the basic decision to go to war had been taken. Nevertheless, the nuclear deal concluded at the private meeting at Sèvres is interesting for three main reasons. First, it shows that the French were determined to go to war at almost any price. Secondly, it reveals the full extent of the incentives the French were prepared to give Israel in order to induce it to play the part assigned to it in the war plot against Egypt. Third, it confirms the impression that Israel did not face any serious danger from Egypt at that time but nevertheless colluded with the European powers to attack Egypt for other reasons. Taken together, the two private conversations at Sèvres thus drive a coach and horses through the official version, which says that Israel went to war only because it faced an imminent danger of attack from Egypt.

The tripartite war plot was now embodied in a formal document, the Protocol of Sèvres, which the representatives of the three parties were called upon to sign. Pineau did so for France, Ben-Gurion for Israel, and Patrick Dean for Britain. Dean made it clear that he was signing *ad referendum,* subject to the approval of his government. Although the protocol had to be ratified by all three governments, Ben-Gurion made no effort to conceal his excitement. He studied it, folded it carefully, and thrust it deep into the pocket of his waistcoat.

The Protocol of Sèvres gave Ben-Gurion the guarantee he desperately wanted against British betrayal, but it also constituted the smoking gun of the tripartite collusion. There were three copies. The British copy was destroyed on Eden's orders, the French copy was lost, and the Israeli copy was kept under lock and key in the Ben-Gurion Archive in Sede-Boker for forty years. In 1996 the original French text of the protocol was released for the first time, for a BBC documentary on the Suez crisis.[77]

The Protocol of Sèvres consisted of seven articles. The first simply stated that Israel would launch a large-scale attack in the evening of 29 October with the aim of reaching the Canal Zone the following day. Article 2 described the Anglo-French appeals to the belligerents to stop fighting and to withdraw their forces to a distance of ten miles from the canal. Egypt alone was asked to accept the temporary occupation of key positions on the canal by the Anglo-French forces. This demand was inserted in order to ensure that Egypt could not possibly accept the appeal. Article 3 stated that if Egypt failed to comply within twelve hours, the Anglo-French attack on the Egyptian forces would be launched in the early hours in the morning on 31 October. This article abandoned the pretence to evenhandedness. No military action against Israel was envisaged.

Article 4 noted the intention of the Israeli government to occupy the western shore of the Gulf of Aqaba and the islands of Tiran and Sanafir in order to ensure freedom of navigation. The British and French governments did not undertake to support this plan, but neither did they express any opposition to it. In Article 5 Israel promised not to attack Jordan during the period of hostilities against Egypt, and Britain promised not to help Jordan if it attacked Israel. The purpose of this provision was to minimize the risk of a military clash between Israel and Britain on the Jordanian front. Article 6 required all three governments to keep the provisions of the accord strictly secret. Finally, Article 7 stated that the provisions of the protocol would enter into force as soon as they had been confirmed by the three governments.[78]

During the three days he spent at Sèvres, hatching the war plot against Egypt, Ben-Gurion completely reversed his position. He arrived at the villa swearing that he would have nothing to do with "the British plan" and insisting on an equal partnership with the European powers. He left the villa having accepted a modified form of this plan. Mordechai Bar-On attributes this reversal to three factors: the pressure of the French and Ben-Gurion's own desire to consolidate the unwritten alliance with France, Dayan's psychological skills in enabling Ben-Gurion to overcome his fears

and suspicions, and the fact that the piece of paper itself arose out
of a face-to-face meeting with the British foreign secretary and
was signed by a senior British official.[79]

Abba Eban has remarked, "At Sèvres, the three groups of leaders decided on a grotesquely eccentric plan."[80] Nothing, however,
was more eccentric than the big plan that Ben-Gurion tried to sell
the French leaders at their first meeting in the suburban villa.
Mordechai Bar-On remembers the embarrassment he felt at hearing his leader present a plan that was so bizarre and so remote from
the immediate purpose for which they had come.[81] The other
Israeli participants also regarded the plan as a long shot and an example of the old man's political imagination running away with
him. Ben-Gurion himself disarmed criticism by calling his plan
"fantastic." Yet his own diary reveals that he was deadly earnest
about it and thought it had a realistic chance of being put into
practice.[82]

The plan is thus highly revealing of Ben-Gurion's inner
thoughts about Israel, the European powers, and the Arab world.
It revealed his craving for an alliance with the imperialist powers
against the forces of Arab nationalism. It exposed an appetite for
territorial expansion at the expense of the Arabs and expansion in
every possible direction: north, east, and south. And it exhibited
a cavalier attitude toward the independence, sovereignty, and territorial integrity of the neighboring Arab states.

THE SINAI CAMPAIGN

Upon their return home Dayan prepared the IDF for war, while
Ben-Gurion prepared the government. He informed first the
Mapai and Ahdut Ha'avodah ministers and then those who represented the National Religious Party and the Progressive Party. He
did not inform the representatives of Mapam until the last moment, because he knew they would be opposed and he feared they
would leak the news. A cabinet meeting was convened on 28
October, the day before the campaign was due to be launched.
Ben-Gurion had not planned to inform the cabinet about the
agreement with the French and the British, but the Ahdut
Ha'avodah ministers insisted that he did. The cabinet approved the
proposal to go to war with Egypt by a large majority. Only the two
Mapam ministers voted against it: they objected to the link with
the colonial powers. They decided, however, to stay in the government and to share in the collective responsibility for the deci-

sion. Menachem Begin, the Herut leader, lent the war plan his enthusiastic support when he heard about it from Ben-Gurion.

On 29 October, in the afternoon, the IDF launched the Sinai Campaign with a paratroop drop in the Mitla Pass. On 30 October, before the IDF forces reached the Suez Canal, Britain and France issued their pre-arranged ultimata to Israel and Egypt, demanding that they withdraw their forces to a distance of ten miles from the canal. Israel accepted the ultimatum; Egypt, as expected, did not. Britain and France began aerial bombardment of the Egyptian airfields during the evening of 31 October instead of at dawn as planned. Ben-Gurion was so anxious and so angry about the delay that he threatened to call off the attack. Despite the vacillation and delays that continued to characterize the military operations of the allies, the IDF achieved a complete military victory within a few days. The Egyptian forces in Sinai and the Gaza Strip withdrew in haste across the Suez Canal, leaving nearly six thousand prisoners and large quantities of military equipment in Israeli hands. By giving the order to withdraw, Nasser minimized the losses to his army. Gaza was captured on 2 November and, by 5 November the whole peninsula was in Israeli hands (see map 6). For the British and the French the Suez escapade ended in a hasty and humiliating retreat. Strong pressure from the superpowers made them halt the attack. John Foster Dulles led the pack against them, and against their Israeli proxy, at the United Nations. American economic pressure forced the British government to turn tail, leaving the French in the lurch.

Although Ben-Gurion had been confined to his sickbed during the entire campaign, he was drunk with victory when it ended. In a cable he sent to the Seventh Brigade following the capture of Sharm el-Sheikh, he wrote, "Yotvata, or Tiran, which until fourteen hundred years ago was part of an independent Jewish state, will revert to being part of the third kingdom of Israel." In his victory speech at the Knesset on 7 November, he hinted that Israel planned to annex the entire Sinai peninsula as well as the Straits of Tiran. Once again he laid a historical claim to the island of Tiran or Yotvata and even quoted from the ancient chronicler Procopius in Greek in support of his claim. In the speech he affirmed triumphantly that the armistice agreement with Egypt was dead, that Israel would not hand over Sinai to foreign forces, and that Israel was ready for direct negotiations with Egypt. The arrogant tone of the speech caused much anger and antipathy outside Israel, not least among American Jews.

Pride comes before the fall. Ben-Gurion's euphoria about the

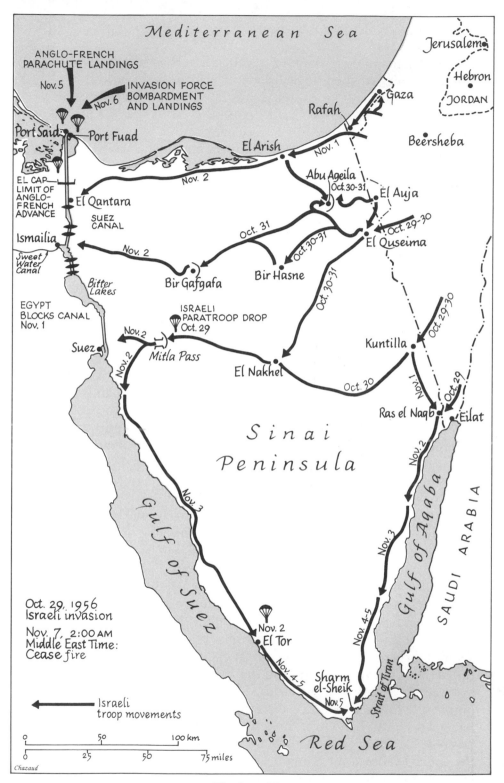

The Suez War

speed and scope of Israel's military victory was short-lived. No sooner had the campaign ended than Israel was subjected to heavy pressure from both superpowers to withdraw immediately and unconditionally from the Sinai peninsula and the Gaza Strip. On 5 November, Nikolai Bulganin, the Soviet premier, sent letters to Britain, France, and Israel threatening them with rocket attacks and promising volunteers to help the Egyptian army. The letter to Ben-Gurion was particularly brutal in its language. It accused the government of Israel of "criminally and irresponsibly playing with the fate of the world" and of placing in question the very existence of the State of Israel. In his diary Ben-Gurion recorded that the letter could have been written by Adolf Hitler.[83] The letter was accompanied by a war of nerves and rumors of preparations for Soviet military intervention. Yosef Avidar, the ambassador to Moscow, who was in Israel at the time, assured Ben-Gurion that Bulganin was bluffing.[84] Ben-Gurion, however, could not discount the risk that the crisis might escalate overnight to a potential global war for which Israel would be held responsible.[85] He dispatched Golda Meir and Shimon Peres to Paris to obtain the French assessment and, if possible, an assurance of assistance. Golda Meir quickly discovered that Christian Pineau took the Soviet threat seriously and that, although sympathetic, was unable to assure Israel of any assistance. She brought up an idea that Ben-Gurion had mentioned at Sèvres: joint oil production in Sinai on equal terms. By her own account Pineau looked at her as if she were crazy and said, "Soviet pilots are flying over Syria's skies. The Russians want to intervene in the Middle East, and you are still thinking about the oil in Sinai?"[86]

Ben-Gurion briefly toyed with the idea of turning to the United States for protection, although President Eisenhower was fuming with anger at having been deceived by the three nations. He thought that at a private meeting he could persuade Eisenhower to see things his way, but Abba Eban advised him that in the current climate it was pointless even to suggest a meeting. The Eisenhower administration insisted on unconditional Israeli withdrawal. Privately Eban was told that if Israel did not withdraw, all official aid from the U.S. government and private aid from American Jewry would be cut off and that the United States would not oppose the expulsion of Israel from the UN. These economic sanctions were threatened after the United States had already removed Israel's—as well as Britain's and France's—protective shield against possible Soviet retaliation. Ben-Gurion was bitterly disappointed, but he agreed to withdraw. He had grossly misread the international situation and now had to pay the price.[87]

The cabinet spent seven hours on 8 November in fraught and tense discussions. There was a genuine fear that a world war would break out as a result of the Soviet rocket rattling. The level of anxiety was unprecedented in Israel's history, and it paralyzed the cabinet. Its decision was—to leave the decision to Ben-Gurion. He decided to withdraw from Sinai—in principle.[88] He was on the point of announcing Israel's immediate and unconditional withdrawal when Eban intervened with a suggestion. His idea was to make Israeli withdrawal conditional on satisfactory arrangements being made for a UN force to take over. Ben-Gurion was in a panic because Israel was completely isolated in face of the Soviet threats. Pressure from the UN reached its climax that morning when the secretary-general spoke of dire consequences for Israel. In the end Ben-Gurion adopted Eban's suggestion, although he considered it rather risky. Ironically, Ben-Gurion, the proponent of the view that it does not matter what the Gentiles say, seemed very frightened of what the Gentiles were saying on this occasion. Eban, the disciple of Moshe Sharett, had the correct reading of the international situation, and it was he who stepped in to pick up the pieces.[89]

At half past midnight on 8 November, a weary and dejected prime minister announced the decision to withdraw in a radio broadcast to his people. The euphoria of the victory speech had disappeared without trace. To underscore Israel's isolation he read the letters he had received from Bulganin and Eisenhower and his replies to them. He also recounted the other events of the day: the UN resolutions, the cabinet meeting, and the decision to withdraw the Israeli forces from all occupied territory upon conclusion of satisfactory arrangements with the UN in connection with an international force. The third kingdom of Israel had lasted three days.

The struggle to salvage something from the political wreckage of the Sinai Campaign lasted four months and was brilliantly masterminded by Abba Eban. The directive he received from Ben-Gurion was to concentrate on two aims: to ensure Israel's freedom to navigate the Straits of Tiran and the Red Sea and to ensure that the Negev would not be exposed again to terrorist raids from Gaza. In his memoirs Eban confesses that he "felt exhilarated at being able to pursue these difficult but attainable goals without the impediment of attachment to an Anglo-French connection expressed in the ludicrous accord reached at Sèvres." Ben-Gurion did not really want to keep the Gaza Strip, because it contained 350,000 disgruntled and disorderly Arabs. He wanted to use Israel's occupation of Gaza as a bargaining card for retaining Sharm el-Sheikh. In the end Israel was forced to withdraw from Sharm el-Sheikh as well as the Gaza Strip. For Moshe Dayan this was a bitter pill to swallow. He gave orders to destroy all the Egyptian military installations in Sinai before the final withdrawal in early March 1957. Eban, on the other hand, felt that both of Ben-Gurion's objectives had been achieved when he read Dulles's memorandum of 11 February. The United States promised to support Israel's right to send its own ships and cargoes without impediment through the Straits of Tiran; to acknowledge that if Egypt renewed the blockade, Israel would be entitled to exercise its "inherent right to self-defense under Article Fifty-one of the UN Charter"; and to maintain UN forces in Sharm el-Sheikh and Gaza until such time as their removal would not lead to the renewal of belligerency.[90]

In drawing up the balance sheet of the Sinai Campaign, one must distinguish between its concrete operational objectives and its broader political aims. There were three operational objectives and three political aims. The three operational objectives were to defeat the Egyptian army, to open up the Straits of Tiran to Israeli shipping, and to put an end to fedayeen attacks across Israel's southern border. All three objectives were achieved to some extent. First of all, the Israeli army won a clear military victory. The Egyptian army was defeated, but not destroyed, as a result of its timely withdrawal from Sinai. Yet the damage to Egypt's army was slight and quickly repaired. Nevertheless, the Sinai Campaign raised the morale and prestige of the IDF and established it as the strongest military force in the Middle East. The second objective was also achieved. The international waterway that passes through the Straits of Tiran was opened up to Israeli shipping. An American assurance was obtained that the closing of the straits would constitute a casus belli. This assurance turned out to be rather hollow when Nasser closed the straits again in May 1967, but that could not have been foreseen in 1956. There was a hope that the campaign would also lift the ban on Israeli shipping through the Suez Canal, but this hope was not realized. The third objective was achieved more fully. The fedayeen bases in Gaza were destroyed, and fedayeen attacks across the border ceased. Moreover, the Egyptian army did not return to its bases in Sinai. The Sinai peninsula thus became effectively demilitarized. Israel was to enjoy eleven years of relative security and stability along the border with Egypt.

The three political aims behind the Sinai Campaign were the overthrow of Nasser, the expansion of Israel's borders, and the establishment of a new political order in the Middle East. None of these aims was realized. The tripartite aggression not only failed to bring about Nasser's downfall; it greatly increased his prestige and influence in the region and in the Third World. Nasser snatched a most spectacular political victory out of the jaws of military defeat. Israel, on the other hand, paid a heavy political price for ganging up with the colonial powers against the emergent forces of Arab nationalism. The collusion seemed to provide the decisive proof of the reactionary and expansionist character of the Zionist movement. Israel's reputation was seriously tarnished. Its own actions could henceforth be used as proof of the long-standing claim that it was a bridgehead of Western imperialism in the midst of the Arab world.

Second, it was hoped that the Sinai Campaign would enable Israel to extend her borders, and some of these territorial ambitions were even recorded in the Protocol of Sèvres. The highest priority was attached to Sharm el-Sheikh and a land link with it, but there was also a desire to retain the whole of the Sinai peninsula, and Ben-Gurion said as much in his victory speech. None of these ambitions was realized. Israel was forced to disgorge all the territory it had conquered, and the status quo ante was restored. The only minor change concerned the demilitarized zone in El-Auja. Israel no longer recognized its special status and treated it from now on as if it belonged to Israel. In general, the initiators of the Sinai Campaign planned it as the last battle of the 1948 war—a battle to achieve satisfactory borders. Yet the actual result was the exact opposite of these intentions. The Sinai Campaign was the last battle of the 1948 war in the sense that it confirmed and consolidated the territorial status quo that had been reached at the end of that war.

The third aim was to create a new political order in the Middle East. This was Ben-Gurion's "fantastic" plan or grand design. The two strands to this grand design were the territorial and the political. Neither of them came anywhere near realization. The territorial strand called for Israel's expansion to the Suez Canal and Sharm el-Sheikh in the south, to the Jordan river in the east, and to the Litani River in the north. The political strand of the grand design was closely related to the territorial strand. Here the thinking was that a Christian Lebanon would of its own accord make peace with Israel; that Iraq would be allowed to take over the East Bank of Jordan on condition that it made peace with Israel; and that a defeated, humiliated, and occupied Egypt would be compelled to make peace on Israel's terms. This was all pie in the sky.

Despite all the political miscalculations and failures of those who planned the Sinai Campaign, it is their version that became firmly entrenched in the mind of the overwhelming majority of Israelis. The popular perception of the 1956 war in Israel is that it was a defensive war, a just war, a brilliantly executed war, and a war that achieved nearly all of its objectives. This version of the war was propagated not only by members of the Israeli defense establishment but by a host of sympathetic historians, journalists, and commentators. However deeply cherished, this version does not stand up to scrutiny in the light of the evidence now available. It is a striking example of the way in which history can be manipulated to serve nationalist ends. The official Israeli version of the 1956 war, like that of the 1948 war, is little more than the propaganda of the victors.

The Sinai Campaign was a major watershed in Israel's relations with the Arab world. In the years 1953–56 a great internal battle raged between the moderates and the activists, between the proponents of diplomacy and the proponents of military force, between the school of negotiation and the school of retaliation. In June 1956 Ben-Gurion forced Sharett's resignation in order to give himself the option of launching a war against Egypt. In October 1956 he exercised this option. Any prospect Sharett might have had of making a political comeback was now irreversibly shattered. Sharett had advocated an alternative to the hard-line policy of Ben-Gurion. This alternative policy was not given a chance. It was defeated by the Israeli defense establishment. The Sinai Campaign drove the last nail into the coffin of the moderate alternative represented by Sharett. Ben-Gurion failed to topple Nasser but he succeeded in toppling Sharett.

5

The Alliance of the Periphery

1957–1963

THE SUEZ WAR did not produce permanent territorial changes in the Middle East, but it had profound repercussions for the balance of power between Israel and the Arab world, between East and West, and between the conservative and radical forces within the Arab world. Israel was the clear winner in the military contest with Egypt, and the result was to boost national self-confidence, enhance the deterrent power of the IDF, and confirm Israel as a major military power in the Middle East. On the other hand, the change in the power relations between East and West worked in favor of the Arabs. The Suez War undermined the cohesion of the Western alliance, caused the collapse of British and French influence in the Middle East, and paved the way to further Soviet advances in the region.

Less immediately obvious but no less significant was the shift in the balance of power within the Arab world. Side by side with the global Cold War between East and West, an Arab cold war had been going on between the radical forces and the conservative forces. The Suez War was a decisive victory for the radical forces, led by Egypt, against the conservative and pro-Western forces, notably Iraq and Jordan. Gamal Abdel Nasser emerged as the undisputed leader of the Arab world in the aftermath of the war, which was seen as an imperialist-Zionist plot against the Arab nation. Nasser's own attitude toward Israel hardened as a result of the war. Suez confirmed his worst fears and suspicions about Israel.

After Suez he identified Israel and the European powers as one enemy and repeatedly stated that the Arabs had to fight both Israel and the powers that stood behind it.

Another consequence of Suez was to deepen Nasser's involvement in the Palestine question. Ever since the Arab League had been founded in 1945, the two main items on its agenda were Arab unity and the Palestine question. The Suez War prompted, or at least enabled, Nasser to merge these two subjects into one. His aim was to forge a cohesive, active, and militant Pan-Arab movement, and he started to present the liberation of Palestine as the principal goal of this movement. In the past he used to talk about the need to find a solution to the problem of the Palestinian refugees, whereas after 1956 he began to talk about the liberation of Palestine and took the lead in establishing the Palestine Liberation Organization (PLO) in 1964. He gave the Palestine problem a Pan-Arab dimension and called for mobilizing all the resources of the Arab world for the fight with Israel and countries that supported it. The containment of Israel became a Pan-Arab goal.[1]

REASSESSMENT AND REALIGNMENT

The conventional wisdom maintains that the Sinai Campaign gave Israel eleven years of peace. This is true in the limited sense that Nasser kept the border with Israel quiet while working to change the military balance of power in favor of the Arabs. But the conventional wisdom is wrong inasmuch as the Suez War further envenomed and deepened the conflict between the Arab world and Israel.

On the Israeli side the undisputed leader and the principal decision maker in defense and foreign affairs was David Ben-Gurion.[2] His prestige and political power were greatly enhanced by victory over Egypt in 1956. He could command a majority for almost anything he proposed in his party, in the cabinet, and in the Knesset, although on controversial matters he would sometimes resort to a threat of resignation in order to have his way. Some sensitive issues, such as a defense pact with the United States and the development of a nuclear capacity, he did not refer to the cabinet at all. His power was so great that his coalition partners used to joke that he submitted proposals to the cabinet only when he wanted them to be defeated.[3]

In Golda Meir, Ben-Gurion had a foreign minister after his own heart, and he liked to boast that she was the only man in his cabinet. Golda, as she was popularly known, had no distinctive views of her own on the Arab-Israeli conflict. She was Ben-Gurion's disciple and followed his lead on all major policy issues. There was constant tension, however, between Golda and Shimon Peres. Peres was the chief architect and chief advocate of a European orientation in Israel's foreign policy, whereas Golda was committed to an American orientation. But the real source of tension was Peres's conduct of the diplomacy relating to the acquisition of arms without consulting or informing the foreign minister. Ben-Gurion was more interested in results than in correct procedures and departmental jurisdictions, yet from time to time he would intervene to smooth Golda's ruffled feathers.

Ben-Gurion experienced no difficulty in asserting his authority over the IDF after the controversial withdrawal from Sinai. Moshe Dayan continued to hold independent views and to exert a strong influence in matters of high policy, but he was succeeded as chief of staff by Major General Chaim Laskov in January 1958. Laskov was a straightforward officer who had served in the British army during World War II and who did not meddle in politics. He concerned himself only with the military aspects of the Arab-Israeli conflict and went about his job in a thoroughly professional manner, winning the respect and affection of his political master. In the period 1957–63 Ben-Gurion thus enjoyed a near-monopoly in the making of foreign and defense policy.

The main lesson that Ben-Gurion drew from the Suez War was that Israel could not realistically hope to expand its territory at the expense of its neighbors. He learned the hard way that in the modern world military conquest did not necessarily confer the right to retain territory, and he came to accept the territorial status quo enshrined in the 1949 armistice agreements as permanent. As an alternative to territorial expansion, he adopted a strategy of deterrence. The aim of this strategy was to deter Arab parties from trying to change the status quo by force; the means was to equip the IDF with the most advanced weapons in order to maintain its qualitative superiority over the Arab armies.

While deterrence was one major theme in Ben-Gurion's post-Suez strategy, the quest for external guarantees of Israel's security was another. He was acutely aware of Israel's international isolation in the aftermath of Suez, especially in the face of the growing danger represented by the Soviet Union. Bulganin's letter of 5

November 1956 gave startling evidence of the shift in the Kremlin's attitude toward Israel. Although the Anglo-French expedition was halted as a result of American pressure rather than Soviet threats, the Soviets received most of the credit in the Arab world. Ben-Gurion feared that the Soviet Union would try to extend its influence in the region by supporting and arming the radical Arab regimes most hostile to Israel. Against this danger there was a limit to what Israel could do on its own. Israel was up against a world power and therefore had to have a world power on its side.

David Ben-Gurion turned to America, the other main protagonist in the Cold War. From America he hoped to obtain arms, political backing, and a security guarantee. He couched his appeals for help in Cold War rhetoric about the dangers posed by international communism, rhetoric calculated to appeal to John Foster Dulles in particular. His appeals for help were usually accompanied by the suggestion of a common stand against the Soviet Union and its Arab allies. The Americans, however, remained cool and distant. Their policy was to keep the military balance of power from being upset, and since, in their estimate, Israel was already stronger than its neighbors, they declined to become its chief arms supplier. Political considerations also accounted for their coolness. They wanted Arab support for their global policy of containment against the Soviet Union and thought they had a better chance of achieving this on their own than in alliance with Israel. Oil was another factor: the Americans kept Israel at arm's length in order to ensure easy access to Arab oil.

The Eisenhower Doctrine, proclaimed on 5 January 1957, gave Israel an opening for improving relations with the United States. This doctrine promised military aid and cooperation to Middle Eastern countries, Israel included, against overt aggression from any nation "controlled by international Communism." Middle Eastern states were invited to associate themselves with the Eisenhower Doctrine. Official opinion in Israel was divided. Mapai, the ruling party, represented the mainstream in favoring an association. Mapai's left-wing coalition partners, Mapam and Ahdut Ha'avodah, balked at an open identification with one side in the Cold War, especially as there was no concrete advantage in doing so. Ben-Gurion was for accepting the invitation, although it fell well short of a formal American security guarantee. In the end a compromise was reached, and the government issued a deliberately vague statement of support for the Eisenhower Doctrine.

Deepening Soviet involvement in Syria in the summer of 1957

gave Israel an opportunity to put the Eisenhower Doctrine to the test. Syrian politics took a sharp pro-Soviet turn when an arms deal was concluded between the two countries. At the same time tension built up along the Syrian-Israeli border as a result of incidents in which several Israeli civilians were killed. Ben-Gurion thought there was a real possibility that Syria would become a "people's republic" and join the Eastern bloc and thus put Israel face-to-face with the Soviet Union. He disputed Dayan's assessment that an Arab attack on Israel was unlikely. In his opinion, the Soviet Union was preparing an attack on Israel through Syria. He saw Soviet references to Israeli troop deployment on the northern front as an attempt to procure an alibi for an attack or a provocation.[4]

Ben-Gurion did not think of a preventive war, but when intelligence reached him that the Americans were encouraging a coup in Syria, he wanted to join in the act. In August, Isser Harel, the head of the Mossad, wrote to Allen Dulles, the director of the CIA, to suggest joint action to prevent further Soviet penetration of the Middle East. The American reply came in the form of a letter from John Foster Dulles to David Ben-Gurion. Dulles ignored the suggestion of joint action and instead asked for assurances that Israel would not take independent action against Syria. Ben-Gurion replied immediately, to stress the dangers to the free world in general and Israel in particular if international communism was to establish a base in the heart of the Middle East, to renew the plea for joint action, and to assure Dulles that Israel could be relied upon to behave discreetly and responsibly. At the end of August, Harel received a reply from Allen Dulles, who had been abroad. The reply was evasive and essentially negative. The Americans were ready to listen to the views of Israel and to receive intelligence from it, but they were anxious to avoid any active cooperation with Israel in relation to the Arab world.[5] Ben-Gurion got the hint and was from then on careful not to embark on any ventures against Arab countries without clearing them with the Americans in advance.

But the lack of an explicit Western security guarantee continued to worry Ben-Gurion, and in the autumn of 1957 he embarked on a diplomatic campaign to associate Israel with the North Atlantic Treaty Organization (NATO). The aim of the campaign was not official membership, which was clearly out of the question, but close association and coordination of defense plans. Dayan was opposed to the idea not because he did not want cooperation with NATO but because he thought it would be demeaning to beg. His views were rejected. Ben-Gurion was so desperate to find shelter under the NATO umbrella that he sent Golda Meir to talk to Dulles and special emissaries to plead Israel's case in Paris, Bonn, and The Hague. The French were sympathetic. But in December 1957, under strong pressure from America, the NATO Council rejected Israel's request for association.

Even after this humiliating rebuff, Ben-Gurion continued his efforts to persuade the Americans to issue a statement that they would come to Israel's aid in the event of a Soviet or Soviet-backed attack. He explained his motives to an American visitor: "When we are isolated, the Arabs think that we can be destroyed and the Soviets exploit this card. If a great power stood behind us, and the Arabs knew that we are a fact that cannot be altered—Russia would cease its hostility toward us, because this hostility would no longer buy the heart of the Arabs."[6]

Since the American position remained unchanged, the Israelis turned to Western Europe in their search for allies and new sources of arms. The honeymoon in the relations between Israel and France continued after the Suez expedition. France continued to serve as Israel's chief arms supplier, and there was close cooperation between the two countries in the cultural as well as the political, military, and intelligence spheres. Ordinary Israelis had a sense that in France they had found a genuine and loyal friend. Ben-Gurion, however, had his doubts about the wisdom of relying exclusively on the French. He recognized that French policy could change either as a result of a change of government in France or because of developments in North Africa. Britain agreed to sell Israel tanks, armored troop carriers, and even submarines, but it expected payment in full. Although the horrors of the Holocaust were still fresh in Israeli minds, Ben-Gurion therefore began to turn to Germany as the most promising source of arms and of economic help in meeting Israel's heavy defense burden.

The Federal Republic of Germany had already concluded a reparations agreement with Israel in 1952. In the autumn of 1957 Shimon Peres went on a secret trip and persuaded the German government to add military assistance to the economic aid it had been giving. Peres termed the friendship with Germany as "friendship for a rainy day." This was an indirect reference to the possibility that the flow of arms from France would cease. Ben-Gurion, for his part, spoke of "a different Germany" that had emerged after the defeat of Nazi Germany. He and Peres were united by the conviction that the support of the new Germany was crucial to Israel's security in the long term. They therefore cultivated this "friendship for a rainy day" in the teeth of very strong opposition in the government, in the Knesset, and among the public at large.

Israeli unity was restored in February 1958 when Egypt and Syria merged to form the United Arab Republic (UAR). The initiative for the union came from a group of Syrian leaders who wanted to stop the drift toward communism at home. But the pro-Western regimes in the Middle East saw the union as a threat to their security. Iraq and Jordan formed a loose Hashemite union, the better to protect themselves against the spread of the Nasserist tide. In Israel the Egyptian-Syrian union was viewed somewhat differently, as an attempt to encircle the country and to intensify Arab pressure on it. Ben-Gurion saw the union as a nutcracker, closing in on Israel from above and below. In fact, the merger did not change the military balance between the Arabs and Israel. But Yehoshafat Harkabi, the director of military intelligence, overreacted to this development. He considered it a serious danger to Israel's security, and Ben-Gurion was influenced by his assessment.[7] Harkabi always proceeded on the basis of worst-case scenarios not only because it was his professional duty but also because of his character. Like Ben-Gurion, he was diminutive in stature and, like him, was haunted by fear and foreboding about Israel's prospects of survival. On one occasion he said to Ben-Gurion, "What we have in common is that neither of us believes that the State of Israel really exists." Ben-Gurion's response consisted of a grunt, which Harkabi was left to interpret any way he liked.[8]

THE ALLIANCE OF THE PERIPHERY

One of the most important, interesting, and overlooked developments in Israel's policy toward the Arab world in the decade after the Suez War was the alliance of the periphery.[9] The basic idea was to leapfrog over the immediate circle of hostile Arab states by forming alliances with Iran, Turkey, and Ethiopia. Iran and Turkey were Islamic but non-Arab states, while Ethiopia was a Christian country in Africa. What all these states had in common was fear of the Soviet Union and of Nasser's brand of Arab radicalism. The alliance of the periphery rested on the principle "My enemy's enemy is my friend." Its two main aims were to check Soviet advances in the Middle East and to curb the spread of Nasser's influence in Asia and Africa.

The idea of the alliance of the periphery was developed by Ben-Gurion and his close advisers after it became clear that territorial expansion was not possible and that an American security guarantee was improbable. The alliance aimed not to change the status quo but to preserve the status quo against subversion by radical forces. It was an attempt to strengthen Israeli deterrence, to reduce Israel's isolation, and to add to its influence and power as an actor on the international stage. But the alliance of the periphery was not an alliance in the conventional diplomatic sense of the word. In fact, Israel did not have normal diplomatic relations with any of the countries involved. The alliance was an informal one, consisting for the most part of secret and clandestine contacts. Although the Foreign Ministry and the IDF were given support roles, the Mossad had the primary responsibility for developing the alliance.

The two individuals most instrumental in promoting the alliance of periphery were Reuven Shiloah and Isser Harel. Shiloah was the main architect and the driving force behind it. He had been head of the Mossad in 1948–52 and counselor at the Israeli embassy in Washington in 1953–57. In September 1957 he was appointed political adviser to Golda Mcir and head of a political planning committee that consisted of senior officials from the Foreign Ministry and representatives from the IDF and the Mossad. Throughout his career he operated behind the scenes and avoided the limelight. His particular approach to strengthening Zionist power in the pre-Independence period was to cultivate powerful friends and allies, to develop Jewish intelligence services, and to plan special operations. In the 1930s he began to explore avenues for intelligence and strategic cooperation, first with Britain and later with America. His long-term aim was to turn the State of Israel, with the help of world Jewry, into a major intelligence force in regional and international politics and to persuade the Western powers that Israel was a strategic asset. His real strength lay not in the conduct of operations but in political planning, in devising strategies suited to Israel's peculiar conditions as a small state surrounded by enemies. After his return from Washington, his fertile political mind continued to work in the same direction. He helped lay the conceptual foundations for Israel's strategy in world politics. The two main pillars in his conception were the alliance of the periphery and the alliance with the United States.[10]

For Shiloah the alliance of the periphery was not just a political strategy but an ideological response to Nasser's doctrine of the three circles. Nasser's doctrine portrayed Egypt as standing at the center of three circles—the Arab, Islamic, and African circles. It was a monolithic concept of the Middle East that posited Egypt as the dominant power and Pan-Arabism as the dominant ideology. The alliance of the periphery challenged this concept at two levels. At the political level it sought to build an outer ring of states linked to Israel; at the ideological level it put forward the idea of a pluralistic region that was not organized by Pan-Arabism or Pan-Islam.

The other major promoter of the alliance of the periphery was Isser Harel, who had succeeded Shiloah as head of the Mossad in 1952. Whereas Shiloah was given to flights of fancy, Harel was a dour and down-to-earth intelligence chief whose strength lay not in analysis but in the conduct of operations. Born in Russia in 1912, Harel emigrated to Palestine in 1931 but retained a strong anti-Soviet sentiment, which made him an enemy of the left-wing parties inside Israel and a staunch supporter of the United States in the Cold War. Like Shiloah, Harel wanted to turn Israel into an ally of America in the global contest against the Soviet Union and in the regional contest against the Arab radicalism.

It was America's rejection of Harel's offer of secret cooperation to block the expansion of Nasser's influence that led him to embark on the creation of a belt of states around the periphery of the Middle East and Africa. He viewed Nasser as a dangerous dictator who, in the style of Hitler, sought to extend his personal influence abroad by the use of agents, assassination squads, subversion, and propaganda. His aim was to erect a dam against the Nasserist-Soviet flood. And since Nasser's main instrument—like that of communism—was subversion and organizing fifth columns, it was essential to take effective measures in the sphere of internal security. Harel therefore devoted considerable efforts to assisting these countries in organizing efficient intelligence and security services and a military force capable of withstanding any sudden internal or externally inspired coup attempt.

Contacts with the countries of the outer ring were developed in the military sphere, with the IDF providing advice, equipment, and training. Israel also cemented its relationship with these countries by providing technical assistance, especially in the fields of agriculture, the management of water resources, and medical care. Through these allies Israel even tried to promote political stability in Arab countries that were officially at war with Israel. Several leaders of Arab states were saved from assassination by Nasser's agents thanks to warnings by the Mossad. This intelligence was conveyed to the intended victims either through friendly Western states or through Israel's contacts in the periphery. Harel had no doubt at all that "this blessed activity of ours stopped the triumphal march by Nasser and his Soviet masters across the Arab Middle East and into Black Africa."[11]

Israel began to cultivate bilateral relations with Iran, Turkey, and Ethiopia long before the Suez War. But the formation of the UAR in February 1958 and the overthrow of the monarchy in Iraq five months later alerted these countries to the danger of Arab radicalism and formed the real backdrop to Israel's efforts to go beyond tentative bilateral relationships and try to develop some kind of a grouping.

Iran was the jewel in the crown of the alliance of the periphery. Its common border with the Soviet Union made Iran a front-line state in the Cold War. Traditional hostility between Iran and the Arab world also facilitated cooperation with Israel. In March 1950 Iran recognized Israel de facto and permitted it to maintain an unofficial low-level representation in Tehran. Iran also supplied oil to Israel. In the aftermath of Suez this low-level economic relationship was transformed into a close political and strategic partnership. General Taimur Bakhtiar, the head of the newly created SAVAK internal intelligence organization, took the initiative in establishing contact with the Mossad in September 1957. These contacts were extended to include the military and intelligence services of the two countries. Israeli representatives began to visit Tehran and to meet with the shah, his prime minister, and other senior officials. The Israelis regularly transmitted to the Iranians reports on Egypt's activities in Arab countries and on Communist activities affecting Iran. Economic relations between the two countries expanded considerably as Israeli experts provided help with a large number of development projects. The shah had an exaggerated notion of the influence wielded by Israel in Washington, and he began to turn to Israel to help him improve his public image there and to plead his case with the administration. In the spring of 1959, with the personal approval of the shah and Ben-Gurion, an agreement was concluded between the two countries on military and intelligence cooperation. This was maintained until the fall of the shah in 1979.

Relations with Turkey followed a similar course. Like Iran,

Turkey was a pro-Western front-line state in the Cold War, with a generally low opinion of the Arabs and their military capability. Turkey recognized Israel de facto in March 1949, and an Israeli legation was established in Ankara with Elias Sasson as its first head. In December 1957 Sasson, who had in the meantime become Israel's ambassador to Italy, met Adnan Menderes, the Turkish prime minister, and Fatin Zurlu, his foreign minister, and reached agreement to step up cooperation against the Soviet and Egyptian threats. Following the republican revolution in Iraq, Menderes agreed to meet his Israeli opposite number in secret. Ben-Gurion flew to Ankara on 28 August 1959 and met Menderes the following day. The two leaders reached an agreement on economic, political, and military cooperation and on the regular exchange of intelligence. Ben-Gurion also undertook to support Turkey's efforts to obtain economic aid from America, while Menderes for his part agreed to back Israel's efforts to get arms from America and to join NATO.

Iran and Turkey were closely allied to America and formed part of the "northern tier" designed to check Soviet advances southward. Both countries were also concerned by the northern thrust of Nasser's activities. This encouraged the Israelis to try to place their relations with Iran and Turkey on a trilateral basis. According to a CIA report on the Israeli secret services captured during the revolt against the shah in Tehran in 1979, the Mossad set up toward the end of 1958 a triangular organization with the Turkish National Security Service and the Iranian SAVAK. The purpose of this organization, code-named Trident, was to exchange intelligence on a regular basis, to mount joint operations, and to provide Israeli training and technical advice on counterintelligence matters to the other two members.[12]

Israel's third major ally in the periphery was Ethiopia. Ethiopia was an isolated Christian state on the east coast of Africa, by the Red Sea. There was a conflict of interest between Ethiopia and Egypt that had to do with the water of the Nile River and the status of Sudan, which served as a buffer between them. Ethiopia felt threatened by Nasser's Pan-African ambitions. In 1955 Emperor Haile Selassie put out feelers for Israeli military and development assistance, but at that stage he was not ready to establish formal diplomatic relations. In 1957, however, the foundations were laid for a close practical relationship. Israeli experts were sent to train the emperor's army and reorganize his intelligence services; the Israelis helped the emperor consolidate his rule at home and resist expansionist pressures from Sudan. Ben-Gurion, who had acquired a taste for secret diplomacy, hoped to visit the emperor but the plan had to be abandoned. He therefore wrote a personal letter to Haile Selassie on the anniversary of his coronation. In this letter Ben-Gurion dwelled on the growing danger the military clique in Cairo posed to the independence of their neighbors and stressed Israel's readiness to continue to assist the countries in Asia and Africa that were threatened by this danger. He promised that Israel's representatives would explain to governments and public opinion in other countries that the Nile belonged not just to Egypt but also to Sudan and Ethiopia. And he expressed his appreciation for Haile Selassie's efforts to promote unity among the leaders of the Umma Party who were fighting for the independence of Sudan.[13]

Israel had its own links with the Umma Party going back to Moshe Sharett's days as prime minister, and some attempts were later made to fit this country into the framework of the alliance of the periphery. The Umma Party was pro-British, whereas its main rival, the National Unionists, had leftist and pro-Egyptian leanings. There was also a division between the Muslim, Arabicized north and the less advanced peoples from the south of the country, and periodic revolts broke out in the south against the imposition of central rule. Some of the rebels approached Israel for help, and Israel responded by providing money and arms and by introducing agents into southern Sudan, sometimes in cooperation with Ethiopia, which also supported the rebels.

In the late 1950s Israel also began to develop friendly relations with the black African countries that were in the process of gaining independence from colonial rule. The list of black African countries cultivated by Israel included Senegal, Mali, Guinea, Liberia, Ivory Coast, Ghana, Togo, Nigeria, the Central African Republic, Chad, Congo, and Zaire. The African offensive was led by Golda Meir, and a special department for international cooperation was set up within the Foreign Ministry. The opening of the Red Sea to Israeli shipping facilitated these contacts and the establishment of normal economic relations. The fact that Israel was a small and young state, untainted by the brush of colonialism, made it more acceptable to other Third World countries. Israel extended technical assistance on a large scale in economic planning, building infrastructure, establishing educational, medical and social welfare facilities, and developing the armed forces.

At first Golda Meir was reluctant to ask for official American support in financing Israeli development projects in Africa. Israel either bore the costs by itself or received help from rich American Jews. Israel also tried to persuade the Swedish government to embark on joint projects in Africa, with Sweden providing the funding and Israel the expertise and the training facilities. But the scale of the operation was so vast that Golda Meir had to turn to America for help. By getting close to the governments of the African states and to their intelligence services, she argued, Israel would be serving American interests as well as its own. The Americans saw the strength of this argument and agreed to meet some of Israel's costs on a project by project basis. By the mid-1960s Israel had established on the African continent a considerable presence, which greatly enhanced Israel's international standing, especially at the United Nations. There was also considerable enthusiasm at home for the idea of Israel's serving as a light to the Gentiles. It diverted attention from Israel's ongoing conflict with its immediate neighbors and demonstrated that, despite their enmity, Israel was not a nation that dwelled alone.[14]

While America saw an advantage in the Israeli presence in Africa, it could not be persuaded to support the alliance of the periphery. Late in 1958 Isser Harel tried, through Allen Dulles, to get the moral and political backing of the Eisenhower administration for Israel's activities in the periphery. He argued that these activities contributed more than any other plan to strengthen Western positions in the region. After a long wait he received a polite but negative reply from Allen Dulles. Ben-Gurion agreed with Harel that they should continue to draw on their own limited resources in carrying out this vital strategic mission.[15]

In the final analysis, the alliance of the periphery did not achieve all of its objectives. It was an original and enterprising venture, which spread Israel's influence far and wide. But it did not change the attitude of the Arabs toward Israel or make them reconsider their refusal to come to terms with Israel. Nor was it fully translated from an idea into a political reality. This does not mean that the effort was not worth making. In politics one cannot always be certain in advance what the results will be. It made perfect sense for Israel to develop its bilateral relations with all the countries in the outer ring. It was the idea of bringing them together into one group with Israel at its center that proved overambitious. Another problem was the blatantly exaggerated propaganda designed to enlist American support. The Americans had good relations with Iran and Turkey, and they did not need Israel's help.

Yet, at the psychological level, the alliance of the periphery did make a difference. It boosted the morale of the Israelis and made them feel that they had something to offer for a change. In the words of one Israeli official, "It contributed to the feeling that we are a great power. This feeling began with the Sinai Campaign, which put Israel on the map as the strongest military force in the region. Now we had contracts from Iran to Ethiopia. So we are not just a beggar sitting in a trench and getting fired upon from all directions."[16]

The 1958 Crisis

In 1958 the Middle East was convulsed by a series of crises involving Lebanon, Iraq, and Jordan. A contributory factor was the political fallout from the Suez War, which had tilted the balance of power in the Arab world against the conservative regimes associated with the West and in favor of the radical, pro-Nasser and pro-Soviet forces. In May a civil war broke out in Lebanon between the predominantly Christian and strongly pro-Western regime of President Camille Chamoun and the predominantly Muslim Socialist National Front, which wanted to join the UAR.

On 14 July a group of Iraqi Free Officers led by Brigadier Abdul Karim Qasim captured power in Baghdad in a swift and savage military coup. The young King Faisal II, the regent, Abdul Illah, and the prime minister, Nuri al-Said, were murdered, and there was talk of turning Iraq into a people's republic. The defenestration of Britain's allies in Baghdad changed the strategic map of the Middle East, since Iraq was a major oil producer and the linchpin of the Baghdad Pact. The coup threatened to unravel the whole system of Western control over the Middle East and its oil resources. There was a real danger that Jordan, which was ruled by the other branch of the Hashemite dynasty, and Lebanon might also be overwhelmed by the Arab nationalist tide. The rulers of these countries felt this danger most acutely. President Chamoun requested military aid from the United States under the Eisenhower Doctrine. King Hussein of Jordan appealed to Britain for help.

The Eisenhower administration decided to put on a general show of force and sent marines into Lebanon within forty-eight hours of the Baghdad coup to help prop up the tottering regime of President Chamoun. The British government, headed by

Harold Macmillan, also resolved on a general show of force, provided it could be carried out in the closest cooperation with the United States. It decided to send immediately by air around 1,500 troops from Cyprus to Amman and asked Israel for permission for overflight across its territory.

The Israeli response to the crisis was hesitant, cautious, and rather muddled. Since, strictly speaking, the coup in Baghdad was an internal matter that did not affect the regional status quo, Israel adhered to a policy of nonintervention. This reduced Israel to an essentially passive role, to giving advice to outside powers. Its hope was that the Western powers would intervene by force against the rebels in Iraq, but it quickly became clear that this was not a realistic option. The decision to assist Lebanon was well received in Israel as a demonstration that America was faithful to its commitments. On the British request, however, the cabinet was divided, with Mapai's left-wing coalition partners opposing the request. The Mapam ministers had a neutralist orientation and did not wish to side with Britain against the Soviet Union. The Ahdut Ha'avodah ministers believed that the monarchy in Amman was doomed, with or without British help, and they did not want to miss a chance to capture the West Bank.

The IDF experts were also concerned about the future of Jordan. Their intelligence suggested that the coup in Iraq had been well prepared and carried out with the help of the UAR, and they feared a similar coup in Amman because of its proximity to Israel's vulnerable strategic points. Various contingency plans had been prepared for the capture of the entire West Bank, or parts of it, in the event of a Nasserist coup in Amman. On the evening of 14 July, the chief of staff, Chaim Laskov, proposed the capture of Hebron, of the area around Jerusalem, and of the high ground all the way to Nablus. Ben-Gurion was unconvinced. "This time the Arabs will not run away!" he wrote in his diary.[17] The demographic problem was important because there were nearly a million Arabs on the West Bank, compared with only 1.75 million Jews in Israel. But it was not the only one. Another consideration was the strong opposition that Israeli expansion into the West Bank was likely to encounter from the Western powers and from the international community. Also, in common with the foreign policy establishment, Ben-Gurion regarded the survival of the Hashemite monarchy in Amman as essential to Israel's security. They all recognized that the preservation of the status quo in Jordan against further encroachment by Nasser was a vital Israeli interest. As Golda Meir told Selwyn Lloyd, "We all pray three times a day for King Hussein's safety and success."[18] It was one thing to preserve Israel's freedom of action in the event of Hussein's fall; it was quite another to seize by force parts of his kingdom while he was still sitting on his throne.

Given the divisions in the cabinet, Ben-Gurion decided to turn to America for advice before replying to the British request. America supported the British plan to fly troops to Amman. It also sought permission to use Israel's airspace itself because it intended to fly over Lebanon, Jordan, and Iraq to project strength and determination. Before the positive Israeli reply was conveyed to Britain, however, RAF planes began to fly over Israel on their way to Amman.[19] A total of four thousand paratroopers were airlifted to Amman, as well as military equipment and fuel. After securing the royal palace and other installations in Amman, the British forces stayed for several months and withdrew only when the danger seemed to have passed. King Hussein was grateful for Britain's help and for Israel's part in facilitating it. The situation in Jordan became ominous, as he recalled many years later:

> Suddenly, we found ourselves isolated; our oil tankers were caught up in Iraq and couldn't come through; the Syrian border was closed. Nasser straddled both Syria and Egypt, the Saudis would not permit overflights or the supply of food. . . . So we were totally cut off and we needed oil, and there was only one way: to fly across Israel into Jordan. We did not have any direct negotiations over that. The British and Americans did, and we certainly appreciated it.[20]

Israel was not being asked to do anything to help Jordan, except to permit the use of its airspace. Nevertheless, Ben-Gurion earnestly hoped to get something in return for helping the Western powers. He gathered his advisers and told them, "We now have to act with all our energy to obtain arms from the United States, to demand to be involved in political and military discussions relating to the Middle East, and to bring closer together the Middle Eastern states that are opposed to Nasser."[21] As the crisis evolved, four distinct objectives emerged: to persuade Britain and America to supply arms to Israel, to obtain a public American security guarantee, to integrate Israel into the Western plans for the defense of the Middle East, and to secure American support for the alliance of the periphery.

Ben-Gurion summoned the British ambassador for a talk on 18 July. His main purpose was to propose a working partnership between the United Kingdom and Israel along the lines of that already existing between Israel and France. Nasser, said the prime minister, threatened not only Israel but Saudi Arabia, Iran, Turkey, and Sudan as well. He suggested a partnership between equals based on common interests and common values and asked that his proposal be considered at the highest level.[22] A couple of days later Macmillan sent a friendly but noncommittal letter to Ben-Gurion. He expressed the hope that the current situation would be the beginning of a fruitful stage in the development of the relations between their two countries. As a result of the crisis the British became less inhibited about the supply of arms to Israel, but they were reluctant to assume any long-term political commitments.

Ben-Gurion pinned his greatest hopes on a change of attitude in Washington. He therefore mustered all his powers of persuasion in a letter to President Eisenhower on 24 July. His main purpose in writing was to get American support for the alliance of the periphery. He began by painting a very dark picture of the situation in the Middle East after the Iraqi revolution and by describing Arab nationalism as a front for Soviet expansionism. Anyone who had read the writings of Colonel Nasser, he wrote, could not be surprised by what happened in Iraq or regard it as the end of the matter. If Nasser realized his aim of dominating the Arab world with the help of the Soviet Union, the consequences for the West would be serious, warned Ben-Gurion. Next came an account of Israel's efforts to strengthen its relations with the outer ring of the Middle East—Iran, Turkey, Sudan, and Ethiopia—"with the object of establishing a strong dam against the Nasserist Soviet torrent."

Ben-Gurion dwelled on the possibilities of enhancing freedom and mutual help in the outer ring of the Middle East. He pointed out that although Israel's resources were limited, it was able to assist these countries in many fields and that the fact that Israel was not a great power made it less suspect in the eyes of other countries. The implication was that Israel was better placed than the United States to organize the containment of Nasser because it did not arouse suspicions of neocolonialism. Ben-Gurion made it clear that he was talking not about a far-off vision but about a design whose first stages were already in the process of fulfillment. He also stressed that the outer ring would represent a source of strength for the West. Two things, however, he deemed essential: American political, financial, and moral support, and a clear indication to the other four countries that Israel's efforts had the backing of America. Ben-Gurion concluded his letter with an affirmation of faith that, with Eisenhower's help, they could safeguard the independence of this vital part of the world and with a request for an early meeting to discuss this matter further.[23]

Eisenhower replied to Ben-Gurion promptly. His letter, like that of Harold Macmillan, was friendly but noncommittal. It contained a fairly anodyne assurance, stating that Israel could "be confident of United States interest in the integrity and independence of Israel" and promising that Dulles would write to him in more detail.[24] Dulles wrote to Ben-Gurion on 1 August, but his letter was typically woolly and evasive, with few details and no commitments. He confirmed that America, like Israel, was interested in strengthening the security of the nations in the Middle East that were determined to resist the expansionist forces at work in the area, and he referred to recent action by America to strengthen its relations with Turkey, Iran, and Pakistan. With regard to Israel's security, all he said was that they were prepared to examine the military implications of this problem with an open mind.[25] In no way did he commit the United States to come to Israel's aid in the event of a Soviet attack.

The Soviet Union, which had played no visible role in the crisis of 1958, suddenly loomed large in the eyes of the Israeli ministers with the arrival of a Soviet note on 1 August. The note protested against the overflight of Israel by U.S. and UK aircraft, associated Israel with their aggressive acts, and spoke of perilous consequences for Israel's own national interest. The note provoked strong demands in the cabinet to withdraw permission for the overflights. Ben-Gurion felt that he had no firm basis for continuing to resist this pressure, and he informed America and Britain that the flights had to stop, unwisely giving the Soviet note as the sole reason for this decision. Dulles immediately summoned Abba Eban and spoke to him sternly about his and the president's shock at learning that Israel had caved in to the Soviet demand without even consulting them. When Eban tried to explain that Israel was in a precarious position because it lacked a formal security guarantee, Dulles stated that the Eisenhower Doctrine made it clear that the United States would come to the support of Israel should it be attacked by a Communist power. For future guidance he wanted to know whether Israel felt so menaced by the USSR that it would do whatever the Soviet Union requested.[26]

Ben-Gurion immediately reversed his decision again, permitting the airlift to Jordan to continue until 10 August and denying that there was any link between the Soviet note and his earlier decision. He took Eban's advice to delay his reply to the Soviet note and to assure the Americans in the meantime that Israel was second to none in its steadfastness in the face of pressures and intimidation from Moscow. In truth, Ben-Gurion felt very bitter at what he saw as American hypocrisy in exposing Israel to the risk of retaliation from another superpower while denying it a formal defense guarantee and a part in the formulation of Western plans for the defense of the region. The resentment was mutual. Dulles resented the constant pressure to which the Israelis subjected him, especially during the crisis. In his public utterances he was careful not to show his true feelings, but in private Anglo-American exchanges he called Israel "this millstone round our necks."[27]

The Middle East crisis gradually subsided. In Lebanon, Camille Chamoun's extremely pro-American government was replaced by a neutral one headed by General Fouad Chehab. In Jordan, contrary to all local expectations, King Hussein survived and finished the year more firmly on his throne than he had started it. Ben-Gurion achieved only one of the four objectives he had set himself when the crisis erupted: Britain revised its previous policy of restricting the supply of arms to Israel. America was still reluctant to become Israel's main arms supplier, but it began to provide "shooting weapons," as opposed to defensive military equipment. The other three objectives were not achieved. Britain and America refused to give Israel a formal defense guarantee. They also politely brushed aside Ben-Gurion's proposals for a close political and military partnership. Finally, the Americans could not be drawn to make any commitment, even a purely verbal one, to the alliance of the periphery. These results were rather disappointing when measured against Ben-Gurion's initial expectations of using the 1958 crisis as a stepping stone to a strategic partnership with the Western powers against the forces of radical Arab nationalism.

BEN-GURION AND THE BOMB

The 1958 crisis was followed by several years of acute instability in the internal politics of the Arab states and in inter-Arab relations. But along Israel's borders with its neighbors, except for that with Syria, a general relaxation of tension prevailed. There seemed to be a marked improvement not only in Israel's day-to-day security but also in its basic security. This was reflected in growing public confidence in the IDF's ability to deal effectively with any Arab attack. Although Ben-Gurion helped foster this mood of confidence, he did not share in it himself. Only too well aware of the superiority of the Arabs in numbers, space, and financial resources, he was haunted by the fear that one day they would overwhelm Israel. Victory in the Sinai Campaign did not allay his anxiety about Israel's future. His greatest fear was an attack on all fronts. In the late 1950s, he told an aide, "I could not sleep at night, not even one second. I had one fear in my heart: a combined attack by all the Arab armies."[28] The solution to this problem had been lurking at the back of Ben-Gurion's mind for years: Israel had to develop a nuclear capability. Nuclear weapons would provide the ultimate deterrent against an Arab attempt to annihilate the State of Israel. It is no exaggeration to say that Ben-Gurion became obsessed with nuclear weapons. He felt that in the long run they constituted the only counter to the numerical superiority of the Arabs and the only sure guarantee of Israel's survival.

After Ben-Gurion returned from Sede-Boker in 1955, the development of Israel's nuclear power was one of his main goals. On this we have the testimony of Yuval Ne'eman, the deputy head of the IDF intelligence branch, who later became a leading nuclear scientist. In July 1956 Ne'eman was given responsibility for liaison with the French security and intelligence services. Although his mission was confined to the military sphere, Ben-Gurion, in his briefing, stressed nuclear capability as the long-term goal to strive for.[29] At the conference of Sèvres, Shimon Peres had succeeded in getting a high-level French commitment to provide Israel with a nuclear reactor. The negotiations with the French were for a small nuclear reactor for civilian purposes. Nothing was said at that stage about possible military applications of this nuclear technology, but that was Ben-Gurion's ultimate aim—to produce nuclear weapons. A year later, in October 1957, when Maurice Bourgès-Maunoury was prime minister, the French signed a secret agreement to supply Israel with a nuclear reactor that had twice the capacity previously promised. The package included a facility for separating plutonium, the material needed for the production of nuclear weapons. All the members of Israel's Atomic Energy Commission, except its chairman, resigned because they thought that Israel's nuclear program should be oriented toward economic rather than defense needs.

In 1955 President Eisenhower had offered Israel assistance in nuclear research under the Atoms for Peace program. The offer was to help Israel build a small research reactor of the "swimming pool" variety with a capacity of one megawatt. Israel undertook to use this reactor only for research purposes, and a group of Israeli nuclear scientists were trained in America to operate it. Ben-Gurion decided to go forward with the Americans and the French at the same time. Consequently, in 1958 work began on the construction of two nuclear reactors: a one-megawatt reactor in Nachal Soreq, fifteen miles south of Tel Aviv, and a twenty-four-megawatt reactor fueled by natural uranium in Dimona, between Beersheba and the Dead Sea.

The nuclear facility in Dimona was constructed behind the thickest imaginable veil of secrecy. The reason for this secrecy was that the project was designed to create the expertise and the infrastructure that would enable Israel eventually to produce nuclear weapons. In pursuing the nuclear option, Ben-Gurion was extraordinarily single-minded and secretive. He needed to be single-minded because the nuclear program was very costly and finding the funding for it a daunting and difficult task. He opted for secrecy in order to protect the project, especially in its early stages. Premature disclosure was certain to provoke American pressure on Israel to desist and Arab efforts to acquire their own nuclear weapons. Ben-Gurion went to great lengths to prevent any publicity, and even acted in an undemocratic and unconstitutional manner. He did not bring this matter before the Knesset, or the Knesset Committee on Defense and Foreign Affairs, or the cabinet, which was collectively responsible for all the actions of the government.[30]

Discussion of the nuclear issue proceeded quietly outside these formal political institutions among senior politicians, military leaders, and officials. The question was not whether Israel should base its defense on conventional weapons or on nuclear weapons. It was clear to everyone that Israel was bound to continue to defend itself by conventional weapons. Rather, the debate was about defense priorities, about the allocation of scarce resources, and about the pace of the nuclear program. On one side were those who believed that Israel should invest heavily in developing the capacity to produce nuclear weapons. Their aim was to ensure that, if nuclear weapons were introduced into the region, Israel would not be left without the capacity for nuclear deterrence. On the other side were those who believed that the danger of the Arabs' overtaking Israel in the technological and nuclear spheres was very remote and that the bulk of the defense budget should be invested in strengthening the IDF.[31] This was the view of the great majority of Israel's senior soldiers. It was also the view of Yigal Allon, the Ahdut Ha'avodah leader and former military commander. Allon had a very low opinion of the military capability of the Arabs, he continued to dream about territorial expansion, and he emerged as the most outspoken defender of the traditional doctrine of conventional deterrence.

In the decisions about Dimona, however, Ben-Gurion consulted only a handful of senior colleagues from his own party. In the November 1959 general election, Abba Eban, Moshe Dayan, and Shimon Peres were all elected to the Knesset on the Mapai list. Eban entered the new government as minister without portfolio, Dayan became minister of agriculture, while Peres was promoted from director general to deputy minister of defense. Golda Meir, who stayed on as foreign minister, strongly resented the young upstarts and feared their encroachment on her patch. Levi Eshkol carried on as minister of finance and Pinhas Sapir as minister of commerce and industry.

Mapai's ministers were divided in their attitude toward the nuclear project at Dimona. One group believed that this project had to be developed at any price. It included Ben-Gurion, Peres, and, after some skepticism, Dayan. A second group, while not going as far as outright opposition, questioned whether a nuclear plant on the scale of Dimona was really necessary and warned that the cost would be astronomical and possibly crippling to the Israeli economy. This group included Eshkol and Sapir. A third group wanted to use Dimona for the purpose of bargaining with the Americans. The idea was to signal to the Americans that Israel might be driven to go down the path of nuclear deterrence unless America agreed to supply Israel with advanced weapons in sufficient quantities to sustain the conventional balance of power between it and its Arab enemies. This group included Golda Meir and Abba Eban, who were in broad agreement with the senior officials in the Foreign Ministry. Eban once described the reactor as "an enormous alligator stranded on dry land."[32] Despite the internal opposition and reservations, Ben-Gurion and Peres went ahead with the development of the nuclear reactor in Dimona and with the production of long-range missiles, which were also necessary for a credible nuclear option.

The first challenge to Israel's nuclear ambition came in

December 1960, in the twilight between the Eisenhower and the Kennedy administrations. In Israel there was tight military censorship, but Western newspapers started buzzing with rumors that Israel was building a nuclear reactor that would enable it to start producing nuclear weapons within about five years. American U-2 spy planes discovered that the plant in Dimona, officially described as a textile factory, was a large and tightly guarded nuclear facility. The press reports caused surprise and suspicion in official quarters and provoked condemnation in the Arab states. The U.S. government wanted to know whether Israel was planning to produce nuclear weapons.

Ben-Gurion responded by making a carefully worded statement in the Knesset on 21 December. He acknowledged, for the first time and to the surprise of the Israeli public, that Israel was engaged in the construction of a research reactor with the capacity of twenty-four thermal megawatts, but he emphasized that the reactor was "designed exclusively for peaceful purposes," and he estimated that the construction would take three or four years to complete. He dismissed the report that Israel was building a bomb as a "deliberate or unwitting untruth." The statement was truthful as far as it went. At the time it was made, Israel was certainly not producing nuclear weapons. But it was significant that Ben-Gurion gave no pledge of any kind about the future. He did not say that Israel had no intention of producing nuclear weapons. Nor did he offer to submit the Israeli reactor to the safeguard system of the International Atomic Energy Agency. His statement was designed to give as little information as possible and to keep all the options open.

The Americans reacted by probing for more information and by trying to clarify Israel's long-term intentions. John F. Kennedy was committed to a global policy of nonproliferation, and he adopted at the outset a tough stand designed to elicit a pledge from Israel not to produce nuclear weapons and to open Dimona to international inspection. Kennedy and Ben-Gurion had a private meeting at New York's Waldorf Astoria Hotel on 30 May 1961. There was growing domestic opposition to Dimona, from Levi Eshkol and Isser Harel among others, so Ben-Gurion had come fearing the worst. But the meeting with the young American president went much better than expected. After a brief exchange of courtesies, the two leaders plunged into a discussion of Israel's nuclear reactor. Israel had invited two distinguished Jewish-American physicists to visit Dimona, and Kennedy described their report as very helpful. He seemed to be satisfied that the reactor was intended exclusively for peaceful purposes, and he simply suggested that just as "a woman should not only be virtuous, but should also have the appearance of virtue," Israel's purposes should not only be peaceful but should be seen as such by other nations.[33]

Several other matters were discussed at the meeting. Ben-Gurion gave a survey of Israel's security problem, emphasizing its unique character. Nasser's officially declared aim, he said, was to destroy Israel. The security problem of Israel was thus unparalleled in the world. At stake was not just the independence of the country and the control of its territory but the very lives of its people. For if Nasser were to defeat Israel, he would do to the people of Israel what Hitler had done to the six million Jews of Germany. Ben-Gurion asked Kennedy specifically for the supply of surface-to-air Hawk missiles. The skies were decisive to Israel's security, he explained, because its territory was small and narrow and because it had only three airfields, compared with twenty-six airfields in the UAR. Kennedy replied that the United States was committed to Israel's security under the terms of the Tripartite Declaration and therefore had an interest in ensuring that Israel was not placed in a situation that invited aggression. As far as weapons were concerned, America's policy remained unchanged. It wanted to stay out of this area as a major arms supplier. The danger of supplying missiles to Israel was that the other side would get missiles and that there would be missile escalation. The situation would be different if Israel were placed at an imperiling disadvantage. So although Kennedy could not grant the request for Hawk missiles, he promised to keep the military balance between Israel and its enemies under constant review.

Ben-Gurion next suggested a joint U.S.-USSR declaration guaranteeing the existing borders in the Middle East. Kennedy replied that the Soviets were unlikely to agree to such a joint declaration, not least because the current borders were unacceptable to the Arabs. Kennedy then raised the question of the Palestinian refugees. He was moved by their plight, and he hoped that an Israeli gesture would open the road to a settlement of the Arab-Israeli dispute. The UN Palestine Conciliation Commission (PCC), he observed, would soon approach the countries concerned for a solution that would include some repatriation, resettlement in the Arab countries, and migration of refugees to countries outside the Arab world. Ben-Gurion stated firmly that the commission would fail because the Arab states did not care what happened to the refugees. "They regard them simply as the best weapon to fight us," he said. "If they succeed in getting the refugees back into Israel, it would create a critical situation. We are surrounded on all sides and they can destroy us. This is what they want." Kennedy conceded that it was possible that the Arab states would not agree to anything realistic, but he preferred that the responsibility for failure should not appear to rest on Israel. The discussion ended on a happy note of agreement with the president saying "blessed is the peacemaker" and the prime minister responding that, if peace was achieved, it would be easy to solve the refugee problem.[34] Overall the meeting was a success from the prime minister's point of view. The nuclear reactor had been saved, at least for the time being.

In the summer of 1962 Kennedy reversed his decision against the sale of Hawk surface-to-air missiles to Israel. He hoped that this would discourage Israel from seeking to develop a nuclear option, and he wanted to signal to the Arabs more clearly than in the past that the United States was committed to the defense of Israel. Kennedy and his advisers intended to use the supply of Hawk missiles to induce Israel to show more flexibility on the refugee question. They regarded the Palestinian refugees as a central factor in the Arab-Israeli equation, and they held strong views on the need to settle this problem. Dr. Joseph Johnson, a former State Department official, was asked to handle this matter, and in August 1961 he was also appointed special representative for the PCC. After a visit to the region, Johnson came up with the idea of polling a representative sample of refugees to determine how many would want to return to their homes if given the choice between return and compensation. Israel disliked the idea and asked for endless clarifications.

Myer ("Mike") Feldman, Kennedy's special assistant on Jewish affairs, had a secret meeting with David Ben-Gurion and Golda Meir on 19 August 1962. Feldman began by announcing the president's decision to make Hawk missiles available to Israel but cautioned that there was a long lead time. He also told them that Nasser would be informed of the decision, in the hope of preventing an arms race. Ben-Gurion replied that he would gladly agree to no missiles at all if Nasser would accept arms limitations. Feldman then raised the Johnson plan and met with a severely skeptical response. But rather than assume responsibility for defeating the plan, Ben-Gurion demanded prior commitments by

Nasser that he knew to be unrealistic. He and Golda Meir felt so strongly about this issue that they would probably have forfeited American economic and military assistance had it been made conditional on their acceptance of the Johnson plan. They wanted peace in order to solve the refugee problem but were convinced that the Arab states wanted resettlement in order to destroy the State of Israel. Ben-Gurion need not have worried. In the end Syria publicly rejected the plan, while the other Arab states concerned gave ambiguous replies. Israel was let off the hook.[35]

Despite the inflexibility displayed by Israel, Kennedy continued to tilt America's Middle Eastern policy in Israel's favor. He received Golda Meir on 27 December 1962 at his family home in Palm Beach, Florida. Golda gave him a long lecture on Jewish history and the dangers of another Holocaust. He listened attentively and then gave her his own assessment. He said that America had a special relationship with Israel comparable to the Anglo-American special relationship but that she also needed to cultivate other pro-Western states in the region. This way she could make it clear to the Arabs that she was committed to friendship with Israel and to upholding Israel's security. Kennedy indicated that, in the event of an Arab invasion, America would use its Sixth Fleet in the Mediterranean and come to Israel's aid. He wanted Israel to understand that its security depended not only on America but on its own behavior toward the Arabs. In effect, Kennedy spoke of a partnership between America and Israel and of an unwritten alliance. In September 1963 he confirmed this new American policy in a letter to Israel's new prime minister, Levi Eshkol.[36]

THE END OF THE BEN-GURION ERA

As Ben-Gurion grew older, he became more crotchety, inflexible, and authoritarian, and his style of decision making grew more personalized and idiosyncratic. He relied increasingly on young and dynamic aides and on personal diplomacy, bypassing the Knesset, the government, and the Foreign Ministry. By his behavior he antagonized his senior party colleagues and especially the previously loyal Golda Meir, who was incorrigibly vain and suspicious and quick to take offense. On a number of occasions he sought to reassure her that he had full confidence in her, but tact was not his strong suit and he usually ended up by making matters worse. In 1960 evidence emerged that Colonel Binyamin Gibli had forged documents in 1954 in order to pin responsibility on Pinhas Lavon for the botched operation in Egypt, which in public could still only be referred to obliquely as "the mishap."[37] Lavon demanded that the prime minister clear his name. Ben-Gurion replied that he could not do so, because he was not a judge. The Lavon affair rumbled on and on, tearing Mapai apart and taxing Ben-Gurion's declining mental faculties to the limit. Behind the Lavon affair was a vicious struggle between two Mapai factions for the succession of "the old man." In one group were "the young ones" like Moshe Dayan, Shimon Peres, and Giora Yoseftal, the minister of housing, who enjoyed Ben-Gurion's erratic support. In the other were the Mapai veterans like Golda Meir, Levi Eshkol, and Pinhas Sapir who made a common cause with Isser Harel, the powerful head of the Mossad. Domestic politics of Byzantine complexity became enmeshed in the debate over the country's foreign and defense policies.

One major bone of contention was the employment of German scientists to develop missiles in Egypt. In July 1962 the world was surprised by Egypt's launching of surface-to-surface missiles that, it was claimed, could hit any target south of Beirut. This was accompanied by press reports that German scientists were also helping Egypt develop unconventional weapons of a radioactive kind. Isser Harel believed that the Egyptian weapons program constituted a lethal danger to Israel's security. He therefore mounted a campaign to harass and intimidate the German scientists—for example, by sending them letter bombs. He also demanded a vigorous diplomatic campaign against the German government, which he suspected of complicity.[38] Harel was supported not only by the Herut opposition party but by Golda Meir and some of her colleagues. Ben-Gurion, on the other hand, considered the reports to be greatly exaggerated and was also reluctant to put at risk the large-scale economic and military assistance that Israel was receiving from the Federal Republic of Germany.

Shimon Peres strongly disputed Harel's analysis and policy proposals. Ben-Gurion also received a report from Major General Meir Amit, the director of military intelligence, which belittled the danger posed by the Egyptian weapons program. Ben-Gurion came out against Harel, with whom he had been working in harmony for the preceding fifteen years. On 25 March 1963 Harel resigned as head of the Mossad, giving as the only reason his differences of opinion with the prime minister over the German scientists working in Egypt. He was succeeded by Meir Amit.

Harel used his newly won freedom to mobilize public and parliamentary opinion against what he regarded as his former chief's policy of appeasement of Germany.[39]

There were also signs of change in Ben-Gurion's attitude toward Nasser, although in public he continued to express his policy in barks of defiance. Building up Israel's deterrent power remained at the top of his list of priorities, but he was on the lookout for signs of change on the Arab side as well. The conviction that had guided his conduct all along was that nothing much could be done about peace until the Arabs had recognized that Israel was unbreakably strong. Now he was trying to assess whether this point had been reached. Nasser held the key. He was undoubtedly the most important leader in the Arab world. If he would agree to reconciliation with Israel, the other Arab leaders would follow suit. But Ben-Gurion could not tell for certain what Nasser's current views were on the fateful subject of such reconciliation.[40] He therefore took the initiative in asking other world leaders, including U Nu of Burma and President Tito of Yugoslavia, to try to arrange a secret meeting between himself and Nasser.

Early in 1963 an unusual opportunity presented itself. Sir Denis Hamilton, the editor of the London *Sunday Times,* interviewed Nasser in Cairo. In that interview Nasser evidently said, not for publication, that "he felt the whole problem could be solved if he (Nasser) and Ben-Gurion were to be locked together in a room alone for three hours."[41] Hamilton reported this conversation to Baron Edmund de Rothschild, who in turn brought it to Ben-Gurion's attention. Ben-Gurion invited Hamilton to visit Israel, and they met on 28 March. He told Hamilton that Nasser was the only Arab leader capable of reaching an accommodation with Israel, and he asked him to go to Cairo and convey his offer to meet secretly anywhere Nasser chose, even in Cairo. Hamilton conveyed the offer, but Nasser refused to meet Ben-Gurion, saying he had no reason to trust him. He cited a long list of events from the preceding fifteen years, including his personal experience in the 1948 war, the Israeli attack on Gaza, and the Sinai Campaign, as evidence that Ben-Gurion could not be trusted.[42]

Just as the hope of a dialogue with Nasser faded away, the fear of a combined Arab attack on Israel returned to haunt Ben-Gurion with a vengeance. In Cairo, on 17 April 1963, Egypt, Syria, and Iraq signed a provisional constitution for an Arab federation. The constitution spoke prominently of "the question of Palestine and the national duty to liberate it." Michael Comay, Israel's permanent representative to the UN, addressed a letter to the president of the Security Council, stating that the expression "liberation of Palestine" meant nothing less than the aim to destroy Israel. He denounced the document as a flagrant violation of the Charter and as a direct threat to international peace and security.[43]

Ben-Gurion's personal reaction to the Arab federation was one of deep, almost irrational, anxiety. He saw the federation as a plan to encircle Israel on all sides and eventually to attack and destroy it. His greatest fear was that King Hussein would be overthrown, that Jordan would fall under Nasser's influence, and that Israel's encirclement would become complete. His idea that Israel should reserve the right to capture the West Bank in the event of an adverse change in the political status quo elicited no sympathy whatever from the Western powers. Although his fears were not shared by his advisers, he decided to address a dramatic personal appeal to the leaders of several major powers, including India, the Soviet Union, Britain, and France. Each letter was worded somewhat differently, but they all ended with the request that they put pressure on the Arab states at the forthcoming meeting of the General Assembly to abide by the principles of the UN Charter and respect the independence and territorial integrity of all the states in the Middle East. The letter to Charles de Gaulle, president of the Fifth Republic, went further in asking for an urgent meeting and for a French guarantee of Israel's security.

The most important letter, and the most revealing of Ben-Gurion's state of mind, was sent to President Kennedy on 26 April. Ben-Gurion, who had always identified himself completely with the destiny of the Jewish state, was in a gloomy mood in the last months of his premiership, and the letter may have been intended as some kind of political testament. That, at any rate, was the impression of Gideon Rafael, who helped him prepare the English version of the letter. The Hebrew draft reflected Ben-Gurion's somber mood. In it he dealt extensively with Nasser and his evil designs. He wrote that after what had happened to the Jews during World War II, he could not dismiss the possibility that this might occur again if the Arabs continued to pursue their policy of belligerency against Israel. Then came the sentence that shocked Golda Meir and her officials: "It may not happen today or tomorrow, but I am not sure whether the state will continue to exist after my life has come to an end." Golda asked Rafael to try to persuade Ben-Gurion to delete this prophecy of gloom and doom but, as always, he was adamant about matters that were of great importance to him.

In his letter to Kennedy, Ben-Gurion recalled that the civilized world did not take seriously Hitler's statement that one of his aims was the worldwide extermination of the Jewish people. Ben-Gurion had no doubt that a similar calamity could befall Israel if Nasser succeeded in defeating its army. To avert this calamity Ben-Gurion made the astonishing proposal that the United States and the Soviet Union issue a joint declaration that "any country in the Middle East that refuses to recognize the territorial integrity and to live in peace with any other country in the area would receive no financial, political or military aid from the two powers." He then proposed two measures to ensure peace and security in the Middle East: the complete demilitarization of the West Bank to remove the danger to Israel from any change of regime in Jordan, and the conclusion of a bilateral security agreement between the United States and Israel, with which allies of the former would be invited to associate themselves. Finally, he expressed willingness to fly to Washington for a discussion with the president without publicity.[44]

Kennedy did not share Ben-Gurion's interpretation of the tripartite federation, and he rejected all of Ben-Gurion's proposals, including that for a secret meeting between them. The American view was that the federation was built on sand, that the situation in Jordan was stable, that Israel was in a position to defeat any Arab attack, and that the Arab leaders knew this. The Americans also thought that Egypt's ballistic missile program posed no threat to Israel, and they dismissed the reports that Egypt was developing nonconventional weapons.

For the Americans the most serious worry was Israel's nuclear program. A CIA report warned that Israel's acquisition of a nuclear capability would substantially damage the U.S. and Western position in the Arab world. It would make the Middle East more polarized and unstable, make Israel's policy toward its neighbors more rather than less tough, make Israel feel freer to take vigorous action against border harassments, and turn the Arabs against America and drive them to look to Moscow for assistance against the new Israeli threat.[45] In May, President Kennedy intensified the pressure on Ben-Gurion to agree to regular international inspection of Dimona. This was partly because the reactor was about to become operational and partly because Ben-Gurion himself was pressing for a security guarantee.[46]

Ben-Gurion remained reluctant to open up Dimona to inspection despite a series of letters he received from Kennedy on the subject. Only the United States, the United Kingdom, France, and the Soviet Union had nuclear weapons at that time, and nuclear proliferation was perceived as a major threat to international security. Kennedy therefore pressed Israel very hard on this issue. At first he suggested that the Vienna-based International Atomic Energy Agency should supervise Israel's nuclear activities. Israel rejected this suggestion on the ground that unfriendly states were represented in Vienna. Kennedy then suggested American supervision of Israel's nuclear activities, and there was a good deal of discussion by experts on this but no satisfactory results. "We are *the* experts in argumentation," observed one Israeli official involved in these discussions. "We know how to turn people around and around until they despair. All the time we continued to argue that we have no nuclear weapons; that we have the know-how but that we would not turn it into bombs. Know-how we had to have because tomorrow the Arabs might start developing nuclear weapons. It was then that we invented the formula which said that Israel would not be the first state to introduce nuclear weapons into the Middle East."[47]

On 16 June, Ben-Gurion announced his resignation from the government. The announcement came as a complete surprise to the country and the world. Although his decision seemed sudden and capricious, it was preceded by a long process of wear and tear in which the Lavon affair, the ongoing dispute over the handling of the German scientists, and the differences with the Kennedy administration over nuclear power all played a major role. The nuclear reactor in Dimona, the project he felt most passionately about, was threatened by a combination of internal and external pressures. Golda Meir and Isser Harel did not want to proceed with this project to the point of open confrontation with America, Pinhas Sapir saw in it a touch of megalomania, while Levi Eshkol warned that the project could not be funded for much longer out of the state budget. The Americans continued to demand supervision of Dimona and explicit pledges that Israel had no intention of producing atomic weapons. The issue that finally precipitated Ben-Gurion's resignation, however, was the campaign against the German scientists in Egypt. Golda Meir went to consult with Ben-Gurion on this matter on Saturday night, prior to the cabinet's regular weekly meeting on Sunday morning. She demanded action against the German scientists, and he refused. They had a huge row, and she threatened to resign. Ben-Gurion preempted her by announcing to a stunned cabinet the next morning his own irrevocable decision to resign.

Ben-Gurion was seventy-six years old and a very tired man, an exhausted volcano. He was also a troubled and disillusioned man. He was the founder of the Jewish state and the main architect of its defense policy, yet peace with the Arabs had eluded him. Although in objective terms Israel was much more secure in 1963 than it had been in 1948, he fell prey, in the twilight of his long political career, to inflated and irrational doubts about his country's long-term prospects of survival. He himself was aware that his mental powers were in decline, and this probably contributed to his decision to retire. "The young ones" were left out on a limb. The government fell into the hands of the Mapai old guard, led by Levi Eshkol.

6

Poor Little Samson

1963–1969

LEVI ESHKOL WAS everybody's first choice to succeed Ben-Gurion as party leader and prime minister, including Ben-Gurion himself. When Ben-Gurion retired to Sede-Boker for the first time, in 1953, he wanted Eshkol to succeed him, but the party chose Moshe Sharett. In 1963 there was general agreement in Mapai that Eshkol was their strongest candidate. Eshkol's main qualifications were in economic affairs. He had served as minister of agriculture and development and as minister of finance. But he was no newcomer to defense, having served as "finance minister" of the Haganah and in effect as Ben-Gurion's deputy in the Ministry of Defense in 1948. In defense matters Eshkol was Ben-Gurion's disciple, but in his views on the Arab world he was rather closer to Sharett than to Ben-Gurion. Following Ben-Gurion's example, Eshkol assumed the defense portfolio on becoming prime minister. As minister of defense, his achievements in some ways surpassed those of his more illustrious predecessor. Eshkol steadily built up the deterrent power of the IDF, giving priority to the armored corps and to the air force. That the IDF was so well prepared for war in June 1967 was largely due to him.

Levi Eshkol did not like to make irrevocable choices. He was a man of consensus and compromise. His preference for compromise is illustrated by the story of the waiter in a restaurant who asked Eshkol whether he wanted coffee or tea. "Half and half" was the reply. Eshkol was also noted for his sense of humor and for the witty phrases in Yiddish that frequently spiced his conversation. In 1965, Ezer Weizman, the commander of the air force, was sent to Washington with a long shopping list, which included a good number of Skyhawks as well as forty-five A-6 Intruders. Weizman went to see the minister of defense to ask for help with a small problem. On the one hand he had to exhibit a certain degree of weakness, to persuade the Americans to sell the planes. On the other hand he had great confidence in the ability of his pilots and did not want the Americans to get the idea that they were dealing with a feeble little air force. Eshkol did not hesitate for a moment before proffering his famous advice: "Present yourself as *Shimshon der nebichdicker!*"—as poor little Samson, or a pitiful Samson.[1]

PERSONALITIES AND POLICIES

Levi Eshkol was born in Ukraine in 1895 as Levi Shkolnik. In 1914, at age nineteen, he immigrated to Palestine as part of a contingent representing the youth movement Hashomer Hatzair (the Young Watchman). Membership in this left-wing youth movement helped form his general outlook toward the Arabs. His attitude was liberal, humane, and sympathetic, and it was accompanied by a belief in the possibility of Jewish-Arab coexistence. In Palestine he worked as a common farm laborer, a watchman, an operator of a pumping station, and a trade union leader. He was also a founding member of Degania Bet, one of the country's first kibbutzim, or collective settlements, and the founder of the Mekorot water company. He was no ideologue and made no distinctive contribution to the Zionist debate on "the Arab problem." An unassuming son of the soil, all of whose instincts were peaceful and positive, he was happiest when he could dig his fingers into the practical work of building a homeland. His attitude toward the Arabs was one of live and let live. Like Moshe Sharett, he saw the Arabs not just as an enemy but as a people. Like Sharett, he did not think that Israel was doomed to live forever by the sword. And like Sharett, he saw the value of dialogue and patient diplomacy in pursuit of the long-term goal of peaceful coexistence between Israel and its neighbors. Although Eshkol did not explicitly identify himself with Sharett's political line, his rise to power could be expected to herald the gradual reassertion of the Sharettist trend in Israel's foreign policy following Ben-Gurion's resignation.

The composition of the government remained largely unchanged. Golda Meir stayed on as foreign minister, Pinhas Sapir
became minister of finance, Zalman Aran replaced Abba Eban as
minister of education and culture, and Eban was appointed minister without portfolio and deputy prime minister. Ben-Gurion's
departure increased the tensions between the Mapai old guard
and "the young ones," who tried but failed to secure the defense
portfolio for Moshe Dayan. Dayan stayed on as minister of agriculture and Shimon Peres remained as deputy minister of defense,
but they resigned later to join their old chief in forming a party
that broke away from Mapai.

On 24 June 1963 Eshkol presented his government to the
Knesset, stressing the continuity in policy. From its infancy, he
said, the Zionist movement was imbued with the faith that peace
and cooperation expressed the true interests and aspirations of all
the people of the Middle East. This faith also inspired his government. But peace could be based only on mutual respect for the independence and territorial integrity of all the states in the area. A
strong Israel, he said, was a guarantee for the prevention of war in
the Middle East and also, ultimately, for the achievement of peace
in the area. Direct negotiations between Israel and its neighbors
offered the only road to peace. While striving for peace, his government's top priority would be to consolidate the country's security by acquiring the latest military hardware and by cultivating
relations with friendly countries. There was thus nothing original
or arresting in the Eshkol government's Arab policy at the declaratory level.

The change at the top was more noticeable in the way the government went about its work. Eshkol's style was relaxed and informal. He was a good listener and a good team player. In the
cabinet he acted as first among equals, as a chairman of the board
whose task was to reconcile conflicting points of view and promote
consensus. He not only sought advice from his colleagues but
shared his powers and responsibilities with them. The cabinet's
defense committee began to meet more regularly, receive more information, and participate more actively in the making of policy. In
addition, Eshkol resorted to frequent ad hoc consultations with a
group of ministers whose opinions he particularly valued. The
group included Golda Meir, Abba Eban, Moshe Haim Shapira
(the leader of the National Religious Party), and Israel Galilee and
Yigal Allon (the leaders of the Ahdut Ha'avodah).

Another influential adviser was Yitzhak Rabin, who became

chief of staff on 1 January 1964. Rabin was close to Ahdut Ha'avodah and especially to Allon, who had been his commanding officer, but he never joined the party. Rabin was the IDF's most experienced field commander and an excellent staff officer who combined military professionalism with sound political judgment. His working relationship with Eshkol was close and harmonious. Eshkol left him considerable freedom of action and gave him full backing but expected to be fully informed on all important defense matters. The new prime minister would often bombard his colleagues with questions. These could be irksome, but for Eshkol they served two purposes. First, the questions were designed to elicit more information before he committed himself irrevocably, and sometimes the additional information led him to change his mind. Second, they were designed to make the interlocutor a party to the decision.[2]

On the aims of Israel's defense policy, the prime minister and the chief of staff were in complete agreement. The first five-year plan for the IDF worked out under Rabin's direction, reflected a broad consensus that "the State of Israel can realize fully its national goals within the borders of the armistice agreement." The clear implication was that Israel did not require more territory than it already possessed. Another implication was that Israel would not take the initiative in starting a war with any of the Arab states. In the event that war was imposed on Israel, the plan required the IDF to move swiftly into the enemy's territory in order to destroy the infrastructure for waging war.

One of the first issues that required a high-level decision was the future of Israel's nuclear program. On July 4, a week after he was sworn in, Eshkol received a letter from President Kennedy about Dimona.[3] Some of the ministers urged outright rejection of the American demands, but Eshkol decided to follow in the footsteps of his predecessor. He convinced Kennedy that the reactor in Dimona was intended exclusively for peaceful purposes, and he agreed in principle to visits by American experts but not to a regular or intrusive system of inspection. Kennedy seemed satisfied with these assurances and with the verbal clarifications that Eshkol conveyed to him through the American ambassador in Tel Aviv. By agreeing to visits, whose scope and nature remained deliberately vague, Eshkol assured Kennedy that Israel was not about to take a political decision to cross the threshold and start producing nuclear weapons. Eshkol did not, as his critics were to claim, abandon the nuclear option or freeze the nuclear program.[4] What he did was refrain from adopting a nuclear strategy, as Ben-Gurion had done before him. In return Eshkol obtained a clearer American political commitment to Israel's defense, strategic talks between the experts of the two countries, and access to America's conventional arsenal. It was a classic Eshkol compromise, in which he obtained much more than he conceded.

Israel's relations with America continued to improve when Lyndon Johnson became president following Kennedy's assassination. As congressman and vice-president Johnson had taken a consistently pro-Israeli line, and he continued to display strong support for Israel after assuming the presidency. In early June 1964 Eshkol went on a state visit to the United States, an honor that had been denied to Ben-Gurion. In psychological terms the state visit represented a major step forward. The two main topics were Israel's arms needs and water desalination, and Johnson promised substantial help on both.[5] At the end of the visit, a joint statement was issued against the use of force and aggression. The statement also mentioned the need to preserve the territorial integrity of all states; this marked the final abandonment of any American plans for a change in the 1949 armistice agreements. Eshkol returned home with his stature as a national leader greatly enhanced.

In his report on the visit to the Mapai Secretariat, Eshkol said that Johnson gave the impression of being genuinely interested in Israel's security and welfare. No less important than the contribution the visit made to Israel's power of military deterrence, said Eshkol, was the enhancement of its capacity for political deterrence. It demonstrated to the Arabs that Israel did not stand alone.[6] The visit thus carried Israel a significant step closer to the goal that had persistently eluded Ben-Gurion, namely, an American guarantee of the country's territorial integrity.

At home Eshkol consolidated his power base by negotiating a merger between Mapai and Ahdut Ha'avodah, which resulted in a new grouping known as the Alignment. The merger was a shrewd move in the power struggle inside Mapai between the young men in a hurry whom Ben-Gurion had left behind and the party's old guard. Ahdut Ha'avodah could offer a group of young leaders with considerable experience in defense matters, such as Israel Galilee, Yigal Allon, and Moshe Carmel, who had commanded the northern front in the War of Independence. It is true that these leaders did not share Eshkol's restraint and moderation in dealing with border incidents. But they were firmly on his side, and on the side of his chief of staff, in the debate about nuclear strategy. Their basic premise was that the IDF had to retain the capacity to deal with any conceivable Arab challenge by conventional means alone. They were therefore happy with Eshkol's decision to give priority to strengthening the capacity to fight a conventional war over accelerating the nuclear program.[7]

The merger with Ahdut Ha'avodah offered Ben-Gurion an opportunity to render his successor's life uncomfortable, which he did by resuscitating the "Lavon affair." One possible explanation for Ben-Gurion's behavior was that he was jealous of his successor's success and wanted to replace him as he had replaced Sharett in 1955. Whatever his motives, Ben-Gurion turned against his longtime friend with unprecedented vehemence and venom, declaring him unfit to govern. Ben-Gurion accused Eshkol of unspecified security failures. His young lieutenants explained in private that Eshkol jeopardized the nuclear option by giving in to American demands for inspection of Dimona. These claims were inaccurate, to say the least. Before precipitating the final split, Ben-Gurion made an open bid to unseat Eshkol at a party conference. In June 1965, after the bid had been defeated, Ben-Gurion created his own splinter political party, Rafi (Reshimat Poalei Israel, Israel Workers' List). Moshe Dayan and Shimon Peres reluctantly resigned from the government and the ruling party and followed their old chief into the political wilderness.

Rafi's critics called it the pro-nuclear party on account of the obsession with the bomb. As a party Rafi did not have a coherent or agreed social and economic philosophy. Its leaders were united by the thirst for power and by the desire to see a more aggressive policy prevail in the conflict with Israel's neighbors. The party seemed to want to revert to the hard-hitting policy of military reprisals practiced by the Ben-Gurion-Dayan duo in the early 1950s. Eshkol's moderate policy toward the Arabs was denounced as dangerous appeasement. His calls for peace were said to weaken the deterrent power of the IDF. At that time Habib Bourguiba, the Tunisian president, created a great stir by calling on his fellow Arabs to abandon hope of destroying Israel and to make peace with it on the basis of the 1947 UN partition borders and the return of the Palestinian refugees. Eshkol welcomed the note of realism sounded by the Tunisian president, and especially the suggestion that the Arab-Israeli dispute be resolved by peaceful means, although he could not accept the details of the proposed program. But even this cautious welcome was too much for the Rafi leaders. They seized on it as proof of the illusions of peace har-

bored by the Eshkol government. Their attacks became more strident and more vicious in the lead-up to the general election.

In the election held on 2 November 1965, Eshkol trounced
Ben-Gurion. The Alignment won 45 seats in the Knesset; Rafi, a
mere 10. Mapam won 8 seats. Just before the election Herut had
merged with the Liberal Party to form Gahal, but the new party
won only 26 seats. As the price of the merger, Herut agreed to
drop its claims to the whole Land of Israel. Some members of the
Liberal Party ran on a separate ticket as the Independent Liberal
Party and won 5 seats. Two months after the election Eshkol assembled a coalition with a majority of 75 in the 120-member
Knesset. The coalition consisted of the Alignment, Mapam, the
National Religious Party, the Independent Liberal Party, and two
smaller parties. The opposition included Gahal, Rafi, and Agudat
Israel.

Golda Meir stepped down as foreign minister, and it was generally assumed that this would be the end of her political career,
but a year later she was called to serve as secretary-general of the
Alignment. She was replaced as foreign minister by Abba Eban.
On relations with the Arab world, they differed markedly, for she
belonged to the hawkish wing of the party whereas he was a leading dove. In his memoirs Eban gives the following summary of his
views:

> In the 1960s Israel's security doctrine was rooted in the idea
> of an independent deterrent power. I supported this defini-
> tion. I believed that our strategy toward the Arab world would
> have to have an attritional stage. First they would have to be
> driven to despair of causing our downfall and liquidation. At
> that stage they would perhaps see the advantage and compul-
> sion of "doing a deal." My experience and reading had told
> me that those who most ardently wanted peace were not al-
> ways those who obtained it. At the same time, I wrote and said
> that even if we built a wall against attack or intimidation, we
> should have a door in the wall in case the attrition was suc-
> cessful and our neighbors came to seek accommodation. Our
> immediate task was to maintain a sufficient deterrent balance
> to bring the Arab states, or at least some elements in their
> leadership, to a realistic preference for compromise.[8]

In his views on relations with the Arabs, Eshkol was closer to the
new than to the outgoing foreign minister. The two men could

hardly have come from more dissimilar backgrounds, but they had in common a quiet confidence that Israel could look after itself, a desire to explore every possible avenue for reconciliation with the Arabs, and an optimistic outlook on the future. The working relationship between the two men was smooth and uninhibited, and they complemented each other to a remarkable degree, with Eshkol providing the bedrock of common sense and Eban the professional diplomatic polish. Eshkol admired Eban for his skill in presenting Israel's case to the world, but he felt that he was rather detached from the reality of Israel's day-to-day security problems. He was confident that Eban could always come up with a good speech, less confident that he could come up with the right solution. In his good-humored way, he even called Eban the clever fool. Eban respected Eshkol for his open-mindedness, his capacity to balance conflicting considerations and points of view in the making of foreign policy, and his skill in sustaining domestic support behind the government's external policy.

The importance of the last skill should not be underrated, because party politics, personal rivalries, and domestic power struggles constantly impinged on the conduct of the country's external relations. Rafi, for instance, used Eshkol's moderate Arab policy as a stick with which to beat him. To this can be added the example of an Egyptian peace feeler that remained unanswered because of personal political rivalries within the Israeli defense establishment.

The two main figures involved were Meir Amit and Isser Harel. Amit had been appointed head of the Mossad by David Ben-Gurion upon Isser Harel's resignation in March 1963. Amit was close to Rafi and particularly to Dayan, who had been his commanding officer in the IDF. Harel was appointed adviser for intelligence affairs to Eshkol in September 1965, largely as a result of pressure from Golda Meir and Yigal Allon. Rafi conducted a campaign against Harel in the media, claiming he had been mobilized by Eshkol to help him in his political fight against Ben-Gurion. Relations between Harel and Amit were extremely tense and acrimonious, and the entire intelligence community felt the ructions and reverberations.

Toward the end of 1965 Amit received an invitation to go to Cairo for a secret meeting with Abdel Hakim Amer, the first vice-president and deputy commander in chief of the Egyptian armed forces. Since Amer was Nasser's close personal friend, it was highly unlikely that the invitation could have been issued without Nasser's knowledge. Amit himself thought that this was an opportunity for contact with Nasser and that it should be seized.[9] Egypt at that time was in dire economic straits. Amer wanted Israel to help procure American economic aid for Egypt. In return he could promise that Egypt would tone down its anti-Israeli propaganda, reduce the scope of the economic boycott of Israel, and allow Israeli goods to pass through the Suez Canal, though not under the Israeli flag.

Levi Eshkol was in favor of allowing the visit and even informed the Americans about it. He also wanted Amit to be accompanied by Zvi Dinstein, the deputy minister of defense in charge of economic affairs. Harel opposed the visit, warning that the invitation was a trap. Some ministers were persuaded by Harel that Israel had nothing to gain from a maneuver allegedly designed to improve Egypt's relations with the United States. Fresh objections were raised every time the matter came up for discussion. In the end Amit and Dinstein stayed at home.[10] This was not Eshkol's finest hour. He allowed bureaucratic politics to dictate Israel's response, or rather nonresponse, to an invitation to meet the number two man in the Egyptian hierarchy. Whether anything would have come out of the meeting, there is, of course, no way of telling. All one can say for certain is that the Egyptians issued an invitation to a high-level meeting and the Israelis turned it down.

Eshkol was rather more successful in establishing a secret channel for communications with King Hussein of Jordan and in insulating it from the vagaries of domestic politics. The purpose of these contacts was to exchange views on day-to-day security, facilitate practical cooperation, and explore the possibilities of a settlement. A key figure on the Israeli side was Dr. Yaacov Herzog, the director general of the prime minister's office and a trusted political adviser. Herzog met King Hussein in London on 24 September 1963 in the clinic of the king's Jewish physician, Dr. Emmanuel Herbert. It was the first in a long series of meetings between the king and Israeli officials. King Hussein took the initiative in arranging this meeting, and he later explained his reasons:

> One had to break that barrier and begin a dialogue whether it led anywhere immediately or not. But it was important to have it direct and firsthand and not to let other players manipulate us. And by chance I had a very, very good friend who looked after my health here, Dr. Herbert, and . . . I think he made the offer of the possibility of some contact, and I said "fine." That is how it started. Trying to explore, trying to

find out what the other side of this issue was like. What was the face of it?[11]

Dr. Herzog told the king that Israel fully understood and shared his interest in avoiding border clashes. He went on to assure the king, "Israel regards the integrity of the kingdom of Jordan and its sovereignty as its interest. And we have reason to believe that Nasser has taken into account that a crisis in Jordan could touch off Israeli intervention." The king took a long-term view of their relations: "Since the attainment of a final settlement would require a great deal of time, it is our historic duty to develop in an appropriately discreet manner avenues of cooperation directed at the final settlement." He also expressed his gratitude for assistance rendered by Israel in the past in alerting him to plots against his regime.[12]

At the next meeting with King Hussein, which took place in Paris in 1965, Israel was represented by Golda Meir, who was accompanied by Yaacov Herzog. Relations between the Arab world and Israel were then at a low ebb following a decision by the Arab League to divert the headwaters of the river Jordan. Nevertheless, recalled King Hussein,

> It was a good meeting. It was really a meeting of breaking the ice, of getting to know one another. And we talked about our dreams for our children and grandchildren to live in an era of peace in the region, and I think she suggested that maybe a day will come when we could put aside all the armament on both sides and create a monument in Jerusalem which would signify peace between us and where our young people could see what a futile struggle it had been and what a heavy burden it had been on both sides. Essentially, it didn't go beyond that. There wasn't very much indeed that happened, just an agreement to keep in touch whenever possible.[13]

These early meetings paved the way for greater intelligence cooperation between the two countries. The Israelis passed on to the Jordanians intelligence on subversive activities and plots to assassinate the king. The two sides agreed to abide by the water quotas allocated to them by Eric Johnston. Jordan departed from the Pan-Arab position in agreeing to Israel's diversion of water to the Negev, while Israel approved Jordan's various water conservation projects. Israel agreed to support King Hussein's request for

American military assistance, but only on the clear understanding that American tanks would not be deployed on the West Bank. Thus, de facto peace prevailed between Israel and Jordan in the first three years of the Eshkol government despite the activities of irregular Palestinian forces operating from Jordan's territory and a limited number of retaliatory raids by Israel.[14]

THE SYRIAN SYNDROME

The Egyptian front was even quieter than the Jordanian front. Its involvement in the war in Yemen was one reason for the care Egypt took to avoid border clashes with Israel. Nasser's assessment that Israel was militarily stronger than all the Arab states put together was another. In line with this assessment, Nasser consistently urged his allies to guard against the danger of a military confrontation with Israel before they had sufficiently built up their military capabilities. Palestinian irregulars were stopped from operating against Israel from the Gaza Strip so as not to give Israel any excuse for taking military action against Egypt.

The only problematic front in the 1960s was the Syrian front. There were three principal sources of tension between Israel and Syria: the demilitarized zones, water, and the activities of the Palestinian guerrilla organizations. The conflict in the DMZ had been going on intermittently since 1949, with Israel trying to assert control by military force and Syria resisting with military force. To this ongoing dispute was added the struggle over water. Israel had been forced to abandon its plan to divert water from the Jordan in the central DMZ to the Negev in 1953. In 1959 it began instead to build the National Water Carrier to convey water from Lake Kinneret to the Negev, and this project was completed in 1964. The Arab states, with Syria at their head, resolved to frustrate Israel's plans by diverting the headwaters of the river Jordan, and the result was a series of violent clashes in which Israel gained the upper hand. Having been defeated in the water war, the frustrated Syrians began to sponsor attacks on Israel from their territory by Palestinian guerrilla organizations. Of the three sources of conflict, the last two were the most important. They fed the tension that finally exploded in a full-scale war.

The river Jordan is formed by the confluence of three rivers: the Banias, which flows down from Syria; the Hazbani, which flows down from Lebanon, and the Dan, which emerges in northern Israel. Roughly 50 percent of the Jordan waters come from the Banias and the Hazbani and the other 50 percent from the Dan. Eshkol, a former director of the Mekorot water company, was steeped in the water question. He participated personally in many discussions and agreed that without control over the sources of water the Zionist dream could not be realized. Without water there could be no agriculture, and agriculture was the basis for the existence of the Jewish people in the land of Israel, he said.

The IDF generals were naturally more interested in the military than the economic aspect of the water dispute, and they had many old scores to settle with the Syrians. Brigadier General Israel Lior, Eshkol's aide-de-camp, suspected that the never-ending chain of action and reaction would end up in all-out war:

> In the north a pretty heavy war was conducted over the water sources. The war was directed by the chief of staff, Yitzhak Rabin, together with the officer in charge of the northern command, Dado Elazar. I had an uneasy internal feeling on this matter. All the time it seemed to me that Rabin suffers from what I call the "Syrian syndrome." In my opinion, nearly all those who served along the front lines of the northern command . . . were affected by the Syrian syndrome. Service on this front, opposite the Syrian enemy, fuels feelings of exceptional hatred for the Syrian army and people. There is no comparison, its seems to me, between the Israeli's attitude to the Jordanian or Egyptian army and his attitude to the Syrian army. . . . We loved to hate them.
>
> Rabin and Dado were very aggressive in combat operations over the headwaters in the north. Incidents over these headwaters and over control in the demilitarized zones became an inseparable part of the daily routine.[15]

In January 1964 an Arab League summit meeting convened in Cairo. The main item on its agenda was the threat posed by Israel's diversion of water from the north to irrigate the south and the expected reduction in the water supplies available to Syria and Jordan. The reaction of the summit to this threat was deadly serious. The preamble to its decisions stated,

> The establishment of Israel is the basic threat that the Arab nation in its entirety has agreed to forestall. And since the existence of Israel is a danger that threatens the Arab nation, the

diversion of the Jordan waters by it multiplies the dangers to Arab existence. Accordingly, the Arab states have to prepare the plans necessary for dealing with the political, economic, and social aspects, so that if the necessary results are not achieved, collective Arab military preparations, when they are completed, will constitute the ultimate practical means for the final liquidation of Israel.[16]

This was the first time that the Arab states collectively declared in an official document that their ultimate aim was the destruction of the State of Israel.[17] The preamble was followed by specific and highly significant decisions: to divert the headwaters of the Jordan River in Syria and Lebanon, to establish the Palestine Liberation Organization (PLO), and to set up a unified Arab military command. The PLO was formed several months later, and Ahmad al-Shuqayri was appointed its first chairman. The PLO was set up as a political organization under the auspices of the Arab League, with Egypt playing the dominant part in directing its activities. But the PLO had a military arm, the Palestine Liberation Army (PLA), whose units were dispersed in various Arab countries and were subordinate to their military commands. Gradually, a number of semi-independent Palestinian guerrilla organizations emerged on the scene in addition to Fatah, which had been in existence since 1958.[18]

Israel's leaders took the decisions of the summit very seriously, although they were aware of the divisions and rivalries in the Arab camp. They knew that Jordan and Lebanon perceived the United Arab Command, which was to be headed by an Egyptian general, as a threat to their own independence. Golda Meir told a party forum that even though some Arab states went along rather reluctantly with the summit decisions, Israel had to assume that the United Arab Command would not be a mere paper organization.[19] Yitzhak Rabin thought that the summit marked a turning point in the history of the Arab-Israeli conflict. According to him, the origins of the Six-Day War could be traced to the Cairo summit conference.[20]

A second Arab summit conference was held in Alexandria from 5 to 11 September 1964. This summit approved the detailed plans that had been worked out for the diversion of the headwaters of the Jordan and the joint military plan for the defense of this project. The council issued a proclamation calling for the liberation of Palestine from Zionist imperialism and stressing the need to utilize all Arab potentialities and concentrate all Arab energies against the common enemy. The council welcomed the establishment of the PLO as a support for the Palestine entity and a vanguard of the joint Arab struggle to liberate Palestine.

Once again Israel took a very grave view of the decisions of the Arab summit. In a note to the Security Council, Michael Comay, Israel's permanent representative to the UN, drew attention to the above proclamation. "The clear purport of this proclamation," he wrote, "is that thirteen member-States of the United Nations have set themselves the aim of liquidating another member-State, have declared that to be a central policy objective guiding their collective actions, and have determined to concentrate all their national potential on the attainment of this aim." The Alexandria decisions were said to be in naked conflict with the Charter of the United Nations and with every accepted principle governing the relations between states.[21] Eshkol explained to the Knesset, in a statement on 12 October, that the summit decisions marked a shift in the center of gravity from empty national slogans to careful preparation for the ultimate confrontation with Israel. Israel, he emphasized, was determined to protect its vital interests and to proceed with its plan to draw from Lake Kinneret the quantities of water that had been allocated to it under the Johnston plan.[22]

Although the cabinet was united in its determination to prevent the Arab diversion plan, there were various views about the appropriate means. Moshe Dayan thought that Israel could not prevent the diversion by any means short of war. He even published an article in which he argued that if the Arabs went ahead, war would be inescapable. Israel Galilee and his colleagues suggested that Israel might use an incident in the DMZ to seize some Syrian territory around the Banias River and hold on to it for as long as there was a threat of resuming the water diversion work. This suggestion appeared too provocative to Eshkol, who came down in favor of a suggestion made by the chief of staff. Rabin suggested preventing the diversion by destroying the heavy machinery that the Syrians started to assemble near the border.[23]

On 13 November, Eshkol was called upon to make an instant decision. The Syrians opened fire on an IDF patrol, which they claimed had crossed their border, and there was a major conflagration around Tel Dan. Rabin called Eshkol to request permission to send the Israeli Air Force (IAF) into action against the Syrian positions. The air force had not been used in border clashes since 1951, for fear of provoking war, and Eshkol recognized the risks involved. He knew that the introduction of the air force would constitute a major act of escalation. He was not opposed in principle to retaliation, but he was discriminating in the use of military force and careful not to make matters worse when this could be avoided. On this occasion, with so much at stake, he authorized the use of the air force against the Syrian sources of fire. This act signaled a new and severe policy toward Syria and anyone else involved in the water diversion project.[24]

In the following year Rabin and his men perfected the techniques for fighting the new kind of war: the war against tractors, bulldozers, diggers, and dredgers. At first they used tanks to shell the engineering equipment across the border, but the tanks had a short range and frequently missed their target. They therefore improved the accuracy of the tanks and increased their range from 700–800 meters to five kilometers. In the spring and the summer of 1965, the Israelis initiated a series of incidents with a view to hitting the Syrian tractors that were being moved farther and farther away from the border. Israel's aim was to force the Syrians to choose between abandoning the diversion project and risking war.[25] In the end the Syrians abandoned work on the diversion of the Banias, while the Lebanese abandoned their halfhearted preparations for diverting the Hazbani.

At the third Arab summit conference, in Casablanca in September 1965, the secretary-general of the Arab League reported that the diversion work had to be stopped because of Israeli aggression. The Syrian representative vowed to keep up the fight against the Zionist enemy, but Nasser injected a characteristic note of caution by warning against resuming the diversion work before the Arabs had improved their land and air defense capabilities. He hinted that if Syria acted unilaterally, it would not be able to count on his assistance. In effect he conceded that Israel had won the water war.

The next challenge Israel had to confront was attacks by Fatah guerrillas who acted independently of the PLO. The first guerrilla raid, on 1 January 1965, was aimed at blowing up the pipes of Israel's National Water Carrier at Ain Bone, on the west bank of the Jordan River. Fatah's general strategy was to drag the Arab states into war with Israel by stoking up the fire along the borders. It tried to use all the confrontation states as staging bases for the operations against Israel, but Syria was the only country that gave the Fatah fighters assistance and encouragement. The Egyptian authorities firmly prevented Fatah from operating against Israel from the Gaza Strip and Sinai. Jordanian opposition to Fatah was even firmer, but it was not always possible to prevent small units from crossing the border into Israel.

On 13 November 1966 Israel abruptly departed from the pattern of small, almost symbolic retaliation against Jordan by launching a devastating attack on the village of Samu, south of Hebron on the West Bank. Staged in broad daylight by a large force with tanks, the attack resulted in the death of dozens of Jordanian soldiers and the destruction of forty-one houses. Israel had been pointing an accusing finger at Syria, so the attack on Jordan came as a complete surprise both at home and abroad. The reason given by the IDF spokesman was that the saboteurs who had planted mines on the Israeli side of the border had come from the Hebron area, but no satisfactory explanation was ever given for the scale or ferocity of the attack.

Inside Jordan the effects of the raid were highly destabilizing. It exposed King Hussein's military weakness and touched off large-scale unrest and protest against his regime. Hussein felt personally betrayed by the Israelis because their action contradicted their previously expressed commitment to the safety and stability of Jordan. The raid occurred on his birthday and killed one of his close friends:

> It really created a devastating effect in Jordan itself because again the action, if it had been an action from Jordan, was not something that Jordan condoned or sponsored or supported in any form or way. And to my way of thinking at that time, I couldn't figure out if a small irrigation ditch or pipe was blown up—assuming it was, which I didn't necessarily know for sure—why the reaction in this way? Was there any balance between the two? Why did the Israelis attack instead of trying to figure out a way of dealing with the threats in a different way, in a joint way? So it was a shock, and it was not a very pleasant birthday present.[26]

Yitzhak Rabin was also shocked by the consequences of the Samu raid. He had repeatedly emphasized that whereas in Syria the problem was the regime, in Jordan the problem was the civilians who assisted Israel's Palestinian enemies. The plan of action he had proposed to the cabinet was intended not to inflict casualties on the Arab Legion but to serve as a warning to the civilian population not to cooperate with the Palestinian saboteurs. The damage greatly exceeded the estimate he had given the cabinet, and he later admitted that Eshkol had good reason to be displeased with him. "We had neither political nor military reasons," he said, "to arrive at a confrontation with Jordan or to humiliate Hussein."[27]

Rabin came under considerable criticism in the cabinet, in the Knesset, and in the press for his part in the Samu affair, and Eshkol gave him no support. Miriam Eshkol, the prime minister's wife, recalled his bitterness toward the IDF leaders at that time. Miriam, who had been the librarian of the Knesset, was Eshkol's third wife. They were married in 1964 when he was sixty-nine and she thirty-four. In sharp contrast to the mild-mannered Eshkol, she was belligerent and confrontational and terrified his aides. Even the toughest army generals used to quake in their boots when she was around. She expected the generals to respect her husband's moderate line toward the Arabs, and she also kept a diary. During the controversy over the Samu raid, her husband said to her, "Write down that, unlike my predecessor, I am not the representative of the army in the government!"[28]

The Samu raid was a terrible blunder, and the IDF leaders knew it. Thereafter they reverted to targeting Syria, which was undergoing a process of radicalization. An extreme left-wing Ba'th regime had assumed power in Damascus in February 1966 and embarked on a fierce anti-Zionist ideological offensive. It called for a popular war for the liberation of Palestine and sponsored Palestinian guerrilla attacks on Israeli targets. This new form of warfare did not endanger Israel's basic security, but it greatly exacerbated the mutual hostility between Israel and Syria. The changes of regime and policy in Damascus served to reinforce the Syrian syndrome that afflicted so many of Israel's senior officers. They were determined to retaliate. In early 1967 they resumed cultivation of land in the DMZ in a manner calculated to provoke clashes with the Syrians. The general trend was to retaliate forcefully against low-level Syrian aggression and to escalate the military contest in order to compel the Syrian regime to desist from its hostile activities.

A major landmark in the spiral of violence was an air battle on 7 April 1967 in which six Soviet-made Syrian MiGs were shot down by the IAF. The Syrians opened fire on a tractor plowing the land in the DMZ near Kibbutz Ha'on, on the eastern shore of Lake Kinneret, and the Israelis returned the fire. The Syrians started shelling other Israeli settlements in the area. Israeli tanks went into action but could not reach all the positions from which the Syrians were firing. So the chief of staff requested and obtained the prime minister's permission to use the IAF. As the Israeli planes went into action to silence the Syrian guns, they were intercepted by Syrian MiGs and an aerial engagement took place. Previous restrictions were removed in allowing IAF planes to roar over Damascus. This was the first time that the IAF penetrated all the way to the Syrian capital. Two of the Syrian MiGs were in fact shot down on the outskirts of Damascus, turning Syria's military defeat into a public humiliation. All the Israeli planes returned safely to base. The shooting down of the six Syrian MiGs started the countdown to the Six-Day War.

Israel's strategy of escalation on the Syrian front was probably the single most important factor in dragging the Middle East to war in June 1967, despite the conventional wisdom on the subject that singles out Syrian aggression as the principal cause of war. It is an article of faith among Israelis that the Golan Heights were captured in the Six-Day War to stop the Syrians from shelling the settlements down below. But many of the firefights were deliberately provoked by Israel. Support for this revisionist view came in 1997 from an unexpected quarter: Moshe Dayan. Dayan had died in 1981, so the support was from the grave. In a series of private conversations in 1976 with a young reporter named Rami Tal, Dayan talked about mistakes he had made in the course of his political career. Twenty-one years later, with the approval of the celebrated military commander's daughter, Yael Dayan, Tal published his notes of the conversations in the weekend supplement of *Yediot Aharonot*. Dayan confessed that his greatest mistake was that, as minister of defense in June 1967, he did not stick to his original opposition to the storming of the Golan Heights. Tal began to remonstrate that the Syrians were sitting on top of the Golan Heights. Dayan interrupted,

> Never mind that. After all, I know how at least 80 percent of the clashes there started. In my opinion, more than 80 percent, but let's talk about 80 percent. It went this way: We would send a tractor to plow someplace where it wasn't possible to do anything, in the demilitarized area, and knew in advance that the Syrians would start to shoot. If they didn't shoot, we would tell the tractor to advance farther, until in the end the Syrians would get annoyed and shoot. And then we would use artillery and later the air force also, and that's how it was. I did that, and Laskov and Chara [Zvi Tsur, Rabin's

predecessor as chief of staff] did that, and Yitzhak did that, but it seems to me that the person who most enjoyed these games was Dado [David Elzar, OC Northern Command, 1964–69].

In retrospect, Dayan could not point to a clearly formulated strategic conception that governed Israel's behavior in the DMZ between 1949 and 1967. All he suggested was that he and some of his fellow officers did not accept the 1949 armistice lines with Syria as final and hoped to change them by means that fell short of war, by "snatching bits of territory and holding on to it until the enemy despairs and gives it to us." This may have been naive on their part, said Dayan, but at that time they did not have much experience in diplomacy among sovereign states.[29]

Dayan's 1976 comments on Israel's behavior were rather sweeping and simplistic. They may have been colored by his disgrace and resignation as defense minister following his failure to anticipate the Arab attack in October 1973. This failure thrust him into the political wilderness and led him to question the official Israeli version of the conflict. Being a man of extremes, he now exonerated the Syrians and placed most of the blame for the conflict on the Israeli side. Nevertheless, Dayan's 1976 comments are of significance to the historian of this period. They confirm that some of Israel's top military leaders were afflicted by the Syrian syndrome and that this led to aggressive and provocative behavior and to local skirmishes that eventually culminated in a full-scale Arab-Israeli war.

THE ROAD TO WAR

Of all the Arab-Israeli wars, the June 1967 war was the only one that neither side wanted. The war resulted from a crisis slide that neither Israel nor her enemies were able to control. Israel inadvertently unleashed this avalanche by issuing a series of threats to act against the Syrian regime unless it stopped its support for Palestinian guerrillas who were operating against Israel. On 12 May 1967, in an interview to a newspaper, Yitzhak Rabin threatened to occupy Damascus and overthrow the Syrian regime. His words caused a storm. They contradicted the official line that Israel did not interfere in the internal politics of the Arab states but only acted in self-defense against Arab aggression. Several ministers criticized the chief of staff at the next cabinet meeting, and the prime minister reprimanded him. But Eshkol himself stated on 13 May that there could be no immunity to a state aiding saboteurs and that Israel "may have to teach Syria a sharper lesson than that of 7 April." Other public figures also used strong language that was widely interpreted in the Arab world as a signal of Israel's intent to overthrow the Syrian regime by force. Abba Eban remarked in his autobiography, "If there had been a little more silence, the sum of human wisdom would probably have remained intact."[30]

The Israeli leaders did not grasp the importance that the Soviet Union attached to the survival of the Ba'th regime in Syria. Concern for this regime prompted the Soviet leaders to intervene in the crisis, and they too lost control of the situation. They sent a report to Nasser that Israel was concentrating forces on its northern front and planning to attack Syria. The report was untrue and Nasser knew that it was untrue, but he was in a quandary. His army was bogged down in an inconclusive war in Yemen, and he knew that Israel was militarily stronger than all the Arab confrontation states taken together. Yet, politically, he could not afford to remain inactive, because his leadership of the Arab world was being challenged. Since the Samu raid the Jordanians had been accusing him of cowardice and of hiding from the Israelis behind the skirts of the UN Emergency Force in Sinai. Syria had a defense pact with Egypt that compelled it to go to Syria's aid in the event of an Israeli attack. Clearly, Nasser had to do something, both to preserve his own credibility as an ally and to restrain the hotheads in Damascus. There is general agreement among commentators that Nasser neither wanted nor planned to go to war with Israel. What he did was to embark on an exercise in brinkmanship that was to carry him over the brink.

Nasser took three steps that were intended to impress Arab public opinion rather than be a conscious prelude to war with Israel. The first step was to send a large number of troops into Sinai. The second was to ask for the removal of the UN Emergency Force from Sinai. The third and most fateful step, taken on 22 May, was to close the Straits of Tiran to Israeli shipping. For Israel this constituted a casus belli. It canceled the main achievement of the Sinai Campaign. The Israeli economy could survive the closure of the straits, but the deterrent image of the IDF could not. Nasser understood the psychological significance of this step. He knew that Israel's entire defense philosophy was based on imposing its will on its enemies, not on submitting to unilateral dictates by them. In closing the Straits of Tiran to Israeli shipping, he took a terrible gamble—and lost.

Israel hesitated on the brink. The government, paralyzed by

fear and by conflicting currents of opinion, took two weeks to reach a decision. These two weeks were a traumatic experience for the Israeli public, and they went down in history as "the period of waiting." During this period the entire nation succumbed to a collective psychosis. The memory of the Holocaust was a powerful psychological force that deepened the feeling of isolation and accentuated the perception of threat. Although, objectively speaking, Israel was much stronger than its enemies, many Israelis felt that their country faced a threat of imminent destruction. For them the question was not about the Straits of Tiran but about survival. Weak leadership was largely responsible for permitting this panic to spread from the politicians to the people at large. Eshkol and Rabin, who had done so much to prepare the IDF for war, proved unequal to the task of leading the nation in a crisis that involved a high risk of war. Faced with a crisis of the supreme magnitude, they fumbled and faltered and Rabin suffered a temporary breakdown.

Eshkol's performance was impaired by crisis-induced stress, by his own relative lack of experience in foreign affairs, and by domestic political pressures. His former party colleagues who had split off to form Rafi in 1965 had become his most outspoken critics and now conducted a merciless campaign to undermine his authority. David Ben-Gurion, Shimon Peres, and Moshe Dayan, who had been languishing in opposition, tried to make political capital out of the crisis by persistently drawing attention to Eshkol's shortcomings. Of the three, Dayan was the most devious, manipulative, and power hungry. His greatest ambition was to replace Eshkol as minister of defense. Eshkol refused to step down as prime minister in favor of Ben-Gurion but was eventually forced to hand over the defense portfolio to Dayan.

The domestic political crisis was resolved on 1 June by the formation of a national unity government, which included the two main opposition parties—Gahal and Rafi. Dayan entered the government as minister of defense, while two Gahal leaders, Menachem Begin and Yosef Sapir, entered it as ministers without portfolio. Dayan was brought in despite strong opposition from Golda Meir, the Alignment's secretary-general. She proposed to give the defense portfolio to Yigal Allon, and most of her party colleagues supported her. But the National Religious Party threatened to quit the coalition unless a national unity government was set up with Dayan as minister of defense. Dayan's appointment was a painful personal blow to Levi Eshkol, but it helped restore the public's and the army's confidence in the government.

One of the consequences of the Rafi campaign against Eshkol was to undermine Rabin's self-confidence and to weigh him down with a sense of guilt. Rabin was Eshkol's principal military adviser, and during the crisis he carried a heavy burden of responsibility, made even heavier by his being constantly called to attend meetings of the cabinet, the cabinet defense committee, and the Knesset Committee on Defense and Foreign Affairs. Following the Egyptian troop movement into Sinai, Rabin proposed a partial mobilization of the reserves as a precautionary measure. Dayan criticized Rabin at a meeting of the Committee on Defense and Foreign Affairs for having contributed to the crisis by ill-considered actions such as the attack on Samu and the air battle over Damascus. Following the closure of the Straits of Tiran, Rabin thought that Israel should respond immediately with military force in order to protect the deterrent power of the IDF, but this time Eshkol decided to defer action until all the avenues for a diplomatic solution had been exhausted.

Rabin felt the need to talk to Ben-Gurion, but instead of fortifying his spirits, the Old Man gave him a dressing down. "I very much doubt whether Nasser wanted to go to war, and now we are in serious trouble," said Ben-Gurion. He claimed that the mobilization of the reserves had been a mistake. Rabin replied that he had recommended mobilization in order to make sure they were ready. "In that case, you, or whoever gave you permission to mobilize so many reservists, made a mistake," repeated Ben-Gurion. "You have led the state into a grave situation. We must not go to war. We are isolated. You bear the responsibility."[31] The words struck Rabin like hammer blows and contributed to the breakdown he suffered on the evening of 23 May. The next day he stayed at home and received medical attention. Acute anxiety incapacitated him for twenty-four hours, after which he returned to full activity.

Military pressure on the cabinet to agree to immediate military action against Egypt steadily intensified. Before agreeing to it, Eshkol and the majority of his ministers wanted to ascertain the current American view of the pledge that Dulles had given Eban ten years earlier. On 23 May the cabinet decided to send Eban on a mission to Paris, London, and Washington to secure international action to reopen the Straits of Tiran. He returned three days later empty-handed. His most important meeting was with President Lyndon Johnson. Johnson told Eban that it was the unanimous view of his military experts that there was no sign that the Egyptians were planning to attack Israel and that if they did attack, the Israelis would "whip the hell out of them." Johnson promised to act with other maritime powers to open the Straits of Tiran to Israeli shipping, and he warned against the initiation of hostilities by Israel. He repeated several times, "Israel will not be alone unless it decides to go it alone."[32] Eban's report to the cabinet on the disappointing results of his trip reopened the debate on the proposal for military action. By a majority that included Eshkol, the cabinet decided on 28 May to wait two or three weeks.

That evening Eshkol met with the General Staff to explain the decision of the cabinet. The meeting was very stormy. The generals used blunt language in charging the civilian leadership with weakness, muddle, and confusion. For the generals the central problem was not the right of passage through the Straits of Tiran but the deployment of the Egyptian army in Sinai. They did not believe that the maritime powers would pull Israel's chestnuts out of the fire. Some argued that the maritime powers should not even be allowed to break the Egyptian blockade, that the IDF had to do it on its own, and that this was the only way to restore the deterrent power of the IDF. All the speakers stressed that time was of the essence because the longer they waited, the heavier would be the price of victory in terms of casualties. Eshkol disputed that the only way to achieve deterrence was by launching an immediate attack, and he elaborated on his reasons against preventive war. "Would we live forever by the sword?" he asked, his voice rising in anger. The atmosphere became so intolerable that the meeting had to be adjourned, and he left in a huff. What was said on "the night of the generals" was so blunt and so harsh that it could be seen as verging on an open rebellion. Eshkol, according to his aide-de-camp, regarded what he heard as a vote of no confidence in himself and in his government.[33]

The military certainly had no confidence in Abba Eban or in his report of the American position. It therefore suggested that Meir Amit, the director of the Mossad, be sent to the United States on a secret mission. His task was to clarify how the Americans saw the situation, whether they planned to act, and how they would react if Israel seized the military initiative. Amit's arrival coincided with a change in American policy. Lyndon Johnson had told Eban that America planned to organize an international armada to open the straits and therefore asked Israel to wait. By the time Amit arrived, American policy had shifted in favor of unleashing Israel against Nasser. Amit shifted the emphasis from the legal issue of the straits to the strategic issue of the

Egyptian forces in Sinai. He told Robert McNamara, the secretary of defense, that Israel was considering going to war. He asked for three things: American diplomatic support at the UN, American backing in the event of Soviet intervention, and, if the need arose, American replenishment of Israel's military arsenal. McNamara recognized that America had a moral responsibility to open the straits, but he preferred that Israel to do it by itself because America was tied down in Vietnam and because the CIA estimated that Israel could defeat the Egyptian army without any outside help. In effect he gave Israel a green light to take military actions against Egypt.[34]

Amit reported on the result of his mission to a small group of advisers who met in the prime minister's house on the evening of Saturday, 3 June. Amit indicated that the Americans would welcome an independent Israeli strike to shatter Nasser. Yet, surprisingly, Amit suggested waiting a week in order to test whether Israel had a casus belli by sending a ship through the straits. Dayan, for whom this was the second day at his new post, pressed for immediate action and refused to wait a day or two. Yigal Allon, the minister of labor, agreed with him. They were the most fervent advocates of military action. The next day, Sunday, 4 June, the full cabinet met and took the decision to go to war.[35]

The Six-Day War

The Six-Day War was the most spectacular military victory in Israel's history. It was launched on 5 June 1967 with a surprise air strike on enemy airfields and ended on 10 June with Israel in occupation of the entire Sinai peninsula, the West Bank, and the Golan Heights. The Egyptian air force was wiped out on the ground in the early hours of 5 June, but false information was given to Egypt's allies to encourage them to join in the fighting. At noon the air forces of Syria, Jordan, and Iraq started to attack targets inside Israel. Within two hours the Syrian and Jordanian air forces were also wiped out, as was the Iraqi airbase at H-3, near the Jordanian border. In all, four hundred enemy planes were destroyed on the first day of fighting, and that in essence sealed the fate of the Arab armies. The speed and scale of Israel's military victory led some observers to suspect that Israel launched the war not in self-defense but in order to expand its territory. Arab observers, in particular, were inclined to believe that Israel deliberately provoked the Six-Day War in order to fulfill its long-standing territorial ambitions. This view is without foundation. The Six-Day War was a defensive war. It was launched by Israel to safeguard its security, not to expand its territory. The main enemy was Egypt. The chief aims were to open the Straits of Tiran, to destroy the Egyptian army in Sinai, and to restore the deterrent power of the IDF. Political and territorial objectives were not defined by the government when it gave the IDF the order to strike. War aims emerged only in the course of the fighting in a confused and contradictory fashion.

Moshe Dayan was highly critical of the government precisely because it had no political plan for the conduct of the war. A few days after the victory, Dayan launched a scathing attack on the conduct of the war at a meeting of the Knesset Committee on Defense and Foreign Affairs. This was the least-planned of Israel's wars, he said. In the Sinai War the moves were determined in advance. In the Six-Day War moves were not determined in advance in relation to Jerusalem or the West Bank or Syria. There was no clear political plan, with guidelines to the army on how far to go. There was operational planning by the army but no political planning. In some cases the government simply trailed behind events; in others it exploited opportunities. The prime minister gave the army an order for a war of seventy-two hours only, and the Straits of Tiran were not included in the original plan he approved. "It's absurd," said Dayan.[36]

What Dayan omitted to say was that he himself gave the army most of the orders during the war and that he did not always consult the cabinet or the prime minister. Israel Lior, Eshkol's aide-de-camp, was unable to fathom Dayan's intentions, hard as he tried. Lior thought that Dayan's decisions needed to be examined by a psychologist no less than by a historian: "Their fickleness was extraordinary—but maybe ordinary for Moshe Dayan."[37]

Eshkol's conception of the war was defensive and limited: to remove the Egyptian threat to Israel's security by military means once all the diplomatic efforts had been exhausted. The Operations Branch of the General Staff prepared two war plans. One plan, named Atzmon, called for the capture of the Gaza Strip and the southern flank of El-Arish. The second plan, named Kardom, called for the capture of the eastern part of the Sinai peninsula up to Jebel Libni. Both plans envisaged holding the territory until Egypt agreed to open the Straits of Tiran. The allocation of forces for the northern and eastern fronts was only for defensive purposes. On 24 May, the day Rabin was ill, Major General Chaim Bar-Lev, who was soon to be appointed deputy chief of staff, presented the two plans to Eshkol. Eshkol followed Bar-Lev's advice and approved the second plan.[38] On becoming minister of defense, Dayan made two changes in the second plan. One was to expand the area to be captured and add to it Sharm el-Sheikh. The other was to make the destruction of enemy forces the war's primary aim. Dayan thus changed the underlying conception from limited war to total war without consulting or informing the cabinet.[39]

Once Dayan had changed Kardom, Rabin suggested that, from the military view, the most logical place for their forces to stop would be the Suez Canal. Dayan thought it would be political madness to advance all the way up to the canal and gave an order to stop some distance from it. He reasoned that the canal was an international, not an Egyptian, waterway and he also feared getting entangled with the Soviets. When told, on the morning of 7 June, that an IDF patrol had reached the canal, he ordered its immediate recall. That evening, however, Dayan canceled his own order because he heard that the Security Council was about to call for a cease-fire, and he wanted to improve Israel's bargaining position. IDF commanders made a dash for the canal and stayed there.

Decision making in relation to the northern and eastern fronts was even more haphazard. Prior to the outbreak of war, the IDF contingency plans called for minor modifications in the borders with Syria and Jordan. They called for the capture of the demilitarized zones on the border with Syria and for linking Jerusalem with the Israeli enclave on Mount Scopus. Eshkol and his party colleagues had a positive image of the Hashemite dynasty and continued to nourish hope of a settlement with Jordan. "There was nothing here," noted Abba Eban, "of the inhuman virulence which marked the attitude of other Arab nationalists toward Israel's existence. Even in wars, an unspoken assumption of ultimate accord hovered over the relations between Israel and Jordan."[40] In May–June 1967 Eshkol's government did everything in its power to confine the confrontation to the Egyptian front. Eshkol and his colleagues took into account the possibility of some fighting on the Syrian front. But they wanted to avoid a clash with Jordan and the inevitable complications of having to deal with the predominantly Palestinian population of the West Bank.[41]

The fighting on the eastern front was initiated by Jordan, not by Israel. King Hussein got carried along by the powerful current of Arab nationalism. On 30 May he flew to Cairo and signed a defense pact with Nasser. On 5 June, Jordan started shelling the Israeli side in Jerusalem. This could have been interpreted either as a salvo to uphold Jordanian honor or as a declaration of war. Eshkol decided to give King Hussein the benefit of the doubt. Through General Odd Bull, the Norwegian commander of UNTSO, he sent the following message on the morning of 5 June: "We shall not initiate any action whatsoever against Jordan. However, should Jordan open hostilities, we shall react with all our might, and the king will have to bear the full responsibility for the consequences." King Hussein told General Bull that it was too late; the die was cast. Hussein had already handed over command of his forces to an Egyptian general. He made the mistake of his life. Under Egyptian command the Jordanian forces intensified the shelling, captured Government House, where UNTSO had its headquarters, and started moving their tanks into the West Bank.

Had King Hussein heeded Eshkol's warning, he would have kept the Old City of Jerusalem and the West Bank. No one in the cabinet or the General Staff had proposed the capture of the Old City before the Jordanian bombardment began. By throwing his lot with Nasser so ostentatiously and by his defiant response to Eshkol's suggestion, Hussein himself rekindled irredentist aspirations on the Israeli side.

In the evening of 5 June, the cabinet convened in the air raid shelter of the Knesset. Allon and Begin argued that Jordanian shelling gave Israel a historic opportunity to liberate the Old City of Jerusalem. Eshkol deferred a decision until Dayan and Rabin could be consulted. On 6 June, Dayan allowed members of the IDF General Staff to encircle the Old City, but he ordered them not to enter it. He was worried about damage to the holy places and wanted to avoid fighting in a built-up area. He also thought that international pressure would force Israel to withdraw from the Old City after the war, and he did not want to pay a heavy price in casualties. A report that the UN was about to call for a cease-fire made him change his mind. Without clearing it with the cabinet, he gave the IDF the order to move into the Old City. By 10:00 A.M. on 7 June it was in Israeli hands. Three hours later Moshe Dayan, Yitzhak Rabin, and Uzi Narkis, OC Central Command, entered the city through the Lions' Gate. Standing by the Wailing Wall, Dayan declared, "The IDF liberated Jerusalem this morning. We reunited divided Jerusalem, the bisected capital of Israel. We have returned to our holiest places, we have returned in order not to part from them ever again."

General Shlomo Goren, the chief rabbi of the IDF, wanted to go much further than Dayan and blow up the Mosque of Omar, also known as the Dome of the Rock because it is the site of the Sacred Rock from which the Prophet Muhammad had purportedly ascended heaven. The Mosque of Omar is located in what the Jews call Temple Mount, for it is the site of the Second Temple, which was razed by the Romans in 70 A.D. Only the Western Wall of the temple survived, and it became known as the Wailing Wall. Shortly before his death in 1997, Uzi Narkis revealed the details of a conversation he had with General Goren on 7 June 1967 as they were standing on Temple Mount after the ritual blowing of the horn by the Wailing Wall. There was an atmosphere of spiritual elation. Paratroopers were milling around in a daze. Narkis was standing for a moment on his own, deep in thought, when Goren went up to him and said, "Uzi, this is the time to put a hundred kilograms of explosives in the Mosque of Omar—and that's it, we'll get rid of it once and for all." Narkis said, "Rabbi, stop it." Goren then said to him, "Uzi, you'll enter the history books by virtue of this deed." Narkis replied, "I have already recorded my name in the pages of the history of Jerusalem." Goren walked away without saying another word.[42]

Decisions on the West Bank were also taken in stages. They were dictated by military developments, not by a political master plan. The Israeli reaction to the Jordanian shelling was restrained in the hope that Hussein would desist after satisfying Jordan's honor. After the Old City was captured, Dayan ordered his troops to dig in on the slopes east of Jerusalem. When an armored brigade commander, on his own initiative, penetrated farther east and reported having Jericho in his sight, Dayan angrily ordered him to turn his force around. It was only after military intelligence reported hours later that King Hussein had ordered his forces to retreat across the river that Dayan ordered the capture of the entire West Bank. That evening Dayan met with senior officers to consider these unexpected developments. "How do we control a million Arabs?" asked Yitzhak Rabin with reference to the inhabitants of the West Bank. "One million, two hundred and fifty thousand," corrected a staff officer. It was a question to which no one had an answer.[43]

Narkis stressed the resistance of the government to military action in the sector for which he was responsible throughout the pre-crisis period. The Mapai leadership, according to him, was intent on preserving the status quo with Jordan. Military intelligence believed that Jordan would not join the battle. The Hussein-Nasser pact hit them like a bolt from the blue. Despite the pact, Rabin refused to allow Narkis to retain an armored division in reserve, because he persisted in thinking that there would be no fighting in that sector. Even after the Jordanians opened fire, all the proposals made by Narkis—to capture Latrun, for example— were turned down. Only when Government House was captured, did the Israeli military machine start to roll. There was a serious threat to Jerusalem's security, so he was allowed to send troops to Mount Scopus. Narkis summed up: "First, the Israeli government had no intention of capturing the West Bank. On the contrary, it was opposed to it. Second, there was not any provocation on the part of the IDF. Third, the rein was only loosened when a real threat to Jerusalem's security emerged. This is truly how things happened on 5 June, although it is difficult to believe. The end result was something that no one had planned."[44]

Rabin agreed that the final outcome was determined not by political war aims but by military contingencies: "The war developed as a result of its own inner logic, and this development enclosed all the forces of the Jordanian army in Judea and Samaria and willy-nilly led to the capture of the natural border of the Land of Israel—the river Jordan."[45]

Nowhere was Moshe Dayan more erratic and unpredictable than in relation to Syria. Here too the government had no clearly defined war aims. The IDF was deployed in a defensive mode on the Syrian front, as it was on the Jordanian, when the war against Egypt was launched. Syria for its part, wanted to stay out of this war. True, its air force made a sortie and its artillery bombarded Israeli settlements along the front line on 5 June, but these were limited hostilities and they ceased after Israel's devastating counterattack on Syria's air force. There was no need for Israel to open a second or third front. David Elazar, OC Northern Command, exerted all the pressure he could for all-out war against Syria, but Dayan kept him on a very tight leash.

On the night of 5–6 June, Dayan and Rabin discussed the possibility of further military action on the Syrian front. Dayan ruled that the IDF must not cross the international border but that it should take over all the demilitarized zones. This ruling was confirmed by a decision of the ministerial defense committee on 6 June. The following day Eshkol held a consultation with Allon,

Rabin, and Elazar. Eshkol proposed a much larger operation whose aim would be the capture of the sources of the Banias and Tel Azaziat, a fortified Syrian position on the Golan Heights. All the other participants supported this proposal. Rabin and Elazar wanted to go farther than Tel Azaziat, and Allon insisted that they be given permission to do so. There was much criticism of Dayan behind his back.

The settlers from the north added their voice for the capture of the Golan Heights. A whole settlement lobby sprang into action and they found in Eshkol a sympathetic listener. He even invited three representatives of the settlers to put their case directly to the ministerial defense committee, which met in the evening of 8 June. By this time the Egyptian and Jordanian armies had disintegrated and Israel could turn its undivided attention to the Syrian front. The representatives of the settlers pleaded not to be left at the mercy of the Syrian guns. Their words made a strong impression on all those present, except Dayan.

Dayan was determined not to run the risk of Soviet military intervention on the side of Syria. He was also worried that their forces would become overextended. "We started the war in order to destroy the Egyptian force and open the Straits of Tiran," he said. "On the way we took the West Bank. I do not think that it is possible to open another campaign against Syria. If the idea is to go into Syria and change the border in order to make life easier for the settlements, I am against." Dayan pointed out that the Syrians would never accept the loss of their territory, and the result would be never-ending conflict. Rather than trying to move the international border, he proposed moving ten settlements to a distance of fifteen kilometers from the border. Allon and Eshkol were outraged by this suggestion. Allon, a member of Kibbutz Ginossar in the north, said that the entire Galilee panhandle did not amount to fifteen kilometers and that they could not give up part of the country. Eshkol, speaking as a former farmer, said that the idea of uprooting settlements and moving them elsewhere was completely out of the question. The committee decided to defer decision on action on the Syrian front for two or three days and to ask the chief of staff to prepare an operational plan.[46] No one except Dayan could have blocked single-handedly a proposal that enjoyed such strong political and military support.

Dayan's next move completely astounded his colleagues. Early in the morning on 9 June, a few hours after Syria requested a cease-fire, Dayan called General Elazar directly, bypassing the chief of staff, and ordered him to go to war with Syria. It was up to the chief of staff to give operational orders, but on this occasion Rabin had "no desire to quibble when the Syrians were about to get their just deserts for malicious aggressiveness and arrogance."[47] Eshkol did not receive the news with the same equanimity. He suspected that Dayan was trying to steal all the glory for himself and even considered canceling his order. "What a vile man," he muttered in the presence of his aide-de-camp.

What prompted Dayan to change his mind so suddenly was a message from Gamal Abdel Nasser to the Syrian president, Nur al-Din al-Atasi, which was intercepted on the night of 8–9 June by Israeli intelligence. The message said,

> I believe that Israel is about to concentrate all its forces against Syria in order to destroy the Syrian army and regard for the common cause obliges me to advise you to agree to the end-ing of hostilities and to inform U Thant [the UN secretary-general] immediately, in order to preserve Syria's great army. We have lost this battle.
> May God help us in future.
> Your brother, Gamal Abdel Nasser.

Dayan claimed that this message completely changed the situa-tion and led him to give the order to storm the Golan Heights and capture even more territory than had been proposed the preced-ing day. His order was "Do whatever can be done." In the margin of the text of Nasser's message, Dayan scribbled,

> Eshkol,
> 1. In my opinion this cable obliges us to capture the maximal military lines.
> 2. Yesterday I did not think that Egypt and Syria (the politi-cal leadership) would collapse in this way and give up the con-tinuation of the campaign. But since this is the situation, it must be exploited to the full.
> A great day.
> Moshe Dayan.[48]

Having changed his mind, Dayan prosecuted the war on the Syrian front with characteristic vigor. But he greatly underestimated the strength and determination of the enemy. He told Elazar that the Syrian units were crumbling and that their soldiers had begun to flee even before the IDF assault. In fact the Syrian units fought obstinately and with all their strength, but by the evening of 10 June, when the cease-fire that Israel had persistently disregarded went into effect, the Golan Heights were in Israeli hands.

Although Dayan got most of the glory for the victory over Syria, he himself later regarded the decision to go to war against Syria as a mistake. In his 1976 conversations with the journalist Rami Tal, Dayan confessed that on the fourth day of the June War he had failed in his duty as minister of defense by agreeing to the war with Syria. There was really no pressing reason to go to war with Syria, he said. The kibbutz residents who pressed the government to take the Golan Heights did so less for security than for the farmland. Dayan admitted that these civilians had suffered a great deal at the hands of the Syrian soldiers. "But I can tell you with absolute confidence, the delegation that came to persuade Eshkol to take the heights was not thinking of these things. They were thinking about the heights' land." This confidence was unjustified. The protocol of the meeting of the ministerial defense committee shows that the kibbutz leaders spoke only about the nightmarish security situation and made no mention of land.

The allegation that Israel went to war against Syria because the kibbutz residents coveted Syrian land provoked strong indignation in Israel. There was even greater anger at Dayan's allegations from the grave that Israel's security was not threatened by the Syrians. For it became an article of faith among Israelis that the Golan Heights were seized in 1967 to stop the Syrians from shelling the settlements down below. When Rami Tal tried to make this argument, Dayan cut him short: "Look, it's possible to talk in terms of 'the Syrians are bastards, you have to get them and this is the right time,' and other such talk, but that is no policy. You don't strike at every enemy because he is a bastard but because he threatens you. And the Syrians, on the fourth day of the war, were not a threat to us."[49]

Dayan's various accounts of the reasons for the war against Syria are so alarmingly inconsistent that one indeed needs to be a psychologist to fathom his behavior. But one thing emerges clearly from all his contradictory accounts: the Eshkol government did not have a political plan for the conduct of the war. It was divided internally, it debated options endlessly, it improvised, and it seized opportunities as they presented themselves. It hoped for a war on one front, was drawn to war on a second front, and ended up by initiating war on a third front. The one thing it did not have was a master plan for territorial aggrandizement. Its territorial aims were defined not in advance but in response to developments on the battlefield. Appetite comes with eating. The decision-making process of the Eshkol government during the war was complex, confused, and convoluted. It did not bear the slightest resemblance to what political scientists like to call the "the rational actor model."

The victors as well as the vanquished in the Six-Day War sustained losses. On the Israeli side 983 soldiers were killed and 4,517 were wounded. Israel lost 40 aircraft and 394 tanks. At least half of these tanks, however, were later repaired and returned to full operational status. In addition, the Israelis captured about 150 Soviet-made tanks and put them into their postwar inventory. Egypt, Jordan, and Syria had 4,296 soldiers killed and 6,121 wounded. Between them they lost 444 aircraft and 965 tanks.[50]

Israel also sustained one major loss on the diplomatic front: the rupture of relations with the Soviet Union. The Security Council first called for a cease-fire on 6 June, and by 9 June Jordan, Egypt, and Syria had agreed to cease hostilities but the Israeli offensive continued. On 8 June the Soviet government issued a statement warning that unless the demand for an immediate cease-fire was implemented, the USSR would review its relations with Israel. On 10 June, Moscow severed diplomatic relations with Israel and threatened military intervention unless Israel ceased hostilities immediately. The Soviet media launched a campaign against the Israelis, accusing them of "barbaric actions." Moshe Dayan was dubbed Moshe Adolfovich (implying that he was Hitler's disciple), and Zionism was variously denounced as a band of gangsters, as a tool of Wall Street, and as a criminal conspiracy directed against all peace-loving peoples.[51] Prolonging the war in order to capture the Golan Heights not only cost Israel its diplomatic relations with the Soviet Union but also prompted Moscow to step up its diplomatic and military support for Israel's Arab enemies in the aftermath of the war.

POSTWAR DIPLOMACY

Victory in the Six-Day War marked the beginning of a new era in Israel's history—an era of uncertainty. The victory reopened the old question about the territorial aims of Zionism. This question had been settled by the 1949 armistice agreements, and the

armistice lines were reconfirmed in the aftermath of the Sinai
Campaign. By 1967 it had become clear that the Zionist move-
ment could realize all its essential aims within the 1949 borders.
Now, following a war seen by the overwhelming majority of
Israelis as a defensive war, as a war of no choice, they were in con-
trol of Sinai, the Golan Heights, and the West Bank (see map 7).
The question was what to do with these territories, and to this
question there was no simple answer.

The national unity government, hastily formed on the even of
the war, was not well placed to answer this question. It consisted
of twenty-one ministers representing seven different parties and a
wide range of ideological positions. Some of the parties were internally divided on the question of what should be done with the
territories. Gahal resulted from a merger of Herut and the General
Zionists. Herut members subscribed to the Revisionist Zionist
ideology, which claimed the West Bank as part of the Land of
Israel, whereas the General Zionists did not. The Alignment had
resulted from a merger of Mapai and Ahdut Ha'avodah. Most of
the Mapai leaders were pragmatic politicians who had accepted
the prewar territorial status quo, whereas Ahdut Ha'avodah's leaders were territorial expansionists. Divisions thus lay not only between parties but within parties.

Despite these differences, there was a general agreement not to
hand East Jerusalem back to Jordan. On 18 June the government
decided to annex East Jerusalem and the surrounding area. On 27
June, Israeli law and administration were extended to Greater
Jerusalem, which included the Old City. The annexation of East
Jerusalem was the first and most dramatic assertion of Israel's claim
to sovereignty over its ancient homeland. Zion, one of the ancient
names for Jerusalem, was at the heart of Zionist dream for the
restoration of a Jewish kingdom in Palestine. The members of the
Knesset who voted for the annexation of East Jerusalem had no
doubt about Israel's moral claim to the whole of Jerusalem. As for
peace, they believed that it could be attained only from a position
of strength—by demonstrating to the Arabs that Israel could not
be defeated. Ze'ev Jabotinsky, the founder of Revisionist Zionism,
had made the case for the creation of such an iron wall against
Arab rejection forty years earlier. In this context the annexation of
Jerusalem was seen as an act of peace insofar as it demonstrated to
the Arabs the unflinching resolve and the power of the Jewish
state.[52] But in another sense the annexation of East Jerusalem represented an abrupt reversal of the policy of the Zionist movement

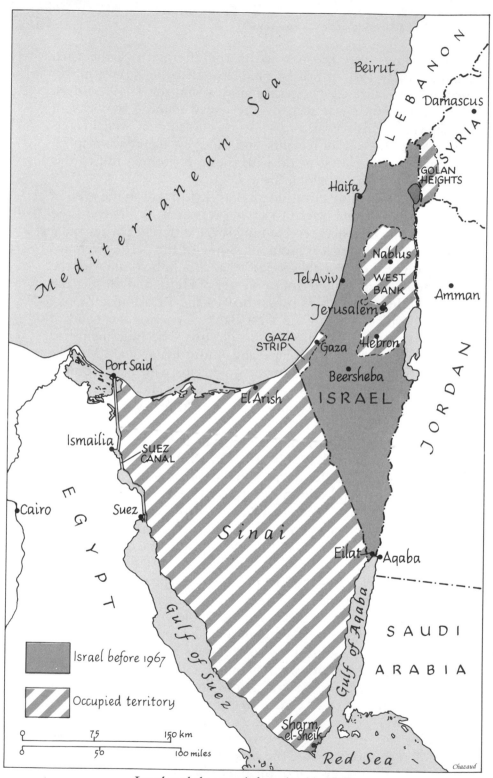

Israel and the occupied territories, 1967

over the preceding three decades. From 1937 until 1967 the Zionist movement was resigned to the partition of Jerusalem, and in 1947 it even accepted the UN plan for the internationalization of the city. But from 1967 on there was broad bipartisan support for the policy that claimed the whole of Jerusalem as the eternal capital of the State of Israel.

Consultations on the future of the new territories started as soon as the guns fell silent. An informal meeting took place in Eshkol's house on 13 June with Abba Eban, Moshe Dayan, Yigal Allon, and Israel Galilee. The main question for discussion was Israel's terms for a peace settlement with its neighbors. A broad consensus emerged in favor of peace with Egypt and Syria on the basis of the international border and withdrawal from heavily populated parts of the West Bank. The first formal discussion of the future of the new territories took place in the ministerial defense committee on the following day. Between 16 and 19 June the whole cabinet discussed the proposals of its defense committee and reached one of the most significant decisions in the annals of Israeli foreign policy.

The decision of 19 June read, "Israel proposes the conclusion of a peace agreement with Egypt based on the international border and the security needs of Israel." The international border placed the Gaza Strip within Israel's territory. Israel's conditions for peace were: (1) guarantee of freedom of navigation in the Straits of Tiran and the Gulf of Aqaba; (2) guarantee of freedom of navigation in the Suez Canal; (3) guarantee of overflight rights in the Straits of Tiran and the Gulf of Aqaba; and (4) the demilitarization of the Sinai peninsula. The decision also proposed the conclusion of a peace treaty with Syria, based on the international border and the security needs of Israel. The conditions for peace with Syria were (1) demilitarization of the Golan Heights and (2) absolute guarantee of noninterference with the flow of water from the sources of the river Jordan to Israel. Finally, the cabinet agreed to defer a decision on the position to be taken with regard to Jordan.[53] The cabinet decision was taken unanimously.

The cabinet decision of 19 June was communicated to Abba Eban in New York, where he had gone to enlist American support for the forthcoming debate at the United Nations. This was very close to the views he had expressed in the earlier sessions prior to his departure. "I was surprised," writes Eban in his autobiography, "by the spacious approach which Eshkol now authorized me to communicate to the United States for transmission to Arab gov-

ernments." Eban met Secretary of State Dean Rusk on 21 June
and outlined to him Israel's proposals for a final peace. According
to Eban's account, Rusk and his colleagues could hardly believe
what he was saying: "Here was Israel, on the very morrow of her
victory, offering to renounce most of her gains in return for the
simple condition of a permanent peace. This was the most dramatic initiative ever taken by an Israeli government before or since
1967, and it had a visibly strong impact on the United States."
Eban goes on to report, "A few days later replies came back
through Washington stating that Egypt and Syria completely rejected the Israeli proposal. Their case was that Israel's withdrawal
must be unconditional."[54] The American record of the meeting
confirms that Rusk considered the Israeli terms as not ungenerous,
but it makes no mention of a request by Eban to transmit these
terms to Egypt and Syria.[55] Nor is there confirmation from
Egyptian or Syrian sources that they received a conditional Israeli
offer of withdrawal through the State Department in late June
1967.[56] One is left with the impression that Eban was more interested in using the cabinet decision of 19 June to impress the
Americans than to engage the governments of Egypt and Syria in
substantive negotiations.

   The cabinet decision of 19 June remained a closely guarded secret in Israel. Even the chief of staff was not told about it. Rabin
only learned about the proposal from his American colleagues after
he had taken off his uniform and become ambassador to
Washington. Moreover, the ministers who made the decision soon
had second thoughts. They quickly concluded that the offer to
withdraw to the international border had been too rash and too
generous and that a higher price should be exacted from Egypt
and Syria for their aggression. Both in private and in public, ministers began to talk about the necessity for retaining some of the
land, especially on the Golan Heights. Military leaders led by
General Elazar made the case on security grounds for keeping a
substantial part of the Golan Heights. The views of the military influenced the politicians. As early as mid-July the politicians started
approving plans for the building of Jewish settlements on the
Golan Heights. In doing so, they reversed their own policy and
embarked on the road toward creeping annexation. The decision
of 19 June became a dead letter even before its formal cancellation
in October.[57]

   If the consensus on complete withdrawal from Sinai and the
Golan Heights was quickly eroded, on the West Bank there was no

consensus at all. With regard to the West Bank there were two main alternatives: to reach an agreement with King Hussein or to give the inhabitants of the West Bank political autonomy under overall Israeli control. The former was called the Jordanian option; the latter, the Palestinian option. The conventional view is that Israel's postwar policy was based on the Jordanian option, on solving the Palestinian problem by restoring to King Hussein most of the territory of the West Bank. According to this view, Israel's leaders were so captivated by the Jordanian option that they failed to consider other political options in their attempt to deal with the postwar situation.

Reuven Pedatzur has convincingly challenged the conventional view. He was allowed to see the relevant protocols of the policy debates of the ruling party, the cabinet, and the cabinet defense committee. His conclusion is that the Palestinian option was the first choice of the Israeli policymakers and that they adopted the Jordanian option only after attempts to realize the Palestinian option had failed.[58]

Eshkol certainly wanted to explore the Palestinian option despite his continuing sympathy for King Hussein and the Hashemite dynasty. He appointed Moshe Sasson, the son of Elias Sasson, special adviser for Palestinian affairs. Moshe Sasson had many meetings with Palestinian leaders from the West Bank and the Gaza Strip and introduced some of them to Eshkol. These discussions were unproductive. Two considerations were uppermost in Eshkol's mind: security and demography. He believed that Israel needed to exercise military control over most of the area up to the river Jordan. On the other hand, he was reluctant to incorporate a substantial Palestinian population into the Jewish state. When Golda Meir asked him what they would do with a million Arabs he replied jokingly, "The dowry pleases you but the bride does not." The problem was how to keep the West Bank without turning Israel into a binational state. His solution was to say that the Jordan River was the border and to give the inhabitants of this area a special status. What he had in mind was "only a semi-autonomous region, since security and the land are in the hands of Israel. I won't mind if in the end they want representation in the United Nations. I began with an autonomous region, but if it transpires that this is impossible, they will get independence."[59]

Other senior policymakers shared Eshkol's inclination toward the Palestinian option, and some even talked in terms of a Palestinian state. The cabinet discussions that led to the decision of 19 June revealed a wide spectrum of opinions regarding the future of the West Bank. Menachem Begin represented one end of the spectrum. He called for the annexation of the West Bank to the State of Israel, arguing that the borders of the State of Israel should correspond to those of the historic Land of Israel. At the other end of the spectrum stood Abba Eban, who was willing to restore the West Bank to Hussein's kingdom. Yigal Allon proposed the annexation of Judea to Israel and the granting of a semi-autonomous status to Samaria, the northern half of the West Bank. He opposed returning the West Bank to Hussein and warned against repeating the mistake made in 1948–49—dalliance with the house of Hashem. Moshe Dayan, like Allon, saw no basis for agreement with King Hussein on the future of the West Bank. But he doubted that Israel could impose a unilateral political settlement on the West Bank, as it had done on Jerusalem, without running the risk of intervention by the great powers. He therefore proposed to proceed in a pragmatic fashion to improve relations with the residents of the West Bank without settling its status.[60]

The person who was perhaps closest to the prime minister in his thinking was the chief of staff. On the one hand Rabin thought that the river Jordan was the best line of defense to the east and that it would therefore be a mistake to restore the West Bank to Jordanian rule. On the other hand he thought that the addition of a million Arabs would spell disaster for the State of Israel. He therefore favored a special status for the West Bank.[61]

Allon and Dayan converged in supporting the Palestinian option but diverged on Israel's security needs in the West Bank. Allon considered control of the Jordan Valley crucial to Israeli security. Dayan deemed control of the mountain ridge from Jenin in the north to Hebron in the south to be much more crucial. Allon moved faster in putting his ideas down on paper. On 26 July he submitted to the cabinet a plan that was to bear his name. It called for incorporating in Israel the following areas: a strip of land ten to fifteen kilometers wide along the Jordan River; most of the Judean desert along the Dead Sea; and a substantial area around Greater Jerusalem, including the Latrum salient (see map 8). Designed to include as few Arabs as possible in the area claimed for Israel, the plan envisaged building permanent settlements and army bases in these areas. Finally, it called for opening negotiations with local leaders on turning the remaining parts of the West Bank into an autonomous region that would be economically linked to Israel. The cabinet discussed Allon's plan but neither adopted nor rejected it.[62]

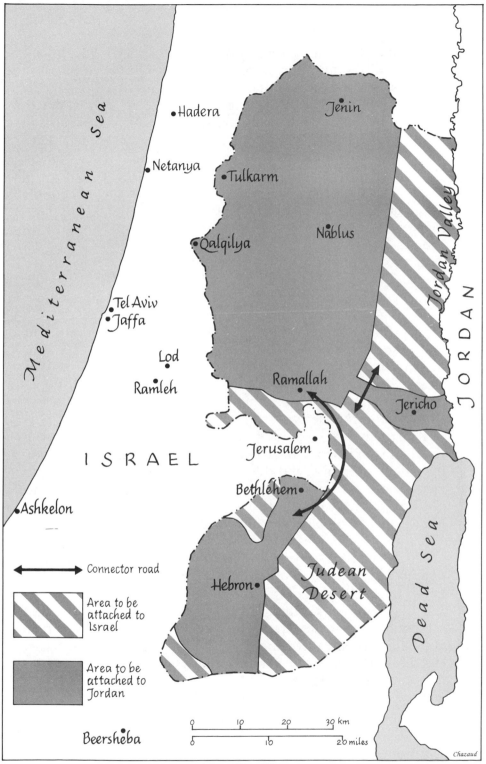

Mediterranean Sea

• Hadera

• Netanya

• Tulkarm

Jenin

• Qalqilya

Nablus

Tel Aviv
Jaffa

Lod
Ramleh

Ramallah

Jericho

JORDAN

Jordan Valley

I S R A E L

Jerusalem

Bethlehem

• Ashkelon

Judean
Desert

Dead Sea

Hebron

Connector road

Area to be
attached to
Israel

Area to be
attached to
Jordan

| 0 | 10 | 20 | 30 km |

| 0 | 10 | 20 miles |

Beersheba

Chazaud

The Allon Plan

Moshe Dayan submitted to the cabinet an alternative to the Allon Plan. Dayan proposed the establishment of what he called "four fists" along the mountain ridge that runs down the middle of the West Bank. Each fist was to consist of large army bases surrounded by civilian settlements connected by convenient roads to Israeli territory inside the Green Line (the prewar border). Each fist was to be located near a large Arab city, near Jenin, Nablus, Ramallah, and Hebron. One of the most salient features of Dayan's plan was the willingness to settle Jews in the heart of the area that was densely populated with Arabs. For the other policy-makers this was the main drawback of the plan. On 20 August the cabinet adopted the military component of Dayan's plan by deciding to establish five army bases on the mountain ridge. It did not adopt the civilian component of the plan.[63] The debate on settlements continued, and here the Allon Plan became the main basis for government policy.

An Arab summit conference was held in Khartoum, the Sudanese capital, between 28 August and 2 September. It was the first meeting of the Arab leaders since their defeat in the June War. Israel's leaders watched with keen anticipation to see what conclusions the Arab leaders would draw from their military defeat. The conference ended with the adoption of the famous three noes of Khartoum: no recognition, no negotiation, and no peace with Israel. On the face of it these declarations showed no sign of readiness for compromise, and this is how Israel interpreted them. In fact, the conference was a victory for the Arab moderates who argued for trying to obtain the withdrawal of Israel's forces by political rather than military means. Arab spokesmen interpreted the Khartoum declarations to mean no formal peace *treaty*, but not a rejection of a state of peace; no *direct* negotiations, but not a refusal to talk through third parties; and no *de jure* recognition of Israel, but acceptance of its existence as a state. President Nasser and King Hussein set the tone at the summit and made it clear subsequently that they were prepared to go much further than ever before toward a settlement with Israel.[64] At Khartoum, Nasser and Hussein reached a genuine understanding and formed a united front against the hard-liners. King Hussein later gave a glimpse of the debate that went on behind the scenes:

At Khartoum I fought very much against the three noes. But the atmosphere there developed into one where all the people who used to support Nasser . . . turned on him and turned on him in such a vicious way that I found myself morally unable to continue to take any stand but to come closer to him and defend him and accuse them of responsibility in things that happened. That was the first collision I had with many of my friends in the Arab world.

But then we talked about the need for a resolution and the need for a peaceful solution to the problem. And his approach was that "I feel responsible. We lost the West Bank and Gaza and that comes first. I am not going to ask for any withdrawal from the Suez Canal. It can stay closed forever until such time as the issue of the West Bank and of Gaza is resolved and the issue of the Palestinian people is resolved. So go and speak of that and speak of a comprehensive solution to the problem and a comprehensive peace and go and do anything you can short of signing a separate peace." And I said in any event I am not considering signing a separate peace, because we want to resolve this problem in a comprehensive fashion.[65]

The Khartoum summit thus marked a real turning point in Nasser's attitude to Israel. At Khartoum, Nasser advised, and indeed urged, King Hussein to explore the possibility of a peaceful settlement with Israel. This was, of course, not known in Israel at the time. As far as Israel was concerned, the Khartoum declarations closed every door and every window that might lead to a peace settlement. On October 17 the cabinet took a decision that amounted to an official cancellation of the decision of 19 June. The new decision, which was adopted by the Knesset following a statement by the prime minister on 30 October, said, "The Government notes with regret the fact that the Arab states adhere to their position of not recognizing, not negotiating, and not concluding peace treaties with Israel. Faced with this position of the Arab states, Israel will maintain the situation fixed by the cease-fire agreements and reinforce its position by taking into account its security and development needs." On the same day that the Knesset adopted this decision, the cabinet took a further decision, which remained strictly secret and was not communicated to the U.S. government. This decision canceled the principle of seeking peace with Egypt and Syria on the basis of the international border. The decision did not specify the areas that Israel needed for security and for settlements. It simply stated that the agreements with Egypt and Syria must give Israel secure borders.[66]

The most significant international pronouncement on the

Arab-Israeli dispute after the Six-Day War was UN Security Council Resolution 242. The preamble to the resolution emphasized the inadmissibility of the acquisition of territory by force and the need to work for a just and lasting peace. Article 1 stated that a just and lasting peace should include two principles: (i) "withdrawal of Israeli armed forces from territories occupied in the recent conflict" and (ii) respect for the right of every state in the area "to live in peace within secure and recognized boundaries free from threats or acts of force." The resolution went on to affirm the necessity for guaranteeing freedom of navigation and for achieving a just settlement of the refugee problem. The resolution supported the Arabs on the issue of territory and Israel on the issue of peace. Basically, it proposed a deal in which Israel would get peace in exchange for returning to the Arab states their territories.

The resolution was a masterpiece of deliberate British ambiguity. It was this ambiguity that won for the resolution the support of the United States, the Soviet Union, Jordan, and Egypt but not of Syria. Israel had many successes on the long road that led to its adoption. It defeated a series of Arab and Soviet proposals that called for withdrawal without peace. Another success was to avoid the requirement of withdrawing from "the territories" or "all the territories" occupied in the recent war. The final wording was "withdrawal from territories," and this gave Israel some room for maneuvering. The cabinet decision of 19 June played a major part in enlisting American support for the Israeli position, but the Americans understood the UN resolution to mean Israeli withdrawal to the international border in Sinai and the Golan.

Israel's interpretation of Resolution 242 also differed from the Arab interpretation. Egypt and Jordan agreed to peace but insisted that the first step be complete Israeli withdrawal. Israel declared that before it would withdraw from any part of the territories, there must be direct negotiations leading to a contractual peace agreement that incorporated secure and recognized boundaries. In fact, Israel did not publicly accept Resolution 242 until August 1970. But on 12 February 1968 Abba Eban informed the UN mediator, Dr. Gunnar Jarring, that Israel accepted the resolution.

Jarring, the Swedish ambassador to Moscow, had been appointed by the UN secretary-general to promote an Arab-Israeli settlement on the basis of Resolution 242. Having rejected 242, Syria declined to participate in his mission. The other Arab states had high expectations of his mission, whereas Israel had none at all.

Jarring was perceived in Jerusalem as personally unimaginative and ineffectual. But the real problem was that Israel had no trust in the impartiality of the UN or in its capacity to mediate. The Israeli tactic was to keep feeding Jarring proposals and documents to which he was to obtain Arab reactions. The aim was to keep his mission alive and prevent the matter from going back to the UN, where Israel would be blamed for the failure. Eban's colleagues were happy to leave it to him to conduct the elaborate exchange of notes with Jarring as long as he did not make any substantive concessions. Eban understood better than any of them both the limits and the possibilities of Jarring's mission. "Some of my colleagues," noted Eban, "did not understand that even a tactical exercise fills a vacuum. Even diplomatic activity that is not leading anywhere is better than no diplomatic activity at all. Activity itself gives Arab moderates an alibi for avoiding the military option."[67] For more purposeful diplomacy Eban went outside the UN framework.

Eban met King Hussein in London in December 1967. He was accompanied by Dr. Yaacov Herzog. The initiative for the meeting came from the king, who had met Herzog on 2 July and twice in November. Eban was not authorized by the cabinet to make any peace proposals. He was empowered only to explore what Jordan's reaction would be to a peace treaty in which Israel kept Jerusalem and some territory along the Jordan River but in such a manner as to restore to the Hashemite kingdom the bulk of the populated areas of the West Bank.[68] Hussein did not reject the idea but wanted Jordan to be compensated for its territorial loss, possibly in the Gaza Strip. The meeting amounted to no more than a very preliminary exchange of views.

The meeting with Hussein was symptomatic of a declining interest among the Israeli policymakers in the Palestinian option. Talks with the Palestinians led nowhere. The traditional West Bank leaders listened politely to Israel's suggestions of limited autonomy, but they wanted real independence, which was not being offered. They were also afraid to be seen as collaborating with Israel and turning their back on the Arab world. The younger generation of Palestinian nationalists looked to the PLO as their leader. They became engaged in a struggle for national liberation and began to organize resistance to Israeli occupation. Externally, too, there was no significant support for a Palestinian option. UN Resolution 242 referred to the Palestinians only indirectly, by calling for a solution to the refugee problem. Jarring had no dealings with the

Palestinians, only with member states of the UN. The United States showed no interest in Palestinian national aspirations and encouraged Israel to negotiate with King Hussein. The Palestinian option had never been formally adopted by the cabinet, nor was it formally renounced, but in the early months of 1968 it was unmistakably on the decline.

An internal development that had consequences for foreign policy was the union of the Alignment with Rafi in January 1968 to form the Israel Labor Party (Mifleget Poalei Eretz Israel, or Mapai). Golda Meir agreed to serve as the secretary-general of the new party. David Ben-Gurion opposed the return of Rafi to the mother party. The 1968 union contributed to immobilism in the foreign policy sphere. The new Labor Party straddled a wide range of views: Mapai's old guard were pragmatic and committed to territorial compromise, Ahdut Ha'avodah's leaders were ideological and committed to the preserving of the whole Land of Israel, while Rafi's leaders stood for an activist defense policy and an expansionist policy on the West Bank. The union created fear of an initiative that would split the new party and caused Mapai's leaders not to use its majority in favor of pragmatic foreign policy decisions.[69]

In April 1968 the new party held consultations on the future of the West Bank. Prior to the meeting Yigal Allon revised his plan. He had more or less given up the hope of reaching agreement on autonomy for the West Bank with the local leaders. The alternative he proposed was to hand over to the Hashemite Kingdom of Jordan the parts of the West Bank that Israel did not need. Allon did not change the map of July 1967, but instead of offering to share the West Bank with the Palestinians, he offered to share it with King Hussein. Although no decision was taken on the revised Allon Plan, Eban was authorized to discuss it in general terms with King Hussein at their scheduled meeting in London in late May 1968. Eban reported to his colleagues on his return that the king was no longer satisfied with a general presentation of their thinking but expected a specific proposal to which he could respond. Only then was it decided to present the Allon Plan to Hussein as the official policy of Israel.

The next meeting was held in London on 27 September. King Hussein was accompanied by his trusted adviser Zeid al-Rifai; Eban, by Yigal Allon and Yaacov Herzog. Eban opened the meeting by describing it as a historic occasion. He said they had been instructed to discuss the possibility of a permanent peace but hinted that if the king rejected the principles presented to him, they would have to find tracks to a settlement with the Palestinians without affinity to Jordan. Allon described the meeting with King Hussein as the happiest moment of his life. He spoke of the dangers of Soviet-Arab cooperation for the Jordanian regime and suggested that an agreement with Israel would serve to guarantee the regime against external intervention and domestic instability. The king responded that his search for a permanent settlement began long before this meeting and that he aspired to devote the rest of his life to achieving it. He admitted that at Khartoum things were said that should not have been said, but he added that at the end of the conference the countries directly involved were charged with working toward a political settlement.

Eban outlined six principles that underlay the Israeli approach to a settlement with Jordan. Allon then presented the map of his plan.[70] According to Eban, "The first reaction of Jordan was one of interest. But when the conception behind our policy found expression in a map attributed to Minister of Labor Yigal Allon, the Jordanian attitude became adamant. It was clear that King Hussein would rather leave Israel under international criticism in possession of all the West Bank than take on himself the responsibility of ceding 33 percent of it to us."[71]

Although the king rejected the plan on the spot, the Israeli ministers proposed another meeting within the next fortnight to give him a chance to reconsider his position. The king did not need a fortnight. A day later Zeid al-Rifai called Herzog to arrange a meeting. There Rifai gave Herzog a document listing his master's six principles in reply to Eban's six principles. The fifth paragraph dealt with secure borders. It gave the king's unambiguous answer to the Allon Plan: "The plan itself is wholly unacceptable since it infringes Jordanian sovereignty. The only way is to exchange territory on the basis of reciprocity." The document served to demonstrate just how wide the gulf between the Israeli and Jordanian positions was. Although the king had rejected the Israeli terms for a settlement, the secret meetings with him did not stop. They continued until the conclusion of the peace treaty between Israel and Jordan in October 1994, and after that there was no need for secrecy.

It was only after the signature of the peace treaty that the king agreed to speak on the record about his meetings with Israeli leaders. About the Allon Plan, which was put in front of him time and again, he remained adamant:

This was totally rejected. And in point of fact in the subsequent period of negotiations and discussions and so on, I was offered the return of something like 90 plus percent of the territory, 98 percent even, excluding Jerusalem, but I couldn't accept. As far as I am concerned, it was either every single inch that I was responsible for or nothing. This was against the background of what happened in 1948 when the whole West Bank was saved, including the Old City of Jerusalem. Yet my grandfather eventually paid with his life for his attempts to make peace. If it were to be my responsibility, I had to return everything, not personally to me, but to be placed under international auspices for the people to determine what their future ought to be. We were perfectly happy with that. But I could not compromise. And so this repeated itself time and time and time again throughout the many years until 1990.[72]

On 26 February 1969 Levi Eshkol died in Jerusalem. He was seventy-four years old and had been suffering from cancer. His hope of translating Israel's territorial gains in the Six-Day War into a permanent political settlement with the Arab world remained unfulfilled. He himself has sometimes been criticized for not showing enough magnanimity at the moment of victory. This criticism is not entirely justified with regard to Egypt and Syria. Initially, he was prepared to make peace with these countries on the basis of the international border, but he failed to communicate specific peace offers to them. The problem with Jordan was more complex because the area between the two countries contained a large Palestinian population. Here the usual criticism is that Eshkol was fixated on the Jordanian option and therefore failed to explore the option of a settlement with the Palestinians. This criticism, too, is not altogether justified. Eshkol initially inclined toward the Palestinian option, and he engaged in serious talks with local leaders from the West Bank and Gaza after the end of the war. Only after concluding that there was no possible Palestinian option did he begin to explore the Jordanian option. He quickly discovered that there was no Jordanian option either. The Palestinians demanded complete Israeli withdrawal and complete political independence, and this Eshkol could not have delivered even if he had wanted to. King Hussein demanded complete Israeli withdrawal, and this, too, Eshkol could not have delivered even if he had wanted to. The real mistake was to occupy and stay in the West Bank. As Eshkol himself pointed out to Golda Meir, there was no way they could have the dowry without the bride.

Dr. Theodor Herzl.

President
Chaim Weizmann.

Prime Minister
David Ben-Gurion.

Ze'ev Jabotinsky.

David Ben-Gurion reading the Declaration of Independence,
14 May 1948.

The Israeli flag is raised as Israel becomes a member of the United
Nations, 11 May 1949. *Right,* Moshe Sharett; *left,* Abba Eban.

Prime Minister Moshe Sharett with David Ben-Gurion at the latter's home in Sede-Boker.

Golda Meir and Pinhas Lavon.

The press conference on the Sinai campaign with Chief of Staff Moshe Dayan.

The Six-Day War, June 1967. Three Egyptian MiG-21s destroyed by bull's-eye hits from Israeli planes during an attack on an Egyptian airfield.

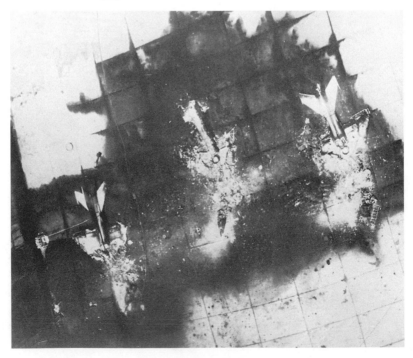

The Six-Day War. Captured Egyptian soldiers in truck *(right)* and
an Israeli armored convoy.

Prime Minister Levi
Eshkol with President
Lyndon Johnson at the
ranch in Texas, 7 January
1968.

Prime Minister Golda Meir and Dr. Henry Kissinger flanked by
Ambassador Yitzhak Rabin and his wife, Leah, 27 February 1973.

The October War, 1973. Israeli prisoners of war supporting each
other after being taken captive by the Egyptian army.

Middle Eastern peace conference in the Palais des Nations, Geneva, 21 December 1973.

Golda Meir makes a point.

Prime Minister Menachem Begin welcoming President Anwar al-Sadat at Ben-Gurion Airport, 19 November 1977.

President Carter, President Sadat, and Prime Minister Begin sitting on the porch of Aspen Lodge at Camp David, 6 September 1978.

President Carter, President Sadat, and Prime Minister Begin signing the Camp David Accords in the White House, 17 September 1978.

Prime Minister Menachem Begin *(right)* shakes hands with President Anwar al-Sadat at the signing of the Israel-Egypt peace treaty in the White House, 26 March 1979.

The Lebanon War, 21 June 1982. Israeli armor lines up on the coastal highway leading to Beirut.

The Lebanon War, June 1982. Israeli armored personnel carriers in the streets of Beirut.

Yitzhak Shamir and Shimon Peres.

Palestinian burning tires in a demonstration in Ramallah during the *intifada*, 3 October 1988.

Jewish settlers demonstrating against the IDF's handling of the *intifada* during the visit of Prime Minister Yitzhak Shamir at Bracha settlement, 12 January 1989.

Destroyed homes in Ramat Gan after an Iraqi Scud missile hit
during the Gulf War, 30 January 1991.

President George Bush addressing the opening session of the
Middle Eastern peace conference in Madrid, 30 October 1991.
Right, Prime Minister Yitzhak Shamir.

Prime Minister Yitzhak Rabin shaking hands with PLO Chairman Yasser Arafat at the signing of the Declaration of Principles in the White House, 13 September 1993.

PLO Chairman Yasser Arafat, Egyptian President Hosni Mubarak, and Prime Minister Yitzhak Rabin meeting during the Cairo summit, 6 November 1993.

King Hussein of Jordan extends his hand to Prime Minister Yitzhak Rabin as President Clinton looks on at the start of a Rose Garden ceremony to sign the Washington Declaration, 25 July 1994.

President Bill Clinton watches Prime Minister Yitzhak Rabin and King Hussein shake hands after the signing of the Israel-Jordan peace treaty, 26 October 1994.

The Nobel Prize laureates for 1994 in Oslo, 10 December 1994.
Right to left, Prime Minister Yitzhak Rabin, Foreign Minister
Shimon Peres, and PLO Chairman Yasser Arafat.

Shell of an egged no. 26 bus in Jerusalem blown up in a terrorist
attack by a Hamas suicide bomber, 21 August 1995.

Prime Minister Rabin and PLO Chairman Arafat sign Oslo II
maps in the White House in the presence of President Mubarak,
President Clinton, and King Hussein, 28 September 1995.

Prime Minister Shimon Peres shaking hands with Nahariya residents during a visit to the city in the midst of Operation Grapes of
Wrath, 15 April 1996.

Prime Minister Binyamin Netanyahu addressing the Knesset,
18 June 1996.

Prime Minister Ehud Barak.

7

Immobilism

1969–1974

GOLDA MEIR WAS seventy-one years old when she was elected to succeed Levi Eshkol as leader of Mapai and prime minister in March 1969. In July of the preceding year, she had resigned from her post as secretary-general of Mapai, and this was taken to mark the end of her political career. She was in poor health, suffering from a serious blood disease, and required constant medical attention. In the autumn of 1968 she was visited in her convalescent home in Switzerland by Pinhas Sapir, who had succeeded her as Mapai's secretary-general. Sapir told her that Eshkol was seriously ill and that she would have to succeed him when he died. Golda agreed to serve as an interim prime minister on condition that there was no change in the composition of the government. To Abba Eban, Sapir explained that Golda would be a caretaker prime minister because she, too, was very ill but that the party needed her in order to prevent a contest between Moshe Dayan and Yigal Allon for the senior post.[1] The sophisticated, Cambridge-educated Eban was not an admirer of Golda Meir. One of his many quips about her was that she chose to use only two hundred words although her vocabulary extended to five hundred.

GOLDA THE INTRANSIGENT

Having been brought out of retirement, Golda ruled her party and her country with an iron rod for the next five years. She had an exceptionally strong and decisive personality, being imperious, overbearing, and intolerant of opposition. Subtlety and ambiguity were alien to her character, and she had a remarkable capacity for simplifying complex problems. She saw the world in black-and-white, without intermediate shades of gray. Her confidence that in any debate her party, her country, and she were in the right was without limits. And it was this burning conviction of always being in the right that made it so difficult to reason with her.

Nowhere was Golda's self-righteousness more conspicuous than in relation to the Arab world. Her attitude to the Arabs was based on emotion and intuition rather than on reason and reflection. As her biographer pointed out,

> Golda was afraid of the Arabs, and these fears were connected with her memories of pogroms and the Holocaust. She may have also been afraid of the quest for revenge that she detected among the Arabs. She could not come to terms with the thought that maybe the Arabs felt that an injustice had been committed against them. She also rejected absolutely the possibility that some of the Arab demands might be justified. She refused to recognize that the Arabs felt humiliated. She did not agree with the assumption that the Palestinian Arabs felt that they were a people without a country. . . . It was very hard for her to face up soberly to the main problem that confronted Zionism: the Arab question. Her position was simple: they or us.[2]

In anything that touched Israel's security Golda Meir was intransigent. After the June 1967 war she considered border adjustments essential to Israel's security and vehemently rejected the claim of the critics that this was evidence of expansionism. In her memoirs she noted,

> And of course, "intransigent" was to become my middle name. But neither Eshkol nor I, nor the overwhelming majority of other Israelis, could make a secret of the fact that we weren't at all interested in a fine, liberal, anti-militaristic, dead Jewish state or in a "settlement" that would win us compliments about being reasonable and intelligent but that would endanger our lives. . . . Israeli democracy is so lively that there were, and are, almost as many "doves" as "hawks," but I have yet to come across any Israeli who thinks that we should turn

ourselves, permanently, into clay pigeons—not even for the sake of a better image.[3]

The differences in temperament between Golda Meir and Levi Eshkol were very striking. She was a fighter; he was a man of compromise. She was dogmatic and domineering; he was open-minded and often hesitant. She was intransigent; he was flexible. But in their thinking about the future of the West Bank they were not all that far apart. Both wanted to preserve the Jewish and democratic character of the State of Israel, and both were therefore opposed to the annexation of the West Bank. Both came around to the view that the most promising solution to the Palestinian problem lay in a territorial compromise with Jordan that would keep the bulk of the Palestinian population outside Israel's borders. The difference was largely one of presentation: Eshkol put the emphasis on what Israel was prepared to concede for the sake of a settlement with the Arabs, whereas she put it on Israel's security-related conditions.[4]

On becoming prime minister, Golda Meir adopted the two principles that formed the bedrock of Israeli policy after 1967: no return to the prewar borders and no withdrawal without direct negotiations and peace treaties with the Arab states. In her first statement to the Knesset as prime minister, on 5 May 1969, she stressed the continuity in policy but also made it clear, in typically forthright language, that Israel would not settle for anything less than contractual peace treaties with its neighbors. The Arab demands for retreat from the cease-fire lines without peace were unacceptable. As long as the Arabs refused to make peace, Israel would consolidate its position along the cease-fire lines. Equally unacceptable were the substitutes for peace treaties that had been suggested over the preceding two years, such as demilitarization, the end of belligerency, and international guarantees. Peace treaties had to be negotiated directly between the governments of the Middle East, not by external powers: "The peace treaties must include agreement on final, secure, and recognized boundaries. The peace treaties must annul claims of belligerency, blockades, boycotts, interference with free navigation, and the existence and activity of organizations and groups engaged in preparing or executing sabotage operations from bases and training camps on the territories of the states signatory to the peace treaties." What the new prime minister refused to spell out, on this and many subsequent occasions, was what she meant by secure boundaries.

In the country at large there was no consensus on policy toward the Arabs. The polarization of public opinion in the aftermath of the Six-Day War was most clearly manifest in the emergence of two ideological movements: the Greater Israel movement and the peace movement. Both were fringe movements dominated by intellectuals, both cut across party lines, both represented traditional currents of thoughts within Zionism, and both emphasized the importance of ideology as a basis of action to a Mapai leadership that prided itself on being pragmatic. The former advocated the incorporation of all the territories occupied in the war into the boundaries of Israel. The latter advocated the return of most of the territories and a conciliatory policy designed to lead to accommodation with the Arabs. As the government seemed to be leading nowhere, each movement stepped up the pressure for the adoption of its policy alternative. And the intense debate this generated had the effect of further eroding the middle ground and sharpening the division within Mapai.[5]

Within Mapai, Golda Meir had always been identified with the activist wing. She was a disciple of David Ben-Gurion and shared his views about the implacable hostility of the Arabs and about the need to deal with them from a position of strength. After 1967, when the terms "activist" and "moderate" began to be replaced by the terms "hawk" and "dove," she continued to be identified with the hawkish wing of the party. Eshkol was a traditional Mapai moderate who had fallen among hawks. Golda Meir was a hawk who listened only to other hawks. She was much closer in her views to the small factions within the labor movement, Ahdut Ha'avodah and Rafi, than to her colleagues in Mapai. She was particularly close to Israel Galilee, who became her principal political adviser and speech writer. To Moshe Dayan she was never personally close, but she allowed him to exercise far greater influence in the making of foreign policy than Eshkol ever did. Galilee was one of the most uncompromising hawks within the united labor movement. Dayan, who doubted that the Arabs could be persuaded to make peace with Israel, became a leading expansionist. The majority in Mapai remained dovish, but the tone was set by this hawkish trio.

In the government, too, the hawks exercised an influence disproportionate to their numbers. Most of the Mapai ministers were doves: Abba Eban, Zalman Aran, Pinhas Sapir, Ze'ev Sharef, Yaacov Shimshon Shapira, and Eliahu ("Elias") Sasson. But they did not form a coalition with the dovish ministers from Mapam, the National Religious Party, and the Independent Liberal Party. They tended to go along with the hawkish coalition, which consisted of Golda Meir, Israel Galilee, Yigal Allon, Moshe Carmel, Moshe Dayan, Yosef Almogi, Menachem Begin, and Yosef Sapir. The last two represented Gahal. Galilee and Dayan had a particular interest in maintaining the national unity government with this right-wing party. The partnership with Gahal gave them a majority on many of the issues that really mattered to them, issues connected with foreign policy, security, and the occupied territories. It enabled them to resist proposals for political initiatives to settle the Arab-Israeli dispute on the grounds that they would divide the nation.[6]

In the cabinet Golda Meir threw all her weight behind the policy of preserving the status quo and avoiding political risks. In fact she epitomized the policy of immobilism, of sitting tight on the new cease-fire lines and refusing to budge until the Arabs agreed to make peace on Israel's terms. She was not a neutral chairperson of cabinet meetings but a strong leader capable of riding roughshod over ministers who disagreed with her even if they were the majority. As prime minister she had ultimate responsibility for defense policy. This responsibility was expressed constitutionally by the prime minister's chairmanship of the cabinet's defense committee. But during her premiership this committee did not meet regularly. Its place was taken by an informal body that came to be known as "Golda's kitchen" because it met in her house.

The regular participants in Golda's kitchen were Israel Galilee, Yigal Allon, Moshe Dayan, Abba Eban, and Pinhas Sapir. From time to time other ministers were invited to participate if a subject in which they were directly involved was on the agenda. The kitchen cabinet usually met on Saturday evening, prior to the cabinet's weekly meeting on Sunday morning. Its main role was to try and establish a united position for the ruling party and to formulate specific proposals for discussion and decision by the cabinet. Sometimes the kitchen cabinet took decisions on its own, and there was a written record of them. But most of the important proposals were submitted to the full cabinet for its approval. Now and then Golda Meir came under criticism for failing to consult the entire cabinet in matters of great importance and for operating in an unconstitutional manner. But throughout her tenure as prime minister, the kitchen cabinet continued to play a crucial role in the making of foreign and defense policy.

Another body that gained in influence under Golda Meir was

the IDF General Staff. The trend had started with the spectacular success of the IDF in the Six-Day War. The chief of staff began to attend cabinet meetings regularly to report and advise. Military intelligence acquired a monopoly over the presentation of national intelligence estimates, marginalizing the Foreign Ministry in the process. Since the cabinet did not have at its disposal an independent body of experts in charge of policy analysis and long-term planning, the estimates of the military were difficult to challenge and acceptance of their recommendations was usually a foregone conclusion.

Golda Meir's assertiveness in relation to her civilian colleagues was matched by a curious subservience toward her military subordinates. She always saw herself as somebody who did not understand defense matters. As foreign minister she once defined her essential task as that of being a weapons procurer for the IDF.[7] As prime minister she displayed an uncritical approach to the advice proffered by the IDF General Staff. Abba Eban regarded this as one of her greatest weaknesses as prime minister. In his view Israel needed a prime minister who was able to disagree with the views of the defense establishment. Ben-Gurion, Sharett, and Eshkol were all capable of not accepting the military point of view. "But Mrs. Meir herself has more or less said that on security matters, 'I would do nothing but blindly accept the military view.' That is not the function of a prime minister."[8]

The growing influence of the senior army officers reinforced a long-standing tendency to view relations with the Arab states from a strategic perspective and to subordinate political and diplomatic considerations to military ones in the making of high policy. It had always been the thesis of the defense establishment that for as long as Israel was in a state of siege, it must have primary responsibility for policy in the entire security field—and that included much of the country's external relations. After the Six-Day War, Israel's bargaining position greatly increased as a result of the acquisition of Arab territories, but the internal constraints on the use of this bargaining power also increased with the passage of time. Lack of consensus on national goals curtailed the government's ability to take political initiatives. International initiatives for a peaceful solution of the Arab-Israeli conflict were invariably deemed by Meir and her advisers as prejudicial to Israel's security. When the Arab states resorted to force in order to dislodge Israel from their land, Israel responded with greater force. Under Meir's leadership, Israel's policy in the conflict consisted essentially of military activism and diplomatic immobility. "Intransigent" was not only her middle name. It was also the hallmark of Israel's policy in the conflict with the Arab world during the five years of her premiership.

THE WAR OF ATTRITION

Failure to bring about Israeli withdrawal from the occupied territories by diplomatic means led Gamal Abdel Nasser to coin the slogan "That which was taken by force can only be recovered by force." Military clashes between Egypt and Israel occurred intermittently from the end of the Six-Day War until the spring of 1969. However, it was the large-scale offensive mounted by the Egyptian army in March 1969, coupled with Nasser's renunciation of the UN-decreed cease-fire, that marked the beginning of the War of Attrition. A formal declaration of intent came later, on 23 June. Nasser's immediate goal was to prevent the conversion of the Suez Canal into a de facto border, while his ultimate goal was to force Israel to withdraw to the prewar border. The military strategy adopted for this purpose consisted of heavy artillery bombardment of Israel's positions on the canal front, occasional air attacks, and hit-and-run commando raids. The idea was to take advantage of Egypt's massive superiority in manpower and Israel's comparative disadvantage in static warfare and well-known sensitivity to casualties in order to exhaust Israel militarily, economically, and psychologically, and thus pave the way to an Egyptian crossing to dislodge Israeli forces from Sinai.

Israel had to decide on a suitable response to the Egyptian challenge. Its traditional military doctrine called for carrying the war to the enemy's territory. And there was a proposal for capturing the west bank of the Suez Canal, but this was turned down, partly because the IDF did not have the necessary amphibious equipment but mainly for political reasons. Israel settled for a defensive strategy of preventing the Egyptian army from crossing the canal and capturing territory on the east bank. The IDF considered two alternatives for the defense of Sinai: a permanent physical presence along the waterline or protection of the canal zone by means of mobile forces deployed in the interior. Chief of Staff Chaim Bar-Lev ruled in favor of the first alternative. The result was the erection of the line of fortifications along the canal that bore his name. Political considerations influenced the decision against flexible defense and in favor of static defense. Gold Meir's basic aim was to preserve the political and territorial status quo and not to yield any ground until Egypt agreed to a peace treaty. Static defense was a more effective means of meeting this political end, but it also presented the IDF with a host of new problems.

In mid-July 1969, after four months of intensive but inconclusive warfare, the Israeli Air Force was used as "flying artillery" in the canal zone. The aim was to gain mastery of the skies, to hit the Egyptian ground forces, and to deter them from planning a new war. Bar-Lev described the new strategy as an attempt to escalate for the purpose of de-escalation but the result was further escalation in the fighting.

A general election was held on 28 October, in the shadow of the War of Attrition. Mapai had merged with Mapam the previous year to form the Alignment. Dayan opposed the merger with the dovish Mapam and even threatened to leave the party unless he could dictate its electoral platform. The platform made no mention of UN Resolution 242 or of withdrawal. Moreover, most of Dayan's demands were incorporated in "an oral doctrine" that was binding on all the members of the Alignment. This doctrine indicated what the party meant by "secure borders." It stated that the river Jordan would be Israel's eastern security border, that the Golan Heights and the Gaza Strip would remain under Israeli control, and that Israel would retain a strip of land all the way down to the Straits of Tiran. Dayan put his own gloss on the Alignment's electoral platform by saying, "Sharm el-Sheikh without peace is better than peace without Sharm el-Sheikh."

The Alignment did not fare well in the election. It won 56 seats, compared with 63 seats won by its component parts in 1965. Gahal won 26 seats, the National Religious Party 12, and the Independent Liberal Party 4. Overall, the right wing increased its power, but the electorate continued to put its trust in the Alignment and its leader. After the election Golda Meir formed a national unity government very similar in composition to the one she had inherited from Eshkol.

The first challenge to confront the new government was an American peace plan. A Republican administration had come to power in January with Richard Nixon as president, Henry Kissinger as his national security adviser, and William Rogers as secretary of state. The State Department had long advocated an "evenhanded" approach to the Arab-Israeli conflict and an active American role in promoting a political settlement based on the principles embodied in UN Resolution 242. On 9 December 1969 Rogers presented his peace plan for the Middle East. The plan was based on 242. It envisaged Israel's return to the international border with its neighbors, with only minor modifications for mutual security, and a solution to the Palestinian refugee problem.

The Rogers plan took Israel's leaders by complete surprise. They saw it as evidence of U.S.–USSR collaboration in trying to impose a peace settlement on them. On 15 December, Golda Meir presented her new government to the Knesset and used the occasion to launch the first of many attacks on the Rogers plan. Relations became even more strained when, on 18 December, Charles Yost, the U.S. representative at the UN, proposed guidelines for a settlement between Israel and Jordan based on the Rogers plan. Yost advocated Israeli withdrawal from most of the West Bank, Jordanian administration for East Jerusalem, and a settlement of the Palestinian refugee problem. Golda termed the plan "a disaster for Israel," ordered a campaign of protest by Israel's friends in Washington, and recalled Ambassador Yitzhak Rabin for urgent consultations. Rabin had been appointed ambassador to Washington following his retirement from the IDF and seemed to regard diplomacy as the continuation of war by other means. At its meeting on 22 December, after hearing Rabin's report, the cabinet decided formally to reject all the American proposals. "If these proposals were carried out," said the cabinet statement, "Israel's security and peace would be in grave danger. Israel will not be sacrificed by any power policy, and will reject any attempt to impose a forced solution upon it."[9]

Having rejected the American peace proposals, Israel returned to wage the War of Attrition. In the last week of December, the cabinet took a fateful decision—to initiate strategic bombing of the Egyptian hinterland.[10] The idea originated with the IDF General Staff and was recommended to the cabinet by the minister of defense. The original proponent of the strategic-bombing idea was Major General Ezer Weizman, who parachuted into the government as a Gahal minister after the general election. Inside the government he continued to press for the use of the IAF to bring an end to the War of Attrition. He had a powerful ally in Yitzhak Rabin, the soldier turned diplomat. Rabin reported to the cabinet that the Nixon administration would welcome deep-penetration bombing in Egypt because it would serve American interests in the region. Abba Eban disputed the ambassador's analysis of the American position. He reasoned that the Americans could not possibly be interested in the extension of the Arab-Israeli conflict, because of the danger of increased Soviet involvement on the Arab side. Rabin's visit helped tip the balance in the cabinet in favor of inflicting massive military blows on Egypt.

Another question on which the cabinet had to make up its collective mind was the likely Soviet reaction to the bombing of the Egyptian interior. Once again Eban found himself in a minority. He estimated that the bombing would step up Soviet military involvement in the region. The majority believed that the Soviets would protest but stop short of physical intervention. The cabinet discussion on this question was cursory, uninformed, and superficial. The result was to miscalculate not only the likelihood of Soviet intervention but also its impact on the Israeli-Egyptian military balance.

The IDF was authorized to start implementing the new policy on 7 January 1970. The military objectives of this policy were, first, to reduce Egyptian military pressure in the forward canal area; second, to deter the Egyptians from planning a full-scale war; and third, to bring the War of Attrition to an end and compel Egypt to observe the cease-fire. The idea was to end the war in such a way as to enhance the deterrent power of the IDF. This goal could not be attained by a negotiated, mediated, or conditional cease-fire. It was thought to require a demonstration of the IDF's capacity to compel the Egyptian army to follow a course of action prescribed for it.

In addition to military objectives, Israel's decision makers hoped to achieve a range of psychological and political objectives. These were not clearly articulated and did not command unanimous agreement, but they played a significant part in producing the decision to embark on deep-penetration bombing. The undeclared aims were to break Egyptian morale, create a credibility gap between Nasser and the Egyptian people, and bring about the downfall of the Nasser regime and its replacement by a pro-Western regime. There was an echo here of the Sinai War. Talk of overthrowing regimes by external military pressure is usually a symptom of confusion, and this instance was no exception. Events were to show—as logic and history and any knowledge of Egyptian politics would have suggested—that, far from undermining the Egyptian will to resist, the bombing would reinforce it; and far from bringing Nasser down, it would rally the people behind him in an upsurge of national solidarity.

The first raid on the Egyptian hinterland was launched on 7 January 1970; the last one took place on 13 April. During those four months, Israel's American-made supersonic Phantom fighter planes struck repeatedly at targets in the Nile delta and on the outskirts of Cairo. All in all, the Israelis flew 3,300 sorties and dropped an estimated 8,000 tons of ordnance on Egyptian territory. What was lacking was a coherent policy. Golda Meir denied that the raids were deliberately intended to topple Nasser but added that if they brought about a change of regime, she would not shed any tears over it. At times she gave the impression that the raids were part of an educational campaign to make Nasser stop lying to his people, as if he were a naughty boy she was taking by the ear to the woodshed.

The conduct of the campaign was not accompanied by any sign of political flexibility. Israel's leaders were simply bent on increasing the military pressure until they succeeded in eliciting from Nasser a public agreement to abide by an unlimited cease-fire. Eban was convinced that the American aim was to bring the fighting to a halt. On 7 February he proposed to the cabinet a political initiative to restore the cease-fire for a limited period as part of a new "peace offensive." His idea was that they should not only declare their policies but also give dramatic expression to their readiness for a temporary cease-fire on the Suez Canal as a first step toward military de-escalation. He argued that there was nothing to lose by exploring the possibility of ending the War of Attrition, and there was some support for his proposal. But Golda Meir turned all her fury against him. Did Eban not recall that Nasser himself had proposed a temporary cease-fire? If this was in Nasser's interest, how could it be in the interest of Israel? Was Eban not proposing a dangerous trap for Israel in contradiction to its stated policy?

Noting that there was no majority for his proposal for a peace offensive, Eban did not wish it to be discredited by a vote. Meir, however, insisted on putting the proposal to the vote. Some ministers implored her to avoid a vote against a peace offensive, but she was insistent and hands were raised to defeat the proposal that was no longer on the table. Eban himself declined to take part in the vote. "This episode," he wrote, "illustrated the difficulty of being a foreign minister in a cabinet that had an exaggerated vision of the role of war in international politics. The triumph of our forces in 1967 had encouraged a belief in an Israeli invincibility that ceased to operate as soon as the Six-Day War came to a halt. It was not Golda at her best. The episode highlighted the centrality of personal rancor in the general system of her thought and emotion."[11]

The deep-penetration bombing inflicted serious damage on

the Egyptian war machine, but it did not bring Nasser to his knees. On 22 January he flew to Moscow for a secret meeting with the Soviet leaders to request urgent help. They responded by providing Egypt with antiaircraft guns, surface-to-air missile batteries, radar systems, and MiG fighter planes, together with a mini-army of technicians to operate the new hardware. Never before had the Soviet Union injected such sophisticated military equipment into a non-Communist country in such a short time. Fifteen thousand men were sent to Egypt, including 200 pilots. The Soviet military effectively took over the defense of Egypt, except for the canal zone.

As a result, Israel's previous absolute air supremacy and freedom to attack targets in the Egyptian interior were severely curtailed. Israel was forced to scale down its air offensive, and in mid-April the deep-penetration bombing came to a halt. During this time Israel's casualties in soldiers and aircraft continued to rise at an alarming rate. In the General Staff there was a willingness to consider the withdrawal of ground forces away from the canal, to place them out of the range of the Egyptian artillery. Golda Meir reportedly opposed this idea, fearing it would encourage the Arabs to renew their demands for complete Israeli withdrawal without negotiations or peace. A presence along the Suez Canal was supposed to give Israel security. But now Israel was clinging to the Suez Canal for political reasons. This situation exposed the flaw in the argument that territory gave Israel strategic depth and that strategic depth straightforwardly enhanced Israel's security.

At home Golda Meir came under criticism for remaining inflexible even when there were growing signs that the Egyptians were interested in a diplomatic solution to the War of Attrition. On 28 April a group of high school students sent a letter to the prime minister. Anticipating their call-up for national service in the IDF, they stated that it would be difficult to persuade them that the war was one of *ein breira*, of no alternative, because of the policy of her government. The backdrop to this letter was an invitation from Nasser for Dr. Nahum Goldmann, president of the World Jewish Congress, to visit him in Cairo. The visit did not take place, because the Israeli government refused to authorize it. Many in Israel thought that this step showed unwillingness on the part of their government to engage in a peaceful dialogue with the enemy. The letter said, "We, the undersigned, are high school students about to be recruited into the IDF. After the government rejected the prospect of peace by refusing Dr. Nahum Goldmann's trip, we do not know whether we would be capable of carrying out our duty in the army under the slogan *ein breira.*" This short letter provoked a prolonged public debate on the question of who was responsible for the continuing state of war.

The War of Attrition continued to rage across the Suez Canal after the bombing of the Egyptian interior had ceased. Nearly all the assumptions that prompted the deep-penetration bombing turned out to be mistaken. Nasser's regime did not collapse under the blows inflicted by the IAF; the Soviet Union intervened physically and not only verbally to parry the blows; and the United States evinced none of the enthusiasm for the bombing that Ambassador Rabin had predicted. Israel had seriously misjudged both the Soviet and the American reactions. It now had to turn to its superpower patron as the only possible source of deterrence against the other superpower. Israel's dependence for strategic support and arms supplies on the United States increased sharply, and with it the susceptibility to American political pressure. Thus, by pressing too far its military advantage against Egypt, Israel helped to defeat its own important postwar objective of keeping the superpowers out of the Middle East as far as possible.

Soviet forces loomed ever larger over the horizon. On 18 April, Israeli pilots encountered Soviet pilots flying an operational mission in the canal zone. On 30 June a dogfight took place near the canal in which the IAF shot down five MiGs flown by Soviet pilots. This victory boosted Israeli morale, but the military experts knew that the Soviets and the Egyptians were steadily moving their surface-to-air missile systems toward the western edge of the Suez Canal and that this would curb Israel's superiority in the air.

The dangers of escalation prompted Secretary of State Rogers to put forward, on 19 June, a second proposal, which came to be known as Rogers B. The proposal had three parts: first, a three-month cease-fire on the Egyptian front; second, a statement by Israel, Egypt, and Jordan that they accepted UN Resolution 242, and specifically the call for "withdrawal from occupied territories"; and third, an undertaking from Israel to negotiate with Egypt and Jordan under Dr. Jarring's auspices as soon as the cease-fire came into force. The proposal also contained an important provision for a "standstill" during the cease-fire: neither Egypt nor Israel would be allowed to move its missiles closer to the canal.

Golda Meir's instinctive reaction was to reject the American proposal. Although Rogers B said nothing about final borders, she suspected that it was simply a ploy for imposing Rogers A. In the IDF there was concern that a temporary cease-fire was not a sufficient guarantee against the renewal of the War of Attrition. But President Nixon advised Israel not to be the first to reject Rogers B, and both Egypt and Jordan accepted the proposal. On 24 July, Nixon sent a letter to Meir in which he stated explicitly that the final boundaries must be agreed between the parties themselves by means of negotiations under the auspices of Ambassador Jarring; that the United States would not exert pressure on Israel to accept a solution to the refugee problem that would fundamentally alter its Jewish character or endanger its security; and that not a single Israeli soldier would have to be withdrawn from the cease-fire lines until a peace agreement satisfactory to Israel had been reached. The letter represented the virtual abandonment of the first Rogers plan. In some quarters it was hailed as a second Balfour Declaration.[12]

Nixon's assurances and promise of economic and military assistance persuaded Golda Meir and her kitchen cabinet to swallow the bitter pill of Rogers B. They made it clear, however, that they agreed only to a cease-fire and the renewal of the Jarring mission, not to the provisions of Rogers A. On 31 July the cabinet voted by a majority of 17 to 6 for accepting Rogers B. Gahal departed from the national unity government because acceptance of the plan implied acceptance of Resolution 242. Not all the Gahal ministers supported the decisions to quit, but Menachem Begin was adamant. The cease-fire on the Egyptian front went into effect on 7 August, ending the War of Attrition.

On the day the cease-fire went into force, Egypt, with Soviet help, violated the standstill agreement by moving its missiles to the edge of the Suez Canal. Israel decided to suspend its participation in the talks due to begin under Jarring's auspices. The war had ended, but the political stalemate continued. Unlike the three wars that preceded it, the War of Attrition ended without anything that might be called a victory for one side or defeat for the other. In effect, the seventeen-month-long war ended in a draw. Israel's political and military leaders differed in their assessment of the outcome. Some, including the minister of defense, the chief of staff, and other generals, pointed out that Egypt failed to make any territorial gains in the course of the war. Others, for different reasons, considered that Egypt was the real victor in the war. A candid study of the positions of the two sides before and after the war led Abba Eban to the conclusion that the psychological and international balance changed to Egypt's advantage.[13] Ezer Weizman was more interested in the military balance. For him the key fact was that the war ended with the Egyptian missile system on the edge of the canal and the consequent loss of Israel's previously undisputed air supremacy. This outcome, argued Weizman, gave the Egyptians a free hand, over the next three years, to prepare for the great war of October 1973.[14]

With few exceptions, Israel's leaders drew the wrong lessons from the War of Attrition. They continued to cling to a defensive military doctrine and its corollary, a static defense system, even though the war had shown it to be costly and ineffective.[15] Mordechai Gur, who became chief of staff in 1974, was later to argue that it was not the easy victory in the Six-Day War that lulled Israel into a false sense of security on the eve of the October War but a wrong reading of the outcome of the War of Attrition. "There is no doubt that our victory in the War of Attrition was very important," wrote Gur in the IDF monthly, "but did only one conclusion follow from it—to sit and do nothing? That we are strong and if the Arabs want peace, they have to come to us on their knees and accept our terms? . . . This was the great political and strategic mistake—the reliance on force as the almost exclusive factor in the formulation of policy."[16]

This was indeed the great mistake of the government headed by Golda the intransigent. It was very rigid in its approach to the Arabs. Its policy after 1969 consisted of offering the Arabs only one of two alternatives: either full contractual peace without full Israeli withdrawal from the occupied territories or continuation of the status quo without any concessions. The War of Attrition, waged at great economic cost and with heavy casualties, was the longest war in Israel's history. After it came to an end, Meir resorted to a diplomacy of attrition in defense of the status quo, and the eventual result was another full-scale Arab-Israeli war.

The War of Attrition also affected Israel's nuclear policy. The atomic weapons debate of the early 1960s continued to the end of the decade. Yigal Allon and Israel Galilee were the main advocates of a conventional strategy. The main advocates of the nuclear option were Moshe Dayan and Shimon Peres. Dayan's power greatly increased after he became minister of defense in 1967. In 1968 the Non-Proliferation Treaty (NPT) was signed. Its 140 members promised to refrain from acquiring nuclear arms, in return for full access to nuclear technology for peaceful purposes. Since Israel refused to sign the NPT, American officials wanted to know whether Israel intended to produce nuclear weapons. The most that the Israelis would say in reply was that they would not be the first to "introduce" nuclear weapons into the Middle East. Pressed for clarification, Ambassador Rabin explained that Israel would not be the first to "test" such weapons or to reveal their existence publicly.[17] This formula satisfied the Americans. They stopped pressing Israel to sign the NPT, and visits to Dimona by the American inspectors ended in 1969.

Moshe Dayan was principally responsible for the decision to move from nuclear potential to the production of a small inventory of nuclear weapons. He took this step partly because he feared that Israel would not be able to maintain indefinitely its conventional superiority over the Arabs and partly in order to reduce Israel's dependence on external powers. The arms embargo imposed by France in 1967 highlighted Israel's dependence on its arms suppliers. The War of Attrition imposed a huge economic burden on Israel and left it more dependent on American arms supplies. It also led to growing Soviet involvement on the side of Israel's enemies. Dayan therefore developed a new formula to which he gave an ominous title—the bomb in the basement. This involved producing the bomb but without testing it and without publicly declaring its existence. Disagreement with other ministers probably produced this compromise formula, which had the advantage of not requiring Israel to adopt an open nuclear strategy while signaling to the Arabs and the rest of the world that there was a nuclear arsenal in Israel's basement.[18]

A Reply to Dr. Jarring

In September 1970 two events distracted attention from the crisis over the reactivation of Dr. Jarring's mission: the civil war in Jordan and the death of Gamal Abdel Nasser. In Jordan the Palestinian guerrilla organizations created a state within a state that posed a challenge to the rule of King Hussein. The king ordered his army to disarm and break the power of these organizations. In the ensuing civil war thousands of Palestinians were killed, and many more left the country. At the height of the crisis, Syrian forces invaded Jordan in what looked like a bid to help the Palestinians overthrow the monarchy. King Hussein sent an urgent appeal for help to Washington. Dr. Kissinger, the national security adviser, conveyed to Golda Meir what he interpreted as a royal request for an Israeli air attack against the Syrian armored force in the north of the country. Kissinger promised that if the Egyptians renewed the fighting in the south, the United States would extend to Israel all necessary military assistance. Israel put its air force on the alert and also mobilized ground forces on the border with Jordan, in readiness to move against the Syrians. But the need to intervene did not arise, because Jordan's army itself went into action against the Syrian invaders. The crisis ended with a Palestinian defeat, a Syrian retreat, and King Hussein sitting firmly on his throne in Amman. Throughout the crisis Israel coordinated its moves very closely with Washington. By its response to the call for help, Israel earned a debt of gratitude from the American president as well as the Jordanian monarch.

The other event was the death of President Nasser on 28 September. The fifty-two-year-old died of a heart attack. He had exhausted himself in the effort to mediate between King Hussein and his Palestinian opponents. Nasser was succeeded by his deputy, Anwar al-Sadat. Sadat was one of the Free Officers who had staged the revolution in 1952. He was considered a political lightweight who would be unlikely to last in power for very long. Toward the end of his life Nasser seemed to have reached the conclusion that the Arab-Israeli conflict could not be resolved by military means. Sadat had kept his opinions largely to himself, so it was difficult to predict what line he would take on the conflict.

At the end of December, following protracted negotiations with the Nixon administration, Israel agreed to proceed to peace talks under the auspices of Dr. Jarring. Jarring was encouraged by the Americans to play a more active role as a mediator than he had done in the past and not to confine himself to serving as a mailbox. His preliminary contacts with Israel and Egypt, however, convinced him that both sides were clinging very firmly to their by now well-established positions. He therefore took it upon himself to try to break the diplomatic deadlock by stating what was needed to move forward toward a settlement. On 8 February 1971 he addressed Egypt and Israel with identical memoranda outlining his own proposals for resolving the dispute between them. Of Egypt he requested an undertaking to enter into a peace agreement with Israel; of Israel, to withdraw to the former Egypt-Palestine international border.

Egypt replied to Jarring's questionnaire on 15 February. The reply stated, "Egypt will be ready to enter into a peace agreement with Israel containing all the aforementioned obligations provided for in Security Council Resolution 242." Egypt made a number of additional demands: an Israeli commitment to withdraw not only from Sinai but also from the Gaza Strip, a commitment to settle the refugee problem in accordance with UN resolutions, and the establishment of a UN force to maintain the peace. The reply marked a breakthrough. It was the first time that an Egyptian government declared publicly its readiness to sign a peace treaty with Israel. The Egyptian reply was welcomed as a positive and far-reaching development by both Jarring and Rogers.

The Israel government was impressed by Egypt's public commitment to make peace but troubled by the conditions and caveats with which Egypt hedged its position. As a matter of fact, Egypt's territorial conditions for peace should have come as no surprise. They were very similar to the decision taken by the Eshkol government on 19 June 1967 in favor of withdrawal to the international border with Egypt and Syria in return for peace. This decision, however, had been canceled by the Eshkol government, and the Israeli position had further hardened in the intervening period.

The Israeli reply, transmitted to Jarring on 26 February, was the result of convoluted discussions in the cabinet. Israel noted with satisfaction Egypt's willingness to sign a peace agreement and expressed again its desire for direct negotiations on all issues relating to a peace agreement. The problem arose over the pledge for complete territorial withdrawal requested by Jarring. Initially, the cabinet was inclined to accept Eban's noncommittal formulation: "Withdrawal of Israeli armed forces from the cease-fire line with Egypt to secure, recognized, and agreed boundaries to be established in the peace agreement." But Israel Galilee, with help from Moshe Dayan, succeeded in persuading the cabinet not to leave any doubt about the boundary issue. The cabinet opted for a categorical refusal to restore the previous boundary, and this gave its reply a peremptory and negative tone. To Eban's withdrawal clause it added a short but highly significant sentence: "Israel will not withdraw to the pre–5 June 1967 lines."[19]

Critics of Golda Meir's government have argued that this sentence spelled the failure of the Jarring mission and the loss of an opportunity for peace with Egypt. Some commentators have argued that if Eban's advice had been heeded and the sentence been omitted, peace could have come about without the tragedy of the Yom Kippur War. Eban himself continued to regret that his formula was not endorsed, because it adequately safeguarded Israel's right to territorial revision. But he found it hard to accept that if Sadat was really ready for a settlement at that stage, he would have abandoned the effort merely because of the wording of the Israeli reply to Jarring.[20] Eban's comment suggests that even he, the most moderate of Meir's ministers, failed to appreciate the full significance of Sadat's statement.

Yitzhak Rabin, the ambassador to Washington, was even more critical than Eban of the Israeli handling of Jarring's initiative. Relations between the ambassador and the minister were rather strained because the ambassador often reported directly to the prime minister, bypassing the foreign minister. In this instance, however, the ambassador and the minister were united in their desire to see a positive response. Rabin returned home for consultations in the wake of Egypt's reply to Jarring. Rabin considered this reply a milestone: "For the first time in the chronicles of the Middle East conflict, an Arab country—indeed, the largest Arab country and the leader of the Arab world—had issued an official document expressing its readiness to enter into a peace agreement with Israel!" He recommended to the cabinet a similar reply: an expression of readiness to sign a peace treaty followed by a detailed exposition of Israel's views on the issues of borders and refugees. The cabinet's reply was no less disappointing to him than to his American colleagues. It "turned out to be a rambling document whose long-windedness was exceeded only by its vagueness. Worst of all, it failed in its main task: presenting Israel's demands in return for peace."[21]

Jarring considered the Israeli reply to his questionnaire unsatisfactory. He had sought an Egyptian commitment to make peace with Israel and an Israeli commitment to withdraw from Egypt's territory; he got an Egyptian but not an Israeli commitment. Whether or not Golda Meir's government missed a real opportunity for a peace with Egypt, it sealed the fate of Jarring's mission. Some Israeli officials laid the responsibility for the failure at the door of the UN mediator. Gideon Rafael wrote, "The Jarring initiative, instead of priming progress, had deepened the deadlock."[22] The same could be said of the Israeli reply. Jarring's mission was not officially terminated, but it was overtaken by a more dramatic initiative.

AN INTERIM SETTLEMENT

The eclipse of the Jarring mission coincided with an initiative by the new Egyptian president, Anwar al-Sadat. Jarring's aim was an overall peace agreement between Egypt and Israel. Sadat's aim was an interim settlement in the first instance. On 4 February 1971, in a speech before the Egyptian National Assembly, Sadat proposed the reopening of the Suez Canal and a partial withdrawal of the Israeli troops on the eastern bank of the canal as the first step in the implementation of Resolution 242. His proposal gave a hint of his plan to shift the emphasis from UN mediation to U.S. mediation and from an overall settlement to an interim one. In his questionnaire of 8 February, Jarring made no reference to Sadat's proposal. For a time the two plans appeared simultaneously on the international agenda, but with the fading of the Jarring mission, Sadat's became the principal basis for further discussions.

Sadat's proposal did not take Israel by surprise. Following the collapse of the cease-fire in August 1970, Moshe Dayan talked to the Israeli press about the need for a new agreement with Egypt. His main concern was to reduce Egypt's motivation for renewing the war, and to this end he was willing to consider a partial settlement. One specific idea he floated was an Israeli pullback from the Suez Canal to enable Egypt to reopen the canal and to rebuild the cities that had been badly damaged during the War of Attrition.[23] On 15 January 1971 Joseph Sisco, the assistant secretary for state for Near Eastern affairs, informed Rabin that Donald Bergus, the American chargé d'affaires in Cairo, had been approached by an Egyptian general close to President Sadat with a proposal to explore the feasibility of reaching a settlement to reopen the Suez Canal. The proposal was for an Israeli withdrawal to a line about forty kilometers from the canal, a limited thinning out of the forces on the Egyptian side, and the reopening of the waterway. Rabin thought this was "a refreshing change from the high-stakes, all-or-nothing atmosphere that surrounded all the 'final settlement' proposals related to Resolution 242. For that reason alone it merited serious thought."[24]

Rabin recommended a positive response. But Golda Meir was far from happy with the Egyptian proposal. She feared that it would lead to an Israeli withdrawal to the old international border without a peace treaty. She responded to Sadat's public announcement of his proposal with angry and negative comments on American television. Undeterred, Sadat sent a message to the State Department that was relayed to Jerusalem. He explained that his purpose was to defuse the prevailing danger and that his proposal was neither a tactical nor an academic exercise. He wanted a serious discussion with Israel conducted through the good offices of the United States, not of the United Nations. Sisco recommended that Golda Meir react to Sadat's initiative in a positive and constructive fashion, as did Abba Eban. In her statement to the Knesset on 9 February, Meir cautiously intimated the government's willingness to discuss the Egyptian proposal under certain stringent conditions. According to Gideon Rafael, "She had adopted this line half-heartedly, more as a tactical accommodation than a desirable objective."[25]

Meir's hesitant and skeptical response to Sadat's initiative invited probing and pressure by the Americans. Although the reopening of the canal carried more advantages for the USSR than for themselves, the idea appealed to the Americans as a means of preventing the resumption of hostilities. In early March, Sisco presented to Israel a paper with preliminary ideas that had been discussed with Sadat. Israel should withdraw its forces to a distance of forty kilometers from the canal; the evacuated area would be demilitarized; Egyptian technicians and up to seven hundred policemen would be allowed into a ten-kilometer-wide strip along the east bank of the canal. Six months after the signature of the agreement, the canal would be opened to shipping, including Israeli shipping. The agreement would constitute a first step toward the full implementation of Resolution 242, and both sides would be free to review the cease-fire after one year.

Golda Meir did not like Sadat's new proposals. The idea of withdrawal without a peace treaty was anathema to her. She remained wedded to the official line that not a single Israeli soldier should be withdrawn from the cease-fire lines before the conclusion of a peace treaty. Second, she objected to the proposed linkage between the canal agreement and the full implementation of Resolution 242, which in Arab eyes meant the evacuation of all the territories occupied in the Six-Day War. Third, she adamantly opposed the stationing of Egyptian military personnel on the east bank of the canal, or even the stationing of seven hundred policemen.[26]

Sadat's new proposals were discussed by the cabinet on 22 March. Moshe Dayan took the lead in the discussion, arguing in favor of a limited withdrawal from the canal in exchange for something less than peace. He proposed that in return for a limited pullback, enabling Egypt to reopen the canal, Egypt should be asked for an end to belligerency, demilitarization of the evacuated area, and the restoration of normal civilian life in the western side of the canal. Another condition was a binding American engagement to long-term military assistance to Israel and to ensuring that the area evacuated by Israel would remain demilitarized. Dayan was ready for a withdrawal of thirty kilometers from the canal, up to the western edge of the strategic Gidi and Mitla Passes. The cabinet accepted the principle of a limited withdrawal of forces in the context of an interim agreement, even without peace.

With this cabinet decision, writes Abba Eban, "a new era in Middle Eastern diplomacy began. The concept of a partial interim settlement replaced the previous 'all or nothing' approach to peace. And the idea of American 'good offices' superseded the previous concept of UN mediation."[27] There was no agreement, however, on the application of this concept. Eban remarks that the fact that Dayan originated the idea played some part in prompting his political opponents to oppose it. Opposition to substantial withdrawal from the canal was expressed by Israel Galilee and Yigal Allon and, more surprisingly, by the moderate Pinhas Sapir. Chief of Staff Chaim Bar-Lev held that the Israeli withdrawal should not exceed ten kilometers from the canal. A limited withdrawal, he argued, would have made it more difficult for Egypt to cross the canal in strength to launch an attack. It would also have enabled Israel to "shoot its way back" to the canal in the event of an Egyptian violation of the agreement.[28]

Internal divisions delayed the formulation of the Israeli counterproposal. This counterproposal was transmitted to the Americans on 19 April, six weeks after they had presented to Israel Sadat's preliminary ideas. The main problem with the Israeli counterproposal was the demand that Egypt renounce the state of belligerency in return for very limited Israeli withdrawal from the canal. Rabin thought this was unrealistic, but the cabinet was adamant and instructed him to notify the Americans that ending the state of belligerency was a sine qua non of a partial agreement. If asked how far Israel was prepared to withdraw, he was to say that he did not know. Israel's demands, on the other hand, were formulated in some detail: the opening of the canal to the shipping of all nations, including Israel; the unlimited duration of the cease-fire; the withdrawal of Israeli forces to a distance to be agreed; no Egyptian military forces in the area to be evacuated by Israel; the thinning out of Egyptian forces on the western side of the canal; and the release of all prisoners of war.

Rabin took the cabinet's paper to Kissinger. Kissinger read it with astonishing speed, and his reaction to the document was equally swift. "What is this?! Where is the new line?" he demanded.

"If that is your proposal, I don't want to have anything to do with it. Take it to Sisco . . . I won't touch it! It indicates a fundamental misconception of both the basic problem and your standing in the United States. It will lead to stagnation and confrontation. So do whatever you want, but leave me alone!" Sisco's reaction to the Israeli document was less hostile; after consulting William Rogers, he said he would present it to Egypt with a request for a positive response.[29]

In early May, Rogers and Sisco traveled to Cairo and from there to Jerusalem in search of a compromise. Rogers was impressed by Sadat's moderation and understanding of Israel's need for security. Golda Meir thought that Rogers was naive, and in the sharp exchanges between them the practical issue was lost from sight. Dayan's subsequent meeting with Sisco was much more constructive. When asked how far Israel would be prepared to withdraw, Dayan outlined two possible approaches. One approach assumed that the fighting might be renewed. It therefore allowed only for a limited withdrawal, of about ten kilometers, to enable the IDF to shoot its way back to the canal. This was the approach the cabinet had taken in its paper. The other approach involved the destruction of the Bar-Lev line, a withdrawal of thirty kilometers to the Gidi and Mitla Passes, and a permanent renunciation of Israeli access to the canal. Dayan did not conceal that he himself supported the second approach. He did not believe that the Egyptians could reopen the canal and rebuild their cities with the Israeli army in such close proximity. Dayan was reprimanded for what some of his colleagues regarded as excessive flexibility. Eban sent him a note asking whether he would put his idea to a vote in the cabinet. Dayan replied that unless the prime minister supported his idea, he would not even bring it up for discussion. Eban always regretted that Dayan "did not show tenacity in support of this imaginative proposal, which could have averted the Yom Kippur War."[30]

Dayan also thought that his proposal could have averted the Yom Kippur War, but he blamed Golda Meir for missing the opportunity. His main aim throughout was to reduce Egypt's motivation to go to war. He believed that the danger of war would decline if Israel pulled back its forces and allowed Egypt to reopen the canal to international shipping and restore normal civilian life in the cities around it. His first step was to ask the IDF General Staff whether the idea was feasible from the military point of view. The General Staff was divided. Some generals, such as

Israel Tal and Ariel Sharon, supported the idea. All along they had advocated a flexible defense of Sinai instead of the static conception of the Bar-Lev line. They believed that a pullback from the waterline to the passes would not endanger Israel's security and, indeed, might actually solve some of its military problems. Bar-Lev and David Elazar preferred a much more limited pullback in order to be in a position to supervise activities in the canal zone. Golda Meir, according to Dayan, was completely opposed to his idea and pleased with the support she got from Bar-Lev and Elazar. The disagreement between Dayan and Meir was not military but political. He hoped that an interim agreement would reduce the tension and pave the way to further negotiations with the Egyptians. She simply did not trust the Egyptians. Given the division of opinion in the IDF and in the government, Dayan thought it inevitable that the prime minister's opinion should prevail.[31]

The Americans regarded the Israeli position as the main stumbling block to an interim settlement. They even suspended the supply of Phantom planes to induce Israel to show some diplomatic flexibility. On 4 October 1971 William Rogers outlined American thinking on an interim settlement in an address to the UN General Assembly. He said that the reopening of the Suez Canal would be a step in the implementation of Resolution 242 and that negotiations for a comprehensive settlement should take place under the auspices of Dr. Jarring. He added that the two sides would have to find a solution to all the technical problems connected with operating the canal, including the presence of Egyptian personnel on the east bank, and he suggested "proximity talks" between them in New York.

Two days later Golda Meir rejected these proposals. She said that the speech by the secretary of state would only encourage the Egyptians to cling to their stubborn positions. Israel's agreement to a pullback was based on the principle that no Egyptian forces would be stationed on the east bank of the canal. Most important, she insisted, the agreement on reopening the canal had to be self-contained, not part of a comprehensive agreement. She repeated these points in a defiant speech in front of the Knesset on 26 October. A few days later she notified the Americans that her government would refuse to consider any further proposals for reopening the canal until they resumed their delivery of Phantoms to Israel.

At the same time, the Americans held discussions with the Soviets on an overall solution in the Middle East. On 5 November,

Kissinger informed Rabin of the existence of a secret proposal that President Leonid Brezhnev had communicated to President Nixon. The proposal was for a settlement in two stages: first an interim agreement for reopening the canal; then, after the 1972 American presidential elections, an overall agreement based on the Jarring document. In Jerusalem everyone agreed that it was vital to reject the Soviet initiative, and Rabin was instructed to inform Kissinger of this decision. Kissinger warned that Israel could not go on rejecting all the proposals that it received without stating which terms were acceptable. He put his finger on the central weakness in the Israeli position: the demand that Egypt waive her military option while rejecting any link between the partial settlement and the overall settlement. The only thing Kissinger and Rabin could agree upon was that the prime minister would come to talks with the president.[32]

Golda Meir had her meeting with President Nixon on 2 December. Her two main aims were to persuade Nixon to abandon the Rogers plan and to resume arms deliveries to Israel, and she achieved both. Nixon also assured her that there would be no American-Soviet deal at Israel's expense. On the idea of partial settlement there was only a general discussion. Nixon had transferred responsibility for handling this matter from the State Department to his national security adviser, and it was with him that she was asked to discuss the details. Having been assured that the Rogers plan was dead and that the delivery of Phantoms would be resumed, Meir was prepared to show more flexibility on the interim agreement. At her meeting with Kissinger on 10 December, she made a number of significant concessions: the Israeli withdrawal would stop short of the western approaches to the Sinai passes; the cease-fire would be limited in duration to eighteen to twenty-four months; there would be a link between the interim settlement and the final one, provided it did not bind Israel to the Rogers plan in any way whatsoever; and a small number of Egyptian soldiers in uniform would be allowed to cross the canal.[33]

Despite these concessions, Meir's basic position remained unchanged. She had insisted all along that a partial Israeli withdrawal could in no way commit Israel to total withdrawal from Sinai in accordance with a predetermined timetable. For her this was the central issue: there could be no commitment, explicit or implied, to return to the pre–5 June 1967 border with Egypt. The new border had to be agreed in negotiations between Israel and Egypt following the implementation of the interim agreement. She reserved Israel's right to demand territorial revision.[34] But agreement in principle to an interim settlement under rigorous conditions was not the same as positive support, let alone enthusiasm for such a settlement.

Major General Aharon Yariv, the director of military intelligence, had a conversation with Mrs. Meir at the Waldorf Astoria Hotel in New York after her meeting with President Nixon. Yariv recommended going the extra mile toward meeting Sadat's demands in order to give him a sense of achievement and to reduce the pressure on him to resort to military action. Yariv saw no harm in allowing Sadat to declare that he had liberated part of the homeland and that the Egyptian flag was flying on both sides of the Suez Canal. The risk involved in an Israeli withdrawal to the passes was not much greater than the risk involved in a withdrawal of ten kilometers from the canal. Their strategic position was excellent, Yariv explained, and they could afford to be generous. Meir remained skeptical. She feared that partial withdrawal would lead to pressures for complete withdrawal from Sinai, and she doubted that the cabinet and the public would support far-reaching concessions to Egypt. Personal considerations also came into the picture. Yariv got the distinct impression that Meir did not want to start the process of withdrawal and go down in Israel's history as the first prime minister who handed over territory.[35] The conversation may have influenced her to show more flexibility at her next meeting with Henry Kissinger, but it did not alter her fundamental attachment to the political, military, and territorial status quo.

The concessions Meir made at her meeting with Kissinger, on 10 December 1971, were not too little, but they were too late. Had they been made six months earlier, they would probably have produced a breakthrough in the search for an interim agreement. But Sadat's position had hardened in the meantime. Although he had not given up the idea of an agreement, he was now insisting that it would only be a stage toward complete Israeli withdrawal from Sinai. In any case, Kissinger did not transmit to Cairo Meir's latest offer.

Kissinger's reasons for this are not entirely clear. One possibility is that the State Department was trying to arrange "proximity talks" between Israel and Egypt and that for tactical reasons he held back the Israeli offer. These talks never got off the ground, because in February 1972 Egypt refused to participate. Another possibility was Kissinger's conviction that the way to an agreement went through Moscow. He knew that Moscow was opposed to an interim agreement, but he was in no hurry. He thought the longer the U.S.-Soviet talks went on without producing results, the more likely Sadat would be to turn directly to the United States. He did not take Sadat's militant public statements seriously and had his eyes fixed on the superpower summit meeting in Moscow in May 1972. By the time the summit took place, the idea of a separate canal settlement had expired and with it the notion of proximity talks.[36]

THE DIPLOMACY OF ATTRITION

Israel's principal aim in 1972–73 was to perpetuate the status quo. Abba Eban summed up both the premise behind this policy and the price Israel eventually had to pay for it:

> All this time, the Israeli defense strategy was frankly attritional. The logic was that if the Arabs were unable to get their territories back by war or by Great Power pressure, they would have to seek negotiation and to satisfy some of Israel's security interests. This view made no provision for a third Arab option—neither docility nor negotiation, but a desperate recourse to war in the hope that even an unsuccessful attack would be more rewarding than passive acceptance of the cease-fire lines.[37]

The strategy of attrition was accompanied, logically enough, by a diplomacy of attrition. If the strategy of attrition was directed at perpetuating the territorial status quo, the diplomacy of attrition was directed a perpetuating the political deadlock and at denying the Arabs any political gains until they accepted Israel's terms for a settlement. Israel's confidence in its ability to preserve the status quo came from two main sources: a favorable military balance and strong support from the United States.

During the presidency of Richard Nixon the relationship between the two countries gradually developed into a close strategic partnership. America's involvement in a costly and inconclusive conflict in Southeast Asia led to the formulation of the Nixon Doctrine. This doctrine laid down that America should avoid direct military engagement in the Third World and rely instead on proxies such as the shah of Iran in the Persian Gulf and Israel in the Middle East. In the context of the Nixon Doctrine, Israel assumed the role of preserving a regional balance of power favorable to American interests. This meant, above all, curbing Arab radicalism and checking Soviet expansionism in the Middle East. Israel's local interest in keeping the Arabs in their place neatly converged with the Nixon administration's interest in expelling the Soviets from the Middle East.

The Middle East had always been caught up in the rivalries of outside powers. It was also a major theater of superpower rivalry since the beginning of the Cold War. But, in contrast to its perception in the 1950s, the United States now perceived Israel as a bastion of regional order and as a strategic asset in the Middle East. The main architect of this policy was Henry Kissinger. Kissinger was critical of the State Department's approach to Israel. The State Department tactic was to withhold arms from Israel in order to induce it to show greater diplomatic flexibility. Kissinger thought that the more insecure Israel felt, the greater would be its resistance to compromise. He also challenged the State Department's fundamental premise that continuing stalemate strengthened the Soviet Union's position in the Middle East. In his view the opposite was the case: the longer the stalemate continued, the more obvious it would become that the Soviet Union had failed to deliver what the Arabs wanted.[38]

Kissinger's attritional strategy was directed mainly against Egypt. It was not applied to Jordan, partly because the Hashemite kingdom was America's ally but also because it was of lesser strategic importance in the Cold War than Egypt. Moreover, Jordan's position on a settlement of the Arab-Israeli conflict was close to the American position. Jordan accepted both Resolution 242 and the Rogers plan of December 1969, and its response to the Jarring questionnaire of February 1970 was positive. Israel could therefore count on American support in exploring the possibilities of a settlement with Jordan. Whereas Jerusalem's contacts with Egypt were mediated by the United States, the contacts with Jordan were direct and at the highest level. Golda Meir was not alone in having meetings with King Hussein in the interwar period, though she was said to be particularly fond of him. Abba Eban, Yigal Allon, Moshe Dayan, and other Israeli officials also met with him, sometimes individually, sometimes in pairs, and sometimes in groups. Sometimes the meetings were held in London, sometimes in a tent in the desert near the border between the two countries, sometimes on the royal yacht in the Gulf of Aqaba, and sometimes in Tel Aviv.

Golda Meir had never shown any interest in the Palestinian option. She regarded the Palestinians as the irreconcilable enemy of Israel. Her views about the Palestinians had been formed in the pre-Independence period and had hardly changed. In November 1947 she and King Abdullah had reached an agreement to partition Palestine at the expense of the Palestinians, and that policy held until early June 1967. After June 1967 she remained unremittingly hostile toward Palestinian nationalism. In fact, she refused to acknowledge that the Palestinians were a nation or that they had any right to national self-determination. As prime minister she was well known for her anachronistic and hard-line views about the Palestinian problem, and she achieved notoriety for her statement that there was no such thing as a Palestinian people. "It is not as though there was a Palestinian people in Palestine considering itself as a Palestinian people and we came and threw them out and took their country away from them," she said. "They did not exist."[39]

Meir saw Palestinian nationalism as a threat not only to Israel but to the monarchy in Jordan as well. This was one of the reasons for her feeling of solidarity with King Hussein. In August 1968 she sent the following message to the king through an American visitor: "I hope your majesty realizes that Israel is your best friend in the Middle East." On his return to Jerusalem, Theodore Sorensen, a former close adviser to President Kennedy, reported that when King Hussein heard the message, he replied with a smile, "There are some people who think that I am Israel's best friend in the Middle East."[40]

Given her hostility toward the Palestinians and her affinity with King Hussein, it was not surprising that Meir wanted to involve him in working out a solution to the Palestinian problem. But there was a historical and a political dimension to her thinking that transcended personalities. Her thinking was explained by Simha Dinitz, who served as director general of the prime minister's office in 1969–73:

> For Golda the only realistic solution to the Palestinian problem, from the demographic and the geographic point of view, was to place them under Jordan's jurisdiction. An attempt to deal with the Palestinian question without linking it to Jordan, in other words, an attempt to create an additional state between Israel and Jordan, would not succeed, because such a state would not have an adequate geographic or demographic base. This was the foundation of her thinking. Consequently, in order to arrive at a solution to the Palestinian problem, a

link with Jordan had to be forged. Hence all the meetings and discussions with Hussein.

Dinitz went on to argue that although a peace agreement was not achieved, the orientation on Jordan was successful in a number of different ways:

> First, the dialogue with Jordan prevented the rise of the PLO as a central force in the Palestinian arena. As long as the dialogue continued, the PLO was prevented from becoming the main spokesman of the Palestinians or the most important spokesman.
>
> Second, the contact yielded all sorts of agreements, ranging from the fight against terrorists to the fight against mosquitoes. These practical and security agreements between Israel and Hussein created a situation of de facto peace, though not de jure peace. On the one hand, there was the policy of open bridges across the Jordan River; on the other hand, there was a coordinated effort to suppress the terrorists who threatened both Jordan and us. There was also cooperation in practical matters such as the division of land, farming, pest control, and irrigation.
>
> Third, the contacts with Hussein created a precedent for a direct dialogue with an Arab leader. They made Sadat's trip to Jerusalem less revolutionary and less incredible than it would have been otherwise. So this chapter in the relations with Jordan was not a waste of time.[41]

King Hussein had his own reasons for cooperating with Israel in the security, administrative, judicial, and economic spheres. As far as he was concerned, however, there was never a Jordanian option in the political sphere. In Israel the much vaunted Jordanian option meant territorial compromise over the West Bank. This was unacceptable to him. Golda Meir favored the Allon Plan as the basis for a settlement, but the king rejected it again and again. She was also prepared to go along with Dayan's plan for a functional solution, the essence of which was that Jordan would administer the West Bank while Israel would be in charge of security. This plan, too, was unacceptable to the king.[42] In March 1972 the king unveiled his own federal plan for a United Arab Kingdom. The federation was to consist of two regions: the region of Jordan, comprising the East Bank, and the region of Palestine, comprising the West Bank and the Gaza Strip. Each region was to have its own government and its separate judicial system. Amman was to be the capital of the federation and of the Jordanian region, and Jerusalem was to be the capital of the Palestinian region. By launching this plan, the king wanted to signal to the Arab world and the international community that he had no intention of abandoning his claim to the West Bank or to the representation of the Palestinians who lived there. The plan was rejected by the PLO, by Egypt, and by Israel.

Meir's rejection of the plan was swift and categorical. In a speech to the Knesset on 16 March, she said that Israel never interfered in the internal structure or form of an Arab regime. If the king of Jordan had seen fit to change the name of his kingdom to "Palestine" and modify its internal structure, she would have raised no objections. But she had strong objections to the king's federal plan because it affected Israel's borders and security. She pointed out that the plan made no mention of willingness to negotiate with Israel or to make peace with her.

Meir's strident rejection of King Hussein's federal plan was music to the ears of Yasser Arafat, the leader of the PLO. Arafat and his colleagues regarded the king's plan as "an attempt to put the PLO out of business." Arafat told his biographer that if Israel had agreed to withdraw from the West Bank, King Hussein would have made peace with her immediately "and the PLO would have been finished. Absolutely finished. Sometimes I think we are lucky to have the Israelis as our enemies. They have saved us many times!"[43]

President Sadat broke off diplomatic relations with Jordan in protest against King Hussein's federal plan. Although both of them belonged to the moderate Arab camp, they eyed each other suspiciously. Sadat suspected Hussein of planning to make a separate deal with Israel over the West Bank, while Hussein suspected Sadat of planning to make a separate deal with Israel over Sinai. Israel was interested in a separate deal with either of them, but not at the price of complete withdrawal from their territories. In July 1972 Sadat dropped a bombshell. With a dramatic flair for which he was to become famous, he announced the expulsion of the fifteen thousand Soviet military advisers in Egypt. The move was not as sudden as it seemed, but it took Washington and Jerusalem by complete surprise.

In Jerusalem the expulsion of the Soviet advisers was interpreted as the fading away of Egypt's military option and as a vindication of Israel's attritional strategy. The general view, in the words of Abba Eban, was that "Sadat had obtained an emotional satisfaction at the expense of his strategic and political power. The disruption of the military organization in which the Soviet officers had played such an important role would surely weaken the Egyptian order of battle along the Suez Canal. Egypt, deprived of the Soviet presence, also appeared less formidable as a political adversary."[44] Gideon Rafael, the director general of the Foreign Ministry, did not share these sanguine interpretations of the Soviet exodus from Egypt or the serene outlook of their authors. He raised the possibility that Sadat regarded the Soviet Union as an inhibiting factor rather than as a supporter of military action, and that he expelled the Soviet advisers in order to regain his freedom of action. Rafael remained in a minority of one.[45]

Eban tended to accept the majority view that Sadat's blow to the Soviets would boomerang, that it would diminish Egypt's strength and fortify Israel's position. But he did not share the opinion that the new situation justified the policy of diplomatic standstill. He warned that a diplomatic vacuum was likely to produce political turbulence in the area.[46] Eban's warning fell on deaf ears. All diplomatic activity concerning the Middle Eastern conflict was suspended in the second half of 1972. In Jerusalem the diplomacy of attrition was the order of the day. Eban himself admitted to the editorial staff of the *Jerusalem Post* that Israel was not planning any peace initiatives: "Israel's best policy at present is to let Egypt's President Sadat 'sweat it out,' with his range of alternatives narrowing all the time, eventually driving him to negotiations with Israel itself."[47] This attritional policy did indeed narrow down Sadat's options, but ultimately it drove him not to the conference table but to the battlefield.

While preparing for war, Sadat made one last attempt to persuade America to put pressure on Israel to accept his terms for a political settlement. He sent his national security adviser, Hafez Ismail, on a secret mission to Washington. Henry Kissinger, who had replaced William Rogers as secretary of state, held a series of meetings with Ismail between the end of February 1973 and the end of May. Two conversations with King Hussein bracketed Kissinger's first meeting with Ismail. On 1 March, Golda Meir had a meeting with President Nixon and followed it up with detailed discussions with Kissinger. Thus, in the early months of 1973, Kissinger was drawn, somewhat against his will, into the labyrinth of Middle Eastern diplomacy.

Kissinger's reluctance to mediate between Arabs and Israelis may have had something to do with the fact that he himself was Jewish and therefore bound to be perceived as pro-Israeli by the Arabs. But Kissinger prided himself on his ability to formulate a foreign policy based on interests, not on ideals or sentiments. The real reason for his reluctance to get involved in diplomacy was that he had adopted the Israeli thesis that the stalemate in the Middle East served American as well as Israeli interests and that it worked against the Soviet Union and its Arab allies.

Hafez Ismail's presentation of Egypt's terms left Kissinger with little reason for optimism. King Hussein was more forthcoming. Kissinger describes the king's predicament with insight and sympathy:

> Hussein repeated his willingness to make peace with Israel. But despite secret contacts he faced an impasse. Hussein symbolized the fate of Arab moderates. He was caught between his inability to sustain a war with Israel and his unwillingness to make a common cause with the radicals. He was prepared for a diplomatic solution, even a generous one, but Israel saw no incentive for negotiations so long as Hussein stood alone. Any return of conquered territories seemed to it less secure than the status quo. And the West Bank with its historic legacy would unleash violent domestic controversy in Israel—the National Religious Party, without which the governing coalition could not rule, was adamantly opposed to the return of *any* part of the West Bank.[48]

The next visitor to the White House was Golda Meir. At her meeting with President Nixon on 1 March, she proclaimed, "We never had it so good," and suggested that the stalemate was safe because the Arabs had no military option. Meir had two objectives: to gain time, for the longer the status quo continued, the more Israel would be confirmed in the possession of the occupied territories; and to obtain Nixon's approval of a new package of military aid for Israel. With respect to negotiations, her attitude was simple. "She considered Israel militarily impregnable; there was, strictly speaking, no need for any change. But given the congenital inability of Americans to leave well enough alone, she was willing to enter talks though not to commit herself to an outcome."[49]

Kissinger's conversations with the Egyptian, Jordanian, and Israeli visitors failed to produce any practical results, but they shed a good deal of light on the positions of the principal protagonists and on the underlying causes of the deadlock in the Middle East. These conversations had little value except as an academic exercise. As a former academic, Dr. Kissinger would have no doubt appreciated the irony in the fact that the adjective "academic" also means futile.

Following the failure of the Washington talks to produce any results, Anwar Sadat and Golda Meir went their separate ways. The talks confirmed Sadat in his view that the United States would make no move if Egypt itself did not take military action to break the deadlock. He concluded that he had no choice but to step up Egyptian preparations for a military showdown with Israel.[50] Golda Meir was pleased with the result of her visit to Washington. She played her customary dual role as an arms procurer and a political procrastinator and was equally successful in both. She was much more interested in American arms than in American mediation. Moshe Dayan once remarked, "Our American friends offer us money, arms, and advice. We take the money, we take the arms, and we decline the advice." This was essentially Meir's policy, although she never underestimated the importance of maintaining good relations with America. On this occasion there was very little American advice, and any pressure was so gentle as to be imperceptible. She therefore returned home confirmed in her convictions that the Arabs had no military option, that Israel's military superiority was guaranteed, and that the status quo could continue indefinitely.

Moreover, on her return home she had to prepare her party for the forthcoming election. She had no desire to add international complications to domestic controversies. As Gideon Rafael observed, "Standstill appeared to her the simplest way of avoiding difficulties. But simplicity was not always the essence of political wisdom. One of its distinguishing marks is foresight."[51] If Golda Meir was the main advocate of political immobilism, Moshe Dayan was the main advocate of territorial expansionism. In the summer of 1973 the Alignment had prolonged debates on the future of the occupied territories. Dayan raised the banner of large-scale Jewish settlement to stake Israel's claim to the West Bank. The task at hand, he argued, was not to explore the prospects for peace with Israel's neighbors but to create facts on the ground, to draw a new map for Israel. On 30 July 1973 he said to *Time* magazine, "There is no more Palestine. Finished." In April 1973, from the peak of Massada, he proclaimed the vision of "a new State of Israel with broad frontiers, strong and solid, with the authority of the Israel Government extending from the Jordan to the Suez Canal."[52]

The moderates, led by Abba Eban and Pinhas Sapir, struggled to save the soul of the party. They tried, without much success, to commit the party to a course that would preserve the option for peace with the Arabs and at the same time preserve the Jewish and democratic character of the State of Israel. Eban warned in a series of speeches and articles that a security doctrine based on unlimited confidence would degrade the tone and quality of their lives and that the impression of durability might be illusory. The political and military stalemate could end in war because, if the Arabs had no hope of gaining something in the diplomatic field, they could not be expected to abstain from military action.[53] Sapir predicted that prolonged occupation would destroy the moral fabric of Israeli society. He thought the whole country lived in a fool's paradise, but he was less outspoken than Eban, for fear of damaging his party's prospects in the forthcoming election.

The task of bridging the gap between the hard-liners and the moderates was entrusted to Israel Galilee, the minister without portfolio, who was himself one of the staunchest hard-liners. In late August, Galilee published a statement by government ministers of the Israel Labor Party on proposed policy in the occupied territories over the next four years. Known eventually as the Galilee Document, it called for reinforcing existing Jewish settlements in the occupied territories and for building new ones; for giving incentives to Israeli industrialists to build factories in the occupied territories; for permitting the purchase of land in the occupied territories; and for building housing units in Yamit, near Rafah, at the southern entrance to the Gaza Strip. The Galilee Document incorporated many of Dayan's demands and it was a major triumph for the hard-liners and the annexationists. Although it did not decree formal annexation of the occupied territories, it provided a powerful boost for the policy of creeping annexation.

The Galilee Document was incompatible with peace with Israel's neighbors. Its supporters argued that there was no realistic possibility of peace with the Arabs in the foreseeable future anyway. Its critics later claimed that it gave Sadat and Hafez al-Assad the final push to go to war. The Syrian-Egyptian decision to go to war, of course, preceded the publication of the Galilee Document. Nevertheless, this document had far-reaching psychological consequences because of its implied contempt for the Arabs. Sadat was particularly sensitive to these manifestations of Israeli arrogance. He watched parties and candidates outbidding each other in their plans for taking over conquered Arab territories. Dayan talked openly of his designs for building the deep-water port of Yamit, which would cut off Egypt from the Gaza Strip. "Every word spoken about Yamit," said Sadat, "is a knife pointing at me personally and at my self-respect."[54]

The annexationist pronouncements of the Alignment politicians combined with supreme confidence on the part of Israel's military leaders to produce a strident national style. Mainstream political and military leaders shared this smug satisfaction with the status quo. Abba Eban continued to make speeches about the need to balance Israel's historic rights with the rights of others, about the dangers of the status quo, and about the moral imperatives of continuing to work for peace, but his was a lone voice in the wilderness. As he himself recalled, "By 1973 the diplomatic deadlock, the failure of the Jarring mission, the strong support given by the Nixon-Kissinger administration to an attrition policy, all created a climate of exuberant self-confidence that began to border on fantasy. There was an obsession with the physical frontiers of the country without regard to its political or moral frontiers. The rhetoric of 1973 is almost inconceivable. Opinion passed from sobriety to self-confidence and from self-confidence to fantasy, reaching a somewhat absurd level in 1973."[55]

This national mood of exuberant self-confidence manifested itself in Israel's Twenty-fifth Anniversary parade in Jerusalem in April 1973. Several months later Eban convened in Jerusalem a meeting of Israeli ambassadors in Europe. Some of the diplomats asked the intelligence chiefs to comment on the possibility of an Arab attack designed not to inflict a military defeat on Israel but to break the political deadlock. The intelligence chiefs were confident that the Arabs would not risk such an attack, which they knew would be suicidal; and even if they did, they would be flung back so swiftly and violently that Israel's deterrent power would become even greater than before.[56] A low opinion of the Arabs' ability to wage modern war contributed to this sanguine outlook. As one former director of military intelligence later confessed, "a mixture of conceit and complacency tended to colour the evaluation of future developments in the area."[57]

THE YOM KIPPUR WAR

At 2 P.M. on Saturday, 6 October 1973, Egypt and Syria launched a combined military attack on Israel. The war that the intelligence chiefs had described as a "low probability" erupted with spectacular suddenness. The day chosen for the attack was the Day of Atonement, the holiest day in the Jewish calendar. It gave the war its portentous title: the Yom Kippur War.

Military history offers few parallels for strategic surprise as complete as that achieved by Egypt and Syria on 6 October 1973. After the war the government appointed a commission of inquiry headed by the president of the Supreme Court, Dr. Simon Agranat, to examine the responsibility of the military and civilian authorities for the failure to anticipate the attack and for lapses in the initial conduct of the war. The Agranat Commission cleared the political leaders and pinned all the responsibility for the intelligence failure on the army. It also recommended the removal from their posts of four senior officers, including the chief of staff, David Elazar, and the director of military intelligence, Eli Zeira.

The intelligence branch of the IDF had exceptionally detailed and precise information about the military capabilities and operational plans of the enemy. Failure to anticipate the Arab attack was caused not by the shortage of information but by the misreading of the available information. The Agranat Commission attributed the intelligence failure to what it called the conception. The conception rested on two assumptions: (a) Egypt would not go to war until it was able to stage deep air strikes into Israel, particularly against its major military airfields, in order to neutralize Israel's air force; (b) Syria would not launch a full-scale war against Israel unless Egypt was in the struggle too.

The Arab attack represented not just an intelligence failure but, above all, a policy failure. Until the early hours of 6 October, the intelligence chiefs did not think that the Arabs planned to go to war. But the very fact that the Arabs decided to go to war at all showed the failure of the status quo policy, for which the politicians bore the ultimate responsibility. This policy was based on the assumption that Israel had the capacity to perpetuate the status quo indefinitely, an assumption that turned out to be incorrect. Both the intelligence failure and the policy failure thus had their roots in overconfidence in Israel's power to deter an Arab attack.

The Arab aim in launching the war was to break the political deadlock and to provoke an international crisis that would force the superpowers to intervene and put pressure on Israel to withdraw from the territories it had captured in June 1967. Egypt's aim was to cross the Suez Canal in force and entrench itself on the east bank of the canal before the diplomatic negotiations began. Syria's aim was to recapture parts of the Golan Heights and to destroy some of the Israeli forces there. Both Egypt and Syria had limited war aims. They had no illusion that they could defeat Israel or dislodge it from all the territories it had captured in 1967. Their aim was primarily political. They followed Clausewitz's dictum that war is the continuation of policy by other means.

Israel's aim in the event of war was "to deny the enemy any military gain, to destroy his forces and military infrastructure, and to give Israel significant military advantages both in terms of the balance of forces and in terms of the cease-fire lines." Achieving this aim was intended to strengthen Israel's deterrent power, to prove again to the Arabs that they had no military option, and to give Israel strong cards in the negotiations to terminate the war.[58] None of these aims were fully achieved.

The October War was the third Syrian-Israeli war and the fifth Egyptian-Israeli war. In all previous wars political deadlock followed the ending of hostilities. The October War was the first war to be followed by a political settlement. Three reasons help explain how this war laid the foundations for the conclusion of a peace treaty between Egypt and Israel five years later.

The first reason was the impressive performance of the Arab armies in the initial phase of the war. The Egyptian army crossed the canal in force, captured the Bar-Lev line, advanced a certain distance into Sinai, and inflicted heavy losses on Israel in tanks, aircraft, and manpower. The Syrian army launched a highly effective armored thrust on the Golan Heights and for a short period seemed unstoppable. Between them the two armies demonstrated that Israel was not invincible, and they cured themselves of the trauma of the June War. They restored Arab pride, honor, and self-confidence. After the war they did not face Israel from a position of hopeless inferiority. This was an important, but not sufficient, condition for progress toward a political settlement.

The second way in which the October War contributed to a political process is connected with Israel's performance. Israel was taken by surprise, it had to mobilize the bulk of its reserves only after the fighting had started, and it suffered very serious setbacks in the initial phase of the fighting. Yet Israel managed to recover from the surprise, to regain its balance, and to launch a powerful counteroffensive. Its most daring move was to cross over to the west side of the canal and cut off the Egyptian Third Army. The war ended with Israeli forces sixty miles from Cairo and twenty miles from Damascus. Having absorbed the first blow, Israel turned the tables on its enemies. If the Arabs won the first round in the military contest, Israel won the second round, and the result was something of a draw. Israel's losses were considerably heavier than they had been in the Six-Day War. Israel suffered 2,838 dead and 8,800 wounded; the Arabs, 8,528 dead and 19,549 wounded. Israel lost 103 aircraft and 840 tanks; the Arabs, 392 aircraft and 2,554 tanks.[59] The final outcome in 1973 was thus very different from that in 1967. In 1967 the Israeli victory was so decisive and the Arab defeat so crushing that the Arabs were reluctant to face Israel across the negotiating table. In 1973 the final outcome was much more balanced, not least at the psychological level. It promoted a more realistic attitude on both sides and established a more promising basis for bargaining and compromise.

The third reason that political negotiations became possible in the immediate aftermath of the war was U.S. engagement. In Henry Kissinger's hands, U.S. policy was largely reduced to support for Israel and for the status quo. Once the status quo had been shaken up, however, Kissinger moved with remarkable speed to develop an Arab dimension to American foreign policy. His aim was to use the fluid situation created by the war in order to move the parties, step by step, toward a political settlement. He himself became personally involved in the process by embarking on the shuttle diplomacy that took him back and forth from Jerusalem to Cairo and Damascus.

Just as Kissinger was getting into his stride, an international conference took place in Geneva. The conference was convened by the UN secretary-general and given the task of discussing the implementation of Resolution 242 and the establishment of just and lasting peace in the Middle East. Its cosponsors were the United States and the Soviet Union. The parties to the conflict were represented by their foreign ministers. Syria excluded itself, and Israel excluded the Palestinians. Prolonged procedural debates preceded the formal opening of the conference on 21 December. Israel was preparing for a general election at the end of the month, and major policy decisions could not be taken in advance of the election. Eban, as usual, made the most eloquent speech. Kissinger spoke in favor of moving quickly into the practical stage of negotiation. He urged the parties to forget their past rancors, quoting an Arab proverb: *Illi fat mat*—"That which is past is dead."[60] The Jordanians, however, quickly discovered that Kissinger did not intend to work toward implementing Resolution 242 in full and on all fronts. They suspected that he was plotting to knock Jordan out of the game once and for all so as to pave the way for a separate deal between Egypt and Israel for which he would claim all the credit.[61] After three days of speeches and working sessions, the conference adjourned. It convened again in the first week of January 1974 but dispersed without fixing a date for another meeting.

Kissinger took charge of the practical negotiations, relegating the Soviet Union to the sidelines. His shuttle diplomacy resulted in two military disengagement agreements. The Israeli-Egyptian disengagement agreement was signed on 18 January 1974; the Israeli-Syrian agreement, on 31 May 1974. The former required Israel to withdraw from all the territory it held on the western side of the Suez Canal. An area thirty kilometers wide on the eastern side of the canal was divided into three zones. Egypt received a zone by the canal, equivalent to its bridgehead, in which it was allowed to keep up to 7,000 soldiers, thirty tanks, and thirty-six artillery pieces. The middle zone was a buffer zone under UN control. In the eastern zone, which extended to the Sinai passes, Israel was allowed to keep the same level of forces as Egypt in its zone. It was explicitly stated that the military disengagement agreement was only the first step toward a just and lasting peace in accordance with UN Security Council Resolutions 242 and 338. Resolution 338, of 22 October 1973, called upon the parties to cease fire and start implementing Resolution 242. Israel made greater concessions in return for a military disengagement with Egypt in 1974 than those it had refused to make in return for an interim agreement in the first half of 1971. It is reasonable to suppose, though this can never be proved, that had Israel made these concessions in 1971, the Yom Kippur War could have been averted.

The Israeli-Syrian disengagement agreement followed the same general outline, but it took Kissinger thirty-two days to broker it. Israel had to withdraw from the Syrian territory it captured during the war. The Golan Heights were divided into three zones: Syrian and Israeli zones with limited forces, and a narrow UN buffer zone between them. The town of Kuneitra was returned to Syria, but Israel retained control of the adjacent hills.

The Israeli election, originally scheduled for October, was postponed because of the war until 31 December 1973. The Meir-Galilee-Dayan trio was bitterly attacked for its entire conduct of foreign and defense policy, for lulling the country into a false sense of security, and for failing to anticipate the Arab assault. Several protest movements sprang up, with a large number of recently demobilized and disillusioned reservists in their ranks. Much of the protesters' anger was directed personally at Moshe Dayan for what was described as the blunder or the breakdown that preceded the war. The Labor Alignment's representation in the Knesset fell from 56 to 51 seats. Much of the protest vote went to the parties of the right. Several months before the election Gahal merged with two smaller right-wing parties to form the Likud, whose name means "unity" in Hebrew. Ariel Sharon, who had left the IDF earlier in the year to go into politics, was the main driving force behind the merger. The Likud won 39 seats in the Knesset, whereas its component parts had won 32 seats between them at the preceding election. Despite its losses, the Alignment remained the largest party, however, and Golda Meir was called upon to form the next government.

Meir kept Moshe Dayan as defense minister in her new government, which had the shortest life span in Israel's history. On 1 April 1974, three weeks after the government was sworn in, the Agranat Commission published its interim report. This report cleared Golda Meir and Moshe Dayan of direct responsibility for Israel's unpreparedness for the 1973 war. It even praised Meir for her decisions on the day war broke out. Its publication provoked public outrage at the manifest injustice of punishing the soldiers and absolving the politicians. Mass demonstrations called for the resignation of the prime minister and the minister of defense. On 10 April, Golda Meir tendered her resignation. Seventy-five years old and wracked by guilt, she decided she could not carry on. The two candidates to succeed her were Shimon Peres and Yitzhak Rabin. By a narrow majority the party elected Rabin. Meir continued as head of a caretaker government until Rabin was in a position to present to the Knesset his own government on 3 June.

Golda Meir's premiership was marked by a stubborn refusal to reevaluate Israel's relations with the Arab world. She personally had no understanding of the Arabs, no empathy with them, and no faith in the possibility of peaceful coexistence with them. This bolstered a simplistic view of the world in which Israel could do no wrong and the Arabs no right. More than most Israeli leaders, she exhibited the siege mentality, the notion that Israel had to barricade itself behind an iron wall, the fatalistic belief that Israel was doomed forever to live by the sword. Meir was a formidable war leader, but her own policy of immobilism was largely responsible for the outbreak of the Yom Kippur War. In her five years as prime minister she made two monumental mistakes. First, she turned down Jarring's suggestion that Israel should trade Sinai for peace with Egypt, the very terms on which the Egyptian-Israeli peace treaty was to be based eight years later. Second, she turned down Sadat's proposal for an interim settlement, thus leaving him no option except to go to war in order to subvert an intolerable status quo. Few leaders talked more about peace and did less to give it a chance to develop. Meir never tired of repeating that she was prepared to go anywhere at any time to meet any Arab leader who wanted to talk about peace. Given her expansionist policies, these statements had a distinctly hollow ring. Even her own officials used to joke about Golda's launderette being open twenty-four hours a day. With her departure from office, a singularly sterile phase in Israel's relations with its neighbors came to an end.

8

Disengagement

1974–1977

YITZHAK RABIN WAS a political novice when he began his first term as prime minister on 3 June 1974. He had been a member of the Knesset for less than six months and minister of labor for only three months. One of his main advantages in the contest to succeed Golda Meir was that he was in no way associated with the blunders of the Yom Kippur War. Rabin was an innovation in the political life of the country. He was the first prime minister to be born in Israel—in Jerusalem in 1922—and the first to rise up from the ranks of the army and not the ranks of the Labor Party. His outlook on the Arab-Israeli conflict was largely shaped by his experience as a soldier and diplomat. A lifetime of soldiering conditioned him to view developments in the Middle East from the perspective of Israeli security. His five years as ambassador to Washington also conditioned him to view them from the perspective of Israel's special relationship with the United States. As prime minister he cared about two issues above all others: Israel's security and Israel's strategic partnership with the United States.

A SPHINX WITH NO SECRETS

Rabin's government had an air of freshness about it. Of its nineteen ministers only seven had served in the preceding government. The average age of its members was lower than that of any previous Israeli administration. Yet it was far from being a united or harmonious team. Many of its problems stemmed from infighting within the ruling party. The Labor Alignment had been formed in 1968, but its constituent parts retained their tribal loyalties. This complicated the task of forming a government. Shimon Peres, who had the support of the Rafi faction and who had come a close second in the contest for the leadership of the Alignment, demanded the defense portfolio. Ahdut Ha'avodah wanted this portfolio for Yigal Allon. Rabin gave it to Peres and the foreign affairs portfolio to Allon. This entailed the removal of Abba Eban, who had by far the best credentials for the post of foreign minister but lacked a power base within the party. Rabin and Peres could hardly cooperate in seeking peace with the Arabs, because they were at war with each other. The suspicious Rabin thought that Peres was constantly plotting against him, and in his memoirs he called him "the indefatigable underminer." Peres tried to subvert Rabin's authority and take his place while continuing to serve as a member of his cabinet. Their mutual antagonism was comprehensive and unremitting and had a debilitating effect on the conduct of government business.

As prime minister Rabin suffered from the additional handicap of presiding over a coalition that had the narrowest of parliamentary majorities: 61 supporters in the 120-member Knesset. The National Religious Party (NRP), which had 10 seats in the Knesset, declined to join the coalition. The NRP had been the Labor Party's traditional ally, and its leaders had served in almost every government since 1948. But after the Six-Day War it became much more nationalistic, opposing the return of any part of the biblical homeland to Arab rule, and it spawned Gush Emunim (Block of the Faithful), a militant, neomessianic settlement movement. In the hope of attracting the NRP, Rabin had at the outset committed his government to hold an election before concluding a peace agreement that involved the surrender of any territory on the West Bank. In September 1974 the NRP joined the coalition. This immediately provoked the departure of the Citizens' Rights Movement, a militantly secular and dovish splinter group with 3 seats in the Knesset. The net effect was to increase the parliamentary base of the government from 61 to 68 but at the same time to curtail seriously Rabin's freedom of action in relation to Jordan and the Palestinians. His party was committed to territorial compromise over the West Bank; the NRP, to keeping the whole of the West Bank—Judea and Samaria—within Greater Israel.

The challenges that faced Rabin's weak and divided government were formidable: to restore the morale and the deterrent power of the IDF, to avert the collapse of the economy, and to continue the process of military disengagement with Egypt and Syria. On 3 June 1974 Rabin presented his government to the Knesset and received its approval. He described his government as one of "continuity and change." The continuity was evident, but the change was more difficult to pinpoint. After several months in power the elements of a new approach could be detected in Rabin's speeches. First, he made it clear that the road to peace entailed risks at least as great as those involved in refusing to budge and that a government that was not prepared to run these risks would be failing in its duty. Second, he stated that the move toward peace did not have to begin with direct negotiations between Israel and the Arabs but could pass through a stage of negotiations involving a third party. Third, he proposed to move gradually by trading small pieces of territory for a political settlement that fell short of peace.

This approach represented a departure from the previous one of freezing the status quo and shunning political risks. It implied willingness to use Israel's bargaining assets in order to reach accommodation with at least some of the Arab states. But when Rabin moved beyond these general principles, the continuity was more striking than the change. He refused to draw a precise map in advance of negotiations. When one added up all the territories he listed as essential to Israel's security, the overall map was not dissimilar to that depicted in the Labor Alignment's oral doctrine of 1969. Rabin was thus a "sphinx with no secrets," as Lova Eliav of the Alignment wittily put it.

The need to gain time occupied a pivotal place in Rabin's thinking about Israel's relations with the Arab world. He depicted the post–October 1973 period as the seven lean years that would be followed by seven fat years. The reasons he listed for the seven lean years were Arab oil power, Europe's dependence on Arab oil, and continuing superpower rivalry in the Middle East. His reasons for the seven fat years were the decline of Arab oil power by the end of the decade, the West's overcoming of its dependence on Arab oil power, and the replacement of the isolationist mood in the United States with a renewed willingness to assume external commitments of which Israel would be the main beneficiary. The problem was how to reach the end of the seven lean years without alienating America and without meeting the two central Arab de-

mands: a return to the borders of 4 June 1967 and the establishment of an independent Palestinian state. In short, the problem
was how to gain time.

Rabin's emphasis on playing for time gave the impression that,
like his predecessor, he wanted to preserve the status quo, that he
preferred to avoid difficult decisions, and that he had no long-
term vision of peace. This impression is not entirely justified.
According to Shlomo Avineri, Rabin had a grand strategy for
bringing about a settlement of the Arab-Israeli conflict. Avineri, a
political theorist at the Hebrew University of Jerusalem, was in
early 1976 appointed by Yigal Allon director general of the
Foreign Ministry. Avineri went to see the prime minister in order
to ask him to explain how he thought peace might be achieved.
Rabin responded with an hour-long lecture:

> Rabin made it clear to me that he had no doubt that an Arab-
> Israeli settlement would involve withdrawal from most of the
> territories that the IDF conquered during the Six-Day War,
> except for Jerusalem, the Jordan Valley, and specific points of
> strategic value. Areas with dense Arab population in the West
> Bank and the Gaza Strip could not remain under our rule for-
> ever, and, in order to assure maximum negotiating flexibility,
> we should refrain from establishing Jewish settlements on
> them. The partner in the negotiations on the future of Judea
> and Samaria ought to be the kingdom of Jordan.
>
> But—and this is the heart of the matter—this process must
> not take place in the shadow of the Yom Kippur War and
> under the pressure of the Arab oil power, which was then at
> its peak. Under no circumstances, said Rabin, should Israel
> withdraw from the territories in a manner that looked as if it
> expressed Israeli weakness. The first task of his government
> was to achieve for Israel a period of time in order to rebuild
> its strategic, diplomatic, and psychological position following
> the trauma of the Yom Kippur War, and only then—he indi-
> cated a period of about five years—from a position of Israeli
> strength, should one strive for arrangements along the lines he
> had outlined.

The crux of the strategy was to remove from Arab minds the idea
that a weak Israel would make concessions. This strategy impressed
Avineri as simultaneously dovish and hawkish: dovish in its aims,
hawkish in its means; generous in concessions that might be made
to the Arabs in the framework of a peace settlement, but stubborn

on the manner in which such a settlement might be reached. Avineri also noted that Rabin could not reveal his true strategy to the public without endangering his chances of carrying it out.[1]

The Rabin government's attitude to Jewish settlements in the occupied territories provides the best illustration of the difficulty in implementing his grand design. On the one hand, he was opposed to the building of Jewish settlements in the heavily populated areas of the West Bank and the Gaza Strip as the logical corollary of his commitment to territorial compromise. Friends as well as enemies widely condemned such settlements as obstacles to peace and as evidence of Israeli expansionism. On the other hand, there was a strong lobby for settlement inside the government, which included Shimon Peres, Israel Galilee, and the NRP ministers. The collective weight of these ministers accounted for the decision to build a new town in the Golan Heights at a time of great financial stringency and for the decision to start building Jewish settlements in Samaria with the approach of the 1977 general election. It also accounted for Rabin's leniency toward Gush Emunim, which openly defied him by setting up illegal settlements on the West Bank. Rabin was infuriated when a group of these religious zealots set up a camp in Sebastia, near Nablus. But his efforts to evict them were undermined by the active support they received from Peres and the passive support of other ministers. Success at Sebastia encouraged Gush Emunim to sponsor more settlements in Samaria in defiance of the divided government. And these squatter settlements struck at the heart of Rabin's undeclared grand strategy for eventually trading the bulk of the West Bank for peace with the Hashemite Kingdom of Jordan.

JORDAN AND THE PALESTINIANS

The military disengagement agreement with Egypt had been signed on 18 January 1974 and the one with Syria on 31 May. Rabin's newly appointed cabinet had to decide how to proceed. But the cabinet was divided between the proponents of "Jordan first" and the proponents of "Egypt first," rather like its predecessor in late 1948–49. Yigal Allon was the main advocate of the "Jordan first" approach. He argued that the next step should be an interim agreement with Jordan, to be followed by an interim agreement with Egypt. He was faithful to the Jordanian option and wanted to give priority to King Hussein in order to strengthen his position in the Arab world. Yitzhak Rabin was the main advo-cate of the "Egypt first" approach. He argued for resuming nego-tiations aimed at an interim agreement with Egypt.

No one advocated negotiations with the PLO. Although the PLO had not participated in the October War, its political stand-ing improved as a result of the war. It also took a step to moder-ate its political program. The Palestinian National Charter called for an armed struggle to liberate the whole of Palestine. The Palestinian National Council (PNC), which convened in Cairo in June 1974, shifted the emphasis from the armed struggle to a po-litical solution by means of a phased program. As a first stage, it ap-proved the establishment of an "independent national authority over any part of the Palestinian territory which was liberated."[2] This was an ambiguous formula, but it conveyed a willingness to consider the possibility of a Palestinian state alongside Israel rather than in place of it.

On the Israeli side, however, the PNC resolution was inter-preted as the result of a change of tactics rather than a change of aims. Frequent references were made to the PLO's theory of stages to make the point that a Palestinian state in part of Palestine would only serve as a base for continuing the armed struggle to liberate the whole of Palestine. The Rabin government adhered to the or-thodox line of refusing to recognize or to negotiate with the PLO. Two moderate ministers, Aharon Yariv and Victor Shemtov, pro-posed a formula saying that Israel would negotiate with any Palestinian body that recognized it and renounced terror. But there was no majority for this formula. Rabin was opposed to it. He wanted to keep the Palestinian question "in the refrigerator." He took the view that Israel must refuse to talk to a terrorist or-ganization that was committed to its destruction. Nor was he pre-pared to consider a Palestinian state alongside Israel; this, he said, "would be the beginning of the end of the State of Israel." For all practical purposes, his position was the same as that of Golda Meir. She denied the existence of a Palestinian people. Although he rec-ognized that a Palestinian people existed and that there was a Palestinian problem, he was not prepared to do anything about it. His position remained firm and inflexible: Israel would never rec-ognize the PLO, enter into any negotiations with the PLO, or agree to the establishment of a Palestinian state.

If personal convictions precluded Rabin from offering any-thing to the PLO, domestic political constraints kept him from of-fering anything of substance to King Hussein. Rabin's American friends urged him to talk to the pro-Western monarch. Two weeks after Rabin was sworn in, Richard Nixon (who was soon to lose the presidency because of the Watergate scandal) came to Israel on a state visit. Nixon urged that the military disengagement agreements with Egypt and Syria be followed up with a similar agreement with Jordan. Kissinger kept warning Israel's leaders that they had a choice of settling with Hussein or Arafat; it had to be one or the other. Kissinger advised Rabin, "For God's sake do something with Hussein while he is still one of the players."[3] Rabin, however, had tied his own hands by pledging to submit any withdrawal on the West Bank to the verdict of the Israeli electorate, and he shied away from putting his ideas to the voters. Consequently, he could offer Hussein nothing, and the negotiations between them came to naught.

Although Rabin was not ready for a deal on the West Bank, he valued the contact with King Hussein. During the three years of his premiership, Rabin had over half a dozen meetings with the king. The king was always accompanied by his prime minister and close confidant, Zeid al-Rifai; Rabin, by Allon and Peres. Israel initiated all the meetings, which all took place on Israeli soil. One meeting was in a guest house in north Tel Aviv; all the others were held in the Arava desert, near the border between the two countries, in an air-conditioned caravan that kept changing its location for security reasons. The king and Rifai would arrive by helicopter and be taken by car or helicopter to the meeting place, near Massada. Each meeting lasted about three and a half hours and included dinner. The meetings would begin with a survey of the regional and global scenes; since both Rabin and Hussein spoke slowly, this would take a relatively long time. On the Israeli side each meeting was carefully prepared in advance by officials who also produced a detailed record of the discussions. Israel had four main aims in these discussions: to explore the possibilities of a deal with Jordan, to solve minor problems that affected both countries, to promote economic cooperation, and to coordinate policy toward the West Bank and the Palestinian guerrilla organizations. Jordan put forward two proposals in these discussions: an interim agreement involving partial Israeli withdrawal on the West Bank, and a full peace agreement in return for complete Israeli withdrawal.[4]

The first meeting took place on 28 August 1974. Allon introduced Rabin and Peres to King Hussein. The king repeated the proposal he had already made to Golda Meir for a military disengagement involving a withdrawal of about eight kilometers on both sides of the Jordan River. This proposal was incompatible with the Allon Plan, which envisaged that the whole of the Jordan Valley would remain under Israeli control. Rabin rejected the proposal out of hand and added that he could not even consider it as an option for the future. Peres then put forward a proposal of his own.

Before the meeting with Hussein, Peres obtained Rabin's and Allon's approval to present his own thoughts on the Palestinian problem. He proposed that a possible solution lay in the creation of three political entities: Israel, Jordan, and a Palestinian entity that would be administered by them jointly. The Palestinian entity, comprising the West Bank and the Gaza Strip, would be wholly demilitarized and fall under no single sovereignty. Instead, residents carrying Jordanian passports would vote for the Jordanian parliament, and those with Israeli citizenship would vote for the Knesset in Jerusalem. The inhabitants of the Gaza Strip, many of whom were stateless refugees, would receive Jordanian passports. The three entities would form a single economic unit, open to the free movement of goods, persons, and ideas. Peres conceded that his plan might seem fantastic, "but fantasy is the only way to solve this situation."

The king remarked impatiently that he wanted to talk about the present, which meant a military disengagement agreement. Allon stepped in to save the meeting from failure. He suggested that the town of Jericho be turned over to the Hashemite Kingdom of Jordan for it to set up a civil administration there. The king was noncommittal because what he really wanted was an Israeli withdrawal along the entire front, as in the case of Sinai and the Golan Heights. The meeting ended without any agreement being reached.[5]

The second meeting was held on 19 October. By this time Hussein had come around to the Jericho plan. However, he asked not just for the town of Jericho but also for an enclave around it that would have given him access all the way to Ramallah. Hussein viewed the Jericho plan as a means to extending his influence on the West Bank. But Rabin, having just brought the NRP into the government, was unwilling to consider even an enclave because he feared the collapse of his fragile coalition.[6] Rabin's reasons for rejecting the Jericho plan were candidly explained by Abba Eban, who was no longer in the government: "If we ask why a Jordanian disengagement was not pursued by the Israeli Government, the answer can only be found in our domestic context. Kuneitra and Suez do not mean elections. Jericho means elections, and one does not want elections—therefore one does not want a disengagement agreement with Jordan. So here we have a very classic case of mutual relationship between international policies and domestic inhibitions."[7]

At the end of October an Arab League summit meeting was held in Rabat, the capital of Morocco. King Hussein suffered a major defeat because the summit endorsed the claim of the PLO to be "the sole legitimate representative of the Palestinian people." The summit also reaffirmed the right of the Palestinian people to set up an independent national authority, led by the PLO, on any part of Palestine that was liberated. The implication of these resolutions was that the territories captured in 1967 should not revert to Jordan but go to the Palestinians to establish an independent state. A month later Yasser Arafat was invited to address the UN General Assembly, which proceeded to pass a resolution affirming the right of the Palestinian people to national self-determination. The Israeli government remained unmoved, however, by the PLO's successes in gaining international legitimacy. It refused to adopt the Yariv-Shemtov formula. Rabin in fact hardened his stance against the PLO by underlining that Israel would deal only with King Hussein.

Viewed from Amman, the Israeli position was far from helpful. The Israeli government consistently refused to throw to Hussein and his government a lifeline in the form of a disengagement agreement. Hussein's position was seriously weakened at Rabat by his inability to point to any success in recovering occupied territory. When the Arab heads of state designated the PLO as the sole legitimate representative of the Palestinian people, he had little choice but to go along with this decision.[8] Hussein was angry with the Israelis and felt that they had let him down. His next meeting with the Israeli leaders did not take place until 28 May 1975. By this time Israel had started negotiating a second disengagement agreement with Egypt. Hussein feared that such an agreement would further weaken Jordan's position in the Middle East, but there was little he could do except to cast doubt on Sadat's reliability. Like the preceding two meetings, this one brought no agreement.

After the Rabat Summit the meetings continued because both sides saw some value in staying in contact. But the emphasis shifted from the discussion of a political settlement to dealing with day-to-day problems. Among the subjects that came up were the combating of terrorist activities by the radical Palestinian factions, ecology, water, aviation, shipping in the Gulf of Aqaba, and border demarcation.[9] On the issues that really mattered, according to King Hussein, "Rabin was very rigid, very polite, very cordial but rigid and impossible to alter." When they met again during Rabin's second term as prime minister, in 1992–95, Rabin said to Hussein, "You were very stubborn," and Hussein replied, "Yes, I was because I could not give an inch of Palestinian territory or an iota of Palestinian rights." Hussein also recalled his last meeting with Rabin in 1976, at which Rabin said, "Well, there is nothing that can be done. Wait for ten years; maybe things will change on the ground." Hussein replied, "Well, too bad."[10]

Overall, Rabin did not display much statesmanship or foresight in relation to Jordan. He subordinated the country's international needs to domestic convenience. He refrained from tackling the big issues in Israel's relations with Jordan because he did not possess the courage to face up to their domestic political consequences. His tactic was to play for time, to postpone difficult decisions until the regional constellation had changed in Israel's favor, to survive politically. For him the problem of Jordan and the Palestinians was neither central nor urgent. On several occasions he repeated that the heart of the Middle Eastern problem was the relationship between Israel and Egypt. So it was not surprising that he chose to give priority to continuing the process of disengagement with Egypt. Nor was it surprising that Henry Kissinger's step-by-step approach coincided with his own preferences, for on the Egyptian front, too, he wanted to avoid the core issues in the conflict for as long as possible. But here at least he was prepared to pay small installments of territory for something less than peace.

SINAI II

The Israeli team for the negotiations on the interim agreement with Egypt consisted again of Rabin, Allon, and Peres. But whereas with King Hussein they negotiated directly, with Egypt they negotiated through a third party, the indefatigable American secretary of state, who resumed his shuttle between Jerusalem and Cairo in March 1975. By this time Richard Nixon had left the White House in disgrace and handed over the presidency to Gerald Ford. Ford and Kissinger agreed with Rabin that an overall Middle

Eastern settlement was beyond their reach and that the next step ought to be an interim agreement between Israel and Egypt. Kissinger had been exposed to Rabin's unconventional diplomatic style during his years as national security adviser to Nixon. This is how Kissinger described Rabin when he was ambassador to Washington:

> Yitzhak Rabin had many extraordinary qualities, but the gift of human relations was not one of them. If he had been handed the entire United States Strategic Air Command as a free gift he would have (a) affected the attitude that at last Israel was getting its due, and (b) found some technical short-coming in the airplanes that made his accepting them a reluctant concession to us.[11]

Prior to Kissinger's arrival the Israeli policymakers discussed among themselves the kind of interim agreement they wanted to reach with Egypt. As in 1971 the military leaders were less fixated on territory than the politicians were. In the IDF General Staff a consensus emerged in favor of new security arrangements in Sinai. The main requirements was a buffer zone that would be as wide as possible and from which the forces of both sides would be excluded. This buffer zone, according to the IDF proposal, could be supervised either by joint Israeli-Egyptian patrols or by UN forces. The proposal represented a major shift from the static conception for the defense of Sinai to a flexible conception. The great advantage of the buffer zone was that any attempt by Egyptian forces to cross it and to move toward the Israeli border would deprive them of their umbrella of surface-to-surface missiles and expose them to attack by Israeli armor and aircraft. The main proponent of this proposal was Lieutenant General Mordechai Gur, who had replaced David Elazar as chief of staff in April 1974. Gur recommended a deep Israeli withdrawal, to the El Arish–Ras Muhammad line. Furthermore, he recommended that this withdrawal not be made conditional on a political agreement with Egypt.

The government did not accept the recommendations of the chief of staff. On the one hand, it was not prepared to effect a complete withdrawal from the Sinai passes and insisted on keeping the early-warning station in Um Hashiba in Israeli hands. On the other, it was determined to exact a political reward for every pull-back.[12] Rabin struck a particularly tough posture. As he explained to President Ford, the step-by-step approach had its own pitfalls.

If Israel were to give "a piece of land" without getting "a piece of peace" in exchange, the process could end with Israel's relinquishing everything it held without achieving its goal. It was therefore imperative for any further agreement to involve a political step toward peace. Rabin held out for the termination of the state of belligerency and the retention of the Mitla and Gidi Passes and the Abu Rodeis oil fields. This struck Kissinger as an unrealistic position when he embarked on his shuttle in early March 1975.

During one of the sessions in Jerusalem, Rabin suggested to Kissinger that he ask Sadat privately whether he would agree to conclude a separate and full peace agreement in return for most of Sinai. The reply he received was that Sadat could not conclude a separate peace agreement. But even in the negotiations on the interim agreement, Rabin kept insisting on conditions that would have effectively taken Egypt out of the war. The main bone of contention was the Sinai passes. Here Rabin's last offer was an Israeli withdrawal to the eastern edge of the passes, provided the Egyptian forces did not advance beyond the western edge. In return he insisted on a nonbelligerency declaration. This was unacceptable to Sadat. Kissinger blamed Israel for the impasse and started to apply heavy pressure on it. He threatened that if Israel persisted in its inflexible position, the Geneva conference would have to be reconvened with Soviet participation. On 21 March, President Ford sent Rabin a very tough message, warning that the failure of Kissinger's mission would have far-reaching consequences for the region and for U.S.-Israeli relations. The message achieved the opposite effect to the one intended. Even the waverers in the cabinet now resolved that the negotiating team must remain adamant in its policy. Kissinger's mission failed, and Kissinger blamed Israel for the failure. Once again, he told journalists on his plane, Israel's hard line had made it miss an opportunity.

Following the failure President Ford officially announced a "reassessment" of U.S. policy toward the Middle East. This heralded one of the most difficult periods in U.S.-Israeli relations. For six months, from March to September 1975, the Americans refused to sign new arms deals with Israel, though they continued to honor contracts signed before the crisis broke out. In June, Rabin paid a visit to Washington to try to clear the air. During the visit the Jewish lobby mounted a public relations campaign in support of Israel. Seventy-six senators signed a letter to the president calling for "defensible borders" for Israel and large-scale economic and military assistance. Ford presented Rabin with two options: a return to the Geneva conference to work out an overall settlement for the Middle East or another attempt at an interim agreement between Israel and Egypt. Rabin preferred the latter but sought payment in American currency for the concessions he knew Israel would have to make to Egypt.

The General Staff had worked out a withdrawal plan to meet Egypt's objections to an Israeli presence at the eastern entrance to the passes. The IDF would remain to the north of the Gidi Pass and the south of the Mitla road and hold on to the eastern ridge running between the two passes. This would enable Israel to control the eastern openings to the passes without occupying them. The plan required the Americans to take over all the early-warning installations in the area of the passes and to operate them on behalf of both Israel and Egypt. Kissinger and Ford were initially taken aback by the idea of an American military presence in Sinai. In early July the administration informed Israel that, although it was not prepared to send military personnel to Sinai, it was prepared to man the Um Hashiba installation as well as to build and man an additional early-warning station on the Egyptian side. Further exchanges with the Americans, who were also in touch with the Egyptians, convinced Rabin that the way was finally open to an interim agreement on terms acceptable to Israel.[13]

The second round of negotiations led by Kissinger lasted from 21 to 31 August. During these eleven days Kissinger steadily inched his way forward to an agreement. His style of negotiating tested to the limit the patience, persistence, and even physical endurance of all the participants. The second Sinai agreement was initialed on 1 September and formally signed in Geneva on 4 September. It was approved by the Israeli cabinet on 1 September and ratified by the Knesset on 3 September by a vote of 70 to 43. Among those who voted against the agreement were Moshe Dayan and two other members from the Rafi faction. Jealousy of Rabin for succeeding where he had failed was the most likely explanation for Dayan's vote.

The agreement between Egypt and Israel—or Sinai II, as it came to be known—followed the general pattern of the first military disengagement agreement of 18 January 1974. But it contained one novel feature: an American role in relation both to the agreement and to Israel. Israel agreed to withdraw from the Abu Rodeis oil fields and the passes, but it was to keep some hills at the eastern end of the Gidi Pass. It was also to keep the sophisticated early-warning station at Um Hashiba, inside the passes. America undertook to build for Egypt a similar station in the passes, and the two stations were to be part of the Sinai Field Mission, manned solely by American civilian personnel. The oil fields and the passes were included in a demilitarized buffer zone under the control of UN forces. On both sides of the UN buffer zone there were limited-force zones, as in the Sinai I agreement (see map 9). In return for these gains Egypt accepted several elements of nonbelligerency but without agreeing to a comprehensive abolition of the state of war. Article 1 stated, "The conflict between them and in the Middle East shall not be resolved by military force but by peaceful means." Article 2 stated, "The parties hereby undertake not to resort to the threat or use of force or military blockade against each other." Article 3 committed the parties to continue to observe the cease-fire on land, sea, and air, while Article 8 spoke of the parties' continuing their efforts to negotiate a final peace agreement within the framework of the Geneva peace conference and in accordance with Security Council Resolution 338.[14]

Rabin made it clear to Kissinger that the cabinet would not ratify the Sinai II agreement unless it was accompanied by an American-Israeli agreement. So they went on to discuss the "memorandum of agreement" between their countries, which detailed U.S. commitments to Israel following from the interim agreement. The conclusive discussion on the bilateral issues was held on the night of 31 August and lasted until 6 A.M. Many of the participants on both sides dropped out of the discussion through sheer exhaustion; by the end it had become a dialogue between Rabin and Kissinger against a chorus of snores all around. The memorandum pledged American support "on an on-going and long-term basis to Israel's military equipment and other defense requirements, to its energy requirements and to its economic needs." More specifically, it promised a positive response to Israel's request for F-16 fighter planes and Pershing missiles with conventional warheads. In a separate "memorandum of agreement," which was kept secret, the United States confirmed that it would not negotiate with or recognize the PLO, initiate any moves in the Middle East without prior consultation with Israel, or diverge from Resolutions 242 and 338 as the sole basis for peace negotiations.[15]

The agreement with America was as important to Rabin as that with Egypt. Israel now had an alliance with America in all but name. The cost of the agreement to the United States was roughly $4 billion annually for the next three years, or 200 percent above the existing level of American aid to Israel. The package was crit-

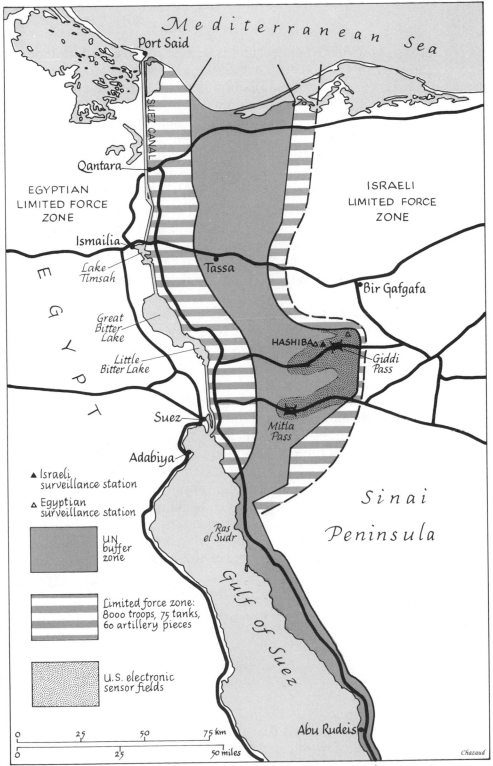

Israeli-Egyptian Sinai agreement, 4 September 1975

icized in some American quarters as being excessive, and even extortionate, in relation to what Israel was required to give up. George Ball wrote that Sinai II amounted to "a vast real estate deal in which the United States bought a slice of the Sinai Desert from Israel for a huge financial and political consideration and then paid Egypt for accepting it."[16]

In Israel the Sinai II agreement was presented as an invaluable step on the road to peace with Egypt. It was Rabin's principal departure from the foreign policy of his predecessor. But in some respects the agreement marked the end of the road rather than a new beginning. Israel relinquished one-seventh of the Egyptian territory it occupied, including the strategic passes and the oil fields. In return, however, it obtained a three-year breathing space during which it would be required to make no drastic political decisions, three years it could use to consolidate the new status quo. Notably absent from the agreement was any commitment by Israel to enter into negotiations over the Golan Heights or the West Bank. True, the agreement contained a reference to continuing the efforts toward a just and lasting peace but only between Israel and Egypt. The memorandum of agreement between the governments of Israel and the United States made it clear that both regarded Sinai II as a separate agreement and not as a first step toward comprehensive peace in the Middle East. Article 12 states, "It is the United States Government's position that Egyptian commitments under the Egypt-Israel Agreement, its implementation, validity and duration are not conditional upon any act or developments between the other Arab states and Israel. The United States Government regards the Agreement as standing on its own." If Kissinger's objective was to drive a wedge between Sadat and the Soviet Union, Rabin's was to widen the rift between Sadat and Syria.

SYRIA AND LEBANON

The Sinai II agreement was widely unpopular in the Arab world. Syria and the Palestinians were not alone in thinking that Sadat had weakened the chances of Israeli withdrawal from the other Arab territories captured by Israel in 1967. The Syrians felt that Sadat eroded the political assets that they, no less than he, had helped gain for the Arab world in October 1973. To compensate for Sadat's "defection" the Syrians tried to create a crescent-shaped coalition, or "banana front," extending from Aqaba on the Red Sea to Naqura on the Mediterranean Sea. The banana front was to consist of Jordan, Iraq, and Lebanon, with Syria as its pivot, and it was to stretch around Israel's eastern and northern flanks. From the Israeli point of view, a successful move by the Syrians to establish themselves in Lebanon would have significantly increased the danger from this front.[17]

At the same time, Syria launched a diplomatic offensive at the UN for an overall solution to the Arab-Israeli conflict and for international recognition of Palestinian rights and of the PLO as the sole spokesman of the Palestinians. Some State Department officials were sympathetic to the view that the Palestinian issue was at the heart of the Middle Eastern problem and that the PLO position could evolve in a moderate direction. In January 1976 President Ford took advantage of a state visit by Yitzhak Rabin to Washington to urge both privately and publicly that further steps be taken to advance peace negotiations. Rabin stated, in an address to a joint session of Congress, that Israel was ready for negotiations with any Arab state but that it was not ready to commit national suicide by meeting with the PLO. In truth, the road to negotiations with Syria lay closed. Kissinger had promised Sadat that once Sinai II had been concluded, he would try to promote a second agreement between Syria and Israel. But he also promised Israel in writing that the United States regarded Sinai II as standing on its own. The United States was therefore obliged to defer to Israel's opinion on the possibility of an agreement with Syria. Israel took the view that there was room only for "cosmetic changes" in the disengagement lines on the Golan Heights. This was of no interest to Syria, so negotiations for a second Israeli-Syrian agreement never got off the ground.[18]

The rift between Damascus and Cairo exacerbated the conflict in Lebanon. Lebanon did not present Israel with a military or strategic problem. The problem stemmed from Lebanon's internal political situation, which revolved around a delicate and shifting equilibrium between four main groups: the Maronite Christians, the Druze, the Shiites, and the Sunni Muslims. A large Palestinian community, consisting of 1948 refugees whose ranks were swelled by the exodus from Jordan after the crushing of the PLO in September 1970, affected both the demographic and the political balance. The PLO leaders and fighters who moved from Jordan to Beirut and southern Lebanon created a state within a state. All the contending groups in Lebanon had outside sponsors

and supporters. The weakness of the Lebanese state and the frag-
mentation of Lebanese society not only permitted but invited outside intervention. Syria and Israel were the main external actors in
the Lebanese drama. The Syrian leaders, for historical reasons, regarded Lebanon not as an independent, sovereign state but as part
of Greater Syria. Israel's links with the Maronite community
stretched back to the pre-Independence period, and after
Independence Israel continued to encourage the trend toward
Christian separatism and Christian hegemony in Lebanon.
Particularly close bonds existed between Israel and the Phalange,
a political party and a militia that was opposed to Pan-Arabism.
What Syria and Israel had in common was the fear that Lebanon
would be dominated by their enemy. Syria wanted to encircle
Israel, not to be encircled by it. Israel could not tolerate the
prospect of Syrian troops on two of its borders. Each country eyed
the other's moves in Lebanon with inevitable suspicion.

In April 1975 the simmering tensions in Lebanon erupted into
a civil war. The first phase of this war, which lasted until January
1976, consisted of firefights and sporadic acts of violence between
the leftist-PLO coalition and the various Christian militias, which
were divided among themselves. The second phase, which lasted
from January until May 1976, witnessed a sharp escalation of the
fighting and the first signs of victory by the leftist-PLO coalition.
The embattled Maronites appealed for help from two very different quarters: Syria and Israel. Syria responded to this appeal by taking a series of steps. First, it tried its hand at political intervention
by summoning the warring factions to Damascus and imposing on
them an agreement designed to shore up the old constitutional
structure of the country with only minor changes. When this did
not work, Syria sent Saiqa, a military organization that owed it al-
legiance, to intervene in the civil war on the side of the Christians.
On 1 June 1976, when the Christian-rightist forces faced an imminent danger of being overwhelmed, Syria sent its regular army
into Lebanon.

The Israeli policymakers were not sure how to respond to the
fast-moving events in Lebanon or to the increasingly desperate
Maronite appeals for help. It was obvious that the status quo could
not last, but the disintegration of the Lebanese state carried with
it dangers as well as opportunities. Yigal Allon tended to dwell on
the opportunities and Yitzhak Rabin on the dangers. Allon was a
strong supporter of an alliance with other minorities to counter
Sunni Muslim dominance in the Middle East. He favored an active

interventionist policy and the forging of close links with Kurds, Druze, and Christians anywhere in the Arab world. His pet scheme since the 1950s was to help the Druze in Syria, in the Golan, and in the Shouf mountains in Lebanon unite and enter into an alliance with Israel. During the October War, Allon wanted the IDF to advance into Syria and help create a Druze state at Syria's expense, but his advice was not heeded. The civil war in Lebanon presented Israel, according to Allon, with a historic opportunity to rectify the mistake of 1973. He envisaged two small minority states linked to Israel, one Druze and one Maronite. Like David Ben-Gurion twenty years earlier, Allon represented the interventionist streak in the Zionist policy toward the Arab world.

Yitzhak Rabin, by contrast, was much more skeptical about the prospect of gains and more concerned about the risks of being sucked into the Lebanese quagmire. He was by nature a cautious and prudent man, not prone to taking political or military gambles. All his instincts tended toward the preservation of the status quo. He wanted to preserve Lebanon as a buffer between Syria and Israel rather than accelerate its demise or turn it into a laboratory for experiments in state making. Unimpressed with the Maronite leaders, he was wary of being drawn into Lebanon to fight their battles for them. Like Moshe Sharett twenty years earlier, he suspected that the Maronites might turn out to be a broken reed. He was not as firmly opposed to intervention as Sharett had been, but he set clear limits beyond which he refused to go. Although he agreed to give the Maronites arms and training facilities, he was not prepared to intervene directly or actively in the conflict between them and the Muslim communities. His approach was to help the Maronites help themselves.

The Maronite call for help, the ascendancy of the PLO and its allies, and Syrian intervention necessitated a reappraisal of Israeli policy in Lebanon. The government considered three options. The first was direct Israeli intervention in the civil war. Rabin came out against this option, fearing that a massive Israeli intervention on the side of the status quo militias might lead to war with Syria and harm the relations with Egypt. The second option was to let Syria take over if the traditional Lebanese entity could not survive. While this was preferable to domination by the PLO and its allies, the drawback was that it was bound to enhance Syria's standing in the region and to require Israel to deter Syria on two fronts.

The third policy option was an intermediate one: accepting Syrian intervention but with certain limitations. The limitations

became known as the "red lines," which the United States conveyed to Damascus. The red lines stipulated that Syria would not
dispatch forces south of Sidon, would not use its air force, and
would not deploy ground-to-air missiles on Lebanon's territory.
This was the option the government adopted.[19] Differently stated,
the red lines meant that Syria could not cross a line on the map
running directly east from Sidon to the Lebanese-Syrian border,
that it could not act against Israel from the air, and that it could
not use missiles against Israel's planes. From the Israeli point of
view this intermediate policy option had a number of advantages.
First, it reduced the risk of a military clash between Israel and Syria
in Lebanon. Second, Syrian intervention was directed against
Israel's enemies in Lebanon, against the PLO and the leftist-
Muslim forces. Third, it enabled Israel to pursue a common policy with the United States in Lebanon. The Americans, like the
Israelis, had come to view Syria as a potentially stabilizing force in
Lebanese politics.

King Hussein played a part in arranging the tacit understanding between Hafez al-Assad and the Israelis. The king advised the
Maronites that if they wanted to survive in the Middle East, they
should turn to Israel. He also agreed to serve as a messenger for
President Assad, who knew about his contacts with the Israeli leaders. One night in April 1976 Gideon Rafael, Israel's ambassador in
London, was asked to meet King Hussein urgently at the house of
a mutual friend. The king was deeply concerned about the mounting tension in the area. It was in their mutual interest, he argued,
to keep the situation under control and to contain the present
fighting in Lebanon. The message he conveyed from Assad to
Rabin was that Syria's intervention in Lebanon was designed to
protect the Christians and that there was no intention of harming
Israel's interests there. Assad promised to keep his forces away
from the Israeli border and asked the Israelis not to intervene. A
few hours later Rafael was on his way to Israel. Rabin appreciated
the message. At a special meeting the cabinet accepted the Syrian
explanation and confirmed its decision to refrain from direct intervention in Lebanon. Rafael flew back to London to convey the
reassuring message to the king, who promptly dispatched it to
Damascus.[20]

Israel established direct contact with the Christian militias in response to their calls for help. Toward the end of March a team of
four intelligence and army officers, headed by Colonel Binyamin
Ben-Eliezer, was sent to assess the military capabilities of the

Christian militias and their prospects in the civil war. Dressed in civilian clothes, they left by gunboat for the port of Jounieh and visited the Christian strongholds in the north of Lebanon. Among the leaders they met were Sheikh Pierre Gemayel and his son Bashir, Camille Chamoun, the former president, and his son Danny. The Christians asked for arms so that they could slaughter the Palestinians. Ben-Eliezer was appalled by the brutality, vindictiveness, and downright dishonesty of Israel's would-be allies. Camille Chamoun invited him and his colleagues to step out to the garden of his villa to inspect some of his female fighters. The young women in combat fatigues were armed with Kalachnikovs, pistols, hand grenades, and commando knives. Ben-Eliezer asked about their achievements. "Show him," said Chamoun to the first one. She produced out of her pocket a transparent plastic bag containing amputated fingers, one finger from each man she had killed. A second woman waved a plastic bag full of earlobes, also war trophies. By this time Ben-Eliezer had seen enough and asked to go back to the house. From the visit he concluded that the Lebanese Christians wanted Israel to capture Lebanon for them and fight the civil war on their behalf. In return they said they would be prepared to sign a defense pact and even a peace agreement with Israel.

The Israeli team presented its report to a special meeting of the cabinet's defense committee. The other participants included Rabin, Allon, Peres, Chief of Staff Mordechai Gur, and Yitzhak Hofi, the head of the Mossad. Ben-Eliezer's report was rather mixed. He described the internal divisions among the Christians and their inflated expectations, but he recommended helping them with arms and military training. Hofi warned against large-scale involvement in Lebanon. He was very cautious and pointed out the risks of getting embroiled. It later emerged that there were two schools of thought in the Mossad. Hofi's school was opposed to excessive involvement. The other school, led by David Kimche, advocated active intervention on the side of the Christians.[21]

Kimche believed that Israel's interests would best be served by enforcing Christian hegemony in Lebanon. He was the main formulator of and driving force behind "the Christian conception," which held that the Christians, the enemies of Israel's Muslim and Palestinian enemies, should not only survive in their traditional enclaves but rule over the entire country. The Christians were perceived both as political allies and as a source of intelligence on Lebanon and the entire Arab world. Kimche's conception ran into considerable opposition from the IDF Intelligence Corps, which argued all along that the Christians were playing a double game and that the intelligence they supplied was worthless. In April 1980 Hofi suspended Kimche from his post as deputy head of the Mossad responsible for external relations. The specific charge against him was that he exceeded his authority in supplying arms to the Christians. It was evident that the close relations Kimche had cultivated with the Christians were not to Hofi's liking.[22]

The first top-level meeting between Israeli and Maronite officials took place in August 1976 on a missile boat anchored just outside Haifa harbor. The participants were Camille Chamoun and Yitzhak Rabin. "Will you intervene?" asked Chamoun pointedly. "Will you ask us to?" retorted Rabin evasively. Rabin proceeded on the basis of a report prepared by Colonel Ben-Eliezer. The report spoke of the divisions in the Maronite ranks and of glaring military shortcomings, but it also stressed their dedication to the struggle against the PLO and the wide popular support for the militias. Rabin assured Chamoun that Israeli arms supplies would be increased. "Our guiding principle is that we are prepared to help you help yourselves," he explained to his elderly Lebanese guest. Following the meeting the Maronites started receiving American rifles, TOW antitank rockets, and antiquated Sherman tanks. It was later estimated that during the government's three-year term Israel invested close to $150 million in building up the Maronite militias in Lebanon.[23]

In addition to the arms and training given to the Maronite forces in northern Lebanon, Israel also extended assistance to the smaller Christian militias in southern Lebanon. The area near the border became an Israeli sphere of influence. Contact with the militias enabled Israel to develop links with other segments of the Christian community. The fence separating the two countries was opened at several points and came to be known as "the Good Fence." The policy of the Good Fence won Israel some friends on the other side and helped expand Israel's sphere of influence, but its strategic value remained rather limited.

While extending its sphere of influence in southern Lebanon, Israel closely watched Syrian moves in the rest of the country. The Lebanese civil war became a major issue in inter-Arab politics. In October 1976 the Arab League legitimized the Syrian presence in Lebanon under the guise of the Arab Deterrent Force. Syria was mandated to restore law and order and to enforce a cease-fire in the name of the Arab League. In pursuit of this mandate Syrian forces pushed PLO units into southern Lebanon. Israel warned Damascus, via Washington, not to cross the red lines. The Syrians responded in a conciliatory manner. They explained that they were not opposed to Israel's Good Fence policy and that their own aim was to disarm the PLO rather than encourage it to act against Israel. Henry Kissinger supported the idea of Syrian deployment in southern Lebanon in order to disarm the PLO. Israel was happy to have the Lebanese government disarm the PLO and restore order in the south, but it would not trust Syria with the task. Yet, as Kissinger pointed out, only the Syrians were capable of bringing the PLO to heel and pacifying the south.[24]

The red line agreement demonstrated that despite the absence of any direct contact between them, Jerusalem and Damascus were able to conduct a strategic dialogue in a pragmatic fashion. Israel's policymakers were well pleased with the results of this agreement, but the new situation was not without its paradoxes. Yitzhak Rabin estimated that within a few months the Syrians killed more Palestinians than the guerrilla organizations had lost in all their operations against Israel and clashes with the IDF over the preceding thirty years. "Even more ironic," noted Rabin, "was the fact that because the Syrians were prevented from moving south of the 'red line,' southern Lebanon became a haven for terrorists. We had foreseen such an eventuality but preferred it to Syrian military control of the area bordering on our territory. But that did not reduce the absurdity of the new situation: PLO terrorists, Israel's sworn foes, found an asylum under an Israeli 'deterrent umbrella' intended against the Syrians."[25] This was to remain Israel's dilemma in southern Lebanon.

DEADLOCK AND DEFEAT

In the search for a settlement of the Arab-Israeli conflict, 1976 was an uneventful year. President Sadat thought that the step-by-step approach had exhausted itself with the Sinai II agreement, and he urged a continuation of the process toward a comprehensive settlement. But he was unable to bring effective international pressure to bear on Israel to move in that direction. In the United States 1976 was an election year, and, as usual, the rival candidates competed with one another in promises of support for Israel in order to win Jewish votes. Prime Minister Rabin had no desire to return to the Geneva conference, because he knew that there was no chance of a comprehensive settlement on terms acceptable to Israel. In the absence of any real pressure from America, he was able to do what he preferred—to play for time.

The only possibility Rabin did wish to explore was that of a separate agreement with Egypt. In the spring of 1976 he approached King Hassan II of Morocco to inquire whether he would be willing to act as a conduit for contacts with Egypt. The king agreed, and Rabin traveled in disguise via France to a meeting with him in Morocco. Rabin asked Hassan to tell Sadat that Israel was seriously interested in direct talks. Hassan sent General Ahmed al-Duleimi, commander of the royal guard, to Cairo to convey the message in person to Sadat. The message suggested direct talks with the ultimate aim of achieving peace, and it carried an Israeli commitment to maintain strict secrecy. Hassan also passed on his personal view that Rabin was serious and his advice that Sadat should stop depending on the Americans and deal directly with the Israelis. Sadat did not take up the offer.[26]

At the beginning of 1977 Hassan Tuhami, Egypt's vice-president, asked Chancellor Bruno Kreisky of Austria to arrange a meeting between himself and Shimon Peres. Tuhami, one of Sadat's oldest friends and closest confidants, had previously served as Egypt's ambassador to Austria. Kreisky, a socialist Jew with a deep personal commitment to resolving the Arab-Israeli dispute, sent one of his confidants to inform Rabin. "Many things in Israel's history might have turned out differently had that proposed meeting gone ahead and had Labour thus embarked on the peace process with Egypt instead of the Likud," writes Peres in his memoirs. "But apparently Prime Minister Rabin was not convinced of the seriousness of the proposal."[27] Rabin's response was that he himself was always ready to meet Sadat and if Sadat wanted to meet him, he knew his address and could approach him directly without intermediaries. Personal jealousy may have played a small part in this episode. Nevertheless, Rabin's main reason for declining the Austrian offer of mediation was that he was unable to make Sadat a far-reaching proposal, in order to tempt him to consider peace with Israel, without running the risk of losing his own parliamentary majority.

Toward the end of 1976 Rabin's hold over power was seriously shaken by a political crisis partly of his own making. The crisis eventually cost him his parliamentary majority, forced him to declare an early election, and reopened the contest between Shimon Peres and himself for the leadership of the Labor

Alignment. The National Religious Party, although in the coalition, abstained in a vote on a motion of no confidence in the government because of the desecration of the Sabbath. The motion was defeated, but Rabin went ahead and dismissed the three NRP ministers from the government. Having lost his majority in the Knesset, he tendered his own resignation. The election date was brought forward to 17 May 1977, and his became a caretaker government. Peres seized the opportunity to renew his candidacy for the leadership of the Alignment, and his bid was defeated by only a very slim majority. The Alignment's position was further undermined by a series of financial scandals. Asher Yadlin, Rabin's candidate for the post of governor of the Bank of Israel, was convicted of taking bribes and sentenced to five years in prison. Avraham Ofer, the minister of housing, was suspected of financial irregularities and committed suicide.

Deadlock on the diplomatic front did nothing to improve the Alignment's electoral prospects. Ever since the October War relations with the United States had been punctuated by crises, some of them deliberately manufactured by the government for bargaining purposes. The Israeli public gained the impression that its government was responsible for mishandling the relations with America. Many members of the public believed that Israel had relinquished significant territories, yet terror continued, peace with the Arabs was no nearer, the whole world blamed Israel, and even its friends were deserting it. All this was seen as evidence of failure on the part of their government.[28]

The feeling that America was turning away from Israel was strengthened by Jimmy Carter's victory in the presidential election. Rabin's government did not expect the new Democratic administration to take any initiatives in the Middle East during its warm-up period in office. But Carter had done his homework on the Middle East prior to his election. He was particularly influenced by a report of a study group of the Brookings Institution that argued that the time had come to move beyond interim agreements to a comprehensive settlement. Some of the authors were appointed to posts in the new administration.

By the time Rabin arrived in Washington in early March 1977, he discovered that the new president had firmly made up his mind in favor of three things: reconvening the Geneva conference; Israeli withdrawal, with only minor modifications, to the borders of 4 June 1967; and recognition of Palestinian rights. Carter was the first American president to call publicly for an almost complete

Israeli withdrawal to the pre-1967 borders. Even more worrisome from the Israeli point of view was his position on the Palestinian issue. At first he expressed support for "a homeland for the Palestinian refugees," but this was soon changed to support for "a homeland for the Palestinians." Carter was thus the first American president to champion the Palestinian right to national self-determination. Convinced that the PLO was ready for compromise, he used the terms PLO and Palestinians interchangeably. He and Rabin were therefore bound to clash not only over procedure and borders but also over the Palestinian issue. At their private meeting Carter was critical of Rabin's absolute rejection of the PLO, even if it were to recognize Israel's legitimacy. The meeting was a serious setback for Rabin's entire strategy of moving step by step toward partial agreements with the Arab states in close coordination with America.

Personal problems came on top of Rabin's political problems. An Israeli newspaper revealed that he and his wife had kept a dollar account in Washington since his days as ambassador there. This was an offense against Israeli currency regulations. The account was formally owned by Rabin's wife, Leah, but he felt responsible for it. On 7 April he announced his resignation. Three days later the Alignment's central committee unanimously elected Peres to take over from Rabin as the head of the caretaker government and as party leader in the approaching general election.

The election of 17 May 1977 resulted in the greatest upheaval in Israel's political history. It put an end to nearly three decades of Labor domination and brought to power the rightwing Likud under the leadership of Menachem Begin. Labor's decline was much more spectacular than the Likud's rise. The Likud emerged as the largest party after it increased its power from 39 to 43 members of the Knesset. The Alignment, on the other hand, went down from 51 to 32 members. The principal beneficiary of the widespread disenchantment with the Alignment was not the Likud but a new party named the Democratic Movement for Change (DMC), led by Professor Yigael Yadin, the former chief of staff and an eminent archaeologist. The DMC, which was billed as a force for "clean politics," received nearly half as many votes as the Alignment, and this translated into 15 seats. Despite this remarkable achievement, the DMC did not hold the balance of power in the new Knesset, because the Alignment's partners did not fare well either. The United Arab List connected with the Alignment lost 2 of its 3 seats, the Citizens' Rights Movement also lost 2 of its 3 seats, and the Independent Liberals lost 3 of their 4 seats. The National Religious Party increased its representation from 10 to 12 seats. This party, the real holder of the balance in the new Knesset, opted to join the Likud. A combination of the Likud, the NRP, the two smaller religious parties, and a couple of other small parties gave Begin a parliamentary majority that was substantially increased when the DMC joined the coalition. The era of Labor domination of Israeli politics was over.

Yitzhak Rabin's first term as prime minister lasted barely three years. Rabin himself regarded it as a period of personal failure. He blamed himself for not stamping his authority firmly enough on his party and his government. On the external front Rabin did not distinguish himself either. He was hesitant, unenterprizing, and excessively cautious. Instead of seizing the initiative, he waited for circumstances to change in Israel's favor. His strategy was to rebuild the iron wall of Jewish military strength to such a point that concessions could not be conceivably interpreted as a sign of weakness. Consequently, during his three years as prime minister, he did little more than play for time. The real lesson from his premiership, as from that of his two immediate predecessors, was that time was not Israel's friend unless used for active diplomacy in pursuit of peace with the Arabs. It was a lesson Rabin acted upon when he returned to power fifteen years later.

9

Peace with Egypt
1977–1981

T HE LIKUD'S VICTORY in the 1977 election was not just a ballot box revolution in Israeli politics but also a watershed in Israel's relations with the Arab world and especially in its approach to the occupied territories. The fundamental difference between the foreign policy of the Labor Alignment and that of the Likud was that the former was pragmatic whereas the latter was ideological. Labor's policy in regard to the occupied territories was governed primarily by security considerations, whereas the Likud's was governed chiefly by ideological considerations. To say this is not to suggest that Labor was indifferent to nationalist ideology or that the Likud was indifferent to security but simply to point out their different priorities.

IDEOLOGY AND FOREIGN POLICY

The Likud's ideology can be summed up in two words—Greater Israel. According to this ideology, Judea and Samaria, the biblical terms for the West Bank, were an integral part of Eretz Israel, the Land of Israel. The Likud categorically denied that Jordan had any claim to sovereignty over this area. Equally vehement was its denial that the Palestinians had a right to self-determination there. *Shlemut hamoledet*, the integrity of the homeland, was an article of faith in the Likud's political creed, as was clearly stated in the party's manifesto for the 1977 election:

The right of the Jewish people to the Land of Israel is eternal, and is an integral part of its right to security and peace. Judea and Samaria shall therefore not be relinquished to foreign rule; between the sea and the Jordan, there will be Jewish sovereignty alone.

Any plan that involves surrendering parts of Western Eretz Israel militates against our right to the Land, would inevitably lead to the establishment of a "Palestinian State," threaten the security of the civilian population, endanger the existence of the State of Israel, and defeat all prospects of peace.[1]

Ze'ev Jabotinsky, the founder of Revisionist Zionism, was the main source of ideological inspiration for the Likud leader Menachem Begin and his colleagues. As a young man in Poland, Begin had been exposed to Jabotinsky's message of national redemption, power, and grandeur. He used to refer to Jabotinsky as "our teacher, master, and father." Begin opposed partition in 1937 and again in 1947. As commander of the Irgun and as leader of the opposition after Independence, Begin remained faithful to Jabotinsky's fundamental political philosophy. The capture of the West Bank in the Six-Day War suddenly gave Jabotinsky's ideas a new lease on life. As minister in the national unity government, Begin was not against relinquishing Sinai and the Golan Heights, but he firmly opposed what he termed the repartition of the historic homeland. His resignation from the government in 1970 was over this very issue.

Begin's life was more tragic and more traumatic than that of Jabotinsky. Jabotinsky died in 1940, before the onset of the Holocaust, in which six million Jews were to perish. Begin lost his parents and brother in the Holocaust, and this searing experience haunted him for the rest of his life. As a result, he saw the world as a profoundly antisemitic, extremely hostile, and highly dangerous environment. He perceived Arab hostility as an extension of the antisemitism that had resulted in the annihilation of European Jewry. Throughout his political career Begin had demonstrated hostility toward the Arabs. The experience of the Holocaust intensified his mistrust of all non-Jews, including the Arabs. It seemed to prove that the Gentiles were out to destroy the Jewish people and that only Jewish military power could protect the Jews against this danger. It strengthened his activist instincts and deepened his commitment to the goal of Jewish control over Jewish destiny. Begin described his generation as the generation of the Holocaust and the redemption. For him and his colleagues in "the fighting family," the lines of cause and effect between the Holocaust and the tenets of Israeli foreign policy were clearer, stronger, and more direct than for any other political group in Israel.[2]

On the link between Jabotinsky's thinking and the foreign policy of the new prime minister, we have the testimony of Eliahu Ben Elissar, the director general of the prime minister's office: "The deterrent power, or in Jabotinsky's language 'the iron wall,' was intended to convince the Arabs that they would not be able to get rid of the sovereign Jewish presence in the Land of Israel, even if they could not bring themselves to recognize the justice of the Jewish people's claim to its homeland." Begin believed that the IDF's primary function was not to go to war but to deter the Arabs from going to war. He derived satisfaction from the thought that the very composition of his government might deter the Arabs from attacking Israel, if they had any such thoughts. "The Arabs would not go to war against us," he told his aides, "when in the government sit military leaders like Moshe Dayan, Ezer Weizman, and Ariel Sharon."[3] Dayan was the foreign minister, Weizman the defense minister, and Sharon the agriculture minister. The Democratic Movement for Change joined the government four months after it was formed. Among its leaders were two former generals, Yigael Yadin and Meir Amit. This confirmed Begin's belief in the power of his government to deter an Arab attack on Israel.

The most important decision Begin made in forming his first government was to offer the Foreign Ministry to Moshe Dayan. Dayan accepted the offer on condition that Israeli sovereignty would not be extended to the territories that had been captured in the Six-Day War so long as peace negotiations with the Arabs were taking place. One of Begin's reasons for offering Dayan this key post was to stress the continuity in Israel's foreign policy. Begin was well aware that outside Israel he was widely perceived as an extremist, a fanatic, and a warmonger. He knew of the widespread fears that his rise to power would cause tension between Israel and its neighbors. To allay these fears, he tried to give the impression of being reasonable and responsible.

On 20 June, Begin presented his government to the Knesset and won a vote of confidence by a majority of 63 to 53. The basic guidelines of the government's foreign policy emphasized that "the Jewish people have an unchallengeable, eternal, historic right to the Land of Israel, the inheritance of their forefathers" and pledged to build rural and urban settlements on this land. The guidelines then stated that the government would actively strive to achieve peace in the region and that all of Israel's neighbors would be invited to engage in peace negotiations without any preconditions. The government also announced its readiness to participate in the Geneva conference on the basis of UN Resolutions 242 and 338. Most significantly, the guidelines promised not to extend Israeli law to the West Bank while negotiations were under way for peace treaties between Israel and its neighbors. Having asserted his government's ideological commitment to the whole Land of Israel, Begin thus made it clear that there was no immediate plan to annex the West Bank or the Gaza Strip. Israel's neighbors were not reassured by these statements. Jordan's leaders were in fact panic-stricken at this point. They feared that the new government would not only annex the West Bank but carry out a large-scale expulsion of Palestinians from the West Bank to the East Bank.

SADAT'S JOURNEY TO JERUSALEM

Very soon after his election Begin sent signals to Washington about his peaceful intentions. The signals from the opposite direction, conveyed from the White House by Jewish American leaders, were that the Carter administration could not accept the ideological claims of the Likud and that if the new government was serious about realizing them, there would be nothing but problems in the relations between Washington and Jerusalem.[4] President Carter was committed to Israeli withdrawal on all fronts to the 1967 lines with only minor modifications. He regarded the Jewish settlements in the occupied territories as illegal and as an obstacle to peace. Unlike his predecessors in the White House, Carter also saw the Palestinian problem as the heart of the Middle Eastern conflict, and he was the first American president to support a Palestinian homeland. Thus, from the beginning, Begin and Carter were on a collision course. The Israeli prime minister was unwilling to accept the principle of withdrawal from the West Bank under any circumstances and was committed to the building of more Jewish settlements there. But even though he felt he could not make any concessions to Carter's point of view on the Palestinian question, Begin was prepared to reconsider Israeli policy toward Egypt and Syria.[5]

Carter took the initiative by inviting Begin to a meeting in

Washington on 19 July. His aim was to bring Israel and the Arabs to Geneva as soon as possible in order to reach a peace agreement. Begin went to the meeting armed with a detailed plan that Moshe Dayan had helped him formulate and that the cabinet had approved. The first part of the paper stated that Israel would be prepared to take part in a conference in Geneva in accordance with Security Council Resolutions 242 and 338. The participants were to be Israel, Egypt, Syria, and Jordan, and they were not to present preconditions of any kind. After the inaugural session three separate mixed committees would be established: an Egypt-Israel, a Syria-Israel, and a Jordan-Israel committee. These committees would negotiate and finalize the peace treaties between Israel and its neighbors.

This part of the paper, on the procedure for convening the Geneva conference, was presented by Begin at the morning meeting with Carter and his aides. A second part of the paper dealt with the substantive question of borders and the West Bank. Begin did not refer to this part in the morning session. He read it to Carter at their first private talk, held after the state dinner. It consisted of three articles. The first stated that in view of the large area separating Israel and Egypt, Israel was prepared, within the framework of a peace treaty, "to make a significant withdrawal of her forces in Sinai." The second, on the Israel-Syria border, said that Israel would remain on the Golan Heights but that, again within the framework of a peace treaty, "we shall be prepared to withdraw our forces from their present lines and redeploy them along a line to be established as the permanent boundary." The third article, on the West Bank, said that "Israel will not transfer Judea, Samaria and the Gaza District to any foreign sovereign authority." Two reasons were given for this position: "the historic right of our nation to this land" and "the needs of our national security, which demand a capability to defend our State and the lives of our citizens."

Following the meeting, the Americans presented a paper for setting in motion the wheels of Arab-Israeli peace negotiations. It contained five principles they hoped would be acceptable to both parties. Israel had no objection to the first three: that the purpose of the negotiations of the Geneva conference was to reach peace agreements, that the basis for the conference was Resolutions 242 and 338, and that the aim of 242 was not just an end to belligerency but the establishment of completely normal relations. Israel, however, was not prepared to accept the last two principles,

one of which called for Israeli withdrawal from all fronts and the
other for self-determination for the Palestinians in their future status.[6]

While the Americans continued to work for the convening of
the Geneva conference, Begin and Dayan began to explore the
prospect of a bilateral agreement between Israel and Egypt. With
the Likud in power, the Jordanian orientation in Israel's foreign
policy was replaced by an Egyptian orientation. But before issuing
any peace feelers to Egypt, Dayan arranged a secret meeting with
King Hussein in London on 22 July. Dayan asked Hussein about
his intentions regarding the Palestinians of the West Bank. Hussein
was still bitter about the decision of the Rabat summit to recognize the PLO as the sole authorized representative of the
Palestinians and to withdraw that role from him. He explained
that he was now concentrating on administering his own kingdom and that he had no intention of taking any initiative in matters relating to the Palestinians. He felt a deep obligation to help
them but was no longer their representative and would not try to
force himself upon them. Dayan then asked the king whether he
would agree to a peace treaty with Israel based on the division of
the West Bank between Jordan and Israel. By his own account,
Dayan received not only an unequivocal answer but an instructive
lesson. The king rejected the idea out of hand, saying that he, as
an Arab monarch, could not propose to the people of even a single village that they cut themselves off from their brother Arabs
and become Israelis. Agreement to such a plan would be regarded
as treachery. He would be charged with "selling" Arab land to the
Jews so that he could enlarge his own kingdom. The meeting contained no surprises. Dayan received the answers he expected, and
he reported them to Begin. The answers simply confirmed Begin's
view that the king would not agree to the division of the land. On
many subsequent occasions Begin would quote the king's own
words that such a division was "totally unacceptable."[7] Territorial
compromise between Israel and Jordan was now ruled out by both
sides. Begin and Dayan felt free to explore the Egyptian option.
They stepped up their diplomatic efforts to persuade President
Sadat that Israel wanted to begin negotiations.[8]

On 25 August, Begin visited Anwar Sadat's good friend
President Nicolae Ceausescu of Romania. Begin impressed on his
host that he was serious about peace and that his first goal was
peace with Egypt. Ceausescu conveyed the message to Sadat. A
more important channel for contacts with Egypt was King Hassan

II of Morocco. On 4 September, Dayan embarked on the first of three secret visits to Morocco. His principal purpose was to try to secure Hassan's help in arranging a meeting between Israeli and Egyptian representatives. Dayan explained to the king that there seemed to be two contradictory problems. On the one hand, no Arab country was willing to make a separate peace with Israel. On the other, it was impossible to achieve a simultaneous peace arrangement with all the Arab states. They were thus caught in a vicious circle, and Dayan proposed to break out of it by a high-level meeting between Israel and Egypt.

King Hassan moved with remarkable speed to arrange a meeting between Dayan and Dr. Hassan Tuhami, the Egyptian vice-president, who had asked President Ceausescu earlier in the year to arrange a meeting for him with Shimon Peres. On 16 September, Dayan made a second secret trip to Morocco, this time to meet Tuhami. Tuhami was guided by one overriding principle: peace in return for complete Israeli withdrawal from all the territories it had occupied since the Six-Day War. He said that Sadat was prepared to open a dialogue with Israel but that only after Begin agreed to the principle of total withdrawal would Sadat meet Begin and shake his hand. Dayan made no commitments. Hinting that complete withdrawal from Sinai might be possible, he gained the impression that this might open the path to a separate arrangement between Egypt and Israel. The meeting ended with an understanding that both parties would report immediately to their heads of government and receive their agreement to a further meeting in two weeks' time for which peace documents would be prepared. Begin agreed to a further meeting and to the drawing up of proposals for a peace treaty for mutual study. But he was not prepared to make a commitment to complete withdrawal from Sinai in advance of a meeting with Sadat.[9]

Having reported to Begin, Dayan proceeded to the United States to talks with President Carter and his secretary of state, Cyrus Vance, on the Geneva conference. He made no mention of his meeting with Tuhami. The Geneva conference was of no real interest to either Begin or Sadat. Begin wanted bilateral negotiations with Egypt, Syria, and Jordan, in that order. He was prepared to discuss the Geneva conference because the Americans saw it as the only way forward. Sadat thought that the Geneva conference was essentially about procedure rather than substance, and he was also concerned about the Soviet role as co-convenor. On 1 October the United States and the USSR surprised the world by issuing a joint statement on the reconvening of the Geneva conference. Sadat was angry. "We kicked the Russians out of the door and now Mr Carter is bringing them back through the window," he thundered.[10] Begin was furious because the statement contained a reference to "the legitimate rights of the Palestinian people."

Dayan held further talks with Carter and Vance in an effort to limit the damage. The result was a joint American-Israeli working paper headed "Suggestions for the Resumption of the Geneva Peace Conference." Begin approved the working paper in a telephone conversation with Dayan, but three of his close aides were critical of it. Article 1 said, "The Arab parties will be represented by a unified Arab delegation, which will include Palestinian Arabs." Article 3 was the most controversial, stating, "The West Bank and Gaza issues will be discussed in a working group to consist of Israel, Jordan, Egypt and the Palestinian Arabs." This was the first time that Israel agreed to the representation of Palestinian Arabs in official negotiations. The critics objected even more strongly to this than to the idea of a unified Arab delegation. The full weight of Begin's authority was required to secure cabinet approval of the working paper. In the Knesset debate Labor opposition spokesmen took the view that Israel should hold talks only with Jordan and that the representatives of the West Bank and Gaza Arabs should be merged with the Jordanian delegation. Labor's resolution was defeated by 41 votes to 28, and the controversial working paper received parliamentary approval.[11] Syria and the PLO rejected the working paper; Egypt was prepared to accept it, but only on condition that the PLO be explicitly mentioned; King Hussein was prepared to include West Bankers in his delegation and saw no need for PLO representation.

For Sadat the Syrian reaction was the last straw. If the Geneva conference had to take place, he wanted the Arabs to appear in separate delegations. President Assad of Syria insisted that the Arabs be represented by a single unified delegation. President Carter pressed Sadat hard to accept Assad's proposal, and Sadat reluctantly agreed, after which Syria announced its out-and-out opposition to the Geneva conference. Sadat felt he had to act alone. He decided to sit face-to-face with Israel and did not inform either the Americans or the Israelis of the dramatic political initiative on which he had set his mind. On 9 November, in an address to the Egyptian parliament, he dropped his bombshell. "I am prepared to go to the ends of the earth for peace, even to the Knesset itself," he announced.

The ball was now firmly in Israel's court. Four days later Begin extended a verbal invitation to President Sadat, on behalf of the Israeli government, to come to Jerusalem to conduct talks for a permanent peace between Israel and Egypt. An official invitation was sent to Sadat through the American embassy in Tel Aviv, and it was promptly accepted. In the Israeli press unnamed military experts were quoted as saying that Sadat was talking about peace but preparing for war. Chief of Staff Mordechai Gur said in a newspaper interview that there were signs that Sadat's peace initiative might be a cover for military action by Egypt. Deputy Prime Minister Yigael Yadin suggested a partial mobilization of the reserves to avoid a repeat of the October 1973 surprise. Ezer Weizman, the minister of defense, publicly reprimanded Gur and rejected Yadin's suggestion. Although Weizman had been a leading hawk in the IDF, he was convinced that Sadat's intentions were honorable, and he became one of the strongest supporters of peace with Egypt.

Sadat arrived at Ben-Gurion Airport in the evening of Saturday, 19 November, shortly after the end of the Jewish Sabbath. He was received with a red carpet, national flags flying, national anthems played by a military band, an honor guard, and a long line of prominent public figures who came to welcome him. It was a moment of high drama for the invited guests and for the millions of Israelis and others around the world who watched the ceremony on their television screens. Anwar Sadat, the man responsible for the October War, arrived in an Egyptian civilian aircraft and landed at Israel's international airport as the guest of the Israeli government. Sadat coined the slogan "No more war," and this simple message had a powerful emotional impact on the Israeli public. One of Sadat's aims in embarking on his dramatic trip to Jerusalem was to break down the psychological barrier that in his view made up a large part of the Arab-Israeli conflict, and in this respect he was brilliantly successful.

On Sunday afternoon, 20 November, Sadat arrived in the Knesset. He was received with prolonged applause. The speaker of the Knesset welcomed him and invited him to deliver his address. Sadat's speech was crafted to justify his decision to visit Jerusalem, a decision that had infuriated the Arab world. To counter the impression that he was interested only in recovering Egypt's land and that he was prepared to make a separate peace with Israel, he reiterated the standard Arab positions. He called for "an overall peace" based on justice and said that this would involve full Israeli withdrawal to the 1967 borders and recognition of the right of the Palestinians to their own state and their own entity. But he also ac-

knowledged Israel's right to exist as a sovereign state in the Middle
East, to be officially recognized by its Arab neighbors, and to have
guarantees of its security.

Begin spoke after Sadat. It was clear that he was unable to rise
to the historic occasion. His tone was hectoring and his reply notable for its harshness and lack of generosity. He delved into the
past, ancient and recent, and compiled a long list of Israeli grievances against the Arabs. He did not move beyond Israel's well-
established positions and made no promises. The president of
Egypt, he said, knew before coming to Jerusalem that Israel's views
on permanent boundaries differed from those of Egypt. What he
proposed to Sadat was negotiations without any preconditions.
Begin ignored the Palestinian issue completely and implied that
Israel had no intention of giving up control over the whole of
Jerusalem. His speech contained nothing to encourage optimism.

The real breakthrough was achieved at a meeting between
Begin and Sadat at midnight that day, after the state banquet. No
officials were present at this meeting and no minutes taken of the
conversation. But according to Dayan's account the two leaders
agreed to three principles: no more war between the two countries;
the formal restoration of sovereignty over the Sinai peninsula to
Egypt; and the demilitarization of most of Sinai, with limited
Egyptian forces to be stationed only in the area adjoining the Suez
Canal, including the Mitla and Gidi Passes.[12] A joint statement
was issued at the end of the visit. It made no mention of the agreement in principle on Sinai or of the unresolved differences on
Sadat's demands for total withdrawal and for a Palestinian state. At
the press conference the two leaders reiterated time and again the
slogan that Sadat had made popular: "No more war."

Shortly after Sadat's return from his visit to Jerusalem, he decided to convene a "peace conference" in Cairo and invited representatives of the Arab states, the PLO, the United States, the
United Nations, and Israel. Sadat gave no details about the agenda
or level of the participants, but his intention was clear: to signal to
the Arab world that he was not moving toward a separate agreement with Israel. A separate peace agreement was precisely what
Begin and Dayan were hoping for, so they were taken aback by
Sadat's proposal. A few days later, however, came Sadat's reassuring request that Dayan meet Tuhami once again in Morocco. So
on 2 December Dayan left for his second meeting with Tuhami.
This time he flew directly to Marrakesh in an IAF plane, but, at
Sadat's request, this meeting too was kept secret.

For the second meeting Dayan set down on paper Israel's ideas for an agreement with Egypt. The paper assumed that there would be a full peace treaty between the two countries and that this would involve complete normalization of the relations between them. A second assumption was that the peace treaty would be concluded quickly and not be conditional upon the conclusion of peace treaties between the other Arab states and Israel. Dayan stressed that the ideas he was presenting had not been brought before the cabinet for approval and that the object of the meeting was to discover Egypt's response to them. King Hassan, who hosted the meeting, and Tuhami read and reread the paper. Their main worry was Arab suspicion that Egypt was preparing to make a separate deal with Israel. After the discussion of the Israeli paper, Tuhami read from a handwritten document in Arabic setting out a four-point message from Sadat. The first and most important point was that the agreement they reached would need to include a resolution of the conflict with all the other Arab states and should therefore not be presented as an exclusively bilateral agreement. The other three points dealt with Egyptian-Israeli issues. Reflecting on the day's talks, Dayan was unhappy about the lack of clarity on Egypt's position. He did not think that Sadat would retreat from the course on which he had embarked, but he suspected that he was not quite sure how to advance: Sadat knew what he wanted but not how to achieve it.[13]

One question to which the participants gave different answers concerned the timing of the commitment given to Sadat that Israeli would withdraw completely from Sinai: before his visit to Jerusalem, during his visit, or after his visit. Tuhami claimed that the promise was made by Dayan to him at their first meeting in Morocco. Dayan claimed that the promise, in principle, was made by Begin to Sadat at the end of the latter's visit to Jerusalem. Eliahu Ben Elissar, the director general of the prime minister's office, suggests that the promise was made by Dayan at his second meeting with Tuhami. According to Ben Elissar's account, Dayan proposed that the parts of Sinai east of the Mitla and Gidi Passes be demilitarized and that joint patrols operate in them until the year 2000, when the situation would be reviewed. Dayan indicated that he was in favor of the former Egyptian territories all the way to Ras Muhammad having 100 percent Egyptian sovereignty, under UN supervision, but stressed that if quoted, he would deny any such statement. This, says Ben Elissar, was the first time that an authorized Israeli representative spoke in front of an Egyptian representative of his willingness to see the entire Sinai peninsula under Egyptian sovereignty.

Tuhami is said to have replied that the Egyptians had no interest in a separate agreement and that the solution to the Palestinian problem would have to be in line with the aspirations of the Arab world. The Israeli settlements in Sinai would have to be removed not immediately but in accordance with a plan and a timetable; otherwise it would be partition, not peace. Demilitarization was acceptable to Tuhami, but joint patrols were not. Dayan confessed that he did not believe that King Hussein would join the process. "Hussein is a coward, and he is not prepared to wet his fingers. He would not move without Assad," said Dayan to Tuhami and King Hassan. The Moroccan king volunteered his own assessment of the PLO. "The PLO is the cancer in our midst," he said. "Their fate does not concern me at all."[14]

Sadat's preparatory conference, which opened in Cairo on 14 December, turned out to be an unmitigated failure. Not a single Arab state accepted his invitation. The plan went ahead with only four delegations, those from Egypt, Israel, the United States, and the United Nations. The dialogue between the Egyptian and Israeli delegations was unproductive. The Egyptians presented a list of principles as the basis for peace, but the Israelis rejected them out of hand. Agreement was not reached on a single issue, not even on procedural matters. "Both sides," observed Dayan, "knew they were only going through the motions of conferring, and the game they were playing was like a dialogue between two deaf people who could not yet lip-read."[15] Two other events coincided with the Cairo conference. One was the conference of the rejectionist Arab states in Tripoli, the capital of Libya. These states were opposed to any recognition of or negotiation or compromise with Israel. The presidents of Syria, Algeria, South Yemen, and Libya issued a statement denouncing Sadat for "grand treason" and announcing their intention to form a "steadfastness and confrontation front." Their states were joined by the PLO in declaring an economic and diplomatic boycott on Egypt because of its negotiations with Israel. The other event was Begin's visit to Washington.

PLANS FOR PALESTINIAN AUTONOMY

Begin's purpose in the trip to Washington was to balance the tremendous impression made by Sadat's visit to Jerusalem. He sought a meeting with Carter in order to present Israel's plans for a peace with Egypt and for autonomy for the Palestinian Arabs.

Sadat asserted not only an Egyptian claim to the whole of Sinai but also a Palestinian claim to national self-determination. This second demand posed a truly acute dilemma for Begin. It forced him to choose between his lifelong ideological commitment to the integrity of the homeland and his desire for peace. Begin grappled with this dilemma and, with the help of Moshe Dayan, came up with a solution in the form of a plan for Palestinian autonomy on the West Bank and Gaza. The essence of the plan was that it was nonterritorial. In other words, autonomy was to apply not to the land but only to the people who lived on it. The inspiration for this plan came from Ze'ev Jabotinsky, who had recognized the need to concede certain rights to the Palestinian Arabs after the erection of the iron wall. For Begin the autonomy plan had two principal attractions. First, it enabled him to remain true to his principle of not allowing foreign sovereignty west of the river Jordan. Second, it did not compel either of the contending parties to renounce their claims and aspirations regarding this area. Decision on sovereignty was postponed for a later date. By leaving the question of sovereignty open, Begin hoped to achieve the two aims he had set himself and his government: preservation of the integrity of the homeland and the attainment of peace.[16]

Begin drafted his own autonomy plan after extensive consultations with his foreign minister, the attorney general, Aharon Barak, and the IDF General Staff. A special think tank was set up in the Ministry of Defense under the chairmanship of Major General Avraham Tamir, the head of the General Staff Planning Branch. Tamir's team independently reached the same conclusion as the prime minister: the only practical solution that all sides could live with was the abolition of Israeli military government on the West Bank and Gaza and its replacement by Palestinian autonomy. Before leaving for Washington, Begin convened a special meeting of the ministerial security committee to discuss the plans he was going to present to Carter. Some ministers, including Ariel Sharon, expressed the fear that autonomy would evolve in the direction of a Palestinian state. But the committee approved the plan with certain amendments.

Begin's autonomy plan consisted of twenty-six articles. It envisaged the abolition of Israeli military government and its replacement by administrative autonomy of the residents of the West Bank and Gaza for an initial period of five years. The Arab residents would elect an eleven-member administrative council with offices in Bethlehem. This council would have competence in all administrative affairs relating to the residents. It would have eleven departments dealing with education; religious affairs; finance; transportation; construction and housing; industry and commerce; agriculture; health; labor and social welfare; refugee rehabilitation; and the administration of justice and supervision of local police forces. Security and public order were to be Israel's responsibility. The Arab residents would be allowed a free choice between Israeli and Jordanian citizenship, and this choice was to determine where they would have to vote. A joint committee of Israel, Jordan, and the administrative council would review and amend existing legislation. Another committee would determine norms of immigration, including immigration by refugees. Israeli citizens were to be permitted to purchase land and to settle in Judea and Samaria and in Gaza. Residents of these territories who opted for Israeli citizenship would be permitted to purchase land and settle in Israel. These principles would be subject to review after a five-year period. Article 24 stated Israel's position on the vital question of sovereignty: "Israel stands by its right and its claim of sovereignty to Judea, Samaria and the Gaza District. In the knowledge that other claims exist, it proposes, for the sake of the agreement and the peace, that the question of sovereignty in these areas be left open."[17]

Begin presented his proposals for Palestinian autonomy to President Carter and his aides on 16 December. The Americans were already familiar with the broad outlines of Israel's proposals for peace with Egypt, but the autonomy plan was new to them. Begin stressed the risks involved in withdrawal from Sinai and in granting autonomy to the Palestinians. Carter welcomed Begin's proposals for peace with Egypt but had serious reservations about his plan for Palestinian autonomy. Despite these reservations, Begin pleaded with Carter to convey to Sadat his interest in a face-to-face meeting to discuss the Israeli proposals. Begin's aim in visiting Washington, and then London, was to gain international legitimacy for his approach. He thought that if Carter accepted the proposals, it would be more difficult for Sadat to turn them down. In his statement to the press, Begin came close to saying that President Carter had endorsed his plan. Official spokesmen in Washington reacted by saying that this plan was an Israeli proposal, and it was for Israel and the Arabs to deliberate and decide on it.

On 25 December, Begin, Dayan, Weizman, and their advisers flew to a meeting with the Egyptian president in Ismailia. Begin regarded this as a historic occasion, comparable to Sadat's visit to Jerusalem. But there were serious differences between Weizman and the other ministers, especially Dayan, on the extent to which Sadat considered himself bound to a solution of the Palestinian problem. Weizman argued that the faster they understood Sadat's problems and responded to his demands, the less would be required to satisfy him. In the deliberations that preceded the trip to Ismailia, Weizman took the view that all Sadat wanted on the Palestinian issue was a general declaration of principles, which would scarcely be binding on anyone. "He wants a fig leaf," Weizman repeated over and over again. "If we don't give it to him now, the Palestinian problem will become a branch, and then it will grow into a tree." The other ministers may have enjoyed Weizman's botanical imagery, but they did not heed his advice. Dayan contended that Sadat would want something far more concrete. Weizman thought that Sadat would be satisfied with an autonomy scheme, provided it was proper autonomy. But Weizman did not regard the scheme they were proposing as proper autonomy: "By the restrictions and qualifications they had imposed, Begin and the others had reduced the autonomy plan to a caricature of genuine self-rule."[18]

The Ismailia summit attracted much attention from the international media, including one hundred reporters from Israel alone. But the atmosphere at the summit was far from congenial. The face-to-face encounter between the high-level delegations was accompanied by endless misunderstandings and even the trading of insults. The Egyptians were incensed by the new settlements that the Israelis busily started constructing in the Rafah salient. The fate of the existing Israeli settlements in Sinai had not been determined yet, and to the Egyptians this looked like a very crude attempt to present them with faits accomplis. To the Israelis it appeared that Sadat's subordinates did not share his commitment to peace and that they were deliberately placing obstacles in his path. The Egyptians saw Begin himself as the main obstacle to progress. Boutros Boutros-Ghali, the minister of state for foreign affairs, included the following snapshot of the Israeli team at Ismailia in his *Egypt's Road to Jerusalem:*

> Begin's stony personality was apparent in every word he uttered and every movement he made. This man, who was a statesman and a diplomat, was bellicose and struck me as a danger to peace and the peace process. On the other hand,

Weizman, who was a great military man, charmed us with his lighthearted style, and his presence eased the atmosphere. Dayan was unpredictable. One moment he would be arrogant and bitter; the next he would propose creative solutions and move the process forward.[19]

Begin set forth his peace proposals, and Sadat said that they were not acceptable and that Egypt would present counterproposals. He insisted on total Israeli withdrawal, the right of self-determination for the Palestinians, and no separate peace. Begin and Sadat were poles apart, and the tension between them steadily increased. Their aides could not draft an agreed communiqué, so two separate statements were given at the press conference. One read, "The position of Egypt is that a Palestinian State should be established in the West Bank and Gaza Strip." The other, "The Israeli position is that the Palestinian Arabs residing in Judea, Samaria and the Gaza District should enjoy self-rule."[20]

The only achievement of the Ismailia summit was Sadat's agreement to Begin's proposal to set up two working parties—one for political and civil affairs, the other for military affairs. The political committee was to convene in Jerusalem, with the Egyptian and Israeli foreign ministers alternating as chairmen, while the military committee was to meet in Cairo, with the defense ministers alternating as chairmen.

On 28 December the Knesset held a political debate. Begin reported on his talks in Washington and London and on the summit meeting in Ismailia. He read out the full text of his autonomy plan for the Palestinian Arabs and outlined his proposals for peace with Egypt. At the end of the debate on the prime minister's statement, the government's autonomy plan and guiding principles for peace between Egypt and Israel was approved by a majority of 64 to 8, with 40 abstentions. The most vociferous opposition to the government motion came not from the Labor benches but from the members of the ruling party. Nevertheless, Begin now had parliamentary as well as cabinet endorsement for his peace plan. He could have followed Charles de Gaulle's example by turning his back on his party and proceeding according to his own convictions. Begin, however, lacked the courage of his peaceful convictions. Faced with an open revolt inside his party and a determined challenge by Gush Emunim to build more settlements in Sinai, he took refuge in nationalistic rhetoric of which he was a past master, and he began to change his own peace plan in a way that was bound to reduce further what little credibility he enjoyed in Arab eyes. He said he had never intended to allow the Sinai settlements to come under Egyptian control. He also denied any intention of giving away the Israeli airfields in Sinai. Then, out of the blue, he came up with the statement that Resolution 242 did not apply to the West Bank and Gaza. Thus, he practically preempted any conclusion that the two committees set up in Ismailia might reach through negotiations.

The political committee opened its proceedings in Jerusalem on 17 January 1978, and these resulted in another setback. Egypt's delegation was headed by Muhammad Ibrahim Kamel, the newly appointed foreign minister. His predecessor, Ismail Fahmy, had resigned in protest against Sadat's peace initiative. Some progress was made on the first day, but a speech Begin made at a dinner in Kamel's honor wrecked the atmosphere. Begin began by saying, "The foreign minister of Egypt was still very young when the Holocaust was inflicted on the Jews by the Nazis, so he does not realize how badly they needed the return to the safety of their historical home." His tone then became more truculent: "The Arabs have enjoyed self-determination in twenty-one Arab countries for a very long time. Is it too much for Israel to have one country among twenty-one? NO, I declare in my loudest voice, NO to withdrawal to the 1967 lines, NO to self-determination for the terrorists."[21] Later that night Kamel called Sadat and reported that Begin had foreclosed meaningful negotiations. Sadat ordered Kamel and his men to pack their bags and return home. The military committee continued its discussions in Cairo under the leadership of Ezer Weizman and his opposite number, General Abdel Ghani Gamassi. The atmosphere in Cairo was much more calm and cordial than that in Jerusalem. Weizman established warm personal relations with the Egyptian leaders, especially with Sadat. But no real progress could be made after the political negotiations had been suspended. The committees represented the last serious attempt at bilateral negotiations between Egypt and Israel. The Americans subsequently had to step in to prevent the collapse of Sadat's peace initiative.

Sadat gave an interview to the Egyptian weekly *October*, in which he bitterly attacked Israel and said he had lost hope that he would be able to reach agreement with it on the foundations of peace. Israel was no less a rejectionist state than Syria. Israel had sown the wind and would therefore reap the whirlwind. He, by his visit to Jerusalem, had given Israel the prospect of peace, security, and legitimacy, but he had received nothing in return. He had risked not only his political future but also his life, yet he had believed that by doing so he had put an end to the Arab-Israeli conflict. Israel, however, was refusing to agree to the peace principles he had proposed, which called for Israel's return of Sinai, the West Bank, and the Golan Heights and endorsed the Palestinian's right to statehood. By agreeing to this, Israel would get Arab recognition as well as normal relations with its neighbors. Put simply, he added, Israel had to choose between territories and peace. There was no middle road.[22]

Sadat failed to grasp Begin's real aims and aspirations. As Eliahu Ben Elissar observed, Begin had also set himself an ambitious goal but in the opposite direction. He wanted to remove Egypt from the circle of war and was prepared to pay a high price for this. But he had no intention of including in the price any territory outside the Sinai peninsula. While Sadat regarded his trip to Jerusalem as earth-shattering, Begin viewed it from a more practical perspective. Sadat's often repeated statement that the psychological barrier made up 70 percent of the Arab-Israeli conflict implied that only 30 percent remained for negotiation after his visit. Begin was a tough politician and as such was not willing to pay with material assets for an initiative, however brilliant, that aimed to break psychological barriers. Ben Elissar's assessment was that Sadat had failed to fathom in Israelis the depth of their fear of what they regarded as an Arab determination not to permit Jewish independence in the Middle East: "Sadat did not understand the extent of the reluctance of the overwhelming majority of Israelis to part with 'the iron wall,' whether they were familiar with this article by Jabotinsky or not. Territory was also part of 'the iron wall.' "[23]

Sadat was in despair. On 3 February he flew off to the United States and appealed directly for Carter's support. Carter, who shared Sadat's exasperation with Begin's hard line on Sinai and the West Bank, could not have been more sympathetic. Sadat's visit was also a media triumph. He aroused the sympathy of the American public and even managed to convince some Jewish leaders that Begin was being unreasonable. Begin went to Washington on 21 March to try to balance the effect of Sadat's visit. His visit was delayed because on 11 March a group of Palestinian terrorists attacked a bus on the Haifa–Tel Aviv coastal road, killing thirty-five passengers and wounding seventy-one others. Three days later Israel retaliated by launching Operation Litani. A large IDF force combed the whole of southern Lebanon up to the Litani River to wipe out PLO bases. This was not one of the IDF's more effective military engagements. Most of the PLO fighters fled to the north, and the civilian population bore the brunt of the Israeli invasion. Villages were destroyed, some war crimes were committed, and thousands of peaceful citizens fled in panic from their homes.

By the time Begin's team arrived in Washington, many questions were being asked about the scope, purpose, and methods of the Israeli operation in southern Lebanon. The Americans regarded the operation as an overreaction to the massacre on the coastal road, with implications for the quest of peace. The peace quest was the main item on the agenda for the Carter-Begin meeting. Carter recalled that this was Begin's third visit to Washington. Previously he had been full of hope, but now he berated Begin for refusing to give up the settlements in Sinai, for refusing to yield political control over the West Bank, and for refusing to give the Palestinians the right to choose, after a five-year period, between joining Jordan, joining Israel, or continuing the status quo. "Though Carter spoke in a dull monotone, there was fury in his cold blue eyes, and his glance was dagger-sharp," recalled Dayan. "His portrayal of our position was basically correct, but it could not have been expressed in a more hostile form."[24] Begin later admitted to his aides that this was one of the most difficult moments of his life. He returned home in a state of shock, with American accusations ringing in his ears.

American pressure on Begin was unrelenting. Shortly after his return home, the Americans sent an official document containing a list of questions about the future of the West Bank and Gaza at the end of the five-year transition period. Begin, whose political problems were compounded by ill health, was unable to formulate his reply to these questions until the second half of June. His reply, in essence, was that after the five years Israel would not be prepared to discuss the future of the territories or the question of sovereignty over them but only "the character of future relations" between itself and their residents. Even this evasive formula was approved by the cabinet only after an acrimonious argument.

Armed with this decision, Moshe Dayan proceeded on 17 July to a meeting at Leeds Castle in England with Muhammad Ibrahim Kamel and Cyrus Vance, the American secretary of state. Kamel and Dayan presented position papers, but the attempt to bridge the gulf between them ended in failure. Without being authorized by the cabinet, Dayan gave his personal view that if Israel's proposal for Palestinian autonomy was accepted, Israel would be prepared at the end of five years to discuss the question of sovereignty over the West Bank and Gaza. Begin was displeased with Dayan for exceeding his authority, but he nevertheless went to some trouble to secure cabinet approval for the new formula. The new formula was nothing but a fig leaf, however, and as such was turned down by Sadat. On 27 July, Sadat ordered Israeli participants in the military committee to leave Cairo. His only remaining hope for saving his peace initiative was American pressure on Israel.

In early August, Cyrus Vance visited Israel and Egypt in order to settle the crisis. He brought with him an invitation to a summit meeting in the United States at the level of heads of government—Carter, Sadat, Begin. Sadat accepted Carter's invitation to the presidential retreat at Camp David, in Maryland, with alacrity and without any preconditions. There was no demand for a prior Israeli commitment to total withdrawal or to Palestinian self-determination, but he expected Carter to back him on those demands at Camp David. Sadat urged that Begin and he be empowered not only to discuss but also to take on-the-spot decisions in the name of their governments and that each bring with him his trusted advisers.

Begin, too, accepted the invitation without setting any preconditions. Although he was still under strong attack from the hard-liners in his party for making too many concessions, the mood in the country had shifted in the opposite direction as a result of Sadat's success in breaking down the famous psychological barrier. In early March a group of some 350 reserve officers signed an open letter urging the prime minister to change his priorities and to accept an exchange of territories for peace. In the wake of this letter a new movement emerged that called itself Peace Now. It organized mass demonstrations and rallies to entreat the government not to miss the chance for peace, and it won the endorsement of thirty Knesset members from six parties. The Camp David summit opened on 5 September. On the eve of the departure of the Israeli delegation, Peace Now organized a demonstration in the central square in Tel Aviv with about 100,000 participants. It was the largest political demonstration in Israel's history and a remarkable display of popular yearning for peace.

THE CAMP DAVID ACCORDS

Menachem Begin went well prepared to the summit meeting at Camp David. He took with him a large group of aides and advisers, including his foreign and defense ministers. All his advisers held more pragmatic and more flexible views than he did. The composition of the delegation and the large number of experts indicated that he wanted the conference to succeed. So did the fact that he got the cabinet to empower the ministerial team to make decisions on the spot without reference back. He knew that tough decisions would have to be made, and had he wanted to avoid them, he would not have asked the cabinet to delegate its authority. At the same time, though, Begin had his own red lines. On the status of Jerusalem he was not prepared to compromise in any way. A second red line was his claim of sovereignty over the West Bank: there was to be no compromise over this claim. A third red line was the quality of peace: there was to be no full withdrawal from Sinai without full peace with Egypt.[25] In short, Begin went to Camp David to work for peace, but it had to be his kind of peace—a peace that guaranteed his vision of Greater Israel.

Moshe Dayan gave the following overview of the course of the Camp David conference and of the relations between Begin and the other members of the Israeli delegation:

> The Camp David summit meeting lasted thirteen days, starting on 5 September 1978 and ending on 17 September. It proved the decisive, most difficult and least pleasant stage in the Egypt-Israel peace negotiations. The differences between the stands taken by Carter, Sadat and Begin were abundant, wide and basic, and all three parties had to resolve agonizing psychological and ideological crises in order to reach an agreed arrangement. It meant abandoning long-held traditional viewpoints and outlooks and taking up new positions.
>
> The deliberations were marked by sharp and often bitter arguments between us and the Egyptians, and even more so with the Americans. To my regret, even the discussions within our own Israeli delegation were not always tranquil. There were times when only by clenching teeth and fists could I stop myself from exploding. No one disputed Begin's right, as Prime Minister and head of our delegation, to be the final and authorized arbiter of Israel's position in all matters under review. But none of us was disposed to accept, as though they were the Sinai Tablets, those of his views which seemed to us extreme and unreasonable. We were not always at odds, and indeed, on most issues we held identical opinions. But on those occasions when I disagreed with him and questioned his proposals, he got angry, and would dismiss any suggestion that did not appeal to him as likely to cause inestimable harm to Israel.[26]

On the Israeli side Begin was obstinate, while his delegation was flexible and even indulgent. The pattern of negotiations on the Egyptian side was the reverse: Sadat was flexible, while his delegation was rigid, and he used this as leverage when confronting the Americans and Israelis. The strangest member of the Egyptian delegation was Hassan Tuhami, Sadat's astrologer, court jester, holy man, and morale booster. A former army officer, Tuhami turned into a religious mystic, believing that in dreams he received instructions directly from the Prophet. He saw himself as a sort of Egyptian Saladin, with a special mission to recover Jerusalem and defend Islam. Sadat was at ease with him and enjoyed his company, but the other Egyptian officials thought he was mad. Tuhami distributed pieces of ambergris to his colleagues, telling them to dissolve it in their tea, for it would give them the stamina to confront the Israelis. Some of them used this smelly substance from the bowels of the sperm whale, but Boutros Boutros-Ghali declined the offer.

As the days went by, Camp David seemed more and more like a prison camp. To provide a diversion for their guests, the Americans organized a visit to Gettysburg National Military Park, an important battleground in the American Civil War. As they walked over the battlefield, Boutros-Ghali found himself between Moshe Dayan and Hassan Tuhami. The crazed Tuhami asked the Israeli foreign minister, "Are you the anti-Christ?" No answer. Tuhami then declared that he intended to enter Jerusalem riding on a white horse and assume the post of governor of the city. Dayan smiled politely but made no comment, and this only reinforced Tuhami in his delusion.[27]

In the first five days at Camp David, the discussion went in circles and ended in deadlock. Begin had made some concessions but not on Israeli control over the West Bank. On 10 September the Americans presented a paper that served as a basis for the final agreement, but it took twenty-three drafts to get there. The Israelis presented a counterproposal, but the two other players rejected it. Carter applied intense pressure on Begin to moderate his position at every stage in the negotiations. He left no room for doubt that if the summit failed, Begin would get the blame, with catastrophic consequences for U.S.-Israel relations. Sadat also came under strong pressure—from Carter to show more flexibility and from his advisers to stand his ground. Muhammad Ibrahim Kamel resigned at Camp David because he felt that Sadat surrendered on all the essential points relating to the West Bank and Gaza, leaving Egypt isolated in the Arab world. Kamel was the second foreign minister to resign in protest against Sadat's policy.

The two main stumbling blocks in the negotiations were the Israeli settlements in Sinai and Jerusalem. Begin dearly wanted to keep the settlements, including Neot Sinai, where he planned to retire. But the Egyptians were adamant on recovering every square foot of their land, and Begin eventually gave in. The concession was made easier by a telephone call from Ariel Sharon in which the hawkish former general assured the prime minister, at the request of the defense minister, that the evacuation of all the Sinai settlements and bases would not involve unmanageable security risks. Begin, however, made the evacuation of the Sinai settlements conditional on ratification by the Knesset. The differences over Jerusalem were even more fundamental. Sadat wanted to include East Jerusalem with the West Bank. Begin insisted that unified Jerusalem was the eternal capital of Israel. On 17 September, the last day of the conference, the crisis reached its climax with the Egyptian delegation packing its bags to return home. The crisis was settled at the last minute by an exchange of letters. Sadat and Begin gave letters to Carter presenting their position on Jerusalem, while Carter gave Sadat a letter confirming that the United States continued to oppose the annexation of East Jerusalem to Israel.

The Camp David Accords were signed in an impressive ceremony in the White House on 17 September 1978. The two accords were entitled "A Framework for Peace in the Middle East" and "A Framework for the Conclusion of a Peace Treaty between Israel and Egypt." The former stated in its preamble, "The agreed basis for a peaceful settlement of the conflict between Israel and its neighbours is UN Security Council Resolution 242 in all its parts." The framework dealt with the West Bank and Gaza and envisaged nothing less than "the resolution of the Palestinian problem in all its aspects." Egypt, Israel, Jordan, and the representatives of the Palestinian people were to participate in the negotiations, which were to proceed in three stages. In the first, the ground rules would be laid for electing a "self-governing authority" for the territories, and the powers of this authority would be defined. In the second stage, once the self-governing authority had been established, a transitional period would begin. Israel's military government and its civilian administration would be withdrawn; Israel's armed forces would also be withdrawn and the remaining forces redeployed into specified security locations. In the third stage, not later than the third year after the beginning of the transitional pe-

riod, negotiations would take place to determine the final status of
the West Bank and Gaza. These negotiations had to recognize
"the legitimate rights of the Palestinian people and their just requirements."

"A Framework for Peace in the Middle East" was deliberately
ambiguous on many crucial issues in order to make agreement
possible. Nevertheless, it contained a number of principles and
provisions to which Begin had been firmly opposed in the past.
Initially, for example, Begin refused to include the preamble to
Resolution 242, because it emphasized the inadmissibility of the
acquisition of territory by war, but in the end he agreed to
"Resolution 242 in all its parts." Each party could interpret this in
its own way. The withdrawal of armed forces from the West Bank
represented another concession. However, Begin's greatest departure from the tenets of Revisionist Zionism and from the position of all previous Israeli governments lay in his recognition of
"the legitimate rights of the Palestinian people and their just requirements." Semantic devices were used to obscure the significance of the change in the Hebrew text of the accord. Thus the
English text spoke of the West Bank and Gaza, whereas the
Hebrew text spoke of Judea, Samaria, and the Gaza District.
Similarly, the term "Palestinians" appeared in the Hebrew text as
"the Arabs of the Land of Israel." Only the English text of the accord, however, was binding on all the parties.

"A Framework for the Conclusion of a Peace Treaty between
Israel and Egypt" was less complex and convoluted. It envisaged
that a peace treaty would be concluded within three months and
its terms implemented between two and three years after it was
signed. The treaty was to rest on four principles: complete Israeli
withdrawal from Sinai and recognition of Egyptian sovereignty
over this territory, demilitarization of most of Sinai, the stationing
of UN forces to supervise demilitarization and to ensure freedom
of navigation in the Gulf of Suez and the Suez Canal, and full normalization in the relations between Egypt and Israel. The
timetable required normalization to go into effect after Israel's
withdrawal from western Sinai. This meant that for another two
years Israel would retain control of the area east of the line El
Arish–Ras Muhammad with its civilian settlements, army camps,
and airfields.

On his return from Camp David, Begin was received with
demonstrations of support from Peace Now and demonstrations of
protest from the nationalist camp. A group of Herut supporters

waited for him at the gates of Jerusalem with black umbrellas in their hands. They shouted "Chamberlain" and accused him of appeasing Israel's enemies. The critics focused on his surrender of the whole of Sinai and his abandonment of the civilian settlements there rather than on Egypt's agreement to peace and normalization.

Begin needed all his skills as a politician and parliamentarian to secure the ratification of the Camp David Accords. He knew that had he sought approval from his own party, he would not have gotten a majority. He therefore refused to hold consultations within his party and arranged a cabinet meeting for 24 September and a Knesset debate to be held the following day, leaving no time to convene a meeting of the Knesset Foreign Affairs and Defense Committee. The cabinet meeting lasted seven hours. Begin was forthright and forceful in his defense of the accords, turning mercilessly on the critics and the waverers. At the end of the meeting, the cabinet approved Begin's proposal by a large majority. Eleven ministers voted in favor, two against, and one abstained. The religious ministers did not take part in the cabinet vote, because their parties had not had time to formulate their position. The cabinet decision authorized the prime minister to propose to the Knesset a resolution approving the Camp David Accords and authorizing the government to evacuate the Israeli settlers from Sinai.

Begin's address to the Knesset was punctuated by catcalls and heckling. "I bring to the Knesset," he said, "and through the Knesset to the nation, news of the establishment of peace between Israel and the strongest and largest of the Arab states, and also, eventually and inevitably, with all our neighbors." Hecklers accused Begin of presenting the Knesset with a fait accompli. Begin rejected the charge. The agreement reached at Camp David, he said, was subject to Knesset approval. The Knesset could endorse it and thereby turn it into the basis for negotiating a peace treaty with Egypt. Or it could reject it, in which case the agreement would be null and void and no negotiations with Egypt would take place. It was for the Knesset to decide. The leader of the opposition, Shimon Peres, congratulated the prime minister and the government on "the difficult, awesome, but vital decision they had taken to secure peace at a price which had been thought impossible for this government." Peres appealed to his followers to support the agreement as the best current hope for peace. Voting against the government, he said, would be interpreted as spurning the outstretched Egyptian hand as well as America's friendly advice.

All 120 members of the Knesset voted at the end of a debate that lasted seventeen hours. The result was 84 in favor of the government motion, 19 against, and 17 abstentions. Most Labor members voted for the motion, and without their support the motion would probably have been defeated. Most of the members who opposed the motion, or who abstained, came from the Likud and from the National Religious Party. Of the 84 affirmative votes, only 46 came from the ranks of the coalition, and only 29 from the Likud's 43 members. Prominent members of the Likud abstained in the vote, such as Yitzhak Shamir, the Speaker of the Knesset, and Moshe Arens, the chairman of its Foreign Affairs and Defense Committee. With the Knesset vote, the Camp David agreement went into force. In the country at large, support for the agreement was greater and more enthusiastic than in the Knesset. A public opinion poll showed that 82 percent of those questioned were in favor of the agreement.

In some ways Begin's most surprising achievement was his own endorsement of the agreement he tabled before the Knesset. American pressure at Camp David probably pushed him to make greater concessions than he had intended, but he did not cross his red lines. Moshe Dayan and Ezer Weizman, who made a vital contribution to the success of the conference, thought that Begin lived to regret the concessions he had made at Camp David. Arye Naor, who was closer to Begin personally and politically, saw no sign of such regret. According to Naor, Begin suffered protracted agonies over the choice but, once he had made his choice, never wavered in his conviction that it was the right choice. The Camp David Accords, to Begin's way of thinking, were not only necessary for neutralizing Egypt as an active confrontation state, and thus bringing many years of peace and tranquillity to Israel, but also the best guarantee for preventing foreign sovereignty over the western part of the Land of Israel. Begin believed that, in signing the Camp David Accords, he achieved for Israel the two fixed aims of his policy—peace and the integrity of the homeland.[28]

THE PEACE TREATY WITH EGYPT

At Camp David a target of three months was set for finalizing the peace treaty between Israel and Egypt. Begin and Sadat promised each other to try and achieve it in two months, but in the end six months were required to complete the negotiations. The awarding of the Nobel Peace Prize was an incentive to the two leaders to continue along the road on which they had embarked. But domestic political opposition reduced their room for maneuvering. Begin was under constant attack from his own party colleagues for the concessions he had made at Camp David. He now felt that Moshe Dayan and Ezer Weizman were too eager to charge forward to peace with Egypt at almost any price and that it was up to him to apply the brakes.

Sadat came under fierce attack at home and in the Arab world for signing the Camp David Accords. The accords envisaged a role for Jordan and the representatives of the Palestinian people in the negotiations on autonomy for the West Bank and Gaza. King Hussein, despite American entreaties, declined to take part in the negotiations. So did the Palestinians of the territories. The PLO denounced the Camp David Accords and mounted a propaganda offensive against Sadat. An Arab summit meeting was held in Baghdad in November 1978. It confirmed the 1974 Rabat designation of the PLO as the sole legitimate representative of the Palestinian people, and it threatened Egypt with expulsion from the Arab League if it made a separate peace with Israel.

Egyptian national pride and Israeli arrogance compounded the difficulty of reaching agreement. Some of the Israeli negotiators were mindful of the need not to give the impression of dictating a victor's terms. Others, however, behaved as though, since they were conceding Sinai, it was up to the Egyptians to yield on all other points. But the Egyptians were not overwhelmed by a sense of gratitude for this Israeli concession. They took the view that Sinai was Egyptian soil, that Israel had taken it by force, and that it was up to Israel to return it in exchange for peace. Furthermore, the Egyptians did not feel that they had come to the negotiating chamber as a defeated nation. For them the October 1973 war was a source of great national pride: they had broken through the Bar-Lev line, crossed to the eastern side of the Suez Canal, and successfully engaged the IDF in battle. The fact that the JDF later turned the tables on them did not change this perception. Indeed, they saw Israel's earlier withdrawals in Sinai, in 1974 and 1975, as political achievements flowing from their military success.[29]

Negotiations for a peace treaty opened in Washington on 12 October at the level of foreign ministers. The negotiations were protracted, arduous, and punctuated by crises. There were three main obstacles to an agreement. The first was the conflict between the Egypt-Israel peace treaty and Egypt's treaties with Arab states, which required Egypt to join them should they be at war with

Israel. Egypt suggested a general formula that failed to satisfy the Israelis. Israel wanted a clause in the peace treaty stating specifically that this treaty would have priority over Egypt's other obligations. The second obstacle was the question of linkage between the normalization of relations between Egypt and Israel and the negotiations on Palestinian autonomy. Egypt wanted to link bilateral relations with the Palestinian question in order to avoid giving the impression of embarking on a separate peace. Israel was not prepared to make its peace treaty with Egypt part of another agreement. It wanted this treaty to stand on its own. The third hurdle had to do with the establishment of diplomatic relations and the exchange of ambassadors. At Camp David it was agreed that this would be done simultaneously with Israel's withdrawal to the El Arish–Ras Muhammad line. Egypt subsequently suggested a more gradual process, starting with an exchange of chargés d'affaires and ending perhaps with full diplomatic relations after the evacuation of Sinai had been completed. Israel insisted on full diplomatic relations immediately upon the completion of the first phase of its withdrawal.

Israel threw a huge monkey wrench into the works by stepping up settlement activity on the West Bank. President Carter claimed that at Camp David Begin had promised him that the settlement freeze would continue until the negotiations on Palestinian autonomy were completed. Begin retorted that he had promised only a freeze during the three months allocated for negotiating the Egypt-Israel peace treaty and that the freeze did not preclude the "thickening" of existing settlements. In the middle of November the talks broke down, and the two delegations packed their bags and returned home. Cyrus Vance made several attempts to restart the talks, but to no avail. In January 1979 an Islamic revolution toppled the shah of Iran, and this gave both countries food for thought. Egyptians feared that normalizing relations with Israel would bring them into conflict with the radical elements in the Islamic world. For the Israelis, whose oil supplies from Iran were instantly cut off, the relinquishing of the Sinai oil fields seemed fraught with dangers.

The Americans, who also suffered a setback with the fall of the shah, convened a second meeting at Camp David on 21 February 1979. Prime Minister Mustafa Khalil and Foreign Minister Moshe Dayan spent four days going over familiar ground without being able to reach any agreement. Carter decided to travel in person to Egypt and Israel in early March to break the deadlock. He later admitted that the new initiative was "an act of desperation." On 7 March, Carter arrived in Cairo to an enthusiastic welcome and reached an understanding with Sadat on a range of issues. In Jerusalem, Carter had meetings with the cabinet and the Foreign Affairs and Defense Committee and gave an address to the Knesset. But the meetings between Carter and Begin were tense and unproductive. Begin did not help matters by his refusal to initial any agreement with the Americans without first submitting it to the cabinet and to the Knesset for debate and approval. On 13 March, just as Carter was about to abandon his mission, compromise formulas were reached on all the outstanding questions. Carter flew back to Cairo to present the new formulas to Sadat. He met Sadat at the airport and obtained his agreement to all the changes. In Sadat's presence Carter called Begin to announce the breakthrough.

The peace treaty between Egypt and Israel was a detailed implementation of the principles agreed upon at Camp David. The preamble stated that the treaty was an important step in the search for a comprehensive peace in the Middle East and in the settlement of the Arab-Israeli conflict in all its aspects. Article 1 required Israel to withdraw its armed forces and civilians from Sinai to the international border to allow Egypt to resume the exercise of its full sovereignty over the peninsula. Full diplomatic relations were to be established upon completion of the first stage of the Israeli withdrawal. Subsequent articles dealt with security arrangements in Sinai, the stationing of UN forces, freedom of navigation, and the various aspects of normalization. The treaty was accompanied by a memorandum of understanding guaranteeing Israel's oil supplies for the next fifteen years, assuring Israel of American support in the event of violations, and a continuing commitment to be "responsive" to Israel's military and economic requirements. Finally, a joint letter from Sadat and Begin to Carter committed them to start negotiations on autonomy for the West Bank and Gaza within a month of the peace treaty's ratification. This was intended to conceal the fact that Sadat agreed to a separate peace with Israel. In the final analysis Begin got what he wanted: a peace agreement with Egypt that stood on its own.

The cabinet approved the peace treaty with Egypt after hearing a report from Begin and Dayan. Next, Begin turned to the Knesset for its approval of the peace treaty and its appendixes and accompanying letters. Nearly all the members of the Knesset, including the majority of the ministers, participated in the debate, which lasted twenty-eight hours. On 22 March the Knesset approved the peace treaty: 95 voted for and 18 against, 2 abstained, and 3 declared that they were not participating in the vote.

The next day Begin left for Washington at the head of a large delegation that included the negotiating team and representatives from the government and the opposition. The peace treaty was signed on 26 March 1979 in an elaborate ceremony on the South Lawn of the White House in the presence of hundreds of guests and television reporters from all over the world. Speeches were made by Carter, Sadat, and Begin, all of whom underlined the historic significance of the occasion, quoted from the Bible, and paid compliments to one another. Begin praised Carter for the dedication and Sadat for the courage that helped to change the course of history.

Egypt was expelled from the Arab League following the conclusion of the peace treaty with Israel. The main charge against Egypt was that it had broken ranks and struck a separate deal with the enemy. This was compounded by the fear that behind the treaty lurked a secret alliance between Israel and Egypt, with the backing of the United States. Conspiracy theorists held that Egypt would be the political leader, Israel the technological leader, and the United States the financial backer, and together this triumvirate could dominate the Middle East.[30] Despite widespread Arab hostility, the implementation of the peace treaty between Israel and Egypt proceeded smoothly and according to plan. On 26 May 1979 El Arish was returned to Egypt; on 15 November the monastery of Saint Catherine was returned ahead of schedule as a goodwill gesture; and on 25 November the oil fields in Alma were turned over to Egypt. On 26 January 1980 the border between Egypt and Israel was opened, after Israel had retreated to the El Arish–Ras Muhammad line, giving Egypt 80 percent of Sinai. On 26 February diplomatic relations were established, ambassadors were exchanged, and the Israeli flag was raised in the Israeli embassy in Cairo. Considerable progress was also made in establishing normal economic relations, lines of communication by land and air, and tourist facilities.

At the same time, though, real problems arose in dealing with Palestinian autonomy. Begin managed the autonomy talks in such a way that nothing could possibly be achieved. The first sign was Begin's appointment of Dr. Yosef Burg, the minister of the interior, to head Israel's six-man negotiating team. Burg was the leader of the National Religious Party, which saw Israel's right to Judea and Samaria as embedded in Scripture and supported the settlement activities of Gush Emunim. There was something symbolic in entrusting the conduct of negotiations over the West Bank to the minister of the interior rather than the foreign minister. Begin preferred Burg to Dayan, because Dayan wanted the autonomy talks to succeed and had some imaginative ideas on how to carry them forward.

Another sign that Begin did not want the autonomy talks to succeed was the change he made to his own plan. He had always held that autonomy should be given to the inhabitants of the West Bank and Gaza, not to the territory. But when he drew up his autonomy plan, he suggested that the question of sovereignty remain open. The relevant paragraph read, "Israel stands by its right and its claim to sovereignty to Judea, Samaria and the Gaza District. In the knowledge that other claims exist, it proposes, for the sake of the agreement and the peace, that the question of sovereignty in these areas be left open." However, after the peace treaty with Egypt was signed, Begin did not wish to repeat this text and proposed to the cabinet a new version. This one read, "At the end of the five-year transitional period, Israel will continue to maintain its claim to the right of sovereignty in the Land of Israel territories— Judea, Samaria and the Gaza District." The new version also stated explicitly that Israel would not agree to the establishment of a Palestinian state.[31] Dayan knew that the Palestinians could not possibly agree to negotiate on this basis, and he left the whole matter in the hands of Begin and Burg. The last straw for Dayan was the government's decision to expropriate private land on the West Bank to make room for new settlements by the religious zealots of Gush Emunim. On 2 October, Dayan wrote to Begin to tender his resignation from the government. Disagreement with the official line on autonomy and with the manner in which the autonomy negotiations were being conducted was given as the reason for the resignation.

For six months Begin served as his own foreign minister until, in early March 1980, he appointed Yitzhak Shamir to this crucial post. Begin and Shamir had long-standing political differences going back to pre-Independence days when Begin commanded Irgun and Shamir led the more extreme Stern Gang. More recently, Shamir had expressed reservations about the peace policy of the Begin government. Shamir, by his own account, was not a natural candidate for the top post at the Foreign Ministry, the stronghold of the Labor movement: "I was an acknowledged 'hard-liner,' a man who had abstained in the 1978 vote on the Camp David Accords, and again in 1979 in the voting on the Peace Treaty with Egypt, and who, many believed, would probably have voted against both agreements had he felt free to do so. Hardly a recommendation for a Foreign Minister, now that those Accords and Treaty were a cornerstone of Israeli foreign policy."[32] What united Begin and Shamir was a deep ideological commitment to the integrity of the homeland. Whether intentionally or not, Shamir's appointment signaled to Egypt that the era of Israeli concessions was over. It also signaled, at home and abroad, that the pragmatism that had produced the peace treaty with Egypt was at an end and that from now on foreign policy would follow the ideological precepts of Revisionist Zionism.

In a government led by Begin and Shamir, the position of Ezer Weizman became increasingly untenable. Talks on Palestinian autonomy continued to engage Israeli and Egyptian officials but without any discernible progress. Meanwhile, prominent figures from the occupied territories formed the National Guidance Committee, whose main purpose was to fight the Israeli autonomy plan and lead the struggle for complete Israeli withdrawal and the establishment of a Palestinian state. Weizman was inclined to talk with members of the committee and try to persuade them to participate in the negotiations on autonomy. But the tone of the cabinet was now set by the ministers who were opposed to a dialogue with Palestinian nationalists and supportive of the efforts of the Gush Emunim nationalists to build more settlements on the West Bank even when this involved breaking the law. Weizman could not agree to a change in the law to make it possible to expropriate private Arab land for civilian settlement as opposed to security needs. Nor could he agree to the government's allocation of funds for settlements while imposing cuts in the defense budget. By May 1980 Weizman felt compelled to resign from the government in protest against what he regarded as the loss of a historic opportunity to bring about a comprehensive settlement of the Arab-Israeli conflict. On his way out of the prime minister's office, he pulled down a peace poster from the wall and tore it up. "No one here wants peace," he thundered. Weizman coupled his resignation with a scathing public denunciation of the government's indifference to peace. In a subsequent vote in the Knesset on a motion of no confidence in the government, he raised his hand with the opposition. Begin took over the defense portfolio and kept it until he formed his second government.

10

The Lebanese Quagmire

1981–1984

ANWAR AL-SADAT did not read the Israeli political map right. He was right in believing that only Begin's Likud could achieve the peace with Egypt, but he did not grasp that only the Labor Alignment could achieve peace with the Palestinians. Sadat saw Begin as a strong leader who could be relied on to deliver Palestinian autonomy on the West Bank and Gaza. Consequently, Sadat knowingly helped Begin against his Labor opponents in the lead-up to the elections of 30 June 1981. On 4 June, Sadat went to a summit meeting with Begin at Sharm el-Sheikh, which was still in Israeli hands. On the main issue that divided Egypt and Israel—Palestinian autonomy—no agreement was reached except to continue to talk. Many television networks pictured the two leaders in a relaxed mood, sitting on a balcony facing the sea. Israel's electoral law prohibited showing these pictures on the news, so they were included in the Likud's election propaganda. Three days later the IDF launched a surprise attack against the Iraqi nuclear reactor.

OPERATION BABYLON

Operation Babylon was the popular name given to the IAF attack on the Iraqi nuclear plant at Osirak, near Baghdad. Sixteen planes took off from the Etzion airbase, in eastern Sinai, on Sunday afternoon, 7 June 1981. Eight of the planes were F-16 Fighter Falcons, each carrying two 2,000-pound laser-guided bombs. The other eight were F-15 Eagles, carrying air-to-air missiles, electronic countermeasure pods, and extra fuel tanks. Flying low and in tight formation, the planes avoided detection by the radar of Jordan, Saudi Arabia, and Iraq. Not a single Iraqi missile was fired at the IAF planes. The attack lasted two minutes. The Iraqi nuclear reactor, called Tammuz, was destroyed, and all the Israeli planes returned safely to base. This daring and brilliantly executed raid helped the Likud win the general election against heavy odds three weeks later. Both the decision to launch the attack and its timing came under criticism in Israel. Shimon Peres, the leader of the Alignment, opposed the attack, arguing that Iraq could have been prevented from acquiring nuclear weapons by diplomatic means. Other Alignment leaders accused Menachem Begin of deliberately ordering the attack just before the election in order to boost the flagging fortunes of his party. Operation Babylon was viewed by these critics as an electoral stunt. The truth was more complicated.

The Israeli cabinet reached its decision to authorize the operation at the end of a long and agonizing process. Menachem Begin, Yitzhak Shamir, and Ariel Sharon were the strongest supporters of the operation. On becoming prime minister in 1977, Begin was briefed by Yitzhak Rabin on Iraq's plans to develop nuclear weapons and on Israel's efforts to foil these plans. From then on, Begin remained preoccupied with this problem. Nuclear weapons in Iraqi hands raised in his mind the specter of another Holocaust and the destruction of the State of Israel.

On 23 August 1978, shortly before his trip to Camp David, Begin convened a meeting of senior ministers and experts to discuss developments in the nuclear field in the Arab world in general and in Iraq in particular. Begin opened the meeting, invited the director of military intelligence to present his survey, and then asked the ministers for their opinion. All the ministers thought that Iraq should not be allowed to acquire nuclear weapons, but they could not agree on the means Israel should take to this end. These divisions were to persist until the final decision was made. Ariel Sharon proposed the adoption of a policy stating that any attempt by an Arab state to develop or acquire nuclear weapons would be considered a casus belli. Most of the other speakers were not prepared to go that far. They preferred to continue to follow developments without taking any binding decisions. Yigael Yadin, the deputy prime minister and leader of the Democratic Movement for

Change, urged caution in dealing with such a sensitive matter and strongly opposed any idea of taking military action against the Iraqi nuclear plant. Several of the experts, including Shlomo Gazit, the director of military intelligence, and Yitzhak Hofi, the head of the Mossad, agreed with Yadin. They pointed out that the Iraqi nuclear reactor had a long way to go before it became operational and that until then it would not pose a serious danger. Begin concluded the meeting by saying that the danger facing Israel was very serious and by ordering various lines of action to slow down the Iraqi nuclear program. Thus, even while negotiating peace with Egypt, Begin was deeply concerned with the danger from the east. A short time after the outbreak of the Iraq-Iran war, Iranian planes attacked the Iraqi nuclear plant at Osirak. The damage was limited, and Begin concluded from the subsequent intelligence reports that it would not take long for the plant to be repaired and reopened.[1]

On 14 October 1980 Begin convened a meeting of the ministerial security committee and a large number of experts. Although most of the experts were opposed to direct military action to destroy the Iraqi reactor, Rafael Eytan, the chief of staff, was strongly in favor. He had also started preparing an operational plan that entrusted the mission to the IAF. Begin opened the discussion by saying that the government had to choose between two evils: either bombing the Iraqi reactor and risking hostile reactions from Egypt and the rest of the world or sitting with folded arms and allowing Iraq to continue its efforts to produce nuclear weapons. He himself favored the first evil because the Iraq-Iran war had weakened Iraq and slowed down its nuclear program, thereby limiting the risk of radioactive fallout, and because, if Saddam Hussein got the bomb, he would not hesitate to hurl it against Tel Aviv. The risks of inaction, concluded Begin, outweighed the risks of action. Sharon sided with Begin. A strike against the Iraqi reactor, he argued, would have a deterrent effect on other Arab countries with nuclear ambitions and should therefore be carried out at the earliest possible date. Yadin again headed the opposition. He listed the risks of military action, including Soviet retaliation and American suspension of arms delivery to Israel; he made it clear that he would not be willing to share in collective responsibility for a decision to bomb the reactor; and he demanded that the matter be brought before the entire cabinet.

On 28 October, Begin convened a special meeting of the cabinet. He called on the chief of staff and other senior officers to provide a briefing on Iraq's nuclear program. He then gave his own views about the nuclear threat facing Israel, views that soon crystallized into what became known as the Begin Doctrine. Begin gave all the advisers who were opposed to military action the opportunity to explain their reservations. In the course of the discussion, the cabinet divided into two groups, and in the end ten ministers voted for Begin's proposal and six against it.[2]

The decision in principle to bomb the Iraqi nuclear reactor was followed by a series of delays in carrying out the operation. On 30 December, Begin summoned Shimon Peres, the leader of the opposition, and told him in confidence about the decision. Peres sent a secret, handwritten letter to Begin urging him at least to postpone the operation.[3] The operation was postponed until 7 June. That afternoon a special meeting of the cabinet was convened in the prime minister's residence. Begin spoke about his prolonged agonizing over the decision. There was no precedent in world history for what they were about to do, he noted, but they were doing it in the knowledge that this was necessary to save their people and their children from a terrible danger. It was agreed to issue a statement only if an official Arab source announced the destruction of the reactor. Begin prepared the text.

The following day Begin was told that Radio Amman announced that Israel had sent planes to attack vital targets in Iraq. On the spot Begin decided to issue the statement that explained the government's reasons for ordering the attack. The last sentence read, "On no account shall we permit an enemy to develop weapons of mass destruction against the people of Israel."[4] This was the Begin Doctrine. It implied that the destruction of Tammuz was not an exceptional measure but part of an overall policy of preventing any Arab country from producing nuclear weapons. It also hinted at Begin's intention to preserve Israel's nuclear monopoly in perpetuity.

The attack on the Iraqi reactor was greeted by a chorus of condemnation from many countries, including the United States. President Reagan suspended the delivery of aircraft to Israel and announced that he was considering additional sanctions. Begin responded with a personal letter to Reagan, replete with references to the Holocaust: "A million and a half children were poisoned by the Ziklon gas during the Holocaust. Now Israel's children were about to be poisoned by radioactivity. For two years we have lived in the shadow of the danger awaiting Israel from the nuclear reactor in Iraq. This would have been a new Holocaust. It was prevented by the heroism of our pilots to whom we owe so much."[5]

Another letter was sent by Begin to Sadat to justify the Israeli action, but Sadat could not be mollified. His summit meeting with the Israeli premier three days before the attack cast him in Arab eyes as an accomplice in a criminal act. Begin's letter was conveyed to Sadat by the Israeli ambassador, Moshe Sasson. Sadat received Sasson, a fluent Arabic speaker, at 11:00 A.M. on 10 June in the Mamoura rest house in Alexandria, in the garden overlooking the Mediterranean Sea. For the Israeli ambassador this was the most tense and dramatic meeting of his entire diplomatic career. Sadat read Begin's letter very slowly. A long silence ensued. Sadat lit his pipe and seemed deep in thought. He then got up and started pacing back and forth on the lawn, like a caged lion. When he eventually broke his silence, it was to say that what mattered to him most was the peace process in the region and that the Israeli attack on the Iraqi nuclear reactor set history back to the point that preceded his peace initiative. His aim had been to break down the psychological barrier and to help Israel acquire the image of a country with which the Arabs could live in peace. Now Israel appeared in its old, arrogant image as an invincible power, as a power with a long arm that could reach the remotest corners of the Arab world. "Once again," said Sadat, "we face the same Israel that is completely oblivious to what happens in the Arab world and to what the Arab world thinks of it."

Sasson breathed a sigh of relief when Sadat asked him to tell Begin that he himself would tenaciously cling to what remained of the peace process. Sadat then stopped in his tracks and, as if addressing Begin directly, said, *"Allah yasmahak, ya Menachem!"*— meaning, "May God forgive you, O Menachem!" He repeated this sentence several times, shaking his head as he did so. Sadat explained to the Israeli ambassador that he had repeatedly told Begin, "Menachem, preserve Egypt's friendship. The Egyptian people will always stand by you if you preserve this friendship. . . . If you win the friendship of the Egyptian people, you will, in the course of time, also gain the understanding of the Arab world. The Egyptian people are a noble and good-natured people and when they confer their friendship on someone, they do not revoke it unless something terrible happens." Sadat complained that the attack on the Iraqi reactor provided the Soviet Union and Syria with ammunition against Egypt and the peace process. The personal blow was a grievous one, he concluded, but more serious was the blow to the peace process.[6]

Begin had underestimated the political and psychological impact that Israel's military operation was likely to have in the Arab world. So obsessed was he with Israel's security that Arab sensitivities hardly figured in his calculations. His determination to destroy the Iraqi reactor was dictated not by electoral considerations, as his critics claimed, but by a genuine conviction that Israel faced a mortal danger. Once Operation Babylon had been successfully carried out, however, he moved to extract every ounce of electoral advantage from it. He went on the offensive against the Alignment leaders and claimed that it was not his decision but their criticism of it that was motivated by electoral considerations.[7] He even took the unprecedented step of publishing the text of Peres's strictly confidential letter to him. The message he sought to convey to the public was that he had the courage to stage this strike against Israel's distant enemies, whereas the challenger to the premiership sought to dissuade him. The operation was vastly popular with the Israeli public, and Begin and his colleagues received much of the credit for it.

The bombing of the Iraqi reactor tipped the scales in favor of the Likud in the election of 30 June 1981. Three months before the election, a Peres victory seemed certain. The Alignment had a lead of 25 percent over Likud in the opinion polls. In the election itself the two parties polled a roughly equal number of votes. The Likud won 48 seats in the Knesset, compared with the Alignment's 47. The Alignment had increased its representation from 33 to 47 seats, but its traditional allies fared badly, while the Democratic Movement for Change and the Independent Liberals disappeared altogether from the political map. As the leader of the largest party, Begin was invited by President Yitzhak Navon to form the new government. The coalition government he formed had the support of 61 members of the Knesset: 48 from the Likud, 6 from the National Religious Party, 4 from Agudat Israel, and 3 from Tami, a religious party that drew most of its support from the community of North African Jews. For the first time in Israel's history, the entire coalition was drawn exclusively from the right-wing part of the political spectrum. Numerically it was a weak government with a wafer-thin majority. But what it lacked in numerical strength, it more than made up for in political cohesion and ideological fervor.

The composition of the government also reflected the shift of the political center of gravity to the right. Begin's first government had included Moshe Dayan as foreign minister, Ezer Weizman as defense minister, and Yigael Yadin as deputy prime minister. Individually and collectively these men had exercised a moderating and restraining influence on the government's policy toward the Arab world. In Begin's second government no trace was left of this moderating influence. Yitzhak Shamir carried on as foreign minister, while Ariel Sharon, the relentless hawk, prevailed on Begin to hand over to him the defense portfolio. With this trio in charge, Israel's foreign policy was to become more activist, more aggressive, and more uncompromisingly nationalistic.

At the beginning of August, Begin presented his new government to the Knesset. The foreign policy guidelines of this government were blunt and forthright. They affirmed Jerusalem's status as "the eternal capital of Israel, indivisible, entirely under Israeli sovereignty," and the "right of the Jewish people to the Land of Israel, an eternal unassailable right that is intertwined with the right to security and peace." The guidelines contradicted the contract that Begin himself had signed at Camp David. There he had recognized the legitimate rights of the Palestinian people and agreed to grant full autonomy to the inhabitants of the West Bank and Gaza. The 1981 guidelines stated that Israel would assert its claim to sovereignty over all of the land west of the Jordan River at the end of the transition period envisaged in "A Framework for Peace in the Middle East," signed at Camp David. Thus it became official policy to establish a permanent and coercive jurisdiction over the 1.3 million Arab inhabitants of the West Bank and Gaza. The emptying of the autonomy concept of any political content, the building of new Jewish settlements in the most densely populated areas of the West Bank, the expropriation of Arab land and the displacement of its owners, and the strong-arm policy of military repression instituted by the IDF in the occupied territories combined to scotch any possibility of continuing the peace process. "Western Eretz Israel is entirely under our control," proclaimed Begin at the graveside of Ze'ev Jabotinsky. "It will never again be divided. No part of its territory will be given over to alien rule, to foreign sovereignty."[8]

Sadat made one last effort to salvage the faltering peace process at a summit conference with Begin in Alexandria on 26 August. Sadat was anxious to smooth the way for Israel's departure from the remaining part of Sinai, a departure scheduled for April 1982. At the summit the two leaders agreed to renew the stalled Palestinian autonomy talks and to expand commercial, cultural, and tourist exchanges between their countries. It was a valiant attempt on Sadat's part, but Begin's reelection ruled out any prospect of genuine Palestinian self-government. Although Sadat was reluctant to admit it publicly, his peace initiative had not produced the results he had hoped for. On 6 October 1981, the anniversary of the October War, Sadat was assassinated by an Islamic fundamentalist officer in a military parade. Ten days later Moshe Dayan died of cancer. The two main architects of the peace between Egypt and Israel were removed from the scene in the same month. Begin attended Sadat's funeral and met his successor, Hosni Mubarak. Mubarak assured Begin that he would not budge from his predecessor's course. Begin, for his part, assured Mubarak that Israel intended to abide by its commitment to complete the withdrawal from Sinai. But there was an uneasy feeling, at least in some quarters in Israel, that Sadat's vision of comprehensive peace in the Middle East had expired with him.

THE ANNEXATION OF
THE GOLAN HEIGHTS

During Begin's second term in office, Israel moved toward closer strategic cooperation with the United States despite the crisis occasioned by the destruction of the Iraqi nuclear reactor. Ronald Reagan's Republican administration, which came to power in January 1981, replaced Jimmy Carter's regionalist approach to the Middle East with a globalist approach whose main aim was to combat Soviet influence. Alexander Haig, the new secretary of state, tried to create a "strategic consensus" in the Middle East to counter Soviet expansionism. Begin and Sharon embraced eagerly, much more eagerly than any Arab leader, the idea of forming a united front with the United States against the Soviet Union. One of Begin's basic aims after coming to power had been to demonstrate that Israel was a strategic asset for the United States in the Middle East. He had no ideological or political inhibitions about siding openly with one side against the other in the Cold War. On the contrary, he tried to use the global rivalry between East and West in order to gain Washington's official acknowledgment of Israel as an ally and a geopolitical asset. His efforts were crowned with success on 30 November 1981 when the two countries signed in Washington a memorandum of understanding on strategic cooperation.

The memorandum's significance lay as much in its form as in its substance. Formalizing for the first time the concept of American-Israeli strategic cooperation, it read, "United States-Israel strategic cooperation . . . is designed against the threat to peace and security of the region caused by the Soviet Union or Soviet-controlled forces from outside the region introduced into the region."[9] The memorandum carried a number of advantages for Israel. First, it established channels for closer military and intelligence coordination. Second, it provided for the prepositioning of American military equipment in Israel, this enhanced the confidence of Israelis that they would not be left alone in an emergency. Third, it called for cooperation in defense research and development. Israel, for its part, undertook to cooperate with the United States in emergency situations and to make available its facilities for the speedy deployment of American power.[10] For the first time the Soviet Union was described in an official Israeli document as a confrontation state, and the possibility was raised of using the IDF for missions unrelated to the defense of Israel.

When the terms of the memorandum for strategic cooperation became known, leaders of the Labor Alignment attacked the government for entering into such far-reaching commitments without parliamentary debate and approval. They pointed out that the United States assumed no commitment to rush to Israel's aid in the event of an Arab attack beyond its role as guarantor of the Camp David Accords and the Egypt-Israel peace treaty. Rather, it was Israel that was obliged to support the United States in any emergency in the Middle East and the Persian Gulf that involved Soviet forces or Soviet proxies. In the event of a Soviet-supported coup in Saudi Arabia, for example, Israel was obliged to assist the United States even if its own security was not directly threatened.

If Begin was the ideological father of this controversial memorandum of understanding, he was also the man who came close to destroying it. Toward the end of November, Begin slipped in his bath and broke his hipbone. The pain he suffered was excruciating, and he had to be hospitalized. In the days that followed, the pain and the painkillers may have affected his judgment. His behavior, in any case, became more erratic and impulsive than usual. While recuperating in hospital, he made up his mind to annex the Golan Heights. The international situation seemed propitious. The superpowers were preoccupied with a crisis in Poland. Egypt was expecting the return of the rest of Sinai the following spring. In Israel a pressure group was conducting a vigorous political campaign for annexation of the Golan Heights. This pressure group included supporters of the Alignment, because on the Golan there were settlements that identified with the Alignment. Begin himself was being criticized by the Alignment for giving preference to the

West Bank over the Golan, which was crucial to the security of the Galilee, while right-wingers from his own and other parties were lobbying against the dismantling of Jewish settlements in Sinai. Begin perceived an opportunity to confound his critics by a move that was likely to attract a broad national consensus: the annexation of the Golan Heights. The foreign and defense ministers were told in confidence about the plan. On his last day in hospital, Begin summoned Moshe Nissim, the minister of justice, and ordered him to prepare the necessary legislation within twenty-four hours.

On the next day, 14 December, Begin summoned the cabinet to a morning meeting in his residence. Most of the ministers were surprised to hear what the prime minister had to say. Sitting in an armchair, with his ailing leg on a footstool, he informed them of his decision to annex the Golan Heights and to push the necessary legislation through the Knesset on the very same day. This extraordinary proposal entailed squeezing into one day three readings of a bill that would extend Israeli law, jurisdiction, and civil administration to the area that had been under military occupation since 1967. He stressed that immediate action was necessary in order to prevent the United States and the United Nations from applying pressures on Israel.

Begin arrived in the Knesset in a wheelchair to present his bill. For generations, he stated, the Golan Heights had been part of Palestine, and only an arbitrary decision of the colonial powers in the aftermath of World War I excluded it from the area of the British mandate for Palestine. From the historical point of view, the Golan Heights were accordingly part of the Land of Israel. Another of Begin's justifications for the bill was Syria's implacable hostility to Israel and denial of its right to exist within any borders. Finally, Begin denied that annexation would foreclose the option for negotiations with Syria: "If the day comes when there is someone to talk to in Syria, I am convinced that it would not be this step that would prevent negotiations."[11] The Knesset adopted the Golan Heights Law by a majority of 63 to 21. Among those who voted in favor were 8 members of the Alignment.

The annexation of the Golan Heights constituted a violation of the principles of international law, of Resolution 242, of the Israeli-Syrian disengagement of forces agreement of May 1974, and of the Camp David Accords. It also constituted a departure from the policy of all Israeli governments since 1967 of keeping open all options for a negotiated settlement with Syria. A number of reasons

combined to prompt Begin to propose this step, reasons that related to domestic, regional, and international politics. First, by asserting Israeli sovereignty over the Golan Heights, Begin could
pacify the Israeli right. Second, he probably wanted to test Hosni
Mubarak's commitment to the peace treaty that his predecessor
had signed. Third, the passing of the Golan Heights Law sent a
message to the world at large that there would be no further Israeli
territorial withdrawals following the completion of the withdrawal
from Sinai. In other words, by annexing the Golan Heights, Begin
sought to stop the momentum toward a comprehensive Arab-
Israeli peace.[12]

The annexation of the Golan Heights provoked loud protest
throughout the Arab world. It was taken as proof that Israel was
more interested in territory than in peace. It put great strain on
Israel's relations with Egypt and left no room for hope that something real might grow out of the Palestinian autonomy talks. On
the Golan itself, the normally quiet Druze population of about fifteen thousand staged riots in protest of the demand that they
should carry Israeli identity cards. Syria reacted angrily to the annexation of its territory. The Syrian defense minister said that force
would be the best response to the Israeli decision. On 17
December, Syria also complained to the Security Council, which
unanimously adopted a resolution that reaffirmed the principle
that the acquisition of territory by force was inadmissible and
called on Israel to rescind its decision forthwith.

The U.S. representative voted in favor of this resolution. In
Washington there was disappointment and dismay at Israel's failure to consult before taking such a far-reaching step. The Reagan
administration announced the temporary suspension of the memorandum of understanding on strategic cooperation and of $300
million in projected arms sales to Israel. Begin summoned Samuel
Lewis, the American ambassador to Israel, and read out a statement to him. This was the harshest and most undiplomatic statement about the United States ever made by an Israeli prime
minister. Temporary suspension of the agreement, roared Begin,
meant its cancellation. Israel, he told Lewis, was not an American
"vassal state" or a "banana republic." "This leg may be broken,"
he said pointing at the leg that was resting on a footstool, "but my
knees are not bent and they will not bend!"

On his way out Lewis saw the chief of staff and a group of senior officers, maps in hand. They had come to attend a cabinet
meeting that was to discuss the options in the event of military ac-

tion by Syria. The assembled ministers heard a repeat of the prime minister's lecture to Lewis. Begin attached so much importance to his act of defiance that he instructed the cabinet secretary to issue to the press the text of what he had said to Lewis. Although Begin had been presenting the agreement on strategic cooperation with the United States as a major achievement, he was unwilling to ask the Americans to adhere to it. In fact, it was he who chose to interpret a temporary suspension of the agreement by America as a cancellation. The cabinet secretary had the impression that Begin, having invested so much effort in institutionalizing U.S.-Israeli relations, now welcomed the opportunity to reassert Israel's freedom of action. An insight into Begin's motives was given during a later visit to the White House when he explained the meaning of the term "protected Jews." The expression referred to Jews who received a promise of protection from the Gentile landlord against assailants. Zionism, said Begin, quoting the words of Ze'ev Jabotinsky, put an end to this dubious status. Even with their friends, Begin stressed, Israelis would deal only as equals, on the basis of reciprocity. Reagan allowed six months to pass before he invited Begin to a working visit in Washington to renew the strategic dialogue between their two countries. In the intervening period a war in Lebanon erupted.[13]

ARIEL SHARON'S BIG PLAN

Two strands in Israeli policy led to the full-scale invasion of Lebanon in June 1982: the alliance with the Lebanese Christians and a desire to destroy the PLO. Menachem Begin strongly supported both strands of this policy. During his years in opposition Begin developed a political-strategic conception that resembled in some respects that of his great rival, David Ben-Gurion. This conception stressed the interests that were common to Israel and the non-Arab or non-Muslim countries and minorities in the Middle East and in its periphery. Within this broad conception the Christians of Lebanon held a special place because they allegedly faced the danger of destruction at the hands of their Arab and Muslim opponents. Begin was determined not to repeat the mistakes of the Munich conference of September 1938, at which Britain and France abandoned Czechoslovakia to Adolf Hitler's tender mercies. Begin likened Israel to the Western powers, the Maronites to the Czechs, and the Syrians and Palestinians to Nazi

Germany. He felt that Israel had a moral duty to defend its Maronite allies. At the same time, he was committed to waging war against the PLO because of the attacks it launched across the border from Lebanon. Retaliation was not enough in his view; Israel had to seize the initiative, destroy the guerrilla bases in southern Lebanon, and drive the guerrillas to the north of the country, as far away as possible from Israel's own border. This was the basic conception that determined the goals Begin hoped to achieve by invading Lebanon.[14]

The real driving force behind Israel's invasion of Lebanon, however, was Ariel Sharon, whose aims were much more ambitious and far-reaching. From his first day at the Defense Ministry, Sharon started planning the invasion of Lebanon. He developed what came to be known as the "big plan" for using Israel's military power to establish political hegemony in the Middle East. The first aim of Sharon's plan was to destroy the PLO's military infrastructure in Lebanon and to undermine it as a political organization. The second aim was to establish a new political order in Lebanon by helping Israel's Maronite friends, headed by Bashir Gemayel, to form a government that would proceed to sign a peace treaty with Israel. For this to be possible, it was necessary, third, to expel the Syrian forces from Lebanon or at least to weaken seriously the Syrian presence there. In Sharon's big plan, the war in Lebanon was intended to transform the situation not only in Lebanon but in the whole Middle East. The destruction of the PLO would break the backbone of Palestinian nationalism and facilitate the absorption of the West Bank into Greater Israel. The resulting influx of Palestinians from Lebanon and the West Bank into Jordan would eventually sweep away the Hashemite monarchy and transform the East Bank into a Palestinian state. Sharon reasoned that Jordan's conversion into a Palestinian state would end international pressures on israel to withdraw from the West Bank. Begin was not privy to all aspects of Sharon's ambitious geopolitical scenario, but the two men were united by their desire to act against the PLO in Lebanon.[15]

Chief of Staff Rafael Eytan was another enthusiastic supporter of military action against the PLO. The IDF had prepared plans for the invasion, code-named Operation Pines, in two versions, a little one and a big one. Operation Little Pines called for the uprooting of the guerrillas from southern Lebanon. Operation Big Pines envisaged a thrust up to the Beirut–Damascus highway, a landing by sea to surround Beirut in a pincer movement, and the possibility of another landing at Jounieh to link up with the Christian forces in the north. Its ultimate target was the destruction of the PLO command centers and infrastructure throughout Lebanon, including Beirut. Operation Big Pines was first brought before the cabinet on 20 December 1981, soon after the annexation of the Golan Heights. This was the meeting at which Begin reported the scathing comments he had just made to the American ambassador following the suspension of the agreement on strategic cooperation. The ministers had hardly recovered from the shock when Begin surprised them a second time by introducing the plan for going to war in Lebanon. Sharon explained that the idea was not to clash with the Syrians in the Golan Heights but to seize the opportunity to achieve their strategic objectives in Lebanon. "If the Syrians start anything," he said, "we'll respond in Lebanon and solve the problem there." Eytan then presented, with the help of a map, the operational plan for reaching Beirut and beyond. The ministers were astonished by the scale of the proposed operation, and several of them spoke against it. Begin abruptly terminated the discussion without putting the proposal to a vote when it became clear that it would be defeated by a large majority.[16]

Sharon and Eytan, realizing that there was no chance of persuading the cabinet to approve a large-scale operation in Lebanon, adopted a different tactic. They started presenting to the cabinet limited proposals for bombing PLO targets in Lebanon, expecting that the guerrillas would retaliate by firing Katyusha rockets on Israel's northern settlements and that this would force the cabinet to approve more drastic measures. The idea was to implement Operation Big Pines in stages by manipulating enemy provocation and Israel's response. A number of confrontations took place in the cabinet as a result of these tactics. Ministers opposed to a war in Lebanon opposed the more modest proposals for bombing targets in Lebanon because they recognized where these proposals were intended to lead.[17]

Sharon was not deterred from pursuing his preparations for war or his contacts with the Maronites. The Maronites were not a unified group. They were divided into various militias headed by rival warlords; family ties were more significant than religion. Among these militias the Phalange, established in 1936 by Pierre Gemayel on the lines of the Nazi Youth movement, had the closest links with Israel. In January 1982, with the agreement of the prime minister, Sharon paid a secret visit to Beirut to confer with

Bashir Gemayel to assess what could be expected from the Phalange in the event of war. At this meeting the capture of Beirut was explicitly mentioned, and the division of labor between Israel and the Phalange was discussed. Begin himself received Bashir Gemayel in Jerusalem on 16 February. At this meeting Begin stated that Israel would enter Lebanon if terrorist activities continued and that, if this happened, its forces would proceed northward as far as possible.[18]

The relationship with Bashir Gemayel and the Phalange was always controversial. Mossad operatives, who developed this relationship and enjoyed the personal contact involved, had a generally positive view of the political reliability and military capability of the Phalange. However, military intelligence had grave doubts on both scores. From the start the IDF experts were cool about the relationship and regularly exposed the shortcomings of the Phalange. In contrast to the Mossad, they did not regard the Phalange as an asset, nor did they trust its leaders. Major General Yehoshua Saguy, the director of military intelligence, was convinced that even if Gemayel were to be elected president of Lebanon, he would turn toward the Arab world. Saguy repeatedly warned his superiors that Gemayel was only trying to use Israel for his own purposes and that, given the close links between Lebanon and the Arab world, he would not be able to make peace with Israel.

Ministers were explicitly warned by the heads of the intelligence community, at a meeting in Begin's home in April 1982, against the idea of trying to secure Bashir Jemayel's election to the presidency. On this occasion the head of the Mossad, General Yitzhak Hofi, sided with Saguy. Both of them cautioned against assuming that it would be possible to engineer Gemayel's election through the good offices of the IDF and then turn around and withdraw from Lebanon a few weeks later.[19] But by this time the personal relationship between Sharon and Gemayel was so intimate and their joint plans were so far advanced that the opinion of the experts was brushed aside and their warning against interference in the Lebanese political process was not heeded. The influence of the experts began to decline as soon as the Phalangists found their way directly to Sharon's ranch in the Negev.

Sharon and Eytan were constantly on the lookout for an excuse to launch an operation in Lebanon. At the beginning of March, Begin convened at his home a meeting of several ministers and the chief of staff. Sharon and Eytan surprised the ministers by sug-

gesting a new reason for an operation in Lebanon: Israel's commitment to Egypt to withdraw from eastern Sinai, including the
town of Yamit, on 26 April. Once the withdrawal from Sinai was
completed, they said, the Egyptians might cancel the peace treaty;
an operation in Lebanon would test their intentions. Yitzhak
Shamir, Yosef Burg, and Simha Erlich recoiled from this suggestion. They said that the peace with Egypt stood on its own and
should not be linked to Lebanon. Begin agreed with them, and the
suggestion was rejected.

The final phase of the withdrawal from Sinai was carried out in
the face of powerful domestic opposition. Professor Yuval
Ne'eman, leader of the small ultranationalist Tehiya party, and
Moshe Arens, a prominent member of the Likud and chairman of
the Knesset's Foreign Affairs and Defense Committee, led the opposition. Ne'eman, Arens, and some of their colleagues wanted to
revoke the treaty before it was time for Israel to withdraw its forces
and evacuate the civilian settlements between the El Arish–Ras
Muhammad line and the international border. They tried to persuade the Israeli public that, with Sadat gone, the Egyptians would
wait until all Sinai was in their hands, then renounce the peace
treaty with Israel and rejoin the Arab world.[20] Begin resisted this
pressure, all the more strongly after President Mubarak wrote to
reassure him that Egypt would continue to uphold the peace treaty
and the Camp David Accords after the Israeli withdrawal.

As minister of defense, Sharon was responsible for implementing the withdrawal. The most painful and problematic part of the
process was the evacuation of the Israeli civilians who had made
their homes in Sinai. Generous financial compensation was offered
to these settlers, but many of them refused to leave of their own
accord. Political extremists from the rest of the country infiltrated
into Sinai to demonstrate their solidarity and sabotage the withdrawal. Resistance to the withdrawal lasted several days and was accompanied by heartbreaking scenes on television. But in the end
the IDF succeeded in evacuating all the settlers and demonstrators
without bloodshed. Sharon ordered the IDF to destroy the town
of Yamit to its foundations instead of surrendering it intact to the
Egyptians as envisaged in the peace treaty.[21] He claimed that the
Egyptians themselves had requested the destruction of Yamit, but
this claim later turned out to be untrue. Sharon's real motives for
carrying out this barbaric act was a subject for speculation. One
suggestion was that Sharon deliberately made the whole process
more traumatic than it needed to be so that the Israeli public

would balk at the dismantling of any other settlements even for the sake of peace. What the whole episode proved was how ruthless Sharon could be in pursuit of his own designs and how little he cared for the opinion of his ministerial colleagues who had not approved the destruction of Yamit. Begin was well pleased with the energetic and efficient manner in which the evacuation was carried out. He, too, did not regard this as a precedent. Indeed, he proposed a resolution, which found a majority in the Knesset, intended to make it impossible for future governments to sign an agreement that involved withdrawal from the Land of Israel or the removal of Jewish settlements from this land.[22]

THE ROAD TO WAR

Once the Sinai issue was settled, Sharon concentrated even more single-mindedly on his grand design for Lebanon. He knew that the cabinet would not approve a war for the purpose of making Bashir Gemayel president of Lebanon and that it was anxious to avoid a clash with the Syrians, but he was confident of obtaining its consent for an offensive against the PLO. He told the cabinet what it wanted to hear while keeping the pressure on the IDF General Staff to prepare for a major war. Most of the officers on the General Staff accepted Yehoshua Saguy's forecast that a clash with the Syrians would be inevitable, that the Phalangists would remain largely passive, and that the PLO would be defeated but not destroyed. These doubts and reservations, however, were not reported to the cabinet.

One reason for the cabinet's reluctance to go to war in Lebanon was the fear of antagonizing the United States. In July 1981 Philip Habib, a senior American diplomat of Lebanese ancestry, had succeeded in brokering a cease-fire agreement between Israel and the PLO. The two parties, however, interpreted the agreement in different ways. The PLO considered that the agreement applied only to the Lebanese-Israeli front. The Israelis maintained that it required a complete halt to the terrorist attacks on all Israel's fronts, inside Israel, and anywhere in the world. The Americans held that the agreement meant precisely what it said: "There will be no hostile activities from Lebanon directed at targets in Israel [and vice versa]." In accordance with this interpretation, the Americans repeatedly warned the Israelis not to imperil the cease-fire.

The Americans knew much more about Sharon's plans than he realized. Samuel Lewis was one of the few foreign diplomats who understood that Sharon's ultimate aim was to cause the collapse of the Hashemite regime and its replacement by a Palestinian state on the East Bank of the river Jordan and that this was linked to his plans for Lebanon. Bashir Jemayel made no secret of his wish to expel the Palestinians from Lebanon, and Lewis put two and two together. Lewis also suspected that Sharon hoped that the defeat of the PLO in Lebanon would enable him to dictate his own terms in the negotiations on the future of the occupied territories and give Israel unchallenged control over the West Bank.

Sharon himself displayed the same deviousness in his relations with the Reagan administration as he did in his relations with his cabinet colleagues. He fed the Americans selective information that was intended to prove that the PLO was making a mockery of the cease-fire agreement and to establish Israel's right to retaliate. On 5 December 1981, for example, Sharon told Philip Habib, "If the terrorists continue to violate the ceasefire, we will have no choice but to wipe them out completely in Lebanon, destroy the PLO's infrastructure there. . . . We will eradicate the PLO in Lebanon." Habib was appalled by the brutality of Sharon's demarche. "General Sharon, this is the twentieth century and times have changed," he blurted out. "You can't go around invading countries just like that, spreading destruction and killing civilians. In the end, your invasion will grow into a war with Syria, and the entire region will be engulfed in flames!"[23]

In late May 1982, after the cabinet had reached a decision in principle to retaliate massively to the next PLO violation of the cease-fire, Sharon invited himself to Washington. His brief was to ascertain the likely response of the Reagan administration to an Israeli offensive in Lebanon. Sharon met Alexander Haig and his advisers in the State Department on 25 May. According to Haig's subsequent account, General Sharon shocked a roomful of State Department bureaucrats by sketching out two possible military campaigns: one that would pacify southern Lebanon and one that would redraw the political map of Beirut in favor of the Christian Phalange. It was clear to Haig that Sharon was putting the United States on notice: one more provocation by the Palestinians, and Israel would deliver a knockout blow to the PLO. Haig claims that in front of his advisers, and later in private, he repeated to Sharon what he had said many times before: unless there was an internationally recognized provocation, and unless Israeli retaliation was proportionate to any such provocation, an attack by Israel into Lebanon would have a devastating effect in the United States. "No one," retorted Sharon, "has the right to tell Israel what decision it should take in defense of its people."[24]

Sharon professed himself to be well pleased with the result of his mission. On his return to Israel he claimed that the Americans had tacitly agreed to a limited military operation in Lebanon. This is precisely what Haig feared Sharon might say. To avoid any misunderstanding Haig wrote to Begin, on 28 May, to underline his concern about possible Israeli military actions in Lebanon. In his own name and in the name of President Reagan, he urged Israel to continue to exercise complete restraint and to refrain from any action that would further damage the understanding underlying the cease-fire. In reply Begin employed language that demonstrated the depth of his feelings: "You advise us to exercise complete restraint and refrain from any action . . . Mr. Secretary, my dear friend, the man has not been born who will ever obtain from me consent to let Jews be killed by a bloodthirsty enemy and allow those who are responsible for the shedding of this blood to enjoy immunity."[25]

Haig and Reagan were in fact Israel's strongest supporters within the administration. Least friendly to Israel was Secretary of Defense Caspar Weinberger, who had purged the memorandum of understanding on strategic cooperation of many of the advantages it could have given Israel and insisted on its suspension and on punitive measures following Israel's annexation of the Golan Heights. Whereas Weinberger regarded Israel as a liability for the United States in its relations with the Arab world, and especially the oil-producing countries of the Persian Gulf, Haig regarded Israel as a strategic asset in the fight against Arab radicalism and international terrorism.

Toward Menachem Begin personally, Haig showed more tolerance and understanding than any of his colleagues. A tough and unsentimental former general, he sensed that Begin's aggressiveness sprang from a feeling of vulnerability. "Begin certainly believes that Israel is besieged," wrote Haig in his memoirs, "but his entire motive is to preserve the lives of Jews. He has no 'complex'—only an inescapable memory of the Holocaust." Begin once wrote to Haig that in his generation millions of Jews perished for two reasons: "(a) because they did not have the instruments with which to defend themselves, and (b) because nobody came to their rescue." Begin was fiercely determined that this must not happen again: "His letters, his conversation, his speeches—and, unquestionably, his thoughts—were dominated, when he was prime minister, by the sense that the lives of his people and the survival of Israel had been personally entrusted to him. He once said, when asked what he wanted to be remembered for, that he wished to be known to history as the man who established the borders of the state of Israel for all time."[26] Against this background it is not difficult to see why Haig's letter to Begin, following Sharon's visit, was so gentle or why it conveyed no threat of punishment. The letter certainly did not give Israel the green light to invade Lebanon, but neither did it project an unambiguously red light. Begin concluded that the United States accepted Israel's right to retaliate to an indisputable provocation by the PLO. He did not even bring Haig's letter to the attention of the cabinet.

On 3 June the casus belli that the hard-liners had been waiting for materialized. A group of Palestinian terrorists shot and grievously wounded Shlomo Argov, Israel's ambassador to London, outside the Dorchester Hotel. The gunmen belonged to the breakaway group led by Abu Nidal (Sabri al-Banna), Yasser Arafat's sworn enemy. Abu Nidal was supported by Iraq in his struggle against Arafat's "capitulationist" leadership of the PLO. Abu Nidal customarily referred to Arafat as "the Jewess's son." The PLO had passed a death sentence on Abu Nidal for assassinating some of its moderate members who advocated a dialogue with Israel. Mossad sources had intelligence to suggest that the attempt on Argov's life was intended to provoke an Israeli assault on Arafat's stronghold in Lebanon in order to break his power.

Begin was not interested in the details of who had shot Argov and why. An emergency meeting of the cabinet was summoned for the morning of 4 June. Ariel Sharon was on his way back from a secret trip to Romania. Begin was visibly agitated. "We will not stand for them attacking an Israeli ambassador!" he said. "An assault on an ambassador is tantamount to an attack on the State of Israel and we will respond to it!" Avraham Shalom, the head of the General Security Service, reported that the attack was most probably the work of the faction headed by Abu Nidal and suggested that Gideon Machanaimi, the prime minister's adviser on terrorism, elaborate on the nature of that organization. Machanaimi had hardly opened his mouth when Begin cut him off by saying, "They are all PLO." Rafael Eytan was equally dismissive of this detail. Shortly before entering the conference room, an intelligence aide told him that Abu Nidal's men were evidently responsible for the assassination attempt. "Abu Nidal, Abu Shmidal," he sneered; "we have to strike at the PLO!"[27]

Eytan recommended that the air force be sent to attack nine PLO targets in Beirut and in southern Lebanon. He pointed out that the likely PLO response would be to shell settlements along Israel's northern border. What he did not reveal was the intelligence in his possession that the PLO had issued orders to its front-line artillery units to respond automatically to an IAF attack on the Beirut headquarters with barrages against the Israeli settlements. Some reservations were expressed in the discussion about the scope of the proposed bombing in Beirut, especially because of the risks of civilian casualties and a hostile American reaction. Eytan assured the cabinet that precautions were being taken to avoid civilian casualties. The ministers approved the operational plan with a heavy heart, for they knew that the air strike would escalate into a full-scale war in Lebanon. Under the circumstances, however, they felt unable to stop the snowball from starting to roll.[28]

In the early afternoon Israeli jets hit the PLO targets in Beirut and in southern Lebanon. They bombed the sports stadium in Beirut, exploding the ammunition dump the PLO had established beneath the grandstand. Two hours later the PLO reacted precisely as it was expected to. It launched an artillery barrage along the entire border, targeting twenty villages in the Galilee and wounding three civilians. President Reagan sent a message to Begin, urging him not to widen the attack after the stadium bombing. Yasser Arafat was in Saudi Arabia, and the Saudis told the Americans that he was willing to suspend cross-border shelling. It was too late. Begin was in no mood to listen. His deepest emotions had been aroused. "Military targets . . . are completely immune," Begin wrote. "The purpose of the enemy is to kill—kill Jews, men, women, and children."[29]

To the cabinet ministers who convened at Begin's residence in the evening of 5 June, after the end of the Jewish Sabbath, it was clear that the moment of reckoning was at hand. Begin opened the cabinet meeting by saying,

> The hour of decision has arrived. You know what I have done, and what all of us have done, to prevent war and bereavement. But our fate is that in the Land of Israel there is no escape from fighting in the spirit of self-sacrifice. Believe me, the alternative to fighting is Treblinka, and we have resolved that there would be no more Treblinkas. This is the moment in which a courageous choice has to be made. The criminal ter-

rorists and the world must know that the Jewish people have
a right to self-defense, just like any other people.

What Begin proposed was a war to remove once and for all the
threat hanging over the Galilee, a war along the lines of the plan
for Operation Little Pines. In a letter to Reagan the following day,
he stated that the IDF would not advance more than forty kilometers into Lebanon. Ariel Sharon, who had returned from
Romania in the meantime, was invited by Begin to explain the operational plan to the cabinet. Sharon made no mention of the "big
plan." On the contrary, he spoke explicitly of a limit of forty kilometers and stressed that there was no intention of clashing with the
Syrian forces in Lebanon. Sharon and Eytan conveyed five principles to the cabinet: (1) the IDF would advance into Lebanon
along three main axes; (2) Beirut and its surroundings were not
among the targets of the operation; (3) the scope of the operation—up to forty kilometers from the international border; (4)
the duration of the operation—twenty-four to forty-eight hours;
and (5) there was no plan to have a showdown with the Syrians,
and the IDF would accordingly take care to keep a distance of at
least four kilometers from the Syrian lines.

However, Sharon did say that a showdown with the Syrians
could not be entirely ruled out, but that his intention was to
outflank them and threaten them without opening fire so as to
force them to retreat from the Bekaa Valley, along with the PLO
artillery. He did not say that in his own view, and in that of the
IDF experts, a clash with the Syrians was inescapable. This was
also the view of Sharon's deputy, Mordechai Zippori, who was
present at the meeting. A former brigadier, Zippori was the only
member of the cabinet apart from Sharon to have held a senior
rank in the IDF. Zippori told the cabinet in plain language that
the proposed plan would inevitably lead to a clash with the
Syrians. Begin took no notice of Zippori's warning. Simha Erlich
asked whether there was any intention of reaching Beirut. He
was assured by both Sharon and Begin that Beirut was completely
outside the scope of the proposed operation. Begin added that
this war, unlike some of their previous wars, would see no devi-
ations from the plan without an explicit decision by the cabinet.
Fourteen ministers, including Zippori, voted for the operation
while two abstained.[30] Begin himself drafted the cabinet communiqué, and it was he who changed the code name from Operation
Pines to Operation Peace for Galilee. The cabinet took the following decisions:

1. To instruct the Israel Defense Forces to place all the civilian population of the Galilee beyond the range of the terrorist fire from Lebanon, where they, their bases, and their
   headquarters are concentrated.
2. The name of the operation is Peace for Galilee.
3. During the operation, the Syrian army will not be attacked
   unless it attacks our forces.
4. Israel continues to aspire to the signing of a peace treaty
   with independent Lebanon, its territorial integrity preserved.[31]

Both Eytan and Sharon were later to claim that the cabinet knew
in advance that the scope of the operation would not be limited to
forty kilometers. Eytan writes in his memoirs that at the meeting
of 5 June they presented the "big plan" and that the cabinet approved it. He further insists that the decision was to destroy the
terrorists and that no limit was set to the IDF's advance. The maps
he unfolded in front of the cabinet, he claims, had arrows pointing as far north as the Beirut–Damascus highway, and there was no
room for misunderstanding what was being proposed.[32] All these
claims are contradicted by the record of the cabinet discussions and
by the text of the decision that was not made public. This text
stated that the cabinet approved the proposal brought by the minister of defense and the chief of staff. The proposal explicitly mentioned a limit of forty or at most forty-two kilometers, extending
to the south of Sidon. But in practice the war was conducted in accordance with the "big plan," which was submitted to the cabinet
only once, on 20 December 1981, and was decisively rejected by
it. Eytan's ploy, as he told some of his colleagues, was to obtain
permission for Operation Little Pines and to implement Operation
Big Pines.[33]

   Sharon conceded, in a lecture he gave five years after the event,
that the cabinet decision of 5 June 1982 spoke only in general
terms about placing the Galilee outside the range of enemy fire.
But he claimed that the political objective of the war required the
destruction not only of the PLO infrastructure in southern
Lebanon but also of its command posts and bases in Beirut and
south of Beirut. According to Sharon, "Everyone involved—in
the government, in the public at large, and in the IDF—knew exactly what was meant by the general formulation of the objectives." Yet none of the ministers who took the decision could
confirm this understanding. Sharon himself had specifically told

them that Beirut was outside the scope of his plan. It was he who chose to interpret the cabinet decision of 5 June as approval of the first stage of Operation Big Pines, and it was on the basis of the questionable interpretation that he ordered the IDF to prepare to capture all of the area up to Beirut, to cut the Beirut–Damascus highway, to link up with the Christian forces, and to destroy the Syrian forces.[34] Sharon knew from his experience in the army and the government that once the IDF hit its stride, it would be difficult to assert political control over its actions.

THE LEBANON WAR

On Sunday, 6 June 1982, four Israeli armored columns crossed the border into Lebanon, and seaborne forces landed south of Sidon (see map 10). On the first day of the war, they captured Nabatiyeh, surrounded all the Lebanese coastal towns up to Sidon, attacked the PLO forces wherever they could find them, and blocked their route of escape to the north. On the second day of the war, Sharon ordered the IDF to prepare to fight the Syrian forces on their eastern flank and to move toward the Beirut–Damascus highway. On the night of the third day, Bashir Gemayel came by helicopter to the IDF forward command post to meet Rafael Eytan. The leader of the Phalange was told that the IDF would link up with his forces and that he should prepare to capture Beirut and to form a new government in Lebanon. The conversation was not reported to the Israeli cabinet.[35] At this stage there was a broad national consensus, which included the Labor opposition, in support of Operation Peace for Galilee. On 8 June, Begin assured the Knesset that Israel did not want war with Syria and that all fighting would come to an end as soon as the IDF had cleared a zone of forty kilometers from Israel's northern border. "From this rostrum," declared Begin in dramatic tones, "I appeal to President Assad to direct the Syrian army not to attack Israel's soldiers and then they will come to no harm."

The view from Damascus was very different. Syria and Israel were engaged in a long-term contest for hegemony in the Levant. From Assad's perspective, Begin's appeal must have seemed like a challenge. As Assad's biographer has written,

Asad and Begin, champions of irreconcilable visions, came to blows, as they were bound sometime to do, over Lebanon in

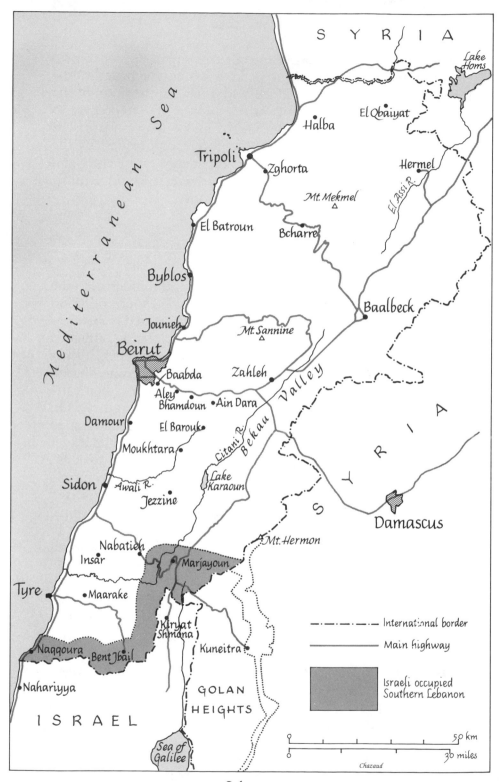

Lebanon

what was to be the goriest engagement in the struggle for the
Middle East. Lebanon in the 1980s was the hapless arena for
the collision between the dominant and expanded Israel which
Begin was determined to build and the rival regional order
with which Asad tried to stop him. Each man recognized the
other as the principal enemy who could put at risk everything
he held dear. In shorthand terms, "Greater Israel" went to war
against "Greater Syria," both controversial concepts of un-
certain definition but which certainly ruled each other out.
The struggle, in a way the climax of their political lives, very
nearly destroyed them both.[36]

Even as Begin was speaking, the IDF was engaged in fighting
Syrian forces in the central sector near Jezzine. To the cabinet
meeting on 8 June, Sharon proposed two alternatives: a frontal attack on the Syrian forces or a flanking maneuver designed to bring
about their voluntary retreat. The option of staying away from the
Syrian positions was not even mentioned. The cabinet approved
the flanking maneuver, which inevitably involved a major clash
since the Syrians stood their ground. To signal that they had no intention of retreating, the Syrians also moved surface-to-air missile
batteries into Lebanon. This was a defensive move, but Sharon
presented it to the cabinet as an offensive move and obtained its
permission to attack the SAM batteries. This decision, taken in
the morning of 9 June, changed the whole character of the conflict.

No sooner had the politicians given the green light than over
a hundred Israeli jets swept over the Bekaa Valley in what was to
be one of the biggest air battles in world history. The IAF attacked
the SAM-6 sites on both sides of the border, destroying them all.
It also shot down twenty-three Syrian MiGs without losing a single Israeli aircraft. At the same time the IDF armored columns
continued to pound the Syrian forces on the ground. The Syrians
fought tenaciously and brought in reinforcements, and the central
sector became the main battleground between the two armies.
Israeli forces advanced along the coast to Damur and to Lake
Karoun, in the Bekaa Valley. Their aim was to reach the
Beirut–Damascus highway and to cut off the Syrian forces from
the Lebanese capital, but they failed to achieve this aim before the
American-sponsored cease-fire came into effect on 11 June. Some
of the IDF commanders blamed the failure on the salami tactics by
which Sharon sought to transform a small operation into a big

operation. Every time Sharon wanted to go beyond what the cabinet had approved, he had to turn to Begin for permission. By telling Begin each additional change in the war plan was necessary in order to save the lives of Israeli soldiers, Sharon usually obtained Begin's permission, but the process took time. Begin himself later confirmed that Sharon kept him informed of every move made by the IDF—sometimes before it was taken, sometimes afterward.[37]

By the time the cease-fire came into force, the IDF had reached the southern outskirts of Beirut, a distance considerably longer than forty kilometers. Even after the cease-fire went into effect, the IDF continued to creep forward toward Beirut. That night Sharon flew to Jounieh for a meeting with Bashir Gemayel. Different conceptions of the character of the conflict quickly rose to the surface. Sharon wanted the Phalangists to move against the Palestinians who were cooped up in West Beirut and under heavy pressure. Gemayel was content to sit back and let the Israelis do all the fighting. It began to dawn on Sharon that the Lebanese Christians were not going to play an active role in the war against the PLO, yet he had no intention of abandoning this war. On his orders the IDF continued to proceed by stealth until it reached the Beirut–Damascus highway and linked up with the Christian forces. Within the ranks of the IDF there was much resentment of Sharon's methods, of the mounting level of casualties they entailed, and of the false statements made by their official spokesman. But by 13 June the ring around Beirut was closed and Sharon had achieved several of his objectives: the PLO was trapped in Beirut, his forces had linked up with Christian forces, and the Syrian units in Beirut had been isolated from the main body of Syrians in the Bakaa Valley. Operation Peace for Galilee had evolved into an Israeli-Syrian war and then into a siege of an Arab capital.

The next Israeli objective was to eradicate the PLO quasi-government from Beirut. The Christian forces were not prepared to undertake this task despite the offers of support from Israel. Yet for the IDF to capture Beirut in street-to-street fighting would have involved an unacceptable level of casualties. The method chosen was a combination of military pressure and psychological warfare to persuade the PLO that its only alternatives were surrender and annihilation. Air attacks, naval guns, and artillery barrages, as well as loudspeakers and leaflets, were used in a campaign of pressure and intimidation. The campaign was directed against the PLO positions, but it inflicted immense suffering and heavy casualties on the Palestinian population of Beirut.

During the next two months the siege of Beirut was steadily intensified. On 4 July the IDF cut off the water and power supplies to the city but restored them a few days later, following a protest from President Reagan. Four hundred Israeli tanks and a thousand guns kept up the bombardment of Beirut. By the end of the first week in July, five hundred buildings had been destroyed by shells and bombs. On 1 August the Israeli forces stepped up their artillery, aerial, and naval bombardment of Beirut. A paratroop unit occupied Beirut's international airport, while Israeli tanks entered the southern outskirts of the city. The methods used provoked unrest within the army, political protest at home, and mounting international criticism. President Reagan lost patience with Israel and joined in the criticism. He demanded of Begin an immediate halt to the shelling of Beirut and threatened to review U.S.-Israeli relations. Begin replied with a telegram to Reagan that was bizarre in the extreme and suggested that he lived in a different world:

> Now may I tell you, dear Mr President, how I feel these days when I turn to the creator of my soul in deep gratitude. I feel as a Prime Minister empowered to instruct a valiant army facing "Berlin" where amongst innocent civilians, Hitler and his henchmen hide in a bunker deep beneath the surface. My generation, dear Ron, swore on the altar of God that whoever proclaims his intent to destroy the Jewish state or the Jewish people, or both, seals his fate, so that which happened once on instructions from Berlin—with or without inverted commas—will never happen again.[38]

The text of the telegram, which was published in the *Jerusalem Post,* shocked many Israelis, who felt that the memory of the Holocaust should not be invoked to justify the Lebanon War or the siege of Beirut. They were also disturbed by the palpable signs that their prime minister had lost touch with reality and was merely chasing the ghosts of the past. Chaika Grossman, a left-wing member of the Knesset who had actually fought in the Warsaw Ghetto, implored Begin, "Return to reality! We are not in the Warsaw Ghetto, we are in the State of Israel." The writer Amos Oz, who had described Operation Peace for Galilee as "a typical Jabotinskyian fantasy," conveyed a similar message to the prime minister: "This urge to revive Hitler, only to kill him again and again, is the result of pain that poets can permit themselves to use, but not statesmen . . . even at great emotional cost personally, you must remind yourself and the public that elected you its leader that Hitler is dead and burned to ashes."[39]

Alexander Haig, one of the few people who thought that Begin did not suffer from a "Holocaust complex," was himself a victim of Israel's war in Lebanon. During the siege of Beirut he thought that the moment had come to move all foreign forces—Syrian, Palestinian, and Israeli—out of Lebanon and to return the country to the Lebanese under suitable international protection and guarantees. His strategy was to use the shock of the Israeli attack to force the PLO out of Beirut.[40] But toward the end of June he was forced to resign amid allegations that he had placed his country in an untenable position by tacitly approving the Israeli invasion of Lebanon. He was replaced by George Shultz, one of whose first acts as secretary of state was to send Philip Habib to negotiate an end to the fighting around Beirut. Yasser Arafat let it be known that he was prepared to withdraw his men from the city, if appropriate terms and guarantees could be worked out.

The withdrawal of the PLO was now only a matter of time, but one problem was that its members had nowhere to go. Ariel Sharon came up with a suggestion. He asked an Egyptian intermediary to persuade Arafat to lead the PLO back to Jordan and said that, if Arafat accepted, Israel would force King Hussein to make way for the organization. "One speech by me," boasted Sharon, "will make King Hussein realize that the time has come to pack his bags." The message was conveyed to Arafat, who asked the intermediary to give Sharon an immediate reply: "1. Jordan is not the home of the Palestinians. 2. You are trying to exploit the agony of the Palestinian people by turning a Palestinian-Lebanese dispute into a Palestinian-Jordanian contradiction." Arafat also suggested that Sharon wanted to provoke Jordanian-Palestinian conflict to give Israel an excuse for occupying the East Bank of the Jordan. When Sharon heard Arafat's reply, he responded with an obscene curse in Arabic.[41]

Philip Habib's aim was an arrangement whereby the Palestinian and Syrian forces would withdraw from Beirut, Israel would not try to enter the city, and the Lebanese government would regain complete control over its capital. The American and French governments agreed to assign troops to a multinational force whose task would be to supervise the evacuation. Begin and Sharon reacted very differently to the American offer to send Marines to Beirut. Begin wanted a political agreement and was ready to enter into negotiations with the Lebanese government. Sharon wanted to change the regime in Lebanon in accordance with his "big plan" and was fearful that American soldiers would get in his way.[42] On 10 August, Habib submitted a draft agreement to Israel. At this point Sharon, impatient with what he regarded as American meddling, ordered unprecedented saturation bombing of Beirut in which at least three hundred people were killed. Reagan was outraged and made another call to Jerusalem. "Menachem," he said, "I think we've been very patient. Unless the bombing ceases immediately, I'm fearful of grave consequences in the relations between our countries." If Begin's trust in Sharon was being eroded, the cabinet had no trust at all. At its meeting of 12 August, the cabinet stripped the minister of defense of most of his powers, such as the power to order the use of the air force, the armored force, and the artillery, and vested them in the prime minister in the event that the cabinet was unable to meet.

Habib eventually succeeded in arranging for the withdrawal of the PLO to Tunisia. A first contingent of fighters left by sea on 21 August. Arafat left on 30 August aboard a Greek merchant ship with the U.S. Sixth Fleet providing cover. Altogether, 8,500 men were evacuated by sea to Tunisia. Another 2,500 men made the journey by land to Syria, Iraq, and Yemen. Egypt, Saudi Arabia, and the Persian Gulf sheikhdoms refused to accept PLO evacuees. After seventy-five days of heavy fighting, the PLO was banished from its stronghold in Lebanon to the periphery of the Arab world, a good deal more than forty kilometers from Israel's border. Begin was pleased with the outcome and announced that Operation Peace for Galilee had achieved most of its objectives.

To Sharon it seemed that the stage was now set for implementing phase two of his "big plan": the creation of a new political order in Lebanon. The Lebanese presidential election was scheduled for 23 August, and the weeks of the siege were used for political pressures and manipulations behind the scenes. The Israelis wanted the deputies to the parliament, who elect the president, to feel that national survival depended on choosing a candidate acceptable to Israel. Bashir Gemayel needed Israel's help to obtain the two-thirds majority required by the constitution because a large proportion of the deputies lived in areas under Israeli control. A united front consisting of Muslim as well as rival Maronite deputies decided to boycott the election on the grounds that it was being held in the shadow of Israeli guns. The Israelis had a list of all the deputies, and they did what they could to assist Gemayel's supporters and to impede his opponents from arriving at Beirut to cast their vote. Bashir Gemayel was elected president by 57 out of the 62 deputies who attended the session. When the result of the vote became known, there was ecstatic rejoicing in the Maronite quarters of Beirut. Israelis, too, joined in the jubilation. One group of Mossad men fired a full case of ammunition into the air, convinced that their patience and perseverance had finally paid off.[43]

The telegram from Jerusalem to the victorious candidate read, "Warmest wishes from the heart on the occasion of your election. May God be with you, dear friend, in the fulfilment of your great historic mission, for the liberty of Lebanon and its independence. Your friend. Menachem Begin." Begin, Sharon, and Shamir made no bones of their expectation that, free from Syrian toils, Lebanon would sign a peace treaty with them. Any Syrian obstruction to this program, Shamir declared, would be "a brutal, insolent threat to peace." Bashir Gemayel himself called for the withdrawal of all foreign armies from Lebanon—Syrian, Israeli, and Palestinian. In Syrian eyes he committed the heinous crime of putting Syria on the same footing as Israel.[44] Having received from the Israelis a leg up in mounting the presidential horse, Gemayel was anxious to demonstrate his independence, to widen his domestic political base, and to emphasize the Arab rather than the Israeli orientation of his foreign policy. But the more evasive he appeared, the more insistently the Israelis demanded an early discharge of his political debt. The Israelis wanted nothing short of a peace treaty and full diplomatic relations with Lebanon, as they had previously achieved with Egypt. What the Israelis seemed unable to understand was that, unlike Egypt, Lebanon was too small and too weak to defy the entire Arab world.

On the night of 1 September, Bashir Gemayel was summoned to a secret meeting with Begin in Nahariya, a coastal resort in northern Israel. Begin kept him waiting for two hours. The fragility of the understanding between them did not take long to manifest itself. While Begin demanded open normalization in the relations between Israel and Lebanon and the signing of a peace treaty, Gemayel pleaded for time to consolidate his position and merely mentioned the possibility of a nonaggression pact. Another bone of contention was the future of Major Sa'ad Haddad, the Christian militia leader in southern Lebanon who was financed by the Israelis. Begin remarked that Haddad at least knew which side his bread was buttered on and held him as an example to be emulated. Gemayel countered that he was going to put Haddad on trial for desertion from the Lebanese army. When Begin cut in with the suggestion that Haddad be appointed chief of staff, the meeting disintegrated into a shouting match. The loudest voice in the room was that of Sharon. Sharon reminded Gemayel that Israel had Lebanon in its grasp and told him he would be well advised to do what was expected of him. Gemayel held out both arms to Sharon. "Put the handcuffs on!" he cried. "I am your vassal." The meeting ended abruptly and acrimoniously and without any agreement being reached.[45]

On the day that Begin met Gemayel, President Reagan unveiled a new peace plan for the Middle East. He said that the departure of the Palestinians from Beirut dramatized more than ever the homelessness of the Palestinian people. His plan was for self-government by the Palestinians of the West Bank and Gaza in association with Jordan. He ruled out both a Palestinian state and annexation by Israel. Additional Israeli settlements in the territories would be an obstacle to peace, said Reagan, and the status of Jerusalem had still to be decided. The message was clear: the United States rejected the Israeli claim for permanent control over the West Bank and Gaza. Equally clear was another message: the United States did not think that Israel was entitled to exploit the recent carnage in Lebanon to implement its grand design for Greater Israel. Reagan and his advisers grasped the ultimate territorial purpose of Sharon's big plan, and they firmly rejected it. They acknowledged that Israel was entitled to security along its northern border, but not that it had a right to territorial expansion at the expense of the Palestinians. Small wonder that Begin rejected the Reagan peace plan with all the vehemence he could muster or that he was supported in striking this defiant posture by a large majority of his fellow parliamentarians.

On 14 September, three weeks after his election, Bashir Gemayel was assassinated in his party headquarters, most probably by agents of Syrian intelligence. The assassination knocked out the central prop from underneath Israel's entire policy in Lebanon. With Gemayel's violent removal from the scene, Sharon's plan for a new political order in Lebanon—a plan predicated from the start on Bashir Gemayel personally—collapsed like a house of cards. Sharon feared that the leftist militias and a couple of thousand PLO men allegedly still at large in Beirut would destroy the prospect of a stable, pro-Israeli regime in Lebanon. The assassination was used as the pretext for sending Israeli forces into West Beirut the following day to take up the areas formerly held by the

PLO. Sharon ordered the IDF commanders to allow the Phalangists to enter the Palestinian refugee camps Sabra and Shatila, on the south side of Beirut, in order to "clean out" the terrorists who, he claimed, were lurking there.[46]

Inside the camps the revenge-thirsty Christian militiamen perpetrated a terrible massacre, killing hundreds of men, women, and children. Israel estimated the number of dead at seven to eight hundred, while the Palestinian Red Crescent put the number at over two thousand. The carnage went on from the evening of Thursday, 16 September, until Sunday. Already on Thursday evening, not long after dropping their Christian allies outside the camps, Israeli soldiers got wind of the massacre but did nothing to stop it. Begin heard about the massacre when listening to the BBC on Saturday afternoon. He called Sharon, who promised to get a report from the IDF. At first official spokesmen tried to obscure the fact that the Christian militia men entered the refugee camps with the knowledge and help of the IDF commanders. Begin himself said, more than a touch self-righteously, *"Goyim* [non-Jews] are killing *goyim,* and the whole world is trying to hang Jews for the crime." Nevertheless, as Rabbi Arthur Hertzberg, a liberal American-Jewish leader, prophetically observed, Menachem Begin could not remain in office "if he has squandered Israel's fundamental asset—its respect for itself and the respect of the world."[47] The sense of shock and revulsion in Israel and the international outcry forced the government to appoint a commission of inquiry under Supreme Court Justice Yitzhak Kahan.

In the months after the massacre, Israel continued to sink deeper and deeper into the Lebanese quagmire. The appointment of Amin Gemayel to succeed his younger brother as president did nothing to restore Israel's sagging fortunes in Lebanon. For whereas Bashir had maintained close links with Israel, Amin had always been regarded as Syria's man in Lebanon. Amin Gemayel predictably declined to collaborate with Israel in forging a new political order in Lebanon. The balance sheet of Israel's relationship with the Maronite community was thus singularly disappointing. Within the space of a few months, in the second half of 1982, Israel learned, the hard way, that "Bashir Jumayyil did not fully represent the Phalange, that the Phalange did not represent the whole Maronite community, that the Maronite community did not speak for all Lebanese Christians, and that Lebanon's Christians were no longer assured of their ascendancy."[48] It was no end of a lesson.

The Kahan Commission presented its report on 7 February 1983. It concluded that Israel bore indirect responsibility for the massacre at Sabra and Shatila, inasmuch as the Phalange entered the refugee camps with the knowledge of the government and with the encouragement of the army. It recommended the removal of the minister of defense and a number of senior officers from their posts. Sharon immediately announced his rejection of the findings and the recommendations of the Kahan Commission. On 14 February the cabinet decided, by a majority of sixteen against Sharon's single vote, to accept the recommendations of the Kahan report. Sharon remained in the cabinet as minister without portfolio. He was replaced as minister of defense by Moshe Arens, the ambassador to the United States.

Arens, a former professor of aeronautical engineering at the Technion, was a Herut hard-liner. Yet he understood that neither the public nor the army would put up with a prolonged and purposeless presence in Lebanon or with the daily attrition in casualties. Under his direction, David Kimche, a senior Mossad official and a strong supporter of the Christian conception that had guided Israeli policy in Lebanon, conducted negotiations with representatives of the Lebanese government. The negotiations required over thirty-five sessions and high-level American involvement, including a ten-day shuttle by George Shultz. On 17 May 1983 Israel and Lebanon signed an agreement that formally terminated the state of war and recognized the international border between them as inviolable. The parties undertook to prevent the use of one country's territory for terrorist activity against the other country. Israel was to withdraw its forces to a distance of forty to forty-five kilometers from the international border to an area defined as a "security zone." The area north of the security zone was to be under the control of the United Nations Interim Force in Lebanon. The agreement also affirmed that Major Sa'ad Haddad's militia would be recognized as a Lebanese "auxiliary force" and accorded proper status under Lebanese law. There was one inherent flaw in the agreement: it was conditional on Syria's withdrawing its forces from Lebanon, and Syria did not oblige.

In the summer of 1983 the decision was taken to withdraw Israeli troops from Lebanon in stages without waiting for a concurrent withdrawal by Syria or the implementation of the 17 May agreement by the Lebanese. Once Israel began to withdraw unilaterally and unconditionally, the diplomatic concept underlying the agreement fell away. Moshe Levi, the new chief of staff, was not interested in the political in-fighting that had been part and parcel of the war in Lebanon. He wanted to reduce the size of the army committed to Lebanon, and he wanted his troops redeployed so as to reduce casualties. He and Arens persuaded the cabinet to agree to the withdrawal of Israeli troops from the outskirts of Beirut to the more easily defendable line along the Awali River. The pullback was twice postponed at the request of the Americans, who wanted to give the Christians a chance to consolidate their position. But in August the Israeli forces began their withdrawal from the Shouf mountains.[49] This move did not adversely affect their security. But it had two grave consequences for Lebanon. First, it permitted Syria to regain control over the Beirut–Damascus highway and to reassert its grip over the Lebanese capital. Second, it provoked a fresh round in the age-old struggle for hegemony in the Shouf between the Druze and the Christian militias. The Druze easily gained the upper hand and went on to sack and destroy entire Christian villages, turning thousands of their inhabitants into refugees. The retreating Israelis were caught in the cross fire. Even the Shiites, who had originally welcomed Israel's entry into Lebanon because of the tensions between themselves and the Palestinians, now turned all their fury against the Israeli forces of occupation and against the Christians. Intercommunal fighting was nothing new in Lebanon, but now all the communities had a common enemy—Israel.

Moreover, the war in Lebanon had a very negative effect on Arab perceptions of Israel. By honoring its commitment to withdraw from Sinai, Israel had gained much credit in Egypt and some credit in the rest of the Arab world. Egypt could hold its head high and show the skeptics that the peace with Israel yielded tangible benefits. By invading Lebanon, Israel dissipated all the credit and placed Egypt in a highly uncomfortable position. The massive force that Israel deployed in Lebanon, the scale of the suffering it inflicted, the siege of Beirut, and the massacre in Sabra and Shatila stunned the entire Arab world, and above all the Egyptians. The Egyptians were convinced that Israel's aim was to impose on Lebanon a separate peace by force. While they had an interest in other Arab countries following in their footsteps and making peace with Israel, they utterly rejected the means employed by Israel to this end. The Egyptians did not renounce the peace treaty with Israel, but they recalled their ambassador from Tel Aviv, froze the process of normalization, and took refuge in what Minister of State Boutros Boutros-Ghali was first to term a "cold peace."[50]

THE END OF THE BEGIN ERA

On 28 August 1983 Menachem Begin announced to his cabinet his intention of resigning from the post of prime minister and retiring from political life. The cabinet was completely unprepared for the announcement, and some of his colleagues tried to dissuade him, but to no avail. The only reason Begin gave the cabinet for his decision was a personal one: "I cannot go on." For a number of weeks Begin looked increasingly gaunt, withdrawn, and almost listless. Rumors had been circulating about his poor health and poor performance. But his aides had been doing their best to conceal from the public the full extent of his physical and psychological exhaustion. That evening hundreds of people gathered outside the prime minister's residence. They included right-wingers who called on him to carry on and supporters of Peace Now who congratulated him on his courageous decision.

After his resignation Begin became a recluse. He retreated to his home a man broken in body and spirit. The reason for his resignation remained something of a puzzle, since he himself never explained why he could no longer carry on. Psychologically, he had always tended to swing from high elation to deep depression, and the death of his wife, Aliza, in September 1982, plunged him into deep depression. On the political plane the war in Lebanon was probably the main cause for his disappointment and despair. The war that Begin said would last two days was now in its second year, with no end in sight. The cost of the war in human lives, to which Begin was particularly sensitive, was mounting all the time. A group of demonstrators outside his house carried a sign on which the number of casualties was constantly updated. At the time of Begin's resignation, over five hundred Israeli soldiers had lost their lives in Lebanon. Bereaved parents blamed Begin for the senseless death of their loved ones. One father sent Begin a harrowing letter that ended with the following words: "And if you have a spark of conscience and humanity within you, may my great pain—the suffering of a father in Israel whose entire world has been destroyed—pursue you forever, during your sleeping hours and when you are awake—may it be a mark of Cain upon you for all time."[51] Begin did have a spark of conscience and humanity in him, at least when it came to Jewish lives, and the burden of guilt finally overcame him.

The Likud's Central Committee elected Yitzhak Shamir to succeed Begin. The contrast of temperament, personality, and style could hardly have been greater. One was volatile and mercurial; the other, solid and reliable. One was charismatic and domineering; the other, dull and dour. One was a spell-binding orator; the other could hardly string two sentences together. Shamir's grayness of character and lack of charisma may actually have helped him get elected. Some Likud members saw him as a sort of Israeli Clement Attlee, as a safe pair of hands, and a welcome antidote to the drama and passions of Begin's Churchillian style of leadership.

In terms of outlook and ideology, however, the difference between Shamir and Begin was not all that great. Both were disciples of Ze'ev Jabotinsky. Both were dedicated to the Land of Israel. Both subscribed to the lachrymose version of Jewish history, seeing it as a long series of trials and tribulations culminating in the Holocaust. Both were suspicious of outside powers, and both were strong advocates of Israeli self-reliance. In some ways Shamir was more intransigent than Begin. For Shamir there could be no retreat from any territory, not just the territory of the Land of Israel. That was why he opposed withdrawal from Sinai and why he supported the annexation of the Golan Heights. He was generally unreceptive to the idea of bargaining and compromise, his natural instinct being to stand firm in the face of external pressure.

By 10 October, Shamir had formed a coalition that comprised many of the same ministers and parties as before, and the Knesset approved the guidelines of its policy. The new government's main task was to get the IDF out of Lebanon under the best possible conditions and with the least possible risk to Israel. Soon after assuming office, Shamir was handed a paper by the IDF planning division. The planners saw no prospect of Syrian withdrawal from Lebanon and accordingly recommended unilateral Israeli withdrawal. This recommendation ran counter to the trend toward confrontation with Syria that was manifesting itself in Washington under the leadership of George Shultz. Shultz had come to the conclusion that Syria was not amenable to diplomatic pressure and persuasion and that the only language it understood was military force.

The strategic dialogue between the United States and Israel was renewed during Shamir's visit to Washington in November 1983. Shamir agreed not to initiate another unilateral withdrawal as long as U.S. Marines remained in Lebanon and not to initiate a major act of war against Syria without prior consultation with Washington. The allies also agreed to act jointly to exert "constant tactical and strategic pressure on Syria" to force it to enter into negotiations with Amin Gemayel about the withdrawal of its forces from Lebanon. This policy of toughness, however, failed to achieve its objectives. The Syrians had no intention of honoring the 17 May agreement, which completely ignored their interests. The American-Israeli axis was not equal to the task of deterring Syria or keeping President Gemayel's domestic opponents at bay. In March 1984 he was summoned to Damascus and ordered to abrogate the 17 May agreement. Israel's policy shifted as a result from reliance on the Lebanese government and army to seeking security arrangements in southern Lebanon in collaboration with its Christian proxies there. Under Shamir's leadership Israel thus remained involved in the protracted and costly, but inconclusive, conflict in Lebanon.

The political results of the war could hardly have been more disappointing, especially when measured against the expectations of Ariel Sharon, the war's chief architect. Sharon's "big plan" was based on a series of assumptions that collapsed like a row of dominoes when put to the test. The greatest misconception, and the one underlying all the others, lay in thinking that Israel's military superiority could be translated into lasting political achievements. In fact, the exchange rate between military power and political gains has never been favorable in Israel's case, and the Lebanon War was no exception. Sharon misread the Israeli political map by not realizing that national consensus was bound to fracture, given the offensive and expansionist character of this war. In his planning for the destruction of the PLO, Sharon underestimated the organization's resilience and the nonmilitary sources of its strength. Sharon also misread the Lebanese political map and deluded himself in believing that Maronite hegemony could be asserted in the face of all the opposition. Sharon counted on political change inside Lebanon to start a chain reaction that would eclipse all of Israel's enemies and catapult it into a position of unchallengeable regional mastery. The political change that Sharon sought in Lebanon could only be achieved over Syria's dead body. Sharon realized, though he never admitted this to his cabinet colleagues, that the expulsion of the Syrian forces from Lebanon was essential if Israel was to emerge as the dominant regional power. But, once again, he underestimated Syria's tenacity and resilience. Syria suffered serious military setbacks during the Lebanon War, but, like Gamal Abdel Nasser in the Suez War, Hafez al-Assad snatched a political victory out of the jaws of military defeat.

While Sharon was the main driving force behind the war in Lebanon, Begin bore the ultimate political responsibility for it.

Although his expectations were not as grandiose as Sharon's, Begin was also a victim of wishful thinking. By dealing a mortal blow to the PLO in Lebanon, Begin hoped not only to achieve peace for the Galilee but also to defeat the Palestinian claim to statehood in what he and his party regarded as the Land of Israel. Once the PLO had been crushed in its stronghold in Lebanon, so the argument ran, all effective Palestinian resistance to the imposition of permanent Israeli rule in the West Bank and Gaza would come to an end. In short, for Begin no less than for Sharon and Eytan, the war in Lebanon was a war for the Land of Israel. But it was absurd to assume that the Palestinian problem would be solved by military action in Lebanon, since the roots of the problem did not lie in Lebanon. Far from relegating the Palestinian problem to the sidelines, the war in Lebanon, and especially the massacre in Sabra and Shatila, served to focus international attention on the need to find a solution to this problem. Far from reducing international pressure on Israel to withdraw from the occupied territories, the war triggered a shift in American policy from acceptance of autonomy for the Palestinians in accordance with the Camp David Accords to the Reagan plan, which called for Israeli withdrawal from the West Bank and Gaza to make way for a Palestinian homeland in association with Jordan. And far from adding a peace treaty with Lebanon to the one with Egypt, the invasion of Lebanon strained the relations with Egypt almost to the breaking point.

Any pretension to a strategy of working toward comprehensive peace with the Arab world that Begin may have entertained until June 1982 was finally and irrevocably destroyed by the invasion of Lebanon. The war in Lebanon was intended to secure Israel's hold over Judea and Samaria. This was not the war's declared aim, but it was the ideological conception behind it. All Israel's previous wars, with the exception of the Suez War, had been wars of no choice, wars that were imposed on Israel by the Arabs. Even the Suez War enjoyed complete national consensus because it was seen as a legitimate response to Arab provocation, was short, and did not involve high casualties. The war in Lebanon, on the other hand, by Begin's own admission was "a war of choice." War was not imposed on Israel by its Arab enemies. The war path was deliberately chosen by its leaders in pursuit of power and some highly controversial political gains. Much of the credit that Begin received for making peace with Egypt in his first term in office was thus wiped out by the ill-conceived and ill-fated war for which he was responsible during his second term.

Begin's premiership provides an interesting illustration of what students of international relations sometimes call the security dilemma. In the absence of a world government, individual states are driven to acquire more and more power in order to escape the impact of the power of others. But the quest for absolute security is self-defeating because it generates insecurity on the part of one's enemies and prompts them to resort to countermeasures that they see as self-defense. The result is a vicious circle of power accumulation and insecurity. In the case of Begin the trauma of the Holocaust produced a passionate desire to procure absolute safety and security for the Jewish people, but it also blinded him to the fears and anxieties that his own actions generated among Israel's Arab neighbors. By invading Lebanon in 1982, Begin thought he would turn the corner, defeat all Israel's enemies once and for all, and achieve perfect security for his people. But there are no corners in a vicious circle.

11

Political Paralysis

1984–1988

EMBROILMENT IN THE Lebanese quagmire and a rapidly worsening economic crisis furnished the backdrop to the general election of 23 July 1984. Against this backdrop, with inflation running at 400 percent, the Labor Alignment was expected to win by a landslide, but the actual result was more like a draw. The Alignment, under the leadership of Shimon Peres, went down from 47 to 44 seats in the Knesset, while the Likud, under the leadership of Yitzhak Shamir, dropped from 48 to 41 seats. Peres was unsuccessful in his efforts to form a narrow coalition because the religious parties preferred the Likud. With some reluctance he therefore adopted the alternative of a grand coalition embracing the Likud. The new government was called a government of national unity, but this was a misnomer, given that the two parties were separated by a yawning ideological gap, with the Likud still firmly wedded to the integrity of the homeland and the Alignment pledged to seek territorial compromise.

Whereas national unity governments had existed before in Israel's history, the rotation agreement worked out by Peres and Shamir was entirely novel and even bizarre. Peres was to serve as prime minister, with Shamir as deputy prime minister and foreign minister in the first twenty-five months in the life of the government; during the remaining twenty-five months the two men were to swap positions. Yitzhak Rabin was to serve as minister of defense throughout the two halves of the government's life. On 13 September, following protracted negotiations and horse-trading, Peres presented the new government to the Knesset. In addition to the Alignment and the Likud, the government comprised the National Religious Party, Shinui, Shas, Morasha, and Agudat Israel. There were twenty-five ministers, six of whom were ministers without portfolio. The cabinet included one former president, three former prime ministers, four former defense ministers, and three former chiefs of staff.

The power of the two main parties was roughly equal. Mapam left the Alignment and went into opposition, but Ezer Weizman, who had run on an independent ticket and won three seats, eventually decided to join the Alignment. Altogether the government had the support of ninety-seven members of the Knesset. An inner cabinet was established, consisting of five members from the Alignment and five members from the Likud. The smaller parties were not represented. This inner cabinet assumed the powers formerly exercised by the ministerial defense committee and was to make all the major decisions. A majority was required to reach a decision or to make a recommendation to the full cabinet. What this meant in practice was that each party had a veto over policy proposals by the other party. And since the two parties were so deeply divided in their attitudes to the Arabs and to the peace process, this was a recipe for political paralysis.

The basic guidelines of the government's program had thirty-three points. On the foreign policy front the main points were withdrawing the IDF from Lebanon while ensuring the security of the northern settlements; consolidating the peace with Egypt; continuing the Camp David peace process; a call to Jordan to begin peace negotiations; the rejection of a Palestinian state in the West Bank and of negotiations with the PLO; no annexation of the West Bank during the life of the government; the establishment of five or six new Jewish settlements on the West Bank within a year and more settlements at a later date; and the preservation of united Jerusalem under exclusive Israeli sovereignty, with free access to their holy places to members of all faiths. These basic guidelines represented the lowest common denominator among all the parties to the coalition. The two main parties wielded the power of veto over specific policy proposals, even if they corresponded to the basic guidelines.[1]

THE ODD COUPLE

Peres and Shamir were both born in Poland, but they were poles apart in temperament, style, and attitude toward the Arabs. Peres was flexible and open-minded; Shamir was rigid and dogmatic. Peres was a technocrat who relied heavily on the advice of scientists and experts; Shamir was an ideologue whose commitment to permanent retention of all of the Land of Israel was unshakable. Peres was sensitive to the slightest sign of change in Arab attitudes to Israel; Shamir believed that any change in Arab attitudes was merely tactical and that the ultimate aim of all Arabs was the destruction of the State of Israel and the throwing of the Jews into the sea. This belief was encapsulated in his often repeated saying "The Arabs are the same Arabs, and the sea is the same sea." Peres believed that the status quo in the occupied territories could not be sustained for very long; Shamir regarded the preservation of the status quo as the supreme national interest. The foreign policy styles of the two men were also markedly different. Peres was predisposed to debate and dialogue with political opponents, to cultivating international contacts, to exploiting opportunities and making deals. He combined extraordinary talent for persuasion and conciliation with dogged tenacity. Shamir, by contrast, was sullen and suspicious, prone to seeing only dangers and traps, contemptuous of compromises, and steadfast in his resistance to international pressures to make peace. The two-headed government they formed was bound to be at cross-purposes and to speak with more than one voice. The arrangement they worked out for sharing the premiership was certainly odd, and they themselves were described, not inaccurately, as the odd couple.

Despite the unwieldy character of his government, Peres was a remarkably effective and successful prime minister during his two-year term in office, especially on the home front. He had three main priorities: to bring inflation under control, to get the IDF out of Lebanon, and to revive the Middle Eastern peace process. Peres came to the premiership well prepared. A team of young academics, known as the 100-day team, had worked out a detailed set of proposals for action in domestic and foreign affairs in the expectation of an Alignment victory at the polls. The team was headed by Dr. Yossi Beilin, a thoughtful and imaginative political scientist and a former spokesman of the Alignment who combined uncommonly dovish views on relations with the Arabs with complete personal loyalty to Peres. Beilin was appointed cabinet secretary and continued to work very closely with Peres. Dr. Nimrod Novik, another member of the team, became the political adviser to Peres. Avraham Tamir, a former general who had been head of the IDF planning division, became the director general of the prime minister's office. Peres was well served by this team of professionals. His first achievement was to conquer hyperinflation, stabilize the economy, reduce unemployment, and regenerate economic growth.

Peres's second achievement was to get the IDF out of Lebanon. The war in Lebanon had cost Israel 660 dead, exacerbated its economic difficulties, subverted the national consensus on security, and tarnished Israel's image abroad. The war also spawned a new militant group named Hizbullah (Party of God) which, with Iranian and Syrian support, conducted a fierce guerrilla war to drive Israel's soldiers out of Lebanon. All the efforts to obtain the withdrawal of Syrian forces from Lebanon in return for withdrawing Israel's forces had failed. The IDF chiefs favored an orderly unilateral withdrawal in order to cut their losses in Lebanon. Yet most of the Likud ministers remained unconvinced of the necessity to withdraw. In the struggle to persuade the cabinet to agree to disengage from Lebanon, Peres found in Yitzhak Rabin a strong ally. Rabin presented a detailed plan to the inner cabinet for a phased withdrawal that would leave the IDF patrolling a narrow security zone along the border in collaboration with its proxy, the South Lebanon Army (SLA). The Likud ministers, led by Shamir, opposed the plan, but their ranks broke when David Levy, the minister of housing, voted for the plan. This meant that the plan could be recommended to the full cabinet. On 14 January 1985 the cabinet approved the plan. Nearly all the Likud ministers, including Shamir, Sharon, and Arens, voted against, but the decision was reached with the votes of Levy, the Alignment, and the smaller coalition partners. A public opinion poll showed that over 90 percent of the population supported the decision. The withdrawal from Lebanon was carried out in stages between February and June. The bulk of the troops returned to their bases inside Israel. Small forces remained in the security zone and coordinated their activities with the SLA, commanded by General Antoine Lahad. From time to time the IDF forces clashed with guerrilla units, especially from Hizbullah, and Katyusha rockets were occasionally fired on Israel's northern settlements.

Nevertheless, the tension eased, and there was a general sense of relief that the nightmare was over.

While working to extricate Israel from Lebanon, Peres made a general effort to rebuild Israel's reputation in the international arena. The previous government had forfeited a great deal of international sympathy by its invasion of Lebanon and by the diplomatic intransigence it displayed in relation to the Palestinians and Jordan. When Peres came to power, the peace process was almost dead and a sustained effort was required to convince the Arabs and the world that peace in the Middle East was not a lost cause. With characteristic vigor Peres threw himself into the task of changing the climate surrounding Israel's relations with its neighbors. He projected himself as a statesman with vision and Israel as a rational and reasonable actor with a genuine interest in regional stability and peace.

Relations with Egypt had been severely strained by the invasion of Lebanon, by the building of new settlements on the West Bank, and by the unresolved dispute over the beach resort of Taba, near the head of the Gulf of Aqaba. The Begin government retained this 1.2 square kilometers of seashore at the time of its withdrawal from Sinai in April 1982 and subsequently permitted the building of a luxury hotel and holiday village on it, although it was claimed by Egypt. Some Israeli officials were prepared to admit privately that this tiny piece of Sinai was retained not because it was thought that Israel had a valid title to it but to avoid setting a precedent for total withdrawal that could be invoked in future negotiations over the West Bank. President Mubarak, however, was adamant that the dispute had to be resolved before he would meet with Peres. The Israeli-Egyptian peace treaty laid down that any dispute that could not be resolved by negotiation should be resolved either by conciliation or submitted to arbitration.

Mubarak pressed for a decision to submit the matter to arbitration and as an incentive offered a package that included the return of Egypt's resident ambassador to Israel and a resumption of the process of normalization in areas such as commerce, tourism, transport, and culture. Peres was prepared to accept this package. But the inner cabinet was split down the middle on this issue. The five Likud ministers would not budge. Their leader, Yitzhak Shamir, brought to bear on this relatively minor issue all of his considerable reserves of stubbornness. He probably wanted to deny Peres a diplomatic success and to keep the stumbling block on the road to peace talks firmly in place. The argument went on and on in the inner cabinet until eventually David Levy moved toward the Alignment's position, as he had done over the withdrawal from Lebanon. On 12 January 1986 Peres submitted to the full cabinet his proposal for referring the Taba dispute to arbitration and threatened to bring down the government if Shamir and his colleagues continued to resist. The meeting lasted twelve hours and had to be adjourned several times when it was on the point of getting out of control. The Likud ministers hurled insults at the prime minister, and he accused them of sabotaging the peace process. At dawn the decision was reached to submit the matter to arbitration, but the Likud ministers succeeded in delaying the implementation of this decision by another nine months. The arbiters eventually found in favor of Egypt, and in March 1989 the beach was returned to Egyptian sovereignty.[2]

In his memoirs Shamir wrote, "It wasn't a happy moment for me; I remained unhappily convinced that if we had held out united we could have kept Taba—without forfeiting anything—and I thought it was ironic that I, and those who like myself resist handing over bits of land to Israel's enemies, should be castigated for 'fanaticism' while no one at all protested or even paid any attention (except the Likud) when the Egyptians, risking peace itself, clutched at Taba solely for reasons of national prestige. Of course nothing changed after Taba; it was as though nothing had happened."[3] These comments merit close attention for a number of reasons. First and most striking is the fact that Shamir referred to Egypt as an enemy, although it had signed a peace treaty with Israel a decade earlier. Then there was Shamir's disregard for international law and for the rights of other states. Last but not least, these comments betrayed a complete inability on the part of Shamir to comprehend any point of view except his own.

RETURN OF THE JORDANIAN OPTION

Shimon Peres's greatest ambition was to settle the Palestinian problem in a separate deal with Jordan. This was the most consistent strand of policy that he pursued during the life of the national unity government, first as prime minister and then as foreign minister. During the preceding seven years of Likud rule, there had been no high-level contact between Israel and Jordan. Peres felt that the annexation of the West Bank, the Likud's long-term goal, would be a disastrous error, because it would undermine the democratic and Jewish character of the State of Israel. Continuing Jewish military occupation was not a satisfactory solution either, because there were 1.5 million Arabs in the West Bank and Gaza and, since their birth rate was higher than that of the Jews, the demographic balance was bound to change in their favor. The only alternative was the Jordanian option—a territorial compromise with King Hussein that would restore to his kingdom the heavily populated areas of the West Bank and Gaza and leave the strategically important areas in Israel's hands. This had been the Labor Party's preferred option since 1967.

Yitzhak Rabin was in complete agreement with Peres on this. "The Jordanian option is even more important than the rebuilding of the economy," he said to his colleagues during the election campaign. "This is the main matter with which the labor movement should concern itself when it is in power." Peres and Rabin directed the team of experts headed by Yossi Beilin to explore the Jordanian option and the means by which it could be realized. They ordered them to replace the question mark around the Jordanian option with an exclamation mark. The team's recommendation was to follow the Camp David model—that is, direct negotiations between Israel and Jordan with the involvement and help of the United States, and with the support of Egypt. So, virtually from his first day in office, Peres began to work through private channels to renew the dialogue with Jordan.[4]

The response from Amman was guarded but encouraging. King Hussein seemed willing to explore ways of starting negotiations without assurances regarding the final outcome. In the past he had always demanded an agreement in principle about the final outcome before agreeing to the official opening of negotiations. Now he was prepared to consider commencing negotiations without preconditions, but he faced two problems. First, the Arab League summit, in Rabat in 1974, had endorsed the PLO as the sole legitimate representative of the Palestinian people. So he could not enter into official negotiations with Israel without the approval of the PLO. Second, the Arab League summit at Fez, Morocco, in 1982 had endorsed the idea of negotiations with Israel but only within the framework of an international conference. So he could not embark on separate negotiations with Israel without the Arab world turning against him, perhaps fatally. To overcome these problems Hussein proposed an international conference with the participation of the five permanent members of the UN Security Council and of all the parties to the conflict, including the

Palestinians. An international conference, he hoped, would enable him to remain within the limits of the inter-Arab consensus while providing a cover for the direct talks that the Israelis wanted so badly.

In Israel, however, the idea of an international conference was extremely unpopular. An international conference was equated with an externally imposed solution, and this was rejected by all the mainstream parties. The Labor Party had always resisted the idea, preferring direct talks with individual Arab states. Peres was not prepared to allow outside powers to have a say in determining Israel's borders, and he feared that at an international conference the most extreme Arab parties would set the tone. The Likud regarded an international conference not as a forum for negotiations but as a code for forcing Israel to relinquish the occupied territories. Shamir was especially vehement and vocal in his rejection of an international conference in any guise or form. He maintained that an international conference would imperil Israel's very existence. The reasons were set out in his memoirs: "I thought that we would all too soon find ourselves more and more isolated, under the kind of intensive international pressure that we might be unable to withstand, and forced to yield to Arab demands (backed by almost everyone else) that would return Israel to the untenable territorial situation in which we had lived prior to 1967."[5] The challenge facing Peres was to find a formula to enable King Hussein to open talks with Israel under an international umbrella and to set up a Jordanian-Palestinian team for the talks, bypassing the PLO.

King Hussein had to maintain a difficult balancing act and accordingly proceeded with the caution of a tightrope walker. First he needed to gain legitimacy for negotiating over the future of the West Bank from his nemesis—Yasser Arafat. On 11 February 1985 he and Arafat concluded an agreement on a common approach to a peace process involving Israel. The aim was Palestinian self-determination exercised through a Jordanian-Palestinian confederation, and the method was a Jordanian-Palestinian delegation to negotiate with Israel at an international conference and an "out at the beginning, in at the end" formula for PLO participation. The three conditions that the PLO was expected to meet in order to qualify for participation at a later stage were to accept Resolution 242, to recognize Israel's right to exist, and to renounce violence. These were the conditions that Henry Kissinger had laid down in 1975 for talks between the United States and the PLO. The

Reagan administration continued to insist that the PLO pass this entrance exam for admission to the diplomatic process. The administration was unenthusiastic about the idea of an international conference, because it involved Soviet participation on an equal footing with the United States, but it was more than willing to try and devise some sort of international cover for Jordanian-Israeli negotiations.

Israeli efforts to pave the way for talks with Jordan were stepped up following the disengagement from Lebanon. In July 1985 Avraham Tamir presented a long memorandum to Peres arguing that during the preceding year the conditions for renewing the peace process had ripened. He listed four reasons. The first concerned the Iran-Iraq war. This focused Iraq on containing the Iranian-Shiite threat in the Arab world, and as a consequence Baghdad had come to accept Egypt's strategy of accommodation with Israel. Second, the position of the PLO had changed as a result of the loss of its military infrastructure in Lebanon. This change accounted for the Hussein-Arafat pact, for the splits in the PLO between the radicals and the moderates, for the decision of the moderates to seek a solution to the Palestinian problem in partnership with Jordan, and for their willingness to consider the acceptance of Resolution 242. Third, Egypt's regaining of its traditional position of primacy in the Arab world strengthened the trend in favor of the peaceful resolution of international disputes. Fourth, the policies of the Israeli government had helped create a better climate for negotiations. These included the withdrawal of the IDF from Lebanon, the freeze on the building of settlements on the West Bank, the improvement in the living conditions of the Arab population of the West Bank, progress toward the settlement of the Taba dispute by arbitration, and willingness to enter into negotiations with Jordan without preconditions concerning the final outcome. Peres, Rabin, and their aides agreed with this analysis. Peres's strategy was to concentrate on the construction of a framework for negotiations and to leave all the substantive issues to a later stage.[6]

Peres met King Hussein in London on 19 July 1985, their first face-to-face meeting in ten years. The meeting took place in the king's house in Palace Green, Kensington, which was conveniently located a few doors away from the Israeli embassy. The king and the prime minister agreed to move forward in stages. In the first stage a joint Jordanian-Palestinian delegation would meet with Richard Murphy, the U.S. assistant secretary of state for Near Eastern and East Asian affairs; in the second the PLO would meet the American conditions for a dialogue; and in the third the peace negotiations would begin. There was one point, however, on which they were unable to agree. The king wanted the joint delegation to include some supporters of the PLO; this was unacceptable to the prime minister.[7]

However, Peres was sufficiently interested in the king's scenario to ask the Americans to give it a try. As George Shultz reveals in his memoirs, on August 5, Simha Dinitz, a former Israeli ambassador to Washington, came to his home with some startling news. He had been sent by Peres, without the knowledge of the cabinet, to report on his meeting with King Hussein. But in addition to reporting on the progress made at that meeting, Dinitz informed Shultz of something that Peres had apparently not told the king: if some PLO supporters were included in the delegation to the preliminary talks with Richard Murphy, Israel would have to live with it although stating its objections publicly. Shultz received a rather different message from Shamir through the Washington attorney Len Garment. Garment said that Foreign Minister Shamir did not want Richard Murphy to meet *any* Palestinians. Shamir questioned their judgment in even considering such a meeting, which he felt would break the letter and spirit of their 1975 commitment not to meet with PLO members until the PLO accepted their conditions, break apart the Israeli government, and jeopardize U.S.-Israeli relations. It was only one more example of the government of national unity speaking with two voices but a rather arresting one. Shultz consulted Ronald Reagan, who ruled that there should be no ambiguity about their refusal to deal with anyone even vaguely connected with the PLO.[8]

Israel's position regarding the PLO was much closer to that of the United States than to that of Jordan. Jordan argued that the PLO was relatively weak and could therefore be pressed to make concessions. Israel replied, much like America, that if the PLO was weak it should be excluded altogether from the diplomatic process. This divergence with regard to the PLO was a major factor in the failure to get peace talks off the ground. As one student of Israeli-Jordanian relations observed, "For Peres and the Labor Party, the higher the profile of the PLO in any negotiations, the harder to create a political majority for the process in Israel. For Hussein and the Hashemites, the higher the profile of the PLO, the fewer the risks in any negotiations, both in the regional and in the Jordanian domestic framework. Hussein felt he could not proceed without the PLO; Peres could not proceed with it."[9]

In the summer of 1985 the PLO stepped up its attacks on

Israeli targets from Jordan. Force 17 within the mainstream Fatah group, also known as Arafat's bodyguards, was active in the eastern Mediterranean. In September, Force 17 killed three Israelis, thought to be Mossad agents, aboard a yacht in the harbor at Larnaca, Cyprus. Ariel Sharon publicly demanded that Israel retaliate against "the terrorist headquarters in Amman." Sharon evinced no interest in renewing the dialogue with Jordan. He had always opposed the Jordanian option, and he pointed to the pact between Hussein and Arafat as evidence that Hussein was not a suitable partner for peace talks. Peres and Rabin had no intention of satisfying Sharon's demand to undertake an operation inside Jordan, but they could not afford to appear "soft" compared with the Likud half of the administration.[10] They therefore proposed to the inner cabinet a strike by the IAF on the PLO headquarters in Tunis. All the members of the inner cabinet, except Ezer Weizman, supported the proposal. The main reason Weizman gave for his opposition to the raid was the damage it was likely to cause to Israel's relations with Egypt.

On 1 October eight Israeli F-16s carried out the raid against Hamam el-Shaat, the military compound in the PLO headquarters in Tunis, killing fifty-six Palestinians and fifteen Tunisians and wounding about a hundred others. Arafat narrowly escaped being blown up. This was another demonstration of Israel's long reach. Tunis was 2,460 kilometers from Israel. The flight lasted five and a half hours, and the planes had to be refueled in midair. The Security Council and many countries condemned the raid, but the United States condoned it as a legitimate response to terrorism. Reagan sent Peres a message expressing his satisfaction with the operation. Reagan himself was to order an air strike against Libya the following year, again as part of the fight against international terrorism.

On 5 October, four days after the raid on Tunis, Peres had another meeting with King Hussein in London. The king was increasingly leaning toward the American view that the PLO had to change its policy before it could be allowed to play a part in the peace talks. The prime minister was growing more confident of his ability to persuade the Israeli public of the need for some sort of an international gathering if the PLO could be excluded. The king surveyed his contacts with the PLO and his efforts to set up a joint Jordanian-Palestinian delegation for peace talks with Israel. He stressed that the negotiations would have to be part of an international conference. The prime minister surveyed his country's complicated domestic political scene in order to underscore the importance of speed. He would have to change places with Shamir in a year's time, he said, and then it would be harder to move toward peace because of the nationalist ideology of Shamir and his party. The king expressed concern that the government of Israel, as a result of its unusual structure, was paralyzed and incapable of reaching difficult decisions. The prime minister responded by saying that if and when the moment of decision arrived, and the Likud ministers were seen as the final obstacle to peace negotiations with Jordan, he would not hesitate to dismantle the coalition. The two leaders exchanged views about the speeches they were due to give later that month at the annual session of the UN General Assembly. The meeting, which lasted two hours, ended with a handshake and an agreement to meet again "to advance the peace process."[11]

Peres delivered his speech to the General Assembly on 21 October. He announced to the world that Israel intended to negotiate peace with its neighbor to the east—the Hashemite Kingdom of Jordan. The objective of these negotiations was to reach peace treaties between Israel and the Arab states, as well as to resolve the Palestinian issue. The negotiations were to be based on UN Resolutions 242 and 338 and on willingness to entertain suggestions proposed by other participants. The negotiations between Israel and Jordan were to be conducted directly between an Israeli delegation on the one hand and a Jordanian—or a Jordanian-Palestinian—delegation on the other.[12] Not once in his speech did Peres use the magic words "international conference," but he did allow for the support of an international forum in initiating bilateral negotiations, and that represented a change in Israel's foreign policy.

The international response to Peres's diplomatic initiative was generally favorable, although at home there was some muted right-wing criticism. A week later he repeated the essential points, including the acceptability of an international forum, in a statement to the Knesset. Once again there were some protests from members of the Likud and from members of parties farther to the right, but the Knesset endorsed the plan. Peres was delighted with the result, but he underestimated the real strength of the opposition. Although Shamir and his colleagues were deeply opposed to the plan, they feared that if they made an issue of it, Peres would refuse to carry out the rotation agreement. Shamir knew that a political crisis over this issue would lead either to the formation of a narrow government headed by Peres or to new elections that Peres was expected to win. Consequently, Shamir bided his time both in order to regain power and to be in a better position to subvert his political opponent's plan.[13]

Behind the scenes Richard Murphy was active in preparing the ground for peace talks. Murphy knew the Arab world intimately, having been U.S. ambassador to Syria and to Saudi Arabia. He also won the confidence of the Israelis. George Shultz thought he had perfect qualifications for this difficult diplomatic mission: "Murphy could sit with unblinking attention while Arab representatives elaborately used hours to get to the point. And he had steely nerves that steadied him as Israeli representatives got instantly to the point and tried to stab him with it."[14] Murphy shuttled for weeks on end between Jerusalem and Amman, and in January 1986 his efforts were crowned with success. He obtained King Hussein's agreement to a ten-point document on the procedure for negotiations. There was to be an international conference, but it was to be pro forma, without any real powers. The negotiations were to take place in bilateral committees that were to be independent of one another. And no party could participate in the conference unless it accepted Resolutions 242 and 338 and renounced violence.

This document was a major achievement for Peres. He had obtained Hussein's agreement to an international conference that would be largely ceremonial, a "castrated" conference, as his aides privately called it. But they remained divided on three key issues. The first question was what would happen if the PLO accepted the conditions for participation in the international conference. Israel's opposition to talks with the PLO remained unconditional, whereas Hussein was bound by his pact with Arafat to bring the PLO on board. The second question concerned the Soviet Union. Peres wanted Soviet participation to be made conditional on restoring diplomatic relations with Israel (which had been broken off in June 1967) and on opening the gates to the emigration of Soviet Jews to Israel. Hussein saw no reason why he should be bound by these conditions, especially the second one. The third question concerned the right of referral back to the conference in the event of deadlock in the bilateral committees. Hussein insisted that this right be preserved, whereas Peres thought that the outside powers should have no power to intervene in substantive matters. As he saw it, the outsiders should attend the opening session of the conference and then disperse, leaving the parties to the conflict to conduct a series of parallel bilateral negotiations. These differences were never resolved.[15]

Meanwhile, Jordan's relations with the PLO continued to deteriorate. On 19 February 1986 King Hussein, in a speech that lasted three and a half hours, announced that he was ending his effort to construct a joint peace strategy with Arafat and the PLO. He characterized Arafat as untrustworthy and said that the problem lay in Arafat's unwillingness to accept unconditionally Resolutions 242 and 338. The speech from the throne drew the curtain on this act of the peace process, and the responsibility for its premature ending was laid fairly and squarely at Arafat's door. The rift between Hussein and Arafat revived hopes in the Peres camp that the Jordanian option might be realized after all through negotiations with a delegation of Jordanian and pro-Jordanian Palestinians from the West Bank. Hussein launched an ambitious five-year plan for improving economic conditions on the West Bank. The Israeli government supported Hussein both in his efforts to obtain American funding for his plan and in his efforts to rebuild his political influence on the West Bank. However, the PLO's assassination of Zafir al-Masri, the pro-Jordanian mayor of Nablus, on 3 March 1986, sent a strong signal that it intended to fight for its position as the sole representative of the Palestinian people.

Yitzhak Rabin met King Hussein near Strasbourg, France, in March 1986. They had last met in 1977, when Rabin was prime minister. Now he was minister of defense with responsibility for the occupied territories. Rabin expressed his concern about the increase in PLO guerrilla activity and asked Hussein to curb the PLO leaders who lived in Jordan. Hussein said he had no intention of allowing the PLO to step up their attacks on Israel. He, for his part, asked for Israel's help in strengthening the economic and institutional links between the Palestinian population of the West Bank and the Jordanian government. The Strasbourg meeting was a great success from the Israeli point of view. Soon after his return home Hussein ordered the closing down of the PLO offices in Amman and the expulsion of Khalil al-Wazir (Abu Jihad), the PLO chief of operations and Arafat's deputy. Tension between Jordan and the PLO reached new heights as a result of these measures.

Rabin and Peres paid a secret visit to Hussein at his holiday house in Aqaba in July. It was a short distance by speedboat from Eilat to Hussein's private wharf at the mouth of the Gulf of Aqaba. They were accompanied by Chief of Staff Moshe Levy because the fight against Palestinian terrorism was one of the topics on the agenda. Prime Minister Zeid al-Rifai was also in attendance. The talks went on for over four hours, and it was well past midnight

when the Israelis set off on their journey back home. The question
of an international peace conference inevitably came up for discussion. Peres said that he would continue to work on this after he
stepped down to become foreign minister and that Rabin would
also represent an element of continuity in the Israeli team. Hussein
agreed with the Israelis that there was no sense in waiting for the
PLO to adopt a single, unified, and realistic stance. He said that he
would try to cultivate moderate leaders from the occupied territories as an alternative to the PLO. The discussion then turned to
Jordan's five-year plan for the economic development of the West
Bank. The Israelis promised to use their good offices in
Washington, but the American response was disappointing. Jordan
was looking for $1.5 billion for the five years, but Congress allo-
cated only $90 million. Regarding the West Bank, the Israelis reaf-
firmed their policy of providing economic incentives and
encouragement to the pro-Jordanian elements. This policy was
publicly stated by Rabin in an interview to a newspaper in
September: "The policy of Israel is to strengthen the position of
Jordan in Judea and Samaria and to strike at the PLO."[16]

There was a flurry of diplomatic activity in the last few months
of Peres's premiership. On 22 July, Peres arrived in Morocco on
an official visit as the guest of King Hassan II. The visit was accompanied by a great deal of publicity. Peres had been to Morocco
twice before as leader of the opposition, but this visit was different; it was a public visit by an Israeli prime minister to an Arab king
who was famous not only for his hospitality but also for his keen
interest in promoting peace in the Middle East. Since the precise
purpose of the visit was not stated, there was a great deal of speculation in the Israeli media. Some commentators thought that
Peres was seeking a diplomatic breakthrough at any price in order
to avoid having to step down in favor of Shamir. Some of Peres's
followers were certainly urging him to ditch the Likud and try to
form a narrow coalition in which the Alignment would be the ruling party. But if that was Peres's plan, the visit to Morocco did little to advance it. King Hassan and his guest had three rounds of
talks but failed to reach any significant conclusions.

Peres followed this with a meeting with President Mubarak in
Alexandria on 11 September, shortly after the two countries signed
the document that permitted the Taba dispute to go to arbitration.
Peres spent two days in Alexandria and met with Mubarak for
three hours of talks. The joint communiqué noted the agreement
on Taba, reiterated the commitment of Israel and Egypt to comprehensive peace in the Middle East, and proclaimed 1987 as "a

year of negotiations for peace." Both leaders indicated their support for an international conference but differed on the role of the
PLO and on the solution to the Palestinian problem.[17]

In the end Peres honored the rotation agreement with Shamir.
Although he had no confidence in Shamir, he felt that his own
credibility would suffer if he reneged on the agreement. In a statement to the Knesset, on 7 October 1986, he justly took pride in
the achievements of his twenty-five-month-old administration: the
lowering of domestic tensions, economic recovery, withdrawal
from Lebanon, new coexistence in the territories, improvement in
the relations with Egypt, and progress in the peace process. The
choice, said Peres, was between negotiations without preconditions and preconditions without negotiations. His preference was
for the former. He hinted that discussions were under way with
Jordan, via the United States, for preparing peace negotiations:

> At this stage what is lacking, from the Arab point of view, in
> order to commence negotiations, is an international forum on
> the one hand and agreement on the composition of a
> Palestinian delegation on the other. Israel does not need an in-
> ternational forum. But Jordan has stated that without such ac-
> companiment it will not be able to take part in negotiation.
> Egypt supports the Jordan stand. We can . . . conduct negoti-
> ations without an international forum but we cannot conduct
> negotiations without Jordan and without a Palestinian element
> in its delegation. For this reason we agreed to an international
> forum that will enable negotiations to get under way.[18]

This was a fair summary of the understandings that had been
reached with Jordan up to that point. But it omitted to mention
the remaining differences on the right of referral and Soviet participation. Clearly, Peres intended to continue his efforts to resolve these problems. On 20 October 1986 he handed over the
premiership to Yitzhak Shamir and moved to the Foreign Ministry.
The handshake between the incoming and the outgoing prime
ministers sealed the fate of the peace process, but this did not become clear until six months later.

COVERT DEALINGS WITH IRAN

Israel was distracted from the single-minded pursuit of the
Jordanian option both by the change at the top and by the

Irangate scandal. In November 1986, a couple of weeks after Yitzhak Shamir had become prime minister, the American media carried a series of startling stories about the covert supplies of arms to the regime of Ayatollah Khomeini in Iran in exchange for the release of American hostages held in Lebanon. Israel was said to have taken the initiative in the spring of 1985 in secretly selling American-made weapons to Iran and in subsequently involving America in the sordid swap of arms for hostages. George Shultz and Caspar Weinberger had categorically rejected the idea of trading arms for hostages when it was first mooted. They also rejected the spurious strategic guise in which this idea was dressed up— namely, that by supplying modest amounts of arms, America would help the moderates prevail against the radicals in the Khomeini regime and then win back Iran for the West.

The Israelis, it was revealed, conspired with officials in the CIA and the National Security Council (NSC) despite the opposition of Shultz and Weinberger. Robert McFarlane, Reagan's national security adviser, and Oliver North, an NSC staff aide, secretly delivered arms to Iran and used the proceeds to fund one of the president's pet projects, aid to the Nicaraguan Contras, which Congress had prohibited. The upshot was to make the Reagan administration a party, if a slightly muddled one, to this transaction and to give Israel political cover for its ongoing arms shipments to Iran. Israel was immediately thrown on the defensive by the exposure of its trafficking in arms, covert support for the most anti-Western country in the Middle East, and manipulation of the American government. Israel chose not to deny specific allegations but to concentrate on damage limitation with the administration, Congress, and the public.

The revelation of covert Israeli support for Iran came as a great surprise because the Islamic Republic of Iran was the most extreme ideological opponent of the Jewish state. There was more than one reason for this support. In the first place, Israel had an interest in maintaining at least a subterranean relationship with Iran after the Islamic revolution in order to help Iranian Jews. But there were also bigger geostrategic considerations. The Iran-Iraq war had been going on since 1980. Ideally, the Israelis would have liked both sides to lose this war. The second-best scenario was for Iran and Iraq to demolish one another in a long, drawn-out war of attrition. The supply of arms to Iran, which had been under a strict American embargo since the revolution, was one way of fueling the war and sustaining the stalemate. As long as Iraq re-

mained bogged down in this conflict, it could not join forces with
Syria or Jordan to form an eastern front against Israel. Israel's policy in the Persian Gulf, however, was at odds with its policy in the
Middle East. In the Middle East, Israel was in tacit collaboration
with Jordan and in open conflict with Syria. Yet Jordan had close
relations with Iraq whereas Syria supported Iran. So in the Gulf
conflict Israel found itself, indirectly, on the same side as Syria and
on the wrong side of Jordan.

An even greater contradiction lay at the heart of Israeli policy,
and it concerned the tricky topic of terrorism. Israel had won wide
acceptance, not only in the United States, for its version of the
Arab-Israeli dispute: the violence of its opponents was "terror"; its
own was "legitimate self-defense." Moreover, Israel was in the
vanguard of the crusade against international terrorism. Binyamin
Netanyahu, Israel's ambassador to the United Nations, had become a compelling spokesman for a tough counterterrorist policy
for the West. In 1986 Netanyahu published the proceedings of a
conference held in Washington by Israel's Jonathan Institute under
the title *Terrorism: How the West Can Win*. By its scathing attacks
on the PLO, Libya, and Syria, this book fostered the impression
that Israel's enemies were also America's, that the Arabs who used
violence against Israel were terrorists, that the countries that sponsored violence against Israel were terrorist states, and that brute
force against them was not only legitimate but desirable. "If a government has harbored, trained, and launched terrorists," wrote
Netanyahu, "it becomes the legitimate object of a military response."[19] The book had a major influence on American attitudes
during Reagan's second term at the White House. Reagan himself
was greatly impressed by the book and recommended it to his senior staff.

The Iran-Contra scandal, however, revealed a fatal contradiction in Israel's own policy on terrorism. Israel was denouncing
Syria because of its terrorist record while secretly shipping arms to
Iran in spite of its terrorist record.[20] By contradicting its own precepts, by maintaining the flow of arms to Khomeini's Iran at a
time when that country was the chief sponsor of anti-Western terrorism, Israel sank into the morass of the Iran-Contra affair and
dragged America along into it.

The damage of the Iran-Contra affair in America was enormous. It came close to destroying the Reagan presidency in the
manner that Watergate had destroyed the Nixon presidency. While
the damage of Watergate was largely confined to the domestic

scene, the Iran-Contra damaged major aspects of Reagan's foreign policy as well as undermining the morale of his administration. This was how George Shultz described the damage at the time:

> After years of work, the keystone of our counterterrorism policy was set: No deals with terrorists. Now we have fallen into the trap. We have voluntarily made ourselves the victims of the terrorist extortion racket. We have spawned a hostage-taking industry. Every principle that the president praised in Netanyahu's book on terrorism has been dealt a terrible blow by what has been done.
>
> We have assaulted our own Middle East policy. The Arabs counted on us to play a strong and responsible role to contain and eventually bring the Gulf War to an end. Now we are seen to be aiding the most radical forces in the region. We have acted directly counter to our own major effort to dry up the war by denying the weapons needed to continue it. The Jordanians—and other moderate Arabs—are appalled at what we have done. And our hopes of getting united allied action against Syria have foundered as the allies see us doing precisely what we have relentlessly pressured them not to do.[21]

The Israeli-inspired initiative also inflicted grave damage on Shultz, the most loyal supporter of Israel in the Reagan administration, next to the president himself. In the vicious bureaucratic infighting that followed the exposure, there was an attempt to turn him into a scapegoat, and he was forced to fight for his political life. He was understandably angry with the Israelis for having gone behind his back to plot with officials in the White House whom he regarded as ignorant, gullible, and irresponsible. Peres offered profuse apologies and sent him one terse message that said, "Hello. Don't go." But Shultz was not mollified and even began to tilt toward Shamir, who sent him several messages of support and encouragement through Netanyahu. It was possibly as a result of the fallout from the Iran-Contra affair that Shultz did not throw his full weight behind the London Agreement.

THE LONDON AGREEMENT

Once Shamir had rotated into the top job, he was as indefatigable in scuppering diplomatic initiatives as Peres was in promoting them. Becoming foreign minister in no way weakened Peres's urgent sense that the Jordanian opening had to be pursued with vigor and determination. The Jordanians would proceed to bilateral negotiations with Israel only under the cover of an international conference, but Shamir flatly rejected the idea. The Americans, too, remained cool to the idea of convening an international conference, because they did not want the Soviet Union to be involved in Middle Eastern diplomacy. As the official diplomatic channels produced no movement, Peres tried to reach a breakthrough by means of a secret summit. He approached Lord Victor Mishcon, a prominent British Jew who was also a friend of King Hussein, and asked him to set up a meeting. The time and place were fixed: Saturday, 11 April 1987, at Lord Mishcon's home in central London. Peres told Shamir about the meeting and received his consent. On Friday, Peres took off for London aboard a small executive jet, accompanied by Yossi Beilin, the political director general of the Foreign Ministry, and Efraim Halevi from the Mossad.[22]

King Hussein came to the meeting with Zeid al-Rifai. It lasted from morning till evening and included lunch with the hosts. The domestic staff had been given a day off, and Lady Mishcon cooked and served a delicious meal herself. The king was in sparkling form, weaving amusing anecdotes into his pithy political assessments. When the meal was over, he suggested that Peres and he go into the kitchen to help with the washing up. At 2 P.M. they settled down to serious business, and their discussion was to continue for seven hours. It began with a survey of the events of the preceding year. The conversation flowed smoothly and pleasantly and gradually turned to the real issues.

King Hussein thought that the Reagan administration was thoroughly confused as to what it was trying to achieve in their region, but he reserved his sharpest comments for members of the PLO. They were ambiguous in their basic political positions, he said, but theirs was not a constructive ambiguity but rather one that reflected vague and indeterminate political thinking. The PLO continued to engage in terror and effectively rejected all openings for productive negotiations. The king stressed that his vision of an international conference did not embrace the PLO as long as it continued to reject Resolutions 242 and 338. Peres felt that they were on the same wavelength. Neither Israel nor Jordan, he said, could regard the PLO, committed by its charter to seek the destruction of Israel, as a partner for peace. Israel certainly did not want to see Yasser Arafat ruling Amman, he added pointedly. Peres reported that a Soviet envoy turned up at a Socialist International meeting in Rome specifically to see him and that his message was that Moscow accepted the concept of a "noncoercive" international conference. The king observed that Soviet policy-making was undergoing very real and positive changes even though many of the officials remained the same.

The two leaders found themselves in agreement on many, though not all, of the key issues. They agreed that the time was ripe to move toward a resolution of the conflict. They also agreed that an international conference should be convened to launch the process, but should not itself impose solutions. Their idea was that the conference should assemble once and that every subsequent session would require the prior consent of all the parties. They agreed, too, that there should be a joint Jordanian-Palestinian delegation, which would not include avowed members of the PLO. Finally, they agreed that after the opening session, negotiations would be carried out face-to-face in bilateral committees consisting of Israelis and their Arab opponents. Rifai said that he, too, agreed with the key points that Peres had articulated.

"Well then," said Peres, "why don't we try to write down our agreement?" The king said he could not do this, since he had another engagement that would take him one hour. He suggested that in the meantime the Israelis draft two documents: one detailing the principles and procedures of the proposed international conference, and the other setting out the agreements and understandings between Israel and Jordan. The king and Rifai left, and the Israelis quickly got down to work. By the time the king and Rifai returned, the two papers were ready. They read them carefully and Rifai started suggesting changes, but Hussein stopped him, saying the two drafts accurately reflected the agreements they had reached. They decided, finally, to transmit the paper to the Americans and ask them to present it as an American paper. The meeting ended on a note of high hope. Both leaders were deeply gratified with the results of the day's work.

The Peres-Hussein agreement was unsigned, but it had the date and venue at the bottom and came to be known as the London Agreement. Typed in English on a single sheet of paper, it was divided into three parts. The first part proposed that the UN secretary-general should invite the five permanent members of the Security Council and the parties to the Arab-Israeli conflict to negotiate a peaceful settlement based on Resolutions 242 and 338 "with the object of bringing a comprehensive peace to the area, security to its states, and to respond to the legitimate rights of the Palestinian people." The second part proposed that the conference should invite the parties to form bilateral committees to negotiate on issues of mutual interests.

The third part was key, for it summarized all the points on which Jordan and Israel had agreed:

> 1. The international conference will not impose any solution or veto any agreement arrived at between the parties. 2. The negotiations will be conducted in bilateral committees directly. 3. The Palestinian issue will be dealt with in the committee of the Jordanian-Palestinian and Israeli delegations. 4. The Palestinians' representatives will be included in the Jordanian-Palestinian delegation. 5. Participation in the conference will be based on the parties' acceptance of Resolutions 242 and 338 and the renunciation of violence and terrorism. 6. Each committee will negotiate independently. 7. Other issues will be decided by mutual agreement between Jordan and Israel.

Finally, it was stated that this paper was subject to approval by the respective governments of Jordan and Israel and that it would be shown and suggested to the United States.[23]

That the PLO was not mentioned anywhere in the document was bound to upset the Palestinians. An international conference, however impotent, was also bound to upset right-wing Israelis. It would be less difficult for Hussein to sell the idea to the Arabs than for Peres to sell it to his countrymen if it appeared to come from the United States. Hence the decision to turn to the United States for help. Not long after his return home, Hussein contacted George Shultz and explained what had been agreed, urging the secretary of state to give his blessing. Peres acted with greater dispatch by sending Beilin to Helsinki to intercept Shultz, who was on his way to Moscow to arrange a summit meeting between Ronald Reagan and Mikhail Gorbachev.

Peres himself called on Shamir as soon as he got home, early on Sunday morning. They arranged to meet alone, after the weekly cabinet session. Peres gave Shamir a full account of his talks with King Hussein and read to him the text of the document. Shamir asked Peres to read it again, and Peres did so. But when Shamir asked for a copy of the document, Peres refused. He told Shamir frankly that he was afraid of leaks not by the prime minister but by his staff. Peres added, a bit disingenuously, that since the arrangement was for the Americans to put forward the plan as their idea, it would be better if Shamir received it directly from the Americans. Shamir said nothing.[24] He and his colleagues did not trust Peres, and although the London Agreement dealt only with procedures, they suspected that Peres had made secret concessions on substance. The fact that Hussein, who in the past had always insisted on knowing the outcome before official negotiations could start, now agreed to negotiations without any preconditions seemed to them to support these suspicions. Besides, even though the London Agreement did not formally commit Israel to anything of substance in advance, Shamir feared that it might open the door to the territorial compromise favored by the Alignment.

In Helsinki, Beilin gave Shultz a full account of the London meeting, describing it as a historic breakthrough and urging him to adopt it as an American plan. "Don't let it evaporate," Beilin said. "It's in your hands now." Shultz had no difficulty with the idea of a carefully controlled international conference that would meet to propel the parties into direct, bilateral negotiations. Yet he thought it extraordinary for the foreign minister of Israel's government of national unity to ask him to sell to Israel's prime minister, the head of a rival party, an agreement made with a foreign head of state. The problem was compounded by the fact that Shamir, in his Passover message to President Reagan on 1 April, had stated that it was "inconceivable that there may be in the U.S. support of the idea of an international conference, which will inevitably reintroduce the Soviets into our region in a major role."[25]

On 22 April, Shultz telephoned Shamir to tell him that he had been informed of the London Agreement by his foreign minister and by the king of Jordan and to say that he was ready to come to the Middle East to go forward with him in the peace process. Shamir replied that he wanted to think the idea over for a day or two, but Shultz could sense that he was dead against it. Two hours later, Elyakim Rubinstein, Shamir's aide, called from Jerusalem to give Shamir's answer. Shamir did not want to say this directly, but the London document did not appeal to him and he would not welcome a visit by the American secretary of state. An international conference would build pressure on behalf of the Arabs on Israel. If the United Nations was involved, there was no way for the PLO not to be involved. On the next day, 23 April, word came from Peres: he was pleased with the way Shultz had handled the

issue with Shamir; he recognized that he would have to risk breaking the government over this; he would not be a party to Israel's
missing this opportunity. "In London, Israel and Jordan had been
in direct negotiations and had achieved agreement. Would the
Israeli prime minister now turn away from this opportunity?" Peres
asked.

A tug of war was taking place between the foreign minister
and the prime minister for the attention of the secretary of state.
It was as if the two men were pulling the stocky American by the
arms in opposite directions. On 24 April, Moshe Arens turned up
at Shultz's office, sent by Shamir without the knowledge of his
foreign minister. Arens said bluntly that the prime minister and
his party were opposed to the holding of an international conference on the Middle East and that if Shultz visited Israel to
present the Peres-Hussein agreement, he would find himself embroiled in an internal Israeli political debate. Shultz described to
Arens in great detail exactly how a conference could work and be
kept under control, but Arens would not budge. Nothing could
go forward, Arens concluded, until Shamir and King Hussein
met face-to-face. The conversation ended on this sober note but
with what amounted to a request for help in arranging such an
encounter.[26]

All the Likud ministers shared Shamir's hostility to the London
Agreement. David Levy was not prepared to break ranks over this,
as he had done over withdrawal from Lebanon. Ariel Sharon did
not want any peace negotiations with Jordan, with or without an
international conference. On 6 May, Peres presented to the inner
cabinet a detailed proposal based on the London Agreement and
met with unanimous opposition from the Likud ministers. He
could have put the matter to a vote, but he decided not to do so,
because the outcome was certain to be a five-five split.[27] After the
meeting Peres continued to lobby for an international conference
at home and abroad, arguing that there was no cabinet decision
against it. Shamir held that Peres was exceeding his powers since
there was no cabinet decision for it. Peres considered resigning,
but this would have entailed giving his reasons in public and thus
violating his pledge of secrecy with King Hussein at their meeting
in London.

King Hussein was as disappointed as Peres that nothing came
of their joint plan. He tended to think, in retrospect, that Peres
had underestimated the strength of the domestic opposition he

would face and overestimated his capacity to mobilize American support for the plan:

> The London Agreement floundered on two levels. Shimon Peres came as foreign minister, and we reached an agreement in London and initialed it. He said he would go back and he would send it immediately to George Shultz, and within forty-eight hours it would come as an American addendum to the Reagan plan. Peres also said that the agreement would be accepted by Israel, and I promised it would be accepted by Jordan. So he left. Two weeks later nothing had happened. And then a letter was sent by Shultz to the Israeli prime minister at the time, Yitzhak Shamir, telling him that this is the agreement that Peres and I had reached and asking him for his views. And of course Shamir took a negative stand against it, and the whole thing fell apart. I cannot say what happened in Israel, but Peres, as far as I was concerned, was the Israeli interlocutor. I talked with him. I agreed with him on something, and he couldn't deliver.[28]

After scuppering the London Agreement, Shamir sought to arrange a meeting with King Hussein. It was far from clear what the point of the meeting would be since the king's overriding aim was to recover the territory he had lost in June 1967, whereas Shamir was adamant that this territory belonged to Israel. In an address to the Likud Central Committee, Shamir overlooked this obstacle and stressed that the road was open to cooperation between Israel and Jordan in matters of common concern such as water, ecology, tourism, and so on.[29] In any case, Shamir did succeed in arranging a meeting with King Hussein; it took place in England on 18 July 1987.

The Israeli prime minister and the Jordanian monarch gave George Shultz rather different assessments of the meeting. Shamir's report was conveyed in the greatest confidence by a senior aide, Dan Meridor. The king had been host in his country house in Surrey. He provided a kosher meal for Shamir. The meeting went on for five hours, beginning formally, ending warmly. Shamir put forward a long list of cooperative steps that could be taken jointly by Israel and Jordan and went over the interim arrangements for Palestinian self-rule that had been launched at Camp David. This was the way to proceed, said Shamir, not by way of international conference. Shultz tentatively raised the possibility of a cosmetic international conference that would lead to direct negotiations and then disperse. "We are against an international conference," Meridor said. It was obvious that Shamir wanted to focus on his own private contacts with the king. The two had agreed, Meridor said, that Shamir would send an emissary to Amman soon. Was there a chance here, Shultz wondered, that Shamir had caught a mild case of peace fever? Might he want to compete with Peres as peacemaker but do it in his own way—secretly with King Hussein and without the backdrop of an international conference?

The report from Amman gave no grounds for optimism on this score. Hussein sent word about his meeting with Shamir, but his description of it diverged dramatically from Meridor's. In effect, Hussein was saying that Shamir was hopeless, that he could not work with him, while Shamir was claiming that he could work directly with Hussein and did not need any help from outside. Each insisted that Shultz not reveal his assessment of the encounter to the other. Shultz specifically asked Hussein for permission to reveal to Shamir that he had received his readout of the session. The answer was no. Both parties seemed to discount the importance of the United States in all this.[30]

Since the parties made no headway on their own, Shultz came up with the idea of linking Middle Eastern peace talks to the Reagan-Gorbachev summit that was due to take place in Washington at the end of the year. His idea was that Reagan and Gorbachev, as an adjunct to their summit, would invite Hussein and Shamir, as well as representatives from Egypt, Syria, and Lebanon, to meet in the United States under U.S.-Soviet auspices and with the UN secretary-general in attendance. Ronald Reagan, who was growing weary of the Middle East and the incessant maneuvering of its leaders, gave the go-ahead. "But the first guy who vetoes it kills it," he said. In mid-October, Shultz flew to Israel to put the idea to Shamir. Shamir asked dozens of questions, all implying that, on reflection, he could not say yes. "Okay," said Shultz, "I don't want to waste your time. Just say no." Shamir wanted time to think and to consult. Their next session was brief. "Well, Mr. Secretary," Shamir concluded, "you know our dreams and you know our nightmares. We trust you. Go ahead."

The next evening Shultz tried out his idea on King Hussein at his residence in London. The king and his advisers were taken aback by the idea and astounded to learn of Shamir's agreement. Hussein also needed time to think and consult. By the time they met the next day, he had made up his mind: his answer was no. He gave two reasons. His nerves were raw at the very mention of

Shamir. "I can't be alone with that man," he said in an aside to Richard Murphy. Hussein did not believe that Shamir would ever permit negotiations to go beyond the issue of "transitional" arrangements for those living in the West Bank and Gaza. And he also did not believe Shamir would ever give up an inch of territory or work on a "final status" agreement for the territories. So no, and that was that, said the king.[31]

Shamir himself was getting weary of the incessant maneuvers to find a peaceful solution to the Arab-Israeli dispute. "The presenting and rejecting of peace plans," he wrote in his memoirs, "went on throughout the duration of my Prime Ministership; not a year passed without some official proposal being made by the United States, or Israel, or even Mubarak, each one bringing in its wake new internal crises, expectations and disappointments—though I had become more or less immune to the latter." These plans rarely contained new elements, Shamir complained; what they amounted to was "peace in exchange for territory; recognition in exchange for territory; never 'just' peace."[32] Underlying these comments was the assumption that Israel was entitled to be served peace with its Arab neighbors on a silver platter, without having to exert itself or make any concessions.

By his own lights Shamir was a successful prime minister. He believed that time was on Israel's side, and he successfully played for time. He did not like the London Agreement and managed to scupper it. He was opposed to an international conference in any shape or form, and that conference was not convened until 1991. He was committed to maintaining the status quo in the occupied territories, and it was maintained, at least on the surface. Below the surface, Palestinian frustration and despondency were increasing all the time. All the hopes that the London Agreement had raised in the occupied territories had come to nothing. A feeling of hopelessness took hold as the Palestinians watched more and more of their land being swallowed up by Israeli settlements. Economic conditions remained as miserable as ever, while Israel's military government was becoming more intrusive and more heavy-handed. The occupied territories were like a tinderbox waiting for a spark.

The Palestinian War
of Independence

The spark that ignited the Palestinian uprising, or *intifada,* was a traffic accident, on 9 December 1987, in which an Israeli truck driver killed four residents of Jabaliya, the largest of the eight refugee camps in the Gaza Strip. It was falsely rumored that the driver deliberately caused the accident to avenge the stabbing to death of his brother in Gaza two days earlier. The two men were unrelated. Nevertheless, the rumor inflamed Palestinian passions and set off disturbances in the Jabaliya camp and in the rest of the Gaza Strip. From Gaza the disturbances spread to the West Bank. Within days the occupied territories were engulfed in a wave of spontaneous, uncoordinated, and popular street demonstrations and commercial strikes on an unprecedented scale. Equally unprecedented was the extent of mass participation in these disturbances: tens of thousands of ordinary civilians, including women and children. Demonstrators burned tires, threw stones and Molotov cocktails at Israeli cars, brandished iron bars, and waved the Palestinian flag. The standard of revolt against Israeli rule had been raised. The Israeli security forces used the full panoply of crowd control measures to quell the disturbances: cudgels, nightsticks, tear gas, water cannons, rubber bullets, and live ammunition. But the disturbances only gathered momentum.

The outbreak of the *intifada* was completely spontaneous. There was no preparation or planning by the local Palestinian elite or the PLO, but the PLO was quick to jump on the bandwagon of popular discontent against Israeli rule and to play a leadership role alongside a newly formed body, the Unified National Command. In origin the *intifada* was not a nationalist revolt. It had its roots in poverty, in the miserable living conditions of the refugee camps, in hatred of the occupation, and, above all, in the humiliation that the Palestinians had to endure over the preceding twenty years. But it developed into a statement of major political import. The aims of the *intifada* were not stated at the outset; they emerged in the course of the struggle. The ultimate aim was self-determination and the establishment of an independent Palestinian state, which had failed to emerge forty years previously despite the UN partition resolution of 29 November 1947. In this respect the *intifada* may be seen as the Palestinian war of independence. The Israeli-Palestinian conflict had come full circle.

The *intifada* took Israel by complete surprise. Political leaders and the entire intelligence community were oblivious to processes taking place under their very noses. They were surprised by the outbreak of the *intifada* because they blithely believed in a conception that was out of touch with reality. This conception had a political aspect and a military aspect. The politicians, for the most part, assumed that time was on their side; that the residents of the

territories depended on Israel for jobs; that there was tacit acqui-
escence in Israeli rule; and that, consequently, Israel could continue the process of creeping annexation without running the risk
of a large-scale popular revolt. The military experts not only assumed but were confident that their traditional methods would enable them to deal effectively with any disturbances that occurred
and that any manifestations of violence by the inhabitants of the
occupied territories could be swiftly nipped in the bud.[33]

It took about a month for Israelis to realize that the disturbances were not just a flash in the pan and that they could not go
on ignoring the twenty-year-old problem. Israeli society was forced
to consider seriously alternatives to the status quo, but the result
was bitter divisions and a shift toward extremes at both ends of the
political spectrum. On the left there was a growing realization that
a political solution had to be found to the Palestinian problem
and that this would probably mean negotiations with the PLO
and the eventual emergence of an independent Palestinian state
alongside Israel. On the right, where ideas of territorial compromise had never been popular, the conviction crystallized that only
brute force could bring the trouble to an end. The immediate result of the unrest was a tilt to the right. This was reflected in the
growing number of voices calling on the IDF to employ an iron
fist in order to smash the *intifada* once and for all.

The *intifada* also accentuated the divisions inside the national
unity government. The Likud and the Alignment, the main parties
in the government, faced a high level of internal dissent. Neither
party was able to devise a clear and consistent policy for dealing
with the *intifada*. Within the Alignment, Shimon Peres tilted toward a political initiative and Yitzhak Rabin toward the use of
force. Peres resurrected the "Gaza first" idea, originally advanced
during the Palestinian autonomy talks with Sadat's Egypt. He suggested to the Knesset Foreign Affairs and Defense Committee in
mid-December that the Gaza Strip be demilitarized but remain
under Israeli supervision and that the thirteen Jewish settlements
there be dismantled. He proposed the dismantling of settlements
not as an immediate or unilateral Israeli move but as part of an
overall peace settlement. Shamir attacked the suggestion, calling
Peres "a defeatist with a scalpel who wants to put Israel on the operating table so he can give away Gaza today, Judea and Samaria
tomorrow and the Golan Heights after that." It was Peres and his
party, claimed Shamir, who were to blame for the unrest because
they encouraged the Arabs to resort to violence.[34] The real prob-

lem, according to Shamir, was not a territorial dispute that could be solved through territorial concessions, but a threat to the very existence of the State of Israel.

Yitzhak Rabin, who as minister of defense had the primary responsibility for dealing with the disturbances, was rather closer in his views to Shamir than to Peres. When the disturbances broke out, he greatly underestimated the gravity of the situation and went ahead with a scheduled visit to the United States. On his return he veered to the other extreme, ordering the use of force on a massive scale to defeat the uprising. "Break their bones," he was reported to have said while directing his troops in the field during the early weeks of the *intifada*. These three words gained him international notoriety. He later denied having uttered them. But the image of Rabin the bone breaker stuck. Rabin's aim was to drive home to the residents of the occupied territories the notion that they would not be allowed to make political gains as a result of violence. He also wanted to leave no doubt in their minds as to who was running the territories. To this end he exhorted his troops to use "might, force, and beatings." But it was precisely this kind of arrogant and aggressive attitude that had provoked the uprising in the first place. In the end it was the residents of the territories themselves who demonstrated to Rabin that military force was part of the problem rather than a solution.

On orders from above, the IDF resorted to a whole range of draconian measures in order to crush the uprising. Among its measures were deportation of political activists, political assassination, administrative detention, mass arrests, curfews, punitive economic policies, the closing down of schools and universities, and the breaking up of communal structures. Thousands of Palestinians were arrested on suspicion of conspiring to subvert public order and incitement to violence, and special detention camps had to be hastily constructed to accommodate all the detainees. These extreme measures did not bring the uprising under control. By the end of the first month, it was clear that the IDF's policy was completely bankrupt. Senior army officers began to admit that there was no return to the pre-December 1987 status quo and that the uprising might continue indefinitely.

Academics were quicker than either the politicians or the soldiers to grasp the true nature of the phenomenon that Israel was facing. Yehoshua Porath, a leading expert on Palestinian history, noted, "This is the first time that there has been a popular action, covering all social strata and groups. . . . The whole population is

rebelling, and this is creating a common national experience."
Urban as well as rural areas were participating in the uprising in
an exceptional demonstration of national cohesion. In Porath's estimate, the *intifada* accomplished more in its first few months
than decades of PLO terrorism had achieved outside the country.
Professor Shlomo Avineri, a prominent Labor Party intellectual,
observed, "The West Bank and Gaza under Israeli rule are a
threat against which the whole might of the Israeli army may not
suffice. . . . An army can beat an army, but an army cannot beat
a people. . . . Israel is learning that power has limits. Iron can
smash iron, it cannot smash an unarmed fist."[35]

Events in the occupied territories received intense media coverage. The world was assailed by disturbing pictures of Israeli
troops firing on stone-throwing demonstrators, or beating with
cudgels those they caught, among them women and children.
Israel's image suffered serious damage as a result of this media
coverage. The Israelis complained the reporting was biased and
that it focused deliberately on scenes of brutality in what was a normal effort to restore order. But no amount of pleading could obscure the message that constantly came across in pictures in the
newspapers and on the television screens: a powerful army was
being unleashed against a civilian population that was fighting for
its basic human rights and for the right to political self-
determination. The biblical image of David and Goliath now
seemed to be reversed, with Israel looking like an overbearing
Goliath and the Palestinians with the stones as a vulnerable David.
British visitors naturally took the side of the underdogs. David
Mellor, a minister of state at the Foreign Office, gave vent to his
abhorrence at the conditions in the Gaza refugee camps: "I defy
anyone to come here and not be shocked. Conditions here are an
affront to civilized values. It is appalling that a few miles up the
coast there is prosperity, and here there is misery on a scale that rivals anything anywhere in the world." Gerald Kaufman, the Labor
Party's spokesman on foreign affairs, himself a Jew and a long-
standing supporter of Israel, remarked that "friends of Israel as well
as foes have been shocked and saddened by the country's response
to the disturbances."[36] Within a short time of the outbreak of the
uprising, Israel's standing sank to its lowest ebb since the siege of
Beirut in 1982.

Israel became the target of outspoken international criticism,
from official as well as unofficial sources. The United Nations
strongly condemned Israel's violation of human rights in the ter-

ritories, as it had done many times in the past. To this was now added specific condemnation of the IDF for the "killing and wounding of defenseless Palestinian civilians." The Security Council called for an investigation, and Marrack Goulding, the UN undersecretary-general for special political affairs, visited the occupied territories in January 1988. He met with Foreign Minister Peres, but Prime Minister Shamir refused to see him, because he was "interfering in Israel's internal affairs." Goulding was dismayed by what he saw. He reported that he had witnessed Israel using "unduly harsh" measures in the territories and that, although the IDF had the right to maintain order, it had "over-reacted" to the demonstrations. During the 1988 session of the General Assembly, nearly a score of resolutions were passed, condemning Israel and calling on it to abide by the Geneva Convention for the protection of civilians in times of war. Israel's delegate to the UN complained that the organization was so biased that "even if we threw rose petals at the Molotov-cocktail throwers, this body would find a way to condemn us."[37]

By far the most serious fallout from the *intifada* was its effect on U.S.-Israeli relations. While the Reagan administration abstained from, or vetoed, many of the UN resolutions condemning Israel, it was privately critical of the Israeli handling of the uprising. The uprising brought about a fundamental change in U.S. policy toward the Arab-Israeli conflict, culminating by the end of 1988 in recognition of the PLO as a legitimate party in the negotiations. There was a marked shift in American public opinion away from its traditional support for Israel. The uprising sparked sympathy for the Palestinians at all levels of American society. It even prompted some of the leaders of American Jewry to raise questions about the wisdom of Israel's policies and the morality of its methods, for the first time since the war in Lebanon. In government circles there was concern that close American association with Israel despite its defiance of world opinion could have negative repercussions for American interests throughout the Middle East and the Persian Gulf.[38] Earlier attempts to organize an international conference had floundered because no solution could be found to the problem of Palestinian representation and because Likud leaders had opposed the whole idea. America's response to this opposition had been rather mild. With the *intifada* gathering momentum, George Shultz became personally involved again. The result was the first major U.S. effort to solve the Arab-Israeli conflict since the Reagan plan of 1982.

Shultz made two trips to the region in search of fresh ideas and then produced, on 4 March 1988, a package that came to be known as the Shultz initiative. The package followed in the path of the Camp David Accords in calling for Palestinian self-rule but with an accelerated timetable. There was also an important new element: an "interlock," a locked-in connection between the talks on the transitional period of self-rule and the talks on final status. This was intended to give assurances to the Palestinians against Israeli foot-dragging. Events were expected to move forward at a rapid pace. First, the secretary-general of the UN would convene all the parties to the Arab-Israeli conflict and the five permanent members of the Security Council to an international conference. This conference would not be able to impose solutions on the participants or to veto any agreements reached by them. Second, negotiations between an Israeli and a Jordanian-Palestinian delegation would start on 1 May and end by 1 November. Third, the transition period would start three months later and last three years. Fourth, negotiations on final status would begin before the start of the transition period and have to be completed within a year. In other words, negotiations on final status would start regardless of the outcome of the first phase of negotiations.

Shimon Peres supported the Shultz initiative and said so publicly. So did President Mubarak. King Hussein, despite some reservations, appealed to the other Arabs not to reject it out of hand. The Palestinian response added up to a chorus repeating the old refrain that the one and only address for any proposals was the PLO in Tunis. And the PLO leaders in Tunis had no intention of letting the "insiders" steal the show by meeting with the American secretary of state.

If Shultz was disappointed with the response of the Palestinians, he was utterly dismayed by the response of Israel's prime minister. Shamir, who had initially given Shultz encouragement, was now singing a different tune. He blasted the idea of an international conference and rejected the interlock concept as contrary to the Camp David Accords. Even more shocking was the discovery that Shamir's interpretation of Resolution 242 did not encompass the principle of "land for peace." He said he was ready to negotiate peace with King Hussein, and with any Palestinians he might bring along with him, but that he was not ready to relinquish any territory for peace. When Shultz brought up the name of Faisal Husseini, a prominent moderate among the local Palestinian leaders, Shamir would say only, "We have a file on him!" Shultz admitted that he did not know the man but suggested that it be kept in mind that he might serve as a partner in future negotiations. "It's a very heavy file," Shamir repeated to stress his point. "Yes," said Shultz, reemphasizing his own point, "but the question is what one *does* with the file." The Shultz initiative was stalled, and its author thought that the main reason for that was Israel's prime minister. He did not say so openly, but he and his aides had a feeling that America's policy in the Middle East had fallen hostage to Israel's intransigence or inability to make decisions.[39]

The *intifada* refocused the attention of the Arab world on the Palestinian problem. At the Arab League summit in Amman in November 1987, the Palestinian problem had been relegated to the sidelines. The *intifada* broke out the following month, and the indifference shown by the Arab world to the fate of the Palestinians was one of the reasons behind it. Now the courage of the Palestinians in resisting Israeli occupation put the rest of the Arab world to shame. In June 1988 an extraordinary summit of the Arab League was convened in Algiers. The summit reaffirmed the role of the PLO as the representative of the Palestinian people in any negotiations and pledged its financial and diplomatic support for the *intifada*.

The two principal losers from the *intifada* werc Israel and Jordan. King Hussein was forced to reevaluate Jordan's position. On 31 July 1988 he suddenly announced that Jordan was cutting its legal and administrative ties with the West Bank. Jordan had continued to pay the salary of about a third of the civil servants on the West Bank during the preceding two decades of Israeli occupation. Many East Bankers felt they got nothing but ingratitude for their efforts to help the Palestinians and that the time had come to cut their losses. The king himself felt that Jordan was fighting a losing battle in defending positions that had already fallen to the PLO. After two decades of trying to blur the distinction between the East Bank and the West Bank, he concluded that the time had come to assert that the East Bank was not Palestine and that it was up to the Palestinians to decide what they wanted to do with the West Bank and to deal with the Israelis directly over its future. As he later put it,

> It was the *intifada* that really caused our decision on disengagement from the West Bank. It was again our lack of ability to get any agreement with our Palestinian brethren. I wish

to God they had been frank enough about what they wanted, and they would have got it a long time before. But we were torn apart trying to get all the pieces of the jigsaw together to help them. However, suspicions and doubts got in the way. But, beyond that, we recognized there was a definite trend which started before the Rabat resolution of 1974 and continued all the way through. They could give, they could take, they could do whatever they liked. They could probably give more than we could, but they decided that they wanted to have their say regarding their future, and I simply tried to help them by that decision.[40]

In a press conference on 7 August, the king said that never again would Jordan assume the role of negotiating on behalf of the Palestinians. This statement was probably not meant to be as final as it sounded. But by closing out the idea of a Jordanian-Palestinian delegation and of a West Bank in some manner affiliated with Jordan, the king's decision appeared to the American secretary of state to mark the end of his initiative. A few weeks after the king had announced his decision, he asked the State Department to pass a message to Shimon Peres: the decision to remove Jordan from the peace process was taken in the hope that it would cause the PLO to "see the light and come to terms with reality."[41]

This private message, however, could do no more than soften the blow that the king's latest move was bound to inflict on his partner in the abortive London Agreement. The effect of the public message was to strengthen the position of the PLO and to undermine the Alignment's so-called Jordanian option. The king himself had never liked the term "Jordanian option," for it implied an agreement between Israel and Jordan over the heads of the Palestinians. In his speech and press conference he therefore cleared the air. He said, in effect, that if a Jordanian option for settling the Palestinian problem had ever existed, it was now definitely dead.

From Israel's standpoint the king's speech marked the collapse of a very popular idea. It meant that Jordan was no longer prepared to deliberate the Palestinian problem with Israel; the only issue it would discuss was the question of its own borders. The Israelis were stunned by the speech and initially interpreted it as no more than a tactical move by the king to get the Palestinians to say that they still wanted him to represent them. But when the king asked his supporters on the West Bank not to sponsor petitions urging him to relent, the Israelis were forced to recognize that disengagement was a strategic move, not a tactical one. Even Likud leaders had reason to regret this move, because they realized that the forecasts of all the prophets of doom had come true: Israel now found itself all alone in the arena with the PLO.[42]

Another consequence of the *intifada* was the birth of Hamas. The name is an Arabic word meaning zeal, and also an acronym for the Islamic Resistance Movement. Hamas was founded in Gaza in 1988 by Sheikh Ahmed Yassin, a paralyzed religious teacher, as a wing of the long-established Muslim Brothers in Palestine. To obtain a permit from the Israeli authorities, the movement was obliged to pledge that its fight for Palestinian rights would be conducted within the limits of the law and without the use of arms. Ironically, the Israeli authorities at first encouraged Hamas in the hope of weakening the secular nationalism of the PLO. But the Palestinian uprising had a radicalizing effect on Hamas, and its members began to step outside the bounds of the law. Although the Israelis repeatedly cracked down on the organization, the roots it put down sprouted again, giving rise to more violence each time. In 1989 the Israelis arrested Yassin and kept him in prison until 1997. Hamas, however, continued to shift from the use of stones to the use of firearms. In 1994 it began, through its military wing, to launch suicide bombs inside Israel. The suicide attacks were undertaken out by individual members of Hamas who carried explosives on their body and detonated them in crowded places such as buses and markets. Israel's tactic of "divide and rule" had backfired disastrously.

While radicalizing Hamas, the *intifada* had a moderating effect on the secular Palestinians. On the one hand, the *intifada* raised the morale and boosted the pride and self-confidence of the Palestinian community. On the other, it did not end Israeli occupation, and living conditions deteriorated in the course of the struggle. Local leaders realized that a Palestinian peace initiative was essential. They were worried that the *intifada* would come to an end without yielding any concrete political gains. Consequently, they started putting pressure on the PLO chiefs in Tunis to meet the conditions that would enable them to enter into negotiations with Israel. Over the years the PLO mainstream had moved toward more moderate positions, but it avoided a clear-cut statement of these positions for fear of alienating the militant factions of the organization. The local leaders now threw all their weight behind the

moderate mainstream. They urged the PLO chiefs in Tunis to recognize Israel, to accept a two-state solution, to declare a
Palestinian state, and to establish a government-in-exile.

The *intifada* also called for a reevaluation of Israel's policy toward the Palestinians, but this was not an easy task, given the
snarled state of the country's political system. Public opinion was
divided. Some people thought that the *intifada* was an unwinnable
war and that Israel should therefore seek a political solution that
would put an end to the occupation. Others urged the use of
greater force in order to smash the *intifada*. Both views were represented inside the government of national unity, which consequently tended to cripple itself every time the issue came up.
Whenever the government seemed to be making progress, its
wheels immediately jammed. Each time it took a step forward, internal forces pulled it two steps back. The government tended to
deal with the most pressing operational questions and postpone
discussions of the longer-term questions raised by the *intifada*.[43]
Thus, in terms of dealing with the Palestinian problem, the government of national unity once again proved to be a government
of political paralysis.

12

Stonewalling
1988–1992

THE GENERAL ELECTION of 1 November 1988 was fought in the shadow of the *intifada*. One of the consequences of the *intifada* was to focus attention on the fundamental issues of national importance, such as security, peace, and the future of the occupied territories. The Labor Alignment's campaign made peace the central theme. Shimon Peres talked about the London Agreement, about the Jordanian option, and about an international conference. His aim was to persuade the voters that he could negotiate a settlement that would bring peace without harming Israel's security. He drew a clear distinction between his vision of the future and that of his political opponents. The *intifada*, however, made security the key issue and bolstered the position of the right-wing parties that advocated an "iron fist" policy to restore law and order in the territories. Likud politicians castigated Labor politicians both for their soft approach to the *intifada* and for their willingness to resolve the Arab-Israeli conflict by exchanging territory for peace.

The Likud's manifesto underlined the gulf between the two parties with regard to the future of the territories. "The right of the Jewish people to Eretz Israel," it stated, "is eternal and indisputable, and linked to our right to security and peace. The State of Israel has a right and a claim to sovereignty over Judea and Samaria and the Gaza District. In time, Israel will invoke this claim and strive to realize it. Any plan involving the handover of parts of western Eretz Israel to foreign rule, as proposed by the Labor Alignment, denies our right to this country." During the campaign Yitzhak Shamir constantly reiterated that the *intifada* was not about territory but about Israel's very existence and that the suppression of the *intifada* was therefore a matter of life and death for Israel.

The election did not produce a clear victory for either the Likud or the Alignment, though Likud emerged with one seat more that the Alignment. The Likud's representation in the Knesset fell from 41 to 40, while that of the Alignment fell from 44 to 39. Both lost seats to the smaller and more ideologically defined parties on the extreme right and left of Israel's political spectrum. Fifteen parties received enough votes to gain Knesset representation. On the extreme right were three parties: Tehiya (Renaissance), headed by Professor Yuval Ne'eman, which won 3 seats; Tsomet (Crossroads), a breakaway group from the Tehiya led by the former chief of staff Rafael Eytan, which gained 2 seats; and Moledet (Motherland), a new party headed by the former general Rehavam Ze'evi, which called for the mass expulsion of Palestinians and which also won 2 seats. On the extreme left, the New Communist List won 4 seats, while the Progressive List won a single seat. The religious parties did especially well, increasing their representation from 12 to 18 seats, thus becoming the holder of the balance in the new Knesset.

President Chaim Herzog called on Shamir, as the leader of the largest party, to form a government, and he recommended another national unity government. Shamir tried but failed to form a narrow government with the religious parties. After fifty-two days of negotiations, the Likud and the Alignment reached agreement on a national unity government. This time, however, there was no rotation: Shamir would be prime minister throughout the government's four-year term. Peres relinquished the post of foreign minister to become vice premier and minister of finance. Yitzhak Rabin retained the defense portfolio. Moshe Arens was appointed foreign minister, David Levy deputy prime minister and minister of housing, and Ariel Sharon minister for trade and industry. The coalition agreement was similar to the 1984 agreement in requiring the consent of both parties on controversial policy issues, such as territorial compromise and the modalities of the peace process. Yet in this coalition the Alignment was clearly the junior partner.

THE ENIGMA OF YITZHAK SHAMIR

For Yitzhak Shamir it was the peak of his political power. He owed his first term as prime minister to Menachem Begin's sudden decision to retire from public life. During his second term Shamir's power was severely curtailed and his style cramped by the rotation agreement with Peres. Now, for the first time, he was almost master in his own house. Yet, despite his prominence in public life throughout the 1980s, Shamir remained something of an enigma. Twenty years underground, as a member of the Irgun, a leader of the Stern Gang, and, from 1956 until 1965, in the Mossad, helped to mold Shamir into an uncommunicative, secretive, and highly suspicious individual. Losing his family in the Nazi Holocaust was another formative experience, which could only reinforce his stark, Hobbesian view of the world. Although he rarely mentioned the Holocaust in his public utterances, the experience seared itself on his psyche and continued to color his attitude to his people's other great adversary—the Arabs. In Shamir's monochromatic picture of the world, "the Arabs" featured as a monolithic and implacable enemy bent on the destruction of the State of Israel and on throwing the Jews into the sea. Mistrust in peace and refusal to pay any concrete price for it was part and parcel of this deeply entrenched view of a hostile world, bad Arabs, and permanent danger. Amos Elon gave this description of Shamir:

> He is a man of few words and short simple sentences but when he speaks of the Land, the homeland, in his grinding bass voice, the deep almost Wagnerian sound resonates through his small frame. His unassuming figure, short, muscular, and stocky, combines with a pair of hard grey eyes to convey an impression of bullish determination, tenacity, and resolve.[1]

Political analysts in Israel and abroad have long speculated on the complicated makeup of Shamir's personality. Some saw him as the *simplificateur terrible*. Others regarded him as a hardheaded realist and shrewd judge of the prevailing power balance. One explanation of the Shamir enigma, which gained wide currency among American Jews, held him to be a tough bargainer but one who was also genuinely interested in peace and therefore ideally suited to represent Israel in negotiations with the Arabs. Shamir's impeccable nationalist credentials, so the argument ran, would be his greatest asset in negotiating a settlement with the Arabs and in dealing with domestic opposition to such a settlement. Just as Begin was prepared to withdraw from Sinai in return for a peace treaty with Egypt, Shamir, it was argued, could ultimately be relied upon to trade land for peace on Israel's eastern and northern fronts. This view of Shamir, however, was based on little more than wishful thinking.

The key to unraveling the Shamir enigma is contained in an interview he gave in 1985. "I'm seventy years old today," said Shamir. "I have been in the Land of Israel for fifty years and I have been fighting for our principles for sixty years. Do you think I'll give up these principles for anyone?"[2] Avishai Margalit, a keen observer of the Israeli political scene, underlined the rigidity of Shamir's basic stand:

> Shamir's success with many American Jews seems based on their confidence that he is essentially a tough bargainer—a Jewish Assad. But Shamir is not a bargainer. Shamir is a two-dimensional man. One dimension is the length of the Land of Israel, the second, its width. Since Shamir's historical vision is measured in inches, he won't give an inch. He will not bargain about the Land of Israel or about any interim agreement that would involve the least risk of losing control over the occupied territories.[3]

In Shamir's worldview power was the paramount factor. To achieve its goals, Israel needed to be strong. In the opening of his article "Israel's Role in a Changing Middle East," in the prestigious American journal *Foreign Affairs,* Shamir wrote, "Traditionally, the twin goals of Israel's foreign policy have always been peace and security—two concepts that are closely interrelated: Where there is strength, there is peace—at least, shall we say, peace has a chance. Peace will be unattainable if Israel is weak or perceived to be so. This, indeed, is one of the most crucial lessons to be learned from the history of the Middle East since the end of the Second World War."[4]

To Shamir's way of thinking, the weak could not command respect in the harsh world of interstate relations. Arab voices calling for peace with Israel were to Shamir nothing but "noises." They were either a sign of weakness or a ploy to continue the war against Israel by other means. Shamir regarded Egypt's peace policy as a tactic rather than as the reflection of a strategic commitment, and he remained suspicious of King Hussein, who seemed to him to speak with two voices. This suspicion of Arab intentions constituted the rationale for passivity and for the preservation of the status quo. By responding to political initiatives, Shamir warned, Israel would weaken itself and undermine its capacity to command respect and to attain its goals. Willingness to negotiate would be seen by the Arabs as a sign of weakness and would result in harm to Israel's national interests, the most important of which was the preservation of the status quo. Indifferent to questions of morality and justice, Shamir cared passionately about Israel's military power as the only sure instrument for preserving the status quo.

"Peace is an abstract thing," said Shamir in an address on the anniversary of Ze'ev Jabotinsky's birth. "You sign a paper and say, 'Here is peace.' But what if tomorrow you tear up the paper and with one stroke of the pen you abolish the treaty?" The uncertainty involved in signing a peace treaty was less tolerable than that in maintaining the status quo. A peace treaty could be torn up, whereas territory could not be recovered so easily. "We have enough experience," said Shamir, "and we will therefore not give land in return for peace again, but only peace in return for peace." This was an indirect criticism of Menachem Begin, who had given land in exchange for peace with Egypt. In Shamir's view this approach contradicted Jabotinsky's doctrine of the iron wall.[5] It was Shamir himself, however, who was guilty of simplifying and thus distorting Jabotinsky's teaching. Jabotinsky certainly regarded an iron wall as essential for attaining the Zionist goal of statehood, but he also recognized the need for negotiation on Palestinian national rights once Jewish statehood had been secured; Shamir did not. Jabotinsky's iron wall encompassed a theory of change in Arab-Jewish relations leading to reconciliation and peaceful coexistence, whereas Shamir was fixated on the iron wall as an instrument for preventing any change in Arab-Israeli relations.

SHAMIR'S PEACE INITIATIVE

The advent of the Shamir government coincided with a revolution in Palestinian political thinking. The impetus for this revolution came from the *intifada,* and the man who presided over it was

Yasser Arafat. The success of the *intifada* gave Arafat and his followers the confidence they needed to moderate their political program. After years of shilly-shallying, they crossed the Rubicon. At
the meeting of the Palestine National Council (PNC) in Algiers in
mid-November 1988, Arafat won a majority for the historic decision to recognize Israel's legitimacy, to accept all the relevant UN
resolutions going back to 29 November 1947, and to adopt the
principle of a two-state solution. The claim to the whole of
Palestine, enshrined in the Palestinian National Charter, was finally
laid to rest, and a declaration of independence was issued for a
mini-state in the West Bank and Gaza, with East Jerusalem as its
capital.

Israel reacted very sharply to the resolutions of 15 November
1988. Just as the Palestinians were moving toward territorial compromise, Israel, under Shamir's leadership, was moving away from
it. On the same day, Shamir gave his reaction in a written statement: "The PLO's decisions and the declaration of a state are a de-
ceptive propaganda exercise, intended to create an impression of
moderation and of achievements for those carrying out violent
acts in the territories of Judea and Samaria." The Israeli cabinet
was equally dismissive of the Algiers resolutions. Following its
meeting on 20 November, the cabinet made the following announcement: "The PNC declaration is an additional attempt at
disinformation, a jumble of illusions, meant to mislead world public opinion. The PLO has not changed its covenant, its policy, its
path of terrorism or its character."[6]

The PLO followed the Algiers resolutions with a concerted attempt to project a more moderate image. It made a special effort
to gain respectability by dissociating the PLO from terrorism.
Arafat issued a series of statements on the subject, which failed to
satisfy the United States, so in the end the State Department virtually dictated the text that Arafat read at the opening of his press
conference in Geneva on 14 December. "I repeat for the record,"
stated Arafat, "that we totally and absolutely renounce all forms of
terrorism, including individual, group and state terrorism.
Between Geneva and Algiers we have made our position crystal
clear." The statement unconditionally accepted Resolutions 242
and 338 and clearly recognized Israel's right to exist. All the conditions that Henry Kissinger had laid down in 1975 for dealing
with the PLO had now been met. One of the last major foreign
policy acts of the outgoing Reagan administration was to recognize
the PLO and to open a substantive dialogue with it. This dialogue

was conducted by the American ambassador in Tunis. President Reagan stated publicly that the special commitment of the United States to Israel's security and well-being remained unshakable.

To Shamir it was crystal clear, once again, that the PLO had not abandoned the path of terror. For him the PLO had always been and would forever remain a terrorist organization. His response to the momentous changes taking place in the Palestinian camp was a reaffirmation of his previous position: no to withdrawal from the occupied territories, no to recognition of the PLO, no to negotiation with the PLO, no to a Palestinian state. Shamir called the U.S. decision to enter into a dialogue with the PLO a "grave error." He saw it as a threat to the long-standing American-Israeli collaboration in support of the territorial status quo. "For the PLO," explained Shamir, "a Palestinian state is a minimum. Therefore, anyone who engages in negotiations with it in effect accepts this principle. What else can one talk about with the PLO, if not about a Palestinian state?" Vice-Premier Peres described the opening of the U.S.–PLO dialogue as "a sad day for all of us." But he felt that Israel had to come up with its own peace initiative, since it was impossible to preserve the status quo. He thought that the new policy would guide the incoming Republican administration, because it was made with the knowledge and consent of George Bush. Peres indirectly blamed the Likud leaders for this development by suggesting that those who opposed the London Agreement and an international conference paved the way for the PLO. Basically, he said, "something has happened, and we must offer a response."[7]

Yitzhak Rabin played a major part in formulating the Israeli response. The *intifada* had taught him several important lessons. In the first place, he learned that it was not the Jordanians who were going to bring the Palestinians to the negotiating table, it was the other way around. Second, he realized that Israel would have to negotiate directly with the local Palestinians and that this, too, involved a departure from the Jordanian option. Third, he came to the conclusion that Israel's policy could not rest solely on military repression but had to include a political initiative. In his phrase, Israel had to march with two feet, the military foot and the political foot. In January 1989 Rabin floated a four-stage plan, which called for (1) cessation of Palestinian violence, (2) a three to six-month period of quiet prior to elections among the Palestinians, (3) negotiations with the elected Palestinian leaders and with Jordan for an interim form of autonomy, and (4) negotiations on the final status of the territories. The basic idea behind the plan was Palestinian elections and expanded autonomy for an interim period in return for cessation of the *intifada*.

Moshe Arens, the new foreign minister, supported the idea of an Israeli political initiative along the lines suggested by Rabin. Arens was a Herut hard-liner but, unlike Shamir, he placed security above ideology. Arens had a more sophisticated understanding than Shamir of the philosophy of Ze'ev Jabotinsky, realizing that the erection of an iron wall had to be followed with political negotiations. American pressure helped convince Arens that the present situation could not continue forever and that a practical solution had to be formulated. George Bush and his secretary of state, James Baker, were much less tolerant of Shamir's stonewalling than Reagan and Shultz had been. They wanted to hear new ideas on how to revive the peace process. Concerted pressure from the United States and from his own defense and foreign ministers eventually persuaded Shamir to put forward some new ideas.

On 14 May, Shamir presented to the cabinet a peace initiative for discussion and vote. Its centerpiece was a call for elections in the West Bank and Gaza to select non-PLO Palestinians with whom Israel could negotiate an interim agreement on self-government. The plan specified that the negotiations would be based on the principles laid down in the Camp David Accords and that there would be no participation by the PLO and no Palestinian state. The debate went on for hours. There was some opposition from the left, from those who felt that the plan did not go far enough. Most of the opposition, however, came from the right. Ariel Sharon argued that the plan would spell disaster for Israel; it would encourage terrorism and lead to another war. At the end of the debate, twenty ministers voted for the plan and six against. What had once seemed impossible thus came to pass: Yitzhak Shamir launched a peace initiative.

Washington's public response to Shamir's peace initiative was sympathetic, although its private prognosis was that without Israel's prior agreement to the principle of peace for territories there could be no real peace process and thus no peace.[8] On 22 May, James Baker spoke at the annual convention of AIPAC (the American-Israel Public Affairs Committee) in Washington. AIPAC was a powerful pressure group, which mobilized the support of the American Jewish community and of many non-Jews on behalf of the State of Israel. In his opening remarks Baker highlighted the shared commitment to democratic values and the strong strategic partnership between America and Israel. He then welcomed the Shamir initiative as "an important and positive start down the road toward constructing workable negotiations." But when he came to the heart of the matter, the fate of the occupied territories, he dropped a bombshell. Interpreting Resolution 242 as requiring the exchange of land for peace, Baker referred to "territorial withdrawal" as the probable outcome of negotiations. Then, in a pointed reference to Shamir's ideology, Baker said, "For Israel, now is the time to lay aside, once and for all, the unrealistic vision of greater Israel. Israeli interests in the West Bank and Gaza—security and otherwise—can be accommodated in a settlement based on Resolution 242. Forswear annexation. Stop settlement activity. Allow schools to reopen. Reach out to the Palestinians as neighbors who deserve political rights." Baker's speech was not well received by his large American-Jewish audience, and it raised worries in Israel. It marked a shift toward a more active effort by the Bush administration to redesign the Shamir initiative into something that might be acceptable to the Palestinians.[9]

In its original form Shamir's initiative was unacceptable to the Palestinians, inside and outside the territories. The Unified National Command issued one of its periodic leaflets, which rejected the plan because it envisaged elections in the shadow of occupation and because it allegedly aimed at the liquidation of the *intifada*. The leaflet added that there was no alternative to the PLO and that a settlement could be reached only within the framework of an international conference with full powers. The PLO accepted the idea of elections but only on condition that Israel carried out a partial withdrawal of its forces from the occupied territories prior to the election and that a timetable was fixed for complete withdrawal.

The fiercest opposition to Shamir's initiative, however, came from within the ranks of his own party. Ariel Sharon, David Levy, and Yitzhak Moda'i began a rebellion against Shamir, accusing him of leading Israel down the road to destruction. They came to be known as "the constrainers," for they claimed that, like the hoops of a barrel, they were going to constrain Shamir. Following Baker's speech, they created an uproar, which was resolved by a decision to bring the peace initiative before the party's Central Committee for an in-depth discussion in early July. At the meeting they tabled a motion incorporating four "additional" principles with which they hoped to hobble the original initiative: the *in-*

tifada should be crushed; the Arabs of East Jerusalem should be prohibited from participating in the elections; there must be no division of the western part of the Land of Israel; and there should be no contact with the PLO.[10]

Shamir did not put up a fight for his plan. On the contrary, he allowed this coalition of ambition to constrain him and to destroy his initiative. The prospect of a clash in the Likud's Central Committee was more daunting for Shamir than the certainty of a clash with America and the daily clashes with the Palestinians in the occupied territories. By knuckling under to his rivals in the Likud, Shamir in effect repudiated the initiative that bore his name. "Thus by a neat sleight of hand, the master magician Yitzhak Shamir managed in rapid succession to launch and shoot down his own peace plan, making it look suspiciously like a clay pigeon devised for nothing more than a bit of harmless sport."[11] The new conditions sealed the fate of the American efforts to bring about a dialogue between Israel and moderate Palestinians without the participation of the PLO. Baker was furious. He informed the House Foreign Affairs Committee that "with such an approach there would never be a dialogue on peace." If Israeli officials were not going to adopt a positive attitude, he added, "I can only say 'Take this number: 202-456-1414. When you're serious about peace, call us.' " The number was that of the White House switchboard.

In September 1989 President Mubarak floated his own ten-point plan. Seven points dealt directly with the procedures for Palestinian elections; one point referred to the land-for-peace formula; another called for the cessation of settlement activity; and a third upheld the right of Arabs of East Jerusalem to participate in the elections. The plan provoked a crisis in the national unity government. The Alignment ministers pressed for a positive response on the grounds that the plan did not call for the PLO to play a role, or for the creation of a Palestinian state, nor did it mention a return to the 1967 borders. Likud ministers, on the other hand, objected to many points in the plan and held that it was designed to bring in the PLO through the back door. There were thus two plans, and the Alignment ministers preferred the Mubarak plan to the Shamir plan because it seemed more likely to provide a way out of the impasse.

In October, James Baker proposed that Israeli-Palestinian talks take place in Cairo, and he put forward a five-point plan covering the procedure for selecting the Palestinian participants and the scope of the talks. Mubarak was keen to host the dialogue in Cairo, and the Palestinians were prepared to go along with Baker's plan despite its firm exclusion of the PLO. Israel's national unity government was divided, with the Alignment ministers again urging a positive response. Shamir regarded Baker's five points as nothing but a ploy to make Israel sit down with the PLO, and his intuition dictated digging in. Yet the Sharon-Levy-Moda'i trio mounted another noisy mutiny against what they claimed was capitulation by the Shamir-Arens faction to the demands of the United States.

As 1989 turned into 1990, Baker became increasingly frustrated by the infighting among the Israelis and by the intransigence of their government. Shamir and Arens, who were accused by their militant colleagues of being weak-kneed, were the ones who insisted that before they could proceed with negotiations with the Palestinians, two conditions had to be met: first, an agreement not to allow the PLO any say in the negotiations; and second, an agreement that the Arab population in Jerusalem would not participate in the Palestinian elections. These conditions were considered by the Alignment ministers as unrealistic, and the coalition began to teeter on the verge of collapse.

On 13 March 1990 Shamir told the cabinet, "Mr Peres asked me to bring about the dissolution of the Unity government and undermined its existence by unjustly charging that this Government is not trying to advance the peace process—its principal task; this leaves me no choice but to terminate his service with the Government."[12] The other ten Alignment ministers tendered their collective resignation and walked out of the cabinet. Two days later the Alignment put on the agenda in the Knesset a motion of no confidence in the government. The motion was carried by 60 against 55 votes. Shamir became the first prime minister in Israel's history to have fallen as a result of a parliamentary vote of no confidence. President Chaim Herzog gave Peres a mandate to form a new government, but six week later Peres was forced to confess his inability to put together a coalition.

Shamir took another six weeks to put together a narrow coalition with the support of the religious parties and two small secular ultranationalist parties, Tehiya and Tsomet. This was the most right-wing government in Israel's history and certainly the most hard-line when it came to relations with the Arabs. Moshe Arens became minister of defense. Shamir's arch-rivals were given key posts in the new government: David Levy became foreign minister, Ariel Sharon was made minister of housing, and Yitzhak

Moda'i took over the finance ministry. Tehiya's Professor Yuval Ne'eman became minister of energy and infrastructure, while Tsomet's Rafael Eytan became minister of agriculture.

On 11 June, Shamir presented his government to the Knesset. He described it as "united by the concept that the Land of Israel is an idea, not merely an area." The basic guidelines of government policy reflected its ideological complexion: no Palestinian state; no negotiations with the PLO; Jerusalem to remain united under Israel's sovereignty; new settlements to be created and existing ones broadened; and talks with the Arab states and non-PLO Arabs to proceed on the basis of the 1989 initiative.[13] Following the departure of the Alignment, Shamir regained some of his freedom of action—or rather freedom of inaction. In a heart-to-heart talk, Arens told Shamir that the dialogue in Cairo was inescapable and that they would be free to say no in Cairo whenever necessary. Shamir did not respond except to say that he was not even sure that a dialogue with the Palestinians was really essential. Arens was unable to discover then or subsequently how his party leader envisaged a resolution of the Arab-Israeli conflict without meaningful contact with the Palestinians. One idea that Arens did put to Shamir on a number of occasions was that Israel should abandon the Gaza Strip because it had become a liability, but he was rebuffed by him every time. "Gaza is part of the Land of Israel," said Shamir.[14]

THE GULF CRISIS

Two major security challenges confronted the Shamir government in the second half of 1990: the ongoing Palestinian uprising and the crisis triggered by Iraq's invasion of Kuwait on 2 August. Initially, the Persian Gulf crisis overshadowed the *intifada*, but it soon caused a serious escalation of the Palestinian-Israeli conflict, pushing it to the brink of intercommunal war. Increasingly, the solution to the crisis became linked in the public debate with a solution to the Palestinian problem, giving rise to a new buzzword—"linkage."

The Iraqi invasion of Kuwait took Israel by surprise, even though Iraq had been identified as a growing threat to the region. After the end of the Iran-Iraq war in July 1988, Israeli intelligence closely monitored the Iraqi military buildup, which included the development of chemical weapons, nuclear weapons and long-range ballistic missile programs, the construction of missile launch sites in western Iraq, and the emergence of an Iraqi-Jordanian military alliance that enabled Iraqi aircraft to conduct surveillance flights along the border with Israel. In early 1990 Saddam Hussein, the president of Iraq, accelerated his nuclear program with the aim of balancing Israel's arsenal of nuclear weapons, which was estimated to consist of 200 nuclear warheads and 47 atomic bombs at that time.[15] In April he made his notorious threat to use binary chemical weapons to devour half of Israel "if the Zionist entity, which has atomic bombs, dared attack Iraq." Various incidents convinced Saddam Hussein that there was an Israeli conspiracy afoot to sabotage his nuclear program and possibly to launch a surgical strike similar to the one that had destroyed the Iraqi nuclear reactor in 1981. His threat was intended to deter Israel.[16]

The combination of verbal threats and the construction of missile launchers led the intelligence experts to take the threat from Baghdad more seriously and to report this concern to their civilian masters. In the summer of 1990 the message from the intelligence community was that Iraq was on the road to becoming a military superpower, that its position on the Arab-Israeli conflict was becoming increasingly inflexible, and that it was developing a long-range strategic capability and nonconventional weapons that could be turned against Israel. General David Ivri, the director general of the Ministry of Defense, warned repeatedly that the Iraqi missiles posed a lethal threat and that Israel had no answer for it, but the ministers did not take these warnings very seriously and one dismissed them as the stories of Little Red Riding Hood.[17]

Following the Iraqi invasion of Kuwait, the IAF was put on alert as a precaution. But officials stated that the movement of Iraqi troops into Kuwait did not in itself threaten Israel and would not provoke a military response. "Kuwait is a long way away," one official observed. Likud leaders used the invasion to drive home their point that Iraq was a greater threat to Middle Eastern stability than the Israeli-Palestinian conflict. They compared Saddam Hussein to Adolf Hitler and the invasion of Kuwait to Germany's acts of aggression in the 1930s. This analogy was usually accompanied by calls on the Western world, and especially the United States, to intervene in order to stop the Iraqi dictator in his tracks. The underlying fear was that unless the Western powers intervened, a showdown between Israel and Iraq would become inevitable sooner or later, and the unstated hope was that Israel's greatest ally would seize the opportunity to defeat Israel's most powerful enemy.

One of the peculiarities of the Gulf crisis was that Israel found itself on the same side as the great majority of the Arab states, including its bitter enemy Syria, in the new lineup. But there was a fundamental difference between the Arab approach to the crisis and Israel's. The Arabs for the most part wanted the reversal of the Iraqi aggression, the restoration of the political status quo, and the containment of Iraq, whereas Israel wanted the destruction of the Iraqi war machine and war-making potential. Syria in particular was worried that the destruction of Iraqi power would tilt the overall Arab-Israeli military equation in Israel's favor. It was precisely for this reason that Israel wanted to see a thoroughgoing devastation of Iraq. Some Israeli experts, including Yitzhak Rabin, were of the opinion that nothing short of nonconventional arms would stop Iraq in the wake of its invasion of Kuwait.

Ten days into the crisis, on 12 August, Saddam Hussein, in what amounted to a rare political masterstroke, suggested that Iraq might withdraw from Kuwait if Israel withdrew from all occupied Arab territory and Syria withdrew from Lebanon. It was this proposal that introduced the concept of linkage into the Middle Eastern diplomatic lexicon. Overnight Saddam Hussein became the hero of the Arab masses and the savior of the Palestinians. The Gulf conflict and the Arab-Israeli conflict, which Israel had labored to keep apart, now became linked in the public mind. A government spokesman dismissed Saddam Hussein's proposal as a cheap propaganda ploy. But the proposal landed the Bush administration on the horns of a dilemma. On the one hand, it did not want to reward Saddam Hussein for his aggression; on the other, it could hardly deny that the long-festering Arab-Israeli conflict also required a settlement. President Bush's way around this dilemma was to deny that there was any parallel between the two occupations but to promise that once Iraq left Kuwait, a settlement of the Arab-Israeli problem would be high on his administration's agenda. In other words, he rejected the simultaneous linkage of the two conflicts in favor of a deferred linkage. This placed Israel once more on the defensive.

After much agonizing, the Israeli government decided to start distributing gas masks to the civilian population on 1 October. For a nation haunted by memories of the Nazi gas chambers, this was a highly sensitive issue. The difficulty of resolving it was compounded by the fact that the IDF had no reliable information whether Iraq was capable of fitting chemical warheads to its Scud missiles. If the issuing of gas masks could be perceived in Baghdad as a prelude to a preemptive strike, the other risk was that it would be taken to imply a purely defensive posture and even a sign of weakness and that Israeli deterrence would be eroded as a consequence. To ensure that this did not happen, Shamir issued a series of public statements of mounting severity, making it clear that any attack on Israel would be met with an Israeli response. His words were carefully chosen, and the adjective "terrible" featured prominently in his characterization of the promised response. Shamir's warnings were widely interpreted by commentators in Israel and abroad to mean that an Iraqi attack on Israel with chemical weapons could provoke an Israeli nuclear response. Shamir did nothing to contradict this interpretation of his statements. He seemed content to let the Western media drive home the message that tangling with Israel might lead to the obliteration of Baghdad.[18]

On the diplomatic front the Shamir government continued to resist all attempts to link the Gulf conflict with the Palestinian issue. The Palestinians shot themselves in the foot by hailing Saddam Hussein as their champion following the invasion of Kuwait. The PLO leadership gave vent to the frustrations that had built up in the Palestinian camp over the preceding two years by openly siding with the Iraqi tyrant instead of standing by the principle of the inadmissibility of acquiring territory by force. The Shamir government seized on this and on the militant anti-Israeli rhetoric that accompanied it as further vindication of its refusal to have any truck with the PLO. The government rejected out of hand a Soviet proposal in early September for the convening of an international conference to deal with all the disputes in the Middle East. The United States also rejected the Soviet proposal. Following a meeting with David Levy in Washington, Secretary of State Baker stated that the Iraqi-Kuwaiti dispute and the Israeli-Palestinian dispute were two separate matters, which had to be treated independently.[19]

This common U.S.-Israeli front against linkage was severely shaken on 8 October by a bloody incident on Temple Mount in the heart of Jerusalem. Temple Mount is the small plateau behind the Western Wall in the Old City that is sacred for Muslims as well as Jews. While the Jews refer to the area as Har Habayit (Temple Mount), Muslims call it Haram al-Sharif (Noble Sanctuary), for it is the site of the Dome of the Rock and the al-Aksa Mosque. A group of Jewish extremists who called themselves "the Temple Mount Loyalists" entered the area to hold public prayers and to assert Jewish control. Muslim worshipers reacted to the provocation by throwing stones. Israeli security forces used live ammunition to deal with a Muslim protest that turned into a riot, killing twenty-one of the demonstrators and wounding more than a hundred. Israel was back in the headlines.

The massacre on Temple Mount unleashed a universal wave of condemnation. Arab governments who had joined in the American-led coalition against Saddam Hussein came under attack for complicity in American double standards in rushing to the defense of Kuwait while doing nothing to end the twenty-three-year-old Israeli occupation of the West Bank and Gaza. The very linkage that Saddam Hussein had failed to achieve was now highlighted by the brutal behavior of the Israeli security forces. America was driven to vote in favor of two UN resolutions condemning Israel. The universal condemnation demonstrated that there was a new equation in the making: an American approach to the Middle East based on an alliance with the Arabs and an Israeli approach to the Palestinians that largely ignored American, Arab, and international opinion. This became the source of persistent tension in U.S.-Israeli relations.

This tension was temporarily relieved on 29 November when the Security Council passed Resolution 687, which authorized the use of "all necessary means" against Iraq unless it withdrew from Kuwait by 15 January 1991. The ultimatum seemed to suggest that America and its allies meant business. Israel's elation was punctured the next day, however, when President Bush offered to go "the extra mile for peace" by inviting Tariq Aziz, the Iraqi foreign minister, to Washington for talks. While careful to avoid the impression that they were goading America to go to war, Israel and its influential friends in Washington questioned the wisdom of a policy of appeasement. Professor Yuval Ne'eman, the leader of the Tehiya party and a leading cabinet hawk, recalled that George Bush had compared Saddam Hussein to Adolf Hitler and said that there was therefore no escape from comparing Bush with Neville Chamberlain.[20]

High-level U.S.-Israeli consultations were stepped up with the approach of the deadline for Iraqi withdrawal from Kuwait. On 11 December, Shamir had a two-hour meeting with Bush at the White House that went some way toward repairing the rift between them. Bush assured Shamir that in the event of an unprovoked Iraqi attack, the United States would come to Israel's aid. Bush stressed that his administration was doing its utmost to avoid linkage between the Gulf crisis and the Palestinian issue and that it was essential for Israel to do the same by refraining from unilateral action against Iraq. Shamir promised not to mount a preemptive strike and to consult Bush before responding to any Iraqi attack. At the end of the month, coordination between the Pentagon and the Israeli military had been stepped up. In return for pledging full consultation with the United States before launching military action against Iraq, Israel was given access to prime U.S. intelligence not normally supplied to other countries. To facilitate cooperation, a hot line, code-named Hammer Rick, was established between the Pentagon Crisis Situation Room and the Israeli Defense Ministry, in Tel Aviv. This provided a significant inducement for Israel to maintain a low profile and refrain from creating unnecessary tensions.[21]

The Gulf crisis also called for a reassessment of Israel's policy toward Jordan. The Labor Party had always regarded the survival of King Hussein's regime in Amman as vital to Israel's security. The Likud, on the other hand, took the line that "Jordan is Palestine" and, consequently, that if the Palestinians overthrew the monarchy and turned Jordan into a Palestinian state, it would not endanger Israel's security and might indeed be a welcome change. Ariel Sharon was the most aggressive advocate of toppling the royalist regime in favor of a Palestinian state and then, little by little, driving the Palestinians of the West Bank across the river. Such thinking inside Israel had played an important part in pushing King Hussein into an alliance with Iraq, an alliance that provided him with his only deterrence against a possible move by the Likud to realize its thesis that Jordan was Palestine. During the Gulf crisis Jordan assumed ever greater importance as a buffer and potential battleground between Iraq and Israel.

Likud leaders suddenly discovered the value of having a stable country under a moderate ruler on their eastern border. The change of tune was unmistakable. Instead of issuing threats, the government began to send, through third parties, soothing messages to Amman to assure the king that they had no plans to attack and to urge him not to allow the entry of Iraqi troops into Jordan.[22] As soon as the crisis erupted, Shamir wrote to Bush to warn that the entry of Iraqi forces into Jordan would be a "red line" from Israel's point of view. Shamir also made it clear that Israel had no hostile intentions toward King Hussein and asked

Bush to discourage the king from serving the Iraqi dictator's aggressive actions.[23] At the start of 1991 there were worrying signs that Jordan was concentrating forces east of the river Jordan and that the king was losing control of the situation. Shamir now sought a more direct channel of communication with Amman.

King Hussein, equally anxious to avoid a military confrontation, invited Shamir to a secret meeting at his house in London on Friday, 4 January 1991. Shamir was accompanied by Elyakim Rubinstein, Yossi Ben-Aharon, the director general of the prime minister's office, and Major General Ehud Barak, the IDF deputy chief of staff. The Israeli officials stayed in the king's house overnight and enjoyed kosher food that had been specially ordered for them. The meeting with the king and his military adviser, General Zeid bin Shaker, took place during the evening of January 5, after the end of the Jewish Sabbath.

According to Shamir, King Hussein opened the meeting with a survey of his difficulties: the Americans had abandoned him, the Saudis were hostile to him, and he was isolated in the Arab world. At home the Palestinians were liable to cause riots if he publicly dissociated himself from the actions taken by Saddam Hussein. He did not want war, he feared its destabilizing effects, and his sole desire was that Jordan not be turned into a battleground between Israel and Iraq. He asked for an Israeli promise not to infringe the territorial integrity of Jordan by land or by air, and he hoped that this would help him procure a similar promise from Iraq.[24]

King Hussein confirmed that a secret meeting took place, but his account of the meeting suggests that it was Shamir who sought assurances that Jordan would not attack Israel:

> At that time, just before the war, there was a suggestion of a meeting with the prime minister, and we met here in London and he had Ehud Barak with him, and he said, "Look, I have a dilemma. In October 1973 our people were not vigilant enough, and the Arab attack took place and caused us a lot of damage. Now you have your troops mobilized and my generals are calling for me to do the same and to have our troops facing yours. There isn't much distance in the Jordan Valley, and it would be totally irresponsible, they say, if I did not take the same measures." So I said, "Prime Minister, you are perfectly within your rights to take the same measures if you feel like, but let me suggest that if that happens then the possibility of an accidental war developing between us is very real."

He said, "Well, what is your position?" I said, "My position is purely defensive." He said, "Do I have your word?" I said, "Yes, you have my word." He said, "That is good enough for me, and I will prevent our people from moving anywhere." And he did. And that was one of the events I will always remember. He recognized that my word was good enough, and this is the way people deal with each other.[25]

The possibility of a clash with Jordan excited some reckless talk in Jerusalem. Some politicians on the extreme right did not share in the sudden conversion to the royalist cause. Ariel Sharon was unimpressed with the argument that Israel had to do its utmost to keep Jordan from getting embroiled in the Gulf conflict. On the contrary, one of his motives for advocating swift and forceful military action against Iraq was his desire to destabilize the regime in Amman. The cabinet continued to receive intelligence briefings on the situation in Jordan, but following the expiration of the ultimatum for Iraqi withdrawal, it redirected its attention to developments farther east.[26]

THE GULF WAR

The allied air offensive against Iraq began at midnight on 16 January 1991. On the night of 18 January, the first barrage of eight Iraqi Scud missiles landed in Tel Aviv and Haifa. After months of uncertainty and bluster, Saddam Hussein carried out his threat to attack the Jewish state, dramatically raising the stakes in the Gulf War. It was the first air attack on an Israeli city since 1948. The material damage caused was limited because the Scud missiles, according to one military expert, were "stone age technology." "Flying dustbins" was how one eye witness described the warheads that fell down from the sky. No one died as a direct result of being hit by a Scud missile, though several people died of heart attacks or because they forgot to open the air valve in their gas mask. Altogether thirty-nine missiles landed in Israel during the war, resulting in only one direct casualty. Nevertheless, the psychological impact of the attack was profound.

An emergency meeting of the cabinet was called for noon on Saturday, 19 January. Feelings were running high, and many of the ministers came ready to approve immediate military action against Iraq. The IAF had prepared a plan for intervention in western Iraq in order to hunt down the Scud launchers. At the cabinet meeting the chief of the IAF pressed for a green light to carry it out, but Chief of Staff Dan Shomron and his deputy, Ehud Barak, did not support him. Moshe Arens, too, felt unable to recommend the implementation of the IAF plan. The ministers were divided. Seven were ready to approve the plan, and seven were opposed to it or at least inclined against it. In general, the military experts were less militant and more cognizant of the importance of close coordination with the United States than the politicians were. Shamir tipped the balance against military action. The starting point for him was the pledge he had given George Bush in December 1990 that Israel would not launch an attack on Iraq except by prior coordination with the United States. Bush called Shamir just before the cabinet meeting to say that he had heard of Israel's plan and demanded that it not be carried out. Shamir closed the meeting by saying that he opposed any action without coordination with the United States.[27] This was to remain his consistent line throughout the war and his principal argument against military intervention.

The loudest voice calling for a military strike against Iraq was that of Housing Minister Ariel Sharon. Sharon made it a habit during the war to visit neighborhoods hit by Scud missiles and to tell the people who had been made homeless that the government was failing to provide them with the protection to which they were entitled. The activities led Gideon Samet, a columnist with the independent daily *Ha'aretz,* to accuse Sharon of "scavenging in the ruins." Inside the cabinet Sharon argued that if Israel did not strike out against Iraq, it would lose its credibility and its power to deter future attacks. Any Arab state would feel free to attack Israel with impunity. Sharon's specific proposal was to send a strong tank column through Jordanian territory into western Iraq. Shamir refused to put Sharon's proposal to a vote in the cabinet. When tens of thousands of Iraqi soldiers surrendered without a fight to the advancing allies during the ground war, the joke among militant Israelis was that the Iraqi and Israeli armies had one thing in common: neither participated in the fighting.[28]

Uncertainty about Iraq's potential for putting chemical warheads on its Scuds was something Israel was destined to live with until the end of the Gulf War. To deter such a move, Israel employed a strategy of threatening ambiguity, of making thinly veiled references to "the bomb in the basement" while carefully eschewing the adoption of an explicit nuclear posture. An American satellite reportedly detected that, following the first Scud barrage,

Israeli missile launchers armed with nuclear warheads were moved into the open and deployed facing Iraq, ready to launch on command. American intelligence picked up other signs indicating that Israel had gone on a full nuclear alert that would remain in effect for weeks.[29]

What the Americans undoubtedly picked up in the media was an increase in the number of Israelis who thought that a chemical attack would justify the use of nuclear weapons. The Americans shrewdly exploited these voices in their own efforts to dissuade Saddam Hussein from using chemical weapons. Richard Cheney, the secretary of defense, stated on 2 February that if Iraq used chemical weapons against Israel, Israel might retaliate with nonconventional weapons. The statement was significant, first, because the warning was issued not in Washington's name but indirectly in Israel's name; second, because it confirmed that Israel was capable of realizing a nonconventional option; and, third, because the warning to refrain from escalation was addressed only to Iraq and not to Israel.[30] The statement was bound to deepen awareness in Baghdad that Israel had nuclear weapons ready for use, and it may well have played a part in Saddam Hussein's decision not to raise the conflict above the conventional threshold.

Nevertheless, missiles continued to be fired on Israel's civilian population—its soft underbelly—from mobile launchers in western Iraq, and the newly arrived Patriot missile batteries with their American crews had only partial success in intercepting them. As a consequence, pressure mounted for sending the IDF into action. On 11 February, Moshe Arens, accompanied by Ehud Barak, made a secret visit to Washington to urge the Americans to step up their air assaults on the targets in Iraq that most concerned Israel and to see whether they would give a green light for an Israeli intervention in the fighting. His most important meeting was with President Bush. Bush claimed that the number of missile launches had significantly declined, and he doubted that Israel could do better than the Americans and their allies. He also referred to public opinion polls in Israel that indicated very wide support for the official policy of restraint. Arens was reminded that Israel could reach Iraq only by passing through the airspace of one of the Arab countries and that such action was liable to damage the coalition. Bush and his colleagues were prepared to meet some of Arens's requests for arms and financial aid, but they showed no sympathy for Israel's desire to intervene and maintained their veto on operational coordination.[31]

At successive cabinet meetings the policy of restraint was reaffirmed. Officially, Israel was "postponing" military response and
keeping its options open, reserving the right to reply at a time and
in a manner of its own choosing. In practice, however, Israel was
beginning to resemble the man who is provoked but wants to be
restrained from having to fight. According to a version released by
Washington when the war was over, after every Scud attack, Arens
would ask Cheney for electronic identity codes for distinguishing
between friend and foe and later for an air corridor through Saudi
Arabia to enable Israeli warplanes to retaliate without overflying
Jordan, but to no avail. Shamir would weigh it all up and sit tight,
and nothing would happen.[32]

By temperament and political outlook Shamir was predisposed
to inaction and immobilism, to resisting outside pressure, and to
defending the status quo. During the Gulf War, therefore, he was
in his element. He presided with great aplomb and gravitas over
the inaction of his country's legendary armed forces. As the leader
of a nation at war, he won no plaudits. What distinguished this war
from all of Israel's previous wars was the inability of its armed
forces to protect the civilian rear. It is this fact, among others, that
turned the six weeks in early 1991 into such a harrowing psychological ordeal for the civilian population. There was a maddening
dichotomy between proven military prowess on the one hand and
a sense of utter impotence on the other.

Shamir's countrymen had become accustomed to heroic feats
from their armed forces, like the raid on Entebbe airport in
Uganda to rescue hostages, and the bombing of the Iraqi nuclear
reactor. They were intelligent enough to understand that this crisis was different, and 80 percent of them supported the official policy of restraint.[33] But they needed a leader to guide them, to inspire
them, and to unite them. All they got from Shamir was a gruff and
stony silence. There was no Churchillian oratory to keep up their
morale. "Maybe we do not deserve someone like Churchill,"
wrote one exasperated journalist, "but do us a favor, Prime
Minister, say something."[34] The only response that this plea
evoked was a prolonged and troubled silence.

Although the public did not know what the diminutive man in
the highest office in the land was thinking, by mid-February, as the
allies were preparing to follow the air offensive with a land war, the
possibility of a change in policy hung in the air. Arens became
convinced that Israel had to retaliate, and he hoped that the land
war would offer a "window of opportunity" for the IDF to weigh

in. His reasoning was that, at this final stage of the war, active resistance to flights over Jordanian airspace was unlikely, the political damage to the coalition would be minimal, and if the Americans were simply informed of an imminent Israeli intervention, they would have to get out of the way. The IDF General Staff had prepared an operational plan and was ready to execute it on command. The chief of staff was now persuaded that the gains of military intervention would outweigh the costs and was, by his own account, itching to go. He discussed with Arens specific scenarios for intervention, but these did not materialize. In the last two weeks of the war, the Iraqis fired only six Scuds, in an apparent attempt to hit the nuclear reactor in Dimona, but they all landed harmlessly in the sands of the Negev.[35] In the meantime, allied ground forces had reached Basra, in southern Iraq. Operation Desert Storm had achieved its two declared aims: the Iraqi forces had been driven out of Kuwait, and the government of Kuwait had been restored. On February 28 President Bush ordered a cease-fire, and Israel lost the opportunity to retaliate.

If the Gulf War was full of contradictions and paradoxes from Israel's point of view, its outcome was not less so. The first and most obvious paradox was that Israel did not participate in the military side of this war, except as a target. Israel was both the strongest advocate of an all-out offensive against Iraq and the most passive party when it came to carrying out this offensive. Its security doctrine was built on carrying the war to the enemy's territory as swiftly and devastatingly as possible, but during the Gulf War all that its army tried to do, with marked lack of success, was to protect its own backyard against attack. Another paradox was that although Israel and Iraq were sworn enemies, Israel was excluded from the coalition of thirty nations assembled by the United States against this enemy, for fear of defection by the Arab members. A third and related paradox was that Israel could make its greatest contribution to the allied campaign to defeat this enemy by staying out and keeping a low profile.

At the beginning of the Gulf crisis, Israel chalked up some impressive gains, but the final outcome fell short of its original expectation. Admittedly, the nightmare scenario did not materialize; for whatever reasons, Saddam Hussein did not withdraw peacefully from Kuwait and had to be ejected by force. But from Israel's point of view, Operation Desert Storm ended too soon. Israel's war aims were threefold: the overthrow of Saddam Hussein, the destruction of Iraq's war machine, and the neutralization of its capacity to develop the weapons of mass destruction. The first aim was not achieved by the Gulf War, and the last two were achieved only in part. Israel's own capacity to deter potential Arab aggressors was probably weakened, on balance, by its deliberate choice to stay on the sidelines in this conflict. Israel had pledged that if attacked it would retaliate. It was attacked, but it did not retaliate. As a consequence, there was a decrease in its capacity for conventional deterrence. Whatever the motive behind the policy of non-retaliation, the result was a diminution in Israel's stature as a military power in its own eyes and in the eyes of its opponents.

The most important consequence of the Gulf War for Israel, however, concerned its special relationship with America. One way of looking at the Gulf War is to say that Israel was the greatest beneficiary because, without having to lift a finger itself, it witnessed the defeat of its most formidable foe at the hands of its most faithful friend. But such a view involves a serious oversimplification. For Israel had traditionally been regarded, not least by itself, as a strategic partner and a strategic asset to the United States in the Middle East. The Gulf conflict was a real eye-opener in this respect. Here was a conflict that threatened America's most vital interests in the region, and the best service that Israel could render its senior partner was to refrain from doing anything. Far from being a strategic asset, Israel was widely perceived as an embarrassment and a liability.

Throughout the Gulf crisis and the war that followed it, there was tension in the triangular relationship between America, Israel, and the Arabs. Gradually but unmistakably, under the impact of the crisis, America continued to move away from reliance on Israel to reliance on its old and new Arab allies in order to attain its objectives in the region. In this important respect, Israel was to emerge from the Gulf conflict not as a winner but as an ultimate loser. Nothing demonstrated this more clearly than the pressure the Bush administration applied on Israel to engage in peace negotiations with the Arabs as soon as the guns in the Persian Gulf fell silent.

THE MADRID PEACE CONFERENCE

The pope, according to a no doubt apocryphal story, maintained that there were two possible solutions to the Arab-Israeli conflict: the realistic and the miraculous. The realistic solution involved divine intervention; the miraculous solution, a voluntary agreement between the parties themselves. A third solution, not foreseen by the pope, involved American intervention. The Middle Eastern peace conference that convened in Madrid on 30 October 1991 represented the most serious attempt ever on the part of the United States to promote a comprehensive settlement of the Arab-Israeli conflict.

Two events of massive significance enabled America to make this attempt: the defeat of the Soviet Union in the Cold War and the defeat of Arab radicalism in the Gulf War. Formally, the Soviet Union was a cosponsor of the Madrid conference, but in practice it was in the final stages of disintegration. The collapse of the Soviet Union as a superpower orphaned Moscow's former clients and pulled the rug out from under the Arab rejection front that had always opposed any peace settlement with Israel. The ending of the global contest between the two principal protagonists thus made possible, or at least conceivable, the ending of the conflict between the Arabs and the Israelis. President Hafez al-Assad of Syria accepted the invitation to Madrid not as a result of a sudden conversion on the road to Damascus to the idea of peace with Israel but because he had lost the support of his old superpower patron and had to make his peace with the sole remaining superpower. The government of Lebanon followed his example. King Hussein of Jordan, having aroused the wrath of the West by his association with Saddam Hussein, was anxious to rehabilitate himself and therefore readily agreed to the formation of a joint Jordanian-Palestinian delegation in order to provide an umbrella for Palestinian participation in the peace talks. The PLO, in the doghouse on account of its support for Saddam Hussein during the Gulf crisis, acquiesced in its own exclusion and successfully exerted behind-the-scenes influence over the Palestinian delegation from the occupied territories.

Yitzhak Shamir was the most awkward customer, and a great deal of arm-twisting was necessary to get him to accept the invitation to Madrid. He warned James Baker that the consequences of any attempt on the part of the United States to force the PLO on Israel would be very serious and that to use the word "conference" might be "provocative."[36] Having consistently rejected any linkage between the Iraqi-Kuwaiti dispute and the Israeli-Arab dispute, Shamir intended to return to the old status quo. To signal his determination to resist pressures for peace talks, he had the moderate Palestinian leader Sari Nusseibeh arrested on spurious charges of spying for the Iraqis; he kept Foreign Minister David Levy on a tight leash; and he drafted into his cabinet the loudmouthed former general Rehavam Ze'evi, the leader of the aggressively jingoistic Moledet party and a notorious advocate of "transfer" or forced deportation of Palestinians.

Much more fundamental was the issue of Jewish settlements in the occupied territories. To give the peace talks a chance, Israel's government was urged on all sides to halt the building of new settlements and new housing. Government spokesmen replied that the demand for a freeze on settlement activity during the peace talks constituted a precondition. This was patently untrue. The truth of the matter was that settlement activity constituted a precondition, for if it continued unchecked, there would eventually be nothing to talk about: the settlements would determine the outcome of the negotiations. Settlement activity was not just incompatible with the peace process; it was intended to wreck it. At a crucial point in the run-up to Madrid, Israeli officials announced plans for a new wave of building calculated to double the Jewish population in the occupied territories in four years. This flatly contradicted the previous promise that no large-scale construction would take place beyond the Green Line.

Shamir did not give in to pressure from the religious and ultrareligious parties that formed a powerful settlement lobby inside his cabinet. He himself belonged to the right wing of his extremely right-wing cabinet. Much of the drive for expanding settlement activity came from Shamir's housing minister and party colleague—Ariel Sharon. Although the two men were political rivals, the policy differences between them were insignificant. The main difference was that Sharon declared openly his intention to create irreversible facts on the ground in order to preclude territorial compromise or Palestinian self-government, whereas Shamir promoted this policy without proclaiming it.

The real debate within the Likud was on whether Israel should enter into peace talks with the Arabs at all and, if so, with whom? Sharon was vehemently opposed to peace talks, whereas Moshe Arens argued that negotiations would not necessarily mean withdrawal. At a meeting of the Likud's foreign affairs and defense committee, Arens recalled the article written in 1923 by Ze'ev Jabotinsky in which he said that negotiations must be carried on with the Arabs, leading to an agreement with them but only after an "iron wall" had been built. Arens posed the question whether the wall had been built, and answered it in the affirmative: the

Jews could no longer be driven out. To the second question—to whom should they talk?—Arens answered that, aside from the Arab states that were at war with them, they should address the grievances and aspirations of the Palestinians and talk to them about a temporary arrangement along the lines of the Camp David Accords.[37] This was hardly a radical proposal, yet it did not suit Shamir's general strategy of evasion and procrastination.

Israel, however, was economically vulnerable. Its dependence on American financial help to absorb large-scale Jewish immigration from the Soviet Union gave George Bush unprecedented leverage. He used it to the full. By withholding the $10 billion loan guarantee requested by Israel, he forced Shamir to the negotiating table. America had given Israel aid totaling $77 billion and was continuing to subsidize the Jewish state to the tune of $3 billion a year. Never in the annals of human history had so few people owed so much to so many. Bush himself felt he owed no debt either to Israel or to American Jewry. He had been vice-president for eight years in the most pro-Israeli administration in American history, yet he won only 5 percent of the Jewish vote in the 1988 presidential election. Bush was thus in a strong position domestically to present Shamir with a choice: keep the occupied territories or keep U.S. support.

The Madrid peace conference was carefully stage-managed by the Americans, with James Baker acting as the chief puppeteer. It was he and his aides, who came to be known as the peace processors, who picked the venue for the conference, issued the formal invitations, provided written assurances to each participant, and stipulated that the basis for the negotiations would be Security Council Resolutions 242 and 338 and the principle of exchanging territory for peace.

What distinguished Madrid from previous Arab-Israel conferences was that the Palestinians were represented there for the first time on a footing of equality with Israel. Madrid registered the arrival of the Palestinians, long the missing party, at the Middle Eastern conference table. The mere presence of official Palestinian representatives in Madrid marked a change, if not a reversal, of Israel's long-standing refusal to consider the Palestinians as a partner to negotiations, as an *interlocuteur valable*. Israel's veto of members of the PLO and residents of East Jerusalem resulted in a Palestinian delegation that was part of a joint Jordanian-Palestinian delegation and an advisory council with Faisal Husseini as coordinator and Dr. Hanan Ashrawi as spokesperson. Ironically, by excluding the PLO, Israel helped the inhabitants of the occupied territories to put forward fresh faces and to project a new image of Palestinian nationalism.

Shamir went to Madrid in a defiant and truculent mood. The opening speeches by the heads of Israeli and the Palestinian delegations faithfully reflected the positions of the two sides. Shamir, like the Bourbons of France, seemed to have learned nothing and to have forgotten nothing. The whole tone of his speech was anachronistic, saturated with the stale rhetoric of the past, and wholly inappropriate for the occasion. He used the platform to deliver the first ever Israel Bonds speech in front of an Arab audience. His version of the Arab-Israeli conflict was singularly narrow and blinkered, portraying Israel simply as the victim of Arab aggression and refusing to acknowledge that any evolution had taken place in the Arab or Palestinian attitude to Israel. All of the Arabs, according to Shamir, wanted to see Israel destroyed, the only difference between them was over the ways to bring about its destruction. His speech, long on anti-Arab clichés, was exceedingly short on substance. By insisting that the root cause of the conflict was not territory but the Arab refusal to recognize the legitimacy of the State of Israel, he came dangerously close to rejecting the whole basis of the conference—UN resolutions and the principle of land for peace.

The contrast between Shamir's speech and the speech of Dr. Haidar Abdel Shafi, the head of the Palestinian delegation, could hardly have been more striking in either tone, spirit, or substance. This single speech contained more evidence of new thinking than all the other speeches, Arab and Israeli, put together. Abdel Shafi reminded the audience that it was time for the Palestinians to narrate their own story. While touching on the past, his speech looked not backward but forward. "In the name of the Palestinian people," he said, "we wish to directly address the Israeli people, with whom we have had a prolonged exchange of pain: let us share hope instead. We are willing to live side by side on the land and the promise of the future. Sharing, however, requires two partners willing to share as equals. Mutuality and reciprocity must replace domination and hostility for genuine reconciliation and coexistence under international legality. Your security and ours are mutually dependent, as intertwined as the fears and nightmares of our children."

Abdel Shafi's basic message was that Israeli occupation had to end, that the Palestinians had a right to self-determination, and that they were determined to pursue this right relentlessly until they achieved statehood. The *intifada,* he suggested, had already begun to embody the Palestinian state and to build its institutions and infrastructure. But while staking a claim to Palestinian statehood, Abdel Shafi qualified it in two significant ways. First, he accepted the need for a transitional stage, provided interim arrangements were not transformed into permanent status. Second, he envisaged a confederation between an ultimately independent Palestine and Jordan.

As the head of the Palestinian delegation was delivering his speech, Israel's stone-faced prime minister passed a note to a colleague. One of the five thousand journalists covering the conference speculated that the note could well have said, "We made a big mistake. We should have insisted that the PLO is the sole legitimate representative of the Palestinian people."

Abdel Shafi's speech in Madrid was both the most eloquent and the most moderate presentation of the Palestinian case ever made by an official Palestinian spokesman since the beginning of the conflict at the end of the nineteenth century. The PLO, for all its growing moderation, has never been able to articulate such a clear-cut peace overture to Israel, because of its internal divisions and the constraints of inter-Arab politics. No PLO official had ever been able to declare so unambiguously that a Palestinian state would be ready for a confederation with Jordan. The whole tenor of the speech was more conciliatory and constructive than even the most moderate statements of the PLO. In the words of Afif Safieh, a PLO official, the speech was "unreasonably reasonable." The principal aim of the speech, an aim endorsed by the PLO leaders in Tunis, was to convince the Israeli public that the Palestinians were genuinely committed to peaceful coexistence. In the international media the speech received every accolade. Even some of the Israeli officials in Madrid professed themselves to be moved by it. The calm and reassuring manner of the elderly physician from Gaza only served to underscore the humanity and reasonableness of his message.

Abba Eban's old gibe against the Palestinians—that they never missed a chance to miss an opportunity for peace—was singularly inappropriate on this occasion and, if anything, could be turned against the Israeli side. Even the composition of the two delegations was indicative of the historic transformation that had taken place on the road to peace. Half the Palestinian delegates to Madrid were doctors and university professors. The Israeli delegation, on the other hand, was led, as the Syrian foreign minister, Farouk al-Shara, reminded the audience, by a former terrorist who in 1948 was wanted by the British for the assassination of Count Bernadotte, the UN mediator to Palestine. "This man," Shara said, brandishing a picture of the thirty-two-year-old Shamir, "killed peace mediators."

Shamir's performance in Madrid raised serious questions whether he and his generation of Likud leaders could ever put the past behind them and work toward a genuine accommodation with the Palestinians. Listening to his speech, one Israeli journalist wondered whether his officials had not by mistake fished out of their files one of Golda Meir's speeches from the early 1970s. Shamir's basic thesis was that the Arabs still refused to accept Israel as a permanent entity in the Middle East. But the peace with Egypt and the presence in the conference chamber around him of representatives from all the confrontation states as well as the authorized representatives of the Palestinians told a completely different story. After the first day of talks, Shamir was asked how it felt to finally sit down face-to-face with all of Israel's Arab adversaries. He answered, "It was a regular day."

If the Palestinians proved to Shamir that he could no longer rely on them to let him off the hook, he had better luck with the foreign minister of Syria. Farouk al-Shara played the old record of rejectionism and vituperation. He was without doubt the most militant and radical Arab representative in Madrid—and also the most isolated. The conference degenerated into an unseemly slanging match between the Israeli and the Syrian. Shamir denounced Syria as one of the most repressive and tyrannical regimes in the world. Shara replied in kind, denouncing Israel as a terrorist state led by a former terrorist, and later refused to answer questions at a press conference from Israeli journalists. Shara was like a bat trying to fly in the daylight. His performance revealed what a closed, dark place Syria still was, notwithstanding its move from the Soviet camp into the American. Against the background of this strident display of Syrian rejectionism, the readiness of the Palestinians to engage in a constructive dialogue with the Israelis was all the more striking.

After the plenary session was over, stage two of the peace process began in Madrid. It took the form of a series of separate bilateral meetings between Israel and each of the Arab delegations. Here, too, the Syrians were the most rigid and intransigent, while the Palestinians seemed more eager than any of the Arab delegations to forge ahead with the talks. As a result of these differences, the common Arab front collapsed. Syria held out for a unified Arab position to back its demand for an Israeli commitment to trade the Golan Heights for peace before the bilateral talks began. Among the Palestinian delegates there was considerable irritation with Syria's attempt to set an overall Arab agenda in the talks. They therefore broke ranks with Syria and not only held their meeting with the Israelis but shook hands in front of the cameras. What the Palestinians were saying, in effect, was that Syria had no power of veto over their own moves and that they would not allow the peace process with Israel to be held hostage to inter-Arab politics.

Another key to the success of the Palestinians in Madrid was the political alliance they formed with the United States, the driving force behind the conference. The emergence of an American-Palestinian axis broke the familiar mold of Middle Eastern politics. The Americans had every reason to be pleased with the performance put on by the Palestinian novices in their debut on the international stage in Madrid. What mattered much more than the polished performance by the novices was the fact that they were a lot closer to the American position in Madrid than the Israelis. They explicitly accepted that the negotiations should be based on UN Resolutions 242 and 338 and the principle of land for peace, whereas Israel did not. They got on board the bus that James Baker told them would come only once, whereas Shamir continued to quibble over the fare, the powers of the driver, the rights of other passengers, the speed of the bus, the route, and the final destination.

This reversal of the Palestinian and Israeli positions in relation to American policy in the Middle East marked a watershed in the history of the Arab-Israeli conflict. The moderation shown by the Palestinians in Madrid made it easier for the Bush administration to tilt farther in their direction and away from Israel. After Madrid the administration kept up the pressure on Israel to negotiate on the central issues of land for peace and self-determination for the Palestinians. When the two sides failed to reach agreement on a date and venue for bilateral talks, the Americans seized the initiative by issuing formal invitations to talks in Washington on December 4, adding for good measure suggestions on matters of substance designed to narrow the gap between Israel and the Arabs.

Yitzhak Shamir and his cabinet colleagues were outraged by

America's failure to consult, by its attempt to force the pace, by its agenda for the Washington leg of the talks, and by its increasingly abrasive and allegedly one-sided approach to the peace process. A meeting in the American capital with all the Arab delegations under the same roof on the same day was not their idea of bilateral talks. The reservations they voiced over technical matters masked deep-seated unease about the content and direction of the entire peace process. They said that they could not start talks until 9 December and insisted that the sole purpose of the meeting in Washington should be to establish the ground rules for separate bilateral talks to be held in the Middle East. America refused to budge. The upshot was that all the Arab delegations arrived for the talks in Washington, but the Israelis were not there.

On the day of the stillborn talks, Shamir made a defiant speech, nailing his colors to the mast of Greater Israel and ruling out the return of even one stone in exchange for peace. "Even as they work day and night for peace," he said, "Israel's leaders cannot conceive of considering ideas aimed at concessions on Jerusalem, the West Bank, Gaza, and the Golan Heights." To underscore the point, another settlement was established near the Arab town of El Bireh in the West Bank.

BILATERAL PEACE NEGOTIATIONS

Five rounds of bilateral talks were held in Washington following the peace conference in Madrid. Through them all, the Likud government continued to rule out the swapping of land for peace and to play for time. A good deal of time was taken up with procedural wrangles, and it was not until Israel agreed to negotiate separately with the Palestinian and Jordanian delegations that the substantive issues could be addressed. Even then the negotiations proceeded at a snail's pace and ended in deadlock. The heads of the Israeli delegations to the bilateral talks were apparently instructed not to budge and to give the impression that real negotiations were taking place and that the peace process was alive and well, but to concede nothing in matters of substance.[38] This posturing was directed primarily at persuading the Americans that Israel was negotiating in good faith and to bring their wrath on the heads of the other side. In Israeli press briefings the same refrain was repeated time and again: "we met and talked and that in itself represents progress." There were certainly no concrete results to report.

On the contrary, profound disagreements over the principles underlying the whole peace process were never resolved. These differences fell into two broad categories. One concerned Israel and two out of the three sovereign Arab states involved in the talks, Syria and Jordan, and the other concerned Israel and the stateless Palestinians. The interstate argument revolved around the interpretation of Resolution 242. The Arabs maintained that this resolution required Israel to withdraw from all the territories it occupied during the June 1967 war—the Golan Heights, the West Bank, the Gaza Strip, and East Jerusalem—just as it did from Sinai. This was the meaning of the principle of exchanging land for peace. The Israeli government's argument was that by returning Sinai to Egypt, it had implemented the territorial provisions of the resolution and now it was up to the Arabs to offer peace for peace. The gap in the intercommunal conflict, between Israel and the Palestinians, was even deeper than in the interstate conflict. Israel and the Palestinians were supposed to negotiate an agreement for "interim self-government" for the Palestinians in the West Bank and the Gaza Strip, leaving the final status of these territories to be negotiated at the end of a transitional period of five years. But the term "self-government" was interpreted very differently by the two sides.

The negotiations between Israel and the Palestinians only highlighted the immense gap between them. The Palestinians started with the assumption that they were a people with national rights and that the interim arrangements under discussion were the precursor to independence and should be shaped accordingly. The Israeli government started with the assumption that the Palestinians were the inhabitants of the territories with no national rights of any kind and certainly no right to independence, not even after the end of the transitional period. At the fourth round of talks, late in February 1992, the two sides presented incompatible plans for the interim period of self-government. The Palestinian blueprint was for a Palestinian interim self-governing authority, or PISGA for short. Israel's counterproposal was for "interim self-government arrangements." Behind the two names lurked irreconcilable positions on the nature and purpose of "interim self-government."

Palestinian negotiators assailed the Israeli plan as one designed to perpetuate Jewish settlements in the West Bank and Gaza, to consolidate Israel's control over the land and water of these territories, and to foster apartheid, or racial separation. They accused

Israel of closing off options, of stalling in order to create "facts on the ground." The Israelis accused the Palestinians of trying to impinge on the final status of the disputed territories by putting forward proposals that looked like building blocks for future statehood. They were both right.

A similar determination to perpetuate the territorial status quo characterized the Israeli approach to the bilateral talks with Syria and Lebanon. Consequently, these talks too went nowhere slowly. The head of the Israeli delegation to the talks with Syria was Yossi Ben-Aharon, the director general of the prime minister's office, who shared Shamir's political outlook and enjoyed his strong backing. In Ben-Aharon's case the ideological commitment to Greater Israel was reinforced by religious conviction, while his contempt for the contemporary Arab world was reinforced by his knowledge of classical Islamic civilization. He was also a dominant personality with a sense of intellectual superiority who set the tone on the Israeli side and exerted influence across the board. Although a civil servant, he saw himself as a policymaker and thought that he knew better than any of the government ministers what was in the country's best long-term interest and how best to deal with the Arabs. All his intellectual and administrative abilities were targeted on the task of ensuring that nothing would change as a result of the talks with the Arabs. A glimpse of what went on behind the closed doors of the Israeli-Syrian talks was provided by Dr. Yossi Olmert, the government spokesman who took part in the first two rounds until removed by Ben-Aharon.

According to Olmert, Ben-Aharon was abrasive and confrontational, deliberately teasing, insulting, and provoking his Syrian counterparts in order to expose their alleged underlying extremism. At the first meeting in Washington, he threw literally in the face of the head of the Syrian delegation a book in Arabic, containing antisemitic remarks, written by Mustafa Tlas, the Syrian defense minister. Some of the experts in the Israeli team were appalled by Ben-Aharon's unprofessional behavior, but they could do little. They would meet in the evening in the bar of their hotel and practice throwing books at a target.

Olmert, an academic specialist in Syrian politics, observed that the willingness to enter into direct negotiations reflected a major change in the Syrian position. His impression was that Shamir, like Israel's first prime minister, David Ben-Gurion, believed that time was on Israel's side and was therefore reluctant to volunteer any concessions unless they were absolutely inescapable. Olmert's verdict was that the Likud government had a real opportunity to advance the peace process with Syria and that this opportunity was missed largely because of the extremism and intransigence of the head of the Israeli delegation.[39]

In the case of Lebanon the imbalance in the power of the two parties was even more pronounced than in the case of Syria, and the consequences of this imbalance were all too evident in the bilateral talks. Some Lebanese politicians, like the former prime minister Selim el-Hoss, took the view that Lebanon should decline the invitation to Madrid and to bilateral talks with Israel and insist on an immediate and unconditional implementation of UN Security Council Resolution 425. This resolution, passed after Israel's March 1978 incursion into Lebanon, called on Israel to withdraw its forces from all Lebanese territory. When Israel withdrew the bulk of its forces from Lebanon in 1985, it declared a security zone in southern Lebanon and continued to control it through a proxy, the South Lebanese Army (SLA). It was inevitable, given the imbalance of power between them, that in any bilateral talks with Israel, Lebanon would be subjected to strong Israeli pressure. If it turned to the UN to demand the implementation of Resolution 425, the answer could be that it was now up to Lebanon to reach a settlement with Israel directly within the framework of the peace process.

In the bilateral talks with Lebanon, the Israelis were as tough and unreasonable as their past record suggested they would be. The plan put forward by Uri Lubrani, the head of the Israeli delegation, seemed to the Lebanese more like a trap than a peace plan. As an experimental measure, the plan envisaged the withdrawal of the SLA from a narrow strip of territory round Jezzine, at the northern end of Israel's self-declared security zone. There was no hint of a complete Israeli withdrawal, which the Lebanese had been hoping for. A second feature that made the plan unacceptable was that it required the government in Beirut to negotiate with General Antoine Lahad, the commander of the SLA, and thus implicitly acknowledge his authority in the southern part of the country. Third, the plan required the Lebanese government to ensure the security and suppress anti-Israeli groups like Hizbullah in this small but troublesome area. The plan thus involved a very tough test for the fragile Lebanese government, virtually placing it on probation without offering any significant inducements. Lebanon's representatives declined the offer, and the situation on the ground in southern Lebanon remained unchanged.[40]

Although the bilateral talks, in Yitzhak Rabin's phrase, were merely grinding water, they unleashed an intense national debate on the future of the occupied territories and Israel's relations with its neighbors. Public opinion polls showed unambiguously that the Israeli public was much more impressed than its government by the signs of moderation on the other side and much more willing to trade land for peace. Even on the eastern front the majority of Israelis were prepared to contemplate territorial concessions of varying magnitudes. It was on this front that the national debate came into focus, both because it touched the core values of the Israeli right and because it was the principal battleground of the *intifada*.

Here Shamir came under fire from two opposite directions. His critics on the left claimed that, by putting land before people and by building more settlements on the West Bank instead of taking proper care of the immigrants from the Soviet Union, he was distorting the Zionist ideal beyond recognition. A related charge was that through his diplomatic rigidity and sheer political incompetence, Shamir was undermining Israel's special relationship with the United States. His critics on the right charged that he was proceeding too far and too fast down the road to Palestinian self-government, the thin end of the wedge of a Palestinian state, and that under pressure from the United States he was preparing to sell out the Land of Israel. To fend off the pressures, Shamir adopted a twin-track strategy: he tried to persuade the Americans that he was in earnest about reaching an agreement with the Palestinians, while at the same time reassuring his right-wing critics that they had nothing to worry about, since he had no intention of making any meaningful concessions to the Palestinians. When charged with dishonesty, Shamir proudly replied that "for the sake of the Land of Israel, it is permissible to lie."[41]

As a result of his lying, Shamir lost credibility both with the Americans and with some of his xenophobic coalition partners. In his memoirs Shamir maintained that the aim of his coalition partners, like that of the Bush administration, was to unseat the Likud: "The small parties to the right of the Likud—Tehiyya, Tsomet and Moledet—blinded by their extremism, though knowing that the Government was committed to uphold the right of Jews to settle everywhere in the Land of Israel—and that I myself was as fervent an advocate of this policy as any of their members—began to distrust and defy me."[42]

In mid-January 1992 Rehavam Ze'evi, the chisel-jawed former general, and Yuval Ne'eman, the superhawkish former colonel, walked out on Shamir, robbing his government of its slim majority in the Knesset and raising further doubts about the future of the regional peace process. "I hope our leaving the government will slow the peace process, which we see as a mortal danger to the state of Israel," Professor Ne'eman said in his letter of resignation.

With the resignation of the far-right ministers, the countdown to the next general election began. As often with the poker-faced Shamir, it was hard to tell whether he was happy or sad. He was certainly not above presenting himself to the electorate as a leader who sacrificed his government for the sake of the peace process, and he seemed confident that he held most of the cards in the domestic political game. The joker in the pack, however, turned out to be the $10 billion loan guarantee, and this card was firmly in the grasp of George Bush.

There was no visible softening of the official line in the peace talks following the departure of Tehiya and Moledet from the Likud-led coalition. As the delegates gathered in Washington for the fourth round of talks, toward the end of February 1992, Shamir declared that the settlement drive would continue and that he himself would not be party to any deals that placed this drive at risk. He specifically rejected any link between the settlement issue and Israel's request for a U.S. loan guarantee. Bush and Baker concluded that Shamir would not alter his policy. So they took the bold step of indicating to the Israeli electorate that, if they wanted American financial support to continue, they should change their government. Bush and Baker's objective was either to bring about the outright defeat of Shamir at the election scheduled for June or to force him into a coalition government with Rabin, the newly elected leader of the Labor Alignment, whom they regarded as far more reasonable.

CONFESSIONS OF A STONEWALLER

The 23 June 1992 election was one of the most important in Israel's history because it focused so sharply on the peace issue and the future of the occupied territories. Yitzhak Shamir represented the Likud's traditional policy of territorial expansion; Yitzhak Rabin, the Labor Party's traditional policy of territorial compromise. In January 1992 Shamir created an uproar by stating that a "big Israel" was now needed in order to settle the Soviet Jews. Abroad this statement was taken as an indication that Israel had opted for the annexation of the occupied territories. Two weeks later, at a meeting with political correspondents, Shamir said that his party would place at the top of its election manifesto "the consistent and serious striving to achieve peace" and that this would also be his chief message in the campaign. When asked whether he planned to achieve this without giving up the territories, he replied unhesitatingly, "Of course. Without giving up the territories of the Land of Israel. We shall march along two tracks: preservation of the Land of Israel and a continuous effort toward peace."[43]

Labor's position was not defined in detail. Labor's campaign managers concentrated their efforts on presenting their seventy-year-old new leader as a credible national leader rather than on spelling out the precise policies that Labor would pursue if it won the election. Rabin himself, however, made three specific points that differentiated him clearly from his right-wing rivals. He promised that, if elected, he would aim to conclude an agreement on Palestinian self-government within six months to a year. Second, he agreed to the inclusion of residents from East Jerusalem in the Palestinian team. Third and most important, he said he would favor a freeze on the building of what he called "political settlements" in the occupied territories.

Given such markedly divergent platforms of the principal contenders, the election became almost a referendum on the peace issue. As they went to the polls, voters were being asked to choose between the expansionist territorial policy of the right and peace based on compromise; between building more Jewish settlements and retaining American support; between absorbing Soviet immigrants within the country's pre-1967 borders and continuing to expend their scarce material resources on the building of Greater Israel. Underlying these choices was an even more critical one: did they want to live in a state that consisted mostly of Jews while respecting the human rights of the Arab minority living within its borders or in a state with a substantial Arab population that was bitterly opposed to Israeli rule and therefore had to be subjected to a repressive military regime and denied the right to vote? The choice was between a democratic Jewish state and a state on the road to becoming binational and undemocratic.

To this series of difficult questions, the Israeli electorate gave an uncharacteristically clear-cut reply. It returned Labor to power with a decisive mandate to put its program into action and relegated the Likud to the opposition. Labor increased its seats in the Knesset from 39 to 44, while Likud's fell from 40 to 32. One has to go back to the 1977 election for a comparable landslide victory.

It would be misleading, however, to explain the Likud's rout simply in terms of its foreign policy. There were other forces at play that were unrelated or only partly related to its foreign policy. The principal reasons for the Likud's defeat may be briefly summarized as follows. First, after fifteen years in government, the Likud bloc presented the electors with an unedifying spectacle of internal discord, corruption, smugness, and lack of leadership. Second, the Likud's record of managing the economy was marred by incompetence, high inflation, and 11 percent unemployment. Third, the evident antagonism of the Ashkenazi elite toward the Moroccan-born David Levy and his associates caused desertion among the Likud's traditional Oriental supporters. Fourth, the Likud's dismal record in coping with the influx of immigrants from the Soviet Union turned many of the newcomers against the ruling party. Fifth, the Likud failed to suppress the *intifada* by military means and was unable to come up with any credible political solution. Sixth, a sizable number of Israelis with middle-of-the-road views had reached the conclusion that the conditions were ripe for a peaceful settlement of the Arab-Israeli conflict and that it was their government that was holding back. Last but not least, many Israelis felt that Shamir had sacrificed the special relationship with America, their lifeline, on the doctrinal altar of Greater Israel and that it was time he made way for a more pragmatic leader.

In defeat Shamir remained as unapologetic and unrepentant about his ideological commitment to the Land of Israel as he had been in power. Many observers suspected that he did not negotiate in good faith and that he used the American-sponsored peace process simply as a smoke screen for consolidating Israel's grip on the West Bank and Gaza. Shamir himself confirmed these suspicions in an interview of blinding candor that he gave to the Israeli newspaper *Ma'ariv* on the morrow of his electoral defeat. In this interview Shamir stressed that the Likud had to be guided by ideology because no political movement could survive unless it was driven by ideology. The centerpiece of his party's ideology, he said, was the Land of Israel, and on this there could be no compromise. "Moderation," he explained, "should relate to the tactics but not to the goal. That is how I acted as prime minister. In my political activity I know how to display the tactics of moderation, but without conceding anything on the goal—the integrity of the Land of Israel. In my eyes, anyone who is not in accord with this, does not belong to the national movement."

Shamir disclosed his secret agenda for the peace talks when asked what he regretted most following his fall from power. "It pains me greatly," he replied, "that in the coming four years I will not be able to expand the settlements in Judea and Samaria and to complete the demographic revolution in the Land of Israel. I know that others will now try to work against this. Without this demographic revolution, there is no value to the talk about autonomy, because there is a danger that it will be turned into a Palestinian state. What is this talk about 'political settlements'? I would have carried on autonomy talks for ten years, and meanwhile we would have reached half a million people in Judea and Samaria." When reminded that, judging by the results of the recent election, there was no majority for a Greater Land of Israel, Shamir retorted bluntly, "I didn't believe there was a majority in favor of a Greater Land of Israel. But it can be attained over time. This must be the historic direction. If we drop this basis, there would be nothing to prevent the development of a Palestinian state."[44]

Shamir's interview was widely reported in the international media and caused outrage among Americans, Arabs, Palestinians, and Israelis alike. The comments angered some of Shamir's ministerial colleagues, who felt they had been tainted by his confession. Moshe Arens, who decided to leave politics in the wake of his party's humiliating defeat, described Shamir's remarks as "a mistake." Labor Party leaders joined in the universal condemnation of Shamir. In Washington eyebrows were raised, particularly in the State Department, where long-standing suspicions that their ally was wasting their time appeared to be confirmed. Israel's neighbors, having had little enough reason to trust Shamir, now had it out of the horse's mouth that, from the very start, and despite all the peace rhetoric emanating from Jerusalem, he had secretly hoped to ensure that the peace talks would fail. This was the grim legacy Shamir left to his Labor successors.

In words as well as in deeds, Yitzhak Shamir was an exponent of the theory of permanent conflict between Israel and the Arabs. All the manifestations of Arab moderation were to him nothing but a mirage. War was more in tune with his inner feelings and his worldview than the possibility of peaceful coexistence. As he saw it, Israel was surrounded by enemies on all sides who were un-trustworthy, inherently vicious, and unalterably committed to its destruction. Waging war was not simply essential to Israel's survival but a commendable way of life. Two days before his electoral defeat, Shamir addressed a memorial meeting of the Fighters of the Freedom of Israel (popularly known as the Stern Gang) in Kiryat Ata. His theme was that nothing had changed since the War of Independence. "We still need this truth today, the truth of the power of war, or at least we need to accept that war is inescapable, because without this, the life of the individual has no purpose and the nation has no chance of survival."[45] The most charitable construction one can put on this statement is that the seventy-seven-year old Revisionist had in mind not war for its own sake but war as a means of defending the Land of Israel, which was always at the center of Shamir's life. His autobiography does not shed much new light on his political career, but the last sentence is highly revealing. "If history remembers me at all, in any way," he wrote, "I hope it will be as a man who loved the Land of Israel and watched over it in every way he could, all his life."[46] History will no doubt remember Shamir as a man who loved the Land of Israel. But it will also remember him as a man who systematically subverted every initiative to resolve the conflict between Israel and the Arabs during his tenure as prime minister.

13

The Breakthrough

1992–1995

W HEN THE LABOR PARTY emerged as the victor in the Israeli
general election of 23 June 1992, a BBC correspondent
asked an Arab janitor in Jerusalem for his reaction. "Do you see my
left shoe," replied the Arab indifferently, "that is Yitzhak Rabin.
Do you see my right shoe, that is Yitzhak Shamir. Two Yitzhaks,
two shoes, so what's the difference?" This feeling that there was
not much to choose between the leaders of Israel's two main parties was not confined to the Arabs. When Rabin served as defense
minister in the national unity government headed by Shamir, there
was a joke in Israel that went as follows: what is the difference between a left-wing Likudnik and a right-wing Likudnik? Answer: a
left-wing Likudnik is a follower of Yitzhak Shamir and a right-
wing Likudnik is a follower of Yitzhak Rabin.

A CHANGE IN NATIONAL PRIORITIES

The traditional foreign policies of the rival parties led by the two
Yitzhaks did display some striking similarities. Both Labor and the
Likud had a blind spot when it came to the Palestinians, preferring
to treat the Arab-Israeli conflict as an interstate conflict. Both parties were deeply opposed to Palestinian nationalism and denied
that the Palestinians had a right to national self-determination.
Both always refused to negotiate with the PLO, and this refusal

was absolute rather than conditional. Both were also unconditionally opposed to the establishment of an independent
Palestinian state.

Yet the differences between Labor and the Likud were quite
profound, in the realms both of ideology and of practical policy.
Shamir's confession that he had no intention of reaching an agreement with the Palestinians had left behind a legacy of mistrust. To
dissociate himself from this legacy, Rabin emphasized the differences and downplayed the similarities between himself and his predecessor. He presented the election results as marking a break
rather than continuity in the country's approach to the peace talks.
"We inherited the framework of the Madrid conference from the
previous government," he told the Knesset. "But there is one significant change: the previous government created the tools, but it
never intended to use them in order to achieve peace."[1]

The composition of the new government also underscored the
sharp break with the legacy of the Likud. If Shamir's government
had been the most hawkish in Israel's history, Rabin's was the
most dovish. Rabin himself was not as dovish as Moshe Sharett or
Levi Eshkol. But his coalition government as a whole was more
dovish than any previous Labor-led coalition. Of Labor's eleven
ministers, at least six could be counted as doves. Its chief coalition
partner was Meretz—a left-of-center party created through a
merger of the Citizens' Rights Movement, Mapam, and Shinui—
which won 12 seats in the Knesset. The other coalition partner was
Shas, a centrist religious party of mainly Oriental Jews that increased its representation from 5 to 6 seats in the Knesset.
Although Rabin's government commanded only a narrow majority of 62 in the 120-member Knesset, it could count on the support of the 5 Arab and Communist members for a moderate
foreign policy.

Rabin thus enjoyed considerable latitude in the making of foreign policy. As the leader of the Labor Party, he was master in his
own house after nearly two decades of debilitating rivalry between
himself and Shimon Peres. The party rallied behind Rabin after he
won the contest for the leadership and fought the election under
the banner "the Labor Party under the leadership of Yitzhak
Rabin." The election results gave him a personal mandate for
change. He emerged with the kind of authority one associates
more with the U.S. president than with the Israeli prime minister.
But Rabin was also the product of the preceding half century of his
people's history. He was the first Israeli-born prime minister and,

to a far greater extent than any of his predecessors, was personally involved at the sharp end of the conflict with the Arabs. His military career spanned the first two decades of statehood, starting as a youthful brigade commander in the War of Independence and reaching its climax as chief of staff in the Six-Day War, in June 1967. This direct involvement in the conflict between Israel and the Arabs, first as a soldier and then as a diplomat and politician, played a decisive part in shaping Rabin's worldview.

Suspicion of the Arabs and a deep sense of personal responsibility for Israel's security were the twin hallmarks of this worldview. For Rabin the Arabs represented first and foremost a military threat, and he consequently tended to view all developments in the region from the narrow perspective of Israel's security needs. His career as a soldier inclined him to proceed with caution, on the basis of "worst-case analysis," and made him reluctant to assume risks. A professional soldier turned politician, he tended to approach diplomacy as the extension of war by other means. As a peacemaker, as he himself recognized, he had not been a notable success during his first term as prime minister, in 1974–77. All he had achieved was the interim agreement with Egypt, whereas his Likud successor achieved the real breakthrough by concluding the peace treaty with Egypt in 1979. Rabin now had his second chance, and he was determined not to miss it. He continued to believe that, to be effective, diplomacy had to be supported by military force, but the emphasis had shifted from the latter to the former. Like the other leaders of the Labor Party, notably David Ben-Gurion, Rabin was influenced by Ze'ev Jabotinsky's theory of the iron wall. But as prime minister in his second term of office, he recognized that the iron wall of Jewish military power had achieved its purpose and that the time had come to negotiate an end to the conflict with the Arab states and with the Palestinians. As a means to that end, however, the Madrid formula had no appeal to Rabin, because it required Israel to negotiate with all its enemies simultaneously. Rather than strive for a comprehensive settlement of the Arab-Israeli conflict, Rabin was a great believer in one peace at a time. The idea behind this approach was to break up the united Arab front, to negotiate with each party separately, and to pay the lowest possible price in terms of territory for each bilateral agreement.

Rabin doubled as prime minister and minister of defense in the new government. He appointed Simon Peres, his old rival, foreign minister, but on the clear understanding that he himself would be in overall charge of the country's foreign policy. Peres's authority was curtailed. He had to agree not to launch any independent foreign policy initiatives and to leave the conduct of relations with the United States in the hands of Rabin. The division of labor between the two men was that the prime minister would direct all the bilateral talks with the Arabs, whereas the foreign minister would direct the less important multilateral talks. Thus, from the very start, Rabin enjoyed a position of towering dominance in the making of his government's foreign and defense policy.

The multilateral talks were set up at the Madrid conference to run parallel to the bilateral talks. They drew on a much wider set of participants and issues. They involved some forty countries, including Israel, all the Arab confrontation states, other Arab states from the Gulf and the Maghreb, the United States, the Soviet Union, the European Union, and Japan. Whereas the bilateral talks were expected to supply the political basis for the resolution of the conflict, the multilateral talks were intended to address problems that cut across national borders and to provide a framework for regional cooperation. Several working groups were set up to deal with water resources, the environment, refugees, arms control, and economic development.[2]

Shimon Peres was exceptionally well suited for the task of overseeing Israeli participation in the multilateral talks. If Rabin was the expert on security, Peres was the statesman intent on changing the course of history. Peres had much more empathy with the Arabs, a better understanding of economics, a clearer appreciation of the declining utility of military force in the modern world, and a vision of a new Middle East. His vision, articulated in his book *The New Middle East*, was inspired by the example of the European Union.[3] A prior condition for the realization of this vision was a comprehensive settlement of the Arab-Israeli conflict. Security, to his way of thinking, had not just military but political, psychological, and economic components. It was a mistake, he thought, for Israel to try to perpetuate the territorial status quo and to continue to base its national security on massive and costly armed forces. The alternative he advocated was Israeli withdrawal from the occupied territories, resolution of the conflict, and open borders that would enable Israel to extend its economic links throughout the region from North Africa to the Persian Gulf. He was a strong believer in the economic dimension of peacemaking. "To construct a political staircase without economic banisters," he remarked, "is to take the risk that people will begin to climb, only to fall off before they reach the top."[4]

Peres's basic position was clear to his close circle of advisers as they set out on their ambitious voyage in the summer of 1992. Since they had effectively lost the "Jordanian option," at least for the time being, they had no choice but to develop a Palestinian option. There was no real prospect of implementing the Palestinian autonomy plan originally proposed by the Likud in 1978. Negotiations on the basis of the Camp David formula had led nowhere in the past. Peres believed that genuine autonomy would involve the handover of the entire West Bank and Gaza to Palestinian rule, but he also knew that most Israelis were not ready for this. Instead, he supported the idea of an interim agreement. If they could not agree at that stage to a map, at least they could try to reach agreement on a timetable, in the hope that conditions would change with the passage of time.

Peres made it clear at the outset that he was entering the government not in order to renew the old rivalry with Rabin but to dedicate himself to the cause of peace. Future relations with Rabin, he said, would be judged by one yardstick—the peace process. If progress was satisfactory, he would be the most loyal of Rabin's ministers; but if the peace process was allowed to grind to a halt, he would not hesitate to raise the banner of rebellion.[5] In the event, the two men succeeded in turning their old rivalry into a close and constructive partnership. Rabin was seventy and Peres sixty-nine, and they united in pursuit of one overriding goal—making peace with the Arabs. President Chaim Herzog, a former general and a member of the Labor Party, was pleasantly surprised by the Rabin-Peres partnership for peace:

> Their political relationship was singular: they did not like each other yet complemented each other like no team in Israel's history. Their success with the Peace Plan was a perfect example. Peres had spent years looking for a link to the Arabs and ultimately decided on Arafat when many thought the choice was lunacy. But Peres could never have carried the plan out without Rabin's strength, cautiousness, and the trust he inspired in the Israeli people. It had been agonizing to watch them vie for power, but such is the nature of politics.[6]

Rabin presented his government and its program in a major speech before the Knesset on 13 July. He grouped the differences between the outgoing and the incoming government under three headings: national priorities, the peace process, and Israel's place in the world. Whereas the outgoing government had lavished money on the territories, Rabin promised to divert resources to the absorption of immigrants, social and economic reforms, the war against unemployment, and better education. As far as the peace process was concerned, Rabin proposed to move from "process" to peacemaking and to give priority to the talks on Palestinian autonomy, implying that Syria would have to await its turn. Peace, however, could not come at the expense of Israel's security. "When it comes to Israel's security," he said, "we will concede not a thing. From our standpoint, security takes precedence over peace."

But the most striking and unexpected part of Rabin's speech concerned Israel's place in the world. Jewish history had traditionally been presented as an endless chain of trials and tribulations, which reached its climax in the Nazi gas chambers. Likud leaders, for their own political purposes, had assiduously cultivated the image of a small and vulnerable Jewish state surrounded by a sea of Arab hostility. Their answer to this sense of permanent threat was to build up Greater Israel as a citadel for the entire Jewish people. Rabin not only discarded this policy but directly challenged the thinking behind it. "No longer are we necessarily 'a people that dwells alone,' " he declared in his historic address to the Knesset, "and no longer is it true that 'the whole world is against us.' We must overcome the sense of isolation that has held us in its thrall for almost half a century." These words constituted a sharp departure from what the American-Jewish historian Salo Baron once called the lachrymose view of Jewish history. It was probably more than a coincidence that they were uttered by the first prime minister born not in the diaspora but in Israel.

FAILURE OF
THE BILATERAL PEACE TALKS

The effects of the new attitude in Jerusalem were felt immediately when the sixth round of Middle East talks got under way in Washington, on 24 August 1992. From the Israeli side came the suggestion of continuous talks, and this round was longer than any of the five preceding ones; it lasted a month with a recess of ten days in the middle. Before embarking on the talks, Israel volunteered a number of confidence-building measures (CBMs) like freeing Palestinian detainees and rescinding deportation orders. The talks opened in a positive atmosphere, with all sides reporting a new tone and a more conciliatory style.

Israel's more relaxed attitude regarding the backstage role of the PLO in directing the peace talks went down well with the Palestinian negotiators. Ever since the Madrid conference Israel had been negotiating indirectly with the PLO because the Palestinian delegation kept in close contact with the PLO leadership in Tunis. Shamir knew this but refused to acknowledge it. He preferred to preserve the fiction that the PLO was completely out of the picture. He opted to bury his head in the sand and play ostrich politics even though, as Abba Eban observed, the posture of the ostrich is neither elegant nor comfortable. Rabin, by contrast, did not care with whom the Palestinian negotiators met or who gave them their instructions. He dealt with facts, not with Likud-manufactured fiction.[7] In December 1992 the Rabin government went a step further and repealed the six-year-old law proscribing any contact between Israeli citizens and the PLO. Rabin made it clear in the Knesset that lifting the ban did not mean that his government was entering into negotiations with the PLO. But it was no longer an offense for Israelis to talk to officials of the PLO.[8]

With so much at stake, Rabin took personal charge of the bilateral talks. He estimated that neither Jordan nor Lebanon was likely to take the plunge in signing the first peace treaty with Israel, because Jordan would be reluctant to preempt the Palestinians and Lebanon would be afraid to preempt the Syrians. That left two parties with which to conclude the first peace agreement: the Palestinians and Syria. To begin with, Rabin planned to concentrate on reaching an agreement on Palestinian autonomy. But he changed his mind. There were several reasons for this change. First, the talks with the Palestinians did not get off to a good start, whereas those with the Syrians did. Second, Rabin was warned by the Americans against leaving the Syrians in the cold, lest they be tempted to obstruct the talks between Israel and the other parties. Third, Hafez al-Assad himself apparently sent messages to Rabin, through President Bush and President Mubarak of Egypt, expressing his interest in a serious dialogue with Israel. Rabin concluded that a settlement with Syria might be feasible after all and that such a settlement, with the second most powerful confrontation state after Egypt, would dramatically change the strategic picture in Israel's favor.[9]

Rabin retained Likud's Elyakim Rubinstein as the head of the Israeli delegation for the talks with the Palestinians. Whether intentionally or unintentionally, this suggested continuity in Israeli policy. Moreover, there were no radically different ideas on offer to counter this impression of continuity. Real dialogue replaced sloganizing, but the positions of the two parties remained wide apart. The sixth round began on 24 August with Israel offering elections to a 15-member Palestinian administrative council, while the Palestinians demanded a 120-member parliament with legislative authority, and this, with some minor relaxation of the Israeli position, was how the talks ended. Israel kept offering to delegate certain tasks, while the Palestinians kept insisting on a meaningful transfer of authority.

During the seventh round, in November 1992, the ambiguity that had obscured the conceptual gap between the Israel and the Palestinian positions since the beginning of the talks finally disappeared. It proved impossible for the two sides to agree on a first step, because they were intent on marching in opposite directions. The Palestinians wanted to end the occupation; the Israelis wanted to retain as much control as possible for as long as possible. The Palestinians tried to negotiate the establishment of a state in the making. They insisted that the interim agreement permit and even lay the groundwork for the development of their sovereign state. The Israelis were equally determined to prevent the interim agreement from resembling the embryo of a Palestinian state. They insisted on keeping sole control of the Jewish settlements and the roads in the occupied territories during the transition period and to share control only of state land.

When the eighth round opened in Washington, on 7 December, in the twilight of the Bush administration, the talks between Israel and the Palestinians were virtually at a dead end. Negotiations about interim self-government were resumed, but Israel continued to focus solely on the interim arrangements while the Palestinians tried, without success, to shift the focus to self-government. To the American sponsors it seemed that the Israeli concept of interim self-government was fundamentally flawed. But in its dying days the Bush administration was not well placed to persuade the Israelis that interim self-government meant precisely what it said—a stage leading to full self-government.

Lack of concrete results from the peace process added to the frustration of the Palestinians in the occupied territories and boosted popular support for the Islamic resistance movement, Hamas, which was opposed to negotiations with the Jewish state. Round eight in the talks was due to conclude on 17 December, but it ended abruptly on the 16th when Rabin announced his government's decision to deport 416 Hamas activists to Lebanon following the kidnaping and murder of an Israeli border policeman. All the Arab delegations angrily suspended their participation in the peace talks and refused to set a date for their resumption.

Rabin was widely condemned but unrepentant. Government policy toward the Palestinians, he said, was two-pronged: fighting violent extremists while talking peace to the moderates. But his deportation order was without precedent and in flagrant violation of international law. It outstripped the toughest measures of the Likud and out-Shamired Shamir. None of the alleged Islamic activists had been charged, tried, or allowed to appeal before being driven blindfolded into exile in Lebanon. This act was intended to curb the rising influence of Hamas, but it had the opposite effect. It discredited the peace talks, strengthened the extremists, and weakened the moderates. Worse than a crime, it was a mistake.

The deportations boosted Rabin's domestic popularity but did not stem the tide of violence. In March 1993 thirteen Israelis were murdered by knife-wielding fanatics. Most of these attacks were carried out by members of the military wing of Hamas, and some of them involved the use of firearms, especially against Israeli settlers and soldiers in the occupied territories. Rabin's response was one of massive retaliation. On 30 March he ordered the closure of Israel's pre-1967 border to workers from the occupied territories. Nearly 120,000 families were punished for the deeds of a handful of killers. The closure achieved its immediate aim of reducing the incidence of violence, but it also had a much deeper significance. It served Rabin's new aim of bringing about Israel's disengagement from the occupied territories. It re-created the 1967 border and led to the economic and social separation of the Jewish and Palestinian communities. Although prompted by short-term security considerations, the closure thus worked against the preceding government's policy of obliterating the Green Line in favor of Greater Israel.

The ninth round of bilateral talks opened in Washington on 27 April, after a hiatus lasting four and a half months. To get the talks restarted, Israel made two minor concessions: acceptance of Faisal Husseini, despite his residence in East Jerusalem, as a negotiator; and approval in principle for a Palestinian police force in the territories. There was also evidence of greater Israeli flexibility on fundamentals. The Israelis were now willing to admit a link between the interim and the final phase of Palestinian self-government. They indicated that the body elected to govern the Palestinians for the five-year interim period could have some legislative powers.

And they affirmed that negotiations on the final status of the occupied territories would be based on UN Resolution 242.

Despite this auspicious beginning, a document presented by the Palestinian delegation in response to the Israeli proposals revealed persistent divergence on three fundamental issues: the application of Resolution 242, the relationship between the interim phase and the final phase, and the nature and powers of the interim Palestinian authority. In an attempt to move the peace talks off dead center, the recently elected Democratic administration headed by Bill Clinton formulated and presented to the Palestinians a working paper that proposed new terms of reference for the talks. The Palestinian delegates, however, detected Israel's thumbprints all over the American paper. Reversing a twenty-six-year-old American policy, the paper accepted the Israeli claim that East Jerusalem and the rest of the West Bank and Gaza were disputed—not occupied—territories. The Palestinian delegation pointed out that the paper deviated from the terms of reference under which the talks were initiated and was therefore unsuitable even as a starting point for talks.

Among themselves the Palestinian negotiators joked that the Americans sent them only "nonpapers" because they looked on them as "nonpeople" and did not respond to most of their memoranda because they regarded them as a "nondelegation."[10] As soon as Bill Clinton entered the White House, the pro-Israeli bias in American policy became more pronounced. The evenhanded approach of the Bush administration was replaced by an "Israel first" approach reminiscent of the Reagan days. Clinton refused to put pressure on Israel and adopted a hands-off attitude to the peace process. The peace process had started with two cosponsors at Madrid, but one, the USSR, no long existed, and the other, the United States, became a spectator.

The American paper failed to move the talks off dead center. The tenth round, from 15 June until 1 July, ended in failure. Little was expected and nothing was achieved. In Israel the Rabin government began to attract criticism for its failure to deliver on its promise of agreement on Palestinian autonomy. Government spokesmen tried to evade responsibility for the deadlock by placing all the blame at the door of the Palestinians. At least one thing was clear at the end of the twenty months and ten rounds of Arab-Israeli peace talks: the Madrid formula was not capable of ushering in a new era of peace in the Middle East, and a new formula had to be found.

Although the Madrid formula involved Israel in indirect negotiations with the PLO, Rabin resisted for a whole year the calls
for formal recognition of the PLO. He saw Yasser Arafat as the
main obstacle to a deal on Palestinian autonomy and did his best
to marginalize him, pinning his hopes on the local leaders from the
occupied territories, whom he considered more moderate and
more pragmatic. Experience taught him, however, that the local
leaders could not act independently of the PLO chairman in Tunis
and that, consequently, if he wanted a deal, he would have to cut
it with his arch-enemy.

The failure of the official talks on the Palestinian track in
Washington left Rabin with two alternatives: a deal with President
Hafez al-Assad of Syria, which entailed complete withdrawal and
the dismantling of Jewish settlements on the Golan Heights, or a
deal with the PLO on interim self-government, which did not en-
tail an immediate commitment to withdraw from the West Bank or
to dismantle Jewish settlements. He opted for the second alternative.

THE OSLO CHANNEL

The decision to hold direct talks with the PLO was a diplomatic
revolution in Israel's foreign policy and paved the way to the Oslo
accord of 13 September 1993. Three men were primarily responsible for this decision: Yitzhak Rabin, Shimon Peres, and Yossi
Beilin, the youthful deputy foreign minister. Rabin held out against
direct talks with the PLO for as long as he could. Peres took the
view that without the PLO there could be no settlement.
Expecting the PLO to enable the local Palestinian leaders to reach
an agreement with Israel, he said on one occasion, was like expecting the turkey to help in preparing the Thanksgiving dinner.
As long as Arafat remained in Tunis, he argued, he represented the
"outsiders," the Palestinian diaspora, and he would do his best to
slow down the peace talks.[11] Beilin was even more categorical in his
view that talking to the PLO was a necessary condition for an
agreement with the Palestinians. He had always belonged to the
extreme dovish wing of the Labor Party. He was the real architect
behind the Israeli recognition of the PLO. Peres backed him all the
way, and the two of them succeeded in carrying their hesitant and
suspicious senior colleague with them.

Beilin not only recognized the need to talk to the PLO but had a clear and coherent long-term strategy for directing the talks. He realized at the outset that to achieve a peace settlement with the Palestinians, Israel would have to pay a high price: a return to the pre–June 1967 borders with only minor modifications, an independent Palestinian state, the dismantling of Jewish settlements, and the granting to the Palestinians of functional control over East Jerusalem.[12] Rabin, on the other hand, had no clear idea of the final shape of the settlement with the Palestinians. He wanted to preserve the Jewish settlements in the occupied territories and to keep Israel's security border along the Jordan River. But he also wanted to end the policing of the large Palestinian cities by the IDF, because it generated endless friction, and he was moving in the direction of a separate Palestinian entity, less than a state, that would run the life of the Palestinian residents of the West Bank and Gaza. It was this policy vacuum at the heart of the government that enabled Beilin to take the lead, to exert an influence that was out of all proportion to his junior position.

Given the deadlock in the official talks in Washington, another avenue had to be found for unofficial talks between Israel and the PLO. Secret talks in Oslo got under way in late January 1993 with the active encouragement of Beilin, who kept Peres fully informed. Altogether, fourteen sessions of talks were held over an eight-month period, all behind a thick veil of secrecy. The Norwegian foreign affairs minister, Johan Joergen Holst, and the social scientist Terge Rød Larsen acted as generous hosts and facilitators. The key players were two Israeli academics, Dr. Yair Hirschfeld and Dr. Ron Pundak, and the PLO treasurer, Ahmad Qurei, better known as Abu Ala. Away from the glare of publicity and political pressures, these three men worked imaginatively and indefatigably to establish the conceptual framework of the Israel-PLO accord. Their discussions ran parallel to the bilateral talks in Washington, but they proceeded without the knowledge of the official Israeli and Palestinian negotiators.

The unofficial talks initially dealt with economic cooperation but quickly broadened into a dialogue about a joint declaration of principles. This was made possible by a change in the PLO's position. In the past the PLO had always demanded that Israel recognize the right of the Palestinians to national self-determination as the price for recognizing Israel. Now the PLO men were prepared to discuss interim arrangements without prior agreement on the final outcome.

In Israel attitudes were also changing. Prolonged closure led to a shift in public opinion in favor of a territorial separation between Israel and the occupied territories. This was especially true of the impoverished and overcrowded Gaza Strip, where anti-Israel feelings always ran very high. Pictures on the television screens of brutal behavior by soldiers against unarmed civilians damaged Israel's image abroad and shocked the public at home. In the wake of the closure, a public debate reopened in Israel on the proposal for a unilateral withdrawal from the Gaza Strip. Many Israelis supported the proposal, viewing Gaza as a millstone around their necks. In May, amid gloom and doom on all sides, Peres took a highly significant decision: he ordered Uri Savir, the director general of the Foreign Ministry, and Yoel Singer, a high-flying attorney who had spent twenty years in the IDF legal department, to join Hirschfeld and Pundak on the weekend trips to Oslo. At this point Peres began to report to Rabin regularly on developments in the Norwegian back channel. At first Rabin showed little interest in this channel, but he raised no objection to continuing the explorations either. Gradually, however, he became more involved in the details and assumed an active role in directing the talks alongside Peres. Since Abu Ala reported directly to Arafat and to Arafat's deputy, Mahmoud Abbas (Abu Mazen), an indirect line of communication had been established between Jerusalem and the PLO headquarters in Tunis.[13]

To tempt Arafat to move forward, Peres floated the idea of "Gaza first." He believed that Arafat was desperate for a concrete achievement to bolster his sagging political fortunes and that Gaza would provide him with his first toehold in the occupied territories. Peres also knew that an Israeli withdrawal from Gaza would be greeted with sighs of relief among the great majority of his countrymen. Arafat, however, did not swallow the bait, suspecting an Israeli plan to confine the dream of Palestinian independence to the narrow strip of territory stretching from Gaza City to Rafah. The idea was attractive to some Palestinians, especially the inhabitants of the Gaza Strip, but not to the politicians in Tunis. Rather than reject the Israeli offer out of hand, Arafat came up with a counteroffer: "Gaza and Jericho first." His choice of the small and sleepy West Bank town seemed quirky at first sight, but it served as a symbol of his claim to the whole of the West Bank.

Rabin did not balk at the counteroffer. All along he had supported the Allon Plan, which envisaged handing over Jericho to Jordanian rule while keeping the Jordan Valley in Israeli hands. But he had one condition: the Palestinian foothold on the West Bank would be an island inside Israeli-controlled territory, with the Allenby Bridge also remaining in Israeli hands. Jordan, too, preferred Israel to the Palestinians at the other end of the bridge. Arafat therefore had to settle for the Israeli version of the "Gaza and Jericho first" plan.[14]

Rabin's conversion to the idea of a deal with the PLO was clinched by four evaluations that reached him between the end of May and July. First was the advice of Itamar Rabinovich, the head of the Israeli delegation to the talks with Syria, that a settlement with Syria was attainable but only at the cost of complete Israeli withdrawal from the Golan Heights. Second were the reports from various quarters that the local Palestinian leadership had finally been neutralized. Third was the assessment of the IDF director of military intelligence that Arafat's dire situation, and possible imminent collapse, made him the most convenient interlocutor for Israel at that juncture. Fourth were the reports of the impressive progress achieved through the Oslo channel. Other reports that reached Rabin during this period pointed to an alarming growth in the popular following of Hamas and Islamic Jihad in the occupied territories. Both the army chiefs and the internal security chiefs repeatedly stressed to him the urgency of finding a political solution to the crisis in the relations between Israel and the inhabitants of the occupied territories.[15] Rabin therefore gave the green light to the Israeli team, and the secret diplomacy in Oslo shifted into higher gear.

Rabin carefully scrutinized every word in the declaration of principles. Yet, despite his caution, Rabin moved a long way in a short time. In June he did not take the Oslo channel at all seriously; in August he wanted to go all the way. In the end, both he and Peres used all their weight to secure a breakthrough in the Oslo channel. On 23 August, Rabin stated publicly for the first time that "there would be no escape from recognizing the PLO." In private he elaborated on the price Israel could extract in exchange for this recognition. In his estimate the PLO was "on the ropes," and it was therefore highly probable that the PLO would drop some of its sacred principles to secure Israeli recognition. Accordingly, while endorsing the joint declaration of principles on Palestinian self-government in Gaza and Jericho and mutual recognition between Israel and the PLO, he insisted on changes to the Palestinian National Charter as part of the package deal.[16]

Peres, in the course of an ostensibly ordinary tour of Scandinavia, met secretly with Abu Ala in Oslo on 24 August and finalized the accord. Since the drafting of the joint declaration of principles had already been completed, the face-to-face discussion between the Israeli foreign minister and the PLO official focused on the other vital element of the accord—mutual recognition. As numerous rumors began to circulate about his secret meeting, Peres flew to California to explain the accord to the U.S. secretary of state, Warren Christopher. Christopher was surprised by the scope of the accord and by the unorthodox method by which it had been achieved. He naturally assumed that America had a monopoly over the peace process. His aides in the State Department had their feathers ruffled because they had been so thoroughly upstaged by the Norwegians. All the participants in the Oslo back channel, on the other hand, had the satisfaction of knowing that they had reached the accord on their own without any help from the State Department. Their success showed that the fate of the peace process lay in the hands of the protagonists rather than in the hands of the intermediaries.

The Oslo accord was presented to the cabinet on 30 August. It was a large gathering attended by, in addition to the ministers, senior officers and intelligence chiefs, Elyakim Rubinstein, Yossi Beilin, Yoel Singer, and Uri Savir. Singer introduced the document. Ehud Barak, the chief of staff, gave his evaluation. Rubinstein, who had been kept in the dark about the Oslo channel, listed twenty-one reservations. Nearly all the ministers who spoke did so in a positive vein and offered their congratulations to the negotiators. The cabinet approved the accord unanimously, with only two abstentions. The text of the accord could not be changed, so a vote against it would have been tantamount to a vote of no confidence in the prime minister and the foreign minister. Nevertheless, the degree of consensus among the ministers in favor of the accord was quite remarkable.[17]

THE OSLO ACCORD

The Declaration of Principles on Interim Self-Government Arrangements was essentially an agenda for negotiations, governed by a tight timetable, rather than a full-blown agreement. The declaration laid down that within two months of the signing ceremony, agreement on Israel's military withdrawal from Gaza and Jericho should be reached, and within four months the withdrawal should be completed. A Palestinian police force, made up mostly of pro-Arafat Palestinian fighters, was to be imported to maintain internal security in Gaza and Jericho, with Israel retaining overall responsibility for external security and foreign affairs. At the same time, elsewhere in the West Bank, Israel undertook to transfer power to "authorized Palestinians" in five spheres: education, health, social welfare, direct taxation, and tourism. Within nine months the Palestinians in the West Bank and Gaza were to hold elections for a Palestinian council that was to take office and assume responsibility for most government functions except defense and foreign affairs. Israel and the Palestinians agreed to commence, within two years, negotiations on the final status of the territories, and at the end of five years the permanent settlement was to come into force.[18] In short, the Declaration of Principles promised to set in motion a process for ending Israeli rule over the two million Palestinians living in the West Bank and Gaza.

The shape of the permanent settlement was not specified in the Declaration of Principles but was left to negotiations between the two parties during the second stage. The declaration was completely silent on such vital issues as the right of return of the 1948 refugees, the borders of the Palestinian entity, the future of the Jewish settlements on the West Bank and Gaza, and the status of Jerusalem. The reason for this silence is not hard to understand: if these issues had been addressed, there would have been no accord. Both sides took a calculated risk, realizing that a great deal would depend on how the experiment in Palestinian self-government worked out in practice. Rabin was opposed to an independent Palestinian state, but he favored an eventual Jordanian-Palestinian confederation. Arafat was strongly committed to an independent Palestinian state, with East Jerusalem as its capital, but he did not rule out the idea of a confederation with Jordan.

Despite all its limitations and ambiguities, the Declaration of Principles for Palestinian self-government in Gaza and Jericho marked a major breakthrough in the century-old conflict between Arabs and Jews in Palestine. Future generations will look back on Monday, 13 September 1993, the day the declaration was signed on the South Lawn of the White House and sealed with the historic handshake between Prime Minister Rabin and Chairman Arafat, as one of the most momentous events in the history of the Middle East in the twentieth century. In one stunning move the two leaders redrew the geopolitical map of the entire region.

Although the Declaration of Principles was signed in

Washington, with President Bill Clinton acting as the master of
ceremonies, it had been negotiated in Oslo and initialed there.
The Oslo accord consisted of two parts, both of which were the
product of secret diplomacy in the Norwegian capital. The first
part consisted of mutual recognition between Israel and the PLO.
It took the form of two letters, on plain paper and without letter-
heads, dated 9 September but signed by Chairman Arafat and
Prime Minister Rabin, respectively, on 9 and 10 September. Nearly
all the publicity focused on the signing of the Declaration of
Principles, but without the prior agreement on mutual recognition
there could have been no meaningful agreement on Palestinian
self-government.

In his letter to Rabin, Arafat observed that the signing of the
Declaration of Principles marked a new era in the history of the
Middle East. He then confirmed the PLO's commitment to recognize Israel's right to live in peace and security, to accept UN
Security Council Resolutions 242 and 338, to renounce the use of
terrorism and other acts of violence, and to change those parts of
the Palestinian National Charter that were inconsistent with these
commitments. In his terse, one-sentence reply to Arafat, Rabin
confirmed that in the light of these commitments, the government of Israel decided to recognize the PLO as the representative
of the Palestinian people and to commence negotiations with the
PLO in the Middle Eastern peace process.[19]

Taken together, the two parts of the Oslo accord fully merit the
overworked epithet "historic" because they reconciled the two
principal parties to the Arab-Israeli conflict. The clash between
Jewish and Palestinian nationalism had always been the core of
the Arab-Israeli conflict. Both national movements, Jewish and
Palestinian, denied the other the right to self-determination in
Palestine. Their history was one of mutual denial and mutual rejection. Now mutual denial made way for mutual recognition,
however grudging. Israel not only recognized the Palestinians as
a people with political rights but formally recognized the PLO as
its representative. The handshake between Rabin and Arafat at the
signing ceremony at the White House, despite the former's awkward body language, was a powerful symbol of the historic reconciliation between the two nations. The old Israeli warhorse was
deeply uneasy about the mammoth step of opening relations with
the PLO, which only weeks earlier he had been calling a terrorist
organization. To his aides he confided that he had "butterflies in
his stomach." Yet he managed to overcome his doubts and reser-

vations and took this gigantic step, knowing full well that there was no turning back.

The historic reconciliation was based on a historic compromise: acceptance of the principle of the partition of Palestine. Both sides accepted territorial compromise as the basis for the settlement of their long and bitter conflict. Partition was not, of course, a new idea. It was first proposed by the Peel Commission in 1937 and again by the United Nations in 1947, but it was rejected on both occasions by the Palestinians, who insisted on a unitary state over the whole of Palestine. Insisting on all or nothing, they ended up with nothing. By finally accepting the principle of partition at the same time, the two sides set aside the ideological dispute over who was the rightful owner of Palestine and turned to finding a practical solution to the problem of sharing the cramped living space between the Jordan River and the Mediterranean Sea. Each side resigned itself to parting with territory it had previously regarded not only as its patrimony but as a vital part of its national identity. Each side was driven to this historic compromise by the recognition that it lacked the power to impose its own vision on the other side. That the idea of partition was finally accepted by the two sides seemed to support Abba Eban's observation that men and nations often behave wisely—once they have exhausted all the other alternatives.[20]

The breakthrough at Oslo was achieved by separating the interim settlement from the final settlement. In the past the Palestinians had always refused to consider any interim agreement unless the principles of the permanent settlement were agreed in advance. Israel, on the other hand, had insisted that a five-year transition period begin without a prior agreement about the nature of the permanent settlement and, indeed, that its purpose be to teach the two sides to work together. At Oslo the PLO accepted the Israeli formula. In contrast to the official Palestinian position in Washington, the PLO agreed to a five-year transition period without clear commitments by Israel as to the nature of the permanent settlement.[21]

The Israeli-PLO accord had far-reaching implications for the interstate dimension of the Arab-Israeli conflict. Originally, the Arab states got involved in the Palestine conflict out of a sense of solidarity with the Palestine Arabs against the Zionist intruders. Continuing commitment to the Palestinian cause had precluded the Arab states, with the notable exception of Egypt, from extending recognition to the Jewish state. One of the main functions of the Arab League, established in 1945, was to assist the Palestinians in the struggle for Palestine. After 1948 the league became a forum for coordinating military policy and for waging political, economic, and ideological warfare against the Jewish state. In 1974 it recognized the PLO as the sole legitimate representative of the Palestinian people. Now that the PLO had formally recognized Israel, there was no longer any compelling reason for the Arab states to continue to reject it.

Clearly, an important taboo had been broken. PLO recognition of Israel was an important landmark along the road to Arab recognition of Israel and the normalizing of relations with it. Egypt, the first to take the plunge back in the late 1970s, felt vindicated and elated by the breakthrough it had helped bring about. When Rabin stopped in Rabat on his way home after attending the signing ceremony in Washington, he was received like any other visiting head of state by King Hassan II of Morocco. Jordan allowed Israeli television the first ever live report by one of its correspondents from Amman. A number of Arab states, like Tunisia and Saudi Arabia, started thinking seriously about the establishment of diplomatic relations with Israel. And the Arab League began discussions on the lifting of the economic boycott that had been in force since Israel's creation. Nothing was quite the same in the Arab world as a result of the Israel-PLO accord. The rules of the game in the entire Middle East had radically changed.

The change was no less marked in Israel's approach to its Arab opponents than in their approach to Israel. Zionist policy, before and after 1948, proceeded on the assumption that agreement on the partition of Palestine would be easier to achieve with the rulers of the neighboring Arab states than with the Palestine Arabs. Israel's courting of conservative Arab leaders, like King Hussein of Jordan and President Sadat of Egypt, was an attempt to bypass the local Arabs, and avoid having to address the core issue of the conflict. Recognition by the Arab states, it was hoped, would help alleviate the conflict without conceding the right of national self-determination to the Palestinians. Now this strategy was reversed. PLO recognition of Israel was expected to pave the way for wider recognition by the Arab states from North Africa to the Persian Gulf. Rabin expressed this hope when signing the letter to Arafat in which Israel recognized the PLO. "I believe," he said, "that there is a great opportunity of changing not only the relations between the Palestinians and Israel, but to expand it to the solution of the conflict between Israel and the Arab countries, and other Arab peoples."

On both sides of the Israeli-Palestinian divide, the Rabin-Arafat deal provoked strong and vociferous opposition on the part of the hard-liners. Both men were accused of a betrayal and a sellout. Leaders of the Likud, and of the nationalistic parties farther to the right, attacked Rabin for his abrupt departure from the bipartisan policy of refusing to negotiate with the PLO and charged him with abandoning the 120,000 settlers in the occupied territories to the tender mercies of terrorists. The Gaza-Jericho plan was denounced as a bridgehead to a Palestinian state and the beginning of the end of Greater Israel. A Gallup poll, however, indicated considerable popular support for the prime minister. Of the 1,000 Israelis polled, 65 percent said they approved of the peace accord, with only 13 percent describing themselves as "very much against."[22]

The Knesset approved the accord, at the end of a debate that stretched over three days, by 61 votes to 50, with nine abstentions. During the debate the right appeared more seriously divided on the peace issue than the center-left coalition backed by five Arab members of the Knesset. Binyamin Netanyahu, who had succeeded Yitzhak Shamir as leader of the Likud, totally rejected the accord and stated that once the Likud returned to power, it would simply cancel it. He compared the accord to Neville Chamberlain's appeasement of Hitler and told Peres, "You are even worse than Chamberlain. He imperiled the safety of another people, but you are doing it to your own people." Rafael Eytan, the leader of Tsomet, said that the government had signed an agreement "with the greatest murderer of Jews since Hitler." The government's margin of victory, much greater than expected, was a boost to Rabin and his peace policy. Given the importance he attached to having a "Jewish majority" for his policy, he was greatly reassured by the fact that more Jewish members voted for than against. The vote gave him a clear mandate to proceed with the implementation of the Gaza-Jericho plan.

Within the Palestinian camp the accord also encountered loud, but ineffective, opposition. The PLO itself was split, with the radical nationalists accusing Arafat of abandoning principles to grab power. They included the Popular Front for the Liberation of Palestine, led by George Habash, and the Damascus-based Democratic Front for the Liberation of Palestine, led by Nayef Hawatmeh. Arafat succeeded in mustering the necessary majority in favor of the deal on the PLO's eighteen-member Executive Committee but only after a bruising battle and the resignation of four of his colleagues. Outside the PLO, the deal aroused the implacable wrath of the militant resistance movements, Hamas and Islamic Jihad, which regarded any compromise with the Jewish state as anathema.

Opposition to the deal from rejectionist quarters, whether secular or religious, was only to be expected. More disturbing was the opposition of mainstream figures like Farouk Kaddoumi, the PLO "foreign minister," and prominent intellectuals like Professor Edward Said of Columbia University and the poet Mahmoud Darwish. Some of the criticisms related to Arafat's autocratic, idiosyncratic, and secretive style of management. Others related to the substance of the deal. The most basic criticism was that the deal negotiated by Arafat did not carry the promise, let alone a guarantee, of an independent Palestinian state.

This criticism took various forms. Farouk Kaddoumi argued that the deal compromised the basic national rights of the Palestinian people as well as the individual rights of the 1948 refugees. Edward Said lambasted Arafat for unilaterally canceling the *intifada,* for failing to coordinate his moves with the Arab states, and for introducing appalling disarray into the ranks of the PLO. "The PLO," wrote Said, "has transformed itself from a national liberation movement into a kind of small-town government, with the same handful of people still in command." For the deal itself, Said had nothing but scorn. "All secret deals between a very strong and a very weak partner necessarily involve concessions hidden in embarrassment by the latter," he wrote. "The deal before us," he continued, "smacks of the PLO leadership's exhaustion and isolation, and of Israel's shrewdness."[23] "Gaza and Jericho first . . . and last" was Mahmoud Darwish's damning verdict on the deal.

Arab reactions to the Israeli-Palestinian accord were rather mixed. Arafat got a polite but cool reception from the nineteen foreign ministers of the Arab League who met in Cairo a week after the signing ceremony in Washington. Some member states of the league, especially Jordan, Syria, and Lebanon, were dismayed by the PLO chairman's solo diplomacy, which violated Arab pledges to coordinate their negotiating strategy. Arafat defended his decision to sign the accord by presenting it as the first step toward a more comprehensive peace in the Middle East. The interim agreement, he said, was only the first step toward a final settlement of the Palestinian problem and of the Arab-Israeli conflict—a settlement that would involve Israeli withdrawal from all the occupied territories, including "Holy Jerusalem." He justified his resort to a secret channel by arguing that the almost two years of public negotiations under U.S. sponsorship had reached a dead end. Some of the Arab foreign ministers agreed with the PLO chairman that the accord was an important first step, even if they were not all agreed on the next step or the final destination.

IMPLEMENTING
THE DECLARATION OF PRINCIPLES

Two committees were set up in early October 1993 to negotiate the implementation of the lofty-sounding declaration signed in Washington. The first was chaired by Shimon Peres and Mahmoud Abbas, the leader who signed the declaration on behalf of the PLO. This ministerial-level committee was supposed to meet in Cairo every two or three weeks. The other, the nuts-and-bolts committee, consisted of experts who were to meet for two or three days each week in the Egyptian resort of Taba, on the Red Sea. The heads of the delegations to these talks were Nabil Sha'ath and Major General Amnon Lipkin-Shahak the number two man in the IDF and head of its military intelligence. The two sides managed to hammer out an agenda and formed two groups of experts, one to deal with military affairs, the other with the transfer of authority.

The IDF officers took a generally tough line in the negotiations. They had been excluded from the secret talks in the Norwegian capital and felt bitter at not having been consulted about the security implications of the accord. Chief of Staff Ehud Barak believed that in their haste to secure their place in history, the politicians had conceded too much to the PLO and that when the time came to implement the agreement, it would be the responsibility of the army to tackle the security problems. Rabin's decision to put army generals in charge of the detailed negotiations with the PLO was due partly to his desire to mollify the generals for their earlier exclusion and partly to his desire to limit Peres's latitude for making further concessions. But, as some of Rabin's own party colleagues pointed out at the time, his heavy reliance on the generals created an unhealthy precedent for the intervention of the military in matters of high policy.

Underlying the labyrinthine negotiations at Taba was a basic conceptual divide. The Israeli representatives wanted a gradual and strictly limited transfer of power while maintaining overall responsibility for security in the occupied territories in their own hands. They wanted to repackage rather than end Israel's military occupation. One way of doing this was to move the bulk of their troops from the big cities to the rural areas, where resistance was more difficult to organize and clashes were less likely. The Palestinians wanted an early and extensive transfer of power to enable them to start laying the foundations for an independent state. They were anxious to get rid of the Israeli occupation, and they struggled to gain every possible symbol of sovereignty. As a result of this basic conceptual divide, the Taba negotiations plunged repeatedly into crisis and took considerably longer to complete than the two months allowed for in the original timetable.

After four months of wrangling, an agreement was reached in the form of two documents—one on general principles, the other on border crossings. The documents were initialed by Shimon Peres and Yasser Arafat in Cairo on 9 February 1994. Although the Cairo agreement was tactfully presented as a compromise solution, it tilted very heavily toward the Israeli position. The IDF had managed to impose its own conception of the interim period: specific steps to transfer limited powers to the Palestinians without giving up Israel's overall responsibility for security. The IDF undertook to redeploy rather than withdraw its forces in the Gaza Strip and Jericho. The Cairo agreement gave the IDF full authority over Gaza's three settlement blocs, the four lateral roads joining them to the Green Line and "the relevant territory overlooking them." The outstanding feature of the agreement was thus to allow the IDF to maintain a military presence in and around the area earmarked for Palestinian self-government and to retain full responsibility for external security and control of the land crossings to Egypt and Jordan. Despite these serious limitations the Cairo agreement formed a first step in regulating the withdrawal of the Israeli civil administration and secret services from Gaza and Jericho.

The process of withdrawal was rudely shaken on 25 February 1994 when Dr. Baruch Goldstein, an American-born settler and member of the racist party Kach, opened fire with an IDF-issued Galil assault rifle on Muslim worshipers in the Tomb of the Patriarchs in Hebron, killing twenty-nine before being bludgeoned to death by the survivors. A preliminary report by a commission of inquiry appointed by the government revealed monumental incompetence and systematic failure to enforce the law against armed Jewish settlers on the part of the Israeli security forces. But the

Hebron massacre also revealed that the Israeli concept of security in the occupied territories was basically flawed because it catered only to Jews while ignoring the needs of the Palestinian inhabitants. Israeli settlers had the army, the police, and the border police to protect them, as well as being heavily armed themselves. The Palestinian inhabitants of the occupied territories, on the other hand, were left to the tender mercies of the settlers and the Israeli security services.

The PLO angrily suspended its participation in the peace talks in response to the massacre and demanded the removal of the four hundred or so militant settlers from Hebron and the disarming of the rest. Hamas, the Islamic resistance movement that had been bitterly opposed to the peace talks with the Jewish state from the start, vowed to exact revenge. Sympathy for the settlers sharply declined inside Israel after the massacre both because of their attempts to derail the peace process and because they threatened to embroil their own countrymen in a vicious cycle of violence and bloodshed.

The Israeli government came under strong pressure to crack down on the militant settlers. The majority of ministers were prepared to remove the settlers from Hebron, but the prime minister was not. He refused to remove the settlers from Hebron, as he had refused to remove the settlers in Gaza, on the grounds that the Oslo accord did not oblige Israel to dismantle any settlements during the interim period. Instead, the government outlawed Kach and detained without trial some of its leaders. It also acceded to the PLO's demand for a temporary international presence in Hebron to assist in promoting stability and restoring normal life in the city. Calls from the PLO and other quarters to put the whole question of settlements on the table were rejected by the government on the grounds that it was not obliged to do so by the original accord until the beginning of the third year of the transition period. The government did promise, however, in a joint communiqué it issued with the PLO in Cairo on 31 March, to accelerate its withdrawal from Gaza and Jericho and to be guided by the target dates set in the Declaration of Principles.

These concessions were just enough to induce the PLO to resume its participation in the peace talks, and another round of negotiations resulted in an agreement signed by Rabin and Arafat in Cairo on 4 May. The Cairo agreement wrapped up the Gaza-Jericho negotiations and set the terms for expanding Palestinian self-government to the rest of the West Bank. Expansion was to take place in three stages. First, responsibility for tourism, education and culture, health, social welfare, and direct taxation was to be transferred from Israel's civil administration to the Palestinian National Authority. Second, Israel was to redeploy its armed forces away from "Palestinian population centers." Third, elections were due to take place throughout the West Bank and the Gaza Strip for a new authority.

The Cairo document was billed by both sides as an agreement to divorce after twenty-seven years of unhappy coexistence in which the stronger partner forced the weaker to live under its yoke. This was true in the sense that Israel secured a separate legal system and separate water, electricity, and roads for the Jewish settlements. It was not true in the sense that the document gave the stronger party firm control over the new relationship.

The Cairo document stressed repeatedly the need for cooperation, coordination, and harmonization in the new relationship. A large number of liaison committees, most of which were to have an equal number of representatives from the two sides, gave a superficial appearance of parity. But this parity was undermined in favor of the stronger partner by the fact that Israeli occupation laws and military orders were to remain in force unless amended or abrogated by mutual agreement. This meant in practice that any issue that could not be resolved by negotiation would be subject to the provisions of Israeli law rather than those of international law. This was at odds with the Palestinian demand that international law, particularly the Fourth Geneva Convention, be the source of legislation and jurisdiction during the transition period.

A week after the Cairo document was signed, a token force of thirty Palestinian policemen entered the Gaza Strip from Egypt to assume control for internal security from the retreating Israelis. This was the first tangible evidence that Israeli occupation was winding down. Until then all the movement had been unilateral, as the Israeli army redeployed its forces so as to provide continuing protection for the tiny community of Jewish settlers in the strip. Now a new Palestinian police force was to take charge of the nearby Palestinian population centers in accordance with a prearranged division of labor. The Israeli withdrawal was greeted with great joy and jubilation among the Gazans. As the last Israeli soldiers pulled out of their military camps in Rafah and Nusairat to a final barrage of stones, the Israeli flag was replaced by the flag of Palestine. A twenty-seven-year-old experiment in imposing Israeli rule over two million recalcitrant Arabs was symbolically and visibly nearing its end.

The government's policy of controlled withdrawal from Gaza and Jericho enjoyed broad popular support. Hard as they tried, the leaders of the opposition failed to arouse the nation against the decisions of the government. As far as the government was concerned, the real paradox was that it needed a strong PLO to implement the Gaza-Jericho settlement, but a strong PLO could only reinforce the determination of the Palestinians to fight for a state of their own. The Israeli prime minister had not mastered the art of gracious giving; the PLO chairman could be every bit as ungracious, and undignified, in fighting over every issue, however small, to extract the last possible concession.

Yasser Arafat's long-awaited arrival in Gaza on 1 July showed how much horror and revulsion he continued to evoke among Israelis even after his historic handshake with their prime minister. Arafat's visit thus marked a moment of truth in Israel's domestic politics. Likud leaders saw the visit as an occasion for a mighty show of strength, joining hands with the leaders of the far-right Tsomet and Moledet parties. Their anti-Arafat rhetoric reached hysterical levels. But a rally organized by "the national camp" in Jerusalem's Zion Square turned into a rampage by some ten thousand right-wing rowdies against Arab bystanders and property in the Old City. The ensuing orgy of violence did nothing to endear the hard-liners to the Israeli public. Far from arousing the nation against the policy of the government, the rally backfired against its organizers, providing ministers with a welcome opportunity to denounce right-wing extremism.

The government maintained its commitment to peace with the Palestinians despite the protests from the right and despite the terrorist attacks launched by Hamas and Islamic Jihad with the aim of derailing the peace talks. On 28 September 1995 the Israeli-Palestinian Interim Agreement on the West Bank and the Gaza Strip was signed in Washington by Yitzhak Rabin and Yasser Arafat in the presence of Bill Clinton, Hosni Mubarak, and King Hussein of Jordan. It became known popularly as Oslo II. This agreement, which marked the conclusion of the first stage in the negotiations between Israel and the PLO, incorporated and superseded the Gaza-Jericho and the early empowerment agreements. The Interim Agreement was comprehensive in its scope and, with its various annexes, stretched to over three hundred pages. From the point of view of changes on the ground, it was highly significant. It provided for elections to a Palestinian council, the transfer of legislative authority to this council, the withdrawal of Israeli forces from the Palestinian centers of population, and the division of the

West Bank into three areas—A, B, and C. Area A consisted of Palestinian towns and urban areas; area B consisted of Palestinian villages and less densely populated parts; and area C consisted of the lands confiscated by Israel for settlements and roads. Area A was placed under exclusive Palestinian control and area C under exclusive Israeli control, and in area B the Palestinians exercised civilian authority while Israel continued to be in charge of security. Under the terms of this agreement, Israel yielded to the Palestinians civilian control over nearly a third of the West Bank. Four percent of the West Bank (including the towns of Jenin, Nablus, Kalkilya, Tulkarem, Ramallah, Bethlehem, and Hebron) was turned over to exclusive Palestinian control and another 25 percent to administrative-civilian control (see map 11). In the Gaza Strip, Israel retained control over 35 percent of the land, containing the Jewish settlements and the roads leading to them, and the rest was turned over to the Palestinian Authority. Oslo II thus marked an important point in the process of ending Israel's coercive control over the Palestinian people.

On 5 October, Yitzhak Rabin gave the Knesset a comprehensive survey of Oslo II and of the thinking behind it. His speech was repeatedly interrupted by catcalls from the benches of the opposition. Two Likud members opened black umbrellas, the symbols of Chamberlain's appeasement of Hitler at Munich. In the course of his speech, Rabin outlined his thinking for the permanent settlement: military presence but no annexation of the Jordan Valley, retention of the large blocks of settlements near the 1967 border, preservation of a united Jerusalem with respect for the rights of the other religions, and a Palestinian entity that would be less than a state and whose territory would be demilitarized. The fact that Rabin sketched out the principles of the permanent settlement in a session devoted to the interim settlement suggested a strong interest in proceeding to the next stage. Rabin was not unduly troubled by the prospect of a Palestinian entity with most of the attributes of an independent state. But first he wanted the Palestinian leaders to prove that they could be relied upon to act responsibly, especially in dealing with Islamic terror. A gradualist approach was in tune with his temperament. The right-wing opposition parties, on the other hand, felt that their initial fears were now confirmed. The dream of the undivided Land of Israel was clearly dying. The Knesset ratified the Oslo II agreement by the narrowest of majorities: 61 votes for, 59 against.

On the Palestinian side, too, there was bitter disappointment

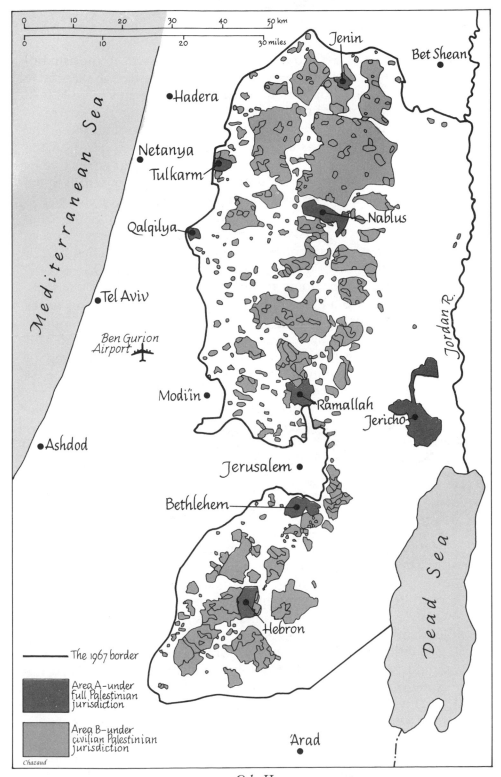

Mediterranean Sea

• Bet Shean

Jenin

• Hadera

Netanya
Tulkarm

Nablus

Qalqilya

Tel Aviv

Jordan R.

Ben Gurion
Airport ✈

Modi'in •

Ramallah
Jericho

Ashdod

Jerusalem •

Bethlehem

Dead Sea

Hebron

——— The 1967 border

Area A–under
full Palestinian
jurisdiction

Area B–under
civilian Palestinian
jurisdiction

'Arad •

Chazaud

Oslo II

with the results of Oslo II. The accord was based on the assumption that the enmity between the two warring tribes would subside during the transition period, paving the way to an equitable final settlement. This did not happen. On the contrary, the extremists on both sides did everything in their power to undermine the agreement. There was a serious drop in living standards on the West Bank and Gaza, caused in part by the frequent Israeli border closures. Moreover, there was no significant gain in human rights to compensate for the rising unemployment, poverty, and material hardship. Human rights were continually sacrificed in the name of "security" by both Israel and the Palestinian Authority. Worst of all, Israeli settlements continued to be built on Palestinian land in palpable violation of the spirit, if not the letter, of the Oslo accord. In the Gaza Strip, home to only five thousand Jewish settlers, Israel controlled a third of the land and most of the scarce water resources desperately needed by its one million Palestinian inhabitants. In the West Bank, Israel retained control over the water resources and over three-quarters of the land. The building of settlements throughout the West Bank and especially in East Jerusalem continued unabated, and a network of bypass roads seemed designed to preempt the possibility of Palestinian statehood. In all these different ways, the Oslo process actually worsened the situation in the occupied territories and confounded Palestinian aspirations for a state of their own.[24]

THE SYRIAN TRACK

Negotiations on the Syrian track proceeded in parallel to those on the Palestinian track. Rabin's strategy was to decouple the Syrian track from the Palestinian, Jordanian, and Lebanese tracks. He controlled the pace of the negotiations with Syria according to what was happening on the other tracks. When he came to power, he identified two candidates for a breakthrough in the bilateral negotiations: the Palestinians and Syria. He felt strongly that Israel should proceed with only one peace at a time, but he had no strong preferences as to who should be the first partner.

The Americans had a preference for Syria and offered their good offices in trying to broker a settlement with it. The cultural gulf between Israel and Syria was much deeper than that between Israel and the Palestinians, and the need for an external mediator was correspondingly greater. With the consent of both parties,

American officials played an active role in managing the talks on the Syrian track. President Clinton had two meetings with President Assad, and Secretary of State Warren Christopher made several working visits to the region, shuttling between Jerusalem and Damascus. Active though it was, the American role did not measure up to Rabin's expectations. Rabin expected America to use its leverage to move Syria toward a settlement, whereas Christopher more or less confined himself to carrying messages back and forth.

In Hafez al-Assad, Rabin encountered a formidable opponent. Assad's political career was dominated by the desire to regain the Golan Heights, which Syria had lost to Israel when he was minister of defense in 1967 and by the wider geopolitical contest with Israel for mastery in the region. The essence of his strategic thinking had always been that the Arabs should strive to muster sufficient deterrent power to hold Israel in check. Failing that, they would have no choice but to submit to its dictates. Assad's concept of a comprehensive peace grew out of much the same root as his aspiration for "strategic parity." In his view peace was indivisible. Only a comprehensive settlement could protect the Arab environment form Israeli encroachment and prevent Israel from picking off the weaker Arab parties one by one.[25] Assad agreed to participate in the peace process started at Madrid but insisted all along on a unified Arab front leading to related peace treaties based on UN resolutions and the principle of land for peace. As far as Syria was concerned, the formula he adopted was "full withdrawal for full peace."

When the Syrians talked about full Israeli withdrawal from the Golan Heights, they meant withdrawal to the armistice lines of 4 June 1967. The Israelis, on the other hand, preferred, as a point of reference, the international border that had been agreed between Britain and France in 1923. The difference between the two borders was small in terms of territory, but the former involved Syrian presence along the northeastern shore of the Sea of Galilee as well as control over the al-Hamma region south of the lake.

The first meeting between Israeli officials representing the Rabin government and Syrian officials was held in Washington on 24 August 1992. The Syrian delegation to the talks was headed by Muwaffaq al-Allaf; the Israeli delegation, by Itamar Rabinovich, a professor of Middle Eastern history at Tel Aviv University and a personal friend of Yitzhak Rabin. The two delegations met in a State

Department conference room, and there were no handshakes as they entered. Since there was no chairperson, Rabinovich decided to open the discussion. In his opening speech, which had been approved by Rabin, he said that Israel not only wished to negotiate peace but also understood that it would have to return land for peace. He announced that his government recognized that UN Resolution 242 in all its parts applied to the negotiations with Syria. This announcement constituted a fundamental shift in Israel's position. Whereas the Shamir government had rejected the principle of trading territory on the Golan Heights for peace, the Rabin government accepted it.

In 1991 Rabinovich had published a book on post-1948 Arab-Israeli peace negotiations entitled *The Road Not Taken*. Just before the meeting, Rabinovich inscribed a copy of this book. The dedication read, "To Ambassador Allaf, hoping that this time the road will be taken." When Rabinovich finished his opening speech, he took it to Allaf and stretched out his hand. Allaf took the book and shook Rabinovich's hand. It was an excellent start.[26] Bushra Kanafani, spokesperson for the Syrian delegation in Washington, praised the new Israeli approach as "constructive" and reflecting a fresh "political mentality."[27] Rabin, however, refused to enter into a territorial discussion with the Syrians before they committed themselves to full diplomatic relations, open borders, and normalization. The two delegations continued to meet, but on the core issues, the Syrian definition of peace and the extent of the Israeli withdrawal, they made little progress.

When Rabin finally realized that the Syrians would not discuss any of the other elements of a peace settlement before they were convinced of Israel's intention to carry out a full withdrawal, he made the opening. At his meeting with Christopher in Jerusalem, on 3 August 1993, he raised for the first time, and without consulting his cabinet or foreign minister, the possibility of full withdrawal from the Golan Heights. Rabin was extremely cautious and cagey. He was afraid that Assad would seize the territorial commitment and then find excuses to delay the peace settlement. Rather than commit himself, Rabin posed a question: "Would Syria be prepared to sign a peace agreement with Israel if its demands for full withdrawal are met? . . . Would they be prepared for real peace, including open borders and diplomatic relations?" Citing the peace treaty with Egypt as a precedent, Rabin said that Israel would need certain elements of peace to be in place before completing the withdrawal: embassies, open borders, and security arrangements. He added that Israel would need five years to complete the withdrawal from the Golan Heights, omitting to note that the withdrawal from Sinai had been effected in three years. Toward the end of the conversation Rabin told Christopher, "This is an assumption that you can raise in front of them, but it would be your assumption." In short, without making any direct commitment, Rabin wanted Christopher to explore the Syrian response to a suggestion of full peace with Israel leading to full Israeli withdrawal from the Golan Heights over a period of five years.

Christopher saw Assad on 4 August and returned to Jerusalem the following day to report to Rabin on the meeting. Christopher thought that Assad had reacted positively to Rabin's overture inasmuch as he accepted the "basic equation" of peace in return for withdrawal. Rabin, however, was deeply disappointed with Assad's response, for although Assad seemed to agree to contractual peace in return for full withdrawal, he expressed some significant reservations and conditions. He did not agree to give Israel some of the elements of peace before the withdrawal had been completed. Nor did he agree to the proposed timetable of five years to completion, suggesting six months instead. Assad also told Christopher that he was uncomfortable with the term "normalization," and he turned down Rabin's request to establish a direct and secret channel of communication. Since Assad's response did not measure up to his expectations, Rabin gave Peres the green light to complete the negotiations with the Palestinians through the Oslo channel.

Three months later, on 12 November 1993, Clinton told Rabin that the Syrians expected Israel to reaffirm its commitment to full withdrawal. Rabin did not like the term "commitment" and preferred to call it a deposit, meaning a conditional promise that could be withdrawn. During the conversation there was no specific mention of the lines of 4 June 1967. Over the next few months the Syrians made it absolutely clear that full withdrawal meant withdrawal to the lines of 4 June 1967, not the 1923 international border that lay farther east. On 2 May 1994 Christopher reported to Rabin that Assad was adamant on the lines of 4 June: unless this was agreed, the negotiations could not continue. The critical conversation regarding these lines was held on 18 July 1994. Christopher said it was essential for him to be able to tell Assad what to expect if he met Rabin's conditions. Rabin said, "You can tell him that he has every reason to expect that this would be the outcome, but the Israelis will not spell it out before all our needs are met. You can tell him that this is your understanding but that he would not be able to get this if he does not meet our demands." Christopher remarked, "I'll keep it in my pocket, not put it on the table." On the basis of this remark, the code for the talks on the 4 June 1967 lines became File Pocket.[28]

The Syrians were later to claim that in July 1994 they received a commitment to full Israeli withdrawal to the 4 June 1967 lines and that this was the basis for the reopening of negotiations at the ambassadorial level in Washington. Itamar Rabinovich, who had in the meantime been appointed ambassador to Washington, continued to head the Israeli delegation to the talks with Syria. He was a protégé and close confidant of the prime minister and reported directly to him on the talks with Syria, without going through the Foreign Ministry. The head of the Syrian delegation was now Walid al-Moualem, ambassador to Washington since 1990.

Moualem reviewed the negotiations in an interview of unusual depth and candor for an official of the tightly controlled Syrian regime. According to Moualem, it took a whole year to finalize the agreement on full withdrawal to the 4 June 1967 lines, but this agreement made possible the opening of negotiations on the other elements of a peace settlement—what Prime Minister Rabin used to call "the four legs of the table." Besides withdrawal, the other three legs were normalization, security arrangements, and a timetable for the implementation of the various measures on which agreement was reached.

The main point of discord on the security front was Israel's request to keep an early-warning station on the Golan after the withdrawal. Syria claimed that this would be an infringement of its sovereignty. Second, Israel asked that the Syrian forces along the border be thinned out. Third, Israel insisted that the demilitarized zone reach just south of Damascus. The Syrians refused all these demands. They considered Israel's security fears to be greatly exaggerated, given the advanced technology at its disposal, the size and quality of its armed forces, and its nuclear arsenal.

Syria also rejected Israel's proposals for normalization, and Moualem explained the reasons: "The wanted *us* to convince *their* public that peace was in their interest. We prepared our public for peace with Israel. Many things changed in our media. But they wanted us to speak in the Israeli media to prepare Israeli public opinion. They wanted us to allow Israelis to visit Syria. We considered such insistence a negative sign: When you do not prepare your own public for peace with your neighbor, this means you do not really have the intention to make peace." The Israelis also wanted open borders and open markets for their goods. The Syrians were afraid to expose their economy and nascent industries to Israeli penetration when their per capita income was $900 per annum while that of the Israelis was $15,000 per annum. Yet Moualem denied that Syria was responsible for the slow pace of progress in the talks. Israel, he claimed, moved very slowly and cautiously until after the Oslo II agreement with the Palestinians had been concluded. "Rabin was reluctant, suspicious, very cautious," Moualem observed. "He moved very slowly, inch by inch."[29]

As a token of their serious interest in the talks, the Syrians sent their chief of staff, Hikmat Shihabi, for talks with his opposite number, Ehud Barak, in Washington in December 1994. The talks did not go well. For one thing, the Syrians felt that the Israelis did not appreciate the significance of their sending such a senior figure to the talks. The Syrians were also put off by Barak's arrogant manner and tendency to lecture. Nor did the Syrians like the heavy-handed security arrangements that Barak presented to them. Shihabi argued that Syria had much more reason to fear Israel than the other way around and that peace was the best answer to all their security problems: if you have peace, you do not need elaborate security arrangements. But the most serious problem resulted from the fact that Rabin had not informed Barak of his conditional agreement to the 4 June 1967 lines. On the contrary, Rabin had instructed the IDF to make plans only for a partial withdrawal from the Golan Heights. The Americans attributed this contradiction to Rabin's bargaining tactics and to his desire to keep both options open. But the Syrians began to suspect that the Americans had deliberately misled them about Rabin's position in order to draw them deeper into the negotiations.

Following the failure of the meeting, Clinton wrote two letters to Assad aimed at renewing the talks between the chiefs of staff. Assad replied that it was up to the politicians to determine the principles and establish the framework for negotiations. Accordingly, the Americans took the lead in drafting a paper in close consultation with Walid al-Moualem and Itamar Rabinovich. On 22 May 1995 Syria and Israel agreed to the final version of the paper "Aims and Principles of Security Arrangements" and deposited it with the State Department. The paper was important because it established the principle of equality and mutuality. It laid down that the security of one side must not come at the expense of the security of the other side.[30]

The agreement on principles made possible the resumption of talks at the level of chiefs of staff. In late June 1995 Hikmat Shihabi had two days of talks at Fort McNair in Washington with Israel's new chief of staff, Amnon Lipkin-Shahak. Shahak, like his predecessor, wanted an early-warning station to remain on the Golan even after a peace settlement had been concluded. Shihabi remarked that the head of the Israeli delegation no doubt knew the final line of withdrawal, alluding to the lines of 4 June 1967. Shahak replied that he knew nothing about it.[31] One of Shahak's aides presented the IDF plan for a security regime. Shihabi rejected the plan on principle, without dwelling on the details, because it was not based on the assumption of withdrawal to the 4 June lines. Shihabi took the view that Israel's demands in the security sphere were inflated and unjustified. He repeated his conviction that peace itself was the best guarantee of security. No agreement was reached on any specific points. Nevertheless, the Israelis left Washington with the impression that they had opened a real dialogue with the Syrian military establishment.[32]

According to Moualem, Rabin all along dictated the pace of negotiations with Syria on the basis of his shifting priorities in relation to the other Arab parties involved in the peace process. When he moved on the Palestinian track in September 1993, for example, he sent a message to say that he could not proceed on the Syrian track, because the Israeli public needed time to digest the Oslo accord. So he suspended the talks. In 1994 he moved on the Jordanian track and claimed that the Israeli public needed time to digest the peace treaty with Jordan. Again the talks with the Syrians were suspended. It was only after the Israelis had signed the Oslo II agreement, in late September 1995, that they turned to the Syrians and said they wanted to move very quickly.

Precisely what Rabin had promised the Syrians cannot be determined with any degree of certainty. One reason for the uncertainty is that Rabin communicated with Assad not directly but through the good offices of the American secretary of state. In his eagerness to achieve a breakthrough on the Syrian track, Warren Christopher may have gone further than he should have by disclosing Rabin's bottom line. This would account for the subsequent Syrian claim that Rabin had definitely agreed to Israeli withdrawal to the lines of 4 June 1967. But a review of the negotiations on the Syrian track does not disclose a clear commitment by Rabin to withdraw to these lines, and there was certainly nothing in writing to this effect. The most likely explanation is that

Rabin himself deliberately sent conflicting signals to Damascus as part of an elaborate bargaining strategy. On the one hand, he told the Americans that, under certain conditions, he would be prepared to consider a retreat to the 4 June 1967 lines. On the other, through his chiefs of staff, he was less specific on the line of withdrawal and held out for Israeli presence on the Golan even in the context of a peace settlement.

To suggest that an opportunity for peace between Israel and Syria had been missed during Rabin's premiership would therefore go well beyond what the available evidence would support. At no point did the Syrians come near to accepting Rabin's conditions on normalization and security. Syria's unyielding terms for a peace settlement made Rabin skeptical of the chances of reaching an agreement. His priorities in the bilateral talks were to implement the Oslo accord and then to work for a peace treaty with Jordan. But while Rabin was not optimistic about the prospect of achieving peace with Syria, he did not want to incur the responsibility for the failure of the talks. He and Assad, in fact, had a great deal in common. They were both very tough and suspicious former generals. Rabin was obsessed with preserving Israeli security; Assad, with restoring Syrian sovereignty over every last inch of the Golan. Both men were shrewd, slow, and stubborn negotiators. Both were as hard as nails.

PEACE WITH JORDAN

Initially Rabin had an open mind as to whether the first peace agreement should be with the Palestinians or with Syria. But after the Oslo accord was signed, he was quite adamant that Israel's second partner in peace should be Jordan and not Syria. All along he adhered to the principle of one peace at a time, in contrast to Shimon Peres, who wanted to move forward simultaneously on all four tracks toward the ultimate goal of a comprehensive peace in the Middle East.

Jordan was more directly affected by the Israel-PLO accord than any other Arab country. A day after the accord was presented to the world, in a much more modest ceremony in the State Department, the representatives of Jordan and Israel signed a common agenda for detailed negotiations aimed at a comprehensive peace treaty. The common agenda constituted the blueprint for the peace treaty. Its main components were borders and territorial matters, water, security, and refugees. The document bore the personal stamp of King Hussein, who had been deeply involved in the quest for peace in the Middle East for the preceding quarter of a century. The Jordanian-Israeli agenda was ready for signature in October 1992, but the king preferred to wait until progress had been made between Israel and the Palestinians. He was therefore greatly angered when it came to light that the PLO chairman had been conducting his own secret negotiations with Israel.

Even after the king had studied the Israel-PLO accord and given it his public endorsement, his attitude remained somewhat ambivalent. On the one hand, he felt vindicated, having argued all along that the Arabs would have to come to terms with Israel. On the other, the new unholy alliance between the PLO and Israel could threaten Jordan's traditional position as "best of enemies" with Israel. If Israel and the Palestinian entity became close economic partners, the result could be inflation and unemployment on the East Bank, leading to political instability. More than half of Jordan's 3.9 million people were Palestinian. If, for whatever reason, there was an influx of Palestinians from the West Bank to the East Bank, the pressure could grow to transform the Hashemite Kingdom of Jordan into the Republic of Palestine. In short, Jordan's very survival as a separate state could be called into question.

The Israel-PLO accord also had implications for Jordan's progress toward democracy. This process got under way with the elections of November 1989 and provided the most effective answer to the challenge of the Islamic fundamentalists. Another election was scheduled for 8 November 1993. Arafat's deal, however, meant that some Palestinians could end up voting for two legislatures, one in Amman and one in Jericho. Mustafa Hamarneh, a constitutional expert, explained the situation to a foreign journalist: "These are extremely challenging times for Jordan. Yasser Arafat did not pull a rabbit out of his hat, but a damned camel."[33]

Under the initial shock of the Israel-PLO accord, King Hussein gave a clear signal of his intention to postpone the elections. Israeli assurances, given at a secret meeting, lay behind the subsequent decision to go ahead as planned. Personal diplomacy had always played a crucial part in the conduct of relations between Jordan and Israel. Countless meetings had taken place across the battle lines between the "plucky little king," as Hussein used to be called, and Israel's leaders. On this occasion the political overture for a high-level meeting came from the Israeli side. The Israeli daily newspaper *Ma'ariv* quoted intelligence reports that said that the king felt "cheated and neglected" over the accord. "King Hussein's political world has collapsed around him and the most direct means are required to calm him down," the Israeli prime minister was reportedly advised. A longtime advocate of coopera- tion with Jordan, Rabin heeded this advice. He spent several hours aboard the royal yacht in the Red Sea resort of Aqaba on Sunday, 26 September, conferring with the king and his advisers. Rabin as- sured the king that Israel remained firmly committed to uphold- ing his regime, that Jordanian interests would be protected in dealing with the Palestinian issue, and that future peace strategy would be closely coordinated with Jordan.[34]

The general election held on 8 November 1993, the first mul- tiparty election since 1957, yielded what King Hussein carefully planned for: a strengthening of the conservative, tribal, and inde- pendent blocs and a resounding rebuff to the Islamic Action Front, whose principal platform was opposition to the peace talks with Israel. This result gave Hussein a pliant parliament for proceeding with the task of Arab-Israeli peacemaking. It also gave rise to spec- ulation that the signing of a Jordanian-Israeli peace accord was imminent.

In the negotiations that led to the peace treaty, the four prin- cipal players were King Hussein, his younger brother, Crown Prince Hassan, Yitzhak Rabin, and Shimon Peres. The Americans encouraged and supported progress on the Jordanian track but did not play an active mediating role, as on the Syrian track, because the leaders enjoyed direct channels of communication. On the Jordanian side King Hussein was the chief decision maker. To the talks with the Israelis he brought rich experience of regional and international affairs, a sense of realism, and renowned social skills that helped create a positive, problem-solving atmosphere. Prince Hassan also played a major role in the conduct of peace negotia- tions. He combined expertise in economic affairs with a wide range of intellectual interests, including medieval Jewish theology. He would surprise and delight the Israeli negotiators by giving them copies of his erudite articles and books with a dedication in Hebrew, a language he had studied at Oxford.[35]

Hussein's attitude toward Peres was ambivalent. He respected his energy, his commitment to the cause of peace, and the imagi- native ideas he constantly generated. On the other hand, Hussein could not forget that Peres had let him down over the London Agreement of April 1987. He saw Peres as both a dreamer and a

publicity seeker and could not fully trust him. For Rabin the king
had considerable respect, which only grew with the passage of
time, because he spoke with the precision of a military man and because he was usually as good as his word. Personal trust between
the king and the prime minister was the key to progress on the
Jordanian track. "We had a unique relationship," said the king
wistfully after Rabin's death. "I felt he had placed himself in my
position many times. I placed myself in his position. We did not try
to score points off each other. We tried to develop something that
was workable, that was acceptable to both our people, something
that was balanced, something that was reasonable. And that's the
approach we had and that's how we managed to get there."[36]
Rabin and Hussein took the lead in the political negotiations,
while Peres and Hassan were largely responsible for the economic
aspects of the peace process.

A trilateral Israel-Jordan-U.S. economic committee was established on 1 October 1993 at a meeting at the White House between Bill Clinton, Prince Hassan, and Shimon Peres. This forum
convened first in Washington and then periodically in the region.
Subgroups were established to discuss specific issues such as trade,
finance, banking, civil aviation, and Jordan Valley joint projects.
Whereas the meeting in the White House was public, on 2
November Peres met Hussein secretly at the Hashemiyah Palace,
on the outskirts of Amman, to review the political as well as the
economic aspects of the prospective peace deal. Peres greatly exaggerated the results of the meeting with the man he once referred to as "His Royal Shyness." He returned to Israel in a
euphoric mood, dropping hefty hints that a peace treaty with
Jordan was imminent. "Put 3 November in your calendars as an
historic date," he told journalists. "All that's needed is a pen to
sign it." The Jordanians were upset by Peres's indiscretion.
Hussein warned Rabin that there would be no more secret meetings if they could not be kept secret. Rabin was also furious with
Peres and decided to keep peacemaking in his own hands.[37]

Meanwhile, the Trilateral Economic Committee continued its
work, and it was the Jordanians who suggested that it should move
from Washington to the region. Their aim in suggesting this move
was to educate public opinion about the potential benefits of
peace. The fifth meeting of the committee was held at Ein Avrona,
along the border north of Aqaba and Eilat, on 18–19 July 1994.
The following day a public meeting took place between Peres and
the Jordanian premier and foreign minister, Abdul-Salam Majali,

at the Dead Sea Spa Hotel in Jordan. They discussed plans for a Red–Dead Sea canal, joining their electricity grids, and turning the barren Wadi Araba desert into a "Valley of Peace," with thriving farming, industrial, and tourist centers. "The flight," said Peres, "took only fifteen minutes but it crossed the gulf of forty-six years of hatred and war."

The Israelis proposed a peace treaty and even submitted a draft toward the end of 1993, but the Jordanians refused to discuss it. They asked instead for "position papers" with Israel's various proposals to protect themselves against criticism from the Arab world in the event of a leak. King Hussein moved cautiously and covered his flanks. He and Rabin had a series of meetings. The first involved an overnight stay in the king's palace in Aqaba on 6–7 October 1993. The king impressed on his guest the importance that he attached, as a Hashemite monarch, to his position as the guardian of the Muslim holy places in Jerusalem. It was at this meeting that the two leaders began a process of working on what turned out to be the Washington Declaration.

On 28 May 1994 Rabin met Hussein at the latter's house in London to review the progress made by their aides. At this meeting Hussein heard for the first time that Israel would be prepared to grant Jordan a privileged position in looking after the Muslim holy places in Jerusalem in any future peace settlement. This was the turning point in the talks. Hussein agreed to a joint declaration of principles that would be followed by detailed negotiations for a peace treaty. He also agreed to a public meeting with Rabin in the White House in October, and Rabin in return promised to recommend to the American president and Congress the cancellation of Jordan's debts to the United States.[38] Hussein himself presented the decision to go public as a joint decision that arose naturally from the progress in the talks:

> The fact that we did not announce peace contacts publicly all through the past was due to a mutual agreement. At first we were so far apart that there would have been no benefit in announcing the meetings. These meetings enabled us to get to know each other. They enabled us to examine our positions every now and then to see if there was any chance of progress. They certainly changed the atmosphere, but it was a mutual agreement from the word go that we keep them quiet until we had something of substance so that when we reached the right moment all this would not be lost.

I returned home and gathered parliament and told them that we decided to meet. I also made a statement in the United States that I was not against a public meeting with Rabin. That's the way people do business; there is no other way. And we prepared the document that turned out to be the Washington Declaration. At first I wanted the first meeting to be held in Wadi Araba. But when we told the Americans, President Clinton invited us to the White House and both of us felt that the Americans had been our partners in trying to get somewhere for so long, particularly President Clinton. So we accepted. And we went with the paper agreed to its last detail, and we gave it to the President's Office at the last possible moment in the evening so it could not get into the newspapers until it was ratified by us the next morning.[39]

The much publicized meeting took place in the White House on 25 July 1994. Out of this meeting emerged the Washington Declaration, signed by Prime Minister Rabin and King Hussein, with President Clinton serving as master of ceremonies and witness. The Washington Declaration terminated the state of belligerency between Jordan and Israel and committed the two countries to seek a just, lasting, and comprehensive peace based on UN Resolutions 242 and 338. Israel formally undertook to respect the special role of the Hashemite Kingdom of Jordan in the Muslim holy shrines in Jerusalem and to give priority to this role when negotiations on final status take place. This was a serious blow to Yasser Arafat, who regarded control of the holy places as a Palestinian prerogative and claimed Jerusalem as the capital of a future Palestinian state. Finally, various bilateral measures were announced, such as the establishment of direct telephone links, joint electricity grids, new border crossings, free access to third-country tourists, and cooperation between the two police forces in combating crime and drug smuggling.

In a speech during the summit, Rabin named all the officials who had played a part in this historic turnabout in the relations with Jordan. Peres was not mentioned. The snub was intended to highlight Rabin's role as a peacemaker in his own right. As this was supposed to be only the second meeting between Rabin and Hussein, Clinton was mildy surprised to see how well acquainted they seemed. "Tell me, how long have you known one another?" he asked. "Twenty-one years, Mr. President," Rabin replied. Hussein corrected him with a benign smile: it was "only" twenty years.

The Washington Declaration, which fell just short of a peace treaty with Jordan, was overwhelmingly popular across the Israeli political spectrum. The Knesset approved it by 91 votes to 3. Many Israelis jokingly said that they would welcome Hussein as their king too. So enthusiastic was the popular response that even the Likud was forced to drop the slogan "Jordan is Palestine," popularized by Ariel Sharon and encapsulating the extreme right's favored solution to the Palestinian problem: replacement of the Hashemite regime on the East Bank by a Palestinian state. Binyamin Netanyahu praised the Washington Declaration publicly and told Crown Prince Hassan privately that Sharon's position was not shared by him personally or by his party.

Following the signing ceremony in Washington, teams of experts from the two sides got down to work on the sensitive issues of water allocation, border demarcation, and mutual security. Most of the meetings took place in the house of Crown Prince Hassan in Aqaba. Toward the end of September the Israelis submitted a peace treaty in draft form, and this served as a basis for the final round of negotiations. Rabin and Hussein had to be called in to resolve outstanding problems. They met in the Hashemiyah Palace with their aides on the evening of 16 October and worked through the night.

The thorniest problem was border demarcation because Israel had expanded its eastern frontier in the late 1960s by an estimated 360 square kilometers, some of which had become farmland. Rabin and Hussein got down on their hands and knees to pore over a huge map laid out on the floor. Together, they worked out the whole line from Eilat and Aqaba in the south to the point of convergence with Syria in the north. In some areas they agreed to land exchanges. In other areas Hussein agreed, with characteristic magnanimity, to allow Israeli farmers to continue to use the land they had been cultivating after it reverted to Jordanian sovereignty. As for water, it was decided that the Jordanians would get 50 million cubic meters a year more from Israel and that the two countries would cooperate to alleviate the water shortage by developing new water resources, by preventing contamination, and by reducing wastage. An important element of the treaty from Israel's point of view was Hussein's undertaking not to allow a third country to deploy forces in Jordan in a way that could threaten Israel. Israel's commitment to respect Jordan's special position in Jerusalem was incorporated into the treaty. Finally, the two parties agreed to work together to alleviate the position of the Palestinian refugees who had found refuge in Jordan.[40]

The Israel-Jordan peace treaty was signed by Prime Minister Rabin and King Hussein on 26 October 1994 at a border point in the Arava desert that had been a minefield just a few days before. In attendance were President Clinton, the foreign ministers of the United States, Russia, and Egypt, and representatives from several other Arab countries. The event was telecast to a vast audience around the world. It was the second treaty concluded between Israel and an Arab state in fifteen years and the first to be signed in the region. Rabin, who had displayed by his body language so much angst when shaking Yasser Arafat's hand in the White House a year earlier, was now in a positively festive mood. He and Hussein seemed to enjoy the carnival-like setting as thousands of balloons were released into the air and senior Israeli and Jordanian officers exchanged gifts. Rabin said it was time to make the desert bloom, and Hussein promised a warm peace, unlike the cold peace with Egypt. The Knesset endorsed the peace treaty with Jordan by a majority of 105 to 3, with 6 abstentions.

Rhetoric aside, the Israel-Jordan treaty carried the potential for building peace in the full sense of the word. Jordan was the second Arab country to sign a peace treaty with Israel, but in one respect it was the first: no other Arab country preceded it in offering a warm peace. Professor Shimon Shamir, who served as Israel's ambassador to both Egypt and Jordan, emphasized the uniqueness of the Jordanian approach to peace. The peace with Egypt was concluded under the pressure of renewed hostilities, in the teeth of opposition from the other Arab countries, and in a world dominated by the Cold War. Security arrangements in Sinai were consequently at the center of this peace treaty, while normalization was merely a bargaining card for the Egyptians. The peace treaty with Jordan, on the other hand, was concluded after years of quiet dialogue and tacit understandings, with legitimacy provided by Madrid and Oslo, and in a world whose beacons were globalism, interdependence, and the market. Accordingly, the treaty said little about security and a great deal about economic cooperation. Jordan's leaders preferred the term "peacemaking" to "normalization" because it denoted a joint enterprise for the benefit of both countries.

King Hussein saw peace as the crowning achievement of his long reign and hoped to see its fruits in his own lifetime. Whenever it was suggested to him that the pace of progress in peacemaking should be controlled, he replied that, on the contrary, cooperation should be accelerated and expanded in order to consolidate the peace. He realized that the peace treaty took his people by surprise, that many of his Palestinian subjects found it difficult to accept, and that the Islamic and radical opposition would do everything in their power to subvert it. But he also knew that, in the final analysis, the peace would be judged by its practical results. Hence the importance he attached to turning the peace with Israel into an economic success story whose benefits would reach the ordinary person in the street.[41] The cold peace that characterized the relations between Egypt and Israel was alien to his entire way of thinking:

> I can't understand the term "cold peace." I don't understand what it means. You either have war, or a state of no war and no peace, or you have peace. And peace is by its very nature a resolution of all problems. It is the tearing down of barriers between people. It is people coming together, coming to know one another. It is the children of martyrs on both sides embracing. It is soldiers who fought each other coming together and exchanging reminiscences about the impossible conditions they had faced in a totally different atmosphere. It is people getting together and doing business. Real peace is not between governments but between individuals who discover that they have the same worries, the same concerns, that they have suffered in the same way, and that there is something they can both put into creating a relationship that would benefit all of them.[42]

Progress in peacemaking did not match this vision. The economic benefits of the peace for Jordan were marginal. Resistance to normal relations with Israel ran much deeper than Hussein expected, and the new reality for which he yearned failed to materialize. The king had hoped to turn the peace with Israel into the people's peace, but it was widely perceived in Jordan as the king's peace. On the Israeli side, the peace with Jordan remained immensely popular, as did the king himself. Both Rabin and Peres recognized the importance of delivering the economic dividends of peace. But the bureaucrats under them moved slowly and cautiously, and the promise presented by the treaty for developing real peace remained largely unfulfilled.

14

The Setback

1995–1996

IN THE PROCESS of implementing the Oslo accord, Yitzhak Rabin began to treat Yasser Arafat as a partner on the road to peace. The two leaders had rather different visions of the Oslo accord. Rabin envisaged a gradual disengagement from those parts of the occupied territories that were not strictly necessary for either Israeli security or Israeli colonization, ending with the formation of a demilitarized Palestinian entity. Arafat envisaged Israeli withdrawal from nearly all the occupied territories followed by the establishment of a sovereign Palestinian state with East Jerusalem as its capital. The Rabin government's policy of expanding Israeli settlements on the West Bank during the interim period compounded the difficulty of reconciling these two visions. The negotiations to determine the final status of the occupied territories were scheduled to start on 4 May 1996. How Rabin would have handled these negotiations is impossible to tell, because he fell victim to a political assassination.

ASSASSINATION OF A PRIME MINISTER

Three bullets fired from a pistol at close range on Saturday evening, 4 November 1995, put an end to the life of Yitzhak Rabin at the conclusion of a peace rally in Tel Aviv's largest square. A right-wing Jewish fanatic shot the prime minister. Rabin was rushed to hospital, where he died an hour later from his wounds. He was seventy-three years old. In his jacket pocket was found a neatly folded sheet of paper with the words of a song he had sung in the rally—"The Song of Peace." It was stained by his blood and pierced by one of the assassin's bullets.

At the rally a crowd of some 150,000 people had demonstrated their support for the peace policy of the Rabin government. It was the largest mass demonstration that Tel Aviv had witnessed since the accord with the PLO had been signed in September 1993. The normally gruff and lugubrious Rabin looked radiant and elated. For the first time in public, he shed the ambivalence he had felt about making peace with the PLO. His relations with members of Peace Now had been uneasy in the past, but on this occasion he displayed his unreserved gratitude for their support. Another arresting scene took place on the podium that evening: Rabin put his arm around Peres in front of the cheering crowd.

Rabin made a short and powerful speech. He began on a personal note: "I was a soldier for 27 years. I fought so long as there was no prospect of peace. I believe that there is now a chance for peace, a great chance, which must be seized." He pledged that his government would exhaust every opening, every possibility to achieve a comprehensive peace. He voiced his belief that even with Syria it would be possible to make peace. And he ended with a clarion call: "This rally must send a message to the Israeli public, to the Jews of the world, to the multitudes in the Arab lands and in the world at large, that the nation of Israel wants peace, support peace—and for this, I thank you."[1]

Israel was stunned by the news of the assassination of the prime minister, and the nation went into mourning. More than a million people filed past the coffin, which was placed in front of the Knesset. Tens of thousands of youths made their way to the square in which Rabin had been gunned down. They lit candles, laid flowers, and sang songs in memory of the man who ended his life as a martyr in the struggle for peace. After seven days of mourning, the square was renamed Yitzhak Rabin Square.

Rabin was buried with full military honors on Mount Herzl, Israel's national cemetery. Leaders from over eighty countries gathered in Jerusalem on a day's notice to pay homage to the fallen leader. Several Arab countries were represented: Egypt by President Mubarak; Jordan by King Hussein; Oman, Qatar, Tunisia, and Morocco by their foreign ministers. The funeral showed the world that Israel was no longer a nation that dwelled alone, that it was well on the way to being accepted as part of the Middle East. Bill Clinton spoke at the graveside, ending his eulogy with two Hebrew words, *Shalom, haver,* "Peace, friend."

King Hussein mourned his friend with a eulogy that was both eloquent and rich in historical resonance. More than any of the other Arab guests, the king felt the poignancy of the moment. He was in Jerusalem for the first time since 1967 to pay homage to the commander who had led Israel's forces in the June War. "We are not ashamed," said the king, "nor are we afraid, nor are we anything but determined to continue the legacy for which my friend fell, as did my grandfather in this city when I was with him and but a boy."[2]

The one Arab leader conspicuous by his absence from the funeral was Rabin's other partner in the struggle for peace—Yasser Arafat. Arafat wanted to attend the funeral but was told to stay at home for security reasons. He did, however, visit Leah Rabin, the widow, in her house in Tel Aviv, to pay his respects and to offer his condolences. "Yitzhak Rabin was the hero of peace," said Arafat. "I have lost a friend. This is a great loss to the cause of peace and to me personally. I am shocked and horrified by this tragic event." Leah Rabin displayed great honesty and courage in her moment of grief. She refused to shake the hand of Binyamin Netanyahu, the leader of the Likud, when he came to console her, because of the part he had played in the incitement that led to the assassination of her husband. Leah was moved by the sincerity and warmth that Arafat exuded during his visit. "Sometimes," she mused, "I feel that we can find a common language with Arabs more easily than we can with the Jewish extremists. It seems that we live in different worlds." Arafat's handshake, she explained, symbolized for her the hope for peace, whereas Netanyahu's handshake represented no such hope.

The murder brought to the surface the deep divisions that had been developing inside Israeli society in response to the peace with the Palestinians. The murderer, Yigal Amir, was a young messianic Zionist, twenty-five years of age and a law student at Bar-Ilan University, a hotbed of right-wing political and religious extremism. Amir was born to a religious family of Yemenite extraction in the aftermath of the Six-Day War, and, like other young people of his generation on the messianic fringe, he saw Israel's victory as a sign of divine favor and a permanent deed to the land.

The simple ideology that guided Yigal Amir was shared by many others in the religious-nationalist camp. The Jewish people, the chosen people, are the rightful owner of the promised land, the Land of Israel. The Palestinians are aliens in this land and, like all other Arabs, a sworn enemy. When the Palestinians talk of peace, they are not to be trusted. They want the territories that were liberated by Israel in 1967 in order to wage their war of annihilation against the Jewish people and the State of Israel. In the 1992 election Amir had voted for Moledet, the racist-nationalist party that advocated the deportation of Palestinians from the Land of Israel.[3]

At his trial Amir confessed that he murdered Rabin in order to derail the peace process, and he invoked Jewish religious law in support of the murder. He questioned the legitimacy of the government, denied the right of Israel's Arab citizens to play a role in Israeli democracy, and denounced Rabin for abandoning the settlers. Amir told the court that according to *halacha*, a Jew who gives his land to the enemy and endangers the life of other Jews must be killed. He described the Palestinians as unreformed terrorists and held Rabin personally responsible for the killing of Jews by them. Rabin, he claimed, had Jewish blood on his hands. To the commission of inquiry Amir said, "When I shot Rabin, I felt as if I was shooting a terrorist." Amir was sentenced to life imprisonment, but he never expressed any remorse for his deed. On the contrary, he took pride in what he had done and repeatedly claimed to have carried out God's wishes and to have rid his country of a *rodef*, a persecutor.

Amir was not mentally deranged. He was perfectly sane but rather extreme in his political and religious convictions. He combined religious fanaticism with racist nationalism in a very potent mixture. Nor was he a loner. He belonged to a subculture infected by feverish messianism generated by the Six-Day War. He was, in the words of the author Ze'ev Chafetz, "as Israeli as hummus pie. He was trained by his rabbis and, as far as I am concerned, he pulled the trigger for them."

The Six-Day War had a profound effect on the religious camp in Israel and gave rise to "religious Zionism." The conquest of the West Bank, which as Judea and Samaria had formed part of the biblical Jewish kingdom, convinced many Orthodox rabbis and teachers that they were living in a messianic era and that salvation was at hand. The war represented the Divine Hand at work and was "the beginning of redemption." Almost immediately, these rabbis began to sanctify the land of their ancestors and to make it an object of religious passion. They made the sanctity of the land a central tenet of religious Zionism. From this it followed that anyone who was prepared to give away parts of this sacred land was perceived as a traitor and enemy of the Jewish people. In this sense, Rabin's murder was a religious murder, carried out with Orthodox rabbinical sanction.

Gush Emunim, the Bloc of the Faithful, and the settlements it set up in Judea and Samaria were the most palpable expression of the new wave of messianism that swept through considerable segments of Israeli society. Gush Emunim settlers effectively turned the Palestinians into aliens on their own soil. While the Labor Party sponsored settlements in the hope of increasing Israel's share of the disputed land, the parties of the right, both secular and religious, used ideological reasons to support settlement in the entire Land of Israel. The nascent settler movement gained respectability by grafting its cause to the established National Religious Party (NRP). In the NRP, the largest of the religious parties, orthodox rabbis began to set the tone. Under these circumstances the NRP, the historic ally of the Labor Party in government, became the natural ally of the right. When Menachem Begin came to power in 1977, the religious parties were happy to join as junior partners in his government. The religious parties moved steadily to the right, while the Likud became more religious; the result was an ever closer partnership between them.[4]

Yitzhak Rabin fatally underestimated the passion that propelled the religious right and the danger it posed to Israeli democracy. An intensely secular man, he had no real understanding of the beliefs of the religious right and tended to dismiss them as a strident but marginal political group. After the Hebron massacre, his government outlawed the racist parties Kach and Kahane Chai and jailed some of their activists. But he and his security services apparently remained unprepared for violence from others on the extreme edge of the religious right, at least they were unprepared for violence against Jews. Rabin's relationship with the settlers was one of obvious antipathy all along, but the Oslo accord put him on a collision course with them. For a quarter of a century Israel had been avoiding decisions on the future of the occupied territories. In 1993 Rabin chose a path that negated the idea of the integrity of the homeland and of the settlers' efforts to hold it.[5] In 1967 Rabin had been the hero of the religious right for his part in liberating the historic homeland; by 1993 he had become a traitor because of his plan to relinquish part of it. By signing the Oslo accord, Rabin signed his own death warrant.

Israeli politics is habitually rough, but the attacks on Rabin in the aftermath of Oslo scaled new heights in their virulence and venom. Rabin was accused of groveling before foreign statesmen, stabbing the country in the back, and being willing to withdraw to "Auschwitz borders." His effigy, dressed in Nazi uniform, was prominently displayed in opposition rallies. Orthodox rabbis, including two former chief rabbis, called on Israeli soldiers, in the name of *halacha,* to disobey any order to evacuate parts of the West Bank. Their pronouncements were reminiscent of certain *fatwas,* or religious edicts, emanating elsewhere in the Middle East from fundamentalist religious leaders. Leading members of the opposition were saying that Rabin had no mandate for his policies, because his majority in parliament depended on non-Jewish Knesset members who received their orders from Yasser Arafat.[6]

On 5 October, the day the Knesset had endorsed Oslo II by a majority of one, thousands of demonstrators gathered in Zion Square in Jerusalem. The leaders of the opposition were on the grandstand while the demonstrators displayed an effigy of Rabin in an SS uniform. Binyamin Netanyahu set the tone with an inflammatory speech. "Today the surrender agreement called Oslo II was placed before the Knesset," he said. "The Jewish majority of the State of Israel did not approve this agreement. We shall fight it and we shall bring down the government." Netanyahu described the agreement as a security nightmare and added, "Rabin is causing a national humiliation by accepting the dictates of the terrorist Arafat."

Two weeks before the murder, the novelist Moshe Shamir said on a radio program, "Yitzhak Rabin is not a Nazi officer as he was presented in that picture. But Rabin does collaborate with the thousands of Nazi officers whom he brings to the heart of Israel, and he hands it over to them, under the command of their leader, Adolf Arafat, to carry forward the plan of the destruction of the Jewish people."[7]

SHIMON PERES
AND THE NEW MIDDLE EAST

In an unprecedented move, 112 out of the 120 members of the Knesset recommended to the president to assign to Shimon Peres the task of forming a government after Rabin's assassination. This task was carried out swiftly. Peres succeeded Rabin both as prime minister and as minister of defense. Ehud Barak, the former IDF chief of staff, became foreign minister and Yossi Beilin minister without portfolio in the prime minister's office. Peres returned to the helm amid a wave of public sympathy and support. Binyamin Netanyahu was widely regarded as a political corpse. A public opinion poll showed that only 23 percent of the electors would have backed him for the premiership in the immediate aftermath of Rabin's assassination. But the bullet that pierced Rabin's heart also killed something inside Peres. The glint in his eye disappeared and little was left of his former vitality, spark, and fighting spirit.

Peres presented his government to the Knesset on 22 November 1995. There were no significant changes in the basic guidelines of the government compared with those of the Rabin government. In his speech Peres promised to continue along the road the late prime minister had charted since 1992. The central goals of his government, he said, were national security and personal security; safeguarding the democratic character of the state; and the continuation of the peace process through implementation of the Interim Agreement with the PLO and the pursuit of full peace with Syria, Lebanon, and other Arab countries. Peres swore to fight violence and extremism. His slogan was "No to violence, yes to peace." From his teacher and mentor David Ben-Gurion, Peres said he had learned that being "a light unto the nations" is a Jewish vision and an Israeli strategy. It was a stirring speech, but Peres won a vote of confidence with only 61 votes—an early sign of his precarious hold on power.[8]

Nevertheless, having returned to power, Peres continued to promote his vision of peace as the dawn of a new age in the region. Variations on a theme continued to flow from Peres's inventive political mind. "In the past," he explained, "a nation's identity was molded from its people's characteristics, the geography of its land, the unique properties of its language and culture. Today, science has no national identity, technology no homeland, information no passport." "The New Middle East," in a standard Peres utterance, would be "dominated by banks, not tanks, ballots, not bullets, and where the only generals would be General Motors and General Electric."

Most of Israel's neighbors were less than comfortable with this vision. What it added up to, they felt, was a reconstruction of the Middle East with Israel at its center. Their principal fear was that Israel's military domination of the area might be replaced by economic domination. The Syrians saw the new rhetoric emanating from Jerusalem as no more than a cloak for Israel's perennial ambition to dominate the Levant. The Egyptians suspected that Israel wanted to take over their traditional role of political leadership in the Middle East. Mohamed Heikal, the doyen of Arab political commentators, warned that the peace process was tailored to serve Israel's interests alone. The "Saudi era" was over, he announced; the "Israeli era" was dawning. Islamists throughout the Middle East were troubled by the prospect of Israeli-brokered Westernization in their countries. Even Arab intellectuals remained distinctly ill at ease with the vision of the New Middle East.

Syria was the standard-bearer of Arab nationalism. After the defection of Egypt, the PLO, and Jordan, Damascus became the last redoubt of Arab resistance, holding out for complete Israeli withdrawal from the Golan Heights. As foreign minister, Peres had often been critical of Rabin's approach to the talks with Syria. In the first place, Peres thought that focusing solely on the security aspects of an accord with Syria, as Rabin seemed to be doing, was a tactical mistake. By dealing simultaneously with all issues, Israel would have more room for maneuver and, once peace was achieved, the security arrangements would fall into place without too much difficulty. Second, Peres felt that Rabin exaggerated the strategic value of the Golan Heights. The real threat, Peres believed, stemmed from Syria's surface-to-surface missiles, unconventional weapons, and state-sponsored terrorism, and against all these the Israeli presence on the Golan was no defense. Golan was important mainly as a bargaining card for peace. Third, Peres was critical of Rabin for putting too much stress in his public pronouncements on the painful price of peace with Syria and not enough on the prospective payoff: comprehensive peace with the Arab world and the removal of the threat of another Arab-Israeli war.

An hour after Rabin's funeral, Peres met Bill Clinton in the King David Hotel. Clinton wanted to know, and the Syrians too asked him to find out, whether Peres would abide by his predecessor's alleged agreement to withdraw to the 4 June 1967 lines in return for full peace with Syria. Peres, who had been kept in the dark about the talks with Syria, was surprised to discover that Rabin had gone that far. Nevertheless, he told Clinton that he would carry out any undertakings given by Rabin, whether orally or in writing. After the meeting Peres summoned Itamar Rabinovich and the other officials involved in the talks with Syria and demanded to see all the relevant documents. He then replaced Rabinovich with Uri Savir as the head of the Israeli delegation to the talks with Syria. Most important, he decided to make an all-out effort to achieve a breakthrough on the Syrian track.

In mid-December, Peres flew to Washington to present his plan for renewing negotiations with Syria after a hiatus of six months. The plan aimed at comprehensive peace and was inspired by his vision of the New Middle East. Peres told the Americans that he was prepared to open negotiations at the highest possible level, on all subjects simultaneously, and without any preconditions. Peres hoped that the negotiations would be less formal and more practical and that they would be carried out at the fastest possible pace. He expressed a strong preference for opening the negotiations at a summit meeting with Assad, but this was not a precondition, merely a proposal. Peres was in an optimistic mood and in a hurry to get results. He calculated that a peace treaty with Syria, or at least a declaration of principles and a summit meeting with Assad, would help him win the next election, scheduled for October 1996. His optimism, however, was not shared by his foreign minister or by the military chiefs.

The initial noises from Damascus were encouraging, but there was no change in Syria's hard line. Although Assad did not rule out a meeting with Peres during the talks, he refused to give a date. Direct negotiations resumed at the level of officials on 27 December at Wye Plantation in Maryland. All issues were placed on the table simultaneously—borders, normalization, water resources, and security arrangements—but little progress was made. A second round of talks opened at Wye Plantation on 24 January 1996 with the participation of military experts on both sides, but once again they failed to produce any positive results. From Uri Savir's report Peres concluded that there was no chance of reaching an accord with Syria before October of that year. He therefore decided to go for an early election, and the date was fixed for 29 May. His calculation was that he could win a mandate for another four years in power and then renew his bid for an accord with Assad and for a comprehensive peace in the Middle East.

Assad's intransigence during the negotiations came as a bitter disappointment to Peres. His disappointment was all the greater because the priority he had accorded to Assad was at the expense of progress with Arafat. Yossi Beilin had already worked out the basic outline of a "permanent status" agreement in a series of secret meetings in Stockholm. Four academics participated in these meetings, two Israelis and two Palestinians. The Israeli academics were Dr. Yair Hirschfeld and Dr. Ron Pundak, the trailblazers for the Oslo accord; the Palestinian academics were Dr. Hussein Agha and Dr. Ahmed Khalidi. The Israeli academics reported to Beilin; the Palestian academics, to Abu Mazen (Mahmoud Abbas). Beilin did not inform either Peres or Rabin about the Stockholm channel. On 31 October 1995, three days before Rabin's assassination, Beilin and Abu Mazen met in Tel Aviv with their advisers and put the final touches on the "permanent status" agreement. In a book aptly called *Touching Peace*, Beilin describes the meeting with a keen sense of drama:

> Abu Mazen was very excited. When we embraced, I saw that his eyes were slightly moist. Here we touched for the first time on the most sensitive issues in the process. If the Oslo process was the breakthrough and the framework in which we got to know one another, in the Stockholm process we dealt with the heart of the conflict. That which we had postponed at Oslo was the essence at Stockholm. Subjects on which we did not believe we could reach any understanding were agreed here in principle. Apparently, at least, we had in our hands a document with a complete, or nearly complete solution to the 28-year-old conflict and perhaps 100-year-old conflict.[9]

The basic premise of the Beilin–Abu Mazen plan was that there would be a demilitarized Palestinian state. The plan envisaged the annexation by Israel of about 6 percent of the West Bank, where roughly 75 percent of the Jewish settlers resided. The other settlers would be given a choice between compensation and staying on under Palestinian sovereignty. Israel adhered to its claim to sovereignty over the whole of Jerusalem, but the Palestinians recognized only West Jerusalem as Israel's capital. The Muslim holy places in East Jerusalem were to be given an ex-territorial status, but the capital of the Palestinian state would have to be just outside the municipal boundary of the city as defined by Israel.

From the Palestinian point of view, the Stockholm accord represented a giant step forward. They stood to gain a state, 94 percent of the West Bank and compensation for the other 6 percent in desert land south of Gaza, and a capital city in Jerusalem. Hussein Agha called it "the deal of the century." From talking to Yossi Beilin, Agha gained the impression that Rabin was more likely to adopt the plan than Peres, for Rabin had come to accept the inevitability of a Palestinian state, whereas Peres wanted to keep all the options open. The Palestinians suspected that Peres's idea of the final status of the territories was a series of enclaves on which it would be impossible to build a Palestinian state. They regarded Rabin as much more reliable than Peres because with Rabin yes meant yes and no meant no, whereas with Peres both yes and no meant maybe. Although outwardly they enjoyed friendlier relations with Peres than with Rabin, they considered Peres insecure and therefore incapable of taking tough decisions and sticking to them.[10]

A week after Rabin's murder, Beilin presented the plan to Peres, spread out the maps in front of him, and told him the full story of the Stockholm channel. Beilin recommended adoption of the plan both as the basis for the permanent status negotiations that were scheduled to start on 4 May and as the Labor Alignment's platform for the election scheduled for 29 October.[11] But Peres could not be persuaded to endorse the plan, for three main reasons: he wanted future relations between Palestine and Jordan spelled out, he regarded the ideas on Jerusalem as inadequate, and he wanted to retain the Jordan Valley as Israel's strategic border.[12]

In early January 1996 Peres faced another difficult decision. The Israeli General Security Service—Shabak—asked him for permission to assassinate Yahya Ayyash, the so-called engineer, who had personally masterminded several Hamas suicide attacks, which killed 50 and wounded 340 Israelis. The Israeli media presented him as public enemy number one, greatly exaggerating his status within Hamas and omitting to mention that the attacks he organized came as a response to the massacre perpetrated by Dr. Baruch Goldstein in Hebron in February 1994. In mid-1995 Ayyash went into hiding in Gaza, and the Palestinian preventive security service told the Shabak that he would not organize any more attacks on Israelis. But the head of the Shabak, who was about to be removed from his post for his failure to protect Rabin, badly wanted to be remembered for one last spectacular success. Peres gave the green light, thinking that apart from dealing out rough justice, the operation would boost the morale of the nation and of the security services. On 5 January, Ayyash was killed in Gaza by means of a booby-trapped cellular phone. The decision to kill Ayyash turned out to be the greatest mistake of Peres's political career.

Hamas declared Ayyash a martyr and promised revenge. On 25 February, at the end of the holy month of Ramadan, one of

Ayyash's disciples blew himself up on a bus in Jerusalem, killing all the passengers. Three other horrific suicide attacks followed in rapid succession, in Ashkelon, Jerusalem, and Tel Aviv, the last one on 3 March. Sixty Israelis lost their lives in these attacks, and many more were wounded. These attacks seriously damaged the credibility of Peres and his government. For the first time since the murder of Rabin, public opinion polls put Binyamin Netanyahu ahead of Peres. Thousands of right-wingers staged a demonstration against the prime minister and the peace process. Inside his own party Peres came under pressure to show that he could be tough in safeguarding Israel's security, even tougher than Rabin. Peres suspended talks with the Palestinian Authority (which emerged with a high degree of democratic legitimacy as a result of the elections held on 21 January), closed Israel's borders to Palestinian workers from the West Bank and the Gaza Strip, and declared all-out war on the Hamas and Islamic Jihad organizations. Still, he continued to lose popular support. The killing of Rabin by a Jewish fanatic had worked in his favor; the killing of Israelis by Muslim fanatics worked in Netanyahu's favor.

Peres also decided to suspend the peace talks with Syria. This decision, too, was influenced by domestic political considerations. Peres was reluctant to make concessions to Syria in the immediate preelection period and thereby expose himself to attack from his right-wing opponents. By taking a tough line with Assad, Peres hoped to protect his domestic flank during this critical period. The excuse he gave for suspending the talks was that Syria had to choose between harboring terrorist organizations and conducting genuine peace negotiations with Israel. Syria was still on the U.S. State Department's list of states sponsoring international terrorism. The Popular Front for the Liberation of Palestine and the Democratic Front for the Liberation of Palestine had their headquarters in Damascus. Hizbullah, Hamas, and Islamic Jihad had offices there. As Assad had been so unhelpful to him, Peres seized the opportunity to go on the offensive, accusing the Syrian leader of aiding and abetting terrorist organizations.

In a desperate attempt to shore up the Peres government and the peace process, an antiterrorist summit was held in Sharm el-Sheikh on 13 March. Twenty-seven countries were represented at the summit, including several Arab countries and the Palestinian Authority. Syria and Lebanon declined to take part. The proceedings consisted largely of empty words, but they went some way to convey the impression that the Arab world, or parts of it, continued to support Israel's embattled leader on the peace process. Bill Clinton went out of his way to heap praise on Israel, promising unqualified support in the campaign to thwart Islamic violence. Peres's own contribution to the summit was geared to his domestic audience. He lectured the Palestinians on their obligations to crack down on "murderous command centers" in their midst, and he condemned Iran as a country that "initiates, promotes, and exports violence and fanaticism." He stressed the value of joint action against Muslim extremists, but the summit produced no significant results beyond demonstrating international solidarity with Israel in its fight against Islamic terror.

One Islamic country that was forging close defense links with Israel was Turkey. Relations between the two countries had been improving since the start of the American-sponsored peace process in the aftermath of the Gulf War. Although Turkey was a Muslim republic, its secular government recognized an affinity with Israel. They were the only Western-style governments in the Middle East, and both were in the process of establishing closer ties with the European Union. In the late 1950s both Iran and Turkey were included in the alliance of the periphery that Israel tried to develop against the Arab states at the core of the Middle East. Now that the Islamic Republic of Iran was providing material help to Hizbullah and Hamas, Israel made an effort to cultivate Turkey as a counterweight to Iran and to Iran's closest Arab rally, Syria. One other change concerned the American position. Whereas in the late 1950s the United States refused to be drawn into the alliance of the periphery, Turkey became a key player in Washington's Middle Eastern order in the 1990s, and the Clinton administration threw all its weight behind the emerging alliance between its two regional protégés.

A military cooperation agreement was signed by the two countries in February 1996 but not announced until two months later. Turkey allowed the Israeli Air Force to use its airspace and bases. Israel undertook to supply military hardware and to upgrade the Turkish air force's Phantom fighter-bombers. At a stroke Israel vastly enhanced its operational range: it could strike at Syria from two directions, and it could deploy its jet fighters on Iran's doorstep. The accord unnerved the Arab and Islamic countries. Syria reminded Turkey of the Organization of the Islamic Conference resolution, supported by Ankara, that all OIC members should abstain from any military cooperation with Israel while it continued to occupy Arab land. The Arab League described the accord as "an act of aggression" and a direct threat to its members. The Egyptian foreign minister, Amr Musa, said it would create new tensions in the Middle East. The Iraqi press said the accord would "encourage the Zionist entity to continue its policy of occupation and colonization." Libya said the accord gave the Israelis "a dangerous and vulgar breakthrough which would serve their plans to dominate the region."[13] The accord threatened to polarize the region into the "peace camp," composed of those who stood with the United States and Israel, and the "war camp," composed of those who did not.

OPERATION GRAPES OF WRATH

The Turkish-Israeli accord caused undisguised alarm in Damascus. The Syrian regime felt encircled, and its sense of isolation deepened. If there had been any prospect of Syria's coming to terms with Israel, the Turkish agreement ended it. But the first target of Israel's stepped-up "anti-terrorist" campaign was Lebanon. The shaky standoff on the Israeli-Lebanese border had been unravelling for some time. Hizbullah started to launch Katyusha rockets on the settlements in northern Galilee and stepped up its attacks on Israeli units and their client militia, the South Lebanese Army, inside Israel's self-declared security zone in southern Lebanon. The SLA had lost the will to fight. The unwritten rules brokered by the United States in July 1993 stipulated that Hizbullah would not launch missiles into Israel and that Israel would not strike civilian target beyond its security zone. These rules were breached by both sides—each side claiming the other did it first. Hizbullah saw itself as a surrogate target for Israel's frustration over the terrorism of Hamas and other groups. But the main aim of its militancy was to expel Israel from its toehold in southern Lebanon. Israel saw the hand of Iran everywhere, while Syria was disinclined to use its influence to curb Hizbullah so long as there was no movement in the negotiations over the Golan Heights. All this made for a tangled web.

The domestic political situation in Israel made Lebanon a tempting target for military intervention. The Israeli public was thirsty for retribution. The Katyusha attacks gave Peres a chance to prove that he did not shy away from tough military action, and he took the chance, if rather hesitantly. He hesitated because he was well aware, from bitter past experience, of the perils of intervention in Lebanon, but both his generals and his party advisers, for different reasons, urged him to switch from diplomacy to military action. Operation Grapes of Wrath was meant to bring security to Galilee by bombing the Hizbullah guerrillas in southern Lebanon, but its other purpose was to recast Peres as the hard man of Israeli politics ahead of the crucial general elections. The United States tacitly supported Israel's aggression against its defenseless neighbor.

The ultimate target of Operation Grapes of Wrath was Syria. The Israeli military planners and Foreign Minister Ehud Barak, who as chief of staff had presided over the Israeli assault on Lebanon in July 1993, wanted to stampede the bulk of the civilian population from south to north Lebanon in order to clear the area for a massive strike against Hizbullah and to impose on both Hizbullah and Syria a change in the 1993 rules of the game. Their thinking was based on linkage politics of the cruelest kind. The idea was to put pressure on the civilians of southern Lebanon, for them to pressure the government of Lebanon, for it to pressure the Syrian government, and, finally, for the Syrian government to curb Hizbullah and grant immunity to the IDF in southern Lebanon. In short, the plan was to compel Syria to act as an Israeli gendarme in Lebanon.

On 11 April, after the Passover holiday, Israel launched Operation Grapes of Wrath. High-technology destruction was rained on southern Lebanon, on Beirut, and on the Bekaa Valley. Nearly 400,000 Lebanese citizens were driven out of their towns and villages and turned into refugees. A combined air and artillery assault was launched against Hizbullah—2,000 air raids and 25,000 shells. Hizbullah had about 300 full-time fighters. Their most formidable weapon was the Katyusha rockets fired from multiple launchers. They were obsolete, inaccurate, and had a maximum range of about twelve miles. Israel's strategy was the equivalent to using a bulldozer to weed a garden. Yet, despite all the firepower directed against it, Hizbullah continued to fire Katyusha rockets across the border. On 18 April a massacre took place. Israeli shells killed 102 refugees in the UN base in Qana. Israel admitted its error, but the pictures of the massacre, transmitted by the media throughout the world, gave Hizbullah a decisive moral victory. Israel was universally condemned, and the United States intervened to extricate its ally from the quagmire. Having given Israel the green light to break Hizbullah, the United States reverted to urging restraint. Once again U.S. diplomats rushed in to rescue Israel from the consequences of military action that the United States at first encouraged. The American-sponsored cease-fire was signed on 27 April. For all Peres's claims to the contrary, it did not represent any significant improvement on the unwritten rules of July 1993. It merely restored an uneasy truce in Lebanon.

Once again Hafez al-Assad benefited from an Israeli military action of which he was intended to be the victim. The rationale behind Operation Grapes of Wrath, as viewed from Damascus, was to weaken Assad, to make him suffer a military defeat, and to cause him to loosen his grip on Lebanon, the one major card he still had in hand. Although the 1982 and the 1996 Israeli invasions of Lebanon differed considerably in scale and duration, they had much in common. Both were billed as operations to protect northern Israel, both were fraudulently named, and on both occasions the real target was Assad. In Assad's eyes, these two Israeli invasions, waged in turn by Menachem Begin and Shimon Peres, were ambitious exercises in geopolitical engineering designed to restructure the region to Israel's advantage. Both were seen by Assad as reflecting the interventionist trend in Israeli politics that, from the days of David Ben-Gurion's premiership, aimed at hegemony over the Arabs by military means.[14]

Operation Grapes of Wrath was a political, military, and moral failure. Israel seemed to have forgotten what many thought, overoptimistically, it had already learned: that there are limits to what can be achieved by military force and a heavy price to pay for depending on it too heavily. The international community roundly condemned Israel for its ruthless targeting of civilians. The entire Arab world was boiling with anger at Israel's brutal treatment of the Lebanese people. Moderate Arab governments wanted Peres to stay in power, but they were highly critical of the entire operation, and especially of the killing of the refugees in Qana. Suddenly, the much trumpeted New Middle East looked very much like the bad, old one, with arrogant Israel throwing its weight around in the name of security that trampled all before it.

In electoral terms, too, Operation Grapes of Wrath was an unmitigated failure. Peres's attempt to change his image from Mr. Peace to Mr. Security only damaged his credibility. Israel's Arabs felt that the military operation revealed Peres's true face, and many of them threatened to vote against him or return a blank ballot paper at the forthcoming general election. Jewish voters, on the other hand, were unimpressed by Peres's attempt to reinvent himself as a security hawk. Binyamin Netanyahu seized the opportunity to argue that the Labor government had brought peace without security, whereas the Likud, under his leadership, would bring peace with security.

The physical security of Israel's citizens inside the pre-1967 borders was a major concern in the lead-up to the election. The greatest irony was that Netanyahu, the most outspoken spokesman against Hamas, was also the principal political beneficiary of the series of suicide bombings it had carried out in Israel's major cities. These attacks had the effect of shifting public opinion against the Labor-led government and to some extent against the peace process with the Palestinians and in favor of tough right-wing politicians with an uncompromising stand on security. Rabin's assassination had dealt a severe blow to Netanyahu and gave Peres a substantial lead in the opinion polls. When the elections were called in mid-February 1996, Peres was ahead in the opinion polls by a seemingly unassailable 20 percent. But the spate of suicide bombings that followed the assassination of Yahya Ayyash wiped away this lead. Islamic terror worked strongly in Netanyahu's favor.

Personalities played a major part in determining the results of the general election held on 29 May 1996. This was the first election in which the new law providing for the direct election of the Israeli prime minister took effect. Consequently, each Israeli citizen over the age of eighteen had two votes to cast: one for a party and one for a prime minister. The list of political parties competing for preference was as long as usual, but there were only two candidates for the post of prime minister: Shimon Peres and Binyamin Netanyahu.

Peres fought a lackluster campaign. He turned down the suggestion that he make the assassination of Rabin, and the twin dangers of religious fanaticism and political extremism to which it pointed, an issue in the campaign. But neither did he focus sharply on the fundamental policy differences between the Labor Alignment and the Likud. Despite the suicide attacks, the majority of Israelis still wanted to go forward with the implementation of the Oslo accords. It was for Peres to present the voters with a clear choice between the peace policy of his party and the Greater Israel policy of the Likud. But he did nothing of the sort, leaving it to Netanyahu to do all the running. During the election campaign Peres behaved like the Jew in the Jewish joke who was challenged to a duel and sent a telegram to his opponent saying, "I am going to be late. Start shooting without me." A debate on television the night before the election helped tip the balance in Netanyahu's favor. Netanyahu seemed well prepared, vigorous, and incisive: Peres seemed old, tired, and rambling. In the opinion polls they were running neck and neck, but when the results were out, Netanyahu had won by a margin of 30,000 votes. He got 50.4 percent of the votes, while Peres got 49.6 percent. Labor won 34 seats in the Knesset; the Likud, only 32. But under the new electoral law, the task of forming the next government had to be assigned to Netanyahu.

For Shimon Peres, at the age of seventy-three, the election was a matter of political life and death. The perennial loser in Israeli politics, he had his greatest chance to give substance to his vision of a comprehensive peace and of a new Middle East order with Israel at its center. In the epilogue to his book *Battling for Peace,* Peres described himself as "an unpaid dreamer."[15] It was the dream of Shimon Peres that was at stake in the general election of 31 May 1996, and it was dealt a severe blow by his disastrous defeat at the polls.

15

Back to
the Iron Wall

1996–1998

THE RISE TO POWER of Binyamin Netanyahu marked a break
with the pragmatism that characterized Labor's approach toward the Arab world and the reassertion of an ideological hard line
that had its roots in Revisionist Zionism. Netanyahu himself hailed
from a prominent and fiercely nationalistic Revisionist Zionist family. His father, Benzion, was a historian of Spanish Jewry, an adviser
to Ze'ev Jabotinsky, and editor of the Revisionists' daily newspaper, *Ha-Yarden*. In 1962, unable to get tenure at the Hebrew
University, Benzion Netanyahu exiled himself and his family to
the United States, where he became a professor of Jewish history
at Cornell University. At home Binyamin, the second son, im-
bibed both Jabotinsky's teachings and his father's bitterness. The
essence of this inherited dogma was that the Jews had always been
and would always be persecuted by all those around them.

Binyamin was born in 1949, when Israel was one year old.
After completing his high school education in America, he returned to Israel, joined the army, and served for five years in an
elite unit, Sayeret Matkal, rising to the rank of captain. He took
part in the raid on Beirut airport in 1968 and in the storming of
a hijacked Sabena aircraft in 1972. But it was his elder brother,
Jonathan ("Yoni"), who passed into legend, the only Israeli commando to be killed in the 1976 raid to rescue hostages at Entebbe
airport. In memory of Yoni, the family set up the Jonathan
Institute with the aim of mobilizing governments and public opin-

ion in the West for the fight against terrorism. Upon his release from the army, Binyamin studied again in the United States, completing a bachelor's degree in architecture and a master's degree in business administration at the Massachusetts Institute of Technology. His university education completed, he went into business, first in the United States and then in Israel.

In 1982 Binyamin Netanyahu was appointed Israel's deputy ambassador to Washington and two years later its permanent representative to the United Nations, and he was successful at both posts. While serving in the United States, he also acquired a reputation as a leading expert on international terrorism and became a frequent participant in talk shows dealing with the subject. In 1988 Netanyahu returned to Israel and was elected to the Knesset on the Likud list. He served as deputy foreign minister in Yitzhak Shamir's government and kept a high profile in the media, especially during the Gulf War and the Madrid peace conference. In the contest to succeed Shamir as party leader, he enjoyed financial backing from wealthy American Jews and introduced American-style electioneering. The other contenders were David Levy and Benny Begin, the son of Menachem Begin. Other young Likud "princes," such as Dan Meridor and Ehud Olmert, were deterred from throwing their hats into the ring by Netanyahu's popularity rating. In the primaries Benny Begin called Netanyahu "a man of tricks and gimmicks," a person who lacked political gravitas. Other members of the Likud also regarded Netanyahu as an intellectual lightweight, as shallow and superficial, as little more than a purveyor of sound bites for American television. But on his side he had youth, vigor, good looks, and the power of communication.

THE RESURGENCE
OF REVISIONIST ZIONISM

Binyamin Netanyahu was elected leader of the Likud in March 1993. That year he also published a major book under the title *A Place among the Nations: Israel and the World*. The book was inspired by the teaching of Ze'ev Jabotinsky and Benzion Netanyahu. Its central theme was the right of the Jewish people to the whole Land of Israel. History was rewritten from a Revisionist perspective in order to demonstrate that it was not the Jews who usurped the land from the Arabs, but the Arabs who usurped it from the Jews. Britain was portrayed as no friend of the Jews, and the chapter on the British mandate in Palestine was simply called "The Betrayal." The whole world was perceived as hostile to the State of Israel, and antisemitism was said to be at the root of this hostility.

Netanyahu viewed Israel's relations with the Arab world as one of permanent conflict, as a never-ending struggle between the forces of light and the forces of darkness. His image of the Arabs was consistently and comprehensively negative and did not admit the possibility of diversity or change. His book did not contain a single positive reference to the Arabs, their history, or their culture. Arab regimes were portrayed as ready practitioners of violence against the citizens of their own countries and across their borders: "Violence is ubiquitous in the political life of all the Arab countries. It is the primary method of dealing with opponents, both foreign and domestic, both Arab and non-Arab." In addition, Netanyahu claimed that "international terrorism is the quintessential Middle East export" and that "its techniques everywhere are those of the Arab regimes and organizations that invented it."[1] The Arab world was described as deeply hostile toward the West. Netanyahu conceded that a few Arab rulers were friendly to the United States but warned against the delusion that this reflected the real sentiments of the Arab masses. Such rulers, in his view, "frequently represent only a thin crust lying over a volatile Arab and Islamic society."[2]

Much of Netanyahu's vehemence and venom was reserved for the Palestinians. He launched a fierce assault on the notion that the Palestinian problem constituted the core of the Middle East conflict. For him the Palestinian problem was not a genuine problem but an artificially manufactured one. He denied that the Palestinians had a right to national self-determination and argued that the primary cause of tension in the Middle East was inter-Arab rivalry. For Netanyahu compromise with the PLO was completely out of the question because its goal was the destruction of the State of Israel, and this goal allegedly defined its very essence. This, in his view, was what distinguished the PLO from the Arab states, even the most radical ones. While these states would clearly prefer to see Israel disappear, their national life was not dependent on Israel's destruction: "But the PLO was different. It was constitutionally tied to the idea of Israel's liquidation. Remove that idea and you have no PLO."[3]

A Place among the Nations was published before the Oslo accord saw the light of day. The possibility that an Israeli government could make a deal with the PLO seems not to have crossed Netanyahu's mind. What did trouble him was the thought that Arab "terrorists and totalitarians" would manipulate the Western democracies into besieging Israel on their behalf. His greatest fear was of the Trojan horse: "For the PLO is a Pan-Arab Trojan horse, a gift that the Arabs have been trying to coax the West into accepting for over twenty years, so that the West in turn can force Israel to let it in the gates." And while it was difficult for uninitiated Westerners to imagine the Arabs destroying Israel as the Greeks laid waste to Troy, warned Netanyahu, it was "all too easy for anyone familiar with Israel's terrain to imagine, precisely as Arafat promises, that a PLO state implanted ten miles from the beaches of Tel Aviv would be a mortal danger to the Jewish state."[4]

Chapter 7 in Netanyahu's book is called "The Wall." This is an allusion to Ze'ev Jabotinsky's famous 1923 article that called upon the Jews to build an iron wall that would force the Arabs to accept them. In this chapter Netanyahu expanded on the military value of the dominating heights of the Golan and the mountains of Samaria and Judea. He buttressed his arguments with maps that highlighted Israel's geostrategic vulnerability. Over and over again, he quoted a Pentagon plan dated 18 June 1967 in support of his argument that for Israel to protect its cities, it must retain military control over virtually all the territory west of the Jordan River. There was no mention of the many Israeli generals who took the view that control over the West Bank was not a military necessity. His conclusion was that the whole of western Palestine constituted one integral territorial unit: "To subdivide this land into two unstable, insecure nations, to try to defend what is indefensible, is to invite disaster. Carving Judea and Samaria out of Israel means carving up Israel."[5]

The Oslo accord was signed shortly after the publication of Netanyahu's book. The accord did precisely what Netanyahu had warned against: it recognized the PLO, it conceded that the Palestinian people had a legitimate right to self-government, and it began the process of partitioning western Palestine. In his book Netanyahu had dwelled on the lessons of appeasement of Nazi Germany and of the betrayal of Czechoslovakia by the Western powers for the contemporary Middle East. He compared the Arabs to Nazi Germany, the Palestinians to the Sudeten Germans, and Israel to the small democracy of Czechoslovakia, the victim of Chamberlain's 1938 Munich deal with Hitler. In a op-ed piece in the *New York Times* on 5 September 1993 under the title "Peace in Our Time?" Netanyahu resurrected this analogy. He depicted Israel as the small and vulnerable democracy, pressured into ceding a vital piece of territory without which it would be unable to defend itself against the inevitable future attack.

Netanyahu was unrelenting in his attacks on the Oslo accord. In his 1995 book *Fighting Terrorism* he wrote, "At Oslo, Israel in effect accepted the first stage of the PLO's Phased Plan: a gradual withdrawal to the pre-1967 border and the creation of the conditions for an independent PLO state on its borders."[6] In the lead-up to the May 1996 elections, however, the opinion polls showed that the majority of Israelis continued to support the peace process with the Palestinians and the policy of gradual and controlled withdrawal from the occupied territories, and that they were much less troubled by the prospect of a Palestinian state alongside Israel than were the politicians of the right. Consequently, Netanyahu began to trim his sails to the prevailing wind of public opinion. "The Oslo accord endangers Israel," he said, "but one cannot ignore reality." If elected, he promised not to renege on any of the country's international commitments, but he implied that he would freeze the Oslo process. The real difference, he claimed, was that the Labor leaders had bought peace without security, whereas he would bring peace with security. But he did not explain how he would achieve peace without making concessions or security without peace.

DECLARATION OF WAR ON THE PEACE PROCESS

Although Binyamin Netanyahu was elected by a margin of less than one percent, he had the advantage of being the first directly elected prime minister in Israel's history. Direct election of the prime minister was intended to curb the power of the small parties, but it had the reverse effect of increasing the representation of these parties at the expense of the two large parties, and it greatly enhanced the independence and the influence of the prime minister. Consequently, although the Likud won only 32 seats in the 120-member Knesset, this relatively inexperienced forty-six-year-old politician was invested with vast powers in the making of Israel's foreign and defense policy and in shaping its relations with the Arab world.

The Likud-led coalition formed by Netanyahu included five

partners: the National Religious Party; the United Torah Party; Shas, a religious party of mainly Oriental Jews; the Third Way, a Labor Party breakaway group that sought greater caution in peace-making; and Israel Be'aliya, a Russian immigrants' party, led by Natan Sharansky. Between them the parties of the coalition commanded 66 seats in the Knesset, giving the government a comfortable majority.

All the key posts in the new government were allocated to leaders of the Likud. David Levy became foreign minister and Yitzhak Mordechai defense minister, and Ariel Sharon got the specially created national infrastructure portfolio. But it was clear from the start that these men would not be able to form a happy or harmonious team, because of personal rivalries and political differences. Netanyahu had been Levy's deputy in the late 1980s, and the relations between them were so strained that Yitzhak Shamir eventually moved the former from the Foreign Ministry to the prime minister's office. Sharon and Levy were poles apart politically but close personally. Sharon represented the most hawkish wing of the Likud and Levy the moderate wing, but they still managed to form an electoral pact against Netanyahu. Levy did not take his seat on the government's front bench in the Knesset until Sharon's demands for extra powers had been met. Yitzhak Mordechai was the only senior minister who kept out of the infighting. He was a former IDF general of Iraqi-Kurdish origins who was respected in the defense establishment and popular in the party.

The fact that he was directly elected by the Israeli people was interpreted by Netanyahu as a mandate to introduce American-style presidential government. The cabinet, whose real powers rarely matched its formal powers, suffered a serious erosion of its authority. Netanyahu was not receptive to advice from his cabinet colleagues, he took steps to curb the involvement of the cabinet in the peace process, and he downgraded the role of the Foreign Ministry and the Ministry of Defense in policy-making. Nor was Netanyahu receptive to advice from the security chiefs. He saw them as supporters of the Labor Party's soft line toward the Arabs and expected them to resist his plans to reverse this line. The security chiefs, for their part, had grave doubts about Netanyahu's competence, judgment, and suitability for the post of prime minister. It was not without significance that in the office of the chief of staff there was a picture of Yitzhak Rabin but no picture of Binyamin Netanyahu. Even Benzion Netanyahu publicly doubted his son's suitability for the top job, saying he might do as foreign minister.

In his own mind Netanyahu was unable to distinguish clearly between the making of foreign policy and the presentation of policy. He was essentially a public relations expert. His previous posts had given him ample opportunity to hone his public relations skills but precious little experience in policy-making. Throughout his career, he had stressed the importance of *hasbara,* of explaining Israel's position and policy to the outside world. As prime minister he continued to display more interest in the task of presenting Israel's policy to the media than in presiding over the process of consultation and discussion of foreign policy options. He surrounded himself with a select group of advisers who, like himself, had spent much of their lives outside Israel and had little or no experience in government. Netanyahu had more advisers than any previous Israeli prime minister, but the great majority of these were media and public relations experts with no expertise in dealing with Arabs and limited knowledge of regional affairs. David Bar-Illan, the former editor of the *Jerusalem Post,* became director of policy planing and communications in the prime minister's office. Entrusting the usually separate tasks of policy planning and policy presentation to the same individual was typical of Netanyahu. Dr. Dore Gold, an academic born and educated in the United States, became the chief negotiator with the Palestinian Authority.

The predominant view among Israeli commentators was that Netanyahu would adopt a pragmatic course of action and that he would not attempt to reverse the policy on which his Labor predecessors had embarked by signing the Oslo accord. The Western media also gave Netanyahu the benefit of the doubt. Gaining power, many commentators suggested, would transform him from an ideological hawk into a pragmatic and practical politician. It was precisely his impeccable right-wing credentials, some added, that would place him in a strong position to continue the policy of accommodation with the Arabs.

In his first major address after his razor-thin electoral victory, Netanyahu sought to sustain the impression of continuity in foreign policy. But his first priority, he said, was to unite Israeli society. He stressed that he would be the leader of all Israelis, Jewish and Arab, religious and secular. "First and foremost, peace must be reached at home—peace between us, peace among us," he told his cheering supporters on 2 June 1996. But he also struck a conciliatory tone and held out the "hand of peace" to Israel's Arab neighbors: "I said that peace begins at home, but it must be continued abroad," he declared. "We intend to further the process of dialogue with all our neighbors to reach a stable peace, a real peace, a peace with security." There was no hint of his bitter opposition to the outgoing government's land-for-peace deal with the PLO.

But the basic guidelines of government policy that Netanyahu presented to the Knesset on 18 June, signaled a clear intention to depart from the outgoing government's course at home and in relation to the Arabs. Those who expected the Likud leader, once elected, to start blunting the edges of his opposition to the peace process, found no comfort in this document. The guidelines were those of an ethnocentric religious-nationalist government. The chapter on education promised to cultivate Jewish values and to put the Bible, the Hebrew language, and the history of the Jewish people at the center of the school curriculum. The foreign policy guidelines expressed firm opposition to a Palestinian state, to the Palestinian right of return, and to the dismantling of Jewish settlements. They reserved the right to use the Israeli security forces against terrorist threats in the areas under Palestinian self-rule. They called on Syria to resume peace talks without preconditions but at the same time ruled out any retreat from Israeli sovereignty on the Golan Heights. The assertion of Israel sovereignty over the whole of Jerusalem was explicit and exhaustive. So was the commitment to continue developing settlements as "an expression of Zionist fulfillment." And for good or bad measure, the guidelines made no explicit reference to the Oslo or Cairo agreements.

In his inaugural speech to the Knesset, Netanyahu noted the change in the leadership of the State of Israel, the transfer of power from the founding fathers to the younger generation born after the attainment of independence. He promised that his government would work for national regeneration and follow a new road, one that would carry Israel forward. Relations with the Palestinian Authority and resumption of the talks on permanent status were made conditional by Netanyahu on strict fulfillment of all its obligations and on cooperation with Israel in suppressing Islamic terror. His call on Syria for talks without preconditions was widely seen as an attempt to dissociate himself from the verbal promises made by his predecessors. But there was also an implied warning that Israel would act not only against terrorists but against the sponsors of terror. Finally, Netanyahu declared that Israel's foreign policy would continue to be conducted in close cooperation with the United States. But he added that the United States, like Russia and the European Union, could play only a limited role in the negotiations between the Arabs and Israel, because only the parties that bore the consequences had the right to decide.

After Netanyahu finished his inaugural address, Shimon Peres went to the podium and delivered his first speech as leader of the opposition. "Time is not neutral; it is of critical importance," he said. "There are many warhorses in the region, and it is a mistake to conduct policy like a tortoise that moves slowly and relies on the armor it carries on its back." Looking at Netanyahu, Peres continued, "My friend, the prime minister, I fear that you will discover quickly that the platform on which you were elected cannot serve as a prescription for progress in the peace process. You would have to disappoint many of your voters and partners if you want to achieve any results. Nice slogans cannot serve as a substitute for policy, and coalition formulas will not remove the need for courageous decisions and difficult choices."

The Arab world, still reeling from the shock of Binyamin Netanyahu's election, reacted with even greater dismay to the formation of his government and to his inaugural address to the Knesset. A Damascus newspaper said that the new government, "dominated by rabbis, generals, racists, mass murderers, and advocates of transfer," could be summed up in a single phrase: "Destroying the foundations of peace." Mr. Netanyahu, the newspaper added, was bent on establishing "biblical Greater Israel from the Nile to the Euphrates through terror, repression, and war." Radio Damascus said that Netanyahu had left nothing for the Arabs to negotiate about. The United States also came under heavy fire. As U.S. officials hailed Netanyahu's stated willingness to negotiate without any preconditions, Arabs argued that his policies made a mockery of U.S. attempts to persuade them that he was a man with whom they could deal. His program was "a recipe for wrecking the peace process," said the Saudi-owned newspaper *Al-Hayat*. King Fahd of Saudi Arabia sent a message to President Clinton warning that the freezing of the peace process by the Netanyahu government would cause the Gulf states to freeze the process of normalization with Israel.

Netanyahu made one contribution to the cause of Arab unity: he aroused such alarm that more of their leaders assembled for a two-day summit in Cairo on 22 June than at any other time since the August 1990 summit after Iraq invaded Kuwait. Egypt, Syria, and Saudi Arabia were the main promoters of the Arab League summit, which was attended by thirteen out of the twenty-one heads of state. The aim of the summit was to restore Arab cohesion and send the message to Israel and the United States that unless the new Israeli prime minister reverted to the ground rules of land for peace on which the Arab-Israeli negotiations had been based since Madrid, the peace process would collapse and the region slide into a cycle of tension and violence.

Syria, the chief advocate of Pan-Arab action, suggested that, while reconsecrating peace as the Arabs' strategic choice, the summit should plan for other eventualities, including war. Syria called on the participants to form a united front against the new Israeli government's "aggressive and antipeace" policies. Spokesmen for the Palestinian Authority joined President Assad, their bitter adversary, in describing the Israeli government's policy platform as tantamount to a declaration of war on the peace process. President Mubarak said Arab states would reconsider their position if Israel took a hard line. He called on Israel to continue carrying out all it had agreed upon and resume negotiations without procrastination and precondition. Jordan alone insisted that normalization should continue regardless of any setback to the peace process, because that was the only way to encourage Israel to move at all.

In their final communiqué the heads of state reiterated that a just and comprehensive peace remained their strategic choice. But this required "a firm, unequivocal, reciprocal engagement from Israel." They called on Israel to withdraw from the Golan Heights, Lebanon, and East Jerusalem. Recalling the 1991 Madrid conference and the principle of land for peace that it had enshrined, they said, "Any deviation by Israel from the commitments, obligations, or agreements entered into . . . or any procrastination of their implementation would compromise the peace process." They did not specify the actions they would take if Israel retreated from its commitments, but they hinted that the result would be a freeze on further normalization, leaving it to Israel to decide whether or not to resume meaningful progress. While Israel's neighbors could afford the luxury of a wait-and-see policy, the Palestinians could not.

There was no evidence of the widely predicted flexibility in Netanyahu's attitude toward the Arabs during his first few months in power. On the contrary, official policy was a faithful reflection of the views expounded by Netanyahu in his speeches and publications prior to his election. In a major interview with the independent daily *Ha'aretz,* he restated his deterministic worldview and his conviction that Israel was doomed to live by the sword. The basic reason for the conflict, Netanyahu explained at the outset, was the Arab world's perception of the Jewish state as an alien element that had no right to exist in the Middle East. The Palestinian problem was the consequence rather than the primary cause of this collision. Many Israelis assumed that if they solved the Palestinian problem, they would solve the Arab-Israeli conflict. Netanyahu questioned this assumption, arguing that even if they achieved a stable agreement with the Palestinians, they would not solve the Arab-Israeli conflict in its entirety. The conflict would end only when the entire Arab world became convinced that Israel was a fait accompli.

Asked if he shared the vision of a New Middle East popularized by Shimon Peres, Netanyahu replied that the notion was characteristic of people who live under continuous siege and want to change what is happening beyond their walls by imagining a different reality. "I don't espouse this psychology of the besieged," he said. "I look objectively at what is happening outside and know that in the foreseeable future the readiness of the Arabs to accept the State of Israel and live with it in peace depends on our ability to make it clear to them that we are not a passing episode." Asked whether this meant that Israel had to continue the policy of the iron wall, Netanyahu replied, "Until further notice we are in a Middle East of iron walls. What iron walls do is give us time. The hope is that in the course of this time, positive internal changes will occur in the Arab world that will enable us to lower the defensive walls and perhaps even drop them one of these days. This process is taking place gradually, but in order to complete it we must create in the Arab world an irreversible understanding that we will not vanish."

Netanyahu claimed that there had been an erosion in Israel's deterrent power in recent years. "This was a conceptual mistake made by the previous government," he said. "It believed that peace alone would provide security, so it allowed itself not to cultivate our power." Netanyahu accused the previous government of taking diplomatic and military risks while allowing the decline in national power that went hand in hand with territorial shrinkage. He intended to change this trend because he believed that if Israel was perceived as weak at the negotiations on final status, a pretext would always be found to attack it. "We must realize that peace treaties do help security," he conceded grudgingly, "but they cannot serve as a substitute for deterrence. The opposite is true. Military might is a condition for peace. Only a strong deterrent profile can preserve and stabilize peace."[7]

Netanyahu's evident intention was to refocus peace talks on Israeli security rather than on the concept of land for peace, which was the main thrust of the Labor-led government. His first target was the Oslo accords, which, though not committing Israel to the idea of an independent Palestinian state, pointed in that direction. By making it clear that he remained absolutely opposed to Palestinian statehood, he all but pulled the keystone from the arch of peace. The Oslo accords represented a step away from the previous Israeli doctrine of maintaining control over the Palestinians in the occupied territories. By adopting at the outset hard-line pre-Oslo positions, Netanyahu was reasserting this doctrine. His aim was to preserve direct and indirect Israeli rule over the Palestinian areas by every means at his disposal. He was as uncompromising in his opposition to Palestinian statehood as Yitzhak Shamir and Menachem Begin had been. But, as he saw it, his Labor predecessors had sold the pass, so he had to be more creative in his efforts to regain lost ground. The main elements of his strategy were to lower Palestinian expectations, to weaken Yasser Arafat and his Palestinian Authority, to suspend the further redeployments stipulated in the Oslo accords, and to use the security provisions in these accords in order to reassert Israel's dominant position.

In relation to the Arab states, and especially to Syria, Netanyahu was similarly determined not to proceed any farther down the path of land for peace. He knew that the collapse of the Soviet Union and the defeat of Iraq in the Gulf War left the Arab states with no military option. They could huff and puff, but none of them could bring any military pressure to bear on behalf of the Palestinians. Indeed, Netanyahu believed that his tough position would compel the Arab states themselves to compromise further on their rights and leave him in a position to argue when seeking a second term that, unlike the Labor government, he took no gambles with the country's security. But this strategy was fraught with danger, and it revealed a defective understanding of Israel's real position. The assumption that the Arabs would suddenly abandon their long struggle for the recovery of occupied land was not simply naive but also provocative. It created a dangerous tide in the relations between Israel and the Arab world.

THE HEBRON PROTOCOL

During his first hundred days in power, Binyamin Netanyahu fell out with just about everybody with whom he came into contact. He quarreled with his own allies in the government, with the trade unions, and with the Israeli business class. But the most fateful rift developed between him and the hardheaded men who ran Israel's security services, because he did not heed their warnings and repeatedly spurned their advice. The Oslo accords had created a new role for the Israeli security forces and their Palestinian counterparts as guardians of the peace process. Whereas the issue in the past had been their capacity to fight one another, the issue now was their capacity to control the low-intensity conflict that was bound to persist in opposition to the peace process. The prime minister, unlike the security chiefs, did not accept the Palestinians as partners and defaulted on many of the commitments he inherited from the previous government.

Serious deterioration occurred in Israel's relations with the Palestinians as a result of Netanyahu's backtracking. He adopted a "work-to-rule" approach designed to undermine the Oslo process. There was no Israeli pullout from Hebron, no opening of the "safe passage" route from Gaza to the West Bank, and no discussion of the further West Bank redeployment that Israel had pledged to carry out in early September. Instead, Palestinian homes without an Israeli permit were demolished in East Jerusalem, and plans were approved for the construction of new Israeli settlements. The quality of life for the Palestinians deteriorated progressively, and hopes for a better future were all but extinguished. The occupied territories were like a tinderbox. All it required was a spark to set it off.

The spark was provided by Netanyahu with an order to blast open, on the night of 25 September, an archaeological tunnel close to the al-Aksa Mosque in the Old City of Jerusalem. The idea was to open a second entrance to the tunnel used by the Hasmoneans of the second century B.C. to bring water to the Jewish temple. The specific purpose of this tunnel was said to be the easing of the flow of tourists through the popular archaeological site. The new gate emerged at the Wailing Wall and at the base of Dome of the Rock, the holy Muslim site directly above. Of no great import in itself, the new gate constituted a symbolic and psychological affront to the Palestinians and a blatant Israeli violation of the pledge to resolve the dispute over Jerusalem through negotiations, not via the fait accompli.[8] Thus, by giving the order to blast open a new entrance to the 2,000-year-old tunnel, Netanyahu blasted away the last faint hopes of a peaceful dialogue with the Palestinians.

The action set off a massive outburst of Palestinian anger and ignited the flames of confrontation. The large-scale protest and rioting got out of hand and provoked the Palestinian police to turn its guns on the Israeli soldiers. The violence intensified and engulfed the entire West Bank and Gaza. In three days of bloody clashes fifteen Israeli solders and eighty Palestinians died. It was the most violent confrontation since the worst days of the *intifada*. The Israeli public was shocked by the scenes of Palestinian policemen opening fire on their Israeli counterparts. But most outside observers regarded Netanyahu's policy of bogging down the peace process as the underlying cause of this costly and bloody conflict.

A summit meeting in Washington was hastily called by President Clinton in an effort to calm the situation and to prevent progress toward a settlement from unraveling completely. President Mubarak declined the invitation. King Hussein, Yasser Arafat, and Binyamin Netanyahu all responded to the call, but the meeting ended without any agreement being reached. All the Arab leaders expressed their disappointment with the Israeli leader, but King Hussein's disappointment was the most poignant because he was the only Arab who had not joined in the chorus of denunciation following Netanyahu's victory at the polls. There was a personal and a political aspect to the king's disappointment. His relations with Yitzhak Rabin had been based on mutual trust, and he hoped to develop a similar relationship with Netanyahu. But the king's trust was severely tested when Netanyahu sent Dore Gold to see him shortly before the opening of the tunnel, conveying the false impression that the king knew in advance about the plan. More serious was the threat Netanyahu posed to the king's efforts to bring about peace between the Arab world and Israel. Although the king was not an admirer of Arafat, Arafat's peace with Israel laid the foundation for the king's peace with Israel, and now Netanyahu was destroying this foundation. The king therefore spoke very sternly to Netanyahu at the White House, as the press reported at the time and as he confirmed later: "I spoke of the arrogance of power. I spoke of the need to treat people equally. I spoke of the need to make progress." Netanyahu did not respond, but, as they were leaving, he went up to Hussein and said, "I am determined to surprise you."[9]

King Hussein was less ready to stick his neck out in defense of normalization with Israel in the aftermath of the bloody clashes. Nearly all the political parties in his kingdom were calling for an end to all forms of normalization with "the Zionist enemy." Feeling against Israel ran very high throughout the Arab world, from North Africa to the Persian Gulf. The Third Middle East and North Africa Economic Conference, Mena III, was scheduled to open in Cairo in November. For a while it looked as if Mena III would not convene at all. President Mubarak threatened to cancel the summit if Israel continued to renege on its peace commitments. He relented only under intense U.S. pressure.

Mena III opened in Cairo on 13 November in a climate of palpable hostility to the *muharwaluun*. The *muharwaluun*—those who "rush" or "scurry"—had become a key concept in Arab political discourse. The Syrian poet Nizar Qabbani coined the term after the handshake on the White House lawn between Yitzhak Rabin and Yasser Arafat, which he interpreted as a humiliating act of surrender by the entire Arab nation. Qabbani poured his anger into a poem that he called *al-Muharwaluun:*

> *We stood in columns*
> *like sheep before slaughter*
> *we ran, breathless*
> *We scrambled to kiss*
> *the shoes of the killers.*

The rush to normalize relations with the Zionist enemy was now derided by those who saw it as a mark of Arab weakness. Business was at the heart of this normalization, as was evident from these annual conferences. The original aim was to forge a regional economic order of which Israel would be an integral part, and economic cooperation was expected to consolidate Middle Eastern peace. At the conference in Casablanca in 1994 and in Amman in 1995, Israel had led the way in fostering Shimon Peres's vision of a new Middle East that incorporated the Jewish state.

King Hussein used to tell his people that normalization would produce prosperity. Arafat used to say that given the right economic climate, he would turn Palestine into a new Singapore. Another major argument of the "scurriers" was that Arab conciliation would encourage Israel to complete the peace process on the Palestinian, Syrian, and Lebanese fronts. Arab countries not involved directly in the conflict also accepted this logic. Morocco, Tunisia, and Qatar decided to open liaison bureaus in Israel. Qatar even agreed to supply Israel with natural gas.

The critics of the "scurriers," on the other hand, argued that the Arabs should withhold the economic rewards of normalization as their last remaining means of pressure. Saudi Arabia refused to lift the boycott of Israel until a comprehensive peace had been achieved. Netanyahu's election tilted the balance in favor of the critics. He was held up as the embodiment of just how wrong the "scurriers" had been. The critics asked, "Why should we take part in an international economic gathering supposedly designed to underpin regional peace and security with economic cooperation when Israel rejects peace?" Jordan and the Palestinian Authority sent only medium-level delegations. Qatar delayed the opening of its liaison office in Tel Aviv and suspended its natural gas deal. Other governments told their delegations to make no deals with the Israelis. The Egyptians made it plain that since Israel was going back on the peace process, the Arabs should go back on the basic objectives of Mena I and II, and turn Mena III into a forum for inter-Arab business alone.[10]

The Arab and the American reaction to "the tunnel uprising" compelled Netanyahu to yield some ground to the Palestinians in connection with the other major flashpoint on the West Bank— Hebron. In September 1995 the Labor government had concluded an agreement on redeployment in Hebron, but this was suspended six months later because of the suicide bombings. Following his electoral victory Netanyahu tried to treat Hebron as a separate issue, while the Palestinians tried to tie it to the Oslo process. Netanyahu also tried to limit the American role, but the crisis over the tunnel prompted President Clinton to intervene in order to prevent the total collapse of the peace process. At the end of the Washington summit meeting, Clinton ordered his special envoy, Dennis Ross, to go to the region to help the parties work out arrangements for Israeli redeployment from Hebron. It took the parties three and a half months to reach agreement. The process itself was noteworthy both because of the active part played by the United States and because this was the first time that the Likud government engaged in negotiations with the Palestinians on the basis of the Declaration of Principles and the Interim Agreement.

The Hebron Protocol was signed on 15 January 1997. It was a milestone in the Middle Eastern peace process, the first agreement signed by the Likud government and the Palestinians. The protocol divided Hebron into two zones to be governed by different security arrangements. The Palestinian zone (H1) covered about 80 percent of Hebron, while the Jewish zone (H2) covered the other 20 percent. In the Jewish zone Israel was to maintain full security control during the interim period. Palestinian critics pointed out that this formula for coexistence gave the 450 Jewish settlers (who constituted 0.3 percent of the population) the choicest 20 percent of the town's commercial center, whereas the 160,000 Palestinians got 80 percent subject to numerous restrictions and limitations. The Hebron Protocol also committed Israel to three further redeployments on the West Bank over the next eighteen months.

The Hebron Protocol was submitted to a special meeting of the Israeli cabinet on 14 January. The meeting was full of tension and lasted thirteen hours. The major issue of contention was the provision for further redeployments. At the end of the meeting, the ministers approved the agreement by a majority of eleven to seven. Benny Begin, the minister of science and technology, resigned from the government in protest against the decision, saying that even a small concession in Hebron constituted a dangerous precedent and that he could not square the provision for further redeployment with his oath to perform his duty in good faith. Defense Minister Yitzhak Mordechai helped Netanyahu persuade the cabinet to endorse the Hebron Protocol. In private conversations Mordechai explained that in signing the protocol the government took a calculated risk in order to avert the complete collapse of the Oslo process and reduce the tensions in the Middle East.

On 16 January, Netanyahu made a statement to the Knesset concerning the Hebron Protocol. "We are not leaving Hebron," he said; "we are redeploying from Hebron. In Hebron, we touch the very basis of our national consciousness, the bedrock of our existence." He claimed that this agreement gave Israel better terms than the agreement he had inherited, underlining two points. First, the implementation of the three further redeployments would be determined by Israel and not be a matter for negotiation with the Palestinians. Second, the time frame was much more convenient and enhanced Israel's freedom of maneuver. In short, said Netanyahu, the Hebron Protocol gave Israel peace with security. At the end of debate, which lasted eleven consecutive hours and in which ninety members took part, the Knesset endorsed the Hebron Protocol by a vote of 87 to 17, with 15 abstentions. Most of the opponents belonged to the coalition, and many of the supporters came from the ranks of the opposition.

The Knesset vote reflected a very broad national consensus in favor of continuing the Oslo process. The Hebron Protocol was widely regarded as hailing the end of the Revisionist Zionist dream of the whole Land of Israel, as foreshadowed in the Declaration of Principles of September 1993. Yet, after implementing the redeployment from Hebron, Israel remained in exclusive control of 71 percent of the West Bank (area C) and continued to exercise security control over another 23 percent (area B), while the Palestinian Authority exercised exclusive control over only 6 percent (area A). The principle of the integrity of the historic homeland may have been compromised, but the announcement of the death of the ideology of Greater Israel was somewhat premature.

THE BATTLE FOR JERUSALEM

Having been compelled to take a relatively conciliatory line on Hebron, and having alienated many of his own followers in the process, Netanyahu adopted a confrontational line on Jerusalem. By signing the Hebron Protocol, Netanyahu broke the Likud taboo on handing over land for peace. So he vowed to strengthen Israel's hold over Jerusalem and to resist any compromise or even meaningful negotiations with the Palestinians over the future of the Holy City. He knew that no Arab could accept less than Arafat was demanding—shared sovereignty. But he believed that a forceful unilateral Israeli assertion of control over the city would dispel Arab illusions of recovering control over the eastern part, illusions that he claimed his Labor predecessors had encouraged.

Netanyahu fired the opening shot in the battle for Jerusalem on 19 February with a plan for the construction of 6,500 housing units for 30,000 Israelis at Har Homa, in annexed East Jerusalem. "The battle for Jerusalem has began," he declared in mid-March as Israeli bulldozers went into action to clear the site for a Jewish neighborhood near the Arab village of Sur Bahir. "We are now in the thick of it, and I do not intend to lose." Har Homa was a pine-forested hill, south of the city proper, on the road to Bethlehem. Its Arabic name is Jabal Abu Ghunaym. The site was chosen in order to complete the chain of Jewish settlements around Jerusalem and cut off contract between the Arab side of the city and its hinterland in the West Bank. It was a blatant example of the Zionist tactic of creating facts on the ground to preempt negotiations.

The Har Homa project had been frozen for two years because

the Palestinians warned that it would damage the Middle Eastern peace process and because Rabin and Peres knew how explosive it would be. But it was part of a policy pursued by all Israeli governments after 1967, whether Labor or Likud, or surrounding the huge Greater Jerusalem area with two concentric circles of settlements, with access roads, and military positions. These ramparts enclosed 10 percent of the area of the West Bank, and in it lived up to half of the Israeli settlers in the territory. It was clear, therefore, that the Har Homa project prejudiced not only the negotiations on the future of Jerusalem but those on a final settlement for the West Bank as a whole.

The Israeli bulldozers had to be given armed guards for the task of leveling the hillside for the controversial settlement. The Palestinians staged a general strike in protest against the project and the expropriation of Arab land it involved. Soldiers scuffled with the demonstrators; Bethlehem and Hebron, a few miles away, were declared closed military zones; and joint patrols were suspended. Arafat froze all contacts with Israel and refused to take two telephone calls from Netanyahu. Ahmed Qurei ("Abu Ala"), the speaker of the Palestinian legislative council, declared, "Netanyahu's bulldozers have destroyed any chance for peace."

Britain led Western governments in condemning the move amid mounting concern about the faltering Middle Eastern peace process. "The start of construction can do nothing but harm the peace process," said Foreign Secretary Malcolm Rifkind. "Like all settlements this one will be illegal, and it goes against the spirit of the Oslo agreement." The United States used its veto twice to block Security Council resolutions that were critical of Israel's decision to construct a settlement at Har Homa. An emergency special session of the UN General Assembly passed a resolution calling for a halt in construction in Har Homa and an end to all settlement activities in the occupied territories. Only three countries voted against: Israel, the United States, and Micronesia. Israel's isolation was virtually complete.

At home the Labor Alignment distanced itself from the ruling party and castigated it for failing to achieve either peace or security. Ehud Barak replaced Shimon Peres as leader of the Alignment following its electoral defeat. Barak was a former chief of staff and a security hawk who promised to follow in the footsteps of Yitzhak Rabin. Under his leadership, however, the Alignment continued to move along the course charted by Peres. At its annual convention, in May 1997, a resolution was adopted to delete from the party's electoral manifesto the long-standing opposition to the establishment of a Palestinian state. The new policy was not to support the establishment of a Palestinian state but merely to recognize that the right to statehood was implicit in the right of the Palestinians to self-determination. Public opinion polls showed that the majority of Israelis were resigned to the emergence of an independent Palestinian state as an inevitable outcome of the Oslo process.

Likud leaders denounced the change as one more example of the Alignment's policy of appeasement toward the Palestinians. But in the ensuing debate it was the Likud that was challenged to show how it planned to achieve peace and security without continuing the process of reconciliation with the Palestinians. "Israel cannot afford and should not try to govern over another people," said Barak. "I think we should separate ourselves from the Palestinians. We do not need here either a kind of apartheid, or a Bosnia, and under Netanyahu we might reach both."

In an attempt to outflank Barak, who had been his commander in Sayeret Matcal, the IDF elite unit, Netanyahu presented to the inner cabinet a plan to hand over to the Palestinians about 40 percent of the West Bank in the final settlement. Originally prepared by the army, the plan specified Israel's security interests on the West Bank. Netanyahu did not attach a precise map to his proposal, but he did indicate the areas that would remain under Israeli sovereignty: Greater Jerusalem, which was to be further expanded; the hills east of Jerusalem; the Jordan Valley; the heavily settled areas close to the 1967 border; essential corridors and roads; and the water sources.[11] Netanyahu called his plan "Allon plus," hoping it would attract the support of left-wing voters. Yet there was a major difference between the two plans. The Allon Plan required the retention of approximately 30 percent of the West Bank and the return of the rest to Jordanian rule. Netanyahu's plan claimed around 60 percent of the West Bank for Israel and offered to hand over the remaining 40 percent to the Palestinian Authority.

Netanyahu's plan was aimed at the Israeli public rather than at the Palestinians. There was no chance that the Palestinians would accept the offer, because they expected to recover 90 percent of the West Bank under the terms of the Interim Agreement of September 1995 (Oslo II). Netanyahu's plan limited Palestinian control to two cantons north and south of Jerusalem, centered on Nablus and Hebron, but with no territorial link between the two. The Palestinians in and around Jerusalem were to be isolated from the two cantons. Saeb Erekat, the chief negotiator of the Palestinian Authority, said, "This is not acceptable. Netanyahu is negotiating with himself, or rather with himself and other extremists in his government. He has forgotten he has a partner."

While Netanyahu's plan conformed to the Oslo equation of land for peace, his policies on the ground worked in reverse. Every day the Palestinians had less land and the Israelis less peace. His vision of the future was taking physical shape on the hills of the West Bank. Sales of new homes rose by more than 50 percent, to 1,560, in the first seven months of 1997, boosted by government incentives. The Jewish settler population in the West Bank and the Gaza Strip reached 161,157 by 1997—a 9 percent increase on 1996. Hamas went on the offensive again with two suicide bomb attacks in Jerusalem, on 30 July and 4 September. Netanyahu held the Palestinian Authority responsible for all terrorist attacks originating from the areas under its control, and he demanded mass arrests of Hamas activists. He stated that Israel would not hand over any more territories to the Palestinian Authority if these territories were going to be used as launching ground for attacks by Islamic terrorists.

Was there anything Israel could do to prevent, or at least to limit, the outburst of violence against its citizens? Netanyahu spent his time in power avoiding this question. His security chiefs did not duck the question. The precise question was whether any link existed between Israel's backsliding on the Oslo agreements and Arafat's reluctance to act more decisively against Hamas and Islamic Jihad. Both the head of the General Security Service and the director of military intelligence were of the opinion that Arafat had no incentive to cooperate with Israel in the fight against Islamic terror as long as he believed that Israel was not complying with the Oslo accords. Netanyahu rejected their assessment.[12] He regarded terrorist attacks by extremist Palestinian fringe groups as a strategic threat to the State of Israel and used them to justify the freezing of the political process that was meant to transform Israel's entire position in the Arab world.

The suicide bombings alerted the Clinton administration to the danger that the entire Middle Eastern process would be swept away by a new tide of violence. Madeleine Albright, who replaced Warren Christopher as secretary of state after Clinton's reelection, reversed her policy of benign neglect of the Middle Eastern peace process by paying a visit to the region in early September. For some time the Americans had been harboring suspicions that

Netanyahu's real aim was to derail the peace train that had started at Oslo. They also suspected Arafat of deliberately preserving the terrorist arm of the Islamic resistance front as a means of exerting pressure on Israel. The purpose of Albright's visit was to dispel the smoke screens set up by the two leaders and to put pressure on them to get the peace train back on track.

This was Albright's first visit to the Middle East, and she delighted Israeli officials by placing the immediate onus for salvaging peace on Yasser Arafat. She gave full backing to Israel's insistence that the Palestinian Authority crush militant Islamic organizations as a precondition for the resumption of the Oslo peace process. Security, she said, was at the center of her agenda. At a joint press conference, Arafat repeatedly condemned the use of violence and offered his condolences to the victims of the two recent suicide bombings in Jerusalem. But Albright indicated that she was unimpressed by his attempts to date to catch the orchestrators of violence. Echoing Netanyahu, she called for concerted and sustained action against terrorism rather than a "revolving door" of arrests and releases.

For Israel, Albright had only the mildest of criticisms. She mentioned government confiscation of Arab land, the demolition of Arab houses, and the confiscation of Palestinian identity documents as acts seen by Palestinians as provocative. It was only on the eve of her departure that she suggested that Israel should consider taking a "time-out" in the construction of Jewish homes on Palestinian land. Even then she insisted, "There is no moral equivalence between killing people and building houses." Though self-evidently true, the dismissive reference to "building houses" showed little understanding of the depth of Palestinian bitterness provoked by the ceaseless spread of new Jewish neighborhoods. Ezer Weizman, the Israeli president, was reported to have told Albright that insufficient pressure was being exerted on Netanyahu to stick to the spirit of the Oslo agreements. He urged her to demand further troop withdrawals from the West Bank and limits on the construction of Jewish settlements. He also told her that she should "bang Arafat's and Netanyahu's heads together." Albright did not heed the advice.

The next major crisis in the Middle East occurred only three weeks after the American secretary of state returned home, and it was indisputably of Israel's making. Mossad prepared a plan to kill Khalid Meshal, a middle-level Hamas leader, by injecting a slow-acting poison into his ear as he entered his office in Amman. The plan went disastrously wrong. Meshal was injected but not killed, and his bodyguard captured the two Mossad agents, who were disguised as Canadian tourists. The Israelis, in their introverted way, concentrated on the technical aspects rather than the egregious political folly of the operation. A political battle erupted over who was to blame for the failed assassination bid. The IDF chief of staff and its director of military intelligence were unaware of the mission until they heard reports that two Mossad agents had been apprehended by the Jordanian authorities. The Mossad man in Amman was said to have opposed the mission for fear of damaging relations between Israel and Jordan. But the prime minister gave the go-ahead. He thereby earned himself the dubious distinction of being the first potentate since Hamlet's uncle Claudius to try to kill one of his rivals by putting poison in his ear.

King Hussein, Israel's best friend in the Arab world, said after the assassination attempt that he felt as if somebody "had spat in his face." Three days before the attempt Israeli and Jordanian officials considered together the problem of Islamic terror. The meeting took place in Amman within the framework of the strategic dialogue between the two sides. At the meeting the Jordanian representatives reiterated their commitment to work closely with the Mossad in the fight against terror. King Hussein intervened in the dialogue personally to report an offer of a cease-fire from Hamas. He requested that this offer be conveyed directly to the prime minister. Great was his surprise and anger therefore when he learned that Netanyahu himself had ordered the bizarre operation in Jordan's capital.

A senior Jordanian official remarked that it was easier to predict the course of the mysterious weather system El Niño than the behavior of the Israeli prime minister. Jordanian officials linked the botched assassination attempt to the peace process. They recalled that Hamas had hitherto refrained from mounting terrorist attacks outside the borders of Israel and the occupied territories. They reasoned that by trying to assassinate Meshal outside these borders, Israel intended to create an intolerable provocation. This would have compelled Hamas to react and to extend its operations to new areas. Israel would have blamed Arafat for the new wave of violence, and the peace process would once again have been put on hold.[13]

By ordering the operation in Amman, Netanyahu showed himself to be feckless, irresponsible, and staggeringly shortsighted. The consequences were very grave. The operation weakened King

Hussein, whose peace treaty with Israel remained as unpopular among his own people as it was popular among Israelis. To obtain the release of the Mossad agents, Netanyahu had to deliver Sheikh Ahmed Yassin, the Hamas spiritual leader who had been languishing in an Israeli prison. The release of Sheikh Yassin, and his triumphal return to Gaza via Amman, made it more difficult for Arafat to meet Israel's demands for a mass arrest of Hamas activists. The fact that Israel was forced to release Yassin increased his prestige and that of the organization he had founded. Thus, by his unremitting concentration on Hamas, Netanyahu ended up by raising it to a position of pivotal importance. By his own ill-considered actions, he came close to destroying one of the central planks in his policy toward the Palestinians: the refusal to negotiate until the violence was halted. Just as his opening of the tunnel in the Old City of Jerusalem forced him to reverse his policy of not trading land for peace, the Amman fiasco undermined his case for refusing to implement the Oslo accords until the Palestinian Authority uprooted the infrastructure of Hamas. New ingredients and new uncertainties were added to the Middle Eastern conflict.

The most basic obstacle to the resumption of the peace talks, however, was the Likud government's policy of giving political and financial support for the expansion of Jewish settlements on Palestinian territory beyond the Green Line. The Palestinians feared that the annexation of land by settlements in the West Bank and Gaza was designed to undermine their claim to a national homeland. Inside Israel the official policy of expanding settlements also came under attack. In early March 1998 more than 1,500 reserve officers from Israel's army and police force, including 12 retired major generals, called on the prime minister to abandon his policy of expanding Jewish settlements in Palestinian areas and to choose peace instead. Their published letter said that continued Israeli rule of 2.5 million Palestinians might harm the democratic and Jewish character of the Israeli state and make it more difficult to identify with the path it was following. "A government that prefers maintaining settlements beyond the Green Line to solving the historic conflict and establishing normal relations in our region will cause us to question the righteousness of our path," the letter said.

External pressure focused on the need to honor the commitment to a second redeployment following the one in Hebron. Netanyahu responded to this pressure by negotiating the accession of the most rabidly antipeace party to his coalition. Moledet's 2 seats in the Knesset raised the government's total from 61 to 63 and thus, according to Netanyahu, enhanced the government's ability to make concessions to the Palestinians. But Moledet's platform called for renouncing the Oslo accords and "transferring" the Palestinians across the river Jordan. Notwithstanding Netanyahu's claim to the contrary, the embracing of this racist party as a partner made the government more rigid rather than more flexible in its approach to the Palestinians.

The IDF's conception of Israel's strategic interests had not changed as a result of the political changes at the top. The security map that the General Staff had presented to Yitzhak Rabin was not very different from the one presented to Yitzhak Mordechai. The map indicated that Israel should retain a strip of land along the river Jordan, along the Green Line, and around Jerusalem. To this map of essential strategic requirements the government now added a map of "national interests." The new term was coined by Ariel Sharon in order to include all the Jewish settlements in the occupied territories. The government used it in its efforts to blur the distinction in the public mind between vital security needs as defined by the General Staff and its own ideology, which treated every Jewish settlement in Judea and Samaria as sacrosanct.

The lack of trust between the Palestinian Authority and the Likud government rendered the Oslo process inoperable. In early May 1998 Tony Blair, the British prime minister, invited the Palestinian and Israeli leaders to talks in London to try to break the gridlock. Arafat was persuaded that British-European participation at the peace table alongside the Americans was a good idea. It was Netanyahu, however, who grabbed the headlines with claims that in London he went the extra mile for peace. But he was not committed to producing a breakthrough. On the contrary, he persisted in his rejection of the American proposal that Israel should cede 13 percent of the West Bank as its second "further redeployment" under the terms of the Oslo accords. The London meeting ended in failure. The Israeli-Palestinian peace talks remained in a state of limbo. To the Palestinians, at any rate, it was abundantly clear that a leader who claimed that a withdrawal of 13 percent was a threat to his country's security was unlikely to agree to greater withdrawals in the negotiations on the final status of the occupied territories. These talks, according to the mutually agreed timetable, had to be completed by 4 May 1999. But by the time Israel celebrated its fiftieth anniversary, on 14 May 1998, the talks had not even started.

DEADLOCK ON THE SYRIAN
AND LEBANESE FRONTS

In relation to Syria, Israeli policymakers had long been divided into two schools of thought. One school advocated striking a deal with Hafez al-Assad, even if his terms were stiff, on the grounds that he was a strong ruler and could be trusted to deliver. The other school argued in favor of waiting for the post-Assad era in the expectation that a weaker and therefore more pliant leadership would come to power in Damascus. Netanyahu had been identified with the second school when he was in opposition, but once in power he inclined toward the first. He and his hard-line Likud colleagues seemed to think that Syria could be "squeezed" and isolated and that Israel's aims on the northern front could be achieved even before Assad's disappearance from the scene. Netanyahu criticized Yitzhak Rabin and Shimon Peres for deferring too much to Assad and argued that Syria could be made to accept arrangements that would enhance Israel's security without having to return any territory on the Golan. The stage was thus set for a diplomatic tussle between the old Lion of Damascus and his brash young Israeli challenger.[14]

The basic guidelines of the Likud government called for the resumption of peace talks with Syria but ruled out Israeli withdrawal from the Golan Heights. They stated that "retaining Israeli sovereignty over the Golan will be the basis for an arrangement with Syria." This amounted to a rejection of "land for peace," the basis of all Middle Eastern peace negotiations since the Madrid conference. Netanyahu was quick to make it clear that his government would not honor the commitments made by Rabin and Peres to withdraw to the 4 June 1967 line. In his view these so-called commitments were no more than "hypothetical statements" of a nonbinding character that were never set down in an official document and never signed. "Statements," he said, "made in the course of negotiations, which are not written down are not part of a formal commitment, are *not* formal commitments. . . . I will only honour formal commitments."[15]

The Syrian view was that although the commitment made by Rabin and Peres to withdraw to the 4 June 1967 line was conditional on Syria's meeting Israel's requirements on security and normalization, it was a formal commitment made by an Israeli government and was therefore binding on its successors. Accordingly, the Syrians insisted that if the talks were to resume, they had to pick up where they had left off. In July 1996 Dennis Ross, the State Department's Middle Eastern envoy, tried to revive the Israeli-Syrian talks on the basis of a Syrian formula that suggested continuing "the peace talks with Israel on the commitments that had been reached before." But Netanyahu firmly rejected the formula. "No," he said, "I am only willing to resume the peace talks without any preconditions."[16]

Not content with renouncing publicly the commitment of his predecessors, Netanyahu waged a vigorous campaign behind the scenes to cancel altogether the only tangible result of American mediation in the Israeli-Syrian conflict. This was the paper called "Aims and Principles of Security Arrangements," which the Israeli and Syrian negotiators had deposited in the State Department on 22 May 1995. The paper laid down the basic principles for security arrangements between the two parties in the framework of a peace treaty. It articulated the principles of force reduction and demilitarization on both sides of the border, but it did not draw the border or determine the size of the demilitarized areas. The paper was the product of five months of intensive negotiations following the meeting between the Israeli and Syrian chiefs of staff in Washington in December 1994. Because the paper was not signed, its critics called it "the nonpaper."

Netanyahu and his advisers launched an all-out attack on this paper. The paper incorporated the principles of equality, mutuality, and reciprocity, and they held that these principles would weaken the security arrangements that were vital to Israel. In particular, they thought it was a mistake to accept the principle of demilitarization on the Israeli side of the border following withdrawal from the Golan. Netanyahu thus asked the Americans to confirm in writing that "the nonpaper" had no standing in international law and was therefore not binding on Israel. Warren Christopher obliged. On 18 September 1996 he sent a personal and confidential letter to Netanyahu, saying that the paper in question was not binding from the standpoint of international law but that the United States reserved the right to raise again the issues discussed in this paper.[17] Christopher's response reflected a lawyer's narrow approach to the problem. It ignored the fact that the paper was not meant to be signed, since it was part of a larger package that remained to be negotiated. It threw away the fruits of four years of American diplomacy. And it rendered more difficult the resumption of negotiations between Syria and Israel.

Difficulty in resuming negotiations with Syria was compounded by a Knesset vote in July 1997 on a private bill for confirmation of the 1981 law on the annexation of the Golan. The
government had taken a decision against introducing further legislation. But when the private bill was put on the agenda for a first
reading in the Knesset, the prime minister and the majority of his
cabinet colleagues voted for it. The foreign minister and the minister of defense were not present and later attacked the proposal as
unnecessary and harmful. Netanyahu's volte-face further damaged
his credibility, especially as he had promised David Levy that he
would remove the bill from the order of the day. The Syrian press
denounced the bill as another act of aggression aimed at preventing the resumption of peace talks.

During her visit to the region in September 1997, Madeleine
Albright made a halfhearted attempt to get the Israelis and the
Syrians back to the conference room. Netanyahu told her that he
might be prepared to "take note" of what the Labor leaders had
said without committing himself in any way. He asked her to try
out this formula on Assad. Albright tried to persuade Assad to accept Netanyahu's proposal to start talks "without preconditions."
Start talking and see where you get, she advised Assad. Assad was
unimpressed. "I don't want talks for talks' sake," he told Albright.
For him the matter was one of principle, not procedure.[18]

Tension between Israel and Syria escalated so sharply in the late
summer and autumn of 1997 that a military clash between them
looked possible, if not probable. The tension was fed by a series of
steps taken by the two sides in response to a perceived threat. The
immediate cause of the tension, from the Israeli perspective, was
Syria's redeployment of about one-third of its Lebanon-based
force to within striking distance of the Israeli positions on Mount
Hermon. Israeli defense experts thought that Syria might be planning a "land grab" in the Israeli-held area of the Golan Heights.
A particular concern was voiced that Syria might attempt to capture Israel's sophisticated communications complex on Mount
Hermon and hold it until the UN Security Council called for a
cease-fire, leaving Syrian troops in situ. At one point the cabinet
considered mobilizing the army reserves.

It was later discovered that Israel's assessment of Syria's intentions during this and earlier crises was influenced by false information supplied by a Mossad case officer named Yehuda Gil.
During Gil's trial in a Tel Aviv court on charges of espionage and
theft, it was revealed that in September 1996 he fabricated intelligence suggesting that President Assad had reached a decision to go

to war with Israel. Gil's report, ostensibly derived from a Syrian contact, claimed that Assad had given up hope of getting any concessions from the Netanyahu government and that he consequently resolved to take military action. The redeployment of Syrian forces on the Golan Heights and in the Bekaa Valley were portrayed as the prelude to the launching of a surprise attack.[19] Gil may have had an ideological motive for fabricating the false information for, after retiring from the Mossad, he became the secretary of the extreme right-wing party Moledet, which advocated the removal of Arabs from the Land of Israel. He was strongly opposed to any accommodation with the Arabs in general and Syria in particular. His loyalty was to the Land of Israel, not to the State of Israel. But whatever his motives, his false reports in September 1996 greatly increased the tension between Israel and Syria and pushed the two countries to the brink of war.

The policy of toughness that Netanyahu adopted toward Syria had its counterpart in his policy toward Lebanon. Here, too, he refused to honor unwritten agreements. He ordered the IDF to move from passive defense of the border area to more aggressive tactics and hard-hitting attacks against its Lebanese Shiite opponents. He promulgated a policy of massive retaliation against attacks by Hizbullah and let it be known that the Syrian army would not go unpunished for its part in supporting Hizbullah. At the same time, though, he sought to separate the dialogue with Syria from the dialogue with Lebanon's billionaire prime minister, Rafiq Hariri, whose aim was to restore Lebanon as a business center and playground of the Arab world.

Like previous Israeli governments, the Netanyahu government stressed that it had no territorial ambition in Lebanon. Soon after coming to power, Netanyahu put forward a proposal called "Lebanon first." Under this proposal, Israel was to withdraw from southern Lebanon in return for a commitment by the Lebanese government to dismantle the Hizbullah militia and guarantee the security of Israel's northern border. This was a retreat from the position of previous Labor and Likud governments insofar as Israel no longer insisted on a peace treaty with Lebanon as a quid pro quo for withdrawal. But in making his much canvassed proposal to wind up Israel's self-declared security zone in southern Lebanon, Netanyahu was not proposing to implement UN Resolution 425 of 1978, which called for the immediate and unconditional withdrawal of Israeli forces to their side of the international border. The withdrawal he proposed was neither immediate nor unconditional.

He had in mind a phased withdrawal traded against the disarming of the Lebanese resistance. His offer deliberately omitted any reference to a parallel withdrawal on the Golan. Syria was being asked to acquiesce in negotiations over Lebanon without having its own territorial claim addressed.

The "Lebanon first" proposal was intended to marginalize Syria, but Syria refused to be marginalized and the Lebanese government declined to enter into separate negotiations with Israel in defiance of Syria. The upshot was that Israel remained bogged down in Lebanon, where its predicament increasingly resembled America's in Vietnam: mounting casualties as a result of involvement in an inconclusive and unwinnable war against indigenous guerrilla forces. Like the Americans in Vietnam, the Israelis embarked on large military operations that were costly in treasure and blood but did not produce any lasting results. Between the end of the Lebanon War and the end of 1996, the Israeli losses in Lebanon where about 400 dead and 1,420 wounded. To these were added 73 soldiers who lost their lives when two helicopters collided after takeoff on their way to Lebanon. Israeli columnists began to call Lebanon "our little Vietnam," "that cursed place," "the Valley of Death," and that "Molloch" cruelly and systematically devouring their young men.

Israel had problems with its allies as well as its enemies in Lebanon. The 2,500-man South Lebanese Army, which served as a sandbag between Hizbullah and northern Israel became increasingly demoralized and ineffective. Some of its soldiers defected in order to join the Islamic resistance to Israeli occupation. Hizbullah's success in winning hearts and minds in the Shiite villages in the south called into question the entire rationale behind the security zone. The strangest thing about the zone was that one could rarely spot the "enemy," but its very invisibility was a measure of Hizbullah's effectiveness. Its hit-and-run tactics were particularly effective against the SLA. Consequently, Israelis had to do what their protégés could no longer do for them. They doubled their strength in the zone to 2,000 men, taking over some SLA positions. They spent $10 million improving these—yet they could not stem the bloodletting inflicted by Hizbullah's more sophisticated weapons and more daring tactics. Hizbullah was estimated to have only 400 fighters, but it was strongly supported by Iran, its morale was high, and it was confident in its ability to drive the Israeli intruders out of Lebanon.

Israel was torn between three options: unilateral withdrawal, launching another onslaught north of the security zone to clobber the guerrillas and possibly teach Syria a lesson, and just staying put with its young men continuing to serve as Hizbullah's sitting ducks. In the past the defense establishment had opposed a unilateral pullout from the security zone, arguing that unless the withdrawal was part of an overall settlement with Syria or Lebanon, it would be interpreted in the Arab world as an Israeli defeat. Another argument was that withdrawal would allow Hizbullah to deploy its fighters along Israel's northern border and to press its attacks across the border.

But Hizbullah's ability to operate inside the security zone, to ambush and kill Israeli as well as SLA soldiers there, weakened the argument that the best defense was from inside Lebanon. Some senior officers felt that the IDF had reached a dead end in Lebanon and that the only way out was a political settlement. But since the government was unable to bring about a political settlement, policy-making was left willy-nilly to the military echelon. Amiram Levin, the officer commanding the northern front, took the lead in making the case for a unilateral but phased Israeli withdrawal from Lebanon. He estimated that if Israel withdrew from Lebanon, Hizbullah and Syria would become rivals and the strength of Hizbullah would diminish. He was confident that the IDF could continue to carry out the necessary military operations from its side of the border. And he concluded that the benefits of withdrawal from Lebanon outweighed the benefits of staying there. In short, he concluded that Lebanon was a trap and that the IDF should be pulled out of the trap. Other senior officers, however, continued to think that it would be a mistake for Israel to withdraw from Lebanon unilaterally. The chief of staff did not come down on either side of the argument.

No one disputed that withdrawal coupled with an understanding with Lebanon or Syria was preferable to a unilateral withdrawal. But the option of an understanding with Lebanon did not exist, and waiting for an understanding with Syria on Netanyahu's terms in effect condemned the IDF to stay in Lebanon indefinitely. For as long as Netanyahu ruled out withdrawal from the Golan and offered Syria only "peace for peace," he could not find any Syrians willing to negotiate with him. His much vaunted idea of "Lebanon first" was a nonstarter, because Syria had the effective power to block any settlement in Lebanon that was not to its liking. Netanyahu tried various versions of his "Lebanon first" idea to make it more attractive to the Lebanese, but all of them were vetoed by Syria and rejected by Lebanon. In December 1996 Israel suggested a multinational force consisting of Egyptian, Jordanian, and possibly French troops to replace the IDF troops in southern Lebanon. Lebanon rejected the idea, saying Israel had to withdraw unconditionally. In March 1998 Israel again offered to withdraw, provided the Lebanese government took charge of the evacuated buffer zone and prevented attacks across Israel's northern border. This offer, too, was rejected. In short, Netanyahu's policy of toughness with Syria perpetuated the deadlock on both the Syrian and the Lebanese fronts.

Binyamin Netanyahu was not as bad as he seemed when he stood for election to the top post in Israeli politics on 29 May 1996. He was much worse. During the election campaign he promised that, unlike Labor, he would bring peace with security. But in his first two years in office he halted progress toward peace and brought no improvement in security. Commentators were initially divided into those who thought that his Revisionist Zionist ideology would get in the way of peacemaking with the Arab world and those who believed that pragmatism would prevail. Netanyahu's record, however, showed him to be neither a pure ideologue nor a purely pragmatic politician but a curious mixture of both. His conduct of Israel's external relations was erratic and contradictory, but one trait was consistent—the tendency to overplay his hand. This tendency accounted in large measure for his disastrous record in antagonizing all of Israel's friends as well as opponents in the Arab world. A master of sound bites, Netanyahu took particular pride in one phrase he coined: "We live in a tough neighborhood." But his attempts to achieve peace and security and at the same time hold on to East Jerusalem, most of the West Bank, and the Golan Heights suggested that he lived in a fool's paradise.

EPILOGUE

ISRAELIS CELEBRATED THE fiftieth anniversary of the establishment of their state in May 1998 in a subdued and somber mood. Israeli society was more divided than at any other time since the foundation of the state, and there was no consensus on how to mark the milestone. On the one hand, Israel could boast about some stunning successes: a democratic polity with universal suffrage; a highly developed, some might say overdeveloped, multiparty system; an independent judiciary; a vibrant cultural scene; progressive educational and health services; a high standard of living; and a GDP per capita almost the size of Britain's.

The ingathering of the exiles had worked. Israel's population reached the six million mark in 1998, nearly ten times what it had been in 1948. One-third of the world's Jews lived in the Jewish state, speaking the Hebrew language, which had been confined to liturgy when Zionism was born, a hundred years previously. In its central aim of providing the scattered Jews with a haven, instilling in them a sense of nationhood, and forging a modern nation-state, Zionism had been a brilliant success. And these achievements were all the more remarkable against the background of appalling tragedy: the extermination of six million Jews by the Nazis during World War II.

On the other hand, some failures could be noted. The most pronounced had been Israel's failure to resolve the conflict with the Arabs. Conflict accompanied the Zionist enterprise long before

Adolf Hitler came on the scene. The conflict involved neighboring Arab states but, in origin and in essence, was a clash between two movements for national liberation: the Jewish one and the Palestinian one. In 1948 the Zionist movement realized its aim of Jewish national self-determination in Palestine. But Israel's War of Independence was the Palestinians' catastrophe, *al-Nakba* in Arabic. The moral case for the establishment of an independent Jewish state was strong, especially in the aftermath of the Holocaust. But there is no denying that the establishment of the State of Israel involved a massive injustice to the Palestinians. Half a century on, Israel still had to arrive at the reckoning of its own sins against the Palestinians, a recognition that it owed the Palestinians a debt that must at some point be repaid.

The conflict with the Palestinians, and with the Arab world at large, cast a very long shadow over Israel's life. For the first forty-five years of its independent existence, Israel's leaders were unwilling to discuss the right of the Palestinians to national self-determination. Golda Meir took a preposterous position by denying that a Palestinian people existed at all. But the dilemma had been there all along, and the early Zionists were well aware of it even if they seldom talked about it. The dilemma, in a nutshell, was that the Jewish aspiration to sovereignty in Palestine could not be reconciled with the Palestinian people's natural right to sovereignty over the same country. This was the "hidden question" that the Zionist teacher Yitzhak Epstein addressed in his 1907 article in *Ha-Shiloah*. It was not long before the hidden question was transformed into an open and deeply contentious question.

Ze'ev Jabotinsky was the first major Zionist leader to acknowledge that the Palestinians were a nation and that they could not be expected to renounce voluntarily their right to national self-determination. It was therefore pointless at that early stage in the Zionist enterprise to hold a dialogue with the Palestinians; the Zionist program had to be executed unilaterally and by force. Jabotinsky's prescription was to build the Zionist enterprise behind an iron wall that the local Arab population would not be able to break. Yet Jabotinsky was not opposed to talking to the Palestinians at a later stage. On the contrary, he believed that after knocking their heads in vain against the wall, the Palestinians would eventually recognize that they were in a position of permanent weakness, and that would be the time to enter into negotiations with them about their status and national rights in Palestine.

In a way this is what has happened. The history of the State of

Israel is a vindication of Jabotinsky's strategy of the iron wall. The Arabs—first the Egyptians, then the Palestinians, and then the Jordanians—have recognized Israel's invincibility and been compelled to negotiate with Israel from a position of palpable weakness. The real danger posed by the strategy of the iron wall was that Israeli leaders, less sophisticated than Jabotinsky, would fall in love with a particular phase of it and refuse to negotiate even when there was someone to talk to on the other side. Paradoxically, the politicians of the right, the heirs to Jabotinsky, were particularly prone to fall in love with the iron wall and to adopt it as a permanent way of life. Yet Jabotinsky's iron wall encompassed a theory of change in Jewish-Palestinian relations leading to reconciliation and peaceful coexistence. Yitzhak Shamir, by contrast, conceived of the iron wall as a bulwark against change and as an instrument for keeping the Palestinians in a permanent state of subservience to Israel.

The first serious attempt to transcend the iron wall was made by Yitzhak Rabin following the Labor Party's victory at the polls in June 1992. On the face of it, Rabin was an unlikely candidate for overturning Israel's traditional policy toward the Arab world. He had spent a lifetime as a soldier, building up the iron wall for the dual purpose of deterring and withstanding Arab attacks. As chief of staff in June 1967, he was associated with Israel's most decisive victory over its enemies and the extension of the wall to enclose more of their territories. After the war he sided with the majority in the Labor Party in preferring a settlement with King Hussein to one with the Palestinians. During his first term as prime minister, Rabin remained implacably opposed to any notion of negotiations with the PLO.

During his second term in office, however, after exhausting all the other alternatives, Rabin grasped the nettle—which meant negotiating with the PLO. The upshot was the Oslo accord and the historic handshake with PLO Chairman Yasser Arafat in the White House on 13 September 1993. The Oslo accord was based on a compromise between the two peoples who had been engaged in the struggle for Palestine over the preceding century. This accord amounted to mutual recognition of each other's right to self-determination in separate parts of Palestine and an understanding that the remaining differences between them would be settled by peaceful means.

The logic of the Israeli-Palestinian peace process was founded on incremental momentum toward a Palestinian state. This was not stated openly. But the basic premise underlying the Declaration of Principles was that the resolution of the Israeli-Palestinian conflict had to be effected gradually. The most difficult issues, such as the rights of the Palestinian refugees, the future of the Jewish settlements, borders, and Jerusalem, were left to the last stage of the process, to the negotiations on the permanent status of the territories. Gradual progress was intended to enable the two communities to overcome their fears and suspicions and to learn to live peacefully alongside one another. Normalization between Israel and the Palestinians was also expected to pave the way to normalization between Israel and the Arab states.

The impact of the Oslo accord was nothing less than sensational. A year after his handshake with the PLO chairman in Washington, Rabin signed a peace treaty with King Hussein of Jordan in a colorful ceremony in the desert. It was Israel's second peace treaty with an Arab state and the first signed in the region. Moreover, in contrast to the cold peace with Egypt, King Hussein opted for a warm peace. By the time of the elections of May 1996, Israel had established diplomatic relations with fifteen Arab states, with Morocco and Tunisia leading the way. In the Persian Gulf region Oman and Qatar were the first to do business with Israel. The Arab League began to lift the economic boycott that was as old as the State of Israel itself. The Middle East and North Africa Economic Conference was established as an annual event with Israel as a full and active participant. Israel seemed set on a course leading to integration in the politics and economy of the Middle East. There was still a long way to go to realize Shimon Peres's full-blown vision of the New Middle East, but a dramatic improvement had already taken place in the relations between Israel and the rest of the Arab world.

If Peres was a dreamer, Binyamin Netanyahu was the destroyer of dreams. Netanyahu was a proponent of the Revisionist Zionist program of the undivided Land of Israel, not of peaceful coexistence with the Palestinians in this land. He rejected the Oslo accords and contributed to the incitement against the democratically elected government that culminated in the assassination of Yitzhak Rabin. In the lead-up to the May 1996 elections, Netanyahu toned down his opposition to the Oslo accords for reasons of pure political expediency: public opinion polls showed that two-thirds of the population supported the continuation of the Oslo process. He won the contest against Peres by a margin of less than one percent. But soon after his election he reverted to rejectionism with a vengeance.

A self-proclaimed disciple of Ze'ev Jabotinsky, Netanyahu propounded a version of the iron wall that was starker, more rigid, and more pessimistic. To his way of thinking, genuine peace was not possible with undemocratic states, and Israel consequently had to continue to cultivate its military power as the only safe instrument of deterrence. When he visited Auschwitz during Israel's fiftieth-anniversary celebrations, he said that "Jewish sovereignty and Jewish power are the only deterrents and the only guarantees against the slaughter of the Jews." It was a typically combative and one-sided statement from a leader whose obsession with military power blinded him to the changes taking place on the other side of the iron wall.

Toward the Palestinians, Netanyahu showed hatred and bitter animosity, which constrasted sharply with Jabotinsky's "courteous indifference." Jabotinsky wanted to live and let live; Netanyahu wanted to dominate. Jabotinsky understood the importance of military power; Netanyahu constantly harped on the importance of military power but had no understanding of its limitations. Jabotinsky saw Jewish military power as a means to an end; Netanyahu saw Jewish military power sometimes as a means to achieving security and sometimes as an end in itself. His vision of Israel's historic role seemed to consist of accumulating more and more military power in order to subdue more and more Arabs both inside and outside the Land of Israel.

From his first day in office Netanyahu worked, surreptitiously but systematically, to undermine the Oslo accords. With the exception of the limited pullback in Hebron, he suspended all the further redeployments to which Israel was committed under the terms of these accords. By building new Jewish settlements on the West Bank and more Jewish housing on Arab land in Jerusalem, he violated the spirit of these accords. Under his leadership the confiscation of Arab lands proceeded apace, and the right-wing settlers were given free rein to harm, harass, and heap humiliations on the long-suffering population of the occupied territories. As for the Palestinian Authority, it was treated by the prime minister not as a partner on the road to peace but as a defective instrument of Israeli security. Cooperation in combating terrorism had been an important, though undeclared, element in the Oslo process. Netanyahu endangered this cooperation by pressuring the Palestinian Authority to crack down harder and harder on the Islamic militants even as Israel reneged on its part of the bargain.

The entire Oslo process began to unravel under the heavy-handed pressure applied by the Likud government. The experience of working together only deepened the conflict and exacerbated the mistrust between the two sides. Every Israeli concession, however minor, was made only after exhausting negotiations, deliberate delays, and protracted crises. Every small step forward involved brinkmanship and increased the bitterness felt by both sides. Whereas the Labor government had groped for a positive-sum game in its relations with the Palestinian Authority, the Likud government reverted to a zero-sum game in which a gain by one side necessarily involved a corresponding loss by the other side. The negotiations on the final status of the territories that the Labor government entered into on 4 May 1996, shortly before the Israeli elections, were not even resumed by the Likud government in the three years following its victory. The final status negotiations were due to be completed by 4 May 1999. In the absence of any progress, a despondent Yasser Arafat began to threaten to issue a unilateral declaration of Palestinian independence on the target date.

The damage done by Netanyahu was not confined to bilateral Israeli-Palestinian relations but extended across the board of the country's external relations. Relations with Egypt and Jordan were severely strained. The trend toward normalization between Israel and the rest of the Arab world was abruptly arrested. Morocco and Tunisia quietly withdrew their representatives from Tel Aviv. Oman and Qatar froze their incipient business links with Israel. At the annual meetings of the Middle East and North Africa Economic Conference, Israel became an unwanted and unwelcome participant. Only strong American pressure prevailed on the host countries to invite Israel at all.

What the Likud government did not seem to understand was that the very peace that for many Israelis represented the realization of a dream implied for the Arabs an admission of impotence and defeat. The peace that the Arab states made with Israel was not an ideological peace but a pragmatic one. This kind of peace was by its very nature fragile and susceptible to failure if it did not live up to the pragmatic expectations of the Arabs, chief of which was the recovery of occupied land.

In the case of the Palestinians, the recovery of land was closely linked to the aspiration for political independence and statehood. The Oslo accords carried the kernel of an understanding that Israel would have no peace unless it recognized the Palestinian right to national self-determination. For all their shortcomings, these accords contained the basis for a historic compromise between the two principal parties in the century-old struggle for Palestine. The Declaration of Principles signed in 1993 had the potential to bring about a comprehensive settlement of the conflict between Israel and the Palestinians, provided it was implemented honestly and fairly and in a manner that took into account the legitimate interests of the two sides. By the time of Israel's fiftieth birthday, five years after the signing of the Declaration of Principles, this potential had not been realized.

Yet the Oslo accords should not be adjudged a failure. They did not collapse under the weight of their own contradictions, as critics liked to argue; the process was subverted by Binyamin Netanyahu and his colleagues in the ultranationalist camp. By subverting the Oslo accords, Netanyahu inflicted serious damage not only on the Palestinians but on his own country and on the Middle East as a whole. The Palestinians had made their choice. They offered Israel peace in return for a minimal restitution of what had been taken away from them by force. The ball was now indisputably in Israel's court. Israel had to choose. It could have land or it could have peace. It could not have both.

The events surrounding the Wye River Memorandum demonstrated once again that the Likud government preferred land to peace. Under intense pressure from the Clinton administration, Binyamin Netanyahu agreed to a summit meeting with Yasser Arafat at Wye Plantation in Maryland. In a twenty-seven-hour negotiating marathon, President Bill Clinton succeeded in brokering a landmark deal exchanging Israeli-occupied territory on the West Bank for Palestinian antiterrorist measures monitored by the CIA. King Hussein arrived at Wye Plantation from the Mayo Clinic in Rochester, Minnesota, where he was undergoing treatment for lymphatic cancer, to add his voice for a settlement. Looking gaunt and frail, he exerted all the moral authority he could bring to bear on Netanyahu and Arafat to reach an agreement for the sake of all of their children. It was to be the king's last contribution to the cause of peace in the Middle East, because he lost his battle against cancer three months later.

The memorandum drafted at Wye was signed in Washington on 23 October 1998. It promised to restore momentum to the Israeli-Palestinian peace process begun at Oslo, after nineteen months of stagnation and mounting tension, and to pave the way for comprehensive negotiations aimed at a final peace settlement. Israel undertook to withdraw its troops from a further 13 percent of the West Bank, in three stages over a period of three months, giving the Palestinian Authority full or partial control of 40 percent of the territory. In return, the Palestinians agreed to a detailed "work plan" under which they were to cooperate with the CIA in tracking down and arresting extremists in the Hamas and Islamic Jihad groups. Arafat also undertook to summon a broad assembly of Palestinian delegates to review the 1968 Palestinian National Charter and to expunge the clauses calling for the destruction of Israel.

On his return home, Netanyahu could have turned the Wye River Memorandum into a personal achievement and a political success that would have sustained him in power until the end of his four-year term of office. An opinion poll for Israel's largest-circulation newspaper, *Yediot Aharonot,* gave the deal a 74 percent approval rating. The Labor Alignment was afraid that Netanyahu would garner much popular support by taking on the mantle of a peacemaker, but it could hardly oppose the deal. Real opposition to the deal came from the Likud's coalition partners in the religious and nationalist parties and from splinter parties farther to the right.

The Israeli cabinet grudgingly passed the Wye summit land-for-security deal on 11 November, more than two weeks after the prime minister had signed it at the White House. Passage came at the end of a stormy debate that lasted seven hours. As part of the bargain to get the accord passed by his right-wing coalition government, Netanyahu agreed to announce public tenders for work to begin at Har Homa, the controversial new Jewish neighborhood in annexed East Jerusalem. Despite the further concessions Netanyahu had wrung out of Washington and the Palestinians in order to placate right-wingers, he was still able to muster only eight votes from ministers in support of the Wye accord. There were five abstentions and four votes against in the seventeen-member cabinet.

The Knesset approved the Wye accord on 15 November by 75 votes to 19, and 9 abstentions, underlining once again the unrepresentative character of the government on the issue of land for peace. The vote exposed the split in the government, but it also demonstrated a broad national consensus in favor of carrying the Oslo process forward. Netanyahu, however, opted to try to save his government by veering to the right and by emptying the accord he had recently signed of any real meaning. Both parties had pledged at Wye not to take "unilateral actions" to change the sta-

tus of the West Bank and the Gaza Strip. But some hard-line ministers publicly urged the Jewish settlers to grab more West Bank
land to keep it out of Palestinian hands. The first stage of the
Israeli troop withdrawal was matched by a renewed spurt of land
confiscations for the purpose of building Jewish settlements and a
network of roads between them. These measures discredited Arafat
and soured relations with the Clinton administration.

In sharp contrast to Israeli backsliding, the Palestinians scrupulously adhered to the course charted at Wye. For all the bitter disappointment of the preceding few years, more than 70 percent of
the Palestinians surveyed in early December 1998 said they still
supported some kind of peace process. On 14 December, Arafat
convened a meeting of the Palestine National Council in Gaza. A
show of hands laid to rest the PLO goal of destroying Israel, in a
gesture witnessed and applauded by President Bill Clinton as a
historic moment in Middle Eastern peacemaking. In his address
Clinton thanked members of the PNC for raising their hands and
rejecting "fully, finally, and forever" the ideological underpinning
of the Arab-Israeli conflict. Israel achieved a renewed cancellation
of the offensive clauses in the Palestinian National Charter, but the
real beneficiaries of Clinton's visit were the Palestinians. The visit
represented a significant tilt in America's position toward recognition of the Palestinian aspirations to statehood.

On 20 December the Israeli government took a highly significant decision—to suspend the implementation of the second pullback stipulated in the Wye River Memorandum until the
Palestinian Authority met a list of five conditions. Most of these
were new and were calculated to torpedo the peace process and to
put the blame on the Palestinians. The truth of the matter was that
the Palestinians had honored their obligations for the second stage
of Wye: the PNC ratified the cancellation of the 1968 charter,
while the Palestinian Authority issued orders against incitement
and continued to cooperate with Israel in security matters. Israel,
on the other hand, failed to fulfill its sole obligation for the second
stage of Wye: the transfer of 5 percent of the West Bank from exclusive Israeli control to joint Israeli-Palestinian control.

By turning his back on the Wye accord, Netanyahu renounced
a basic principle that was supposed to guide his policy, at least at
the declaratory level—namely, observance of all of his country's international agreements. In the past he had reneged on international agreements entered into by his predecessors, but on this
occasion he reneged on an agreement he himself had signed. The

State Department spokesman praised the efforts of the Palestinians to implement the Wye accord and stated that Israel must keep its part of the deal regardless of its domestic political difficulties.

Netanyahu's murky maneuvers eventually brought about the downfall of his government. On 23 December the Knesset decided by a vote of 80 to 30 to dissolve itself and hold new elections, although the government had served only two and a half years of its four-year term. During those two and a half years Netanyahu forfeited the trust of his party colleagues, of his coalition partners, of the Israeli public, of the Palestinian Authority, of the Arab world, and of the United States. The decision to hold new elections amounted to an admission by the Likud that Netanyahu had failed as a national leader and as prime minister. The fall of his government was probably inevitable because of the basic contradiction between its declared objective of striving for peace with the Arab world and its ideological makeup, which militated against trading land for peace. Because of this contradiction the Netanyahu government was unable to deal honestly or effectively with the Palestinians. To the outside world the government appeared to be knowingly and deliberately missing the chance to achieve peace with the Palestinians. Netanyahu himself was described by commentators in Israel as an "endemic refusenik" who created a dangerous tide in the relations with the Arab world and an apprehension of more wars and more *intifadas* among ordinary Israelis at home.

It is one of the ironies of Zionist history that Binyamin Netanyahu, the proud standard-bearer of Revisionist Zionism, betrayed the legacy of the founder of the movement by spurning the offer of peace with the Palestinians. Ze'ev Jabotinsky's strategy of the iron wall was designed to force the Palestinians to despair of the prospect of driving the Jews out of Palestine and to compel them to negotiate with the Jewish state from a position of weakness. During Yitzhak Rabin's tragically short premiership, the Labor Party put into action the second part of this strategy and achieved a breakthrough in the relations with the Palestinians. Netanyahu, on the other hand, remained fixated on the first part of his ideological mentor's strategy of the iron wall and consequently undid much of the good work of his predecessors. Under Netanyahu's leadership Israeli society sank into a situation of confusion and disarray that was without parallel in the country's history.

The general election, held on 17 May 1999, was one of the

most vitriolic in Israel's history. The five months of campaigning highlighted the country's bitter internal divisions, including the growing animosity between the secular and religious, Jews and Arabs, immigrants and veterans, and Sephardic and Ashkenazi Jews. The election was critical for both the future of Israel's relations with the Arabs and the future shape of the country's chronically divided society. The underlying question was whether Israel was going to be a liberal, enlightened, Western-orientated society or whether it was going to fall under the growing influence of the fundamentalist parties. Yet the campaign focused on Netanyahu's personality, with many Israelis accusing him of exacerbating the country's divisions by his paranoid personal style, duplicity, deviousness, and inability to get on with his colleagues. Three of his most senior ministers, who had left the cabinet at different times— Dan Meridor, David Levy, and Yitzhak Mordechai—supported his rival, Ehud Barak, for the premiership.

In some ways the campaign of May 1999 was the reverse of the campaign of May 1996. In 1996 the right was united; in 1999 it was bitterly divided. During his short period in power Netanyahu had gone a long way toward alienating his colleagues and destroying his party. In both campaigns the ruling party was overconfident and found the ground crumbling under its feet. The mood of the nation had also changed significantly in the intervening period. Netanyahu's narrow victory over Shimon Peres in 1996 illustrated how evenly the country was split between giving up land for peace and holding on to it at all costs. The shift was in favor of reaching a permanent peace settlement with the Palestinians and giving them a state over most of the land occupied by Israel since 1967. From a fifty-fifty split, the percentage of all Israelis who viewed a Palestinian state as inevitable, and who did not consider it a threat to Israel's security, had increased to over seventy. History may therefore judge the Netanyahu years as a necessary evil: a time when the great majority of Israelis were forced to come to terms with a two-state solution to the conflict with the Palestinians and to abandon the dream of Greater Israel.

Netanyahu had caused much anger on the right for compromising the ideology of Greater Israel, while also causing disappointment at the center and left of the political spectrum by appearing to cling to it despite all the palpable changes that were taking place in the attitude of the Arabs toward Israel. Under Netanyahu's leadership the peace process had ground to a halt, the economic situation deteriorated, and the country became more riven by ethnic divisions. Barak's approach was more pragmatic and conciliatory, and his aim was to recapture the middle ground of Israeli politics and to reunite the country. He reinvented the Labor Party as One Israel, jettisoning much of its ideology and reaching out to groups traditionally ignored by Israel's elite.

During the election campaign Barak stressed that Israel faced some fateful decisions but he was confident that they would lead to security and peace. He himself was a security hawk and a centrist and that was what the Israeli public wanted. As a former chief of staff and as Israel's most decorated soldier, Barak enjoyed credibility as a national leader, as a leader who would not sell his country short in dealing with the Arabs. Barak did not represent Peace Now, the left-wing organization that advocated a return to the 1967 borders. And he did not intend to repeat the mistakes of Shimon Peres by moving forward at a pace most Israelis found frightening. He presented himself as the heir to Yitzhak Rabin, a soldier who spent years of his life fighting the Arabs and then switched to making peace. He promised to follow Rabin down the Oslo path but with caution and without making light of the difficulties that lay ahead. He pledged to implement immediately the Wye River accord and to resume the negotiations on the final status of the territories with the Palestinian Authority. But at the same time he reiterated that Israel would not withdraw to the borders of 1967, that Israelis would control all of Jerusalem, and that large blocs of Jewish settlements in the West Bank and the Gaza Strip would be preserved. Barak also promised to restart the stalled talks with Syria and to reach within a year a peace deal that would include Israeli withdrawal from Lebanon. The difference between Barak and Netanyahu was the difference between a tough negotiator and a nonnegotiator.

In the direct election of the prime minister, Barak defeated Netanyahu decisively. Barak won 56 percent of the votes, against Netanyahu's 44 percent. Barak's Labor party, part of the One Israel umbrella group, lost 8 seats but ended up with 26, making it the largest party. The Likud party dropped from 32 seats to 19, significantly weakening its position on the political map. Shas, representing religious Jews with roots in the Middle East or North Africa, won an astounding 17 seats, up from 10 seats in the outgoing Knesset. The secular leftwing party Meretz, Labor's natural ally, won 10 seats. Shinui, an assertively secular party, won 6 seats on an anti-Orthodox campaign. A new Center party, led by Yitzhak Mordechai, also won 6 seats. The splintered Knesset complicated the formation of a governing coalition. But the strong personal mandate for change that Barak had won placed him in a relatively strong position to mold a coalition to suit his agenda.

Even before the final election results were declared, Netanyahu threw in the towel, wished his successor luck, and quit as leader of the Likud. Netanyahu's dethronement came as a huge relief in Washington and in Arab capitals because it opened up the prospect of reviving the moribund Arab-Israeli peace talks. Like his right-wing rival, Barak dismissed the vision of the "New Middle East" that Shimon Peres cherished. Unlike his rival, Barak was not fixated on the idea of Israel being surrounded by predators. Barak's success at the polls thus marked a new beginning in the search for peace in the Middle East. But at the same time there could be little doubt that Barak intended to govern as he had campaigned—as the political heir to Rabin the soldier-statesman, not Peres, the poet-philosopher.

The election of May 1999 was a major landmark in the history of the Jewish state. Its most far-reaching implication was for the relations between Israel and the Palestinians. Peace between Israel and the Palestinians was not just a pious hope or a distant dream. Israelis had actually touched it. Yitzhak Rabin laid the foundations for this peace with the Oslo accord of 1993 and the Oslo II agreement of 1995. His successor lost the election of 1996 not because the peace project had lost its appeal but largely due to the intervention of the Hamas suicide bombers. As prime minister Netanyahu employed all his destructive powers to freeze and undermine the Oslo agreements, only to discover how irreversible the Oslo process had become. In 1999 the Israeli electorate passed a severe judgment on Netanyahu and gave a clear mandate to Barak to follow in the footsteps of his slain mentor down the potholed path to peace. Barak won by a landslide. His victory entailed the biggest political change since the upheaval of 1977, when the Likud swept to power under the leadership of Menachem Begin. Not surprisingly, the result of the 1999 election was compared to a political earthquake. But it was more than an earthquake. It was the sunrise after the three dark and terrible years during which Israel had been led by the unreconstructed proponents of the iron wall.

NOTES

PROLOGUE: THE ZIONIST FOUNDATIONS

1. Yitzhak Epstein, "A Hidden Question" (Hebrew), *Ha-Shiloah,* March 1907.
2. Theodor Herzl, *The Jewish State* (New York, 1970).
3. Raphael Patai, ed., *The Complete Diaries of Theodor Herzl,* trans. Harry Zohn (New York, 1960), 2:581.
4. The literature on Zionism and the Arab question is extensive. The books I found particularly useful in writing this chapter are Simha Flapan, *Zionism and the Palestinians* (London, 1979); Shlomo Avineri, *The Making of Modern Zionism: The Intellectual Origins of the Jewish State* (New York, 1981); Shmuel Almog, ed., *Zionism and the Arabs: Essays* (Jerusalem 1983); Yosef Gorny, *Zionism and the Arabs, 1882–1948: A Study of Ideology* (Oxford, 1987); and David J. Goldberg, *To the Promised Land: A History of Zionist Thought from Its Origins to the Modern State of Israel* (London, 1996).
5. Theodor Herzl, *Old-New Land* (New York, 1960), 137–41.
6. Ze'ev Jabotinsky, *Writings: On the Road to Statehood* (Hebrew) (Jerusalem, 1959), 251–60.
7. Ibid., 260–66.
8. Ian Lustick, "To Build and to Be Built By: Israel and the Hidden Logic of the Iron Wall," *Israel Studies* 1, no. 1 (Spring 1996).
9. Quoted in Shabtai Teveth, *Ben-Gurion and the Palestinian Arabs: From Peace to War* (Oxford, 1985), 166.
10. David Ben-Gurion, *My Talks with Arab Leaders* (Jerusalem, 1972), 80.
11. David Ben-Gurion, *Letters to Paula* (London, 1971), 153–57.
12. Menachem Begin, *The Revolt,* rev. ed. (New York, 1977), 433.

CHAPTER 1: THE EMERGENCE OF ISRAEL 1947–1949

1. Ezra Danin, "Talk with Abdullah, 17 Nov. 1947," S25/4004, Central Zionist Archives (CZA), Jerusalem, and Elias Sasson to Moshe Shertok, 20 Nov. 1947,

S25/1699, CZA. See also Avi Shlaim, *Collusion across the Jordan: King Abdullah, the Zionist Movement, and the Partition of Palestine* (Oxford, 1988), 110–17.

2. David Ben-Gurion, *War Diary: The War of Independence, 1948–1949* (Hebrew), ed. Gershon Rivlin and Elhanan Orren (Tel Aviv, 1982), 1:97–106.

3. Benny Morris, *The Birth of the Palestinian Refugee Problem, 1947–1949* (Cambridge, 1987), 62–63.

4. Iraq, *Report of the Parliamentary Committee of Inquiry on the Palestinian Problem* (Arabic) (Baghdad, 1949), 131.

5. Provisional State Council, *Protocols, 18 April–13 May 1948* (Hebrew) (Jerusalem, 1978), 40–44. See also Shlaim, *Collusion across the Jordan*, 205–14.

6. Interview with Lieutenant General Yigael Yadin.

7. Ben-Gurion, *War Diary*, 2:427.

8. Simha Flapan, *The Birth of Israel: Myths and Realities* (New York, 1987); Benny Morris, *The Birth of the Palestinian Refugee Problem* and *1948 and After: Israel and the Palestinians* (Oxford, 1990; rev. and exp. ed., 1994); Ilan Pappé, *Britain and the Arab-Israeli Conflict, 1948–51* (London, 1988) and *The Making of the Arab-Israeli Conflict, 1947–51* (London, 1992); Shlaim, *Collusion across the Jordan* and "The Debate about 1948," *International Journal of Middle East Studies* 27, no. 3 (Aug. 1995).

9. Flapan, *Birth of Israel*, 187–99, and Morris, *1948 and After*, 13–16.

10. Among the more revealing sources on the discord and deception inside the Arab coalition are Iraq, *Report of the Parliamentary Committee of Inquiry on the Palestine Problem;* Salih Saib al-Jubury, *The Palestine Misfortune and Its Political and Military Secrets* (Arabic) (Beirut, 1970); and Abdullah al-Tall, *The Palestine Catastrophe* (Arabic) (Cairo, 1959).

11. Interview with Yaacov Shimoni.

12. Ben-Gurion, *War Diary*, 2:453–54.

13. Sir John Bagot Glubb, *A Soldier with the Arabs* (London, 1957), 110.

14. Uri Bar-Joseph, *The Best of Enemies: Israel and Transjordan in the War of 1948* (London, 1987).

15. Interviews with Lieutenant General Yigael Yadin, Major General Moshe Carmel, Ze'ev Sharef, and Yehoshua Palmon.

16. Yehoshua Freundlich, ed., *Documents on the Foreign Policy of Israel (DPFI)*, vol. 1, *14 May–30 September 1948* (Jerusalem, 1981), 632–36.

17. *The Autobiography of Nahum Goldmann: Sixty Years of Jewish Life* (New York, 1969), 289–90.

18. Yehoshua Freundlich, ed., *DFPI*, vol. 2, *October 1948–April 1949* (Jerusalem, 1984), 126–27.

19. In this section I have made extensive use of Yemima Rosenthal's introduction, written in Hebrew, to the volume of official documents she edited on this subject: *DFPI*, vol. 3, *Armistice Negotiations with the Arab States, December 1948–July 1949* (Jerusalem, 1983).

20. Ben-Gurion, *War Diary*, 3:884–87.

21. Patrick Seale, *The Struggle for Syria: A Study in Post-War Arab Politics, 1945–1958* (London, 1965), chap. 5; Miles Copeland, *The Game of Nations: The Amorality of Power Politics* (London, 1969), 42–46; and Wm. Roger Louis, *The British Empire in the Middle East, 1945–1951: Arab Nationalism, the United States, and Postwar Imperialism* (Oxford, 1984), 621–26.

22. Record of Consultation held on 19 April 1949, Box 2441, File 7, Israel State Archives, Jerusalem (hereafter ISA). See also Avi Shlaim, "Husni Zaim and the Plan to Resettle Palestinian Refugees in Syria," *Journal of Palestine Studies* 15, no. 4 (Summer 1986).

23. Ben-Gurion's diary, 16 April 1949, the Ben-Gurion Archive, Sede-Boker.

24. Ben-Gurion's diary, 30 April 1949.

25. Protocol of cabinet meeting, 24 May 1949, ISA.

26. For a comprehensive treatment of the Arab and Israeli positions, see Rony E. Gabbay, *A Political Study of the Arab-Jewish Conflict: The Arab Refugee Problem* (Geneva, 1959).

27. This is explicitly stated in what is probably the most comprehensive decision on this subject, the one taken by the Arab League Council on 23 Sept. 1952. General Secretariat, the League of Arab States, Decisions of the Council from the first session to the nineteenth session (4 July 1945–7 Sept. 1953), p. 103; copy in the library of the Harry S. Truman Research Institute for the Advancement of Peace, the Hebrew University of Jerusalem, Jerusalem.

28. Protocol of cabinet meeting, 29 May 1949, ISA.

29. Ben-Gurion's diary, 14 July 1949.

30. Ben-Gurion's diary, 18 July 1949.

CHAPTER 2: CONSOLIDATION 1949–1953

1. Proceedings of the Knesset, 4 April 1949.

2. Ben-Gurion, *War Diary*, 3:937, entry for 8 Jan. 1949.

3. Proceedings of the Knesset, 4 April 1949.

4. Ibid.

5. Ibid.

6. Ben-Gurion, *War Diary*, 3:958. See also Tom Segev, *1949: The First Israelis* (New York, 1986), 18–20.

7. Interview with Isser Harel.

8. Yeroham Cohen, *By Light and in Darkness* (Hebrew) (Tel Aviv, 1969), 274.

9. Interviews with Lieutenant General Yigael Yadin, Major General Yehoshafat Harkabi, Joshua Palmon, Dr. Walter Eytan, Yaacov Shimoni, and Gershon Avner.

10. Mordechai Bar-On, "Status Quo Before—or After? Reflections on the Defense Policy of Israel, 1949–1958" (Hebrew), *Iyunim Bitkumat Israel* 5 (1995).

11. Interview with Yaacov Shimoni.

12. Interview with Gideon Rafael.

13. Appendix no. 9, "Report on the Activities of the General Secretariat," record of the 11th session of the Arab League's Council, 25.3.1950–17.6.1950, p. 161; copy in the library of the Harry S. Truman Research Institute for the Advancement of Peace, the Hebrew University of Jerusalem, Jerusalem.

14. This account of the Lausanne conference draws heavily on the introduction by Yemima Rosenthal to the volume of documents she edited: *DFPI*, vol. 4, *May–December 1949* (Jerusalem, 1986).

15. Ben-Gurion's diary, 14 Dec. 1949.

16. For a detailed account of these talks see Shlaim, *Collusion across the Jordan*.

17. Interview with Moshe Sasson.

18. Sir Alec Kirkbride, *From the Wings: Amman Memoirs, 1947–1951* (London, 1976), 112.

19. Ben-Gurion's diary, 26 Nov. 1949.

20. The Conference of Ambassadors, 17–23 July 1950, Third Session: "Israel and the Arab World," 36-9, 112/18, ISA.

21. Ben-Gurion's diary, 13 Feb. 1951.

22. Ben-Gurion's diary, 21 and 23 July 1951.

23. Israel and the Arab States, a consultation in the Prime Minister's Office, 1 Oct. 1952, 2446/7, ISA.

24. The main sources used for this section were the introductions and the official

documents in *DFPI* for 1951, 1952, and 1953; Yehezkel Hameiri, "Demilitarization and Conflict Resolution: The Question of the Demilitarized Zones on the Israel-Syria Border, 1949–1967" (Hebrew) (M.A. thesis, University of Haifa, 1978); Nissim Bar-Yaacov, *The Israel-Syria Armistice: Problems of Implementation, 1949–1966* (Jerusalem, 1967); Aryeh Shalev, *The Israel-Syria Armistice Regime, 1949–1955* (Boulder, Colo., 1993); and Moshe Ma'oz, *Syria and Israel: From War to Peacemaking* (Oxford, 1995).

25. Eli Nissan, "Who Is Afraid of Yosef Tekoah?" *Bamahaneh* (IDF weekly), 13, no. 1024 (26 Dec. 1967); and interviews with Gershon Avner, Mordechai Gazit, and Major General Yehoshafat Harkabi.
26. *DFPI,* 1951, 249–50.
27. *DFPI,* 1952, 585–86.
28. Ibid., 592–93.
29. *DFPI,* 1953, introd. and 321–22; Simha Blass, *Water in Strife and Action* (Hebrew) (Ramat Gan, 1973), 183–84; Ben-Gurion's diary, 17 and 23 April 1953; and Shalev, *Israel-Syria Armistice Regime,* 156.
30. *DFPI,* 1952, 396.
31. Interview with Yaacov Shimoni.
32. *DFPI,* 1952, 454–56.
33. Ibid., 575–78.
34. Ibid., 587.
35. Interview with Abdel Rahman Sadeq.
36. *DFPI,* 1953, 82–83.
37. Ibid., 126–27.
38. Ibid., 356–57.
39. Ibid., 395.
40. Ibid., 414–15.
41. Ibid., 729–31.
42. David Tal, "The Development of Israel's Day-to-Day Security Conception, 1949–1956" (Hebrew) (Ph.D. thesis, Tel Aviv University, 1994), 1–4.
43. Benny Morris, *Israel's Border Wars, 1949–1956: Arab Infiltration, Israeli Retaliation, and the Countdown to the Suez War* (Oxford, 1993), 49 and 412.
44. Ibid., 412–16.
45. Interview with King Hussein of Jordan.
46. See, for example, Lieutenant General J. B. Glubb, "Violence on the Jordan-Israel Border: A Jordanian View," *Foreign Affairs,* 32, no. 4, (July 1954), and his autobiography, *A Soldier with the Arabs* (London, 1957), chaps. 13–15.
47. Glubb, "Violence on the Jordan-Israel Border."
48. Minister of Defense to the Prime Minister, 27.2.1952, collection of Jordanian records of the General Investigations, General Security, and Military Intelligence Departments captured by the IDF during the June 1967 war. Private Papers deposited in the Ben-Gurion Archive, Sede-Boker.
49. Ibid., Protocol of a meeting held with district commanders on 2.7.1952 and chaired by Ahmed Sidqi al-Jundi.
50. *DFPI,* 1953, introd.
51. Ibid., 94–95.
52. Ibid., introd.
53. Interview with Gideon Rafael.
54. *DFPI,* 1953, 766–68.
55. Shabtai Teveth, *Moshe Dayan* (London: Weidenfeld and Nicolson, 1972), 211–14.
56. Commander E. H. Hutchison, *Violent Truce: A Military Observer Looks at the Arab-Israeli Conflict, 1951–1955* (London, 1956), 44.
57. *DFPI,* 1953, introd. and editorial note, 769–71.
58. *DFPI,* 1953, companion vol., 451–52.

59. Ariel Sharon with David Chanoff, *Warrior: The Autobiography of Ariel Sharon* (London, 1989), 90–91.
60. Gideon Rafael, *Destination Peace: Three Decades of Israeli Foreign Policy* (New York, 1981), 32–34.
61. Morris, *Israel's Border Wars*, 67.
62. The text of the report was posthumously published in David Ben-Gurion, "Army and State," *Ma'arachot*, 279–80 (May–June 1981).
63. Moshe Sharett, *A Personal Diary* (Hebrew), 8 vols., 1953–57 (Tel Aviv, 1978), entry for 19 Oct. 1953, 1:53–55. Henceforth only the date of entry into the diary will be cited, without volume and page references.

CHAPTER 3: ATTEMPTS AT ACCOMMODATION 1953–1955

1. Quoted in Michael Brecher, *The Foreign Policy System of Israel: Setting, Images, Process* (Oxford, 1972), 253.
2. Gabriel Sheffer, *Moshe Sharett: Biography of a Political Moderate* (Oxford, 1996).
3. Quoted in Zaki Shalom, *David Ben-Gurion, the State of Israel and the Arabs, 1949–1956* (Hebrew) (Beersheba, 1995), 10.
4. Yaacov Erez, *Conversations with Moshe Dayan* (Hebrew) (Tel Aviv, 1981), 33.
5. Brecher, *Foreign Policy System of Israel*, 285.
6. Protocol of the Political Committee, 12 May 1954, Labor Party Archive, Beit Berl, Kfar Saba.
7. David Ben-Gurion, *Vision and Fulfillment* (Hebrew) (Tel Aviv, 1958), 5:125.
8. Ibid., 171.
9. Golda Meir, *My Life* (London, 1975), 239.
10. Pinhas Lavon, *In the Paths of Reflection and Struggle* (Hebrew) (Tel Aviv, 1968), 153–63.
11. Protocol of the Central Committee, 15 April 1954, Labor Party Archive.
12. Sharett's diary, 29 and 30 Nov. 1953.
13. Moshe Dayan, *Milestones: An Autobiography* (Hebrew) (Jerusalem, 1976), 191.
14. Ury Avnery, *Israel without Zionists: A Plea for Peace in the Middle East* (New York, 1968), 133–34.
15. Quoted in Tal, "Development of Israel's Day-to-Day Security Conception," 132 (emphasis in original).
16. Moshe Dayan, "Military Operations in Peacetime," (Hebrew), *Ma'arachot*, May 1959.
17. Moshe Sharett, "Israel and the Arabs—War and Peace (Reflections on the Years 1947–1957)" (Hebrew), *Ot*, Sept. 1966. The talk was given in Oct. 1957 but the text was published only after Sharett's death. An English translation of the text appeared in the *Jerusalem Post*, 18 Oct. 1966.
18. Dayan, *Milestones*, 139.
19. Ibid.
20. Sharett's diary, 31 Jan. 1954.
21. Ibid., 27 Feb. 1954.
22. Ibid., 28 Feb. 1954.
23. Kirsten E. Schulze, *Israel's Covert Diplomacy in Lebanon* (London, 1998), 39–40.
24. Sharett's diary, 31 March 1954.
25. Protocol of the Political Committee, 12 May 1954, Labor Party Archive.
26. Sharett's diary, 17 May 1954.
27. Quoted in Haggai Eshed, *Who Gave the Order?: The Lavon Affair* (Hebrew) (Jerusalem, 1979), 38.
28. Sharett's diary, 31 May 1954.
29. Ibid., 6 June 1954.

30. Protocol of the Political Committee, 27 June 1954, Labor Party Archive.
31. Interview with Yaacov Shimoni.
32. Dayan, *Milestones,* 122.
33. Rafael, *Destination Peace,* 36.
34. Sharett's diary, report dated 12 Jan. 1955.
35. Ibid., 19 July 1954.
36. Record of a meeting on the Anglo-Egyptian agreement for the evacuation of the Suez Canal Zone, 3 Aug. 1954, 2446/8, ISA.
37. Annual Report on Israel for 1954, 18 Jan. 1955, FO 371/115810, Public Record Office (PRO).
38. Sharett's diary, letter dated 26 Oct. 1954.
39. Ibid.
40. E. L. M. Burns, *Between Arab and Israeli* (Beirut, 1969), 41–44.
41. Sharett's diary, letter dated 26 Oct. 1954.
42. Sharett's diary, letter dated 22 Dec. 1954.
43. Sharett's diary, 13 Jan. 1955.
44. Ibid., 18 Jan. 1955.
45. Ibid., 23 Jan. 1955.
46. Interview with Tahseen Bashir.
47. Jack Nicholls to Evelyn Shuckburgh, 14 Dec. 1954, FO 371/111107, PRO.
48. Report by Dan Avni on the situation in Egypt, 10 Oct. 1954, 2409/2, ISA.
49. Interview with Abdel Rahman Sadeq.
50. Gideon Rafael to Moshe Sharett, 19 Jan. 1956, Summary and Lessons of the Contacts and Negotiations with Egypt, 1949–1955, 2454/2, ISA.
51. Sharett to Nasser, 21 Dec. 1954, 2454/2, ISA.
52. Included in Divon to Sharett, 31 Dec. 1954, 2453/20, ISA.
53. Rafael to Sharett, 22 Dec. 1954, 2553/21, ISA.
54. Sharett's diary, 26 Jan. 1955.
55. Ibid., 27 Jan. 1955.
56. Rafael, *Destination Peace,* 39.
57. Sharett's diary, 10 Feb. 1955.
58. Interview with Yaacov Shimoni.
59. Quoted in Eshed, *Who Gave the Order?,* 128.
60. Sharett's diary, 10 Jan. 1955.
61. Rafael, *Destination Peace,* 41.
62. Eshed, *Who Gave the Order?,* 46.
63. Interview with Mordechai Bar-On.
64. Michael Bar-Zohar, *Ben-Gurion: A Political Biography* (Hebrew), 3 vols. (Tel Aviv, 1975–77), 3:1126.
65. Sharett's diary, 20 and 21 Feb. 1955.
66. Ibid., 27 Feb. 1955.
67. Ibid., 6 March 1955.
68. Kennett Love, *Suez: The Twice-Fought War* (New York, 1969), 1.
69. Rafael, *Destination Peace,* 40.
70. Love, *Suez,* 83.
71. Burns, *Between Arab and Israeli,* 20.
72. Protocol of the Political Committee, 16 Oct. 1955, Labor Party Archive.
73. Sharett's diary, 12 March 1955.
74. Interview with Mordechai Bar-On.
75. Ben-Gurion's diary, 3 March 1955.
76. Zaki Shalom, *Policy in the Shadow of Controversy: Israel's Day-to-Day Security Policy, 1949–1956* (Hebrew) (Tel Aviv, 1996), 46–47.
77. Moshe Dayan, *Diary of the Sinai Campaign* (New York, 1967), 5.
78. Love, *Suez,* 85.

79. Ehud Ya'ari, *Egypt and the Fedayeen, 1953–1956* (Hebrew) (Givat Haviva, 1975). This pamphlet contains photographs of a sample of original documents in Arabic and a summary of the findings in English at the end, on pp. 40–42.
80. Moshe Dayan, *Living with the Bible* (Hebrew) (Jerusalem, 1981), 75–76.
81. Sharett's diary, 25 and 27 March, 1955.
82. Ibid., 11 April 1955.
83. Ibid., 4 April 1955.
84. "Israel's Policy toward the Western Powers: Conclusions of the Conference of Ambassadors," 7 June 1955, 2446/8 ISA; and Ben-Gurion's diary, 12 May 1955.
85. "Israel's Policy towards the Western Powers: Conclusions of the Conference of Ambassadors," 7 June 1955, and "Summary of the Prime Minister's Talk at the Conference of Ambassadors on 28.5.1955," 2446/8 ISA.
86. Sharett's diary, 26 May 1955.
87. Ibid., 16 May 1955.
88. Ibid., 28 May 1955.
89. Ibid., 17 May 1955.
90. Ibid., 17, 18, 19 May 1955.
91. Ben-Gurion's diary, 30 July 1955.
92. Ibid., 31 July 1955.
93. Sharett's diary, 31 July 1955.
94. Ibid., 7 Aug. 1955.
95. Ibid., 8 Aug. 1955; and Protocol of the Central Committee, 8 Aug. 1955, Labor Party Archive.
96. Elmore Jackson, *Middle East Mission: The Story of a Major Bid for Peace in the Time of Nasser and Ben-Gurion* (New York, 1983), 40–45.
97. Sharett's diary, 24 Aug. 1955; Dayan, *Milestones,* 150–52; and Bar Zohar, *Ben-Gurion,* 3:1146–48.
98. Sharett's diary, 5 Oct. 1955.
99. Ibid., 12 Oct. 1955.
100. Interview with Gideon Rafael.
101. Sharett's diary, 14 Oct. 1955.
102. Ibid., 19 Oct. 1955.
103. Ibid., 22 Oct. 1955.
104. Ibid., 25, 26 and 27 Oct. 1955.
105. Dayan, *Diary of the Sinai Campaign,* 12.
106. Mordechai Bar-On, *Challenge and Quarrel: The Road to the Sinai Campaign— 1956* (Hebrew) (Beersheba, 1991), 39–41.

CHAPTER 4: THE ROAD TO SUEZ 1955–1957

1. Interview with Colonel Mordechai Bar-On.
2. Yair Evron, "The Interrelationship between Foreign Policy and Defense Policy in the Years 1949–1955," (Hebrew), *Skira Hodshit,* 35, no. 11 (Dec. 1988).
3. Interview with Colonel Mordechai Bar-On.
4. Bar-On, *Challenge and Quarrel,* 45.
5. Interview with Major General Uzi Narkis.
6. Shimon Shamir, "The Collapse of Project Alpha," in Wm. Roger Louis and Roger Owen, eds., *Suez 1956: The Crisis and Its Consequences* (Oxford, 1989), 81–82.
7. Annual Report for 1955 on Israel, 20 Feb. 1956, FO 371/121692, PRO.
8. Dayan, *Milestones,* 162–65.
9. Interviews with Colonel Meir Pail, Major General Uzi Narkis, Major General Meir Amit, and Lieutenant General Chaim Bar-Lev.

10. Dayan, *Milestones,* 165.
11. Dayan, *Diary of the Sinai Campaign,* 13–15; and interview with Chaim Yisraeli.
12. Sharret's diary, 13 Feb. 1955; Hutchison, *Violent Truce,* 109–10; Burns, *Between Arab and Israeli,* 107–8; Hameiri, "Demilitarization and Conflict Resolution," 107; Tal, "Development of Israel's Day-to-Day Security Conception," 329; and Morris, *Israel's Border Wars,* 364–69.
13. Sharett to Ben-Gurion, 27 Nov. 1955, 2454/11, ISA.
14. Sharett's diary, 16 Dec. 1955.
15. Dayan, *Milestones,* 170; and Sharon, *Warrior,* 124–25.
16. Sharon, *Warrior,* 124.
17. Bar-On, *Challenge and Quarrel,* 56–58.
18. Interview with Major General Uzi Narkis.
19. Sharett's diary, 10 Dec. 1955.
20. Sharett to Ben-Gurion, 12 Dec. 1955, 2454/11, ISA.
21. Abba Eban, *An Autobiography* (London, 1977), 199.
22. Sharett's diary, 19 Dec. 1955.
23. Brecher, *Foreign Policy System of Israel,* 380–81.
24. Sharett's diary, 23, 25, 27, and 28 Dec. 1955.
25. Protocol of the Political Committee, 27 Dec. 1955, Labor Party Archive.
26. Rafael, *Destination Peace,* 48.
27. Weekly Survey No. 198, 25 Jan. 1956, probably written by Gideon Rafael, 2454/11, ISA.
28. Interview with Gershon Avner.
29. Memorandum from the Secretary of State to the Under Secretary of State (Hoover), 12 Dec. 1955, *FRUS,* 1955, 14:848–49.
30. Memorandum of a Conversation, Department of State, 13 Dec. 1955, ibid., 856–57.
31. Dayan, *Milestones,* 174–75.
32. Ben-Gurion's diary, 17 Jan. 1956.
33. Interview with Gershon Avner.
34. Sharett to Dulles, 16 Jan. 1956, 2456/3, ISA.
35. The main sources for the following account of the Anderson mission are David Ben-Gurion, *Negotiations with Nasser* (Jerusalem, Israel Information Center, n.d.); Rafael *Destination Peace,* 48–52; Yaacov Herzog, *A People that Dwells Alone* (London, 1975), 237–42; Mohamed Hassanein Heikal, *The Suez Files* (Arabic) (Cairo, 1986), 387–93 and documents, 780–84; Shamir, "Collapse of Project Alpha," 80–81; and interviews with Gideon Rafael and Gershon Avner.
36. Ben-Gurion's diary, 15 Jan. 1956.
37. Isser Harel, *Security and Democracy* (Hebrew) (Tel Aviv, 1989), 395–401.
38. Interview with Gershon Avner.
39. Dayan *Milestones,* 179–82; and Sharett's diary, 18 March 1956.
40. Sir John Nicholls to Selwyn Lloyd, 26 Feb. 1957, "Israel: Annual Review for 1956," FO 371/128087, PRO.
41. Byroade to the Department of State, 9 April 1956, *FRUS,* 1955–57, 15:498–500.
42. Dayan *Milestones,* 200.
43. Interview with Yitzhak Ben-Aharon.
44. Proceedings of the Knesset, 19 June 1956.
45. Ben-Gurion to S. Yizhar, 21 June 1956, 2375/49, ISA.
46. Ben-Gurion's speech of 18 Jan. 1957, quoted in Sharett's diary for that date.
47. Interview with Gershon Avner.
48. Interview with Shimon Peres.
49. Colonel (res.) Yuval Ne'eman, "The Link with the British and the French in the Sinai Campaign," *Ma'arachot* (Hebrew), 306–7 (Dec. 1986–Jan. 1987).

50. Bar-On, *Challenge and Quarrel,* 148.
51. Shimon Peres, *Battling for Peace: Memoirs* (London, 1995), 119–21; Dayan, *Milestones,* 205–7; and interviews with Major General Yehoshafat Harkabi and Colonel Mordechai Bar-On.
52. Ben-Gurion's diary, 29 July 1956.
53. Ibid., 30 July 1956.
54. Ibid., 29 July 1956; and Dayan, *Milestones,* 218–19.
55. Ben-Gurion's diary, 29 July 1956.
56. Peres, *Battling for Peace,* 121–22.
57. Bar-On, *Challenge and Quarrel,* 193–94.
58. Ben-Gurion's diary, 10 Aug. 1956.
59. Ibid., 25 Sept. 1956; Dayan, *Milestones,* 230–31; and Shimon Peres, *David's Sling: The Arming of Israel* (London, 1970), 189–92.
60. Dayan, *Milestones,* 233–40; Peres, *David's Sling,* 192–97; and the diary of the bureau of chief of staff Moshe Dayan for Sept. 1956, written and edited by Mordechai Bar-On. I am grateful to Mordechai Bar-On for putting this part of the diary at my disposal.
61. Anthony Nutting, *No End of a Lesson: The Story of Suez* (London, 1957), 92.
62. Interview with Sir Anthony Nutting.
63. Mordechai Bar-On, "David Ben-Gurion and the Sèvres Collusion," in Louis and Owen, eds., *Suez 1956,* 149–50.
64. Ibid., 150.
65. Ben-Gurion's diary, 18 Oct. 1956.
66. Ibid., 17 Oct. 1956.
67. Interview with Shimon Peres.
68. Ben-Gurion's diary, 22 Oct. 1956; Dayan *Milestones,* 253–55; and Bar-Zohar, *Ben-Gurion,* 3:1229–31.
69. Christian Pineau, *Suez 1956* (Paris, 1976); Abel Thomas *Comment Israël fut sauvé: Les Secrets de l'expédition de Suez* (Paris, 1978); Selwyn Lloyd, *Suez 1956: A Personal Account* (London, 1978); Moshe Dayan, *Story of My Life* (London, 1976); Peres, *Battling for Peace;* "Ben-Gurion's Diary—The Suez-Sinai Campaign," edited and introduced by Selwyn Ilan Troen, in Selwyn Ilan Troen and Moshe Shemesh, eds., *The Suez-Sinai Campaign: Retrospective and Reappraisal* (London, 1990); Donald Logan, "Suez: Meetings at Sèvres, 22–25 October 1956"; and Memorandum by Sir Patrick Dean, 1986. I am grateful to Sir Donald Logan for giving me copies of the last two documents. An edited version of his account was published as "Collusion at Suez," *Financial Times,* 8 Jan. 1986.
70. Bar-On, *Challenge and Quarrel.* Bar-On originally wrote this detailed account of the events leading up to the Sinai Campaign at Dayan's request in 1957 with full access to the official documents. He was only allowed to publish it in Hebrew in 1991. Bar-On also published a book based on his doctoral thesis: *The Gates of Gaza: Israel's Road to Suez and Back, 1955–1957* (New York, 1994).
71. Ben-Gurion's diary, 24 Oct. 1956 (emphasis in original).
72. Ibid., 25 Oct. 1956.
73. Interview with Sir Donald Logan.
74. Ben-Gurion's diary, 25 Oct. 1956.
75. Peres, *Battling for Peace,* 130.
76. Yossi Melman, "A Royal Present," *Ha'aretz,* 11 Oct. 1992.
77. "The Suez Crisis—BBC Version" was shown on BBC 1 on 22 Oct. 1996. Jeremy Bennett was the producer; Keith Kyle and I were the historical consultants. Shimon Peres, who was foreign minister at the time, gave us permission to photocopy the Protocol of Sèvres after protracted negotiations and only after we produced letters from the British and French governments saying that they

had no objection to our request. The protocol is now available at the Ben-Gurion Archive in Sede-Boker and in the Israel State Archives in Jerusalem. S. Ilan Troen, "The Protocol of Sèvres: British/French/Israeli Collusion against Egypt, 1956," *Israel Studies* 1, no. 2 (Fall 1996), reproduces the original French text of the protocol, a translation into English, the annex to the protocol, and the letters of ratification. An English translation of the protocol and the annex also appears in Keith Kyle, *Suez* (London, 1991), appendix A, 565–67.

78. For a fuller account see Avi Shlaim, "The Protocol of Sèvres, 1956: Anatomy of a War Plot," *International Affairs* 73, no. 3 (July 1997).

79. Bar-On, "David Ben-Gurion and the Sèvres Collusion," in Louis and Owen, eds., *Suez 1956,* 154–58.

80. Abba Eban, *Personal Witness: Israel through My Eyes* (New York, 1992), 257.

81. Interview with Colonel Mordechai Bar-On.

82. Ben-Gurion's diary, 17, 19, 22, 24, 25, and 26 Oct. 1956.

83. Ibid., 7 Nov. 1956.

84. Interview with Major General Yosef Avidar.

85. Moshe Zak, *Forty Years of Dialogue with Moscow* (Hebrew) (Tel Aviv, 1988), 180.

86. Bar-Zohar, *Ben-Gurion,* 3:1273–74.

87. Herzog, *A People That Dwells Alone,* 243–48.

88. Michael Brecher, *Decisions in Israel's Foreign Policy* (London, 1974), 287–88.

89. Interview with Gershon Avner; Eban, *Personal Witness,* 277; and Rafael, *Destination Peace,* 62–63.

90. Eban, *Personal Witness,* 279–85.

CHAPTER 5: THE ALLIANCE OF THE PERIPHERY 1957–1963

1. Lecture by Moshe Shemesh, "The Sinai War between Illusion and Reality: Egypt and the Arab States after the War," 21 Nov. 1996, University of Haifa, conference on the fortieth anniversary of the Sinai War.

2. In writing this chapter, I benefited particularly from three books: Bar-Zohar, *Ben-Gurion,* vol. 3; *David Ben-Gurion: The First Prime Minister: Selected Documents, 1947–1963* (Hebrew), editing and historical notes by Eli Shaltiel (Jerusalem, 1996); and David Shaham, *Israel—50 Years* (Hebrew) (Tel Aviv, 1998).

3. Interview with Yitzhak Ben-Aharon.

4. Dayan, *Milestones,* 348–49.

5. Ben-Gurion to Dulles, 22 Aug. 1957, in Shaltiel, *David Ben-Gurion,* 406; and Harel, *Security and Democracy,* 408.

6. Ben-Gurion's diary, 4 Jan. 1958.

7. Interview with Major General Uzi Narkis.

8. Interview with Major General Yehoshafat Harkabi.

9. One discussion of the development is Michael Bar-Zohar, "Ben-Gurion and the Policy of the Periphery," in Itamar Rabinovich and Jehuda Reinharz, eds., *Israel in the Middle East* (New York, 1984) 164–74.

10. Haggai Eshed, *Reuven Shiloah: The Man behind the Mossad* (London, 1997), xxvi–xxxi and 311–14.

11. Harel, *Security and Democracy,* 409–10.

12. Central Intelligence Agency, *Israel: Foreign Intelligence and Security Services Survey* (Hebrew), trans. and ed. Yossi Melman (Tel Aviv, 1982), 57.

13. Ben-Gurion to Emperor Haile Selassie, 6 Nov. 1958, in Shaltiel, *Ben-Gurion,* 418–19.

14. Interview with Gershon Avner.

15. Harel, *Security and Democracy,* 410.
16. Interview with Gershon Avner.
17. Ben-Gurion's diary, 14 July 1958.
18. Selwyn Lloyd to Sir Francis Rundall (Tel Aviv), 12 Aug. 1958, FO 371/134285, PRO.
19. Ben-Gurion's diary, 17 July 1958.
20. Interview with King Hussein.
21. Ben-Gurion's diary, 17 July 1958.
22. Ibid., 18 July 1958; and Sir F. Rundall to FO, 19 July 1958, FO 371/34284, PRO.
23. David Ben-Gurion to Dwight Eisenhower, 24 July 1958, 4316/7, ISA.
24. *FRUS,* 1958–60, 13:74, n. 2.
25. Ibid., 77–79.
26. Ibid., 82–83.
27. Lord Hood to Sir William Hayter, 9 Sept. 1958, FO 371/134279, PRO.
28. Bar-Zohar, *Ben-Gurion,* 3:1364.
29. Yuval Ne'eman, "Israel in the Age of Nuclear Weapons: Threat and Deterrence beyond 1995," (Hebrew), *Nativ* 8, no. 5 (1995). See also Yair Evron, *Israel's Nuclear Dilemma* (London, 1994).
30. Interview with Yitzhak Ben-Aharon.
31. Interview with Simha Dinitz.
32. Peres, *Battling for Peace,* 136.
33. Avner Cohen, *Israel and the Bomb* (New York, 1998), 108.
34. Meeting of President Kennedy and Prime Minister Ben-Gurion, 30 May 1961, 3294/7, ISA.
35. Feldman to Kennedy, 19 Aug. 1962, *FRUS,* 1961–63, 18:64–66; and Meron Medzini, *The Proud Jewess: Golda Meir and the Vision of Israel: A Political Biography* (Hebrew) (Tel Aviv, 1990), 289–91.
36. Medzini, *Proud Jewess,* 282–83.
37. Eshed, *Who Gave the Order?,* 251–55.
38. Shaham, *Israel—50 Years,* 206–8.
39. Harel, *Security and Democracy,* 411–12 and 427–33.
40. Ben-Gurion's diary, 5 Nov. 1962.
41. Ibid., 27 Feb. 1963.
42. Bar-Zohar, *Ben-Gurion,* 3:1526–29.
43. Press release, 29 April 1963, 2454/17, ISA.
44. Rafael, *Destination Peace,* 125–26. Rafael cites 12 May as the date of the letter, but American documents give the date as 26 April. For a summary of Ben-Gurion's letter, see *FRUS,* 1961–63, 18:481–82.
45. Central Intelligence Agency, memorandum for the director, "Consequences of Israeli Acquisition of Nuclear Capability," 6 March 1963, John F. Kennedy Library, copy in the Ben-Gurion Archive.
46. Abba Eban to Chaim Yahil, 30 April 1963, Yaacov Herzog to Gideon Rafael, 5 May 1963, Katriel Katz to Shimshon Arad, 3 June 1963, memorandum "The United States and Israel's Security," 10 June 1963; and consultation on Israel-U.S. relations, 13 June 1963, 3377/6, ISA.
47. Interview with Gershon Avner.

CHAPTER 6: POOR LITTLE SAMSON 1963–1969

1. Ezer Weizman, *On Eagles' Wings: The Personal Story of the Leading Commander of the Israeli Air Force* (London, 1976), 262–63.
2. Interview with Miriam Eshkol.

3. *FRUS*, 1961–63, 18:624–26.
4. Interview with Shimon Peres.
5. Interview with Avraham Harman.
6. Protocol of the Meeting of the Secretariat, 19 June 1964, Labor Party Archives.
7. Interview with Yitzhak Ben-Aharon.
8. Eban, *Personal Witness*, 327.
9. Interview with Major General Meir Amit.
10. Eitan Haber, *Today War Will Break Out: The Reminiscences of Brigadier General Israel Lior, Aide-de-Camp to Prime Ministers Levi Eshkol and Golda Meir* (Hebrew) (Tel Aviv, 1987), 64–65.
11. Interview with King Hussein.
12. Report by Yaacov Herzog to Levi Eshkol, 24 Sept. 1963, quoted in Moshe Zak, *Hussein Makes Peace: Thirty Years and Another Year on the Road to Peace* (Hebrew) (Ramat Gan, 1996), 12 and 41–42.
13. Interview with King Hussein.
14. Shaham, *Israel—50 Years*, 215.
15. Haber, *Today War Will Break Out*, 95–96.
16. Haytham al-Kilani, *Military Strategy in the Arab-Israeli Wars, 1948–1988* (Arabic) (Beirut, 1991), 260.
17. Moshe Shemesh, "The Arab Struggle against Israel over Water, 1959–1967" (Hebrew), *Iyunim Bitkumat Israel*, 7 (1997).
18. Yezid Sayigh, *Armed Struggle and the Search for State: The Palestinian National Movement, 1949–1993* (Oxford, 1997).
19. Protocol of the Meeting of the Secretariat, 27 April 1965, Labor Party Archive.
20. Interview with Lieutenant General Yitzhak Rabin.
21. Meron Medzini, ed., *Israel's Foreign Relations: Selected Documents*, vol. 2, *1947–1974* (Jerusalem, 1976), 671–72.
22. Levi Eshkol, *On the Way Up* (Hebrew) (Tel Aviv, 1966), 314–20.
23. Shaham, *Israel—50 Years*, 238.
24. Haber, *Today War Will Break Out*, 43.
25. Interview with Lieutenant General Yitzhak Rabin.
26. Interview with King Hussein.
27. Interview with Lieutenant General Yitzhak Rabin.
28. Interview with Miriam Eshkol.
29. Rami Tal, "Moshe Dayan: Soul Searching," *Yediot Aharonot*, 27 April 1997.
30. Eban, *Autobiography*, 319.
31. *The Rabin Memoirs* (London, 1979), 58–59.
32. Eban, *Personal Witness*, 386–91.
33. Haber, *Today War Will Break Out*, 194–99.
34. Meir Amit, "The Road to the Six Days: The Six-Day War in Retrospect," *Ma'arachot*, no. 325 (June–July 1992).
35. Ibid.; and Haber, *Today War Will Break Out*, 216–21.
36. Haber, *Today War Will Break Out*, 273.
37. Ibid., 246.
38. Interview with Lieutenant General Chaim Bar-Lev.
39. Zvi Lanir, "Political Aims and Military Objectives in Israel's Wars," in *War by Choice: A Collection of Articles* (Hebrew) (Tel Aviv, 1985), 129–31.
40. Eban, *Autobiography*, 408.
41. Uzi Narkis, *Soldier of Jerusalem* (Hebrew) (Tel Aviv, 1991), 327.
42. *Ha'aretz*, 31 Dec. 1997.
43. Abraham Rabinovich, "Into the West Bank: The Jordanians were Laughing," *International Herald Tribune*, 6–7 June 1992.
44. Interview with Major General Uzi Narkis.

45. Moshe A. Gilboa, *Six Years—Six Days: Origins and History of the Six-Day War* (Hebrew), 2nd ed. (Tel Aviv 1969), 229.
46. Shlomo Nakdimon, "The Secret Battle for the Golan Heights," *Yediot Aharonot*, 30 May 1997.
47. *Rabin Memoirs*, 90.
48. Haber, *Today War Will Break Out*, 246–53.
49. Rami Tal, "Moshe Dayan: Soul Searching"; and Serge Schmemann, "General Dayan Speaks from the Grave," *International Herald Tribune*, 12 May 1997.
50. Trevor N. Dupui, *Elusive Victory: The Arab-Israeli Wars, 1947–1974* (New York, 1978), 333.
51. Alexei Vassiliev, *Russian Policy in the Middle East: From Messianism to Pragmatism* (Reading, 1993), 69–71.
52. Geoffrey Aronson, *Israel, Palestinians and the Intifada: Creating Facts on the West Bank* (London and New York, 1987), 10–12.
53. Dayan, *Milestones*, 490–91.
54. Eban, *Autobiography*, 435–36.
55. Meeting between Dean Rusk and Abba Eban, 21 June 1967, National Security File, Country File, "Middle East Crisis," vol. 7, Cables, 6/67–7/67, Box 109, Lyndon Baines Johnson Library, Austin, Texas.
56. Interviews with Tahseen Bashir and Ismail Fahmy.
57. Reuven Pedatzur, "The June Decision Was Canceled in October," *Ha'aretz*, 12 May 1995.
58. Reuven Pedatzur, "Coming Back Full Circle: The Palestinian Option in 1967," *Middle East Journal* 49, no. 2 (Spring 1995).
59. Protocol of the meeting of the Political Committee, 7 July 1967, Labor Party Archive.
60. Meir Avidan, "19 June 1967: The Government of Israel Hereby Decides," *Davar*, 2 June 1987.
61. Haber, *Today War Will Break Out*, 297.
62. Ibid., 281–82.
63. Reuven Pedatzur, *The Triumph of Confusion: Israel and the Territories after the Six-Day War* (Hebrew) (Tel Aviv, 1996), 195–99.
64. Robert Stephens, *Nasser: A Political Biography* (London, 1971), 523.
65. Interview with King Hussein.
66. Pedatzur, *Triumph of Confusion*, 112–13.
67. Interview with Abba Eban.
68. Eban, *Autobiography*, 416.
69. Yossi Beilin, *The Price of Unity: The Labor Party to the Yom Kippur War* (Hebrew) (Tel Aviv, 1985), 16.
70. Pedatzur, "Coming Back Full Circle."
71. Eban, *Autobiography*, 446.
72. Interview with King Hussein.

CHAPTER 7: IMMOBILISM 1969–1974

1. Medzini, *Proud Jewess*, 351.
2. Ibid., 523.
3. Meir, *My Life*, 312.
4. Interview with Simha Dinitz.
5. Rael Jean Isaac, *Israel Divided: Ideological Politics in the Jewish State* (Baltimore, 1976).
6. Beilin, *Price of Unity*, 53–54.

7. Interview with Avraham Harman.

8. Interview with Abba Eban.

9. Rafael, *Destination Peace,* 211.

10. For a more detailed account see Avi Shlaim and Raymond Tanter, "Decision Process, Choice, and Consequences: Israel's Deep-Penetration Bombing in Egypt, 1970," *World Politics* 30, no. 4 (July 1978).

11. Eban, *Personal Witness,* 485–86.

12. Gad Ya'acobi, *On the Razor's Edge* (Hebrew) (Tel Aviv, 1989), 34.

13. Eban, *Personal Witness,* 482.

14. Weizman, *On Eagles' Wings,* 274–75.

15. Yaacov Bar-Siman-Tov, *The Israeli-Egyptian War of Attrition, 1969–1970* (New York, 1980), 199.

16. Mordechai Gur, "The Six-Day War: Reflections after Twenty Years" (Hebrew), *Ma'arachot,* no. 309 (July–Aug. 1987).

17. William B. Quandt, *Peace Process: American Diplomacy and the Arab-Israeli Conflict since 1967* (Berkeley, 1993), 57–58.

18. Uri Bar-Joseph, "The Hidden Debate: The Formulation of Nuclear Doctrines in the Middle East," *Journal of Strategic Studies* 5, no. 2 (June 1982).

19. Eban, *Personal Witness,* 500–501; and Rafael, *Destination Peace,* 256–57.

20. Eban, *Personal Witness,* 501.

21. *Rabin Memoirs,* 151–52.

22. Rafael, *Destination Peace,* 257.

23. Dayan, *Milestones,* 569.

24. *Rabin Memoirs,* 149–50.

25. Rafael, *Destination Peace,* 258–59.

26. Ibid., 260–61.

27. Eban, *Personal Witness,* 503–4.

28. Ibid., 504.

29. *Rabin Memoirs,* 155–56.

30. Dayan, *Milestones,* 527–28; and Eban, *Personal Witness,* 504–5.

31. Rami Tal, "Moshe Dayan: Soul Searching," *Yediot Aharonot,* 27 April 1997.

32. *Rabin Memoirs,* 159–62.

33. Ibid., 162–64.

34. Interview with Simha Dinitz.

35. Interview with Major General Aharon Yariv.

36. Mordechai Gazit, *The Peace Process 1969–1973: Efforts and Contacts,* Jerusalem Papers on Peace Problems, 35 (Jerusalem, 1983), 92.

37. Eban, *Autobiography,* 488.

38. Henry Kissinger, *The White House Years* (Boston, 1979), 376.

39. *Sunday Times,* 15 June 1969, as quoted in David Hirst, *The Gun and the Olive Branch: The Roots of Violence in the Middle East* (London, 1977), 264.

40. Zak, *Hussein Makes Peace,* 44.

41. Interview with Simha Dinitz.

42. Interview with King Hussein.

43. Alan Hart, *Arafat: A Political Biography,* rev. ed. (London, 1994), 219–20.

44. Eban, *Autobiography,* 479.

45. Ibid.; and Rafael, *Destination Peace,* 277–78.

46. Rafael, *Destination Peace,* 277–79.

47. *Jerusalem Post Magazine,* 27 Oct. 1972.

48. Henry Kissinger, *Years of Upheaval* (London, 1982), 218–19 (emphasis in original).

49. Ibid., 220–21.

50. Anwar el-Sadat, *In Search of Identity: An Autobiography* (London, 1978), 238.

51. Rafael, *Destination Peace*, 280.
52. As quoted in Eban, *Autobiography*, 487.
53. Ibid., 489.
54. Mohamed Heikal, *The Road to Ramadan* (London, 1975), 205.
55. Interview with Abba Eban.
56. Eban, *Autobiography*, 488.
57. Major General Chaim Herzog, *The War of Atonement* (London, 1975), 41.
58. Israel Tal, *National Security: The Few against the Many* (Hebrew) (Tel Aviv, 1996), 166–67.
59. Dupui, *Elusive Victory*, 609.
60. Eban, *Autobiography*, 548.
61. Madiha Rashid Al Madfai, *Jordan, the United States and the Middle East Peace Process, 1974–1991* (Cambridge, 1993), 19–21.

CHAPTER 8: DISENGAGEMENT 1974–1977

1. Shlomo Avineri, "Leader in the Grip of Political Constraints," *Ha'aretz*, 1 Dec. 1995. This article was published a month after Yitzhak Rabin's assassination.
2. Moshe Shemesh, *The Palestinian National Entity, 1959–1974: Arab Politics and the PLO* (London, 1988), 294.
3. Kissinger, *Years of Upheaval*, 976.
4. Yossi Melman and Dan Raviv, *Behind the Uprising: Israelis, Jordanians, and Palestinians* (Westport, Conn., 1989), 127–29.
5. Ibid., 129–30; and Peres, *Battling for Peace*, 165 and 301.
6. Ya'acobi, *On the Razor's Edge*, 174.
7. Interview in *New Outlook* 18, no. 6 (Sept. 1975).
8. Raad Alkadiri, "Strategy and Tactics in Jordanian Foreign Policy, 1967–1988" (D.Phil. thesis, University of Oxford, 1995), 83–96.
9. Melman and Raviv, *Behind the Uprising*, 130–34.
10. Interview with King Hussein.
11. Kissinger, *White House Years*, 568.
12. Shaham, *Israel—50 Years*, 375–76.
13. *Rabin Memoirs*, 198–215.
14. Agreement between Egypt and Israel, 1 Sept. 1975, in John Norton Moore, ed., *The Arab-Israeli Conflict: Readings and Documents*, abr. and rev. ed. (Princeton, 1977), 1209–10.
15. Ibid., 1219–23; and *Rabin Memoirs*, 213–15.
16. George Ball, "The Coming Crisis in Israeli-American Relations," *Foreign Affairs* 58, no. 2 (Winter 1979–80).
17. Avner Yaniv, *Dilemmas of Security: Politics, Strategy, and the Israeli Experience in Lebanon* (New York, 1987), 60.
18. Nadav Safran, *Israel—The Embattled Ally* (Cambridge, Mass., 1978), 561–62.
19. Itamar Rabinovich, *The War for Lebanon, 1970–1983* (Ithaca, 1984), 105–6.
20. Rafael, *Destination Peace*, 363; and Yossi Melman, "Talks amid Hostility," *Ha'aretz*, 2 Aug. 1991.
21. Aryeh Bandar, "Secret Mission to Beirut," *Ma'ariv*, 11 May 1997.
22. Ronen Bergman, "The Gamble," *Ha'aretz*, 3 Jan. 1997.
23. Ze'ev Schiff and Ehud Ya'ari, *Israel's Lebanon War* (London, 1984), 18.
24. Yair Evron, *War and Intervention in Lebanon: The Israeli-Syrian Deterrence Dialogue* (London, 1987), 55–56.
25. *Rabin Memoirs*, 219.
26. Mohamed Heikal, *Secret Channels: The Inside Story of Arab-Israeli Peace Negotiations* (London, 1996), 244.

27. Peres, *Battling for Peace*, 203.
28. Shaham, *Israel—50 Years*, 388.

CHAPTER 9: PEACE WITH EGYPT 1977–1981

1. Quoted in Colin Shindler, *Israel, Likud and the Zionist Dream: Power, Politics and Ideology from Begin to Netanyahu* (London, 1995), 85.
2. Ilan Peleg, *Begin's Foreign Policy, 1977–1983: Israel's Move to the Right* (New York, 1987), 63–73.
3. Eliahu Ben Elissar, *No More War* (Hebrew) (Jerusalem, 1995), 25.
4. Arthur Hertzberg, "Sensing the Danger," *Ha'aretz*, 17 Jan. 1992.
5. Ben Elissar, *No More War*, 27–32.
6. Moshe Dayan, *Breakthrough: A Personal Account of the Egypt-Israel Peace Negotiations* (London, 1981), 17–22.
7. Ibid., 35–37.
8. Ben Elissar, *No More War*, 33–36.
9. Dayan, *Breakthrough*, 38–53.
10. Heikal, *Secret Channels*, 253.
11. Dayan, *Breakthrough*, 70–74; and Ben Elissar, *No More War*, 46–47.
12. Dayan, *Breakthrough*, 91.
13. Ibid., 91–97.
14. Ben Elissar, *No More War*, 104–7.
15. Dayan, *Breakthrough*, 99–100.
16. Arye Naor, *Begin in Power: A Personal Testimony* (Hebrew) (Tel Aviv, 1993), 152–57.
17. Dayan, *Breakthrough*, appendix 4, pp. 359–61.
18. Ezer Weizman, *The Battle for Peace* (Toronto, 1981), 295–96.
19. Boutros Boutros-Ghali, *Egypt's Road to Jerusalem: A Diplomat's Story of the Struggle for Peace in the Middle East* (New York, 1997), 43.
20. Dayan, *Breakthrough*, 105.
21. Heikal, *Secret Channels*, 270.
22. Dayan, *Breakthrough*, 109.
23. Ben Elissar, *No More War*, 116–17.
24. Dayan, *Breakthrough*, 126.
25. Naor, *Begin in Power*, 174–75.
26. Dayan, *Breakthrough*, 153–54.
27. Boutros-Ghali, *Egypt's Road to Jerusalem*, 133–51.
28. Naor, *Begin in Power*, 178.
29. Major General Avraham Tamir, *A Soldier in Search of Peace: An Inside Look at Israel's Strategy* (London, 1988), 53.
30. Boutros-Ghali, *Egypt's Road to Jerusalem*, 239–40.
31. Dayan, *Breakthrough*, 305.
32. Yitzhak Shamir, *Summing Up: An Autobiography* (London, 1994), 109.

CHAPTER 10: THE LEBANESE QUAGMIRE 1981–1984

1. Naor, *Begin in Power*, 218–20; and Shlomo Nakdimon, *Tammuz in Flames: The Bombing of the Iraqi Reactor* (Hebrew), rev. ed. (Tel Aviv, 1993), 87–91.
2. Noar, *Begin in Power*, 220–22; and Nakdimon, *Tammuz in Flames*, 168–77.
3. Peres, *Battling for Peace*, 210–12.
4. Naor, *Begin in Power*, 222–24.
5. Nakdimon, *Tammuz in Flames*, 275–76.

6. Moshe Sasson, *Seven Years in the Land of the Egyptians* (Hebrew) (Tel Aviv, 1992), 145–52.

7. Amos Perlmutter, Michael Handel, and Uri Bar-Joseph, *Two Minutes over Baghdad* (London, 1982), 148–51 and 167–69.

8. *Ma'ariv*, 9 Aug. 1981.

9. Memorandum of Understanding between the Government of the United States and the Government of Israel on Strategic Cooperation, 30 Nov. 1981, in Meron Medzini, ed., *Israel's Foreign Relations: Selected Documents*, vol. 7, *1981–1982* (Jerusalem, 1988), 200–202.

10. Sharon, *Warrior*, 414–15.

11. Naor, *Begin in Power*, 232–33.

12. Peleg, *Begin's Foreign Policy*, 190–95.

13. Naor, *Begin in Power*, 233–35.

14. Ibid., 238–54.

15. Schiff and Ya'ari, *Israel's Lebanon War*, 38–44; and Arye Naor, *Cabinet at War: The Functioning of the Israeli Cabinet during the Lebanon War* (Hebrew) (Tel Aviv, 1986), 32.

16. Avraham Tirosh and Avi Bettelheim, "Begin Proposed War in Lebanon in December 1981 after the Passage of the Golan Law," *Ma'ariv*, 3 June 1983, special supplement entitled "The Unfinished War."

17. Naor, *Cabinet at War*, 33.

18. Sharon, *Warrior*, 437–43.

19. Schiff and Ya'ari, *Israel's Lebanon War*, 53.

20. Tamir, *Soldier in Search of Peace*, 60–61.

21. Ibid., 66.

22. Shaham, *Israel—50 Years*, 441–42.

23. Schiff and Ya'ari, *Israel's Lebanon War*, 65–66.

24. Alexander M. Haig, Jr., *Caveat: Realism, Reagan, and Foreign Policy* (New York, 1984), 335.

25. Ibid., 330.

26. Ibid., 336.

27. Schiff and Ya'ari, *Israel's Lebanon War*, 97–102; and Ian Black and Benny Morris, *Israel's Secret Wars: The Untold History of Israeli Intelligence* (London, 1991), 375–76.

28. Schiff and Ya'ari, *Israel's Lebanon War*, 101; and Naor, *Cabinet at War*, 44–45.

29. Haig, *Caveat*, 336.

30. Naor, *Begin in Power*, 282–87.

31. Israel Cabinet Decision, 6 June 1982, Meron Medzini, ed., *Israel's Foreign Relations: Selected Documents, vol. 8, 1982–1984* (Jerusalem, 1990), 3.

32. Rafael Eytan with Dov Goldstein, *Raful: The Story of a Soldier* (Hebrew) (Tel Aviv, 1991), 210–11.

33. Naor, *Begin in Power*, 287–89.

34. Ibid., 290–91.

35. Naor, *Begin in Power*, 291.

36. Patrick Seale, *Asad of Syria: The Struggle for the Middle East* (London, 1988), 366.

37. Naor, *Begin in Power*, 322.

38. *Jerusalem Post*, 3 Aug. 1982.

39. Shindler, *Israel, Likud and the Zionist Dream*, 150.

40. Haig, *Caveat*, 342.

41. Heikal, *Secret Channels*, 356.

42. Naor, *Cabinet at War*, 113.

43. Schiff and Ya'ari, *Israel's Lebanon War*, 230–33.

44. Seale, *Asad*, 391.

45. Howard M. Sachar, *A History of Israel,* vol. 2, *From the Aftermath of the Yom Kippur War* (New York, 1987), 190–92.
46. Naor, *Cabinet at War,* 150–51, 155, and 158.
47. Shindler, *Israel, Likud and the Zionist Dream,* 161 and 164.
48. Rabinovich, *War for Lebanon,* 168.
49. David Kimche, *The Last Option* (London, 1991), 173–76.
50. Sasson, *Seven Years in the Land of the Egyptians,* 137–42.
51. Shindler, *Israel, Likud and the Zionist Dream,* 170.

CHAPTER 11: POLITICAL PARALYSIS 1984–1988

1. Meron Medzini, ed., *Israel's Foreign Relations: Selected Documents,* vol. 9, *1984–1988* (Jerusalem, 1992), 1–12.
2. Peres, *Battling for Peace,* 302–3; Tamir, *Soldier in Search of Peace,* 89–92; and Michael Bar-Zohar, *Facing a Cruel Mirror: Israel's Moment of Truth* (Hebrew) (Tel Aviv, 1990), 158–59 and 179–80.
3. Shamir, *Summing Up,* 172.
4. Arye Naor, *Writing on the Wall* (Hebrew) (Tel Aviv, 1988), 125–26.
5. Shamir, *Summing Up,* 168.
6. Naor, *Writing on the Wall,* 149–55.
7. Zak, *Hussein Makes Peace,* 201–2 and 263–64.
8. George P. Shultz, *Turmoil and Triumph: My Years as Secretary of State* (New York, 1993), 452–55.
9. Adam Garfinkle, *Israel and Jordan in the Shadow of War* (London, 1992), 113.
10. Melman and Raviv, *Behind the Uprising,* 173; and Shultz, *Turmoil and Triumph,* 457.
11. Melman and Raviv, *Behind the Uprising,* 166–67.
12. Medzini, *Israel's Foreign Relations,* 9:280–83.
13. Naor, *Writing on the Wall,* 155–56.
14. Shultz, *Turmoil and Triumph,* 439.
15. Naor, *Writing on the Wall,* 156–57.
16. Melman and Raviv, *Behind the Uprising,* 172–73; and Zak, *Hussein Makes Peace,* 204–5.
17. Medzini, *Israel's Foreign Relations,* 9:498–99.
18. Ibid., 509–15.
19. Benjamin Netanyahu, ed., *Terrorism: How the West Can Win* (New York, 1986), 221. The institute was named after Netanyahu's brother, who was killed leading the 1976 Entebbe rescue mission.
20. Seale, *Asad,* 483.
21. Shultz, *Turmoil and Triumph,* 790.
22. The account of the meeting is based on two firsthand sources: Peres, *Battling for Peace,* 205–12; and Shayke Ben-Porat, *Talks with Yossi Beilin* (Hebrew) (Tel Aviv, 1996), 89–94.
23. The Peres-Hussein London Agreement, 11 April 1987, in Peres, *Battling for Peace,* 361–62, appendix 2.
24. Ibid., 308–9; and Shamir, *Summing Up,* 169.
25. Shultz, *Turmoil and Triumph,* 938–39.
26. Ibid., 940–41.
27. Naor, *Writing on the Wall,* 177–79.
28. Interview with King Hussein.
29. Noar, *Writing on the Wall,* 180.
30. Shultz, *Turmoil and Triumph,* 942–43.

31. Ibid., 944–48.
32. Shamir, *Summing Up*, 174–75.
33. Aryeh Shalev, *The Intifada: Causes and Effects* (Hebrew) (Tel Aviv, 1990), 42–43.
34. Don Peretz, *Intifada: The Palestinian Uprising* (Boulder, Colo., 1990), 40–41.
35. Quoted ibid., 78–79.
36. David McDowell, *Palestine and Israel: The Uprising and Beyond* (London, 1989), 2.
37. Peretz, *Intifada*, 163–64.
38. Ibid., 167.
39. Ze'ev Schiff and Ehud Ya'ari, *Intifada*, ed. and trans. Ina Friedman (New York, 1991), 297–99.
40. Interview with King Hussein.
41. Shultz, *Turmoil and Triumph*, 1033.
42. Schiff and Ya'ari, *Intifada*, 271–72.
43. Ibid., 315–16.

CHAPTER 12: STONEWALLING 1988–1992

1. Amos Elon, *A Blood-Dimmed Tide: Dispatches from the Middle East* (New York, 1997), 199–200.
2. Naor, *Writing on the Wall*, 37.
3. Avishai Margalit, "The Violent Life of Yitzhak Shamir," *New York Review of Books*, 14 May 1992.
4. Yitzhak Shamir, "Israel's Role in a Changing Middle East," *Foreign Affairs* 50, no. 4 (Spring 1982).
5. Naor, *Writing on the Wall*, 33–36.
6. Meron Medzini, ed., *Israel's Foreign Relations: Selected Documents*, vol. 10, *1984–1988* (Jerusalem, 1989), 999–1000.
7. Ibid., 1054.
8. Shamir, *Summing Up*, 201.
9. Quandt, *Peace Process*, 389.
10. Moshe Arens, *Broken Covenant: American Foreign Policy and the Crisis between the U.S. and Israel* (New York, 1995), 65–67 and 72–73.
11. Schiff and Ya'ari, *Intifada*, 320–21.
12. Shamir, *Summing Up*, 214.
13. Ibid., 214.
14. Arens, *Broken Covenant*, 128–29 and 209–10.
15. Dilip Hiro, *Desert Shield to Desert Storm* (London, 1992), 58.
16. Efraim Karsh and Inari Rautsi, *Saddam Hussein: A Political Biography* (London, 1991), 207–11.
17. "Israel and the Gulf War," *Maariv*, 29 March 1991. This is a special, fifty-page report, on which I have drawn heavily in this chapter.
18. Dan Margalit, "The Name of the Game—There Is No Alternative," *Ha'aretz*, 3 Oct. 1990.
19. *Ha'aretz*, 6 Sept. 1990.
20. *Ha'aretz*, 5 Dec. 1990.
21. *Ma'ariv*, special supplement, 29 March 1991; and Bob Woodward *The Commanders* (New York, 1991), 363.
22. Garfinkle, *Israel and Jordan in the Shadow of War*, 173.
23. Shamir, *Summing Up*, 218–19.
24. Zak, *Hussein Makes Peace*, 35–36, 47–50, and 227–28.
25. Interview with King Hussein.

26. Uri Avnery, "In Israel, Reckless Talk about Jordan," *International Herald Tribune,* 7 Sept. 1990; and Ze'ev Schiff, *Ha'aretz,* 3 March 1991.
27. Arens, *Broken Covenant,* 184; and Amnon Barzilai, "The Fateful Saturday," *Ha'aretz,* 13 Jan. 1995.
28. Elon, *Blood-Dimmed Tide,* 206–7.
29. Seymour M. Hersh, *The Samson Option: Israel, America and the Bomb* (London, 1991), 318.
30. *Ha'aretz,* 3 Feb. 1991; and Ze'ev Schiff, "A Nonconventional Warning in Israel's Name," *Ha'aretz,* 4 Feb. 1991.
31. *Ma'ariv,* special supplement, 29 March 1991; and *Ha'aretz,* 13 Feb. 1991.
32. Hiro, *Desert Shield to Desert Storm,* 332.
33. Meron Benvenisti, *Fatal Embrace* (Hebrew) (Jerusalem, 1992), 100.
34. Gideon Samet, "Even If We Have No Churchill," *Ha'aretz,* 25 Jan. 1991.
35. *Ma'ariv,* special supplement, 29 March 1991; interview with Moshe Arens, *Yediot Aharonot,* 17 April 1991; and Lieutenant General (res.) Dan Shomron, "A Personal Report on the Gulf War," *Yediot Aharonot,* 8 Sept. 1991.
36. Shamir, *Summing Up,* 227.
37. Arens, *Broken Covenant,* 233–34.
38. Ze'ev Schiff, *Ha'aretz,* 19 June 1992.
39. Yossi Olmert's interview with Urit Galili, *Ha'aretz,* 7 Aug. 1992; and Urit Galili, *Ha'aretz,* 28 Aug. 1992.
40. Lecture by Selim el-Hoss entitled "The Middle East after the Madrid Conference," delivered at the Middle East Centre, St. Antony's College, Oxford, 10 Dec. 1991.
41. Yossi Sarid, "Old Lies, New Lies," *Ha'aretz,* 14 Feb. 1992.
42. Shamir, *Summing Up,* 249.
43. *Ha'aretz,* 7 Feb. 1992.
44. Interview with Yosef Harif, *Ma'ariv,* 26 June 1992.
45. *Yediot Aharanot,* 22 June 1992, quoted in Shindler, *Israel, Likud and the Zionist Dream,* 280.
46. Shamir, *Summing Up,* 257.

CHAPTER 13: THE BREAKTHROUGH 1992–1995

1. *Ha'aretz,* 11 Sept. 1992.
2. Joel Peters, *Pathways to Peace: The Multilateral Arab-Israeli Peace Talks* (London, 1996).
3. Shimon Peres, *The New Middle East* (Shaftesbury, England, 1993).
4. Peres, *Battling for Peace,* 324.
5. Ibid., 314 and 320–21.
6. Chaim Herzog, *Living History: A Memoir* (New York, 1996), 388.
7. Hanan Ashrawi, *This Side of Peace: A Personal Account* (New York, 1995), 211.
8. Yossi Beilin, *Touching Peace* (Hebrew) (Tel Aviv, 1997), 74.
9. Yoel Marcus, *Ha'aretz,* 18 Sept. 1992.
10. Ashrawi, *This Side of Peace,* 232.
11. Peres, *Battling for Peace,* 323–24.
12. Avraham Tal, "There Is No Return from the Temporary," *Ha'aretz,* 19 Sept. 1993.
13. Mahmoud Abbas, *Through Secret Channels: The Road to Oslo* (Reading, England, 1995).
14. Nahum Barnea and Shimon Schiffer, "The Norwegian Connection," *Yediot Aharonot,* 3 Sept. 1993.
15. Yoel Marcus, *Ha'aretz,* 15 Sept. 1993.
16. Ibid.

17. Beilin, *Touching Peace*, 141–43.
18. Declaration of Principles on Interim Self-Government Arrangements, Washington, 13 Sept. 1993, in Meron Medzini, ed., *Israel's Foreign Relations: Selected Documents*, vol. 13, *1992–1994* (Jerusalem, 1995), 319–28.
19. Israel-PLO Mutual Recognition, Letters and Speeches, 10 Sept. 1993, ibid., 306–10.
20. Abba Eban, "Building Bridges, Not Walls," *The Guardian*, 10 Sept. 1993.
21. Beilin, *Touching Peace*, 152.
22. *The Guardian*, 16 Sept. 1993.
23. Edward Said, *Peace and Its Discontents: Gaza–Jericho, 1993–1995* (London, 1995), 2.
24. Nicholas Guyatt, *The Absence of Peace: Understanding the Israeli-Palestinian Conflict* (London and New York, 1998), 34 and 42.
25. Patrick Seale with Linda Butler, "Assad's Regional Strategy and the Challenge from Netanyahu," *Journal of Palestine Studies* 26, no. 1 (Autumn 1996).
26. Ahron Bregman and Jihan El-Tahri, *The Fifty Years War: Israel and the Arabs* (London, 1998), 34.
27. Ma'oz, *Syria and Israel*, 225.
28. Itamar Rabinovich, "What Precisely Did Rabin Offer, What Did Assad Reply and What Did the Americans Think?" *Yediot Aharonot*, 6 Feb. 1998; and Ze'ev Schiff, "File Pocket: What Did Rabin Promise the Syrians?" *Ha'aretz*, 29 Aug. 1997.
29. Linda Butler, "Fresh Light on the Syrian-Israeli Peace Negotiations: An Interview with Ambassador Walid al-Moualem," *Journal of Palestine Studies* 26, no. 2 (Winter 1997) (emphasis in original).
30. Ibid.
31. Schiff, *Ha'aretz*, 29 Aug. 1997.
32. Itamar Rabinovich, "Shihabi Talked about the Israeli Capability, Shahak about the Syrian Missiles," *Yediot Aharonot*, 13 Feb. 1998.
33. Nora Boustany, "King Hussein Fears Prospects for Peace Could Raise Premature Hope in Jordan," *International Herald Tribune*, 18–19 Sept. 1993.
34. Jerrold Kessel, "Rabin Soothes King at Secret Meeting," *The Guardian*, 29 Sept. 1993.
35. Elyakim Rubinstein, "The Peace Treaty with Jordan" (Hebrew), *Hamishpat*, no. 6 (Dec. 1995).
36. Interview with King Hussein.
37. David Horovitz, ed., *Yitzhak Rabin: A Soldier for Peace* (London, 1996), 124–27.
38. Zak, *Hussein Makes Peace*, 293–94.
39. Interview with King Hussein.
40. Horovitz, *Yitzhak Rabin*, 129; and David Makovsky, *Making Peace with the PLO: The Rabin Government's Road to Oslo* (Boulder, Colo., 1996), 158–60.
41. Shimon Shamir, "Three Years after the Signature of the Peace Treaty with Jordan: The Desert Is Still Arid," *Ha'aretz*, 22 Oct. 1997.
42. Interview with King Hussein.

CHAPTER 14: THE SETBACK 1995–1996

1. Meron Medzini, ed., *Israel's Foreign Relations: Selected Documents*, vol. 15, *1995–1996* (Jerusalem, 1997), 346–47.
2. Fouad Ajami, *The Dream Palace of the Arabs: A Generation's Odyssey* (New York, 1998), 294–95.
3. Amnon Kapeliouk, *Rabin: A Political Assassination* (Hebrew) (Tel Aviv, 1996), 32.
4. Ibid., 81–82.

5. Horovitz, *Yitzhak Rabin*, 178–79.
6. Elon, *Blood-Dimmed Tide*, 310.
7. Kapeliouk, *Rabin: A Political Assassination*, 61.
8. Medzini, *Israel's Foreign Relations*, 15:363–77.
9. Beilin, *Touching Peace*, 205.
10. Conversation with Dr. Hussein Agha, Ditchley Park, 24 Jan. 1997.
11. Beilin, *Touching Peace*, 205–12.
12. Ze'ev Schiff, *Ha'aretz*, 22 Feb. 1996.
13. Chris Nuttal, "Pact Sours Turkish-Arab Ties," *The Guardian*, 11 April 1996.
14. Patrick Seale, "The Address Is Syria," in Rosemary Hollis and Nadim Shehadi, eds., *Lebanon on Hold: Implications for Middle East Peace* (Oxford, 1996), 19–23.
15. Peres, *Battling for Peace*, 355.

CHAPTER 15: BACK TO THE IRON WALL 1996–1998

1. Benjamin Netanyahu, *A Place among the Nations: Israel and the World* (London, 1993), 102–3.
2. Ibid., 121.
3. Ibid., 232.
4. Ibid., 236–37.
5. Ibid., 287.
6. Benjamin Netanyahu, *Fighting Terrorism: How Democracies Can Defeat Domestic and International Terrorism* (New York, 1995), 102.
7. Ari Shavit, "A New Middle East? What an Amusing Idea," *Ha'aretz*, 22 Nov. 1996.
8. Laura Zittrain Eisenberg and Neil Caplan, *Negotiating Arab-Israeli Peace: Patterns, Problems, Possibilities* (Bloomington, Ind., 1998), 149.
9. Interview with King Hussein.
10. David Hirst, "Arabs to Shun Israel at Economic Summit," *The Guardian*, 13 Nov. 1996.
11. *Ha'aretz*, 29 May, 30 May, and 5 June 1997.
12. Ze'ev Schiff, "The Government against the Intelligence," *Ha'aretz*, 26 Sept. 1997.
13. Ze'ev Schiff, "A Flaw in Strategic Thinking," *Ha'aretz*, 14 Nov. 1997.
14. Seale with Butler, "Assad's Regional Strategy and the Challenge from Netanyahu."
15. Bregman and El-Tahri, *Fifty Years War*, 274.
16. Ibid.
17. Ze'ev Schiff, *Ha'aretz*, 19 and 24 Jan. 1997.
18. Patrick Seale, "Syria and Israel: No Progress towards Peace," *Middle East International*, no. 565 (19 Dec. 1997).
19. Ze'ev Schiff, "The Intelligence That Gil Passed On: The Syrians Will Attack on the Golan," *Ha'aretz*, 8 Dec. 1997.

BIBLIOGRAPHY

ARCHIVES

Ben-Gurion Archive, Sede-Boker
Central Zionist Archives (CZA), Jerusalem
Israel State Archives (ISA), Jerusalem
Labour Party Archive, Beit Berl, Kfar Saba
Public Record Office (PRO), London

NEWSPAPERS

Davar
The Guardian
Ha'aretz
International Herald Tribune
Ma'ariv
Yediot Aharonot

DOCUMENTS AND OFFICIAL PUBLICATIONS

Documents on the Foreign Policy of Israel (DFPI). Jerusalem: Israel State Archives, various dates of publication. Volumes on 1948–53.
Foreign Relations of the United States (FRUS). Washington, D.C.: U.S. Government Printing Office, various dates of publication. Volumes on Middle East, 1948–63.
Iraq. *Report of the Parliamentary Committee of Inquiry on the Palestine Problem* (Arabic). Baghdad, 1949.
Israel's Foreign Relations: Selected Documents, 1948–1996. Edited by Meron Medzini. 15 vols. Jerusalem: Ministry of Foreign Affairs, various dates of publication.
The League of Arab States, Decisions of the Council from the first session to the

nineteenth session (4 July 1945–7 September 1953). Cairo: General Secretariat.

Proceedings of the Knesset, Jerusalem, 1949–98.

Provisional State Council. *Protocols, 18 April–13 May 1948* (Hebrew). Jerusalem, 1978.

SELECT LIST OF PERSONS INTERVIEWED

Interviewee	Principal Posts	Date
Major General Meir Amit	Director of Military Intelligence, Head of the Mossad	5 Aug. 1982
Major General Yosef Avidar	OC Central Command, Ambassador to Moscow	11 Aug. 1982
Gershon Avner	Foreign Ministry	4, 14 July 1982; 6 Sept. 1983
Lieutenant General Chaim Bar-Lev	Chief of Staff	3, 30 Aug. 1982
Colonel Mordechai Bar-On	Moshe Dayan's Chief of Bureau	3, 6, 11, 23, 29 Aug. 1982
Tahseen Bashir	Egyptian Foreign Ministry	23 May 1981
Yitzhak Ben-Aharon	Leader of Ahdut Ha'avodah, Minister of Transport	21 July, 9 Aug. 1982
Major General Moshe Carmel	OC Northern Command	1 Sept. 1983
Simha Dinitz	Foreign Ministry	21 July 1982
Abba Eban	Foreign Minister	11 March 1976
Miriam Eshkol	Wife of Levi Eshkol	31 Jan. 1982
Walter Eytan	Foreign Ministry	28 April, 18 May 1982
Ismail Fahmy	Egyptian Foreign Minister	17 Sept. 1982
Mordechai Gazit	Foreign Ministry	22 Aug. 1982
Isser Harel	Head of the Mossad	13 Aug. 1982
Major General Yehoshafat Harkabi	Director of Military Intelligence	12 Aug. 1981; 11 June, 12, 17 Aug. 1982
Avraham Harman	Ambassador to Washington	25 Aug. 1982
Hussein bin Talal	King of Jordan	3 Dec. 1996
Sir Donald Logan	British Foreign Office	7 Dec. 1996
Major General Uzi Narkis	OC Central Command	20 July, 2, 4 Aug. 1982

Sir Anthony Nutting	Minister of State for Foreign Affairs	12 March 1997
Colonel Meir Pail	IDF	9 June, 19 July 1982
Yehoshua Palmon	Adviser on Arab Affairs to the Prime Minister	31 May, 14 June, 18 Aug. 1982; 26 Sept. 1983
Shimon Peres	Defense Minister, Foreign Minister, Prime Minister	20 Aug. 1982
Yitzhak Rabin	Chief of Staff, Defense Minister, Prime Minister	22 Aug. 1982
Gideon Rafael	Foreign Ministry	17, 27 May 1982
Abdel Rahman Sadeq	Aide to President Nasser	19 Sept. 1982
Moshe Sasson	Foreign Ministry, Ambassador to Egypt	8 Sept. 1982, 23 Sept. 1983
Ze'ev Sharef	Secretary to the Cabinet	24 May 1982
Yaacov Shimoni	Foreign Ministry	26 Aug. 1982; 26, 29 Sept. 1983
Lieutenant General Yigael Yadin	Chief of Staff	18 Feb., 19 Aug. 1982, 30 Aug. 1983
Major General Aharon Yariv	Director of Military Intelligence	30 Aug. 1982
Chaim Yisraeli	Ministry of Defense	3 June, 9 Sept. 1982

Works Cited

Abbas, Mahmoud (Abu Mazen). *Through Secret Channels: The Road to Oslo.* Reading, England: Garnett, 1995.

Ajami, Fouad. *The Dream Palace of the Arabs: A Generation's Odyssey.* New York: Pantheon, 1998.

Alkadiri, Raad. "Strategy and Tactics in Jordanian Foreign Policy, 1967–1988." D.Phil. thesis, University of Oxford, 1995.

Almog, Shmuel, ed. *Zionism and the Arabs: Essays.* Jerusalem: The Historical Society of Israel and the Zalman Shazar Center, 1983.

Amit, Meir. "The Road to the Six Days: The Six-Day War in Retrospect." *Ma'arachot,* no. 325 (June–July 1992).

Arens, Moshe. *Broken Covenant: American Foreign Policy and the Crisis between the U.S. and Israel.* New York: Simon and Schuster, 1995.

Aronson, Geoffrey. *Israel, Palestinians and the Intifada: Creating Facts on the West Bank.* London and New York: Routledge, 1987.

Ashrawi, Hanan. *This Side of Peace: A Personal Account.* New York: Simon and Schuster, 1995.

Avineri, Shlomo. *The Making of Modern Zionism: The Intellectual Origins of the Jewish State.* New York: Basic Books, 1981.

Avnery, Ury. *Israel without Zionists: A Plea for Peace in the Middle East.* New York: Macmillan, 1968.

Ball, George. "The Coming Crisis in Israeli-American Relations." *Foreign Affairs* 58, no. 2 (Winter 1979–80).

Bar-Joseph, Uri. "The Hidden Debate: The Formulation of Nuclear Doctrines in the Middle East." *Journal of Strategic Studies* 5, no. 2 (June 1982).

———. *The Best of Enemies: Israel and Transjordan in the War of 1948*. London: Frank Cass, 1987.

Bar-On, Mordechai. "David Ben-Gurion and the Sèvres Collusion." In Wm. Roger Louis and Roger Owen, eds., *Suez 1956: The Crisis and Its Consequences*. Oxford: Clarendon Press, 1989.

———. *Challenge and Quarrel: The Road to the Sinai Campaign—1956* (Hebrew). Beersheba: Ben-Gurion University of the Negev Press, 1991.

———. *The Gates of Gaza: Israel's Road to Suez and Back, 1955–1957*. New York: St Martin's Press, 1994.

———. "Status Quo Before—or After? Reflections on the Defense Policy of Israel, 1949–1958" (Hebrew). *Iyunim Bitkumat Israel* 5 (1995).

Bar-Siman-Tov, Yaacov. *The Israeli-Egyptian War of Attrition, 1969–1970*. New York: Columbia University Press, 1980.

Bar-Yaacov, Nissim. *The Israel-Syria Armistice: Problems of Implementation, 1949–1966*. Jerusalem: Magness Press, 1967.

Bar-Zohar, Michael. *Ben-Gurion: A Political Biography* (Hebrew). 3 vols. Tel Aviv: Am Oved, 1975–77.

———. "Ben-Gurion and the Policy of the Periphery." In Itamar Rabinovich and Jehuda Reinharz, eds., *Israel in the Middle East*. New York: Oxford University Press, 1984.

———. *Facing a Cruel Mirror: Israel's Moment of Truth* (Hebrew). Tel Aviv: Yediot Aharonot, 1990.

Begin, Menachem. *The Revolt*. Rev. ed. New York: Dell, 1977.

Beilin, Yossi. *The Price of Unity: The Labor Party to the Yom Kippur War* (Hebrew). Tel Aviv: Revivim, 1985.

———. *Touching Peace* (Hebrew). Tel Aviv: Yediot Aharonot, 1997.

David Ben-Gurion, *Vision and Fulfillment* (Hebrew). 5 vols. Tel Aviv: Am Oved, 1958.

———. *Letters to Paula*. London: Vallentine, Mitchell, 1971.

———. *My Talks with Arab Leaders*. Jerusalem: Keter Books, 1972.

———. *War Diary: The War of Independence, 1948–1949* (Hebrew). Edited by Gershon Rivlin and Elhanan Orren. Tel Aviv: Ministry of Defense, 1982.

———. *David Ben-Gurion: The First Prime Minister: Selected Documents, 1947–1963* (Hebrew). Editing and historical notes by Eli Shaltiel. Jerusalem: Israel State Archives, 1996.

———. *Negotiations with Nasser*. Jerusalem: Israel Information Center, n.d.

Ben-Porat, Shayke. *Talks with Yossi Beilin* (Hebrew). Tel Aviv: Hakibbutz Hameuchad Publishing House, 1996.

Benvenisti, Meron. *Fatal Embrace* (Hebrew). Jerusalem: Keter Books, 1992.

Black, Ian, and Benny Morris. *Israel's Secret Wars: The Untold History of Israeli Intelligence*. London: Hamish Hamilton, 1991.

Blass, Simha. *Water in Strife and Action* (Hebrew). Ramat Gan: Masada, 1973.

Boutros-Ghali, Boutros. *Egypt's Road to Jerusalem: A Diplomat's Story of the Struggle for Peace in the Middle East*. New York: Random House, 1997.

Brecher, Michael. *The Foreign Policy System of Israel: Setting, Images, Process*. Oxford: Oxford University Press, 1972.

———. *Decisions in Israel's Foreign Policy*. Oxford: Oxford University Press, 1974.

Bregman, Ahron, and Jihan El-Tahri. *The Fifty Years War: Israel and the Arabs*. London: Penguin Books, BBC Books, 1998.

Burns, E. L. M. *Between Arab and Israeli*. Beirut: Institute for Palestine Studies, 1969.

Butler, Linda. "Fresh Light on the Syrian-Israeli Peace Negotiations: An Interview with Ambassador Walid al-Moualem." *Journal of Palestine Studies* 26, no. 2 (Winter 1997).

Central Intelligence Agency. *Israel: Foreign Intelligence and Security Services Survey* (Hebrew). Translated and edited by Yossi Melman. Tel Aviv: Erez, 1982.

Cohen, Avner. *Israel and the Bomb*. New York: Columbia University Press, 1998.

Cohen, Yeroham. *By Light and in Darkness* (Hebrew). Tel Aviv: Amikam, 1969.

Copeland, Miles. *The Game of Nations: The Amorality of Power Politics*. London: Weidenfeld and Nicolson, 1969.

Dayan, Moshe. "Military Operations in Peacetime" (Hebrew). *Ma'arachot*, May 1959.

———. *Diary of the Sinai Campaign*. New York: Schocken Books, 1967.

———. *Story of My Life*. London: Weidenfeld and Nicolson, 1976.

———. *Milestones: An Autobiography* (Hebrew). Jerusalem: Yediot Aharonot, 1976.

———. *Living with the Bible* (Hebrew). Jerusalem: Edanim, 1981.

———. *Breakthrough: A Personal Account of the Egypt-Israel Peace Negotiations*. London: Weidenfeld and Nicolson, 1981.

Dupui, Trevor N. *Elusive Victory: The Arab-Israeli Wars, 1947–1974*. New York: Harper and Row, 1978.

Eban, Abba. *An Autobiography*. London: Weidenfeld and Nicolson, 1977.

———. *Personal Witness: Israel through My Eyes*. New York: Putnam, 1992.

Eisenberg, Laura Zittrain, and Neil Caplan. *Negotiating Arab-Israeli Peace: Patterns, Problems, Possibilities*. Bloomington: Indiana University Press, 1998.

Elissar, Eliahu Ben. *No More War* (Hebrew). Jerusalem: Ma'ariv, 1995.

Elon, Amos. *A Blood-Dimmed Tide: Dispatches from the Middle East*. New York: Columbia University Press, 1997.

Epstein, Yitzhak. "A Hidden Question" (Hebrew). *Ha-Shiloah,* March 1907.

Erez, Yaacov. *Conversations with Moshe Dayan* (Hebrew). Ramat Gan: Masada, 1981.

Eshed, Haggai. *Who Gave the Order?: The Lavon Affair* (Hebrew). Jerusalem: Edanim, 1979.

———. *Reuven Shiloah: The Man behind the Mossad*. London: Frank Cass, 1997.

Eshkol, Levi. *On the Way Up* (Hebrew). Tel Aviv: Ayanot, 1966.

Evron, Yair. *War and Intervention in Lebanon: The Israeli-Syrian Deterrence Dialogue*. London: Croom Helm, 1987.

———. "The Interrelationship between Foreign Policy and Defense Policy in the Years 1949–1955" (Hebrew). *Skira Hodshit* 35, no. 11 (Dec. 1988).

———. *Israel's Nuclear Dilemma*. London: Routledge, 1994.

Eytan, Rafael, with Dov Goldstein. *Raful: The Story of a Soldier* (Hebrew). Tel Aviv: Ma'ariv, 1991.

Flapan, Simha. *Zionism and the Palestinians*. London: Croom Helm, 1979.

———. *The Birth of Israel: Myths and Realities*. New York: Pantheon, 1987.

Gabbay, Rony E. *A Political Study of the Arab-Jewish Conflict: The Arab Refugee Problem*. Geneva: Librairie E. Droz, 1959.

Garfinkle, Adam. *Israel and Jordan in the Shadow of War*. London: Macmillan, 1992.

Gazit, Mordechai. *The Peace Process, 1969–1973: Efforts and Contacts*. Jerusalem Papers on Peace Problems, 35. Jerusalem: Magness Press, Hebrew University, Jerusalem, 1983.

Gilboa, Moshe A. *Six Years—Six Days: Origins and History of the Six-Day War* (Hebrew). 2nd ed. Tel Aviv: Am Oved, 1969.

Glubb, Sir John Bagot. "Violence on the Jordan-Israel Border: A Jordanian View." *Foreign Affairs* 32, no. 4 (July 1954).

———. *A Soldier with the Arabs*. London: Hodder and Stoughton, 1957.

Goldberg, David J. *To the Promised Land: A History of Zionist Thought from Its Origins to the Modern State of Israel*. London: Penguin Books, 1996.

Goldmann, Nahum. *The Autobiography of Nahum Goldmann: Sixty Years of Jewish Life*. New York: Holt, Rinehart and Winston, 1969.

Gorny, Yosef. *Zionism and the Arabs, 1882–1948: A Study of Ideology*. Oxford: Clarendon Press, 1987.

Gur, Mordechai. "The Six-Day War: Reflections after Twenty Years" (Hebrew). *Ma'arachot*, no. 309 (July–Aug. 1987).

Guyatt, Nicholas. *The Absence of Peace: Understanding the Israeli-Palestinian Conflict*. London and New York: Zed Books, 1998.

Haber, Eitan. *Today War Will Break Out: The Reminiscences of Brigadier General Israel Lior, Aide-de-Camp to Prime Ministers Levi Eshkol and Golda Meir* (Hebrew). Tel Aviv: Edanim, 1987.

Haig, Alexander M., Jr. *Caveat: Realism, Reagan, and Foreign Policy*. New York: Macmillan, 1984.

Hameiri, Yehezkel. "Demilitarization and Conflict Resolution: The Question of the Demilitarized Zones on the Israel-Syria Border, 1949–1967" (Hebrew). M.A. thesis, University of Haifa, 1978.

Harel, Isser. *Security and Democracy* (Hebrew). Tel Aviv: Edanim, 1989.

Hart, Alan. *Arafat: A Political Biography*. Rev. ed. London: Sidgwick and Jackson, 1994.

Heikal, Mohamed. *The Road to Ramadan*. London: Collins, 1975.

———. *The Suez Files* (Arabic). Cairo: Al-Ahram, 1986.

———. *Secret Channels: The Inside Story of Arab-Israeli Peace Negotiations*. London: Harper Collins, 1996.

Hersh, Seymour M. *The Samson Option: Israel, America and the Bomb*. London: Faber and Faber, 1991.

Herzl, Theodor. *Old-New Land*. Translated by L. Levensohn. New York: Bloch, 1960.

———. *The Complete Diaries of Theodor Herzl*. Edited by Raphael Patai and translated by Harry Zohn. New York: Herzl Press and Thomas Yoseloff, 1960.

———. *The Jewish State*. Translated by Harry Zohn. New York: Herzl Press, 1970.

Herzog, Chaim. *The War of Atonement*. London: Weidenfeld and Nicolson, 1975.

———. *Living History: A Memoir*. New York: Pantheon, 1996.

Herzog, Yaacov. *A People That Dwells Alone*. London: Weidenfeld and Nicolson, 1975.

Hiro, Dilip. *Desert Shield to Desert Storm*. London: Harper Collins, 1992.

Hirst, David. *The Gun and the Olive Branch: The Roots of Violence in the Middle East*. London: Faber and Faber, 1977.

Horovitz, David, ed. *Yitzhak Rabin: A Soldier for Peace*. London: Peter Halban, 1996.

Hutchison, E. H. *Violent Truce: A Military Observer Looks at the Arab-Israeli Conflict, 1951–1955*. New York: Devin-Adair, 1956.

Isaac, Rael Jean. *Israel Divided: Ideological Politics in the Jewish State*. Baltimore: Johns Hopkins University Press, 1976.

Jabotinsky, Ze'ev. *Writings: On the Road to Statehood* (Hebrew). Jerusalem: Ari Jabotinsky, 1959.

Jackson, Elmore. *Middle East Mission: The Story of a Major Bid for Peace in the Time of Nasser and Ben-Gurion*. New York: Norton, 1983.

al-Jubury, Salih Saib. *The Palestine Misfortune and Its Political and Military Secrets* (Arabic). Beirut: Dar al-Kutub, 1970.

Kapeliouk, Amnon. *Rabin: A Political Assassination* (Hebrew). Tel Aviv: Sifriyat Poalim, 1996.

Karsh, Efraim, and Inari Rautsi. *Saddam Hussein: A Political Biography*. London: Brassey's, 1991.

al-Kilani, Haytham. *Military Strategy in the Arab-Israeli Wars, 1948–1988* (Arabic). Beirut: Center for the Study of Arab Unity, 1991.

Kimche, David. *The Last Option*. London: Weidenfeld and Nicolson, 1991.

Kirkbride, Sir Alec. *From the Wings: Amman Memoirs, 1947–1951*. London: Frank Cass, 1976.

Kissinger, Henry. *The White House Years*. Boston: Little, Brown, 1979.

———. *Years of Upheaval*. London: Weidenfeld and Nicolson, 1982.

Kyle, Keith. *Suez*. London: Weidenfeld and Nicolson, 1991.

Lanir, Zvi. "Political Aims and Military Objectives in Israel's Wars," In *War by Choice: A Collection of Articles* (Hebrew). Tel Aviv: Hakibbutz Hameuchad Publishing House, 1985.

Lavon, Pinhas. *In the Paths of Reflection and Struggle* (Hebrew). Tel Aviv: Am Oved, 1968.

Lloyd, Selwyn. *Suez 1956: A Personal Account*. London: Jonathan Cape, 1978.

Louis, Wm. Roger. *The British Empire in the Middle East, 1945–1951: Arab Nationalism, the United States, and Postwar Imperialism*. Oxford: Oxford University Press, 1984.

Love, Kennett. *Suez: The Twice-Fought War*. New York: McGraw-Hill, 1969.

Lustick, Ian. "To Build and to Be Built By: Israel and the Hidden Logic of the Iron Wall." *Israel Studies* 1, no. 1 (Spring 1996).

McDowell, David. *Palestine and Israel: The Uprising and Beyond*. London: I. B. Tauris, 1989.

Al Madfai, Madiha Rashid. *Jordan, the United States and the Middle East Peace Process, 1974–1991*. Cambridge: Cambridge University Press, 1993.

Makovsky, David. *Making Peace with the PLO: The Rabin Government's Road to Oslo*. Boulder, Colo.: Westview Press, 1996.

Ma'oz, Moshe. *Syria and Israel: From War to Peacemaking*. Oxford: Oxford University Press, 1995.

Margalit, Avishai. "The Violent Life of Yitzhak Shamir." *New York Review of Books*, 14 May 1992.

Medzini, Meron. *The Proud Jewess: Golda Meir and the Vision of Israel. A Political Biography* (Hebrew). Tel Aviv: Edanim, 1990.

Meir, Golda. *My Life*. London: Weidenfeld and Nicolson, 1975.

Melman, Yossi, and Dan Raviv. *Behind the Uprising: Israelis, Jordanians, and Palestinians*. Westport, Conn.: Greenwood Press, 1989.

Moore, John Norton, ed. *The Arab-Israeli Conflict: Readings and Documents*. Abr. and rev. ed. Princeton: Princeton University Press, 1977.

Morris, Benny. *The Birth of the Palestinian Refugee Problem, 1947–1949*. Cambridge: Cambridge University Press, 1987.

———. *1948 and After: Israel and the Palestinians*. Oxford: Oxford University Press, 1990; rev. and exp. ed., 1994.

———. *Israel's Border Wars, 1949–1956: Arab Infiltration, Israeli Retaliation, and the Countdown to the Suez War*. Oxford: Oxford University Press, 1993.

Nakdimon, Shlomo. *Tammuz in Flames: The Bombing of the Iraqi Reactor* (Hebrew). Rev. ed. Tel Aviv: Edanim, 1993.

Naor, Arye. *Cabinet at War: The Functioning of the Israeli Cabinet during the Lebanon War* (Hebrew). Tel Aviv: Lahav, 1986.

———. *Writing on the Wall* (Hebrew). Tel Aviv: Edanim, 1988.

———. *Begin in Power: A Personal Testimony* (Hebrew). Tel Aviv: Yediot Aharonot, 1993.

Narkis, Uzi. *Soldier of Jerusalem* (Hebrew). Tel Aviv: Ministry of Defense, 1991.

Ne'eman, Yuval. "The Link with the British and the French in the Sinai Campaign" (Hebrew). *Ma'arachot*, nos. 306–7 (Dec. 1986–Jan. 1987).

———. "Israel in the Age of Nuclear Weapons: Threat and Deterrence beyond 1995" (Hebrew). *Nativ* 8, no. 5 (1995).

Netanyahu, Benjamin. *A Place among the Nations: Israel and the World*. London: Bantam, 1993.

————. *Fighting Terrorism: How Democracies Can Defeat Domestic and International Terrorism.* New York: Farrar, Straus, Giroux, 1995.

————, ed. *Terrorism: How the West Can Win.* London: Weidenfeld and Nicolson, 1986.

Nissan, Eli. "Who Is Afraid of Yosef Tekoah?" *Bamahaneh* (IDF weekly), vol. 13, no. 1024 (26 Dec. 1967).

Nutting, Anthony. *No End of a Lesson: The Story of Suez.* London: Constable, 1957.

Pappé, Ilan. *Britain and the Arab-Israeli Conflict, 1948–51.* London: Macmillan, 1988.

————. *The Making of the Arab-Israeli Conflict, 1947–51.* London: I. B. Tauris, 1992.

Patai, Raphael. *The Complete Diaries of Theodor Herzl.* Translated by Harry Zohn. New York: Herzl Press and Thomas Yoseloff, 1960.

Pedatzur, Reuven. "Coming Back Full Circle: The Palestinian Option in 1967." *Middle East Journal* 49, no. 2 (Spring 1995).

————. *The Triumph of Confusion: Israel and the Territories after the Six-Day War* (Hebrew). Tel Aviv: Bitan, 1996.

Peleg, Ilan. *Begin's Foreign Policy, 1977–1983: Israel's Move to the Right.* New York: Greenwood Press, 1987.

Peres, Shimon. *David's Sling: The Arming of Israel.* London: Weidenfeld and Nicolson, 1970.

————. *The New Middle East.* Shaftesbury, England: Element, 1993.

————. *Battling for Peace: Memoirs.* London: Weidenfeld and Nicolson, 1995.

Peretz, Don. *Intifada: The Palestinian Uprising.* Boulder, Colo.: Westview Press, 1990.

Perlmutter, Amos, Michael Handel, and Uri Bar-Joseph, *Two Minutes over Baghdad.* London: Corgi Books, 1982.

Peters, Joel. *Pathways to Peace: The Multilateral Arab-Israeli Peace Talks.* London: European Commission, 1996.

Pineau, Christian. *Suez 1956.* Paris: Robert Laffont, 1976.

Quandt, William B. *Peace Process: American Diplomacy and the Arab-Israeli Conflict since 1967.* Berkeley: Brookings Institution, University of California Press, 1993.

Rabin, Yitzhak. *The Rabin Memoirs.* London: Weidenfeld and Nicolson, 1979.

Rafael, Gideon. *Destination Peace: Three Decades of Israeli Foreign Policy.* New York: Stein and Day, 1981.

Rabinovich, Itamar. *The War for Lebanon, 1970–1983.* Ithaca: Cornell University Press, 1984.

Rubinstein, Elyakim. "The Peace Treaty with Jordan" (Hebrew). *Hamishpat,* no. 6 (Dec. 1995).

Sachar, Howard M. *A History of Israel.* Vol. 2, *From the Aftermath of the Yom Kippur War.* New York: Oxford University Press, 1987.

el-Sadat, Anwar. *In Search of Identity: An Autobiography.* London: Collins, 1978.

Safran, Nadav. *Israel—The Embattled Ally.* Cambridge: Belknap Press of Harvard University Press, 1978.

Said, Edward. *Peace and Its Discontents: Gaza-Jericho, 1993–1995.* London: Vintage, 1995.

Sasson, Moshe. *Seven Years in the Land of the Egyptians* (Hebrew). Tel Aviv: Edanim, 1992.

Sayigh, Yezid. *Armed Struggle and the Search for State: The Palestinian National Movement, 1949–1993.* Oxford: Oxford University Press, 1997.

Schiff, Ze'ev, and Ehud Ya'ari. *Israel's Lebanon War.* London: George Allen and Unwin, 1984.

————. *Intifada*. Edited and translated by Ina Friedman. New York: Simon and Schuster, 1991.

Schulze, Kirsten E. *Israel's Covert Diplomacy in Lebanon*. London: Macmillan, 1998.

Seale, Patrick. *The Struggle for Syria: A Study in Post-War Arab Politics, 1945–1958*. London: Oxford University Press, 1965.

————. *Asad of Syria: The Struggle for the Middle East*. London: I. B. Tauris, 1988.

————. "The Address Is Syria." In Rosemary Hollis and Nadim Shehadi, eds., *Lebanon on Hold: Implications for Middle East Peace*. Oxford: Royal Institute of International Affairs in association with the Centre for Lebanese Studies, 1996.

————. "Syria and Israel: No Progress towards Peace." *Middle East International*, no. 565 (19 Dec. 1997).

Seale, Patrick, with Linda Butler. "Assad's Regional Strategy and the Challenge from Netanyahu." *Journal of Palestine Studies* 26, no. 1 (Autumn 1996).

Segev, Tom. *1949: The First Israelis*. New York: Free Press, 1986.

Shaham, David. *Israel—50 Years* (Hebrew). Tel Aviv: Am Oved, 1998.

Shalev, Aryeh. *The Intifada: Causes and Effects* (Hebrew). Tel Aviv: Papyrus, 1990.

————. *The Israel-Syria Armistice Regime, 1949–1955*. Boulder, Colo.: Westview Press, 1993.

Shalom, Zaki. *David Ben-Gurion, the State of Israel and the Arabs, 1949–1956* (Hebrew). Beersheba: Ben-Gurion University of the Negev Press, 1995.

————. *Policy in the Shadow of Controversy: Israel's Day-to-Day Security Policy, 1949–1956* (Hebrew). Tel Aviv: Ma'arachot, 1996.

Shamir, Shimon. "The Collapse of Project Alpha." In Wm. Roger Louis and Roger Owen, eds., *Suez 1956: The Crisis and Its Consequences*. Oxford: Clarendon Press, 1989.

Shamir, Yitzhak. "Israel's Role in a Changing Middle East." *Foreign Affairs* 50, no. 4 (Spring 1982).

————. *Summing Up: An Autobiography*. London: Weidenfeld and Nicolson, 1994.

Sharett, Moshe. "Israel and the Arabs—War and Peace (Reflections on the Years 1947–1957)" (Hebrew). *Ot*, Sept. 1966.

————. *A Personal Diary* (Hebrew). 8 vols. *1953–1957*. Tel Aviv: Ma'ariv, 1978.

Sharon, Ariel, with David Chanoff. *Warrior: The Autobiography of Ariel Sharon*. London: Macdonald, 1989.

Sheffer, Gabriel. *Moshe Sharett: Biography of a Political Moderate*. Oxford: Clarendon Press, 1996.

Shemesh, Moshe. *The Palestinian National Entity, 1959–1974: Arab Politics and the PLO*. London: Frank Cass, 1988.

————. "The Arab Struggle against Israel over Water, 1959–1967" (Hebrew). *Iyunim Bitkumat Israel* 7 (1997).

Shindler, Colin. *Israel, Likud and the Zionist Dream: Power, Politics and Ideology from Begin to Netanyahu*. London: I. B. Tauris, 1995.

Shlaim, Avi. "Husni Zaim and the Plan to Resettle Palestinian Refugees in Syria." *Journal of Palestine Studies* 15, no. 4 (Summer 1986).

————. *Collusion across the Jordan: King Abdullah, the Zionist Movement, and the Partition of Palestine*. Oxford: Clarendon Press, 1988.

————. "The Debate about 1948." *International Journal of Middle East Studies* 27, no. 3 (Aug. 1995).

————. "The Protocol of Sèvres, 1956: Anatomy of a War Plot." *International Affairs* 73, no. 3 (July 1997).

Shlaim, Avi, and Raymond Tanter, "Decision Process, Choice, and Consequences: Israel's Deep-Penetration Bombing in Egypt, 1970." *World Politics* 30, no. 4 (July 1978).

Shultz, George P. *Turmoil and Triumph: My Years as Secretary of State.* New York: Simon and Schuster, 1993.

Stephens, Robert. *Nasser: A Political Biography.* London: Penguin Books, 1971.

Tal, David. "The Development of Israel's Day-to-Day Security Conception, 1949–1956" (Hebrew). Ph.D. thesis, Tel Aviv University, 1994.

Tal, Israel. *National Security: The Few against the Many* (Hebrew). Tel Aviv: Dvir, 1996.

al-Tall, Abdullah. *The Palestine Catastrophe* (Arabic). Cairo: Dar al-Qalam, 1959.

Tamir, Avraham. *A Soldier in Search of Peace: An Inside Look at Israel's Strategy.* London: Weidenfeld and Nicolson, 1988.

Teveth, Shabtai. *Moshe Dayan.* London: Weidenfeld and Nicolson, 1972.

———. *Ben-Gurion and the Palestinian Arabs: From Peace to War.* Oxford: Oxford University Press, 1985.

Thomas, Abel. *Comment Israël fut sauvé: Les Secrets de l'expédition de Suez.* Paris: Albin Michel, 1978.

Tirosh, Avraham, and Avi Bettelheim. "Begin Proposed War in Lebanon in December 1981 after the Passage of the Golan Law." *Ma'ariv,* 3 June 1983, special supplement entitled "The Unfinished War."

Troen, S. Ilan. "The Protocol of Sèvres: British/French/Israeli Collusion against Egypt, 1956." *Israel Studies* 1, no. 2 (Fall 1996).

Troen, Selwyn Ilan, and Moshe Shemesh, eds. *The Suez-Sinai Campaign: Retrospective and Reappraisal.* London: Frank Cass, 1990.

Vassiliev, Alexei. *Russian Policy in the Middle East: From Messianism to Pragmatism.* Reading: Ithaca Press, 1993.

Weizman, Ezer. *On Eagles' Wings: The Personal Story of the Leading Commander of the Israeli Air Force.* London: Weidenfeld and Nicolson, 1976.

———. *The Battle for Peace.* Toronto: Bantam Books, 1981.

Woodward, Bob. *The Commanders.* New York: Simon and Schuster, 1991.

Ya'acobi, Gad. *On the Razor's Edge* (Hebrew). Tel Aviv: Edanim, 1989.

Ya'ari, Ehud. *Egypt and the Fedayeen, 1953–1956* (Hebrew). Givat Haviva: Center for Arabic and Afro-Asian Studies, 1975.

Yaniv, Avner. *Dilemmas of Security: Politics, Strategy, and the Israeli Experience in Lebanon.* New York: Oxford University Press, 1987.

Zak, Moshe. *Forty Years of Dialogue with Moscow* (Hebrew). Tel Aviv: Ma'ariv, 1988.

———. *Hussein Makes Peace: Thirty Years and Another Year on the Road to Peace* (Hebrew). Ramat Gan: Bar-Ilan University Press, 1996.

INDEX

Page numbers in *italics* refer to photographs.